# THE OTHER POLICY

# THE OTHER POLICY

*The influence of policies on technology
choice and small enterprise development*

Edited by FRANCES STEWART, HENK THOMAS
and TON DE WILDE

IT PUBLICATIONS in association with
APPROPRIATE TECHNOLOGY INTERNATIONAL 1990

Intermediate Technology Publications
103/105 Southampton Row, London WC1B 4HH
Appropriate Technology International
1331 H Street, N.W.
Washington, D.C. USA 20005

ISBN 185339 059 3

Appropriate Technology International (ATI) implements its mission
with public funds made available through the Agency for International
Development. ATI's programme is carried out in co-operation with the
Employment and Enterprise Division of the Office of Rural and
Institutional Development within AID's Bureau of Science and
Technology.

Typesetting by J&L Composition, Filey, North Yorkshire
Printed in Great Britain by SRP, Exeter

# Contents

# III Policies and Rural Industrialization

# IV Policy Experience and Policy Problems

# Preface

When E. F Schumacher published *Small Is Beautiful. Economics as if People Mattered* in 1973, appropriate technology appeared to offer a very promising approach to development. The idea was simple. All developing countries had an abundance of people – the most important production factor. What the people needed were technologies appropriate to their conditions, technologies which would be low on capital, labour-intensive, small-scale, adapted to local skill levels, and that would use local materials and renewable forms of energy. Schumacher's approach became even more relevant after the publication of the Brandt Committee report: *North–South: A Strategy for Survival.*[1]

Yet the strategy put forth in *Small Is Beautiful* has not been implemented on a large scale. The organizations most influential in establishing development policy – the IMF and the World Bank – ignored the concept. Several UN organizations made overtures to explore the idea: one of the results of their efforts was the UN Conference on Science and Technology, held in Vienna in 1979. But the actual experimentation was left to the small appropriate technology organizations around the world such as the Intermediate Technology Development Group (ITDG) in London, Appropriate Technology International (ATI) in Washington, Groupe de Recherche et d'Echanges Technologiques (GRET) in France and German Appropriate Technology Exchange (GATE) in Germany. These organizations supported and worked with local non-governmental organizations and, in some cases, governmental organizations in developing countries to introduce a wide range of appropriate technologies ranging from small-scale production of sugar to fuel-efficient cooking stoves.

Trial and error, which characterized the initial implementation of appropriate technologies, pointed to the need for a more systematic approach. Experience indicated that the characteristics of appropriate technology are not the same for all cases and may change over time; moreover appropriate technologies are not necessarily small-scale or labour-intensive. To determine if a technology is appropriate, the question – appropriate to what conditions – must first be answered.

Appropriate technology cannot be studied in isolation from the socio-economic context in which it is to be used. It needs to be efficient in comparison to other alternatives, including large-scale sophisticated technologies. It needs to meet the demands of the market at local, regional,

vii

national and sometimes international levels. To be appropriate, a technology must fit the potential and limitations of the individual producers. This requires an understanding of the risks the potential entrepreneur must take: the availability of credit; transport costs and other factors involved in getting the product to markets; the availability of spare parts; the availability and reliability of energy sources. Above all, if appropriate technologies are to make sustained progress, they must be profitable.

Just as important, the appropriateness of the technology cannot be assessed without considering the people who will use it. Schumacher's belief that the concept of 'appropriateness' must transcend the economic and technical data and address the human side of production and consumption has begun to receive more attention. Awareness of the multidisciplinary nature of appropriate technology led to the application of an 'open systems' approach to development which has, in some cases, produced encouraging results. High rates of economic survival and increasing prosperity have been achieved. It has become possible to establish profitable small-scale enterprises in rural areas of developing countries which have a more than 50 per cent chance of success, higher than the success rate in many industrialized countries. Yet, such successful appropriate technology projects have remained micro-interventions and their benefits have not expanded far beyond the original project.

One of the founders of Appropriate Technology International, Edgar Owens, recognizing the limitations of such piecemeal interventions, wanted to understand how the socioeconomic context affects the introduction and spread of appropriate technology. He initiated a research programme to study the relationship between macro-policy and the choice of appropriate technology. At a workshop held at the Institute of Social Studies in the Hague in 1982, which he and Frances Stewart organized, the research programme was initiated. Under Frances Stewart's guidance, nine macro-policy studies were undertaken, including among others, a comparison of macro-policies in Taiwan and the Philippines and their impact on technology choice and the economic performance of the rural sector, and a comparison of the decision-making process regarding technology choice in private and public enterprises in Kenya and Tanzania. The studies showed how macro-policies affect micro-level decisions, by manipulating economic incentives and constraints, such as the money supply, interest rates, currency exchange rates, availability of credit for different sectors and even sub-sectors. Direct public investments in infrastructure and human resource development and the tying of foreign aid were shown frequently to favour selection of inappropriate technologies. Despite policy statements to the contrary, the studies pointed out that not only were small-scale and appropriate technologies neglected, but also that the environment affecting choice of technology was usually hostile to them and systematically biased to favour the choice of large-scale capital-intensive technologies.

The results of the studies were presented at a workshop jointly organized by the Overseas Development Council (ODC) and Appropriate Technology International in Washington, DC in 1987 and published in *Macro-Policies for Appropriate Technology in Developing Countries*. Following suggestions that the research be expanded and made more region specific, twenty-seven country-specific case studies on the relationship between macro- and institutional policies and the choice of technology in three continents were added to the research base. The nine original studies and the subsequent region-specific studies were then discussed with policy advisers and decision-makers from both public and private sectors at three regional conferences – in Bangkok (March 1988); Nairobi (August 1988) and Mexico City (October 1988). These conferences were sponsored by the Netherlands Government, International Development Research Centre (IDRC) of Canada and, through ATI, by the US Agency for International Development.

In the regional conferences participants stressed, with increasing urgency, the need to disseminate the information widely and approach international development agencies in an effort to start formulating and implementing national programmes addressing the constraints faced at all levels by appropriate technology and small-scale enterprise development. This resulted in an international conference, organized jointly by ATI and the Intitute for Social Studies, and held at the Hague June 5–7 1989. This publication contains the proceedings of this conference, which reviewed the major policy issues associated with the introduction of policies to promote appropriate technology.

At the national level, in addition to identifying more appropriate macro-policies, the conference suggested programmes of action. Country programmes should review legislation, public expenditures, fiscal and monetary policy. At a regional and institutional level, they would assess banking practices and credit policies, R&D programmes of national and international research institutions, as well as policies of marketing and training institutions. At the local level, the programmes would study existing production systems *vis-à-vis* more appropriate small-scale commercially viable alternatives. Available resources would be identified to start new productive activities in a positive policy climate, where neither the large-scale nor small-scale sector would be subsidized and where the cost of production factors would not be unduly distorted by government or international donor policies.

The policy reforms proposed include some elements which are already part of some World Bank structural adjustment loan packages. But there are also some conflicts with IMF/World Bank policies and some additions that need to be made. At a minimum such changes would remove the hostility toward appropriate technology prevalent in many countries and the bias in favour of large-scale capital intensive industry.

We would like to express our gratitude to the Netherlands Government and the US Agency for International Development; without their support neither the conference nor the book would have materialized. Many people and institutions have contributed to this effort. The organization of the conference was a joint effort shared by the staffs of ATI and ISS. In particular, we would like to thank Nancy Tresp of ATI and Henny Romijn and Karin Felix-Faure of ISS who organized all aspects of the conference operations; Arleen Richman and Eric Hyman of ATI who assisted in preparation of the proceedings and other written materials; and Andy de Graaf of ISS who prepared the velotyped recordings of the meetings.

Frances Stewart
Ton de Wilde
Henk Thomas

# INTRODUCTION

Recently, the problems and promises of small-scale enterprises have received considerable attention. On a global level, the first and second World Conferences on Small-Scale Enterprise were held respectively in June 1988 in Washington DC and in June 1989 in Oslo, Norway. In the United States, during 1988 and 1989, six major conferences and workshops were convened on issues affecting small-scale enterprises. In the Netherlands, in September 1988, a conference was organized in Tilburg to inventory the activities of researchers and practitioners in small and micro-enterprises for the coming years. In February 1989, the Erasmus University in Rotterdam organized a policy conference on the informal sector. In March 1988, the Ministry of Development Co-operation of the Netherlands Government organized an international conference on small-scale enterprise development: 'In Search of New Dutch Approaches'.

Most of these conferences dealt with particular aspects of small enterprise development. In contrast, a conference organized by ATI and the Institute of Social Studies focused on the policy environment which can stimulate or inhibit the choice of appropriate technology and the development of small-scale enterprises. This publication contains the proceedings and papers presented at this conference, held in June 1989 in the Hague. What follows summarizes the key issues presented at the conference which are described in detail in this book.

Frances Stewart was the keynote speaker at the conference, entitled 'Policy Approaches Toward Technology and Small Enterprise Development'. She presented the results of a global research programme that she and a group of researchers conducted in both the First and Third Worlds; this work was commissioned by Appropriate Technology International. Stewart pointed out the hostile policy environment toward the choice of efficient and effective low-cost technologies employed in small-scale enterprises, and elaborated on ways in which this policy environment can be changed. Support is needed for an original and effective choice of technology geared to the purpose of the technology and the conditions under which it must function.

In this context, appropriate technology is defined as the complex of capital goods, products, processes and organizations which make good and efficient use of the means available within a country to achieve that country's development objectives. Widespread experience with micro-interventions – the setting up of specific small enterprises – shows that they have not contributed on a large scale to a country's economic growth. In many instances, this failure can be attributed to existing macro- and meso-policies, which distort the factors of production and support institutions favouring large-scale, capital-intensive production systems rather than fostering a choice of effective, small-scale technologies.

Appropriate technology is characterized by labour-intensive production; a small scale; a preference for rural over urban locations; the use of local raw materials, skills and knowledge; and the production of products important in the satisfaction of the basic needs of the poor majority. Of crucial significance is the efficiency of production and the potential to invest and grow. If it is demonstrated that large-scale production makes more efficient use of scarce resources to achieve the development goals of a country, then it is important to focus on such production systems. However, research results often indicate the contrary. Compared to large-scale production, small-scale production uses a relatively larger number of workers, and less capital; production costs, an indication of efficiency, are in many cases more favourable, and the rate of return on investment has been shown to be higher.

However, a number of factors promote the large-scale production option. First and foremost, most of the decision-making actors prefer large-scale technologies. The results speak to the imagination and are often spectacular. Governments and politicians aim to achieve quick results, especially for their constituencies, and the procedures for large-scale projects are clearly understood. For foreign donors, this happens to be very important. Consequently, a number of policies and rules of an economic nature lead to the promotion of the large-scale option; special tax incentives and subsidies, the availability of credit, the availability and manipulation of foreign exchange. Small-scale production systems have to pay relatively more for their inputs, placing them at a comparative disadvantage.

The market is crucially important to the economic success of small-scale industry which uses appropriate technology. The market is directly related to the division of income and the location of production in rural areas and market towns. In this context, it is important to develop linkages between rural development, the development of specific sectors and sub-sectors, and national and international markets. One of the most promising aspects of such linkages are sub-contracts between large-scale and small-scale production systems. Stewart's research concludes that institutions and organizations that are set up to support appropriate technology are often inadequate. Governments, development banks, and other development organizations have lost more and more of their ability to allow the large target group, the poor majority, to participate in the development process.

Stewart argues that government policies have to be changed significantly.

However, one should not expect very rapid or radical changes. Policies are the result of the influence of certain interest groups. Changing those policies will result in changing spheres of interest. For example, not everyone will benefit from necessary and important land-reform programmes, or the introduction of small-scale animal-driven equipment. However, in many areas, compromises are possible which do not require major changes in the existing power structure. Thus, one has to search for those macro- and meso-policies which, on the one hand are directed to achieve broad-based development objectives, but on the other hand do not require, at least in the short-term, major changes in the vested power structures.

Gustav Ranis, of Yale University, who also played a leading role in the research programme, criticized the fashionable but limited focus on export-oriented market policies. This is seen as an expression of the current neo-liberal orthodox approach, which is supported by many professionals within the International Monetary Fund, and the large international banking systems. Following such a one-sided approach will never lead to a balanced national development. A balanced national development, as explained by Stewart in the definition of appropriate technology, needs to be based upon a solid rural development, with roots in agriculture as well as in other sectors. In order to influence agricultural productivity, this rural development must be characterized by a solid network of linkages. The existence of such linkages is crucial to successful development and to the efficient choice of appropriate technology. We have to study the character and intensity of backward linkages such as demand for agricultural tools and equipment, and forward linkages such as the processing of agricultural produce. However, even more important are the forward consumption linkages, the increase in demand for industrial products resulting from the increase of incomes in the agricultural sector.

More in-depth studies of these aspects of agricultural production will result in the realization that industrialization is not an abstract national phenomenon in itself, but is part of a development process that is linked to rural and agricultural development strategies, in which market towns in more remote areas also play an important role. Ranis based these conclusions on, among other factors, a comparative study of Taiwan and the Philippines. There is no doubt that the development model of Taiwan, characterized by an industrialization pattern which was based on increased agricultural production through important linkages with rural industrialization, has allowed it to become a major competitor in the international world market. In comparison with the Philippines, Taiwan has very strong linkages between the agricultural, industrial and service sectors. Taiwan can also be viewed as an example of the application of appropriate technology. Ranis concludes that the government must understand the complexity of the macro-, meso-, and micro-policy interaction, and continue to aim at consistency in the use of their various policy instruments. Governments in particular, as well as the policies of aid donors, can play a limited but catalytic role in this regard. The policies set by both groups can contribute to organizing small farmers and entrepreneurs, the diffusion of research and development in rural regions and rural areas, and making credit available outside traditional channels to medium- and small-scale enterprises.

Carl Liedholm, of Michigan State University, presented the results of a global research programme involving over 20,000 small enterprises in more than 20 countries, carried out during the last few years. He characterized the conclusions of his research on the results of macro-policies for large and small-scale enterprises with the words: 'The playing field is clearly not level'. For example, in Sierra Leone, subsidies and tariff structure led to an effective rate of protection for large-scale industry of 430 per cent compared with only 29 per cent for small-scale industry. Such differences are the result of policies in a number of areas. Attention to a single aspect of policy is at best a partial solution, and at worst, totally misleading. According to Liedholm's research, national income in most developing countries is, on average, 6 to 18 per cent lower than it would be had a more appropriate technology and small-enterprise strategy been promoted. The inefficient use of capital in large-scale, capital-intensive production systems has major negative effects on the creation of jobs. Too often, unemployment is seen as a permanent, unanswerable problem, and is not treated as an acute crisis. However, if it were, and governments would make direct interventions, this could 'with a stroke of the pen', lead to a more labour-intensive development strategy.

Liedholm also noted the lack of quantitative and qualitative statistical data in-country, which makes it impossible to get feedback on policies and policy changes. The problems of choice of technology in the development of micro- and small enterprises are particularly sector and region specific. Because in-depth knowledge is indispensable, donor agencies could make a crucial contribution by stimulating the discussion, formulation, and implementation of strategies for the implementation of appropriate technology and small enterprise development.

### Three regional conferences

One of the most interesting aspects of the conference were the presentations of six case studies, selected from among the papers presented in regional conferences held in Asia, Africa and Latin America. The case studies analysed in-depth factors that help explain why policies that would promote the use of appropriate technology in small enterprise development were never adopted.

In the case of the Philippines, Romeo Bautista from the International

Food Policy Research Institute (IFPRI) showed that over the past decades, an industrial policy has been implemented promoting large-scale, capital-intensive production; this allowed the highest income classes to consolidate and reinforce their own position. The stagnation of rural development, the concentration of industrial development in a few areas, and entrepreneurs' unequal access to credit and foreign exchange were other reasons why appropriate technology was not implemented, even though it would have resulted in the creation of much more employment, thus providing income for many of the rural poor. The author concludes that unless there is a change in government policy, even the establishment of a number of special projects and organizations designed to promote small and medium industry will have a very limited impact on economic development.

A similar conclusion was reached by Q. K. Ahmad of the Bangladesh Centre for Research and Action on Environment and Development. His presentation noted the distinction among the roles played by policy-makers, the administration, and special interest groups. As a result of policy influence by the higher income classes, capital-intensive technologies are replacing traditional rice processing methods which provided income to the large masses of population. He stated that unless macro-policies are changed, other solutions, such as trying through the application of appropriate technology to increase the productivity of traditional technologies and attempting to create employment through product diversification, can only be second-best solutions.

Information contained in the case studies on Zimbabwe and Tanzania, presented respectively by Daniel Ndlela and S. M. Wangwe, was even more depressing. In both countries, the governments, helped by a lot of aid from foreign donors, established a bureaucratic machinery to promote the development of small-scale industry. However, the results are scarcely noticeable. Industry in these countries is characterized by large-scale production systems, capacity under-utilization and capital-intensive production, the result of national government policy, influenced by foreign financial institutions. Stagnating agricultural development and lack of backward and forward linkages have ultimately resulted in a decrease in demand.

Edwardo Doryan-Garron, Vice-Minister of Science and Technology in Costa Rica, spoke about the significance of the role of the government in establishing a favourable policy climate. Costa Rica's success in stimulating the productivity of small-scale coffee growers points out the importance of facilitating contacts and linkages between the small producers and research institutions and universities to stimulate a national research climate which addresses the small-scale producers' problems. These linkages are especially important in the new area of biotechnology, which will result in important changes in agricultural practices.

## Need for research

Most researchers believe there are plenty of subjects that need to be researched. On the contrary, most governments express their doubts about the need for and policy relevance of research. Research, especially longitudinal research, is often very time-consuming and is only appreciated in the long term. While initial research on macro-policies and appropriate technology has provided answers to many questions that can form the basis for necessary policy change, it also made clear how much is not yet known.

For this reason, the conference reserved time for two workshops to discuss research themes on small-scale industrial policies and rural linkages, including the crucial role of regional analysis, sub-contracting, the importance of market towns and linkages with international markets. Presentations made by Albert Berry of the University of Toronto, Francisco Uribe-Echevarria, and Ashwani Saith from ISS, stimulated intense discussion.

Based on his research in Colombia, Uribe contended that small-scale production needed to be seen in the context of regional industrialization. National policies do not take into account the specific characteristics and differences between urbanized regions, intermediary areas and typical rural regions. This results in policies that are too general and have yielded few positive results. He concluded by arguing that small-scale production must be approached within the perspective of regional and sectoral industrialization and development.

Berry's presentation illustrated the efficiency and dynamics of small enterprises. His research, also based on case studies in Colombia, shows the important role small-scale industry plays in economic growth. From a development perspective, very little is known about the dynamics and relevance of small-scale industry to investments, economic growth, and creation of employment. If small-scale production were really less efficient than medium-scale enterprises in the use of capital and raw materials, these enterprises, at least on economic grounds, would have already disappeared.

Saith, whose research focused on Asia, emphasized that linkages are as important as the location of the enterprise in analysing small industry. He argued that policies in developing countries that emphasize the need for small-scale industry might neglect the real causes of poverty. He concluded that a small-scale enterprise strategy, in many cases, is at best a second-best solution to solving the problems of structural poverty. Discussion in this session centred on the place of demand structures, the importance of appropriate research, and the differentiation between regions within countries as well as between the countries themselves.

'Small-scale industrial policies' characterized the papers presented by Charles Cooper of ISS, E. V. K. FitzGerald of ISS and Jeffrey James from Tilburg University. Cooper argued that more research is needed to understand the linkage between increased income of the poorest of the poor and the resulting demand for goods. He questioned if a direct relationship could be established between increased income of the poor and demand for goods which are produced in a labour-intensive way. He cautioned that goods which are produced by small-scale industry are not automatically produced in a labour-intensive way. In other words, one should not expect that a policy enacted to develop small and micro-enterprises will implicitly contribute to an improved distribution of income or more employment.

FitzGerald touched upon the impact of macroeconomic policies on small-scale industry. In particular, he analysed the potential results of structural adjustment programmes on the development of small enterprises. On the one hand, it is to be expected that a more balanced foreign exchange policy will improve the factor distortions between large and small-scale enterprises. But he also argued that deflationary government measures, reduced government expenditures, and increases in interest rates could have important negative effects on the development of small-scale enterprise. Contrary to the opinions of most development economists, he believed that because large-scale industry is so strong, the negative consequences of structural adjustment policies may be passed on to the weaker small-scale sector.

FitzGerald's second theme was the relationship between large and small-scale enterprises. Is there really direct competition between both sectors, or does the mechanism of sub-contracting make them mutually dependent? In addition he analysed the extent to which small industries are producing 'wage goods', which are consumed by employees of medium and small-scale industry. While one can look at these issues strictly in the theoretical sense, they do raise hard political questions. What is the result of structural adjustment policies? The available information is very controversial. Some economists claim that the IMF structural adjustment loan policy improves the position of small-scale industry. Others argue to the contrary.

James, who based his research on a comparative study of the choice of technology in manufacturing industry in Kenya and Tanzania, showed that even when macro-policies are intended to stimulate the use of appropriate technology, inappropriate technology is invariably selected. What is interesting is that there was very little difference between a freer market-oriented, capitalistic system and a more centrally planned socialistic development model. The choice of technology is strongly influenced by the investors. In this case, foreign donors appear to be instrumental in the promotion of capital-intensive technologies. Bureaucracies and political systems find it difficult to cope with labour-intensive appropriate technology solutions because the results are only apparent in the long term; the projects are less spectacular; and the government bureaucrat does not occupy as significant a position.

From the conference discussions, it was clear that macroeconomic policy has a significant influence on the development of small-scale industry. The results of research presented at the conference provide a basis on which to define necessary policy changes. However, the results also point out that more systematic research is urgently needed. Subjects such as the importance of differentiation between the various types of small industry in policy formulations, the labour environment within small industries, the facts on income, and last, but not least, gender issues in small-scale industry, are expected to be important issues on the research agenda in years to come. Other issues, such as sub-contracting and the dynamics of small-scale industry, including barriers that prevent small-scale industries from graduating to medium-scale industries, require independent analyses.

The last day's presentations and discussions were crisp in their analyses and syntheses and clear and innovative in defining a path forward. This was the day of the politicians and practitioners.

First, Bahman Mansuri, Director of the Africa Programme of the International Fund for Agricultural Development (IFAD), briefly reviewed the lessons learned in a study of five countries: Kenya, Malawi, Niger, Madagascar, and Ghana.

The IFAD study examined the impact of structural adjustment on the rural poor and the importance of non-farm activities in rural areas in African countries. It found that the impact of the reforms depends significantly on the access of smallholders to complementary resources and services. The challenge, therefore, is to support rural services that can effectively reach smallholders and the rural poor. For example, in promoting the development of capital markets, governments and donors generally have emphasized providing formal credit through parastatal banks while neglecting the wider informal market and the mobilization of local savings. Only a small minority of rural households in the countries studied had used formal credit.

In reviewing the role of product markets, it was clear that the private sector and co-operatives have to play an important role in providing services. Unfortunately, the private sector frequently lacks the capacity to effectively fulfil these functions, and the resulting lack of competition has reduced the benefits to rural producers and consumers. Although efforts by the private sector should be encouraged, we must recognize that a whole range of functions can only be carried out effectively by the public sector – ie, the construction of rural infrastructure, assuring national food security, and the provision of health and educational services. The study also showed the important role women played in agriculture in the rural economy in Africa, and how women also dominate many non-farm activities.

The study made a number of recommendations for policy changes. First, structural adjustment packages and structural adjustment programmes should be carefully analysed to ensure that they are conducive to the participation of smallholders and the rural poor. In light of the significant role women play in the rural economy, gender issues should receive more attention in policy analysis. In the institutional area, a number of measures should be taken to address business' common need for infrastructure and a more flexible and responsive financial system. For example, innovative approaches could promote co-operation between informal and formal credit-givers. Government decentralization policies are important tools to promote greater participation by the people. The study showed that in reality achieving this may prove to be more difficult than expected.

Finally, Mansuri showed the need for a consistent and sustained effort to provide services to small and micro-enterprises that need capital ranging from a few hundred dollars to a few thousand dollars. Current efforts of IFC and other institutions such as the African Enterprise Project do not fill this gap.

G de Kalbermatten, who represented the United Nations Capital Development Fund, emphasized the difficulties of formulating and implementing people-focused projects. Since the beginning of the 1980s, the Fund has specialized in delivering grants and loans ranging from $200,000 to $5 m for small-scale capital assistance projects for economic infrastructure, agricultural activities, micro- and small-scale enterprises, and basic needs infrastructure. Based on past experience, the Fund stresses the need for a combination of specialized NGOs and small-scale multilateral investors to develop the kind of appropriate delivery systems that developing countries will require in the 1990s.

The commentators both complimented and criticized the speakers. Questions and comments addressed the need to train government officials and, more importantly, staffs of donor agencies and multilateral organizations, who too often look at development merely as a redistribution issue and not a growth issue. It was argued that the appropriate technology route provides not only equity, but also growth.

In a dramatic intervention, one of the African representatives reminded the participants of the effects of traditional structural adjustment loans on the majority of the people in Africa, and blamed the secret negotiations between multilateral agencies and government officials for street demonstrations and violence. He argued that lending agencies should discuss structural adjustment more freely; this would allow the needs of the informal sector and the use of appropriate technology to be incorporated in Structural Adjustment Loans.

In the closing session of the conference, Ton de Wilde focused on the unprecedented rapid increase in the labour force projected for the 1990s, which requires an additional 1.2 billion jobs to be created between 1989 and the year 2000. He emphasized that in job creation, the size of the enterprise is only a secondary factor; it is the technology utilized by the enterprise that determines the number of jobs created. He ended his presentation with a sketch of programmes which would implement some of the policy recommendations of the conference. First of all, in an effort to create a more competitive environment such programmes would review the efficiency of existing production systems. This would make it more difficult for private and public businesses to continue to use inappropriate technologies. Second, a review of capitalization mechanisms for small and micro-enterprises would examine, among other factors, improving access through simpler administrative procedures and risk-sharing through equity financing. Third, such programmes should improve the institutional infrastructure in support of small and micro-enterprises using appropriate technology. Mechanisms such as grants or fellowships to local universities would support action research focused on the problems of small-scale enterprises, the establishment of a national research council for appropriate technology, and special marketing institutions to focus on the marketing of the products of the small-scale and artisanal sector.

Henk Thomas focused his presentation on often overlooked issues in small and micro-enterprise development, such as the quality of employment, the behaviour and characterization of small industrial firms, and the public–private sector dimensions of small enterprise development. He indicated that most of the research has ignored the special labour market situation of workers in small and micro-enterprises. Too often, it is assumed that a job created in a small-scale enterprise is equivalent to a job created in a large-scale, modern industrial enterprise. In reality, labour markets are heterogeneous and segmented. In discussing the need to understand better the behaviour and characteristics of small-scale enterprises, he focused on the barriers for entrepreneurs to 'graduate' their business. For example, an entrepreneur might find that he can update his business and improve the quality of his product, but that his customers cannot pay more for the better quality product. Thus, the entrepreneur may only be willing to make small investments that can be profitably recovered over the short term. This entrepreneurial behaviour may only allow marginal technological innovations. In the private–public dimension, he stressed the pivotal role of institutions in development. He emphasized the importance of the remarks made by the participants of the conference on the need for institutions supporting small enterprises. These institutions may well prove to be an important investment in fostering economic democracy. He pointed to the current experiments in Hungary and Yugoslavia in the convergence of command and market-type economies. Last, but not least, he indicated both the need for more substantive research in this area as well as the dilemmas which are inherent in such research.

Stewart, in her closing remarks, first restated some of the generally accepted views. She indicated that in contrast to the situation some years ago there was remarkably little debate about the definition of appropriate technology, and whether it is efficient. It was also generally accepted that rural linkages are an important part of the development strategy. Macro- and meso-policies are very relevant to the success of small- and micro-enterprises. There was also general agreement that the current policies in many developing countries have had disturbing effects. The current macroeconomic packages of the World Bank and the IMF contain elements that support appropriate technology and small- and micro-enterprise development, but these are not sufficient.

Yet, while there is significant general agreement, controversy still exists in a number of areas. While the significance of demand was emphasized, the best mechanism for increasing demand was still questioned. Another question still open for further research related to the relationship between demand and the formal and informal sector under various policy settings. Do measures that benefit the formal sector improve the position of the informal sector, and vice versa?

In providing credit for various activities in the small-scale sector there was much support for the idea of structured markets. Some disagreed, but most stressed the need for additional changes in the current structural adjustment package.

Stewart noted that some presenters emphasized the need for structural reform to facilitate income distribution – a traditional debate. While recognizing the importance of the discussion, she indicated also the contributions she and other participants had made to this discussion in the past. However, there was no question that government institutions such as parastatals have not been successful. The role of political economy cannot be emphasized enough. If a first-best solution in a certain economy may be impractical for political reasons, a second-best may have to be used. For example, the best solution to rural poverty in Bangladesh would be land reform, while a programme like the Grameen Bank is a second-best solution.

After defining topics for further research, she pleaded for the urgent need to formulate rural adjustment packages which incorporate the policies discussed at the conference, both at a general and at a country level.

### Adept: Adapt

This was the title of the closing address by Luc de la Rive Box, Head of the Policy Planning Section and Advisory Council Secretariat, Department of International Co-operation, Netherlands Ministry of Foreign Affairs.

After describing a case study on the introduction of a rice husker to the Dominican Republic in which de la Rive Box was personally involved, he laid the basis for the themes of the rest of his presentation. The case study pointed out three key areas which need attention:

- The political economy of technological development has to be viewed in dynamic terms as a complex interaction between economic and technological differentiation;
- National macro-agricultural-sector policies still reflect urban biases: they are loaded against rural priorities such as local employment, local technology maintenance, and local capital accumulation. If development planning exists at all, it should counteract such biases;
- Large development agencies like the World Bank or small ones like Dutch Aid have a double job to do if they are convinced that technological differentiation is needed: work at the top to undo particular biases and work at the technological base to allow technological differentiation.

These themes were elaborated on in the rest of his presentation. He concluded his presentation with the following personal conclusions:

- Differentiation in the small-enterprise sector needs to be a starting point for policy formulation. Some parts of the informal sector are quite dynamic, but others remain stagnant. Macro-policies are needed, but their effects on different sub-sectors will differ. Therefore policies need to take into account the particularities of a given sub-sector. Specialists both in and outside the donor ministry will have to become more involved than in the past if such policies are to become realistically accurate;
- The regionalization of policies also is needed. Differentiation within regions is large, too, but certain problems tend to cluster. Decentralization of development policy-making is therefore needed as well; a larger role will need to be played by local specialists working with national embassies. These people should be able to advise on and evaluate projects in terms of macro- and sectoral policies;
- Donor co-ordination is more than just a cliché. Small countries such as the Netherlands have little influence to counteract the major developments that strangle small-scale enterprises in poor countries. The Dutch contribution in international fora like the EC in Brussels is, and will have to remain, to inform and construct coalitions to improve technology policies. Development policy-making is increasingly an affair of donors who find each other in different coalitions;
- Donors need to engage in structural adjustments of their own policies; that is adjust their policies and programmes to the highly differentiated realities.

This conference clearly showed again that small-scale industry suffers when large-scale development programmes are promoted. Yet, large agencies wish to spend large amounts of money in a little time with few staff. There is therefore a need for structural adjustment 'here' so others 'there' will not have to adjust to our idiosyncrasies;

- Industry linkages should not be taboo. Policy-makers do not produce development; if the policies work well they generate a friendly environment to foster development. In the past, Dutch development policy-makers kept themselves at an unhelpful distance from private enterprise. They should not;
- NGOs will play an even larger role in providing the necessary linkages with small-scale sector interests. Development policy-makers will have to learn to work together with specialized NGOs and evaluate whose interests they serve. This conference brought out the dangers of faddism in NGO-linked approaches. In particular, it was argued that parastatals should not now be forgotten. After all, many donors are at least partly responsible for their existence. NGOs cannot replace some of their functions;
- Basic research in rich countries will continue to be important for small enterprise development in poor countries, provided it is well linked with locally established applied researchers. Development policy-makers need to be informed on both the supply side of technology in rich countries and the demand side in poor countries. Technological adaptation cannot be done in Wageningen alone; nor will it come about by itself in Malang, Ibadan, or San Jose. Development agencies can be brokers, provided their research policy is well informed on both sides. Research brokerage needs to be strengthened for this reason;
- Last, but not least, appropriate technology is at least partially the result of user experimentation in a given ecological and cultural context. This is what Gus Ranis, during our conference, called 'blue-collar innovation'. To me, it is at the root of many technological developments in small-scale industry. We are in need of good empirical studies documenting 'technological biographies'.

De la Rive Box concluded: 'It is we, the adepts, who now have to adapt to the conditions of technological differentation and economic development. It is we, the scientists, who have to adapt to the requests of policy-makers and of small-scale entrepreneurs in the field. It is we, the policy-makers, who must adapt the new insights and results of scientists and those we are supposed to serve. In this way we may be able to do what Jan Tinbergen asked us to consider – to double incomes in the next twenty years.'

# GLOSSARY

| | |
|---|---|
| AT | Appropriate Technology |
| ATI | Appropriate Technology International |
| bc | benefit/cost ratio |
| bn | billion (one thousand million) |
| FAO | Food and Agriculture Organization |
| IDB | Industrial Development Bank |
| IFAD | International Fund for Agricultural Development |
| ILO | International Labour Organization |
| IMF/WB | or the Fund and the Bank – International Monetary Fund and the World Bank |
| ISS | Institute of Social Studies, the Hague |
| LDC | Less Developed Country |
| m | million |
| MI | Medium Industry – firms that employ between 50 and 99 workers Micro-enterprises employ less than 5 workers |
| MNC | Multinational Corporation |
| pbc | private benefit/cost ratio |
| RSIE | Rural Small Industrial Enterprise |
| SAL | Structural Adjustment Loan |
| SECAL | Sectoral Adjustment Loan |
| SI | Small Industry – firms that employ between 5 and 49 workers |
| SMI | Small and Medium Industry |
| UNCDF | United Nations Capital Development Fund |
| USAID | United States Agency for International Development |

# I

# *Policy Approaches*

# Macro-Policies for Appropriate Technology: A Synthesis of Findings

## FRANCES STEWART with GUSTAV RANIS

### Introduction

Most efforts to promote appropriate technology have been concentrated at the micro-level, with finance and assistance devoted to particular interventions in support of particular technologies. The range of technologies is wide – extending, for example, from cooking stoves to windmills, from mini-cement plants to micro-electronic devices for controlling hydraulic systems. The interventions have taken a variety of forms, some involving financial assistance, some technical assistance, and some support for new research efforts.[1] However, although there were some good results, the effects tended to be confined to the particular area where the intervention took place, and were not widely disseminated. Moreover, spontaneous growth of small-scale enterprises and development and dissemination of appropriate technologies, in countries where both were badly needed, were comparatively rare. A generally hostile policy environment appeared to be one of the main factors responsible for this, with interventions at the macro-level often unintentionally preventing micro-interventions from bearing fruit.

This paper explores how the macro- and méso-policy environment has impinged on technology choices and the small-scale sector, drawing on empirical work exploring the relationship between the macro-policy environment and technology choice.

The research was supported by Appropriate Technology International. The initial project in this area, involving seven empirical studies, was published in 1987 as *Macro-Policies for Appropriate Technology in Developing Countries*.[2] Subsequently, three regional conferences were held in Thailand, in Kenya and in Mexico to discuss the findings and to provide regional inputs into the formulation of macro- and meso- policies for AT. For each meeting papers were prepared on the interaction

FRANCES STEWART is senior research officer at Queen Elizabeth House and a Fellow of Somerville College, Oxford. She has also served as a consultant to the World Bank, the Ford Foundation, OECD, and many UN agencies.

GUSTAV RANIS is a Frank Atschul Professor of International Economics at Yale University. He has also served as a consultant for USAID, Ford Foundation, Rockefeller Foundation, World Bank and FAO.

between macro-policies and micro-enterprises, based on experience in the region. Participants at the regional conferences included members of the government and other politicians, civil servants, businessmen, representatives of NGOs and academics.

The main aim of this paper is to provide a synthesis of findings from the empirical work, in order to draw up some broad guidelines on policies which would support appropriate technology. A secondary aim is to consider how far the policy set arrived at is consistent with the sorts of policies countries are pursuing under the auspices of IMF/World Bank structural adjustment programmes and to identify changes that might be needed in these programmes to make them more supportive of appropriate technology. The second aim is of considerable importance because many countries (about two-thirds of the countries in Latin America and Africa) are following structural adjustment programmes and are likely to continue to do so for most of the decade.

This paper is organized as follows: the next section discusses what appropriate technology (AT) is and why it is needed, and presents some evidence on the existence and efficiency of AT. The third section discusses how the policy environment affects the choice of products and of processes. In light of these findings, the fourth section presents a summary chart of the macro- and meso-policies identified as favourable to AT; it discusses political economy obstacles to achieving a move toward such policy change, and considers the consistency of the policies identified as favouring AT with the usual IMF/World Bank policy packages, elucidating some changes in these packages that would help to promote AT.

## Appropriate technology

Defined simply, appropriate technology is the technology which best makes use of a country's resources to achieve its development objectives. These objectives include the desire to achieve sustained economic growth, to secure wide and equitable participation in the process of growth, to enable the whole population to satisfy their basic needs and to protect the environment. AT encompasses *products* as well as *techniques*, that is, it includes products with characteristics best suited to meeting the needs of low-income consumers and producers, as well as methods of production with appropriate characteristics. Defined in this way it is clear that there can be no unique appropriate technology to fit all circumstances. The technology which is appropriate will differ according to the nature of a country, its resources and opportunities. As resources accumulate, techniques and products that best meet its needs will also change, so that the AT will change over time. ATs are likely to encompass some large-scale technologies as well as small-scale and products suitable for export, as well as those designed to meet the basic needs of the population.

4

A technology problem exists because the majority of technologies are developed in advanced countries, with different social, economic and cultural conditions from low-income countries and, therefore, many of the techniques and products currently emanating from developed countries tend to be inappropriate for use in developing countries. Compared with developing countries, developed countries have more abundant capital resources (three to ten times that available per capita in developing countries), larger markets, higher average incomes and therefore different consumption patterns and a greater availability of skills. The use of contemporary technology from advanced countries, unmodified for use in developing countries, can lead to inequalities in work opportunities, incomes and consumption patterns and high levels of un- and underemployment.

In contrast to developed-country technology, AT tends to be more labour-intensive and smaller-scale, is more likely to use local materials and to include techniques and products especially suited for rural production, with product characteristics which are better adapted to the needs of the mass of poor consumers. However, as already noted, some ATs may involve large-scale production, while AT is definitely not only for rural use – the urban sector also needs techniques and products appropriate for its conditions.

It is important to emphasize that AT is a flexible concept: the AT must be *efficient* and relevant to each environment. Sometimes, it is suggested that any technology that is labour-intensive and small-scale is appropriate, irrespective of its efficiency, but it is generally not desirable to sacrifice output by adopting inefficient technologies. (The adoption of a technology with lower output than an alternative may be justified if the benefits go to low-income groups who would otherwise not have access to employment. But in such a case the incomes earned will be very low and thus such a solution will not help poverty alleviation in the long run. It is therefore preferable to seek alternative more efficient technologies.) In brief, an efficient technology is one that maximizes the value of output in relation to resource costs, when resources and output are properly costed, allowing for social opportunity costs and benefits and not merely costs as valued on the market. An inefficient labour-intensive technology will not help those who use it in the long run because it will perpetuate low incomes.

Moreover, ATs also have a *dynamic* dimension. The AT is likely to change over time as capital and skills accumulate and incomes grow. It is also necessary for the productivity of AT to increase over time, so as to raise the incomes of those using the technologies and to permit the technologies to compete with technologies with inappropriate characteristics. ATs should offer potential for accumulation and productivity increase through upgrading and learning. There is therefore a need for an ongoing effort to develop and disseminate ATs, making use of R & D based on the most recent scientific and technological advances. Recently the need to create and improve indigenous technological capability for efficient industrial development has been widely stressed.[3] These conclusions apply especially to appropriate technology. ATs should have dynamic potential as well as appropriate characteristics

A critical question is whether *an efficient technology with appropriate characteristics usually exists*. One view, held fairly widely some years ago, was that efficient technology with appropriate characteristics did not exist, because of the inflexible nature of technological development, and particularly the domination of advanced countries in R & D.[4] There now exists a considerable amount of evidence showing the existence of efficient small-scale and labour-intensive technologies in a large number of industries. These technologies are generally more appropriate than large-scale capital-intensive technologies in countries with relatively more abundant labour and less capital.

**Table 1 Performance of small-scale labour-intensive technologies as a multiple of capital-intensive**

| Efficient small-scale technologies | Capital Output | Labour Output | Capital Labour | Costs per unit of output |
|---|---|---|---|---|
| Sugar Processing, India | 0.71 | 2.94 | 0.24 | 0.84 |
| Kenya | 0.27 | 5.86 | 0.05 | 0.66 |
| Pineapple Canning, Philippines and Taiwan | 0.39 | 3.33 | 0.17 | competitive |
| Rice Mills, Philippines | 0.76[a] 0.61[b] | 1.67 | 0.30 | 0.96[c] 0.88[b] |
| Maize Milling, Tanzania | 0.10 | 5.18 | 0.49 | competitive; social costs of labour-intensive lower |
| Spinning, Thailand | 0.67 | 1.34[d] | 0.50 | 0.76[e] |
| *Questionably Efficient* Dhenki Rice Huller, Bangladesh | 0.42 | 13.54 | 0.06 | 6.78 |
| MOSTI, Bangladesh | 0.003 | 7.50 | 0.06 | 2.79 |

[a] Assumes large mill operates at 97 per cent capacity; small mill at 77 per cent, as observed in survey.
[b] Assuming both rice mills operate at 100 per cent capacity
[c] When capital costs are costed at replacement value.
[d] Assuming labour use is proportionate to labour costs.
[e] Assuming no special promotion policies for the large scale.
Sources: Kaplinsky (1987), Ranis (1987), Biggs and Griffith (1987), Ahmad (1988), Bagachwa (1988), Snatikarn (1988).

In the studies reviewed here, efficient technologies with appropriate characteristics were identified in a number of industries. Five examples are

6

presented in Table 1. In each case, capital cost per person employed is much lower in the small-scale than the large-scale technique. The most extreme difference is in sugar processing in Kenya, where capital costs per head in the open pan sulphitation technique (OPS) are less than 5 per cent those in the large-scale vacuum pan technique (VPS). Capital costs per unit of output are also lower for the small-scale technologies, ranging from approximately 10 per cent in maize milling in Tanzania to 71 per cent in sugar processing in India. Labour use is much larger among the small-scale techniques, with the amount of employment created for the same level of output being as much as five times as great as in the capital-intensive technology in Kenyan sugar processing. The costs per unit of output of the various techniques are shown in column 4, indicating their relative inefficiences. In each case the more labour-intensive technique is lower or competitive in cost compared with the capital-intensive alternative.

It is clear from these examples that there are technologies which are both labour-intensive, skill-saving and efficient. (Data on skill use are not provided in the table, because they are not available on a systematic basis, but most of the evidence shows the larger, more sophisticated techniques require more skills than the smaller techniques.) The alternative technologies also typically produce more appropriate products. For example, in both maize and rice milling, the smaller mills produce a more nutritious, less refined product which costs less and is more appropriate to low-income consumers. In pineapple canning, the more labour-intensive technology produces a less 'high' standard product, the pineapples being more crushed and broken.

Two examples of technology were identified which, while they had appropriate characteristics in some respects, were on balance inefficient and lacked dynamic potential. These were the dhenki (a form of manual rice hulling) and the MOSTI (a manually operated tube well). As can be seen in Table 1, fixed capital costs per head of both technologies are a fraction of the alternatives and labour absorption per unit of output is far greater, but because of very low capital productivity of the technologies, unit costs are far greater. The dhenki and the MOSTI are both purely manually operated, whereas all the other examples involve some machinery: the two are basically traditional technologies which have not been upgraded by modern science and technology, while the efficient technologies embody some modern technological know-how.

Other powerful evidence showing the existence of efficient small-scale technologies comes from the work of Liedholm and Mead and also Pack (see Tables 2 and 3). In studies of seven industries in five countries, Liedholm and Mead found that capital intensity (defined as the ratio of capital services to value added) was systematically higher in large-scale firms than small, the ratio varying from 2.4 to 40.8, while economic profit was *consistently substantially higher* for the small-scale firms, being negative in

**Table 2 Comparative efficiency of small enterprises**

| | Relatively capital-intensity[a] of large-scale, compared with small-scale[b] | Relative economic profit as % of capital stock[c] | |
|---|---|---|---|
| | | Large-Scale | Small-Scale |
| **BOTSWANA (1982)** | | | |
| Sorghum Beer | 3.2 | +130 | +190 |
| **EGYPT (1982)** | | | |
| Clothing | 2.8 | +17 | +42 |
| Metal Products | 12.3 | −3 | +103 |
| **HONDURAS (1980)** | | | |
| Clothing | 2.8 | −21 | +45 |
| Furniture | 7.3 | −26 | +58 |
| Shoes | 13.9 | −22 | +102 |
| Leather Products | 7.1 | −21 | +79 |
| Metal Products | 8.6 | −24 | +23 |
| **JAMAICA (1979)** | | | |
| Clothing | 6.6 | −11.0 | +86 |
| Furniture | 5.7 | −0.4 | +173 |
| Shoes | 7.7 | −6.0 | +247 |
| Metal Products | 2.4 | +16.6 | +56 |
| **SIERRA LEONE (1974)** | | | |
| Clothing | 4.9 | −27 | +59 |
| Bread | 7.3 | −11 | +12 |
| Rice Milling | 40.8 | −30 | +80 |

Source: Liedholm and Mead, 1987.

[a] Relative capital-intensity is calculated by comparing the ratio of capital services to value-added in large and small firms.

[b] Large-scale firms are those employing 50 or more; small-scale those employing less than 50.

[c] Economic profit is defined as value-added less capital services (valued at shadow interest rate) and labour costs (including family labour), valued at the competitive wage rate in the industry)

most of the large-scale activities and high and positive in all the small-scale activities (Table 2).

Pack has shown that efficient AT – defined as the technology which would be most profitable using the prices typical of a poor country – can generate a very large amount of additional employment. He compared employment and capital requirements of the efficient AT with the capital-intensive alternative in nine industries. Fixed capital requirements per worker were as little as 1.1 per cent of the capital-intensive technology in fertilizer production and the maximum ratio was 13.9 per cent in brick-making. Taking the nine industries as a whole, use of the AT would generate over four times as much employment as the capital-intensive technology (Table 3) and also more income per unit of capital.

### Table 3 Employment and capital–labour ratios

| | Employment[a] | | Fixed capital per worker | | |
| --- | --- | --- | --- | --- | --- |
| | Appropriate[b] Technology | Capital-Intensive Technology | Appropriate thousands | Capital-Intensive thousands | Ratio of 3 to 4 |
| | 1 | 2 | 3 | 4 | 5 |
| Beer-Brewing | 7,460 | 4,316 | 12.1 | 18.3 | 1.5 |
| Brick-Making | 29,909 | 2,182 | 3.3 | 45.8 | 13.9 |
| Cotton-Spinning | 10,747 | 4,528 | 2.0 | 14.7 | 7.4 |
| Cotton-Weaving | 10,488 | 2,538 | 8.7 | 37.6 | 4.3 |
| Fertilizer | 772 | 691 | 122.3 | 137.6 | 1.1 |
| Leather-Processing | 4,502 | 2,108 | 15.5 | 36.2 | 2.3 |
| Maize-Milling | 19,231 | 7,574 | 2.9 | 9.7 | 3.3 |
| Shoes | 31,589 | 18,158 | 0.8 | 2.2 | 2.8 |
| Sugar-Processing | 123.980 | 15,925 | 0.8 | 6.2 | 7.8 |
| TOTAL | 238,678 | 58,017 | 5.8[c] | 21.3[c] | 3.7[c] |

Source: Pack, 1982.
[a] For an equivalent level of output.
[b] Appropriate is here defined as the technique which was most profitable using prices typical of a low-income developing country. In fact, more labour-intensive technologies were also available, but these would have only been profitable at shadow prices.
[c] Excluding fertilizer (averages).

A World Bank study conducted by Little *et al* has questioned the efficiency of small-scale industry, suggesting that, when ranked by employment, middle-sized firms (with 20–200 employees) have the highest capital productivity. However, when they rank size of firm by the value of the capital stock, capital-intensity rose monotonically and capital-productivity fell as size increased in both Colombia and Japan. In a detailed study of five industries in India this was also broadly true (see Table 4), with smaller firms showing higher capital productivity and lower capital per worker than large firms in all five industries. Although the optimal size in terms of maximizing capital productivity varied, it was by no means always the smallest size. The findings suggest that intermediate-sized technologies are likely to be the most efficient. Thus the study does not contradict the other findings reported here, but usefully underlines the need to consider efficiency as well as other dimensions, and shows, as suggested above, that not all small and labour-intensive activities are efficient. The study also reports that inter-industry differences in labour-intensity can greatly outweigh intra-industry differences.[5]

9

**Table 4 Capital productivity and capital labour ratios in Indian industries**

| Size by Capital Assets | PRINTING | | MACHINE TOOLS | | SOAP | | SHOES | | METAL CASTING | |
|---|---|---|---|---|---|---|---|---|---|---|
| | $\frac{O}{K}$ | $\frac{K}{L}$ | $\frac{O}{K}$ | $\frac{K}{L}$ | $\frac{O}{K}$ | $\frac{K}{L}$ | $\frac{O}{K}$ | $\frac{K}{L}$ | $\frac{O}{K}$ | $\frac{K}{L}$ |
| Rupees | | | | | | | | | | |
| Under 1,000 | – | – | – | – | – | – | 42.3* | 0.1 | – | – |
| 1,000–5,000 | 4.8 | 1.3 | – | – | – | – | 18.4 | 0.3 | 10.7 | 0.3 |
| 5,000–10,000 | 5.4 | 1.6 | – | – | 4.2* | 2.4 | 9.7 | 0.6 | – | – |
| 10,000–20,000 | 5.8* | 1.9 | – | – | 3.8 | 2.4 | 9.4 | 0.8 | 6.8 | 0.9 |
| 20,000–50,000 | 4.0 | 3.3 | 3.2 | 2.0 | 2.4 | 3.2 | 8.6 | 1.3 | 10.7 | 1.2 |
| 50,000–100,000 | 3.5 | 4.1 | 3.3* | 2.3 | 1.4 | 7.1 | 6.3 | 1.7 | 8.9 | 2.6 |
| 200,000–300,000 | 1.4 | 9.0 | 2.1 | 3.1 | 1.6 | 7.5 | – | – | 6.5 | 1.9 |
| 400,000–500,000 | 1.6 | 11.0 | 1.8 | 4.7 | 2.8 | 3.9 | – | – | 8.4 | 3.3 |
| 500,000– 1 m | 1.4 | 10.7 | 2.2 | 4.8 | 2.4 | 5.4 | 3.4 | 4.3 | 7.8 | 2.7 |
| More than 1 m | 1.1 | 11.7 | 1.8 | 8.8 | – | – | 6.1 | 2.6 | 2.7 | 9.5 |

Source: Little, 1987. K = Capital L = Labour O = Output
* Indicates maximum capital productivity. Note: this does not indicate that the technology is necessarily most efficient, but more labour-using technologies with lower capital productivity would almost certainly be less efficient.

It is clear from the evidence presented here that efficient, small-scale and labour-intensive technologies do exist in many industries, Even in industries where the 'core' technology is capital-intensive, alternative more labour-intensive ancillary activities are often possible.[6] In many cases, these more appropriate techniques also use more locally produced inputs, including locally produced machinery (many of the simple rice mills, for example, are produced in the countries in which they are used), and make greater use of local materials, as well as produce more appropriate products. In some cases, it seems that the appropriate technologies also make greater use of female labour. For example, a survey in Zambia showed that in small-scale enterprises women accounted for 65 per cent of ownership and 55 per cent of employment, whereas women account for only 8 per cent of jobs in the formal sector.[7] The dhenki in Bangladesh used 100 per cent female labour, compared with 19 per cent in the small rice huller and 4 per cent in the large rice huller.[8] In general, the jobs provided by these technologies are accessible to low-income groups and the products are consumed by low-income households. In the case of brewing in Botswana, over half the earnings of the home brewing method went to those in the bottom 65 per cent of the income distribution and 5 per cent to the richest 5 per cent whereas in the factory alternative 29 per cent went to the lowest 65 per cent and 47 per cent of the earnings to the richest 5 per cent.[9]

Despite the superior or equal efficiency of these technologies, the fact that they economize on scarce capital resources and use more abundant labour and have a relatively favourable impact on income distribution, most investment in Third World countries is in large-scale and often inappropriate technologies. For example, recent investment decisions in cotton spinning in Thailand were in the semi-advanced technology, not the more efficient intermediate technology (Santikarn). In the Philippines, a sophisticated, large rice mill was recently introduced which would put out of work hundreds of small village rice mills.[10] In Tanzania, a multinational company chose a large, capital-intensive roller-mill, even though the economic and social profitability was much lower than the smaller, labour-intensive hammer mill (Bagachwa). In Kenya, the OPS technology for sugar processing accounts for only 1.7 per cent of total production (Kaplinsky). Parastatal investments in both Kenya and Tanzania consistently adopt inappropriate technologies (James). These are just a few examples among many. Overall, in the early 1970s employment in manufacturing rose by just 0.02 per cent for every one per cent increase in value-added in Africa, falling by 0.02 per cent in Asia. In the latter part of the decade it fell quite significantly in both areas, providing an aggregate indication of the capital-intensity of investment decisions during that period.[11]

The choice of generally inappropriate technology has thus proceeded in spite of its inability to meet either economic or social objectives. One very important reason for this has been countries' macro- and meso-policy environment. The next section considers how this environment has affected technology choice, and the nature of technology change in inefficient and inappropriate directions.

## The policy environment, technology choice and technology change

Government macro- and meso- policies affect technology choices and the development of technology by determining the environment in which decisions on technology are made. Actual investment decisions on choice of technology are, of course, made at the micro-level by a variety of decision-making units – private firms and farms, large and small, foreign and domestic, parastatals, co-ops, and family enterprises. These different types of decision-makers are described here as 'micro-enterprises' or 'units'. Micro-enterprises are greatly affected by the macro- and meso-policy environment – which helps determine the prices they get for their products, the cost of the factors they use, the availability of alternative technologies and their knowledge about these alternatives, the availability of infra-structure, and so on.

*Macro-policies* are those that affect the aggregates of the economy – the total money supply and credit creation, the level of taxation and public expenditure, the prevailing interest rates, exchange rates and the extent of trade protection. *Meso-policies* are policies that are concerned with the distributional and sectoral consequences of the macro-policies. Thus, meso-policies consist of those policies which determine the distributional impact

11

of the tax system (which income groups and which categories of expenditure are affected by any aggregate level of taxation), the allocation of public expenditure and subsidies, price policy toward different sectors, science and technology policy, the distribution of tariffs and quotas and so on. While macro-policies are concerned with the aggregates, meso-policies are concerned with how these aggregates translate into burdens or benefits for particular sectors or income groups. (In an earlier work[3] the term 'macro-policies' was used for both these categories, but this tends to create some confusion because the term is more commonly used for policies affecting the aggregates. Thus here we follow the terminology used in Cornia *et al*[12], dividing the policies into macro and meso.)

Individual enterprises have certain objectives which they aim to meet, subject to their conditions and constraints. These constraints include the resources and technology to which they have access, and the markets in which they operate. Consequently at the level of the individual enterprise, policies which influence their decisions will include those affecting their objectives, their access to resources, technology availability, and their markets. For the rural sector, rural linkages determine the dynamism of rural activities, and the extent of investments in AT in the rural areas. Policies which impinge on rural linkages are therefore of major significance for rural AT. For the economy as a whole, policies toward the composition of units (ie, the proportion of total investment resources controlled by different decision-making units) greatly influence the nature of technology choices in the economy as a whole. Then, cutting across these factors and operating at various levels in the economy, policies toward organization and institutional choices affect technology choice and change in a variety of ways. In the rest of this section, we shall discuss our findings with respect to each of these categories.

### Objectives

The objectives of each micro-enterprise may consist of profit maximization, satisficing, bureaucratic objectives, employment maximization, or maximizing family income and employment. Objectives vary according to the type of enterprise and the general environment. In principle, if prices broadly reflect scarcities, then profit-maximizing objectives are likely to lead to choice of appropriate technologies, while other objectives may result in overly capital-intensive technologies.

The studies showed three types of decision-making units whose objectives *did not* favour AT. First, Santikarn[13] showed that in Thailand many modern large-scale cotton spinning firms, both foreign and domestically owned, chose more capital-intensive technologies 'than what is actually needed for profit maximization'. She suggests that 'satisficing' motivation may explain these choices. Similar results were found in other industries in Thailand by Lecraw[14] and by Bell and Scott-Kemis.[15] Second, James' study showed *consistently inappropriate technology choice by parastatals in Tanzania and Kenya*, despite the existence of more appropriate technologies and (in Tanzania) government-declared objectives of promoting equality, which should have been supportive of AT.[16] The inappropriate technology choices in the government-controlled firms may seem surprising, in view of government control of their activities. James explained these choices as resulting from *bureaucratic objectives*, which he hypothesized are to increase investment and expand output, leading to greater use of foreign finance and, therefore, foreign technology. Aid agencies formed a third category whose objectives did not appear to favour AT. There were a number of examples of aid-finance for inappropriate technologies – for example the integrated rice plant and tractorization programme in the Philippines, and the capital-intensive sugar technology chosen in Kenya. According to Wangwe and Bagachwa: 'Foreign assistance has encouraged the parastatal sector to continue to invest in new large-scale, capital and import-intensive plants and machinery, despite prevalence of excess capacity in existing plants'.[17] While there were a few cases where aid had favoured more appropriate technologies (eg, aid support for some of the MOSTIs) the balance of aid decisions appeared inappropriate. The objectives of aid donors – to maximize aid flows while minimizing bureaucratic costs, as well as to tie aid to supplies provided by the donor country – seem to be largely responsible.

Two types of policies can affect objectives: those affecting the general environment in which enterprises operate and those impinging on the objectives of particular enterprises. It should be noted that the policies may not necessarily be intended to have the effects noted on technology choice, or even be directed at the technology issue at all.

A more competitive environment makes it more difficult for firms exhibiting non-maximizing behaviour to be successful or even to survive. Greater competition can be induced through a more open trading environment, introducing greater international competition, or through domestic competition policies. In the countries studied neither type of competition was strong, so firms were able to make sufficient profits without choosing the most efficient technologies.

More direct interventions are possible in the public sector – both for parastatals and aid agencies. In most cases parastatals are permitted to make losses and are rarely, if ever, forced out of business. The success of managers running parastatals is not assessed with reference to the profitability of their enterprise. A change in these arrangements, requiring parastatals to generate a surplus and providing greater competition among parastatals, would help shift the objectives away from dominance by 'bureaucratic' man. Changed procedures and smaller, more decentralized units would also contribute to more 'maximizing' behaviour and more appropriate decisions within the public sector.

James[16] found that the heavy reliance on finance from advanced countries among parastatals led to the use of advanced and often inappropriate technology, without any systematic technology search. This tie-up between finance and technology might be reduced by diversifying financial sources (eg, toward other Third World countries) and by reducing project finance in favour of sectoral or programme finance.

Within aid agencies, the objective of achieving large rapid disbursements is partly responsible for inappropriate decisions. This objective should be rejected in favour of the adoption of more appropriate and efficient technologies. Changed procedures, reducing bureaucratic requirements, and making greater use of intermediary institutions to disburse funds to small projects would also be helpful. Aid tying also contributes to inappropriate choices by permitting aid only for capital goods supplied by the donor country. In Tanzania it was suggested that the use of donor consultants for aid projects almost invariably led to recommendations for the use of technology, often inappropriate, supplied from the consultant's own country.[17]

For both parastatals and aid agencies the use of efficient AT should form an explicit part of their objectives.

### Resources

The major policies which influence the price and availability of resources facing the micro-enterprise are: policies toward taxes and investment promotion schemes; credit policies; policies toward international trade and foreign exchange; and labour market policies. In general, as will be seen, prevalent policies are *hostile* to AT.

### Policies toward taxation and investment promotion

Many governments have introduced schemes to promote industrial investment, with tax holidays and tax relief, in the form of accelerated depreciation provisions, as the most important elements. These schemes almost invariably discriminate in favour of the use of capital, and of large-scale producers.

In the cases to be reviewed here, two examples will be discussed: Thailand and the Philippines. These cases are typical of many more.

In Thailand, investment incentives were introduced by the Board of Investment in 1960, with benefits consisting of guarantees (against nationalization, competition from state enterprises); permission (special permission being given to bring in foreign staff, own land, repatriate profits); protection (import bans and surcharges against foreign competition and tariff relief on imports) and tax incentives (exemption from corporate income tax and other taxes). Board requirements on minimum size and capital investment meant that small firms were not eligible for these privileges; the larger the firm the longer the tax holiday.

14

'Consequently, many small agro-processing firms in industrial industries such as rice mills, tapioca processing plants are not promoted'.[13] Among large cotton spinning firms, the majority (25 out of 34) claimed to be unaffected by the policies in their choice of technology. Hypothetical estimates showed that the absence of a capital equipment tax reduced costs of the intermediate technology by 6.8 per cent, and of the semi-advanced technology by 8.5 per cent, but a bigger effect resulted from the interest rate reduction for promoted firms, which reduced costs of the intermediate technology by 29.5 per cent and of the semi-advanced technology by 34 per cent. The overall cost reduction of the promotion policies were 34.6 per cent for the intermediate technology and 38.7 per cent for the semi-advanced. Non-promoted firms, which included almost all small firms, were thereby heavily penalized.[13]

In the Philippines, the Investment Incentives Act of 1967 and the Export Incentives Act of 1970 gave a package of fiscal incentives to manufacturing enterprises registered with the Board of Investments. Nearly all the incentives had the effect of cheapening capital. They included:

○ Tax exemption on imported capital acquired within 7 years from the date of registration of the company. This reduced the cost of imported equipment by 10 to 20 per cent;
○ Tax credit on domestic capital equipment equivalent to 100 per cent of customs duties;
○ Tax deduction of expansion reinvestment.

There were also some incentives favouring labour use, including tax deduction of half the expenses of labour training and a wage subsidy for exporters, although the 1977 ILO Report on the Philippines found these to be generally ineffective.[18]

Analysis of the overall effects of these incentives showed that the user cost of capital was reduced by 49 to 71 per cent while labour cost declined by 3.5 per cent for non-exporting firms and 22 per cent for exporting firms. The estimated effects were a reduction of 35.6 per cent in employment for non-exporting firms and 6.9 per cent for exporting firms (see Gregory, quoted in Bautista[19]). These estimates depend on rather arbitrary assumption of the life of the project, the discount rate and the elasticity of substitution.

**Policies toward credit**
Many governments have provided low-cost credit for selected enterprises as a means of promoting investment. For the most part, this credit has been mainly secured by large enterprises, while most small-scale enterprises have had to finance their investment either from their own savings or by borrowing at very high cost from the informal sector. The allocation of subsidized credit has thus tended to favour large-scale enterprises, while the

relative cheapening of capital has favoured the choice of more capital-intensive technologies by recipient enterprises. The private banking system has also tended to favour large-scale and established firms because of the relatively low risks associated with lending to them and the heavy use of collateral.

In the Philippines, the firms registered with the Board of Investment for fiscal privileges (see above) also have preferential access to low-interest credit, which reduces the cost of capital by 9 to 35 per cent (Mejia quoted in Bautista[19]). Limited access to low-price credit by small enterprises changed the composition of units in favour of the large-scale firms, as did the government's 11 large projects, all highly capital-intensive, which together were estimated to cost $US4bn or 10 per cent of one year's GNP. Subsidized credit was also provided for a tractorization programme in a joint World Bank/Government Programme.

In Thailand, the government subsidizes farm credits through the Bank for Agriculture and Agricultural Co-operatives. Fixed assets are required as collateral, preventing those with very few assets from securing loans. There is a fairly low upper limit to individual loans and the policy has probably not had a very large effect on farm mechanization. In the manufacturing sector in a similar situation to that in the Philippines, 'promoted' firms (see above) receive credit at 9 per cent interest, which, as shown earlier, had significant cost-reducing and capital-cheapening effects.

In Tanzania, 'the domestic capital market has been heavily subsidized by the high rates of domestic inflation and low interest rates'.[17] The real cost of institutional borrowing has been negative since 1978. Official low priced credit is allocated administratively through the Central Bank of Tanzania. This mechanism has led 'to the bulk of loanable funds being allocated to the large-scale public sector, firms which are both the most politically and economically adept of the eligible recipients'.[17] The small-scale sector has been excluded from the institutional market for credit on grounds of higher risks and administrative costs of lending.

In both Bangladesh and Zimbabwe, the small-scale sector has also been largely excluded from borrowing from the established financial institutions at relatively low interest rates. In Bangladesh, Ahmad showed that rural entrepreneurs have extremely limited access to institutional credit – a 1979 survey showed that only 6 per cent of rural enterprises received any credit, and of these only one-fifth got institutional credit. Their limited access to institutional credit is attributed to lack of collateral, lack of knowledge about sources of credit, intricate official formalities, the need for bribes, plus a long gestation period (sometimes 5 months or more) and a substantial cost in time (12 to 20 days) in pursuing the credit allocation.[8]

In Zimbabwe, 'almost all private sector lending by financial institutions

16

goes to well-established firms'.[20] This is attributed to the fact that the banks make their lending decisions on the basis of prior earnings, credit history and balance sheets, all of which operate against new and small firms, and those with little collateral.

Surveys of sources of credit for small firms elsewhere have shown that less than 1 per cent come from formal sources.[21] Small-scale enterprises either finance their investment from their own savings or from the informal money market.

According to a 1975 survey, in two-thirds of developing countries, formal sector nominal interest rates were 10 per cent or less.[22] Rates of interest in the informal sector in contrast often exceed 100 per cent per annum. The huge differences in rates are shown in Table 5.

**Table 5 Real interest rates per annum**

|  | Informal Sector | Formal Sector |
| --- | --- | --- |
| Ethiopia | 66 | 8 |
| Ghana | 64 | 0 |
| Ivory Coast | 145 | 6 |
| Nigeria | 192 | −2 |
| Sudan | 120 | 7 |
| Sierra Leone | 60 | −3 |
| India | 15 | −1 |
| Indonesia | 29 | 3 |
| Malaysia | 58 | 16 |
| Pakistan | 27 | 4 |
| South Korea | 49 | 5 |
| Sri Lanka | 20 | −1 |
| Bolivia | 96 | 5 |
| Brazil | 38 | −7 |
| Chile | 52 | −16 |
| Colombia | 40 | 16 |
| Costa Rica | 20 | 4 |
| Honduras | 37 | 6 |
| Mexico | 57 | 7 |

Source: Haggblade et al, 1986.

The dual credit market has a doubly negative effect on the choice of technology. On the one hand, it generates disproportionate access to funds by the large-scale firms adversely affecting the composition of units. On the other, it cheapens the price of capital and thus favours excessively capital-intensive technology choice among large-scale firms, while the resulting scarce and very expensive capital among small firms may lead to insufficient use of capital in this sector.

17

However, it should be emphasized that the situation is by no means only a result of government provision of subsidized credit. Even in the absence of such action, the small-scale sector would receive a relatively small share of total credit from formal sector institutions because of the requirements for collateral, and bureaucratic procedures. A purely 'market' (ie, no government intervention) solution would not, therefore, be sufficient to get credit to the small-scale sector. <u>Institutional innovation is also needed to overcome the obstacles faced by small enterprises.</u>

## Policies toward international trade

### Exchange rates
Many countries, following an import-substituting industrialization policy, maintained high exchange rates, accompanied by heavy tariffs (and/or quotas) on consumer goods with reduced (or zero) tariffs on capital goods. This was the case, for example, in the Philippines in the 1950s and 1960s, in Costa Rica and Colombia in the 1960s and 1970s and in Zimbabwe and Tanzania.

The combination of overvalued exchange rate and low tariffs on capital goods artificially lowered the price of capital, thus encouraging substitution of capital for labour. In addition, the foreign exchange regime discriminated against exports in favour of the production of import-substitutes for the domestic market. As a result, growth of labour-intensive exports was inhibited. In the Philippines the contribution of labour-intensive exports to total exports was very small in the 1950s and 1960s, but after the exchange rate regime changed in the 1970s and the exchange rate was reduced, labour-intensive exports grew rapidly. According to Bautista:

> Not only would growth have been more sustainable had the foreign trade regime been more neutral: labour employment and use of locally produced imports would have been greater, in view of the country's cooperative advantage in labour-intensive products.[19]

The overvalued exchange rate also discriminated *against agriculture* thereby reducing agricultural growth and potential rural linkages, as was widely documented by most of the studies on Latin America, as well as the Philippines, Thailand and Tanzania.

Trade restrictions and exchange rate overvaluation – sometimes complemented by domestic price controls on food items – were estimated to have reduced domestic agricultural prices relative to non-agricultural goods by over 100 per cent in the 1950s in the Philippines, by 45 per cent in the 1960s and around 20 per cent in the 1970s.[19] However, in the Philippines, like Mexico, where there was a similar discrimination against agriculture by macro-policies, this was at times partially offset by sectoral policies providing irrigation and subsidizing imports and credit (see de

18

## Table 6 Degree of currency overvaluation [percentage]

|  | Year | Indications of degree of currency overvalued |
|---|---|---|
| *Africa* | | |
| Botswana | 1983[a] | 10 |
| Cameroon | 1979[b] | 0 |
| Ghana | 1983[a] | 228 |
| Egypt | 1983[a] | 66 |
| Ivory Coast | 1979[b] | 10 |
| Kenya | 1983[a] | 17 |
| Malawi | 1983[a] | 60 |
| Nigeria | 1983[a] | 45 |
| Senegal | 1979[b] | 40 |
| Sierra Leone | 1983[a] | 37 |
| Sierra Leone | 1976[b] | 15 |
| Tunisia | 1983[a] | 12 |
| Zambia | 1983[a] | 27 |
| *Asia* | | |
| Bangladesh | 1983[a] | 42 |
| Hong Kong | 1983[a] | 0 |
| India | 1983[a] | 28 |
| Indonesia | 1983[a] | 0 |
| Malaysia | 1965[c] | 4 |
| Malaysia | 1983[a] | 1 |
| Pakistan | 1963[c] | 50 |
| Pakistan | 1983[a] | 30 |
| Philippines | 1963[c] | 15 |
| Philippines | 1983[a] | 50 |
| South Korea | 1983[a] | 8 |
| Taiwan | 1965[c] | 20 |
| Taiwan | 1983[a] | 6 |
| *Latin America* | | |
| Argentina | 1958[c] | 100 |
| Argentina | 1983[a] | 11 |
| Brazil | 1966[c] | 50 |
| Brazil | 1983[a] | 37 |
| Chile | 1966[c] | 68 |
| Chile | 1983[a] | 17 |
| Colombia | 1968[c] | 22 |
| Colombia | 1983[a] | 21 |
| Jamaica | 1983[a] | 14 |
| Honduras | 1983[a] | 43 |
| Mexico | 1960[c] | 15 |
| Mexico | 1983[a] | 20 |

Sources: [a] Haggblade *et al* (1986), World Currency Yearbook (1984); black market premiums as of 31 December 1983; [b] Jansen (1980); [c] Healy (1972): cit. Little, *et al* (1970) and Balassa (1971).

Jesus Brambila, p. 2 in Bautista[19]). In Thailand, the exchange rate was estimated to have been significantly overvalued between 1960 and 1984. The combined effects of this, the tariff policy and policies toward agricultural prices was a large (but declining) outflow of resources from the agricultural to the urban sector.[23] In Tanzania, the exchange rate became increasingly overvalued during the 1970s and 1980s, with an estimated real appreciation of 56 per cent between 1970–8, and 120 per cent between 1979–85.[17] The overvaluation caused agricultural prices to be reduced and agricultural output to stagnate.[24]

Estimates of currency overvaluation in 28 countries are shown in Table 6. In recent years, however, many countries have devalued their currencies (usually as part of their IMF programme), while others have in effect depreciated because their currencies are tied to the dollar, so that there has been a major real exchange rate devaluation among developing countries of around 30 per cent over the 3 years from 1984–87, much reducing the extent of currency overvaluation. (See IMF *World Economic Outlook*, April 1988.) It must be noted that any estimates of the extent of overvaluation are arbitrary, since they imply that we know precisely what the 'correct' rate is. We do not. Some considerations argue for a degree of overvaluation compared with a free market rate, especially for primary producers, but there are also strong arguments for avoiding excessive overvaluation and protection from many points of view, including those of promoting AT.)

*Tariff structure*
The tariff structure also typically discriminated against small-scale investors, as many of the machines used by the small-scale sector are classified as *consumer goods* and subject to a high rate of tariff, in contrast to the lower or zero tariffs on large-scale imports of capital goods. For example, in Sierra Leone, sewing machines and outboard motors were classified as consumer goods, subject to tariffs of 35 per cent; in Burkina Faso, import duties on handtools were 72 per cent, and on sewing machines 41 per cent (Haggblade *et al.*).

In many countries, duty-free imports are permitted to the large-scale investors as part of the investment promotion policy; eg, in the Philippines tractors were subject to a zero duty, while power tillers were taxed at 19 per cent.[19] In Argentina, it was estimated that duty-free imports of machinery were equivalent to a subsidy on large-scale production of 40 per cent.[25] In Sierra Leone, it was estimated that duty-free capital imports of the large-scale investors amounted to a subsidy to them of around 25 per cent.[26] The effective tariff protection for large-scale clothing producers was 430 per cent, while the small firms with whom they compete received an effective rate of protection of 29 per cent.[26] The structure of protection in Tanzania 'has also tended to overprotect ... the large-scale inefficient

20

firms at the expense of small-scale efficient firms'.[17] A World Bank study showed that 'while a small-scale firm employing less than 25 workers has an effective rate of protection below 10 per cent, the large enterprise employing over 250 workers enjoys a rate of protection well over 2,000 per cent'.[17,27]

### Administrative mechanisms for allocating foreign exchange

Countries following import-substituting strategies, especially when subject to acute foreign exchange shortages, have usually allocated foreign exchange through administrative controls. This was the case, for example, in both Tanzania and Zimbabwe and also the Philippines. In both cases, the controls tended to favour large-scale producers, at the expense of small-scale producers.

In Tanzania, the system of administrative allocation and import licensing has been 'vulnerable to the lobbying strength of the applicant, the crisis nature of the application and overall foreign exchange available and other political considerations. Because of their political and economic power, parastatal enterprises have been receiving a disproportionate share of allocations of foreign exchange ...'.[17]

In Zimbabwe, foreign exchange is allocated by the government in a way that strongly favours existing firms.[20] The appropriateness of the technology is not a criterion. Both bureaucratic procedures and allocation criteria tend to favour large and established firms and discriminate against the small-scale sector (Ndlela).

Evidence of how administrative allocation of foreign exchange is biased against small-scale producers was also shown in Bhagwati's nine-country study, which suggested that even in countries which believe they favoured the small applicants 'ex post outcomes appear to have been disturbingly concentrated on the large-scale applicants'.[28] Countries showing a bias in favour of the large importers included Ghana, India, and Pakistan. The bias was attributed to factors similar to those found to be significant in Tanzania and Zimbabwe: bureaucratic procedures which favour the large scale; and a bias in favour of known and established producers.

While administrative procedures thus usually do *not* help small-scale producers, market solutions – especially in the context of severe disequilibrium – do not necessarily always help either. In Zambia, administrative allocation of foreign exchange was replaced by allocation through auction in 1985. The result was that the small producers (and the agricultural sector) secured almost *no* foreign exchange, as they lacked the resources to put in a competitive bid. The main beneficiaries were the multinational companies and the parastatals (Ncube *et al*[29]).

Policies to promote AT will not only need to eliminate government-imposed distortions, but may also have to introduce some special mechanisms to ensure adequate access to foreign exchange and credit by small-scale producers during the transitional period.

## Labour market policies

Labour market policies form another 'distortion' that tends to bias technology choice toward capital-intensive technologies. These are policies such as minimum wage laws, social security requirements and restrictions on work hours, which raise the cost of labour in the formal sector and thus tend to reduce employment in that sector. These laws do not extend to the informal sector, where the cost of labour tends to be much lower. Since they raise costs in the formal sector, they increase the competitive edge of the informal sector and may thereby increase total employment, by having a positive effect on the composition of units.[30] These labour market policies are typically not effective in reducing poverty, since while they raise incomes in the formal sector they contribute to depressing them in the rest of the economy, where poverty is usually worse.

From the evidence of these studies and of others,[26] it seems that labour market policies – while they usually do operate to increase labour costs in the formal sector – are only of minor significance in quantitative terms as compared with the many capital-cheapening policies discussed above. In part also these negative substitution effects are offset by the positive composition of unit effects.

In the Philippines, minimum wage legislation and supplementary allowances for workers raise the price of labour, but these are partly offset by a subsidy on labour among promoted firms.[19] In contrast, in Tanzania wage policies have been used to reduce differentials among workers and between urban and rural sectors. Real urban wages have fallen sharply since the late 1970s, but policies restricting employers' authority to lay off workers have encouraged capital-intensive technology choices.[17]

While most evidence shows a large wage gap between large and medium/small enterprises, much of this is not due to labour-market policies but to differences in skills and large firms' desire to reduce labour turnover since many large firms pay wages above the legislated minimum. The increase in formal sector labour costs was estimated to range from 15 to 27 per cent in selected African and Latin American countries in the early 1970s (Haggblade, Table 4). Most observers found these to have had only minor effects (see Berry and Sabot[31]). Large reductions in real wages in the 1980s, with the debt crisis, will have further diminished the significance of these effects.

## Aggregate effects of policies toward resources (labour and capital)

On balance, government policies have acted to cheapen capital to the formal sector through tax and promotional policies, credit policies and exchange rate and tariff policies, while allocation of credit and of foreign exchange has favoured the large-scale formal sector and discriminated against the small-scale sector. Labour market policies have tended to raise the cost of labour in the formal sector. Consequently, relative prices of

22

labour and capital have been altered to favour capital-using techniques in the formal sector. Since the informal sector has faced excessively high prices for capital and low prices for labour it has been encouraged to use too little capital. The composition of units effect of credit and foreign exchange mechanisms have favoured large-scale capital-intensive enterprises, but the labour market effects have worked in the opposite direction. The net effect has undoubtedly strongly favoured the capital-intensive sector. However, as noted in a number of areas, it is not only government policies that have had these effects, but also the institutional arrangements. Thus market solutions (eg, applied to credit and foreign exchange allocation) sometimes need to be supplemented by other policies to secure sufficient allocation of resources for the small-scale sector – to secure what we shall call a 'structured market'.

## Technology

The range of technology known and available to a firm limits its possible technology choice. This range depends on the development of and information about alternative technologies. It is a function of the level and direction of government research and development and information services, as well as enterprises' R & D and access to information.

Policies toward the creation and dissemination of technology include policies toward government financed R & D and dissemination, tax/subsidy policies, and policies toward patents.

The studies showed few attempts to develop technology in an appropriate direction and for the small-scale sector. However, where such efforts were made they succeeded in creating competitive technology. Some examples illustrate the potential significance of R & D for the development of efficient small-scale technologies:

o In the case of the OPS sugar technology, R & D in India increased productivity so that a previously inefficient technology could become competitive with the VPS technology;[32]
o The axial flow paddy thresher, developed for small farmers by the International Rice Research Institute, was rapidly taken up in the Philippines and Thailand, and produced by 70 firms in the Philippines and over 20 in Thailand by 1985. Cumulative sales were 55,000 units in 1984, some in Egypt, Honduras, Ivory Coast, Ghana, Colombia and Mexico;[33]
o In Costa Rica, technology development of traditional lime production permitted cement to be replaced by lime;[34]
o In Guatemala, applied research improved the productivity of wool production by small producers by improving genetic material;[35]
o In Kenya, development of improved cooking stoves (lined stoves), led to production by small private workshops. Production started in 1983 and by mid-1988 about 200,000 stoves had been sold.[36]

Most of these successful examples resulted from R & D efforts which had LDC government public or aid support. But in Colombia, innovations occurred among small firms without public support. These examples all indicate the potential of R & D for increasing productivity of small enterprises, while the low efficiency of the dhenki and the MOSTI underline the need for such improvements. But these examples are rather unusual. More typically, R & D efforts are concentrated in large firms, or on large-scale or inappropriate technologies in the public sector (see eg, Beranek and Ranis, Crane[37]). Thus Rudra indicated that R & D in agriculture in India had been mainly focused on rather high cost, input-intensive technologies. In Bangladesh, despite the fact that 'upgrading the technological base of the economy has been a recurring theme in the successive five year plans ... little progress has so far been achieved', while the 'issue of technology for rural industry has been given a rather low priority ... there is not and never has been a clear-cut policy stance in favour of appropriate technology for rural industries'.[8]

In general, in the countries covered, technology policies do not systematically support appropriate technologies. ATs tend to emerge only as a result of special efforts, usually inspired by outside funding bodies. This is partly due to the institutional and reward structure of the science and technology organizations, partly to the political economy pressures the general environment which favours the development and use of inappropriate technology.

The legal system also appears either not to promote local technological development at all, or to be supportive of only the more sophisticated technologies. In Kenya, for example, patents are still registered in London, which would only be relevant for the more sophisticated technologies – generally only those developed by MNCs. Only the Philippines had the 'utility' system of patenting, used in Japan, which gives legal protection to simple technologies, with lower disclosure requirements and a more limited period of protection, which is applied in a bureaucratically simple fashion.

Technology dissemination also presents an obstacle to the transfer of appropriate technology to producers. There exist few effective industrial extension services anywhere in the Third World. Rural enterprises, especially, have very limited access to technological information, as was reported by participants in each of the three regions.

## Markets and products

Markets are important in determining the type of products produced and the scale of production. Both help determine the technologies used.

Markets may be focused on high-income or low-income households within the domestic market, or firms may sell to international consumers. Policies toward markets encompass trade policies, policies toward income distribution and rural linkages, and direct-products policies (which include policies toward advertisements, information systems, products standards and indirect taxes).

For the most part, high-income consumers require a more 'elite' style product with special characteristics, typically produced by modern capital-intensive technologies. A number of studies showed the close relationship between product standards and choice of technique, with the 'higher' standard products, associated with more capital-intensive technologies, more in demand among high-income consumers. The desire to sustain 'high' standards of product quality was put forward as a justification for capital-intensive technologies, by import-substitution industries in a large number of cases – for example, laundry detergent, bread, oil processing, printing ink, cement, maize-milling and beer in Tanzania.[16,17] Tastes for such products among the elite were developed initially through imports, while the import substitution strategy aimed to replicate the same product standards. Most of the cases cited above were of this type. Here inappropriate consumption standards stem partly from unequal income distribution, which means that even in a poor society there is demand for western style products among the elite, while the mass of the people, for whom different products would be appropriate, lack purchasing power. In this context, policies designed to improve income distribution through taxes, subsidies asset redistribution would be necessary to achieve a radical change in product choice.

The influence of international markets on choice of products and techniques is complex, depending on the type of market being served. On the one hand, countries which compete in international markets on the basis of their relatively cheap labour will tend to sell labour-intensive products, where low price compensates for low quality. Thus, more outward orientation will tend to increase labour-absorption. An example of this strategy is provided by Taiwan, where rapid growth of employment was associated with exporting such items as canned asparagus and mushrooms and textiles. Policies supporting, for example, a competitive exchange rate, make labour-intensive production attractive.

In contrast, other countries justify *capital-intensive* techniques on the grounds that 'high quality' products are necessary for exporting. For example, this was a justification used for the sophisticated rice mill in the Philippines, and for the rather advanced technology chosen in a shoe factory in Tanzania. (The World Bank Appraisal Report of this project stated that 'One fairly modern shoe factory presently produces leather and canvas shoes for the internal market. The output is of acceptable quality within Tanzania, but does not meet international standards. The new shoe factory ... would produce about 4 million pairs of shoes to international standards, primarily for export, but it is expected that a small part of the production will be sold internally' (IBRD, 1977, quoted in James[16]) In

25

these cases 'high quality' is used as a competitive device instead of low price. In neither case, in fact, did exports materialize. However, in pineapple canning in the Philippines, the more capital-intensive technique did result in successful export expansion but Taiwan also managed to export pineapples by selling its lower quality products, produced in a more labour-intensive fashion, to a lower niche of the international market.

The argument that exports require 'high' quality, and therefore choice of capital-intensive technology, is often regarded (as in these cases) as decisive, brooking no further argument. Yet deeper examination suggests the argument can often be misplaced. First, the export argument is often used when in fact exports do not materialize at all, or only in very small quantities, as was the case with both the projects cited here. Second, successful exporting does not necessarily require very high quality. There are no unique 'international' standards – the international market is made up of many markets of varying income levels, sophistication and quality requirements, as was clearly illustrated in the pineapple case. South–South markets and exports to low-income Northern consumers offer a potential for trade in more appropriate products. Low price can normally compensate for low quality in international markets. In some countries, as in the Philippines and Tanzania at this time, high product quality was expected to offset the high costs of production resulting from inappropriate macro-policies, especially overvalued exchange rates. In practice, this rarely happens and, when it does, the exports may not be worth promoting, since they require expensive imported machinery and use little local labour. For labour surplus countries, labour-intensive manufactured exports are more appropriate and these can best be secured by appropriate macro-policies, not by artificially upgrading product quality. Thus the need to serve export markets does not appear to be a justified defence of the choice of capital-intensive technologies.

An effective appropriate technology strategy should aim for the first approach to exporting – the export of labour-intensive goods – and not aim to compete on quality in markets where capital-intensity is necessary for success.

Besides those policies which affect product choice by influencing markets (including policies toward rural linkages, which will be discussed below), there are more direct product policies. The studies suggested that the most important direct product policies were government regulations, and parastatal decisions regarding product standards. Policies toward product development and information dissemination are also potentially important.

One direct product policy is to influence parastatal decisions on product choice. James showed that parastatal choices favour inappropriate product standards in areas where a market for more appropriate products and technologies could have been chosen and would have readily found a

26

market. The search for appropriate products should form an important part of the wider search by parastatals for appropriate technology.

Second, governments frequently influence the nature of private sector investment decisions when they approve technology transfer agreements, license investors to use foreign exchange or borrow domestically, or provide special tariff protection. In all these cases, the appropriateness of the product (and technique) should be taken into account in the technology search and decision-making criteria.

Third, government determined product standards and regulations mostly require inappropriate products and techniques. For example, standards of hygiene in food processing often lead to excessively high standards for a small segment of the population[38], while the majority of the people are unaffected since their food is produced in unregulated conditions. Building standards – including standards for brick and cement manufacture – also tend to capital-intensive choices. These standards were devised for the multistorey buildings used in large cities, and are quite unnecessary for the one- or two-storey buildings prevalent in many developing countries. However, in Tanzania the government banned the production of sembe superior (with an extraction rate of around 80 per cent) in order to encourage the production of sembe standard (with a 98 per cent extraction rate). Appropriate product standards and regulations are needed which are more relevant to conditions and levels of living in poor societies.

Other policies influencing product choice one way or another are indirect taxes and subsidies, policies toward advertising and information dissemination, and policies toward product development.

*Rural linkages*
Rural linkages refer to the connections between agriculture and non-agricultural activities in the rural areas. Where agricultural activity is flourishing and rural linkages are strong, rural industrialization develops rapidly. Since rural non-agricultural activities are typically small-scale and labour-intensive, strong rural linkages are favourable to the adoption of appropriate technology. In the early stages of development especially, strong development of rural industrial activities also promotes agricultural growth, by improving incentives for such growth and stimulating technology change and accumulation in the rural areas. The study of rural linkages in the Philippines and Taiwan showed the importance of rural linkages for AT.[10,39] Rural non-agricultural employment was shown to rise rapidly with expansion in agricultural output because of production and consumption linkages. A one per cent increase in agricultural output led to more than a one per cent increase in non-agricultural output and employment. The extent of rural linkages depends not only on the growth of agricultural output, but also on the agricultural strategy. Very dualistic or

bimodal agricultural development leads to weaker linkages than more egalitarian agriculture because if incomes are more evenly distributed consumption of locally produced goods is greater, and small farmers use more local inputs and local processing.[10, 39]

The comparison between Taiwan and the Philippines indicated the type of policies likely to favour rural linkages.[10] While both countries exhibited significant rural linkages, Taiwanese rural industry grew much faster than that of the Philippines. The first requirement for a dynamic rural sector is a sustained growth in agricultural output. Consequently, policies which favour agricultural growth, including both macro- and sectoral policies, are likely to promote rural linkages. The Latin American case studies revealed many instances where the agricultural sector had suffered from discriminatory macro-policies, especially overvalued exchange rates. In some cases, for example, in Mexico, these had been partially offset by favourable sectoral policies (subsidies for fertilizers, subsidized credit), but for the most part they tended to promote mechanization and support large farmers. The linkage studies showed that the *nature* of agricultural growth was also relevant to the size and nature of rural linkages; more labour intensive farming tended to involve larger local consumption linkages; smaller farms, as in Taiwan, tended to use simpler machines which were more often produced locally in small enterprises. Consequently, policies such as land reform and credit reform, which favour small farms, would tend to promote rural linkages. The institutional environment facing rural enterprises was also found to be important. In Taiwan, rural infrastructure (roads, electricity, and water) is much more abundant than in the Philippines, while rural credit institutions ensure access to credit for small enterprises. For example, in 1975, 26.5 per cent of rural households in the Philippines had electricity compared with almost total coverage of Taiwanese rural households. In Taiwan technology for rural enterprises, especially in agricultural products processing, is disseminated through the farmer associations and the Joint Commission for Rural Reconstruction. However, in the Philippines there are very few institutions which disseminate information to medium and small enterprises, particularly in the rural areas. In Taiwan, technological choice information was dispensed along with rural credit through the co-operative linking system within the farmer association structure. In the Philippine case, the science and technology infrastructure is directed toward urban large-scale and internationally specified objectives, with credit flows equally biased in that direction.

## Composition of units

There are systematic differences among different types of enterprise in the environments they face and consequently the major elements determining their behaviour. As a result, different decision-makers make different types

28

# Table 7 Composition of units and choice of technology

| TYPE OF DECISION-MAKER | OBJECTIVES | RESOURCES | MARKETS | TECHNOLOGY | CHOICE OF PRODUCT | CHOICE OF TECHNIQUE |
|---|---|---|---|---|---|---|
| *INDUSTRY* | | | | | | |
| AID DONORS | Maximize flow of funds: use of foreign technology | Cheap capital | | Advanced countries | | |
| GOVT/ PARASTATALS | Bureaucratic – output/project maximizing | Cheap capital if foreign financed | Local elite | Advanced countries – source of finance | Sophisticated/ inappropriate | K-intensive large scale |
| MULTI- NATIONAL CO | Maximize international profits satisficers | Cheap capital | International & local elite | Parent Co. Normally advanced | " | " |
| LARGE-SCALE CO | Profit maximizers | Cheapish capital | Mainly local elite | Foreign in-house | Mainly inappropriate | " |
| SMALL LOCAL CO (FORMAL) | Profit maximizers | Limited access to cheap capital; Labour cheap | Local elite & middle income | Variety of sources | More appropriate | More labour intensive |
| INFORMAL CO and FAMILIES | Maximize family income and employment | Expensive capital & limited; very cheap labour | Local low income | Primitive; AT support institutions | Appropriate | Very labour intensive & small |
| *AGRICULTURE* | | | | | | |
| LARGE FARMERS | Maximize profits | Cheap credit: subsidized tractors | Urban & inter- national | Government and foreign companies and aid institutions | Cash crops | Mechanized large tractors |
| MEDIUM/ SMALL | Maximize profits | More expensive credit – limited | Urban & rural | Same but more limited | Mainly cash crops | Small-scale machines |
| FAMILY | Maximize family income | Little credit, expensive. Very cheap labour | Mainly rural | Primitive | Mainly locally consumed foods | Mainly local and primitive tools |

of technology choices. Large units (MNCs; parastatals, large domestic companies) usually face lower capital costs, and pay higher wages than small firms. Large units have better and cheaper access to the latest technology, compared with the very limited access of small firms. Large units tend to sell mainly to high-income markets, domestically or inter-nationally. In contrast, most small units mainly sell low-income products to the informal sector. As a consequence of all these differences, the larger units tend to adopt more inappropriate technologies (large-scale, capital-intensive, producing more sophisticated products) than the small. This was illustrated in the studies in a large number of cases: for example, the OPS sugar technology was adopted by small firms while parastatals and multi-nationals adopted the VPS technology. Small farms bought the IRRI thresher, while large farms used tractors and large-scale mechanized threshers. Local companies in Taiwan used smaller-scale and more labour-intensive methods for pineapple canning than the multinationals in the Philippines. In Tanzania, the parastatals adopted the large roller mill technology, while the hammer mills were used by small private enterprises.

These differences between units are summarized in Table 7. As a result of these differences, the *composition of units*, that is the proportion of investment resources controlled by different types of decision-maker, greatly influences the types of technological decision made on balance in the economy as a whole. Policies which influence the composition of units include policies toward credit allocation, asset distribution, distribution of infrastructure, income distribution, and administrative procedures. The earlier discussion indicated the ways in which these policies have, in practice, favoured the large-scale sector, and the sorts of policies necessary to shift resources toward small-scale enterprises identified. Policy reforms would not only shift decisions within each enterprise in a more appropriate direction, but would also shift the balance of investment in the economy as a whole toward enterprises likely to make more appropriate decisions – that is, shift the composition of units.

## Institutions and Organizations

Appropriate institutions are an important feature of policies that favour AT. Institutions are pervasive since all activities take place within an institutional structure. The studies showed that some types of institution are much more favourable to AT than others and that the need for institutional reforms extends to many of the areas already mentioned. For example, many R & D institutions produce few applied results, and where they do these are often mainly directed toward capital-intensive technologies. There is little R & D devoted to upgrading rural tech-nologies. New types of R & D institutions and new incentive systems governing their operation are needed. Similarly, reforms are required in technology dissemination institutions. Institutional reform is an important aspect of getting credit to producers with few or no assets, as shown in the very successful case of the Grameen Bank.

Centralized forms of government appeared to work against appropriate technology, favouring the large-scale and the urban, as we have seen in terms of allocation of credit and of foreign exchange, and also in the allocation of infrastructural investment. It was argued strongly, especially in the Asian conference, that decentralization of the government machine, especially decentralized control over expenditure decisions, would assist in the development of rural enterprise, particularly if NGOs were involved to help in administration and monitoring. Institutional change is therefore needed in the structure of government.

In the same vein, institutional changes are needed in the structure of parastatals if they are to make more appropriate decisions. In the private sector, sub-contracting from large- to small-scale firms can permit efficient and dynamic small-scale enterprises, working in tandem with the large-scale sector, as in industrial development in Japan. Studies in Bangladesh and a number of Latin American countries emphasized the importance of producer organizations among small-scale enterprises, partly to permit sharing of technology and marketing, but more significantly to strengthen the bargaining power of the producers and their influence over governmental decisions. In Bangladesh, for example, small farmer associations were of critical importance for securing appropriate irrigation. In Costa Rica, co-operatives of coffee producers eased access to technology and markets for small producers. In Colombia, producer organizations had exerted pressure to secure technology development which was appropriate for small producers.

The development of appropriate organizations – and the reform of inappropriate ones – was thus found to be of wide significance, with relevance to most of the areas affecting technology choice and change. Yet, this factor has been little studied, compared with most other areas considered here. More research is needed to identify the scope of institutional reform as well as the precise nature of the reforms needed.

## Macro- and meso-policies for appropriate technology

Most prevailing macro- and meso-policies have tended to favour inappropriate technology, as indicated in the previous section. In many countries there have been special schemes to support small-scale industry, but generally the effects of these schemes, and of special interventions supporting AT, have been greatly outweighed by the generally hostile macro- and meso-policy environment.

Table 8 summarizes the policy changes identified as necessary to support AT. (A more detailed discussion of the changes is contained in the Appendix.) This section of the paper considers first the political economy of the policy changes identified and second their consistency with Fund/Bank policy packages.

### Political economy of policies and AT
The discussion above has briefly summarized the sorts of policies needed for AT. Yet, as shown earlier, in most countries these policies are not being

31

# Table 8: Macro and Meso-Policies for AT: A Summary

| Objectives | Resources | Technology | Markets/Products | Rural linkages | Composition of units | Organization/institutions |
|---|---|---|---|---|---|---|
| 1. PRIVATE SECTOR changed through more competitive environment, through<br><br>(a) National competition policies<br><br>(b) International<br><br>2. PARASTATAL OBJECTIVES changed through<br><br>(a) requiring surplus creation, except where specified for specific purpose<br><br>(b) changed procedures to include search for efficient AT<br><br>3. AID OBJECTIVES changed through<br><br>(a) removing rapid aid disbursement as objective<br><br>(b) reduced aid tying<br><br>(c) efficient AT to be included as objective | 1. *Tax and investment* promotion schemes for large-scale to be made more relevant abolished<br><br>2. Subsidized *credit* stopped. New credit schemes for small-scale producers with little collateral (as in Grameen Bank)<br><br>3. *Exchange rates* nearer market determined level; tariffs reformed to prevent discrimination against capital goods for small-scale; administrative mechanisms for foreign exchange allocation reformed to avoid existing biases<br><br>4. *Labour:* policies to raise wages and conditions in formal sector to be avoided 5. Credit and foreign exchange need *structured markets* to ensure adequate access for small-scale. | 1. Reform of *government R & D* institutes to make them more relevant<br>  ○ AT to be specific requirement<br>  ○ special institutions to develop ATs for small-scale and rural sector<br>  ○ new forms of financing<br><br>2. Improved system of *dissemination*, especially in rural areas<br><br>3. Reform of legal system, to include utility model of patenting | 1. Domestically, policies to improve *income distribution* and extend markets for APs, through tax system and asset distribution<br><br>2. Open *trade policies* to encourage labour-intensive exports<br><br>3. *Products policies*, including<br><br>(a) Product standards to be reformed to reflect appropriate standards<br><br>(b) Appropriate products to be considered in technology transfer and other investment decisions<br><br>(c) Parastatals to include appropriateness of products as criterion in decisions<br><br>(d) Information and tax systems to incorporate AP considerations. | 1. Macro and sectoral policies to support *egalitarian agricultural growth* through policies toward<br>  ○ agricultural pricing<br>  ○ agricultural credit<br>  ○ agricultural infrastructure<br><br>2. Support for *infrastructure* for rural industrialization, including<br>  ○ credit<br>  ○ technology dissemination<br>  ○ marketing<br>  ○ utilities and roads | Policies to redirect resources to small-scale and family enterprises:<br>  ○ credit reform (as resources)<br>  ○ asset redistribution<br>  ○ development of co-operatives and decentralized parastatals | Reforms in<br><br>1. Government administration more decentralized expenditure decisions; NGO monitoring<br><br>2. R & D institutions (as in technology)<br><br>3. Encourage sub-contracting from large private firms to small firms<br><br>4. Support for marketing institutions for small-scale<br><br>5. Support for producer organizations among small-scale<br><br>6. Reform of credit institutions (as in Resources) |

32

Cond. on c.id

adopted, but rather a set of policies unfavourable to AT is prevalent. One important reason for this dichotomy arises from the political economy obstacles to the changes proposed. To a very large extent, policies that favour AT tend to favour the low-income and relatively deprived (eg, small farmers and the landless, the informal sector and the unemployed).

The policies in place which favour inappropriate technology tend to benefit the 'haves' of society – the established big businessmen, bureaucrats, foreign technology suppliers, and large farmers. Detailed investigation of the beneficiaries and losers from alternative policies showed that this was the case in almost every example – in the Philippines, in Bangladesh, in India, in Keya, and Tanzania. (See the studies in Stewart[2] and the concluding part of this paper for evidence.) Similar forces seemed to prevail, with similar adoption of policies favouring inappropriate technology, in countries which were apparently very different: for example, in socialist Tanzania and capitalist Kenya; in aid-dependent Bangladesh and more self-reliant India. Thus the defensive forces of the self-interest of powerful groups are likely to present a very serious obstacle to the types of reforms identified above.

However, total pessimism regarding the possibility of adopting better policies is not warranted. In the first place, some elements of the policies advocated were to be found in a number of countries. For example, in Bangladesh the Grameen Bank has succeeded in lending to those without assets, with a very low default rate. The Self-Employed Women's Association has also been successful in India. The degree of exchange rate overvaluation has declined sharply in recent years in some countries. The Philippines greatly reduced the degree of overvaluation in the 1970s and Tanzania has done so in the 1980s, while some countries (eg, Taiwan) did so much earlier. Quantitative controls have been lessened and the differential tariffs on imports of capital goods reduced in several countries. These examples show that the possibility of policy reform cannot be ruled out because of the forces of political economy. There are more degrees of freedom than allowed for in recent analyses. (eg, by Bates[40]).

Second, careful analysis of the gainers and losers from different elements in the policy package shows that the type of political obstacles to be faced are likely to differ according to the policy instrument. An example is presented for rural linkages in the Philippines (Table 9). Thus while some policies are highly confrontational, with the gainers making their gains at the direct expense of other (usually powerful) groups, other policies can confer gains for some without severe losses for others. Land redistribution is an example of the first since, in the short run, all gains for the landless are likely to be at the expense of the large landowners. Technology development is an example of the second. The development of a new efficient and appropriate technology can raise incomes for the poor without reducing incomes of the better off, even in the short run, and in the medium term

33

**Table 9 Matrix of gains and losses from policies to promote rural linkages**

| INTEREST GROUP | POLICY CHANGE | | | | | | | |
| --- | --- | --- | --- | --- | --- | --- | --- | --- |
| | Promote Agric. Prices/ Credit | Investment | Policies within agriculture | | | Rural infra-structure | Forward Link | |
| | | | Land reform | Credit/ mech. | crop composition | Elect./ trans. | Credit | Support small-scale |
| Large landowners/ farmers | G | G | LL | L | N | G | N | |
| Small farmers | G | GG | G | G | G | G | N | |
| Landless labourers | G | G | GG | G | G | G | N | |
| Rural industrialists | G | G | G | G | G | GG | GG | G |
| Elite/cronies | I | I | L | I | N | N | L | |
| Urban workers | LL | I | N | N | N | N | N | |
| Urban, informal | LL | I | N | N | N | N | N | |
| Aid donors | G | G | N | U | N | U | U | U |
| Foreign Cos. | N | N | L | L | N | N | L | |

g: small gain    N: neutral
G: medium gain   U: unknown
GG: large gain

I: small loss
L: medium loss
LL: large loss

34

both groups may clearly gain. The better-off may lose in a very indirect way by not profiting from some technology that might have been developed specifically for them, but this type of hypothetical loss will be much less strongly opposed than a direct loss of land or other assets. Earned profits from a new efficient choice of techniques and products may be larger than the windfall profits under present conditions which permit the 'luxury' of inappropriate technology choice.

Third, the balance of forces of political economy in a society may be changed. New organizations may empower the small producers, as they have in some of the Latin American cases cited. As time proceeds, economic success also breeds political power, so that a shift which initially helps the small-scale sector a little may generate cumulative political forces in its favour. The good policy record of Taiwan was probably due in part to an initially favourable political situation leading to land reform, which had cumulative economic and political effects, together with the unavailability of large windfall rents serving to obstruct reforms. Outside intervention can also influence decisions, that is, through conditionality (to be discussed below), but there has been a mixed record in terms of lasting achievements. However, foreign capital, public or private, can be used to diminish or ease the short run costs of otherwise unpopular policies. One example was the use of generous US aid to ease the macro-policy transition in South Korea and Taiwan in the 1960s. Another was the use of British aid to finance land reform in Kenya after independence.

Three main conclusions follow from our analysis of the political economy dimensions of AT. First, the policy package to be promoted must be selected in the light of the political situation and potential in the particular country, with less confrontational policies being promoted in contexts where other policies do not seem feasible in the short run. Second, organizational changes and education, done in a non-spectacular way, can increase the power of the impoverished, even when major policy change has to wait. Third, aid can be used to ease the short-run costs of policy changes.

## World Bank and Fund conditionality and policies for AT

As a result of the debt crisis, and the chronic foreign exchange problem of many countries, World Bank (WB) and Fund (IMF) policy conditionality currently dominate much policy-making in developing countries. Fund programmes have encompassed the majority of countries in Latin America and sub-Saharan Africa in the 1980s. The proportion of WB resources going to Structural Adjustment Loans (SALs) and Sectoral Adjustment Loans (SECALs) now forms nearly a quarter of all Bank lending. It is therefore important to investigate how far the content of these programmes include, or are in conflict with, the policies identified above as necessary to support AT.

Despite some differences, there has been sufficient homogeneity of Fund programmes to make it possible to pick out the main elements. Three categories of policy have formed part of almost every programme. These are *demand* restraint, *switching* policies and policies related to *long-term supply* or *efficiency*.

*Demand restraint* policies are those aimed at reducing demand in the economy, with the objective of improving the trade balance and moderating inflation. Policy instruments include reductions in government expenditure (or in the planned rate of increase of government expenditure), controls over the money supply and credit creation and policies to hold down (or cut) real wages. Particular emphasis has been placed on reducing subsidies, partly as an instrument of demand restraint, partly because this is regarded as necessary for the promotion of efficiency.

*Switching policies* are those aimed at shifting resources from non-tradables to tradables, by changing incentives. Devaluation is the main policy instrument.

*Long-term supply/efficiency* policies consist of reforms that are believed to raise the long-term efficiency of the economy, and thus assist in long-term adjustment. They include a variety of reforms generally designed to secure a more market-oriented economy, subject to fewer restrictions and less segmentation. Reforms include trade liberalization, financial reforms to raise interest rates in the formal sector and to unify credit markets and price reforms. These policies show considerable overlap with some of the conditions of the WB SALs.

Analysis of the composition of Fund programmes from 1980–84 shows that demand restraint policies were implemented in almost every case. Switching policies – as indicated by exchange rate changes were adopted in 54 per cent of the cases, and price reforms (which can have both switching and long-term efficiency effects) in 40 per cent of the cases. Interest rate reform took place in 27 per cent of the cases and development or restructuring of a sector in 65 per cent. Consequently, demand restraint policies predominated over more supply-oriented policies.

Analysis of World Bank SALs suggests that, like Fund programmes, the broad thrust of the programmes (and of the SECALs) has been common to all SALs.

Like the IMF it stresses monetary and fiscal orthodoxy, appropriate real exchange rates, positive real interest rates, and liberal approaches on external accounts. As far as longer term development strategy is concerned, the Bank urges: export expansion and overall outward orientation as against import-substitution: the liberalization of import barriers and an approach toward unified import incentives; and maximum reliance upon markets rather than government ownership or direction in the domestic economy. Its prime emphasis is on price incentives and 'getting the prices right', and its obvious presumption is

36

that even in a world of pervasive imperfections, markets can normally be trusted to achieve that objective better than governments.[41]

SALs contain more detailed country-specific policy interventions than Fund programmes. SAL policy instruments have been categorized as follows (see Mosley):

○ Mobilization of domestic resources through fiscal, monetary and credit policies, and improved financial performance of public enterprises;
○ Improving the efficiency of resource use throughout the economy: in the public sector, measures include reform, rationalization and privatization; in the private sector, the main measures are price decontrol, reduced subsidies, more competition from imports through trade liberalization and credit reform;
○ Trade policies: liberalization, with import quotas removed and reduced and rationalized tariffs; improved export incentives and some institutional reforms to support exports;
○ Institutional reforms: strengthening the capacity of public sector generally; increased efficiency of public enterprises; improved institutions to support agriculture, exports, energy and transport.

There are some strong complementarities between Fund/Bank programmes and AT policies, but also some inconsistencies and some areas which are omitted from the Fund/WB policy package which would need to be included in an AT package.

The major inconsistencies arise in connection with the deflationary policies of the Fund. Cuts in government expenditure and in total credit normally result in cuts in expenditures on rural infrastructure, technology development and dissemination, and similar areas essential for AT. This conflict was noted on numerous occasions in the Latin American conference, where such cuts had accompanied Fund programmes – for example in Colombia, in Mexico and in Argentina. In the Philippines, irrigation maintenance was heavily sacrificed during the 1984–85 crunch.

Policies toward factor prices, exchange rates and credit markets promoted by the Fund/WB are broadly consistent with those identified as necessary to support AT. However, the strongly non-interventionist market solution favoured by the Bank and Fund is not likely by itself to secure sufficient resources for the small-scale sector. What is needed, as noted earlier, is a 'structured' market – namely, a market solution complemented by special institutional reform which will ensure that the small-scale activities receive an adequate share of credit and of foreign exchange. The pure market solution – in an initial context of considerable disequilibrium – does not secure enough resources for AT. Though it may represent an improvement on the 'administrative' solution, it needs to be complemented by special organizational/institutional measures.

Policies toward improved terms of trade for the agricultural sector, which are usually part of the WB policy package, would help rural linkages, but as noted above additional policies would be needed to ensure strong linkages.

The reforms of the parastatals proposed in the WB policy packages would make some contribution to encouraging them to make more appropriate choices by increasing their accountability and reducing government willingness to finance losses, but other changes in structure and in appraisal techniques are also necessary.

Many AT policies do not form part of the WB package. These include, for example, policies toward science and technology, product policies, reforms in administration and in aid. An effective AT policy usually requires a more egalitarian distribution of income and assets, both to secure markets for appropriate products and to increase rural linkages. But this is not a concern of IMF/WB policy reform.

Consequently, if the Fund/WB policies were to be altered to be more compatible with the AT package, the following changes would be necessary:

o Policies would need to be less deflationary, or where cuts in expenditure were unavoidable, deliberate efforts would need to be made to preserve and increase expenditure in critical areas, ie, infrastructure for the rural areas; science and technology and dissemination for AT. Similarly, any credit restraint would need to be accompanied by a reallocation of financing to increase credit to the small-scale sector;

o Organizational and institutional changes would be needed to ensure that the reforms secure adequate resources of credit, foreign exchange and access to technology for small-scale producers. Special lending procedures are needed to get credit to the low-income, which may (but need not) include new institutions;

o Policies to support more egalitarian asset (especially land) and income distribution;

o Additional policies to support rural linkages, including the support of egalitarian and labour-intensive agriculture and the development of appropriate infrastructure;

o Reform of the parastatals to include a more decentralized structure, new forms of public ownership (on a smaller scale) and the use of appraisal techniques which incorporate AT;

o Product policies, including policies toward the development and dissemination of appropriate products and development of appropriate product standards;

o Policies to support science and technology for AT, including institutional and legal reforms;

o Reform of administration toward greater decentralization.

○ Aid procedures to be changed to support AT, not only in special promotion of small-scale, but also in the 'mainstream' aid disbursements.

## Conclusions

The major conclusion of this paper is that effective support for AT requires support for the formulation, introduction and implementation of macro- and meso-policies that would create an environment in which micro-decision units would choose appropriate technologies. In most developing countries, many of the prevailing policies in fact do the opposite – leading to inappropriate decisions. Micro-interventions are likely to have limited effects without such macro- and meso-policy changes.

Changing the policy environment to favour AT should not only affect the *choice* of technology but also the direction of *technical change*. The latter is of critical importance because technical change determines the parameters of future choice. The relative efficiency of labour-intensive and small-scale technologies today is a product of previous efforts to develop technology. Thus the relative efficiency of future labour-intensive technologies could be greatly increased if efforts to create new and improved technologies were systematically directed to this end, while the current backwardness of some small-scale and traditional technologies is largely a reflection of their neglect in research efforts. This sort of change in direction requires not only national action, which has been dealt with in this paper, but also co-operative international efforts.

In many countries there are specific policies to support small-scale industry – providing, for example, special credit and technology for a few small-scale firms. In the cases studied, such policies were in effect in Tanzania and in Zimbabwe. These policies have had very limited effects; they cover only a very few firms, and those that are specially supported in this way often turn out to be high cost and inefficient. This type of small-scale industry support policy is not likely to be effective so long as the macro- and meso-policy environment is generally hostile to the small-scale sector. It makes no sense to favour a few small firms with subsidized credit, while at the same time favouring the large-scale sector in terms of overall credit and foreign exchange allocation plus government regulations. It needs to be recognized that policies for the small-scale sector must be formulated together with policies toward the large-scale sector. In most countries, removing privileges enjoyed by the large-scale firms would do much more for the small-scale firms than the special schemes and regulations currently adopted to help small enterprises.

39

## Appendix: A summary of policy changes supportive of AT

### Taxation and investment promotion
Typical schemes for the special promotion of investment, involving subsidies, special credit allocations, and tax allowances to a relatively few large firms should be abolished.

### Credit
Subsidized credit to a limited number of large or medium-scale firms should be stopped. Rural credit institutions and branch banks should be established to ensure physical access to credit in the rural areas. New credit procedures should be introduced for collateral and monitoring (as in the Grameen Bank, where groups of villagers act as collateral for one another) to help small enterprises, which lack conventional collateral, to obtain access to loans at reasonable rates of interest. It may be desirable to require the major financial institutions to reserve a proportion of their loans for small enterprises as a transitional measure while better procedures for lending successfully to the small-scale sector are developed.

### International trade
Exchange rates should be brought nearer to the market-determined level, so as to avoid excessive discrimination against the agricultural sector and against exports. Tariffs should be reformed so that capital goods do not receive specially favourable treatment. Capital goods imports destined for the small-scale sector and for the large-scale sector should be taxed at the same rate. Systems of allocating foreign exchange by administrative means should be reformed to ensure that the small-scale sector receives an adequate share of the foreign exchange. This may be achieved by a move to a market system of allocating foreign exchange, possibly combined with a requirement that a certain proportion of the foreign exchange is received by the small-scale sector.

### Labour markets
As long as there is a labour surplus, policies which raise wages and restrict hours in the formal sector, while leaving working conditions untouched in the rest of the economy, should be avoided. Policies toward labour market conditions should be devised which could reasonably be applied and enforced throughout the economy, and which do not excessively increase the price of labour.

### Products policies
First, the idea of 'appropriate' products needs to be accepted as an important element in any technology policy. Development and promotion of appropriate products should then form part of science,

40

technology and dissemination policies, investment appraisal among the parastatals, and in any appraisal of multinational investments. Government *standards* should be designed to incorporate local needs, taking into account their technological implications, and not simply copied from advanced countries. Information services about appropriate products and techniques should be supported and a tax on advertising might be considered. Policies (taxes, employment policies, asset redistribution) which make income distribution more egalitarian will also assist by extending the market for appropriate products.

### Science, technology, dissemination
Government-financed science and technology institutions should be reformed so as to devote more of their resources to developing appropriate products and techniques. This would be promoted by:

- Making the development of appropriate products/techniques a specific requirement;
- Developing special institutions to develop small-scale/rural technologies;
- Changing the system whereby the institutions are financed, so that more of their activities are financed by contracts with local firms;
- Encouraging producer and trade associations, including medium and small-scale enterprises which can exert pressure on research organizations, and possibly finance research;
- Establishing a dissemination network for appropriate technology within a developing country and with links with the rest of the world, needs to be established. (See Reddy[42]).

Reform of the legal system may also be required to encourage local innovation in appropriate directions. This involves the establishment of a system of 'utility' model patents.

### Rural linkages
Macro- and sectoral policies to promote egalitarian agricultural growth include policies toward agricultural pricing, extension and infrastructure as well as land reform; the development of rural infrastructure and of institutions to support rural credit and technology dissemination.

### Parastatals
The environment in which parastatals operate needs to become more competitive (through external or internal competition) so that they have to become more efficient in order to survive. This may mean reducing their special financial privileges; improving their appraisal techniques and making AT an explicit element in their appraisal; reducing the influence of donor finance on their decisions, by seeking alternative sources of finance including their own savings and other donors and generating new

forms of public enterprise more likely to make appropriate decisions, eg, more decentralized firms and co-operatives.

### Aid
Aid tying should be reduced; project aid should be reduced relative to programme and sectoral aid; the use of local intermediary institutions to help dispense funds to small firms with lower administrative costs needs to be encouraged and AT incorporated explicitly into project appraisal; the use of local consultancy firms should be encouraged, along with a reduction of auditing and paperwork requirements to ease the problems of small projects.

### Administration
There needs to be more decentralization of the government administrative machinery, especially with respect to the allocation of overhead expenditure, with block grants to local authorities replacing centrally-determined project priorities.

### Education
There is a need to develop an educational programme which ensures a minimal level of numerical ability as well as literacy among a substantial proportion of the population, in order to encourage a socially-based problem-solving capacity. Also decentralized facilities to provide simple technical, administrative and management skills needed by small rural enterprises should be encouraged.

# Rural Linkages and Choice of Technology*

## GUSTAV RANIS

## *Introduction*

We are all aware of the fact that the field of development economics has been subject to extreme fads. In the 1950s and 1960s, industrialization was identified with successful development and the view firmly held by most of the profession, as well as policy-makers, was that a rapid drive toward industrialization could be counted on to drag the agricultural sector along with it. In the early 1970s, under the impact of the oil crisis, combined with a global food shortage, policy-makers and analysts finally became aware of the fundamental importance of the agricultural sector, but mainly as a source of food or as a way of eliminating the need to deploy scarce foreign exchange for the importation of food in regions which often had been exporters of staple crops before independence.

Since then, the realization has grown further that it is indeed very difficult, if not impossible, to 'pull' a large agricultural sector into modernity without mobilizing its own domestic surpluses and/or foreign exchange earnings, as the case may be, on behalf of the overall development effort. Included in that rediscovery of the importance of agriculture was the fact that the individual farmer was by no means an inert, plodding or necessarily non-optimizing individual, but that he would respond well, given a reasonably secure price environment and access to information about new technologies and required inputs. Thus, food producing agriculture has been assigned an increasingly important support role – along with cash crop export agriculture which was never really dethroned as part of the essential fuel for the national development effort. In other words, there now exists more of a recognition that agriculture should be asked to play an important historical role en route to the modern growth epoch.

While there is some recent evidence that the pendulum may be swinging back toward an industry-first strategy – now that the world has experienced a decade of relatively good harvests – this indeed is progress. But what is still missing is the recognition that what needs to be focused on

Gustav Ranis is Professor of International Economics at Yale University.
* From AR Khan, ed, *Trade, Planning and Rural Development: Essays in Honor of Nurul Islam*, (The Macmillan Company), forthcoming, by permission of the author.

in most LDCs is rural development rather than simply agricultural development, as part of a domestic balanced growth strategy. In other words, while the traditional compartmentalization between the rural and the urban sectors, well established during the colonial era, has been modified to some extent by the greater emphasis on domestic food crops, the realization of the potential importance of rural non-agricultural activities for their own sake as well as a way to maintain productivity change in agriculture proper is still extremely deficient.

This incomplete conversion to realizing the full potential importance of the mobilization of the rural economy has, of course, been exacerbated by current concerns with the LDC debt crisis, a crisis which fixes attention further on the open economy or enclave dimensions of development. Without deprecating for a moment the importance of exports, both of the traditional agricultural and the non-traditional industrial variety – the latter gaining increasing importance over time – the development literature in recent years has had a very strong bias in favour of examining post-colonial relations with the rest of the world, including trade, capital movements and technology transfers. Debate and analysis have focused attention on the industrial import substitution versus export promotion choice, including much concentration on the terms for the importation of foreign capital and technology, all in support of a shift from an inner-oriented to an outer-oriented development strategy. But it is also fair to say that, in that context, the emphasis has been almost exclusively on how to redeploy agricultural surpluses, both those generated domestically and those generated via the retained proceeds from cash crop exports, into export-oriented and away from import-substituting types of urban industrial activities. Very little attention has been paid to the locational dimensions of development, specifically to the importance of rural industrial and service activity as a complement to the sustained growth of agricultural productivity. It is this neglect of the sustainability of rural development by paying more analytical and policy attention to the locational dimension of the overall development strategy on which this paper is focused.

The basic problem that still needs to be fully appreciated is the importance of decentralized industrial and service activities in the rural areas, interacting, on the one hand, with agriculture and, on the other, with both urban industry and the rest of the world. Unfortunately, in most of the developing countries I am familiar with, there still exists a profound lack of faith in the capacity of both entrepreneurs and public officials in the rural areas. Even as peasants have finally been given their due under the pressure of the events of the 1970s, this has not been accompanied by a similar recognition of the human potential for non-agricultural activity, private and public, existing in the hinterland. This potential can be realized in the context of a sustained development effort which recognizes the important spatial dimensions of non-agricultural growth as part of a pattern of vigorous rural balanced growth. Indeed, such balanced growth in the rural areas has to be seen as occurring not at the expense of, but as a necessary support to, the more glamorous and well recognized international dimensions of development focusing on the generation of labour-intensive industrial exports supported by capital and technology inflows.

Continued failure to recognize these spatial dimensions amounts to a serious handicap in the way of solving the problem of development, which I believe really lies below the surface of the current topical concern with the so-called debt crisis. It should indeed be emphasized here that even in the small East-Asian success stories, eg, Taiwan, which is usually characterized as an example of an historically successful labour-intensive industrial exporter, what was really critical was the prior mobilization of the rural economy, both agricultural and non-agricultural, as part of a domestic balanced growth effort. While agricultural productivity increased, initially concentrated in rice and sugar, then in mushrooms and asparagus, providing the main initial engine of growth, it was rural industry and services for the domestic and foreign markets, that was expected to propel further growth. Such rural industry was initially (in the 1960s) largely based on agricultural raw materials, but gradually focused more on a subcontracting relationship with imported raw materials-based industries in the export-processing zones and elsewhere.

What is crucial here, and not yet fully understood, is the importance of agriculture and its relation to dispersed rural industry as a key to both successful domestic growth and the export-oriented performance which is o well known internationally. It is noteworthy, for example, to recall that, in 1951, only 34 per cent of all the industrial establishments in Taiwan were located in the five largest cities, quite low by LDC standards; but even more spectacular is the fact that this proportion was unchanged in 1971 after two decades of rapid growth which culminated in Taiwan's reaching the end of her labour surplus condition. The proportion of the total number of persons in manufacturing employed in the larger cities actually declined, from 43 to 37 per cent of the total, between 1956 and 1966, while the proportion for services also declined, from 41 to 34 per cent. Employment in rural manufacturing, on the other hand, increased from 47 per cent to 52 per cent of the total and that in rural services from 49 per cent to 56 per cent of the total during this decade; the rest were located in small towns.

It is, moreover, fair to say that in most contemporary developing countries, in contrast, colonial or post-colonial compartmentalization of the economy has only been partially removed. Yet successful development clearly requires the mobilization of the rural economy as an integral whole in a balanced, persistent and sustained fashion, simultaneously permitting the urban industrial sector to turn outward and begin to make its contribution to the financing of its own future growth through a labour-intensive export diversification drive of major proportions. This second prong of a two-bladed development strategy is being increasingly well understood by now; labour-intensive industrial exports, along with the contribution of foreign capital, and, hopefully modified, imported technology are required not only to mop up additional unemployment but also so that the constraints imposed on the further growth of the urban industrial sector, ie, its needs for further capitalization and/or debt reduction, can be lifted. But the complementary relationship with the first prong is usually ignored. Indeed, the analysis of the spatial characteristics of successful development has not been a prominent part of the development literature and/or of policy-makers' concern during recent decades, ie, the potential historical role of this sub-sector en route to modern growth has not really been appreciated. It is indeed important not only that people in the rural areas be held in productive employment, both agricultural and non-agricultural, but also that a complementary relationship be established between agriculture and non-agriculture in the rural areas, on the one hand, and between rural and urban non-agriculture, including for export, on the other.

Analysis and policy focusing on this hitherto neglected first prong of an efficient development strategy therefore needs to be resurrected if the not uncommon problem of limping growth, along with secularly worsening poverty and income distribution outcomes, is to be addressed. In fact, this fundamental development strategy problem would have to be addressed even if the very topical contemporary debt problem were removed by fiat overnight.

## Agricultural – non-agricultural linkages, rural–rural and rural–urban

The linkages most frequently cited in the literature are those which flow from agricultural to non-agricultural activities, the latter usually not differentiated by urban and rural. The assumption is customarily made that, somehow, agricultural productivity is rising exogenously, for example via increases in physical inputs, technology change and/or organizational change. Given such an exogenous change in agricultural productivity, three kinds of linkages can be identified:

1. Forward consumption linkages;
2. Backward production linkages;
3. Forward production linkages.

The first of these forward consumption linkages, ie, the demand for additional non-agricultural goods as a consequence of exogenous agricultural income change, has been found in all the previous empirical research on the subject to be quantitatively the most important. However, the size of this linkage effect depends not only on how much agricultural output or income has grown, but also on the distribution of that income, which, in turn, depends on both the initial asset distribution in agriculture, the crop mix in agriculture, and the choice of agricultural technology. It is quite well understood that some crops are intrinsically more labour-intensive than others, ie, asparagus and mushrooms are more labour-intensive than sugar and rice, and that for each and every crop there exists a large number of technology choices both on the international shelf and/or as a consequence of domestic adaptations. The way in which primary incomes are generated in agriculture, due to both original asset distribution and land tenure configurations, combined with process and product choices, clearly determines where the demand for additional non-agricultural output will make itself felt, eg, for mass consumption goods or for luxury goods. Once that demand expresses itself, it either results in new rural linkages, or it is satisfied from production in the urban areas or even abroad, depending on the initial availability of locally-produced consumer goods. The response mechanisms leading to new rural activities are likely to be very positive as long as policy does not in a relative sense discriminate against such activities.

Unfortunately, the history of most non-agricultural activities in the rural areas of LDCs is a sad one. To the extent that production of these goods existed historically, it was often destroyed by colonial imports – unless it was far enough away from the port cities to be protected by distance and transport costs. Later, during the post-independence import substitution era when urban industry was definitely favoured, rural non-agricultural activities were discouraged even more, a trend which has continued to this day. Thus, while forward consumer linkages are likely to be potentially the strongest in a relative sense, the conditions for a vigorous response in terms of expanding rural non-agricultural activity are likely not to be met in many typical development settings.

The second kind of linkage referred to, the backward production linkage, focuses on inputs into agriculture, the demand for which will presumably rise given the same exogenous increase in agricultural productivity. This is an area in which technology choices with respect to the nature of agricultural implements and other inputs – thus the association between traditional and modern technologies and their respective output-generating as well as labour-absorbing characteristics – comes into play. One important consideration here is the quantity and quality of the R & D structure in existence which feeds in and diffuses the information on the range of potential technology options, ie, the supply side of technology process and product choices. On the demand side we have the famous degree of distortion of relative factor prices, in addition to the overall macro-economic setting of exchange rates and trade protection, which affect the prices of alternative input combinations in agriculture and the extent of manageable competitive pressures on the agricultural decision-maker. The most obvious instance is the frequently found subsidization of tractors, which in some countries has exceeded the 50 per cent level, affecting the choice between power tillers and tractors for land preparation as well as the technology governing the extensive number of post-harvest operations. These backward production linkages, in other words, may be weak or strong, ie, impact on the more labour-intensive rural supply of inputs or their more 'distant' and capital-intensive urban (or foreign) counterparts, depending on the overall macro-policy environment as well as the particular institutional infrastructure of the R & D diffusion and dissemination system. In the absence of a disarticulated decentralized information and R & D diffusion system and in the absence of relatively realistic relative prices for final goods as well as inputs, the tendency is great for such backward linkages to have a relatively large effect on distant suppliers, including overseas – rather than to encourage the growth of complementary non-agricultural input activities in the rural areas.

From the point of view of modernizing agriculture through new 'green revolution' types of technology change, inputs embodying new science and technology may well be an important contributor to additional agricultural productivity change. Such inputs can, and are likely to be, produced in medium-sized towns rather than in villages, but the more 'appropriate' mixes of seeds, fertilizer and so on are also more likely to emanate from within the region rather than from distant urban areas or based on relatively unadapted national or even international research findings.

Third, there is forward production linkage, eg, food processing, including the canning of cash crops and the processing of food crops. As in the backward production linkage case, what we encounter here is a very large range of alternative technologies. For example, in rice processing the choice often ranges from the deployment of 18 to 56 man-hours per ton, depending on the specific type of machinery being used. The precise processing choice is, of course, also affected by time or perishability, economies of scale and the quality of the product. But, very often, once again, the range of alternative technologies, defined in terms of both process and product, is not widely known or diffused, on the supply side, and very dependent on the kind of macro-policy setting in which the rural economy finds itself, on the demand side.

The three linkages referred to above, of which the first is quantitatively the most important, at least in the static sense, all run from agriculture to non-agriculture and are fairly well established in the literature – even though they have not been given adequate emphasis in recent years. Also important, but relatively even more neglected, are the linkages which run from non-agriculture to agriculture. These were given some prominence by Ted Schultz, looking at the US in earlier years, as well as the Vanderbilt School of Nicholls and Tang, who believed, as we do, that agricultural output is not only a function of physical inputs, technology and organization tenure arrangements, but also of the proximity in a spatial sense to non-agricultural activities.[1] In other words, the all-important 'exogenous' agricultural productivity change which is required to keep the process going through the various kinds of linkages previously referred to, needs to itself be seen as a function, at least in significant part, of non-agricultural activity and its location. But this strand of thought, and empirical analysis, has virtually disappeared from the literature in recent decades.

Three sub-types of linkages running in that direction may indeed be identified. One, somewhat reminiscent of the aforementioned backward production linkages, relates to the overheads, roads, marketing facilities etc, which surely affect in a direct way the feasibility of contemplating a gradual but sustained further increase in agricultural productivity. A second sub-type, more subtle, and less frequently referred to in the literature, resides in the intrinsic importance of new consumer goods becoming available. Such a new window of opportunity in the form of non-agricultural incentive goods, either domestic or imported, could provide a powerful additional reason, ceteris paribus, for the individual farmer/operator to accept the usually higher risks of a new technology. A third sub-type, even less frequently referred to, including by the Vanderbilt School itself, is the issue of the importance of new investment opportunities becoming available, in a visible and relatively familiar setting, preferably close to home, ie, in the rural areas – once again serving to enhance the willingness of farmers to take risks. This third sub-type of non-agriculture-to-agriculture linkage is, particularly in the early stages of development, important before a more sophisticated financial intermediation network is ready to convince farmers to take more 'distant' risks and channel their savings, through an ever more complicated financial inter-mediation system, to arms' length investors. As long as farmers are still willing to trust only their own family members, which is likely to be a feature of the scene for some time in most developing country contexts, the ability to discern new 'local' investment opportunities, including via expenditures on education, remains an important source of productivity increase in agriculture at its source. Thus, in a number of ways, farmers' attitudes toward risk and innovation are very likely to be substantially affected by contacts, via these various linkages, with the rest of the community, in particular various types of non-agricultural rural activity.

In summary, reviewing the bidding in terms of linkages moving from agriculture to non-agriculture and back to agriculture, the potential importance of such location-specific linkages for a virtuous circle of rural balanced growth needs to be more fully appreciated. Their importance may be overstated in the case of relatively small countries or city states, where it is, of course, geographically easier and more likely to have the stimulus come from the urban 'outside' including from the rest of the world. But in any country with a significant agricultural hinterland these linkages, and especially their longer-term dynamic impact, must be viewed as a key issue. This has proven to be empirically verifiable, even in the context of the relatively small East Asian success cases of Korea and Taiwan, as their recent development experience has shown (see below).

Proceeding to a more detailed analysis of the make-up of these linkages, let us consider that, in most LDCs, we are initially faced with a dispersed agricultural population and a relatively concentrated non-agricultural population, including in the rural areas. In the absence of direct government intervention, the location of industry, urban or rural, will then depend on:

○ Size of that population and its dispersal;
○ Extent to which economies of scale play a role in relevant non-agricultural activities; and
○ Topography plus the stock of social overhead capital jointly determining transportation costs.

Depending on the relative size of the rural and urban sectors at the outset, depending on the size of the population and its dispersal, and depending on the infrastructure in place, the relative importance of the rural balanced growth blade as opposed to the export-oriented blade of an 'optimum' development strategy will, of course, differ, but they will both be important. Regardless of such initial typological differences among developing countries, the rural location of industry and its interaction with agricultural output, both food producing and cash crop, represents an important and underemphasized dimension of the development process. Neither the overall size of an LDC nor its organizational/political choice as between a socialist or market economy path affects this basic point, as the importance attached to balanced rural growth in both Taiwan and mainland China in recent years has fully demonstrated.

A key indicator of the relative success or failure of the rural-balanced growth dimension of successful development is the percentage of non-agricultural income in total rural family income, absolutely and over time. This phenomenon reflects the importance of what has sometimes been termed a 'proto-industrialization' process in the course of early Western European development (preceding the Industrial Revolution) and also goes under the name of off-farm employment opportunities in the contemporary language of development economics.[2]

Table 1 shows the marked difference in this critical statistic across

50

**Table 1 Comparative indicators**

| | Non-agricultural income share in rural families' total income (%) | | | Per capita real income growth rate (%/year) | Income distribution (Gini coefficient) | | |
|---|---|---|---|---|---|---|---|
| | 1950/60 | 1970 | 1980 | 1970–79 | 1960 | 1970 | 1980 |
| Taiwan | 32 (1964) | 45 | 65 | 8.1 | 0.44 | 0.29 | 0.29 (1978) |
| S. Korea | — | 15 | 25 | 7.5 | — | 0.37 | 0.38 (1976) |
| Colombia | 14 (1950) | 9 | — | 3.9 | 0.53 | 0.56 | 0.52 (1982) |
| Philippines | — | 17 | 16 | 3.3 | 0.50 (1961) | 0.49 (1968) | 0.50 (1977) |
| Thailand | — | 37 | 38 | 5.0 | 0.41 (1962) | 0.43 (1968) | — |

countries and over time. Note, for example, the contrast between Taiwan, on the one hand, and the Latin American representative, Colombia, on the other, with South Korea lagging substantially behind Taiwan and Thailand doing much better than the Philippines in the Southeast Asian context.[3] Not only is the proportion of such non-agricultural activity as a share of total rural income initially absolutely much lower in Colombia and the Philippines, but it is also declining over time, while it is rising continuously in East Asia – and continues to rise even after the end of the labour surplus condition had been reached in the early 1970s. We may, of course, expect the proportion of rural non-agricultural in total non-agricultural activity to decline in the modern growth epoch as economies of scale become much more pronounced, which, along with migration and Engel's Law, is more likely to lead to a higher relative concentration of industry in urban areas. But this modern economic growth phenomenon is representative of an epoch still not within reach of most of the countries we are considering here.

The comparative strength of the chain of rural linkages yields substantially different results across developing countries, both in terms of the size of non-agricultural rural activities and aggregate bottom line performance. It thus depends on the:

o  Initial conditions, including the size of country, the importance of cash crops versus food crops, plus the size and dispersion of the population, the state of rural infrastructure, etc, already referred to;
o  Extent of equity of the primary distribution of income, a function, in part, of the initial distribution of land and the tenure arrangements in agriculture, and, in part, of the whole array of macro-economic policies of government affecting the realism of both relative input and output prices;
o  State of the organizational–institutional infrastructure with respect to R & D, information dissemination, credit availability, etc; and
o  Extent of workably competitive pressures affecting both sectors of the rural economy.

Any chain is only as strong as the weakest of its links and the strength of any virtuous (or balanced growth) cycle depends on the strength of these individual links, rather than on the point of initiation of growth, be it agriculture or non-agriculture, nor even on whether or not the initial stimulus comes from outside the rural economy or from within.

The relative importance of the weakest part of these links depends on the stage of development. For example, in the early days, or perhaps of more relevance in today's African or other low income countries, a standard local market may still be nearly self-sufficient. But even there contact with a neighbouring self-sufficient area becomes increasingly crucial if agricultural and non-agricultural productivity increases

52

are to feed on each other. In later stages the proximity effects of intermediate-sized cities and, ultimately, large cities and even the rest of the world, become more important with respect to the increased availability of new types of incentive consumer goods but less important with respect to investment opportunities due to the development of the financial intermediation network.

To measure the results of weak or strong linkages, one could compute for each stage of development the:

○ Ratio of population in the capital city to the total population, which, taking out the effects of such factors on economies of scale in non-agriculture, can be viewed as favourable if relatively low;
○ Size of small and medium cities' populations over the total population, which, for the same reason, can be viewed as favourable if relatively high;
○ Proportion of non-agricultural GDP generated in urban versus rural areas in comparison with the overall population distribution, with, once again, a higher proportion, ceteris paribus, viewed as favourable.

Turning to the important issue of causation, admittedly a tricky business when one deals with a chain of linkages, it seems clear, from work undertaken in the Philippines,[4] not only that forward consumption linkages, agriculture to non-agriculture, make the quantitatively largest contribution overall but also that the non-agriculture to agriculture linkage is of special importance in the poorer upland or rain-fed areas. This is clearly attributable to the more equal distribution of income in such regions as well as the relatively greater importance of linkages running from non-agriculture to agriculture at 'earlier' stages of development.

It is often contended that increasing the relative strength of rural linkages and the resulting balanced growth process in rural areas may have to be purchased at the expense of a lower overall rate of growth. One need only appeal to the historical post-war experience of Taiwan and Thailand to put this criticism to rest. A high population density by itself is, of course, not necessarily helpful for the modernization of agriculture or rural balanced growth generally. Static diminishing returns may be seen as likely to be in conflict with the dynamic linkage effects we have been discussing here. For example, Taiwan, an area with one of the highest population densities in the third world, constituted an unusually successful case of rural balanced growth. In contrast, Java (Indonesia) and Bangladesh, with an even higher population density, have achieved a much less satisfactory record of rural mobilization. A high density of population can contribute to the successful transformation by converting a higher percentage of the rural population into non-agricultural producers thus adding to the growth of standard market areas. As the rural population becomes urbanized, in the

53

sense of small towns growing up as counter-magnets, the area of the individual standard market ultimately begins to shrink because of the increasing relative importance of transport costs as compared to scale economies. In the case of Taiwan, for example, as agricultural labour productivity continued to zoom, this brought about a spatially dispersed industrial location, which, in turn, ultimately generated increased linkages between the rural and urban populations, including via the export processing zones, because of the high volume of low-cost tradeables produced.

On the other hand, if agricultural productivity is relatively low, given an economy's initial conditions, it probably leads to a relatively large market area and a relatively low volume of dualistic exchange. This, in turn, is likely to reinforce agricultural stagnation because it is not conducive to rural–urban interaction. Economies of scale may at some point become sufficient to compensate for the higher transport costs of locating industry in the towns or ultimately even in the large cities.

In summary, the linkage between agricultural and non-agricultural activities thus has important spatial dimensions traceable to population size and dispersion, the scale economies of non-agricultural production, and transport costs. The gradual conversion of rural agriculturalists and non-agriculturalists into modern economic agents, aware of the potential of new agricultural and non-agricultural technologies, experiencing wider consumption horizons and aspiring to accumulate new kinds of assets, can be accomplished only through the strengthening of linkages with small town and, ultimately, urban centres. A modern farmer or modern industrial entrepreneur is bound to become increasingly aware of the possibilities of carrying out all kinds of exchanges, not only with one another, but increasingly with far-away places, including even world markets. This is more likely to result from strengthened rural linkages rather than a concentration of resource flows on import-substituting industrial production targets and/or foreign markets. A spatial perspective permits us to see that such compartmentalization, usually inherited from colonialism, tends to restrict modernization to the export-oriented enclave, which customarily touches only a small portion of the population, leaves much of potential agricultural and non-agricultural activity to one side and thus fails to make its human as well as fiscal contribution to the development process.

When a developing country is small, the task of transition into modern growth is relatively easier because the country can follow the option of attempting to achieve development mainly via the opportunities of foreign trade, foreign capital, and foreign technology – though this may not necessarily be optimal even in that situation. But as soon as there exists a substantial hinterland it is clearly suboptimal to rely excessively on exchanges with far-away and foreign urban centres. While farmers can and should take full advantage of international trade, eg, the asparagus, mushrooms and pineapples of Taiwan, which, incidentally, made these farmers just as entrepreneurial as the industrial exporters of Hong Kong, this can only be a part of a successful development story. The experience of both Taiwan and mainland China has shown that there indeed exist linkages through dualistic exchange between agricultural and non-agricultural activities which can be crucial to the chances of achieving sustained growth. Let us now, finally, turn to the kinds of policies, both macro- and organizational–institutional, which are at the government's disposal in the event it should seek to strengthen the various crucial links in the development chain as outlined here.

## Public policy options

In the light of our earlier analysis, it should be clear that paying attention to balanced rural growth means that the seemingly inevitable primary import substitution sub-phase of development, with all its well-known interventions, should be kept relatively brief and relatively mild. This was certainly the case in East Asia and permitted a good deal of attention to be paid to the rural economy even during this relatively industry- and inward-oriented sub-phase of development. More importantly, once the inevitable export-orientation sub-phase begins, a developing country will be much better off to the extent it does not unduly rely on continued import substitution of the secondary variety, coupled with export promotion, in contrast to the more market-oriented export substitution strategy, shifting from land-intensive to labour-intensive exports. The extent to which that second blade of the development process is utilized then makes the task for the complementary rural-balanced growth blade substantially easier, since the continued massive distortion of factor and commodity prices, protectionism and exchange rate overvaluation etc, clearly hurt the domestic agricultural sector by taxing it 'under the table', discouraging competitiveness and maintaining the early colonial and post-colonial habits of compartmentalization.

Macro-policy-related distortions, which weaken rural linkages, include the customary system of import licensing biased toward urban industry; credit markets similarly characterized by tight credit-rationing in favour of urban industrial activities; tax incentives which usually are available only to firms with direct access to civil servants at the centre; exchange rate overvaluation; direct interventions in the internal terms of trade; plus other direct allocations of rationed scarce resources that are familiar to the reader as part and parcel of the normal import-substituting policy package. Less well-known but undoubtedly as important are the organizational/institutional features of the landscape, which usually hinder

55

the building up of a sufficiently strong set of linkages in the rural areas, as well as, later, between urban industrial activities. These include the usually relatively meagre allocation of infrastructural and other public goods to the rural areas and are further reinforced by the precise composition and quality of the overheads placed there, ie, usually focused on assuring the supply of cash crops for export and luxury agricultural goods for the urban enclave, rather than on the mutual reinforcement of agricultural and non-agricultural activities in the food-producing hinterland. Most frequently, this requires a shift from the construction of main highways from ports to mining areas toward farm to market roads as a priority activity.

Similarly, the R & D institutional infrastructure and annual allocation systems are customarily focused very much on the same export-oriented cash crops rather than on the food crops; the little public sector expenditure on R & D for non-agriculture is likely to be focused on manufactured exports.

Finally, in addition to having a subsidized, heavily rationed credit system, not equally accessible to small-sized rural agriculturalists and industrialists, there is the frequent dearth of institutional or banking 'fingers' in the rural areas capable of reaching the dispersed population and thus preventing any deepening of financial markets. It almost goes without saying that the proximity to modern inputs, fertilizer, seeds, as well as access to new information embodied in either foreign or domestic technology, is likely to be very unequal, especially within the agricultural sector, along with the aforementioned access to credit. In most cases I am familiar with, to the extent there is a meagre overall allocation of resources to the rural areas, priorities as to where public goods are to be allocated are very much set by the central authorities. This is all part and parcel of the usual lack of confidence in rural actors, public and private, in sharp contrast to the rhetoric frequently invoked.

In summary, when dealing with rural development as part of the overall effort at transition to modern growth, both analysts and policy-makers must begin to think of agricultural productivity as a function not only of conventional inputs and technology but also of linkage variables as we have defined them here. In explaining differences in total factor productivity across villages in the Philippines, for example, we found labour inputs, a conventional input, to be significant, along with extension expenditures.[4] But equally significant were such variables as roads per hectare (directly related), the average distance to the nearest urban centre (inversely related) and the number of modern non-agricultural establishments within the same village (directly related). These results fit the notion that investment and consumption incentives in nearby non-agriculture help explain the famous 'residual' in agriculture.

Similarly, with respect to non-agriculture, in addition to conventional

56

inputs and technology change, more attention must be placed on explaining differential performance, especially in rural industry, in terms of both process and product choices related to linkage variables. Earlier work, for example contrasting the experience of Taiwan and the Philippines in pineapple processing and canning,[5] supported the notion that a concentrated industry choice (Philippines) had a much smaller impact on both cash crop and food crop production in the area as compared to Taiwan where 23 dispersed national firms did a good deal of sub-contracting. As a consequence, the capital/labour ratio for pineapple processing in the Philippines was from two to six times higher than that in Taiwan. Instead of reaching out only to the pineapple plantations in a vertically integrated set-up, as is typical of the post-colonial enclave, with minimum impact on the surrounding countryside, the Taiwan organization affected large numbers of small holders and led to a much more equal distribution of income, of substantial consequence in terms of the kinds of demands for industrial goods which were generated. The same sort of contrast can be found in the area of rice milling where we were able to compare and contrast the choice of technology in the concentrated large-scale public sector mills of the Philippines with the smaller-scale and much more labour-intensive dispersed private mills of Taiwan.

Both the choice of appropriate processes and appropriate goods in terms of the specifications for milled rice and for the non-agricultural goods purchased out of increased agricultural incomes can thus show marked differences across developing countries. Public policies which not only reduce the macroeconomic distortions so frequently referred to but also concentrate on shifting public goods expenditures from the support of urban industry to strengthening the various links in the rural-balanced growth chain can be expected to be highly effective. They will, in fact, make it possible not only for the rural-balanced growth blade of a successful development effort to go forward but also, by doing so, accelerate the much needed complementary labour-intensive export orientation drive, en route to mopping up the system's labour surplus and entering the epoch of modern growth.

# The Effect of Policy and Policy Reforms on Non-Agricultural Enterprises and Employment in Developing Countries: A Review of Past Experiences

## STEVE HAGGBLADE, CARL LIEDHOLM and DONALD C MEAD

### Introduction

This paper examines the effects of policies and policy reform on non-agricultural enterprises and employment in developing countries. (Although agricultural enterprises are also important contributors to economic development, they are not included in this review. They are extensively covered in other studies and, indeed, are the focus of a separate agricultural policy project. Agricultural policies do have a powerful effect on non-farm activities, however, particularly those located in rural areas, and their role in influencing these non-agricultural activities is considered in this paper.) Since a multitude of policies affect employment and enterprise development, it is necessary to review a comprehensive array of government interventions, ranging from those affecting the labour market to policies dealing with interest rates, product prices, foreign trade and sectoral growth.

Particular attention is focused on the differential impact of these policies on non-agricultural enterprises of varying sizes and in different localities. Numerous studies have made it clear that enterprises of different sizes and types vary substantially in their capacity to generate employment; some types of producers are far more labour-intensive than others. It is also clear, however, that the strength and economic viability of different types

'STEVE HAGGBLADE is Assistant Professor of Economics at Syracuse University. CARL LIEDHOLM, Professor of Economics, is Director of the Michigan State University Growth and Equity through Microenterprise Investments and Institutions (GEMINI) project. DONALD C MEAD is Visiting Professor of Agricultural Economics at Michigan State University. This paper reports on work supported by Employment and Enterprise Policy Analysis Contract DAN–5426–C–00–4098–00 at Harvard Institute for International Development, subcontracted with Development Alternatives, Incorporated, and Michigan State University. The contract is funded by the US Agency for International Development (Employment and Enterprise Development Division, Bureau for Science and Technology) in Washington, DC.

and sizes of producers is strongly influenced by the policy environment in which they operate. This means that the potential for expanding productive employment through the encouragement of particular categories of producers such as small enterprises cannot be realized if the policy environment is skewed in perverse ways. Yet there is a growing recognition that the policies of many developing countries are biased and discriminatory in their impact. There is a need, then, to examine systematically the nature and extent of these policy biases as well as the types of policy reforms which have proven to be most effective in overcoming them.

There is a close relationship between projects on the one hand, and policies, on the other, in encouraging the growth of different groups of producers. Policies can be viewed as affecting whole categories of enterprises while projects generally operate through individualized relationships between an agency running a project and selected beneficiary enterprises. To the extent that existing policies or projects discriminate against certain types of producers, there is a temptation to establish new projects aimed at offering direct benefits to previously excluded firms, 'evening things out' by creating new and offsetting assistance packages. The result is that projects may be justified by the existence of distortions in the economy, but in turn may create new distortions as well as new occasions for increased government intervention. In such a situation, a first-best solution would often involve seeking to eliminate the original distortions rather than trying to create offsetting new ones. This will generally involve policy reform. In fact, this provides one of the main reasons for an interest in issues of policy reform.

Notwithstanding the increased recognition of the importance of policy change in recent years, it is important to keep its role in proper perspective. It is only one of many determinants of long-term, sustainable and broadly based growth and is generally at most a necessary but not sufficient condition for such growth. If the need for policy change received too little attention in earlier discussions, there is a danger that, as the latest focus of attention in the development field, it may receive too much blame (or credit) today. This is of particularly serious concern if the discussion is restricted to policy change in developing countries, with no recognition of any corresponding need for policy adjustments in developed countries. In such a context, it is easy to conclude that the responsibility both for disappointing past results in the development process and for any needed changes to improve that record in the future lies primarily, if not exclusively, with the developing countries themselves. We hope that this conclusion will not be drawn from our analysis.

In examining this topic, the economic issues of employment and enterprise policy will be examined first. Particular attention is focused on empirical evidence of the magnitude of policy distortions and their effects on the efficiency, employment, and size distribution of enterprises in the economy. The various approaches used to change policies in this area are then examined. Of particular concern are the alternative paths to effect these policy changes and the role of donor agencies in this process.

## Economics of employment and enterprise policy

### The economic and policy setting

Before examining existing policy distortions and their effects on the economy, some background information may be helpful to place these issues in proper perspective. A descriptive profile of non-agricultural activities will first be presented. A possible explanation for some of the observed characteristics of these activities will then be sought through an examination of the workings of factor and product markets in developing countries. This will lead to the establishment of a simple framework to facilitate the consideration of the vast array of policies and the various ways these might influence non-agricultural enterprises of various sizes.

### Descriptive profile of non-agricultural activities

Recent research has shed new light on the characteristics of non-agricultural activities in developing countries, particularly those at the small end of the size spectrum. Small-scale firms, which in this paper are defined as those establishments employing fewer than 50 workers, form a significant component of the non-agricultural sectors of most developing countries. There is no commonly accepted definition of what constitutes a small-scale firm. A survey of 75 countries conducted in 1975 revealed that over 50 different definitions were used. Although the definition used in this paper is somewhat arbitrary, this upper limit was chosen because it would exclude most foreign-owned firms as well as most of those more complex, specialized enterprises that have privileged access to capital or other inputs. Indeed, some analysts use access to formal capital markets as the key discriminating variable.[1] Others suggest an analogous approach, dividing firms based on whether or not they pay minimum wages.[2] While not identical, we believe these three possible grouping rules – based on size, access to capital or wage market status – will result in broadly similar firm groupings. Recognizing that no selection can be perfectly satisfactory, we opt for a size designation based on employment, since the bulk of comparative statistics are available in that form.

A recent review of data from 14 countries reveals, for example, that in all but one case, more than 50 per cent of manufacturing employment was generated by small firms (see Table 1). Although comparable data are generally lacking on the relative importance of employment in small

60

## Table 1 Distribution of employment in manufacturing by firm size (percentage)

| Country and Date | Per Capita Income ($) 1982 | Firm Size | | |
| | | Large Scale | Small Scale | |
| | | 50 or more workers | 10–49 workers | Below 10 workers |
|---|---|---|---|---|
| India–1971 | $260 | 38 | 20 | 42 |
| Tanzania–1967 | $280 | 37 | 7 | 56[a] |
| Ghana–1970 | $360 | 15 | 1 | 84[a] |
| Kenya–1969 | $390 | 41 | 10 | 49[a] |
| Sierra Leone–1974 | $390 | 5 | 5 | 90 |
| Indonesia–1977 | $580 | 16 | 7 | 77 |
| Honduras–1979 | $660 | 24 | 8 | 68 |
| Thailand–1978 | $790 | 31 | 11 | 58[a] |
| Philippines–1974 | $820 | 29 | 5 | 66 |
| Nigeria–1972 | $860 | 15 | 26 | 59[a] |
| Jamaica–1978 | $1,330 | 49 | 16 | 35 |
| Colombia–1973 | $1,460 | 35 | 13 | 52 |
| Korea–1975 | $1,910 | 53 | 7 | 40 |

[a] Computed residually as the difference between total employment recorded in labour force or population surveys (including enterprises of all sizes) and employment in larger firms, as reported in establishment surveys.

Sources: Africa: Tanzania, Ghana, Kenya, Nigeria: computed from Page (1979); Sierra Leone: Chuta and Liedholm (1985);
India: Mazumdar (1980)
Indonesia: computed from Snodgrass (1979);
Honduras: Stallmann (1984);
Thailand: Estimated from data provided by National Statistical Office, Thailand;
Philippines: Anderson and Khambata (1981);Jamaica: Fisseha (1982);
Colombia: Berry and Pinell-Siles (1979);
Korea: Ho (1980).

enterprises in other non-agricultural sectors, it is usually contended that small producers predominate in the trading and service sectors as well.[3] Large-scale enterprises generally predominate in mining and utilities.

Among small-scale non-agricultural producers, manufacturing tends to be the most important component. In a review of non-farm employment in 10 developing countries, it was found that in over two-thirds of the cases, manufacturing generated more employment than either trade or services.[4] Because of manufacturing's relative importance and because data on most other components are generally sparse, much of the subsequent analysis in this paper focuses on the manufacturing sector.

Studies comparing small- and large-scale non-agricultural activities in developing countries have discovered important differences in their production technologies. Virtually all studies indicate, for example, that small manufacturing firms generate more employment per unit of capital (ie, are more labour-intensive) than their larger-scale counterparts.[3,5] Many studies, though not all, find that the smaller firms also produce more output (or value added) per unit of capital and thus generate more output as well as employment for a given investment than do larger firms. Finally, most analysts indicate that large and small non-agricultural firms produce similar though not perfectly substitutable products. Although there is some evidence that the small firms tend to produce somewhat lower quality products for lower income customers, they do serve high income consumers as well.[3,6]

One of the primary explanations for the coexistence of large and small firms producing similar goods using very different labour:capital ratios is the alleged existence of segmented factor markets. This segmentation is said to parallel closely the division between large- and small-scale enterprises. In the labour market, for example, it is claimed there is a wage gap between large and small enterprises, even after adjusting for quality differences. This segmentation forces larger firms to pay a higher price for labour than their smaller-scale counterparts.[7,8] It is also argued that a comparable segmentation exists in capital markets. Large firms are said to be able to obtain funds from institutional sources at rates substantially lower than those facing small firms in the informal credit markets.[4] The segmented factor markets thus are said to cause large and small firms to face differing factor prices, which lead them to employ differing combinations of capital and labour.

These segmented markets have often been either created by or reinforced by governmental policies. Indeed, it is through these factor markets as well as the product markets that most policies ultimately affect the economy. Consequently, in examining the effects of policies on non-agricultural employment and enterprises, a framework that focuses attention on these markets seems particularly fruitful. Such an approach enables one to capture the full range of policy distortions, not only those arising in the factor markets, but also those in the product markets, where policies affecting the level and composition of demand for various products can be scrutinized. (This framework is similar to that developed by Steel and Takagi[1].)

## Policies and their points of impact
A wide array of policies influence non-agricultural enterprises through effects on both input and output markets. (This paper is concerned with government policies. There is also a wide array of enterprise standard operating procedures, which could be referred to as private sector policies, covering such things as labour practices, entrepreneurial customs, and contract procedures. Except to the extent that they are influenced by government policies, these private sector practices are treated as outside the scope of this paper.)

62

## Table 2 Inventory of Policies, by functional groupings

1. Trade Policy
   a. import tariffs
   b. import quotas
   c. export taxes or subsidies
   d. foreign exchange rates
   e. foreign exchange controls

2. Monetary Policy
   a. money supply
   b. interest rate
   c. banking regulations

3. Fiscal Policy
   a. government expenditure
      — infrastructure
      — direct investment in production, marketing or service enterprises.
      — government provision of services
      — transfers
   b. taxes
      — corporate income
      — personal income
      — payroll
      — property
      — sales

4. Labour Policies
   a. minimum wage laws
   b. legislation with regard to working conditions, fringe benefits, etc.
   c. social security
   d. public sector wage policy

5. Output Prices
   a. consumer prices
   b. producer prices

6. Direct Regulatory Controls
   a. enterprise licensing and registration
   b. monopoly privileges
   c. land allocation and tenure
   d. zoning
   e. health

Although conceived in isolation one from another, these policies – labour market, interest rate, trade and agricultural policies, to name a few – cumulate and interact to form a system of incentives to which entrepreneurs respond. Table 2 furnishes an inventory of policies according to standard, functional categories, while Table 3 shows how these policies influence input and product markets. Perhaps the most striking conclusion

**Table 3 A view of the factor and product markets: points of policy intervention influencing production, employment and the size distribution of firms**

*Factor and Other Input Markets*

1. Policies affecting the price and availability of capital
   a. interest rates and credit availability [2b]
   b. import duties and quotas [1a, 1b]
   c. exchange rate and controls [1d, 1e]
   d. capital-based taxes (e.g., accelerated depreciation) [3b]

2. Policies affecting the price of labour
   a. minimum wage laws [4a]
   b. labour legislation [4b, 4c]
   c. public sector wages [4d]
   d. policies toward unions [4]
   e. labour-based taxes [3b]

3. Policies affecting the availability and price of other inputs
   a. import duties [1a]
   b. exchange rates and controls [1d, 1e]
   c. price controls [5b]

4. Regulatory policies affecting the relative profitability of different producers and production techniques
   a. zoning [6d]
   b. licensing and registration [6a]
   c. monopoly privileges [6d]

*Output Markets*

1. Policies affecting demand for domestic products through the price of competitive traded goods
   a. effective rates of protection (import duties on inputs and outputs) [1a, 1b]
   b. exchange rates [1d, 1e]
   c. export taxation [1c]

2. Policies affecting demand through sectoral income distribution (agriculture versus industry; rural versus urban)
   a. differential structure of protection [1a, 1b]
   b. differential export taxation [1c]
   c. differential foreign exchange rates and access [1d, 1e]
   d. differential expenditure on services and infrastructure [3a]
   e. differential taxation [3b]
   f. differential output pricing [3a, 3b]

3. Policies affecting demand through vertical income distribution
   a. fiscal policy, transfers and taxation [3a, 3b]
   b. item 2 above

4. Price controls for finished products [5a]

The numbers in brackets refer to policies listed in Table 2

to be drawn from Table 3 is how wide a range of policies come into play to influence the price of capital, the price of labour, prices of material inputs, the profitability of various categories of production and the structure of demand for non-agricultural products.

In the factor markets, exchange rates, tariffs, import duties and interest rates affect the price of capital faced by firms of different size in the economy. Minimum wage laws and other types of labour legislation,

64

government salary structures and policies governing union activities all affect the price of labour. Tariff rates, exchange rates and price controls affect the price of material inputs. Regulatory policies such as zoning and licensing laws affect the relative profitability of different enterprise groups as well as different commodities.

In the output markets, a range of trade policies affect the demand for domestic products, either through the price of competing imports or the price at which exports can be sold. An even wider array of trade, fiscal and price policies affect the sectoral and vertical distribution of income. It is believed that increased agricultural income, increased rural income, increased export production and increased incomes for the poor will all increase the demand for more labour-intensive products, often produced by smaller enterprises. This implies that a great range of demand side policies can play a potentially significant role in influencing aggregate employment in an economy.

By definition, policy distortions lead to allocative inefficiencies and hence to lower output than would prevail in a distortion-free world. Numerous authors have suggested that these distortions also lead to lower employment, because of the biases common in many trade, credit and fiscal policies. As a first step in examining the validity of these contentions, the empirical evidence relating to the magnitude of these distortions will now be considered. This is followed by a discussion of the extent to which these observed distortions have had an impact on patterns of output and employment in the economy.

### The nature and magnitude of existing distortions
Empirical estimation of the magnitude of distortions is an inherently difficult task. There are a variety of sources of divergences in different parts of a segmented market between prices of factors of production (eg, unskilled labour or capital) or of finished products (eg, shirts). Some of those divergences have a 'real' basis such that they would continue to exist even in a distortion-free world with perfect information; these include such things as quality differences (for labour or finished products), or differences in risk or administrative costs (for capital). It is only after correcting for these 'real' sources of divergences that one could refer to remaining differences as distortions. These in turn might arise from a variety of different sources. For our purposes, we wish to separate them (conceptually, at least!) into those which result from policies, versus all others. The latter category might include price divergences arising from lack of information and/or power of some participants to manipulate markets. What this means is that not all *divergences* between prices in segmented factor or product markets should be called *distortions*, and not all *distortions* arise because of *policies*. Our interest in this paper is in policy-induced distortions. Where possible in the subsequent discussion,

we shall attempt to keep these distinctions clear; needless to say, in the review of empirical data, this is generally virtually impossible. It is for this reason among others that the data must be interpreted with caution and used to indicate rough orders of magnitude rather than precise measures.

Although the existence of policy-induced distortions has been widely recognized in many developing countries, relatively few attempts have been made to quantify them. (The World Bank has recently done a study in which they classified 31 countries according to the degree of distortions in factor prices, product prices, and foreign exchange prices. For sub-categories of each of these headings, the Bank staff used quantitative measures plus their own judgment to classify the extent of distortion as high, medium, or low.)[9] As Krueger *et al* point out in their comprehensive study of trade and employment in developing countries, 'little is known about the probable orders of magnitude ... and their consequences'.[10] With the possible exception of trade effects, the treatment of this topic has been piecemeal and sporadic. This section marshalls the limited evidence that exists on the nature and magnitude of distortions, highlighting those that differentially affect large and small non-agricultural enterprises. Policies affecting the factor market will be examined first, focusing particularly on the labour and capital market distortions and how they affect the relative costs of employing these inputs in enterprises of different sizes. This will be followed by a discussion of distortions influencing the product market.

**Factor market distortions**
Government policies can introduce a variety of distortions, many of which operate through differential impacts on costs of factor inputs facing large and small firms. The primary focus of this section is on the labour and capital markets.

*Labour market distortions*
Labour markets in developing countries are frequently segmented in a fashion that parallels the distinction between large and small enterprises. Empirical evidence of a wage gap along these lines is well documented.[8,11,12] Although the range of wages among small firms is wide, the average real wage for unskilled workers in large-scale firms is often on the order of twice that in small- and medium-sized firms.[13-17] A portion of this gap reflects subtle differences in skill levels and labour turnover, since large firms are more likely to be able to select the most proficient and reliable of the unskilled workers. (Variation in personal attributes such as commitment and stability as well as ability, experience and skill are discussed in Squire[2] and Mazumdar.[18]) Nevertheless, some of the gap may be due to policy intervention that differentially affects enterprises of different sizes. Although such interventions as minimum wage legislation, mandated

fringe benefits, restrictions on the ability to fire workers, and government-encouraged union pressures exist in many developing countries, there is evidence that these are applied primarily only to the larger, more visible enterprises. (Fringe benefits are relatively more important in Latin America than elsewhere and weigh more heavily in larger than smaller firms.[2]) The ubiquitous smaller enterprises are usually either formally exempt from such regulations or escape through lax enforcement.

Minimum wage legislation is one of the main forms of government intervention in the market for unskilled labour and is an important feature in most developing countries. Watanabe's international survey of such legislation indicates that the precise form as well as the effectiveness of implementation of minimum wage legislation varies from country to country.[19-29] In several cases, such as in the Sudan[30], the Philippines [31], and Thailand [32], small and medium firms are specifically exempt from coverage. In other instances, the minimum wage is set sufficiently low that actual wage rates in the small-scale sector exceed the minimum, as in Egypt and Zaire.[13] In most cases, however, the minimum wage is not enforced in small firms.[19] (Puerto Rico is recognized as perhaps the one exception where relatively high minimum wages are effectively applied to enterprises of all sizes.) These findings are consistent with information generated from small firm surveys, which indicate that virtually none of the small entrepreneurs feels directly affected by such legislation.[5] Thus, there is substantial evidence that the labour prices facing small-scale non-farm enterprises are relatively undistorted and closely approximate the opportunity cost of that labour. Frequently, however, the medium-sized and even some large firms find themselves subject to formal or variable enforcement, which can subject them to undue harassment or to pressures for side payments, and thus lead to some distortions.

The accumulating empirical evidence also indicates that even for large firms the effects of minimum wage legislation appear to be limited. In several countries, including Sierra Leone[16], the Philippines[31], and Zaire[13], larger firms pay a higher wage than the mandated minimum wage.[2] Some of this may be traceable to trade union activity (either directly or through public wage tribunals) or the hiring practices of public firms, although the empirical evidence of these effects is mixed. Moreover, since the mid-1960s, legislated wage increases in many countries have been less than increases in the general price level and have tended to follow rather than lead those in large scale private firms.

Evidence on the rough orders of magnitude of the policy induced distortions in the labour market between large and small enterprises in several countries is summarized in Table 4. In the unfettered markets of most Asian countries, labour market distortions are virtually non-existent during the period covered by these surveys. Since the mid-1970s, however, minimum wage and other labour legislation have been imposed in

**Table 4 Magnitude of policy-induced distortions in the labour costs of large-scale non-farm enterprises[a]**

|  | Country | Year | Percentage Increase in Labour Costs |
|---|---|---|---|
| *Asia* | | | |
| | Hong Kong | 1973 | 0 |
| | Indonesia | 1972 | 0 |
| | Pakistan | 1961–64 | 0 |
| | South Korea | 1969 | 0 |
| *Africa* | | | |
| | Ghana | 1972 | +25 |
| | Ivory Coast | 1971 | +23 |
| | Sierra Leone | 1976 | +20 |
| | Tunisia | 1972 | +20 |
| *Latin America* | | | |
| | Brazil | 1968 | +27 |
| | Argentina | 1973 | +15 |

[a] As discussed in the text, most small enterprises operate in essentially undistorted labour markets. The figures in the table reflect the policy-induced percentage increases in the large enterprises' wage rates, compared to those that would exist in an undistorted labour market.
Sources: Ghana: Ingram and Pearson (1981);
   Ivory Coast: Monson, (1981);
   Sierra Leone: Chuta and Liedholm (1985);
   Tunisia: Nabli (1981);
   Hong Kong: Krueger, *et al* (1983);
   Indonesia: Pitt (1981);
   Pakistan: Guisinger (1981);
   South Korea: Hong (1981);
   Brazil: Carvalho and Haddad (1981);
   Argentina: Nogues (1980).

Indonesia and Pakistan; it is unclear whether these labour markets continue to be essentially undistorted today. In a number of Latin American and African countries, minimum wage legislation and mandated social insurance schemes for larger firms frequently cause distortions. The magnitude of the distortions for the countries listed – 20–30 per cent – appears typical for other countries in those regions. Since unskilled labour is a relatively small portion of the total cost of these firms, the effect of these particular distortions may not be large. The empirical evidence seems to support the contention of Berry and Sabot[8], Webb[18], Squire[33], Steel and Takagi[1] and Krueger[34] that the extent and magnitude of labour market distortions are generally rather small.

## Capital market distortions

Three important types of capital market distortions need to be considered. The first stems from distortions that arise from the operation of domestic capital markets. The second stems from the operation of the trade regime. Within the trade regime, both the tariff structure and the operation of the foreign exchange market must be considered. Finally, there are direct taxes and related tax concessions and exemptions that can lead to distortions in the capital market.

### DOMESTIC CAPITAL MARKET DISTORTIONS

Domestic capital markets are segmented in most developing countries in ways that parallel the labour market segmentation previously described. Large firms with established credit ratings are usually able to obtain funds from commercial and public banks as well as other formal sector financial institutions. Small- and medium-scale firms rely almost entirely on traditional sources of funds, particularly personal and family savings and to a lesser extent traders, suppliers of goods, and money lenders. Indeed, the limited extent to which small enterprises rely on formal sources for their funds is striking. In small enterprise surveys in several developing countries, the vast majority reveal that less than 1 per cent of initial investment funds for small producers come from formal sources.[5]

Capital costs in formal and traditional markets are vastly different. In most developing countries, governments either explicitly or implicitly have imposed on the formal banking system interest rate ceilings or credit controls that have tended to keep these interest rates artificially low. The World Bank's review of formal sector interest rates in 34 countries revealed that in over two-thirds of them the nominal interest rates were 10 per cent or less; in several cases real interest rates were negative.[35] (The nominal interest rates in formal financial markets, however, may understate the true effective interest rate; lenders often impose additional administrative charges, special repayment provisions, forced saving requirements or other such conditions on the lender that serve to make the effective rate exceed the nominal interest rate.) Similar results are reported in more recent surveys (see Page, 1979). Faced with an excess demand for funds, banks and other formal sector financial institutions have generally responded by rationing the scarce funds by giving priority to their large-scale clients.

Evidence on the interest rates facing small and medium enterprises in traditional or informal markets indicates that they are substantially higher than these formal sector rates. A comprehensive IMF survey by Wai[36], which reviewed the 'unorganized' money market rates in 25 developing countries primarily during the 1950s, revealed that the 'usual' nominal interest rates ranged from 17 to over 100 per cent with the world-wide average falling between 30 and 40 per cent depending on the weighting

**Table 5 Formal and informal, nominal and real interest rates in selected economies**

| Country | Informal Rates (per cent) | | Fixed Rates (per cent) | |
|---|---|---|---|---|
| | Nominal | Real[d] | Nominal | Real[d] |
| **Africa** | | | | |
| Ethiopia[a] | 70 | 66 | 12 | 8 |
| Ghana[a] | 70 | 64 | 6 | 0 |
| Ivory Coast[a] | 150 | 145 | 10 | 6 |
| Nigeria[a] | 200 | 192 | 6 | −2 |
| Sudan[a] | 120 | 120 | 7 | 7 |
| Sierra Leone[b] | 75 | 60 | 12 | −3 |
| **Asia** | | | | |
| Afghanistan[a] | 33 | NA | 9 | NA |
| India[b] | 25 | 15 | 9 | −1 |
| Indonesia[a] | 40 | 29 | 14 | 3 |
| Jordan[a] | 20 | 15 | 7 | 2 |
| Malaysia[a] | 60 | 58 | 18 | 16 |
| Pakistan[a] | 30 | 27 | 7 | 4 |
| Philippines | 30 | 24 | 12 | 6 |
| South Korea[a] | 60 | 49 | 6 | 5 |
| Sri Lanka[c] | 26 | 20 | 5 | −1 |
| Thailand[b] | 29 | 27 | 9 | 7 |
| Vietnam[a] | 48 | 20 | 30 | 2 |
| **Latin America** | | | | |
| Bolivia[a] | 100 | 96 | 9 | 5 |
| Brazil[a] | 60 | 38 | 15 | −7 |
| Chile[a] | 82 | 52 | 14 | −16 |
| Colombia[b] | 48 | 40 | 24 | 16 |
| Costa Rica[a] | 24 | 20 | 8 | 4 |
| El Salvador[a] | 25 | 23 | 10 | 8 |
| Haiti[b] | 140 | 122 | 15 | −3 |
| Honduras[a] | 40 | 37 | 9 | 6 |
| Mexico[a] | 60 | 57 | 10 | 7 |

Sources:
[a] World Bank, 1975. Formal rates are the average of those charged on various types of loans by agricultural credit institutions. Informal rates are from various credit studies in the reporting countries. Both sets of figures cover the period from 1967–70.
[b] Chuta and Liedholm, 1979. Data are from the period 1970–75
[c] Wai, 1977
[d] Real rates were obtained by subtracting from nominal rates the average annual rate of increase in the consumer price index for 1967–70 for World Bank countries or 1972–75 for Liedholm-Chuta countries.

scheme used. More recent studies have also found similarly high rates in the informal or unorganized credit markets. A World Bank survey, based on studies of informal credit markets in 23 countries during the late 1960s and early 1970s, found that real rates in excess of 100 per cent were not unusual and that the median real interest rate world-wide was 40 per cent.[35] (Wai has also undertaken a follow-up study examining interest rates in informal markets, mostly in the period 1968–71. His figures suggest some decline in these rates over the two decades from the first study to the second. The mean figures declined from 44 per cent to 40 per cent, while the median figures dropped from 33 per cent to 30 per cent. There were many differences in the country coverage of the two studies, however; the first study covered data from 22 countries, the second from a somewhat different list of 33. For the 13 countries for which data were available in both time periods (albeit often based on quite different primary studies), the mean interest rates in informal markets declined from 40 per cent to 30 per cent, while the median dropped from 34 per cent to 28 per cent.[37] In virtually every country, small firms faced real interest rates ranging from three to over ten times those facing their larger-scale counterparts. A summary of the quantitative evidence on the magnitude of the interest rate differentials is presented in Table 5.

To some extent, higher rates in traditional capital markets are simply a reflection of the higher risks and higher transactions costs of providing funds to small enterprises. Differences in the duration of the loans made in formal and informal financial markets may also account for some of the observed differences in interest rates. Loans in traditional capital markets are usually made on a very short-term basis; lending through formal institutions, on the other hand, may be for fixed or working capital purposes, but is generally for longer periods than in informal markets. The effect of this difference on interest rates is unclear. In developed countries, long-term rates generally exceed short-term ones. Yet, in developing countries, the pattern is generally reversed.[37] A partial explanation for this term structure of interest rates in developing countries may lie precisely in the fact that longer-term lending is generally undertaken by formal sector institutions and is more likely to be subject to interest rate ceilings.

It is frequently argued that the administrative costs and risk premiums associated with small loans greatly exceed those associated with larger loans.[13] One of the reasons behind the higher perceived risks of lending to small firms concerns the general lack of information about such borrowers, which makes it difficult and expensive for financial institutions to screen good borrowers from 'lemons'. Consequently, commercial banks and other formal financial institutions act to reduce this perceived risk by insisting on full collateral and by dealing primarily with established, large-scale borrowers. Collateral requirements not only operate to enhance repayment, but also to provide compensation to lenders in the event of default. Informal lenders frequently do not require collateral; they thus lack comparable protection from loss. The result is that their private risk from

71

default would be higher, even if actual default rates were comparable so the default risks to the society (ie, the social risks) were comparable for formal and informal sector lending.

Empirical evidence on this issue has been somewhat sparse in the past, but new evidence is emerging. In a recent review of the literature, Liedholm reports that transaction costs for small-scale loans may be lower than previously imagined.[38] Administrative costs as a per cent of loan value in informal markets in India and in several innovative small enterprise lending schemes are less than 6 per cent. Moreover, the arrears and default rates on many of these schemes compare quite favourably with those of lending schemes to larger borrowers. For many developing countries, probably no more than 10 percentage points of the interest rate differential between the formal and informal markets can·be traced to these administrative and risk transaction costs.[31]

A summary of empirical evidence on the quantitative magnitude of distortions in the domestic capital market for selected countries is presented in Table 7. To the extent possible, adjustments have been made in these figures for administrative and risk differentials between large and small borrowers, so these figures can be described as measures of capital market distortions between these different types of borrowers. Except for Hong Kong these distortions are quite large, exceeding 30 per cent. No significant differences are apparent among different regions of the world. Relative to what would exist in integrated and distortion-free capital markets, the actual cost of capital to large firms is unduly low. That for small firms may be closer to capital's real shadow rate, although in some instances the rate facing small firms may exceed the shadow price of capital. (In Sierra Leone, for example, it was estimated from field surveys that the risk free return to informal lenders was approximately 43 per cent; subtracting 6 percentage points for administrative costs yields 37 per cent as a measure of the informal market rate. When the country's 15 per cent inflation rate was subtracted from this figure, it closely approximated Sierra Leone's assumed shadow price for capital, 20 per cent.[16]) In such a distortion-free financial market, much of the currently-observed interest rate differential would disappear.

FOREIGN TRADE REGIME-INDUCED CAPITAL DISTORTIONS
The tariff structure and the operation of the foreign exchange market also introduce distortions that differentially affect large and small non-agricultural enterprises. In particular, they can do so by distorting the prices facing firms of different sizes for imported capital goods.

The import duty structure introduces enterprise size distortions in two important ways. First, many capital (as well as intermediate) inputs used by small non-farm enterprises are classified as consumer goods. Since in most countries the structure of protection involves relatively high duties on consumer goods and relatively low duties on intermediate and capital goods, the small firms end up paying relatively high duties on these items. In Sierra Leone, for example, items such as sewing machines and outboard motors are crucial capital goods for small producers, but were apparently classified as consumer goods since they were taxed on the order of 35 per cent, the same rate normally levied on imported consumer goods.[16] In Burkina Faso, a similar pattern emerges, with import duties of 72 per cent on hand tools, 63 per cent on electrically powered wood and metalworking tools, and 41 per cent on sewing machines.[39]

Second, in many developing countries, large-scale enterprises are granted industrial investment incentives that enable them to import their capital goods duty-free for an extended period. These concessions are granted by government agencies that administer the investment tax codes to qualified or 'priority' enterprises. Usually, these are large-scale, modern, import-substitution activities considered to be crucial to the country's development, although sometimes 'modern' export activities are included as well (such as in the Ivory Coast[40] or in South Korea[41].) In some countries, the incentive laws specifically exclude firms below a certain size; in most countries, however, small firms are either ignorant of the concessions available or are unable to undertake the protracted bureaucratic procedures required to obtain them.[38]

There are only limited data to measure the magnitude of this distortion in the price of capital due to the differential treatment of imported capital. Nogues estimates that in Argentina investors eligible for duty-free imports of machinery received a subsidy of about 40 per cent of their capital costs.[42] In Sierra Leone, it was estimated that large firms accorded import duty relief on their capital also obtained an implicit subsidy of approximately 25 per cent compared to their smaller-scale counterparts in the same industries. As an additional perspective on the differential treatment created by the import duty relief in Sierra Leone, it was estimated that the effective rate of tariff protection for large-scale clothing producers, all of whom received such relief, was 430 per cent, while for their smaller counterparts in the same industry, the effective rate of protection was only 29 per cent. (The effective rate of protection (ERP) is the rate of protection provided to domestic value added in a particular activity, taking account of tariffs on both outputs and inputs. The higher the value of the ERP, the greater is the protection. In the Sierra Leone case cited above, both large and small firms received identical nominal protection on their output but received substantially different tariff treatment on their inputs.) Thus, these investment concessions coupled with the tariff structure have operated in several countries to create a differential in the cost of capital between large and small enterprises.

Quantitative restrictions on imports through quotas and licensing have also served to create distortions in the price of imported capital between small and large enterprises. Import licensing has been a major instrument of protection in several countries either as a substitute for or an adjunct to the tariff structure. Bhagwati, in his authoritative volume on exchange control regimes, argues that 'the majority of authorities like to think of themselves as biasing access to imports in favour of the smaller applicants and indeed in countries such as India and Pakistan, this . . . was considered one of the benefits of an import control system'.[43] The evidence produced by his nine country studies indicated, however, that 'in point of fact . . ., *ex post* outcomes appear to have been disturbingly concentrated on the large-scale applicants'. For Ghana, Leith indicated a deliberate bias in favour of large importers[44] while in the case of India, Bhagwati and Srinivasan concluded that the control system discriminated against the small-scale sector.[45] For Pakistan, Guisinger reported that 'in the 1960s, few small-scale manufacturing firms in Pakistan had access to import licences, and when they purchased foreign equipment it was through import agents who appropriated the scarcity value of the import licences for themselves'.[46] According to Bhagwati, the reasons for the bias against small producers include:

1. Ease of administration in dealing with smaller numbers of successful applicants;
2. Feeling that larger firms were more reliable;
3. Sense that larger firms would get better terms from foreign suppliers;
4. the greater access (and contacts) of the larger firms to the bureaucracy and politicians in general, and to the licensing authorities, in particular, and;
5. Important edge obtained by the larger firms quite simply because nearly all the authorities tended to allocate to past shares or other quantity-related variables.[43]

What is the magnitude of the differentials created by such a system? Guisinger contends that in Pakistan during the 1960s tariff protection was a far less significant factor in overall protection than import licensing. He estimated that the capital cost differential between large and small firms caused by the trade-regime was approximately 38 per cent. Even when small firms in Pakistan purchased machinery made locally, he felt that 'the prices generally reflected the full scarcity margins and tariff duties on the capital and intermediate inputs used in their production'.[46]

In many developing countries, the operation of the market for foreign exchange also contributes to differentials in the capital prices facing large and small enterprises. The exchange rate in many developing countries is overvalued, so that the market price of foreign exchange in terms of domestic currency is below its equilibrium values. Consequently, the prices of imported capital and other imported inputs are unduly low compared to those with access to foreign exchange at the official rate.

## Table 6 Degree of currency overvaluation

| Country | Year | Per cent of currency overvaluation |
|---|---|---|
| **Africa** | | |
| Botswana | 1983[a] | 10 |
| Cameroon | 1979[b] | 0 |
| Ghana | 1983[a] | 228 |
| Egypt | 1983[a] | 66 |
| Ivory Coast | 1979[b] | 10 |
| Kenya | 1983[a] | 17 |
| Malawi | 1983[a] | 60 |
| Nigeria | 1983[a] | 45 |
| Senegal | 1979[b] | 40 |
| Sierra Leone | 1983[a] | 37 |
| Sierra Leone | 1976[b] | 15 |
| Tunisia | 1983[a] | 12 |
| Zambia | 1983[a] | 27 |
| **Asia** | | |
| Bangladesh | 1983[a] | 42 |
| Hong Kong | 1983[a] | 0 |
| India | 1983[a] | 28 |
| Indonesia | 1983[a] | 0 |
| Malaysia | 1965[c] | 4 |
| Malaysia | 1983[a] | 1 |
| Pakistan | 1963[c] | 50 |
| Pakistan | 1983[a] | 30 |
| Philippines | 1963[c] | 15 |
| Philippines | 1983[a] | 50 |
| South Korea | 1983[a] | 8 |
| Taiwan | 1965[c] | 20 |
| Taiwan | 1983[a] | 6 |
| **Latin America** | | |
| Argentina | 1958[c] | 100 |
| Argentina | 1983[a] | 11 |
| Brazil | 1966[c] | 50 |
| Brazil | 1983[a] | 37 |
| Chile | 1966[c] | 68 |
| Chile | 1983[a] | 17 |
| Colombia | 1968[c] | 22 |
| Colombia | 1983[a] | 21 |
| Jamaica | 1983[a] | 14 |
| Honduras | 1983[a] | 43 |
| Mexico | 1960[c] | 15 |
| Mexico | 1983[a] | 20 |

Sources: [a] World Currency Yearbook (1984); black market premiums as of 31 December 1983. [b] Jansen (1980). [c] Healy (1972), citing Little, *et al* (1970) and Balassa (1971).

What is the extent and magnitude of these currency overvaluations? The empirical evidence, summarized in Table 6, indicates that it is quite widespread and has been important in most countries at some time. In the Krueger *et al* review of trade and employment conditions in 13 countries during the post-war period, only Hong Kong escapes, although South Korea, Brazil, and the the Ivory Coast had rates that were thought to be close to equilibrium for some periods.[10] The estimates of the degree of exchange overvaluation for those countries ranged from 20–40 per cent. In Jansen's review of 14 African economies in 1979, he found that the average overvaluation amounted to 40 per cent, with quite a wide variance ranging from 0 (Cameroon) to 300 per cent (Ghana).[47] Black market foreign exchange rates also indicate a similar pattern of overvaluation.

Since there is an excess demand for foreign exchange at an overvalued exchange rate, the government must employ some rationing mechanism to determine who is allowed to import at the implicitly subsidized rate. In some countries this is done through multiple exchange rates; at the end of 1984, some 25 countries were maintaining multiple exchange rate systems.[48] Usually, only the large firms in priority activities were permitted to obtain foreign exchange at the lowest rates, leaving the smaller enterprises to pay the higher rates and thus creating a differential. Other methods used to ration available foreign exchange are quantitative restrictions and systems of tariffs, both of which were previously seen to create distortions between large and small firms.

The orders of magnitude of capital market distortions caused by currency overvaluation coupled with differential tariffs or licensing systems for various countries are set forth in Table 7. Pakistan, Ghana, Sierra Leone, and Tunisia, the four countries with trade regime capital distortions, were all following import-substitution strategies. In these countries, overvalued currencies, combined with relatively low, often zero, rates of protection on imports of capital goods of larger firms made the capital imports of large enterprises unduly low in price. Sierra Leone and Tunisia relied primarily on tariff rates to regulate the capital inflow, while Ghana and Pakistan relied primarily on licensing. Yet, in all four countries, the order of magnitude of the capital price distortion between large and small enterprises caused by the trade regime ranged from 25 to almost 40 per cent, not an insignificant amount. Distortions of similar magnitude were claimed to exist in Uruguay, Argentina, Chile, and Indonesia.[10] On the other hand, negligible trade regime capital distortions were reported to exist in Hong Kong, South Korea (1975), and Brazil (1968), whose currencies were not greatly overvalued at that time and were following export promotion strategies.

76

Table 7 Policy-induced factor price distortions in large and small non-agricultural enterprises
(Expressed as the per cent difference in large firms' costs relative to small firms)

| Country | Period | Per cent difference in labour costs | Per cent difference in capital cost[a] owing to: | | | Total capital | Per cent difference in wage/capital rental rate |
|---------|--------|------|------|------|------|------|------|
| | | | Trade régime | Interest rate | Taxes | | |
| *Asia* | | | | | | | |
| Hong Kong | 1973 | 0 | 0 | 0 | 0 | 0 | 0 |
| Pakistan | 1961–64 | 0 | −38 | −44 | +22 | −60 | +150 |
| South Korea | 1973 | 0 | −5 | −35 | +10 | −30 | +43 |
| *Africa* | | | | | | | |
| Ghana | 1972 | +25 | −25 | −42 | +26 | −41 | +119 |
| Sierra Leone | 1976 | +20 | −25 | −60 | +20 | −65 | +243 |
| Tunisia | 1972 | +20 | −30 | −33 | NA[b] | NA | NA |
| *Latin America* | | | | | | | |
| Brazil | 1968 | +27 | 0 | −33 | NA | NA | NA |

[a] All capital related figures have been converted into the annual rental value of a unit of capital (or user costs) using a modification of the capital recovery formula presented in Guisinger (1981 p. 329).

[b] NA = Data not Available

Sources: Hong Kong: Krueger, *et al* (1983); Pakistan: Guisinger (1981); analysis based on those large firms receiving special incentives; taxes for large from White (1974) based on estimate of actual tax paid; assumes small pay no tax. South Korea: Hong (1981). Figures adjusted to reflect actual duty paid by small firms; interest rate differential reflects curb market interest rate (adjusted) facing small. Ghana: Ingram and Pearson (1981); analysis based on projection derived from sample of seven large firms (out of a total of 158) receiving investment concessions; also reflects overvaluation of currency and 'real' (adjusted) interest rate differential between large and small firms. Sierra Leone: Liedholm (1985); tax figure estimated from actual tax payments made by large firms as a percentage of before tax profits based on figures in Anderson (1972). Assumes small pay no direct taxes. Tunisia: Nabli (1981); figures compare only public (large) and private (small). Brazil: Carvalho and Haddad (1981).

DOMESTIC TAX-INDUCED CAPITAL DISTORTIONS

The domestic tax policies of developing countries can also create distortions that differentially affect non-agricultural enterprises of various sizes. Among large enterprises, the previously mentioned investment concessions frequently provide not just subsidized capital and import duty relief, but also other tax inducements such as income tax holidays, accelerated depreciation allowances and property tax reductions. These direct tax concessions affect the returns to capital and thus contribute to capital cost differentials between those large enterprises receiving them and those which do not.

The treatment of the direct tax component of the investment concessions package also creates distortions between large and small enterprises. Small enterprises are frequently not subject to direct taxes, which gives them a differential *advantage* over those large enterprises *not* receiving such concessions. Many small firms, the majority of which are unincorporated, are formally exempt from such taxes. In Sierra Leone, for example, no income tax was paid in 1965 if yearly income was below $560, a figure that was four times the country's average per capita income. In other instances, smaller firms may be formally subject to tax, but are able to avoid payment because of lax enforcement and the difficulty of collecting from widely-dispersed small firms. Needless to say, large firms in such environments are also often able to avoid these payments as well.

Data on the magnitude of these direct tax-induced differentials are particularly sparse, but information from a few countries is presented in Table 7. Most of these are probably upper-bound estimates of the distortions, because it is assumed that, except in Korea, small firms pay no direct taxes, and that all direct taxes fall on returns to capital of large firms. (There is continuing controversy concerning the locus of the burden of the corporate profits tax. In the short-run (and assuming that firms operate in a profit-maximizing fashion), the burden of the tax falls on the owners of the capital in taxed (large) firms. In the long-run, however, the burden can potentially be shared by capital owners in the untaxed (small) firms as well as by other groups in the economy.[49] It should be noted, however, that the tax is levied on the firm's 'accounting' rather than on its 'economic' profit and thus is directly imposed on the return to capital of the owner.) The limited evidence indicates that outside the special cases of Hong Kong and South Korea, direct taxes increase the effective capital costs of large over small non-agricultural enterprises by at most 20 to 25 per cent. Investment concessions, special tax provisions, and tax evasion 'enjoyed' by many of the larger enterprises operate to reduce the magnitude of their apparent legal direct tax burden, which sometimes amounts to over 50 per cent of a larger firm's profits. (For example, rough – and probably conservative – calculations from Jamaica indicate that large firms actually paid out only about half of their total tax liability in 1981 (calculated from Wozny[50] and Government of Jamaica, 1981).[51]) The actual tax burden incurred by the larger firms thus partially offsets, but does not eliminate, the overall capital cost advantage they enjoy over smaller non-agricultural enterprises.

In summary, capital market distortions, whether caused by domestic or foreign trade policies, were a significant factor in virtually every country examined (the sole exception being Hong Kong). The difference in capital costs between large and small enterprises ranged from 30 to 65 per cent. The differentials were greatest in countries following import-substitution strategies, where both foreign and domestic policies contributed, often in equal amounts, to the capital price distortion. Yet even in export promotion countries significant distortions existed due primarily to domestic policies. In the majority of instances, most of the distortion came from the unduly low price of capital facing large firms. Capital prices facing the smaller enterprises were closer to their 'shadow' or social prices, although it could be argued that in some instances the actual price of domestic capital facing the small enterprises may have exceeded its domestic shadow price.

## Total magnitude of factor cost distortions

A review of Table 3 above makes it clear that distortions arise in factor markets from a variety of sources. In particular, four major categories of distortions are identified: those arising in capital markets; those working through labour markets; those which affect the availability and price of other inputs; those which operate through regulatory policies, affecting the relative profitability of different producers or different production technologies. Our discussion, of necessity, has focused on the first two of these, since these are areas where it was possible to obtain empirical estimates of the magnitudes of policy-induced distortions. Unfortunately, quantitative data on the differential impact of regulations by firm size is sparse and net effect of such regulations cannot be specified with certainty.

Some tentative hypotheses, based on impressionistic findings, relating to the differential effect of regulations on firm size, might be set forth. These effects would seem to vary depending on the type of regulation. Municipal zoning regulations, for example, appear to have, on balance, a negative effect on small enterprises because of the local nature of their markets and their crucial need to deal directly with pedestrian consumers. Small firms are often excluded from certain urban areas for aesthetic rather than health or safety reasons. Such policies create a bias in favour of larger firms, which tend to be relatively less dependent on close proximity to local markets (see, for example, Kilby's description of such regulations in Kenya[52]). The net effect of registration and licensing requirements, on the other hand, are more problematic. The smallest firms in general do not register and are not licensed with public authorities. When small firms are specifically excluded by law, as they are in some African countries, this would constitute a bias *in favour* of the smaller producers. When the small are formally subject to these rules, however, the scope for haphazard and discriminatory enforcement grows, particularly for the more visible intermediate-sized firms. The degree to which firms are actually affected by these regulations is uncertain and, indeed, is a research topic of some importance. Finally, since licensing and registration fees can be viewed as overhead expenses, per unit of output they fall much more heavily on the smallest firms when levied. On balance, the differential effect of these regulations on firms of different size cannot be stated with certainty.

Looking only at capital and labour market distortions, the orders of magnitude of the resulting distortions between large and small enterprises in selected countries are summarized in Table 7. The figures provide a crude measure of the degree to which the wage/capital rental ratios between such enterprises diverge from those that would have prevailed under well-functioning factor markets.

The evidence indicates that the total effect of the factor cost distortions has been quite sizeable in most of these countries. The labour market, trade regime, and domestic capital market factors have all tended to work in the same direction, to induce higher labour costs and lower capital costs for larger enterprises when compared with their smaller-scale counterparts. Taxes operated in the opposite direction, but they served only partially to offset these other factors. Although each of these sources of pricing disparity between large and small enterprises by itself can be important, operating together the effects are generally magnified. In Sierra Leone, Ghana, and Pakistan, for example, the wage/capital ratio facing large non-agricultural firms was more than twice that facing the smaller enterprises. In Argentina, Nogues estimates that, under certain assumptions, the wage/rental ratio in the modern sector might be as much as eight times that in the traditional sector.[52]

There is no single pattern to the relative importance of the various sources of factor price distortion. Pakistan, which had one of the largest overall disparities, had a relatively free labour market. Ghana, on the other hand, had distortions from all sources, yet had a somewhat lower overall level of factor market distortions. The rank order of the overall level of distortion thus seems to be independent of number of sources of that distortion. There is some evidence, however, that exporting countries such as Hong Kong, South Korea, and Brazil had lower levels of total factor market distortions than did import-substituting countries.

**Product market distortions**
In addition to factor market distortions, government policies also cause product market distortions that affect the pattern of production and employment among firms of different size. Taxes and subsidies on domestic and foreign goods, for example, can alter the production structure that would result from efficient resource allocation. Estimates of the quantitative magnitude of these distortions are even rarer than those relating to factor markets and thus the 'rough order of magnitude' caveat applies with even greater force here.

Although a large number of different types of policies affect production, employment, and the size distribution of firms through their effects on output markets, most of these fall under the heading of trade policies, as Table 3 makes clear. In fact most of the discussion of this section relating to product markets concerns the ways in which trade policies affect these markets. Our discussion follows the same order as that given in Table 3: after a brief overview of alternative trade strategies, we look first at ways in which the trade regime directly affects the competititve position of domestic producers of different sizes. We then examine the ways in which these trade policies affect the pattern of income in the economy and finally explore the links between these income distribution dimensions and patterns of production and employment by firm size.

## Foreign trade regimes: an overview

The foreign trade strategy adopted by a country plays a central role in determining the nature and extent of product market distortions found in the country. Import-substitution regimes, which were dominant in the developing world during the 1960s, usually had the following characteristics:

1. High levels of protection to a number of industries, with a wide range of levels of effective protection;
2. Extensive quantitative controls and bureaucratic regulations, particularly with respect to imports; and
3. Overvalued exchange rates.

Export promotion regimes, by contrast, were generally characterized as having:

1. Minimal or zero levels of protection for local activities;
2. Few quantitative restrictions on imports;
3. Equilibrium exchange rates; and
4. Some subsidization of exports.

Taiwan, South Korea (beginning in 1961), Hong Kong, and Singapore – 'the Baby Tigers' – along with Brazil (after 1967), Colombia (after 1970) and the Ivory Coast (after 1960) are often cited as countries that have adopted export promotion strategies.

Empirical evidence clearly supports these characterizations. In the nine countries studied by the National Bureau of Economic Research, careful calculations were made of each country's effective exchange rate, which corrects the official exchange rate to reflect the duties, subsidies and quota premiums for exports and imports (see Table 8).[53] Only in South Korea did the effective exchange rate for exporters exceed that for importers, indicating that exporters received more in local currency per dollar of foreign exchange earned than importers had to pay. (South Korea as well as Brazil, beginning in the late 1960s, sought to sustain the effective exchange rate for exports over time and prevent it from falling below the import rate, through continuous adjustments of the exchange rate and subsidies.[54]) In all the other countries, all of which followed import-substitution regimes, the biases favoured production for imports over export promotion.

81

## Table 8 Effective exchange rates (local currency per US$)

| Country | Year | Trade strategy | Effective exchange rates exports (EERx) | Effective exchange rates imports (EERm) |
|---|---|---|---|---|
| Brazil | 1964 | IS | 1874.0 | 2253.0 |
| Chile | 1965 | IS | 3.3 | 3.8 |
| Egypt | 1962 | — | 43.5 | 42.9 |
| Ghana | 1967 | IS | 0.8 | 1.5 |
| India | 1966 | IS | 6.8 | 9.2 |
| Korea (S) | 1964 | EP | 281.0 | 247.0 |
| Philippines | 1970 | IS | 5.2 | 8.7 |
| Turkey | 1970 | IS | 12.9 | 24.0 |

Source: Krueger, 1978, p. 73
Note: IS=Import Substitution
EP=Export Promotion

An important feature of the export promotion regimes is the large package of incentives granted to exporters. Several instruments are used, including tax incentives, tariff exemptions, and direct subsidies per unit of sales, all of which operate to introduce special benefits for sales in export markets. Carvalho and Haddad estimated for Brazil that it required only 68 per cent of the sales price abroad to compensate the firm for a loss of sales domestically, once the export inducements were taken into account.[55] For South Korea, Westphal and Kim estimated that exporters received subsidies worth about 30 per cent of the commodity's total value when selling abroad.[56] As these and other studies make clear, the exporting success of a number of these newly industrializing countries, far from arising out of the free play of market forces in a laissez-faire environment, rested heavily on a set of government interventions providing extensive export incentives to designated producers.[57,58]

### Differentials by size of enterprise in tariff protection and export assistance

To what extent has the structure of tariff protection and of export assistance varied according to the size of enterprise receiving this assistance? Unfortunately, most of the trade studies have paid little or no attention to the size issue, so the empirical evidence is particularly scanty. On the import side, one exception is Anderson and Khambata's study of small enterprises in the Philippines.[59] Examining the tariff structure of that country, they found that sectors which provided over two-thirds of small-scale employment had negative rates of effective protection, while sectors where large-scale enterprise predominated possessed effective rates ranging from 25 to over 500 per cent.

Two other studies have also examined the size issue with respect to effective protection. In Indonesia, Hiemenz and Bruch found a negative correlation between the share of small-enterprise production in a particular industry and the effective rates of protection.[60] For Malaysia, von Rabenau demonstrated that average plant size is much higher in highly protected industries (ie, with effective protection rates above 100) than in less protected ones.[61] The limited evidence would thus indicate that the sectors in which small-scale enterprises are found in greater numbers tend to be discriminated against by the tariff structure. Direct evidence of the differential effect of other product market distortions by size of enterprise is conspicuous by its absence.

Turning to the size distribution of enterprises benefiting from export incentives, Krueger et al argued that 'an important feature of export promotion regimes is that these incentives are provided to anyone who exports. They provide a uniform degree of bias among exporting activities'.[10] There is, however, contrary evidence. In Korea, for example, it appears that only the larger exporting enterprises were eligible for subsidies. Frank et al, note that under the Trade Transaction Law of 1957 there were minimum export values, which rose over time, before an exporter could be registered by the authorities and thus be eligible for subsidies.[54] A prerequisite for registration was a minimum export of $5,000 for exporters and a minimum export of $20,000 for importers. To maintain a privileged status, traders also had to sustain annual exports exceeding $20,000 per year for exporters and $100,000 for importers. There is evidence that many small enterprises were unable to meet these volumes and thus that the foreign trade regime may have operated to create a further distortion in the product market between large and small enterprises. Scitovsky argues that, perhaps as a result of this discrimination, large firms have played a major role in Korea's export boom.[57] In Taiwan, on the other hand, where the policy stance has been less discriminating (and for a number of other reasons as well), small firms have played a much larger role in industrial development, including in export production.

### Agriculture and industry
In addition to the direct effects of the trade regime just discussed on enterprises of different sizes, there are also indirect effects operating through the structure of production and income in the economy, working back in this way through the pattern of demand to the level of output and employment among firms of different size. Our discussion here focuses on the sectoral dimension of this reasoning, and in particular, on the impact of

trade regimes on the distribution of income between agricultural and industrial sectors. There is considerable evidence to support the widely-held view that policies in many developing countries have tended to be biased against agriculture in favour of industrial activities. The tariff structure of many developing countries is biased against agriculture, particularly in those countries following import substitution strategies. Industrial and other non-agricultural products in these countries are protected by relatively high tariffs, while agricultural products typically are not. Protection thus acts like a tax on agriculture, raising the price of industrial products in relation to agricultural goods in the domestic market.

**Table 9 Effective rates of protection**

| Country | Year | Trade Strategy | Agriculture | Manufac-turing | Consumer Goods[b] | Inter-mediate Goods[b] | Capital Goods[b] |
|---------|------|---------|-------------|---------|---------|---------|---------|
| Brazil | 1966 | IS[a] | 46 | 127 | 198 | 151 | 33 |
| Chile | 1961 | IS | 58 | 158 | 226 | 150 | 16 |
| India | 1968 | IS | 12 | 95 | 128 | 82 | 78 |
| Korea | 1968 | EP | 18 | −1 | −2 | 1 | 100 |
| Mexico | 1960 | — | 6 | 32 | 50 | 40 | 21 |
| Malaysia | 1965 | — | 22 | 11 | 7 | 17 | 1 |
| Pakistan | 1963 | IS | −19 | 188 | 348 | 160 | 110 |
| Philippines | 1965 | — | 33 | 53 | 72 | 45 | 10 |

Source: Balassa, et al., 1971, p. 55 for all but India and Korea.
 Korea: Westphal and Kim, 1977.
 India: Bhagwati and Srinivasan, 1975.
[a] IS = Import Substitution and EP=Export Promotion for those countries included in the NBER studies [Krueger, 1978 and Krueger, et al, 1983].
[b] Aggregates for consumer, intermediate and capital goods are unweighted averages of the disaggregated area.

Evidence of the differential effect of import protection on agriculture and manufacturing is provided in Table 9, which lists effective rates of protection by sector for several developing countries in the 1960s. In five of the eight countries shown, the effective rates of protection enjoyed by manufacturing was more than double that of agriculture, which in one country faced a significantly negative rate of effective protection.

A broader measure of the magnitude of the bias against agriculture in several countries is provided in the studies of Little et al.[62] In a survey covering six countries in the 1960s (Brazil, Mexico, India, Pakistan, Taiwan and the Philippines), the authors measured the sectoral contribution to these nations' gross national product with and without protection, including an allowance for the overvalued exchange rate. These exchange rates generally penalized agricultural exporters, who tended to be the largest exporting group. Without protection, it is estimated that agricultural value added would have been from 8 to 48 per cent higher, while manufacturing value added would have between 8 and 94 per cent lower.

The relatively high taxes levied on agricultural exports in a wide array of countries tend to magnify the distortions caused by the import duty structure. In Sierra Leone, for example, the price paid to farmers by the marketing board was less than 50 per cent of the market price for several agricultural commodities, including coffee and cocoa.[16] Indeed, such a result is common throughout Africa. After reviewing information relating to major export crops in 13 African countries during the 1970s, the World Bank concluded that African farmers' 'tax burden, defined as the ratio of farmgate producer price to economic value at the farmgate, is on the average in the 40 to 50 per cent range'. Subsidies on inputs to farmers, the Bank contends, 'soften the impact very little, by 10–15 per cent in most cases'.[9] In summary, it is clear that policies of many developing countries have tended to discriminate against agriculture in favour of other sectors, particularly manufacturing.

As suggested above, the main impact of these intersectoral distortions on employment and the size distribution of non-agricultural enterprises arise from forces working through the structure of demand among different income recipients.

**Concluding comment**
This review of the empirical evidence has indicated that a panoply of government policies in the factor and product markets have created significant distortions that fall unevenly on non-agricultural enterprises of different sizes. Unfortunately, the few studies that have attempted to quantify the magnitude of these distortions by enterprise size have generally focused only on single policies. What is needed is a systematic examination of all these distortions arising from the entire array of policies that differentially affect firms of various sizes.

*The impact of policy distortions on the economy*
The pervasive policy distortions just described undoubtedly influence economic efficiency, employment and the size distribution of enterprises. A limited amount of empirical work has been undertaken estimating the impact of these distortions on the economy. However, the scope of coverage varies widely from study to study, with many considering only a segment of the overall policy environment. Much of this evidence consists of ex ante predictions of the effect of policy change based on partial equilibrium (or less frequently, general equilibrium) modelling exercises. A few analysts have also attempted ex post evaluations of the impact of policy

change by directly measuring key economic variables before and after significant policy changes.

In reviewing this disparate evidence, we look first at the economic impact of factor market distortions and then turn to look at distortions in output markets. Of particular concern is the effect of policy on economic efficiency and employment. Where evidence exists, we also assess the impact of policy change on the size distribution of firms. This is particularly important in its effects on employment because of the differing labour intensity in firms of different sizes, and because removal of policy distortions will shift employment in different directions in large and small firms. This means that the net impact of policy interventions on employment is strongly affected by changing market shares of small and large firms.

### Effect of policy-induced factor market distortions

*Efficiency*
The often considerable factor market distortions reviewed above lead to economic inefficiency. Estimating the magnitude of this inefficiency in developed countries has frequently led to very small projected losses, in the range of 1 per cent of GNP.[8] In developing countries, where markets – particularly capital markets – are far more distorted, one might expect considerably larger aggregate inefficiency. Estimates of allocative inefficiency in LDCs vary substantially, because they focus on different countries, in which the magnitude of policy distortions may vary significantly, and on different subsets of the total policy environment. Nonetheless, available evidence does support the expectation of higher costs in LDCs given the larger policy distortions.

Reviewing the performance of labour markets in LDCs, Berry and Sabot conclude that distortions there are normally quite small, with the ensuing resource misallocation normally amounting to less than 2 per cent of GNP.[8] They base this conclusion on partial equilibirum work by Leibenstein[63] and by Clague and Selowsky[64] as well as their own experience in studying LDC labour markets.

More recent estimates of labour market distortions have been higher. A computable general equilibrium (CGE) model for Colombia has estimated urban labour market distortions leading to inefficiencies equal to 2.7 per cent of GDP when capital stocks are assumed to be fixed and 10.7 per cent of GDP if capital is mobile among sectors.[65] This experiment examines a different set of labour market distortions from those previously discussed in this paper; it looks not at segmented labour markets (that is, differing wage rates among firms in the same industry) but rather at variable wage rates across sectors of activity. The higher estimated inefficiency in de Melo's CGE framework stems from his inclusion of interactions between production cost and quantities of both domestically produced and traded output as well as from the CGE inclusion of potential factor migration out of agriculture. Earlier partial equilibrium work makes no allowance for these interactions. Hence one's conclusion about labour market distortions depends not only on the extent to which one considers economic feedbacks and interactions but also on the mobility of factors of production.

Looking beyond labour markets, analysts have commonly found higher efficiency losses. Since most such analyses have lumped together capital and output market distortions, we have no independent assessment of the output reducing effects of capital market distortions alone. The magnitude of the capital plus output market distortions, though, has been computed to be in the range of 6 to 16 per cent of GDP in several LDCs, clearly much larger than distortions arising out of labour markets. Since most of these studies emanate from trade policy reviews, the detailed evidence is presented later under that heading. For the present it suffices to note that, while variable, inefficiency losses due to capital and output market distortions have been found to be larger than those due to labour market distortions alone.

*Employment and size distribution of firms*
Factor market distortions affect employment not only through their effect on output but also via firm-level decisions on choice of technique. Because policy-induced factor price distortions are so common in LDCs, many analysts have tried to estimate the impact of a changing wage/rental ratio on factor utilization in firms. Most have projected the impact by estimating elasticities of substitution between capital and labour. Since the introduction of the Constant Elasticity of Substitution (CES) production function in 1961, analysts have estimated manufacturing elasticities of substitution in at least 25 LDCs.[66] Bruton,[67] Morawetz,[68,69] Steel,[17] and White[66] summarize many of them. In general, these early studies measured elasticities in the range of 0.5 to 1.2.[66] Behrman provides a more recent estimate looking at evidence from 23 manufacturing activities across 70 countries and finds most elasticities of substitution not significantly different from one.[70] Although those studies were based predominantly on large-firm data, some estimates have been made looking specifically at elasticities in the very smallest firms. Chuta and Liedholm, for example, directly estimate a CES production function for a range of small-enterprise activities in Sierra Leone and find elasticities of substitution not significantly different from one.[4] Page, using recent evidence from India, finds elasticities of substitution to be similar for large and small firms.[71] Using a translog production function, for which elasticities of substitution need not be constant, he concludes that substitutability among skilled labour, capital and unskilled labour does not vary systematically by firm size. For large and small firms, he finds the elasticity of substitution

between skilled and unskilled labour between one and 3.7. For capital and unskilled labour, it lies between 0.4 and one; between capital and skilled labour, it lies in the range from 1 to 2.4. Kim also computes elasticities of substitution separately for large and small firms.[72] Using data from South Korea to estimate a CES production function, he finds elasticities of substitution to be significantly different from zero in all industries and for both large and small firms. Elasticities range up to about 0.9 for small- and medium-size firms and to 1.6 for large enterprises. Yet in some industries substitutability appears greater in small firms, while in others large firms appear to exhibit more supple factor substitution.

Some analysts have taken estimates of the elasticities of substitution, along with a knowledge of the magnitude of factor price distortions, to estimate the impact of factor pricing policies on firms subject to those distortions. Akrasanee follows this procedure to estimate the impact of minimum wage legislation on Thai manufacturing.[73] Combining what he believes to be a 26 per cent premium of minimum wages over the shadow wage rate for unskilled labour and knowing the share of unskilled labour by commodity group, he estimates that eliminating the minimum wage would increase employment in manufacturing firms by about 20 per cent. Because of data availability, this estimate is made only for firms employing five or more workers. He does not project these changes to smaller firms, although the impact would presumably be quite small given that few are likely to pay minimum wages. His estimate for the larger firms may well be an overestimate given that some may successfully evade the minimum wage laws.

Hooley has undertaken a similar exercise for the Philippines in which he projects the employment impact of removing capital market distortions embodied in a set of capital-biased trade incentives.[74] Assuming that 25 per cent of all manufacturing firms benefited from capital price subsidies, Hooley estimates that removal of the subsidies would lead to a 5.4 per cent increase in that portion of manufacturing employment generated by firms with five or more workers.

Exercises of this nature must be treated with some caution given the widely acknowledged problems with elasticity of substitution estimates. Gaude,[75] Morawetz,[68,69] O'Herlihy,[76] Pack,[77] Roemer,[78] Steel[17] and White[66] all discuss these shortcomings. Particularly disconcerting is the observation that in the estimating form most commonly used, the indirect CES function regressing value added per worker on wage rates, the direction of causality may move in either direction. Higher wages may not induce capital–labour substitution (or management–labour substitution, as Pack suggests[77]) but may instead merely reflect a rise in wages following increases in worker productivity. Hence, the elasticity of substitution estimates may not assure that removal of policy-induced factor price distortions will in fact lead to higher labour use.

Some analysts have tried a related technique, regressing employment on wage rates, to determine their impact on factor employment. Eriksson[79] and Reynolds and Gregory[29] fall into this category. Summarizing many similar efforts, a Williams College research report says, 'measurement of the effects of wage changes on industrial employment show consistently that higher rates of wage increase are associated with slower growth of employment'.[80] Steel[17] and Wolgin *et al*[81] concur based on observations in Ghana and Malawi, although they do not perform statistical correlations. In a similar vein, Fields concludes, on the basis of a review of seven LDCs, that wage restraint is a necessary ingredient if export-oriented trade strategies are to result in higher levels of employment.[82] On a cautionary note, Reynolds and Gregory[29] and Steel[17] provide illuminating discussions of how correlations between wages and employment may camouflage a variety of other underlying changes that are more important than wages in affecting employment levels. While Steel, Wolgin and Fields offer no employment elasticity of wage rates, Eriksson puts it at about 0.4 indicating that a 20 per cent reduction in wage rates (a common level of policy-induced distortion found in the previous section) would be associated with an 8 per cent increase in employment.[79] Depending on one's view of the direction of causality, this could describe wage-induced shifts in employment in response to factor price changes, or it could be interpreted as wages following gains in worker productivity which enable firms to hire fewer workers.

Although minimum wage and related labour legislation has received substantial attention as a potential source of employment reduction, few direct measurements have been made of its impact on employment. Lipton summarizes the results of one of the very few such attempts.[83] The study he cites measured changes in employment in Botswana's formal sector firms one year after a 80 to 100 per cent increase in minimum wage rates. As testament to the difficulties of attributing casuality in such before–after measurements, Lipton notes that employment actually *increased* by 1 per cent in the year following the wage increase. Of course, the increase was due to general growth in the economy. Employers indicated that employment would have risen even more in the absence of the minimum wage rise. They estimated that the minimum wage hike caused them to reduce employment by 1 per cent overall, although the effects were reduced by 2 to 3 per cent in the sectors where wages increased the full 100 per cent. The 1 per cent overall drop in formal sector employment amounted to a 6 to 10 per cent increase in formal sector unemployment. Lipton emphasizes that those hardest hit were the unskilled workers and the females. But the inescapable conclusion is that even a huge increase in the minimum wage rate had a very small effect in aggregate formal sector employment. In a similar exercise, Pack found that Kenyan factory owners felt a wage rise on the order of 200 to 300 per cent would be necessary before they would reduce their labour force.[77]

Squire, in a modelling exercise, reaches a similar conclusion. He finds that even a 46 per cent drop in minimum wage rates would lead to only a 1.6 per cent increase in total employment. One noteworthy feature of his estimate is that it specifically includes employment shifts in both large and small firms together.[2] Aside from this one calculation, though, we have no estimate of the net effect on employment when the joint impact of factor price changes on large and small firms is considered together.

In addition to the magnitude of employment changes, several authors have also examined the speed at which the changes are made. Lipton, for example, notes that in Botswana one year after the minimum wage increase, hardly any enterprises had replaced workers with machines. Instead they had shifted to the use of more skilled labour. This underlines the potentially significant time lags involved between the introduction of policy changes and their impact on employment and especially on capital utilization. Williamson corroborates this conclusion, estimating short- and long-run changes in factor proportions following a large increase in capital costs that accompanied trade liberalization efforts in the Philippines in 1960.[84] Incorporating a lag into his estimating equation, he finds short-term elasticity of substitution to be around 0.3, while in the long run it is much higher, around 0.8. Thus even if factor substitution is possible, as the weight of evidence suggests, policy-makers must be prepared for a time lag of up to several years between policy implementation and the resulting impact on employment.

Many authors recognize that factor market distortions operate in different directions in small and large firms. The capital subsidies compounded by minimum wage legislation result in lower large firm employment than would be found in a neutral policy environment, while the artificially high capital costs faced by small firms lead them to hire more workers than they would under undistorted input markets. Thus, a removal of factor price distortions would lead to higher large-firm employment and lower employment in small firms. The net impact on employment is, *a priori*, uncertain. It will depend not only on intra-firm factor substitution but also on initial small and large firm market shares and how much they change with a change in relative factor prices. This in turn depends, among other things, on the geographic dispersion of markets, transport costs, substitutability of final outputs, how relative profitability of small and large firms will be affected by changes in input prices, and economics of scale. To date, we have no evidence on how small and large firm market share will change and hence we have no estimate of the net employment effect of factor price changes.

### Effects of policy interventions in output markets
There are a variety of ways in which policy interventions influence the composition of final demand faced by producers of non-agricultural

products and services. Most important are those affecting agriculture, those affecting exports as opposed to imports, and those influencing the distribution of income. We examine, to the extent evidence permits, the effects of each set of policies on economic efficiency, employment and the size distribution of firms.

## Agriculture

Policies designed to enhance agricultural output and income can have important effects on non-agricultural output and employment as well as on the size distribution of enterprises, particularly those located in rural areas. In addition to the factor market linkages, two important demand relationships closely tie agricultural and non-agricultural activities together. The first is the consumption linkage that arises from incomes generated by agricultural households, while the second is the production linkages that stem from the agricultural sector's demand for farm inputs or for processing of agricultural outputs. As a result of these linkages, policies aimed at removing the previously described biases against agriculture can have potentially significant influences on non-agricultural activities.

Quantitative evidence on the magnitude of the relationship between agricultural growth and non-agricultural employment, output or the size distribution of enterprises is unfortunately rather sparse. Few empirical studies have focused on these relationships in a comprehensive fashion in any one country. Typically, only one region or only one facet of the interrelationship is examined. Moreover, the results are dependent on the assumptions used to analyse these relationships and on the underlying quality of the data.

Several studies have used input–output analysis to quantify the direct and indirect employment and output effects of agricultural growth or of alternative agricultural policies. For India, Raj Krishna employed a detailed 77 sector input–output table for 1964–65 combined with detailed farm data from the East Punjab to examine the effects of an increase in agricultural technology.[85] His results showed that a 5 per cent increase in agricultural output leads, through intersectoral and multiplier linkages, to a 5.1 per cent increase in non-farm employment, yielding a non-farm employment-to-agricultural-output elasticity of approximately one. Mellor and Mudahar, using a simulation model built on a three-sector input–output framework for the Indian economy, find that the 'potential' employment growth in non-agricultural sector response to a 4 per cent growth in food grain output is 4 per cent, thus also yielding a non-farm employment-output elasticity of one.[86] Neither size nor location, however, is incorporated into these models.

Rangarajan, in an empirical study of agricultural and industrial performance in India, found that a 1 per cent increase in the agricultural growth rate generated an additional 0.5 per cent to the growth rate of industrial output and a 0.7 per cent addition to the growth rate of national income.[87]

Studies undertaken by Byerlee[88] for Nigeria and Byerlee *et al*[16] for Sierra Leone have attempted to examine the employment linkages to agriculture with location and size of enterprises included in the analysis. Using Nigerian (1950–66) and Sierra Leone (1974–75) data and a general equilibrium simulation model built on an input–output framework, these two studies find that the non-agricultural employment elasticities with respect to increases in agricultural output were 1.2 in Nigeria and 1.6 in Sierra Leone, somewhat higher than those found in India. The employment elasticities varied quite markedly between large and small-scale enterprises, however. In Nigeria, the non-farm employment elasticity coefficient for large enterprises with respect to agricultural output was 1.5, while for small enterprises it was only 1.1; in Sierra Leone, a similar pattern was found, with the corresponding figures standing at 2.0 and 1.5, respectively. Moreover, the urban coefficients were somewhat larger than the rural ones. Finally, the employment coefficients were found to vary with the simulated agricultural policy options. With an agricultural export promotion policy, which tended to benefit larger farmers, small-scale enterprise non-agricultural employment fell, while large-scale enterprise employment rose. With a food crop production campaign aimed at small farmers, however, small-scale non-agricultural employment increased while large-scale production remained virtually unchanged. The implication of these studies is that the type of agricultural policy change can have an important effect on non-agricultural employment and the size distribution of enterprises.

Two other regional studies provide measures of the direct and indirect non-agricultural rural employment effects of agricultural activities. Gibb's study of the growth of non-farm employment in the Gapan area of Central Luzon in the Philippines provides an indication of the magnitude of non-farm employment induced in rural areas by the growth of local agriculture.[89] During the 1960s, a development strategy based on encouraging small-farm agriculture led to rapid increases in agricultural output and incomes, which induced rapid increases in local non-farm employment opportunities. Using actual data on agricultural output and employment in a broad range of non-farm occupations in 1961 and 1971, but with no formal model, he estimated the elasticity of demand for non-farm labour with respect to changes in agricultural incomes. The overall employment elasticity was 1.3, but varied for individual activities from 0.8 for public services to 1.97 for trade, crafts and construction. As with previous studies, the non-farm employment links with agriculture were strong.

A final regional study by Bell, Hazell and Slade attempted to measure the indirect effects generated by an irrigation project in the Muda River

92

region of Malaysia in 1974, using a regional model of the agricultural sector along with a semi-input–output model of the regional economy.[90] This well-specified model, which is built on a detailed data base, localized the indirect effects of the project. The results of their study indicated that for each dollar of income created directly in agriculture by the project, 90 cents of value added was created indirectly in the non-farm economy. Another important finding was that about two-thirds of the indirect rural non-farm activity was due to increased rural household demands for consumer goods and services, while the remaining one-third was due to agriculture's increased demand for inputs, processing, and marketing services.

Recent empirical studies in several countries have revealed a strong positive relationship between increases in rural income and increases in the demand for rural non-farm products. Rural expenditure elasticities for rural non-farm products, for example, were found to be 1.40 in Sierra Leone[16], 1.34 in the Gusau region of Nigeria, and 2.05 in the Muda region of Malaysia.[91]

This review of the empirical relationship between agricultural output and non-agricultural output and employment reveals that the linkages are quite strong. In virtually all the countries examined, the non-agricultural employment elasticity with respect to changes in agricultural output exceeded one. Changes in agricultural policy and agricultural output have important effects on non-agricultural activities, particularly those in rural areas. Those few studies that include size and location into their analysis indicate further that alternative agricultural policies have important differential effects on non-farm enterprises of different sizes and locations.

### Exports versus imports

Trade policies affect economic efficiency to a considerable extent. Balassa *et al*, for example, have computed the cost of distorted output and capital markets which accompany trade protection at 7 per cent of Brazil's 1966 GDP and 6 per cent of Chile's 1961 national income.[92] Using data from Krueger[93], they put Turkey's loss at 7 per cent of GNP. Using a general equilibrium framework, de Melo and Robinson put the cost of trade protection in Colombia at 11 to 16 per cent of GNP, depending on assumptions about the availability of surplus labour.[94] Harberger arrives at a 15 per cent estimate for Chile, demonstrating not only the potentially significant levels of income loss due to policy distortions but also the margin of error incumbent in such analyses.[95]

Employment, too, can be substantially affected by trade policy, first through the impact of policy on efficiency and overall output and secondly through its effect on the commodity composition of output. Reductions in total output decrease employment opportunities in proportion to the decline in output if the commodity mix and production techniques remain unaltered. That is, if the employment elasticity of output is equal to one, employment losses of up to 16 per cent would arise due to the output reducing effect of trade policy distortions reported above.

Several available estimates indicate that output is the most important of the three factors commonly viewed as influencing employment (the other two being output mix and choice of technology used for producing given outputs), and that employment elasticities of output in the range of one are not uncommon. For Taiwan and India, Balassa *et al* decompose changes in employment into the individual effects of changes in manufacturing output, commodity composition of output, and labour productivity (wages).[92] In the case of Taiwan over the period 1961–71, they conclude that the observed 10 per cent increase in manufacturing employment came 18 per cent from increased output, 4 per cent from a shift to increasingly labour-intensive industries, a 4 per cent decline due to increased labour productivity and a further 8 per cent due to cross effects. Similarly for India during the 1960s, they found that the 3 per cent increase in manufacturing employment was due 11 per cent to increases in output, –1 per cent to a shifting composition of output, and –4 per cent to cross effects. This amounts to an output elasticity of employment of 1.8 per cent in Taiwan and over 3 in India over those periods. Eriksson found similar results for Argentina, Brazil, Colombia, Costa Rica and Mexico.[79] He computed employment elasticities of output between 0.7 and 0.9 and determined that these figures were about 30 per cent greater than elasticity with respect to wages and three times as great as the elasticity with respect to the capital/ labour ratio. The much more negative assessments of employment elasticity of output in manufacturing, commonly found in the literature, come from studies which fail to separate the effects of output from the simultaneous infuence of commodity mix and factor price distortions. We conclude that allocative inefficiency induced by trade policy distortions can be an important source of employment loss through decreases in aggregate output.

Trade policy can also influence employment by shifting a country's commodity mix toward more labour-intensive export commodities. A rapidly accumulating body of evidence indicates that, as Heckscher-Ohlin-Samuelson would lead us to expect given the low wage rates prevailing in most developing countries, LDC exports do tend to be more labour using than import substitutes. Studies by Krueger *et al*[10] and Little, Scitovsky and Scott[62] indicate that a shift from import substitutes to export-oriented industries will generally result in increased employment in LDCs. Table 10 indicates the magnitude of the differential labour use in the two types of manufacturing. It shows, for example, that in Argentina one unit of value added in exports provides 30 per cent more employment than does a comparable unit of import substitutes. In all countries in the table (except South Korea where gains from export promotion have already been

**Table 10. Increase in employment obtainable by shifting one unit of value added from import substituting activity to export production**

| Country | Per cent increase in employment |
|---------|--------------------------------|
| Argentina | 30 |
| Brazil | 107 |
| Chile | 34 |
| Colombia | 91 |
| Indonesia | 26 |
| Ivory Coast | 21 |
| Pakistan | 41 |
| South Korea | 0 |
| Thailand | 70 |
| Tunisia | 23 |

Sources: Krueger, *et al*, 1983, p. 180, for all but Thailand.
Krueger, 1978, for Thailand

captured), export promotion promises significant increases in labour use. The increase in labour use in exports compared to import substitutes ranges from 21 to 107 per cent.

Krueger acknowledges that these estimates may be biased, since they are based on technical coefficients taken primarily from large-scale firms.[10] She suggests that the employment gains from export promotion may be understated to the extent that more labour-intensive small firms might participate in an export expansion. Unfortunately, the bias might also work in the opposite direction if labour-intensive small firms supplying local markets are displaced by imports as a result of trade liberalization. While evidence is limited, Ho does note that small enterprises in Korea and Taiwan expanded fairly rapidly during both countries' import substitution phases, but their growth was curtailed in each case by a shift to an export orientation.[96] For example, during South Korea's import substitution phase, employment in the small-size category of firms (those employing 4 to 9 workers) increased at a rate of 6.6 per cent per annum; but after their switch to export promotion, this growth dropped to 0.3 per cent per annum. Similarly in Taiwan, employment in the smallest firms (those employing 1 to 3 workers) grew at 2.3 per cent per annum under import substitution policies but declined to 1.6 per cent per annum under export promotion strategies. Ho speculates that this is due to the importance of economies of scale and small firms growing up through the size distribution, but it could also be explained by large firms' preferential access to export advantages. Berry also notes the importance of the size distribution of firms in export strategies. He indicates that while the Colombian trade liberalization of 1958 did result in a decreased capital intensity in large-scale manufacturing and a modest drop in unemployment, the employment gains were not nearly so substantial as might have been hoped, primarily because labour-intensive small-scale enterprises did not participate in the export growth. He concludes that export-oriented strategies should be accompanied by measures aimed at ensuring the participation of small-scale labour-intensive units and suggests measures such as the institution of marketing arrangements necessary to funnel the small producer output to the export markets.[97]

Fields makes a related observation about the importance of policy interactions. In his study of seven countries that had adopted export promotion strategies, he notes that employment increased only when the trade liberalization was accompanied by wage restraint. Thus, Jamaica, Barbados and Trinidad/Tobago achieved little employment growth as a result of their export growth, because their institutional wage setting mechanisms resulted in substantial wage increases. On the other hand, Taiwan, South Korea, Singapore and Hong Kong achieved rapid export-led employment growth. He suggests that this was because they maintained a tight wage policy.[82]

Overall, the potential impact of export promotion on employment appears substantial. To realize the employment potential of exports frequently requires conditions complementary to liberalization, for example wage restraint, the availability of complementary factors of promotion and possibly mechanisms for including small-scale labour-intensive enterprises in the export growth.

## Income distribution

A final link between output markets and employment has to do with income distribution and its impact on employment. Optimists hypothesize that increased incomes for the poor will shift demand patterns in favour of more labour-intensive products and hence lead to increases in aggregate employment. During the early 1970s, the initial upsurge of interest in income distribution issues led to a spate of studies investigating the relationship between income distribution and employment through changing patterns of demand. Morawetz has summarized the results of 11 such studies undertaken between 1970 and 1974.[68] Eight concluded that low-income groups did indeed consume a more labour-intensive basket of commodities than did the rich. One study dissented[98], and two others made a distinction between long- and short-term effects.[99, 100] Soligo, for example, projected that in Pakistan in the first 3 years after policy implementation, increased income for the rich would lead to higher growth of employment because of a high demand for housing; but in the longer run, that is after the third year, increased income for the poor led to maximum growth of employment. In addition to pointing out the potential complexity in the income distribution–employment relationship, his study underlines the importance of time dimensions which one must consider when evaluating policy changes. In a more recent study, King and Byerlee report that households in the lowest income deciles in rural Sierra Leone have expenditure patterns that lead to more employment per additional dollar of expenditure than do those in the top income decile.[101]

While these analyses generally point in the direction of increased employment due to income redistribution, they estimate the magnitude of the impact to be quite small. Even major redistributions of income, they project, would normally lead to no more than a 5 per cent increase in employment.[68] Another study, not cited by Morawetz, estimates that a huge redistribution of income in the Philippines – one lowering the Gini coefficient from 0.47 to 0.25 – would increase employment by 10 per cent initially but would lead to a 0.5 per cent lower employment growth rate in ensuing years.[102] Few analysts discuss how resource transfers of this magnitude might be accomplished. While some redistribution is possible via government fiscal policy on both tax and expenditure sides, the resource transfers of the magnitude apparently necessary to have an impact on employment would probably require redistribution of assets. This takes us beyond the realm of policy distortions and indicates that, realistically, the opportunities for increasing employment through manipulation of fiscal policy are most likely quite small.

*Summary*
The evidence assembled above leads to several conclusions. First, the magnitude of current LDC policy distortions is considerable in many countries, with capital prices typically more distorted than wage rates.

Second, these distortions lead to allocative inefficiency which can result in substantial reductions in aggregate output. Total policy induced allocative inefficiency has been computed in the range 6–18 per cent of GDP. The estimated level of inefficiency varies greatly by country as well as according to the portion of the policy environment selected for study and the method of estimation used.

Third, the effects of the entire package of policy distortions on the size distribution of firms are not well documented. The limited evidence available suggests that the overall policy environment confers cost advantages on large firms, thereby allowing them to hold a larger market share than they would in a neutral policy environment. Where this is so, it is because the large capital price subsidies have outweighed the higher wages and potential tax liabilities faced by large firms. Investment codes and non-payment of taxes have played a significant role in reducing the tax liability of larger firms.

97

Finally, employment is affected in a variety of ways by policy distortions, but by how much and even in what direction is difficult to say. Decreases in aggregate output induced by policy distortions clearly reduce employment opportunities. So too do policies which discriminate against agriculture and against exports. The factor price distortions faced by large-scale firms clearly lead them to employ fewer workers and more capital than they would in a neutral policy environment. But we have less evidence on the magnitude of counteracting policy influences on labour use in small enterprises, and virtually none measuring the effect of policy on the size distribution of enterprises. Without such evidence, it is not possible to estimate with any degree of confidence the aggregate effect of the policy environment on employment. It is likely that overall policy distortions do lead to reduced employment given their impact on large-firm employment and particularly their impact on employment via efficiency losses in aggregate output. At this stage, however, such a judgment can best be termed informed speculation which needs to be tested by more comprehensive data and analysis.

# Discussion: Macro-Policies for Appropriate Technology

*Q K Ahmad*: I have three comments. First, Mrs Stewart mentioned the need to organize the poor to enable them to make use of some of the existing technology and credit facilities and support systems. But in Bangladesh, for example, this has been found to be an extremely difficult process. Only about 25 per cent of the population is literate, mostly those who are relatively prosperous. Therefore, I think it is necessary to emphasize education. Moreover, training is necessary in addition to literacy. Thus, even in a country like Thailand where primary education is almost universal, there is still a need to organize training for the poor.

My second point concerns the multilateral organizations such as the World Bank. Experience suggests that they do not promote policies and projects that favour the poor. They tend to rely more on market mechanisms. Now that environmental issues are being increasingly recognized as important, perhaps these organizations will view ATs more favourably as they are generally less damaging environmentally.

The third comment concerns Mr Ranis' presentation. In Bangladesh, we have done two major studies on rural industrialization. I had the privilege of directing both studies. One was conducted from 1978–81 and the other from 1984–87. We have found that rural people tend to fall back on non-farm activities to increase family incomes during slack seasons in agriculture when they have no other source of employment. They do not take up these activities as regular sources of income, which could be developed and expanded. Therefore, they are not very interested in technology, productivity and profitability. While rural people can manage resources well, they are not always quite prepared to take up rural industrial or non-farm activities as primary vocations. How does one remedy this situation? To start with I think it is necessary to consider rural industrial and other rural non-farm activities as belonging to a dynamic sector and assist their development in that context.

*F Stewart*: I agree with your first point completely, half with your second. We need more detailed empirical work on the environmental issue in order to establish a point of view. If someone would ask me to prove that small-scale activities do less environmental damage than large-scale ones, it would be very difficult. We are only now beginning to understand the environmental impacts associated with different types of technology.

*G Ranis*: I agree that in many countries, when agriculture fails, people are forced to try other economic activities. But even in successful countries such as in East Asia, it is the poorest, smallest farmers who participate disproportionally in non-agricultural activities. Typically, the smallest farmers earn 90 per cent of their incomes through non-agricultural activities, while the corresponding proportion for the large farmers is only 20 per cent. So small-scale rural industry development often results from pressures to diversify from agricultural activities. The question you raised is: 'how can the small entrepreneur obtain information about and access to improved technologies'? Farmer organizations are very useful in the countries I am familiar with, in non-agricultural as well as agricultural activities. The farmer associations were active in diffusing information on technology. Also, legal devices can be useful in facilitating innovation. Some countries, such as Japan, have established a 'petty' patent system, to stimulate medium- and small-scale firms to innovate.

I think that the conception most people have about research and development, that it is white-collar, and large-scale R & D, is one of the enemies of the level playing field, mentioned by Mr Liedholm. I think that blue-collar R & D takes place everywhere, but is often not counted. It needs to be encouraged, either through information or legal devices, to increase opportunities.

*B Mansuri*: I enjoyed listening to the excellent presentations by the three speakers. I agree with all the definitions given by Mrs Stewart, with respect to the small-scale sector and its characteristics. I would like to introduce one more definition, a very important one that has many implications, both for institutional set-up and the policy environment.

Looking at the pattern of employment and unemployment in the Third World and taking into account the capacity of the agricultural sector to absorb additional labour, small-scale enterprises have a very important role in employment generation and poverty eradication. In reference to this, a very important issue concerns the size of small-scale enterprises that are labour-intensive, capital-saving and efficient. I hesitate to define small-scale enterprises by their size. Michigan State University has catalogued 75 different definitions for small-scale industry. We should attempt to find out what level of capital investment is needed in comparison to the capacity of the poor and whether their incomes are below the national per capita income level or below the absolute poverty level needed to meet the basic needs of a family.

The second observation concerns the role of the aid agencies. Mrs Stewart mentioned that 'the IMF and the World Bank are the most important policy-makers in the world'. She is right, but it should not be so. When we are talking about the policy framework of governments, we have to understand the historical circumstances that could have led to this.

A large number of policies were inherited from the colonial period. There are not only issues of prestige but also of national aspirations which have been frustrated because of a large number of external factors. It is important for governments to internalize the process of policy formation and be encouraged to undertake policy analysis. There is an information gap that cannot be bridged unless governments themselves indentify, analyse and formulate policy. I think this is the direction in which the World Bank and IMF are moving. In a meeting of Joint Consultation on Policy Co-ordination in the UN, it was emphasized that a new mentality now prevails. With respect to the aid approach and its influence on government policy, I should refer to the fact that a number of parastatals have been promoted and financed through external assistance, in particular by the World Bank. They are now trying to reorganize them and resort to market forces completely.

The composition of donor financial assistance is also very important. There are a number of examples where aid policies, in particular bilateral aid on technology, have led to capital-intensive technology and large-scale production. I would also like to add my concern about structural adjustment loans. Often, they are conditioned on a negative list of what foreign exchange cannot be used for, mainly a few luxury items such as perfume and armaments. They do not provide more specific guidance on what should be imported. Thus, there is a tendency to allow imports of items that are in demand by elites, other than those on the restricted list. These goods have a high turnover in trade and are absorbed primarily by the urban sector. The rural sector may very well be deprived of essential goods such as inputs, spare parts, and consumer goods.

Finally, I would like to highlight the importance of two other sectors important to small-scale enterprise development – the agricultural sector and the education and manpower development sector. Agricultural policies profoundly influence the development of SSE. Let me give you one example. The agricultural pricing policy will determine the geographic distribution of processing facilities. A pan-territorial pricing system leads to the over-concentration of processing facilities in or around urban areas. How public funds are distributed within the education and manpower development sector, for example, whether elementary level, secondary level, or vocational training is emphasized, will influence the development of skills for self-employment opportunities.

*G de Kalbermatten*: UNCDF, the investment arm of UNDP, is a capital assistance fund that focuses on small-scale projects benefiting the lower income groups in LDCs. On a modest scale, we are sponsors of the kind of projects that promote appropriate technology, such as manual pumps in

Mali, farm-tool production in Togo, rice mills in Senegal or biogas production in Nepal or Burma. As a micro-level operator, we often find when we evaluate a project that the sustainability of our activities depends upon factors in the macro-policy framework beyond our control. Thus it is necessary to address the policy constraints that have been identifed in the macroeconomic framework for micro-interventions to bear fruit.

I am impressed with how timely this meeting is. In the 1990s, the main issue in the development debate will be how to improve the policy package of structural adjustment programmes, the 'human face' question. In this context, the issue of appropriate technology as a means to empower lower income groups is very important. Bearing this in mind, I wonder what kind of documentary output this meeting should produce. We are reflecting on a serious body of analytical research and on ways to go from theory to practical policies and programmes. I would hope that this meeting focuses enough on the technological issue so as not to repeat the broader reflections on promotion of small-scale enterprise and the informal sector conducted elsewhere. It should also serve as a guidebook for those who would like to bring the issue of appropriate technology into stronger focus; for instance before the governing bodies of multilateral organizations.

*E Doryan-Garron*: One of the purposes of this meeting is to establish a policy framework that could complement the more orthodox set of policies that have been developed in many countries funded by the IMF or the World Bank. I interpreted three things from the three papers.

From Mr Ranis' discussion, I noted that export promotion strategies should be coupled with policies to promote balanced rural growth – that would put more emphasis on the whole issue of linkages. This would be a first building block for that complementary view or policy framework we have been discussing.

Concerning what Mrs Stewart said, I hope I am not misinterpreting her position, that 'getting prices right' without 'structured markets' leaves half of the important issues out of the discussion. It would be as incorrect a medicine as the present distortions. The role of institutions and organizations in relation to getting prices right is an important element.

From Mr Liedholm's paper I understood that dealing with one distortion at a time is not sufficient. A comprehensive array of policies must be considered that can deal with short-term as well as long-term structural issues. By themselves, restrictions to reduce balance of payments deficits and getting prices right are only partial steps to eliminate distortions. These three key comments by our speakers could be the beginning of a complementary macro-policy framework.

*W Rasaputram*: It is very clear from these three presentations that we have to look for policy changes in developing countries that raise productivity, incomes and employment. A government may make a decision to effect policy changes, but these changes may not be felt at the lowest level. There are many bottlenecks at every stage. Bureaucrats may create some bottlenecks to preserve their power. They might not wish to implement policy changes.

Then there are the producers, both large and small. Large producers develop vested interests and may seek to block some policies. The small producers need information and training in business and entrepreneurial development to make them good managers. A good manager will make sure that the firm is profitable, competitive, and in a position to diversify production as demand shifts. In Sri Lanka, export villages were organized. One product grown in some export villages was Chinese ginger. The market for it was good for some time. But when demand fell, the farmers did not switch to other products rapidly enough.

My last comment is on the IMF and World Bank adjustment programmes. Every adjustment process burdens the poorest classes. Therefore, the poorest sector must be safeguarded by income and consumption transfers. A humane approach allows development with a human face. More policy studies are needed to prevent more burdens being placed on the poor.

*G Waardenburg*: I have a question for all the speakers. In the research on the impact of macro- and meso-policies on small enterprises, a distinction between the various sizes of small enterprises would be useful. Micro-enterprises and household enterprises could be affected by various policies in a different way than the larger of the small-scale enterprises. Special policies may be needed to reach the very small enterprises.

*K Kuiper*: Mr Liedholm mentioned quite a number of distortions in developing countries. I think we have these distortions much closer to us than in developing countries. So if we come with policy recommendations, it might be good to change those policies ourselves before we tell developing countries to accept our recommendations that even our own governments do not accept.

*C Liedholm*: I would like to respond to several key issues. The first point is that building up indigenous policy analysis research capacity is indeed crucial if you really want to be sure that policies get changed.

A second point relates to the environmental issue as it relates to micro-enterprises. At Michigan State University, we have begun to accumulate some information from an examination of our data sources. In all the cases where we have looked at the efficiency of natural resource use by enterprise size, the micro-enterprises came out ahead of large-scale enterprises.

The third point is that agricultural strategy is crucial. Preliminary results of several linkage studies indicate that policies geared toward small-scale farmers generate greater demand for the products of rural industries than agricultural strategies focused on larger farmers.

Finally, the differential effects of policies by size of enterprises are important. In several of our studies we have looked at one person enterprises as well as larger ones. We have begun to look at this in a dynamic context – in other words, how firms evolve over time and how policies inhibit or foster their evolution, but more needs to be done in this area.

*G Ranis*: I fully agree with the comments made by Mr Rasaputram. The stroke of the pen to change a policy may be hard to achieve, but that is not the end of the story. You have resistance from bureaucrats and non-compliance. You may have wonderful tax reforms, but few firms pay the taxes anyway. Tariff legislation may create special exemptions for particular interest groups. This is a continuing problem in all those reforms.

On the question raised about micro-enterprises versus cottage industry, you cannot be religious about it. I have done some work in Pakistan, where the most efficient scale is between 10 and 50 employees. In some places, the micro-scale may be ideal while in other places, medium-scale production is more efficient. One should provide access to resources for all sizes of firms, and not prevent them from getting bigger. We might look at earlier European experience with proto-industrialization as instructive to the Third World today.

Finally, the environment is very important and is now attracting attention. Environmental degradation is often very closely related to the problem of poverty. Deforestation is a manifestation of poverty, and the relation between world poverty and the environment is something this community should take into account in promoting small enterprise development.

*F Stewart*: I very much agree with each of the speakers who mentioned the importance of education and training – it should be given more attention. On the issue of implementation, there is a lot of evidence on legal reforms that have not been administered. Where legal rights have been established for the poor, they cannot enforce them for lack of economic power. You cannot enact rights for the poor, you have to make underlying changes as well. Finally, I want to say something about adjustment with a human face. The IMF and the World Bank are now making human noises but very little action has followed. It reminds me of a quotation from Hamlet by a man who murdered his brother. When praying for forgiveness, he said: 'My words go up, my thoughts remain below. Words without thoughts to heaven will never go'. The same is happening with the IMF and the World Bank. First, knowledge on how to create a human face is needed. We can help provide the knowledge, but commitment is also needed in the international community. I hope that we can also play a small part in creating that commitment.

*H Thomas (Chairman)*: I want to thank the speakers and those who have contributed to the discussion. Mrs Stewart in her closing words endorsed what she wrote in the beginning, namely that we should search for further leads for theory, policy, and commitment. Mr Ranis was very clear on the linkages issue. At the same time, I think, we will also discover during this conference that the research that is being undertaken is still quite controversial.

Last, a comment for Mr Liedholm with respect to distortions. My own background is the field of labour studies. Often, labour is blamed for distortions – a view that has been accepted for a number of years in various theories. Papers prepared for this conference provide conclusive and convincing evidence that the distortion is often caused by government policies and not organized labour.

# II

# *Policies and Places*

# Macro-Policies and Technology Choice in the Philippines

## ROMEO M BAUTISTA

### Introduction

Direct ownership of production enterprises has not traditionally been a major form of government intervention in the Philippine economy. The dominant influence of government on technological choice in the Philippines can be found in the nature of policies adopted or, to use the terminology of Stewart,[1] the macro-policies that affect the external environment in which micro-level technological decisions are made. Although the focus of this paper is on macroeconomic, trade and public investment policies,other aspects of the government's role in influencing technology choice by private decision-makers will also be addressed, such as institutional and organizational sources of observed policy biases.

It is important to understand how technological decisions made by private 'micro-productive units' are affected by changes in the macro-environment resulting from government policies. In a positive (or objective) sense, this is necessary because of the intimate link between technological decisions and the pattern of technical change on the one hand and development processes on the other. The manner in which the scarce resources of a developing country are used in production not only affects the quantities and prices of goods produced, but also the present and future distribution of costs and benefits among the population. Normatively, technological choices need to be made that support a country's development objectives and strategy.

This paper first describes the general character of Philippine economic performance since 1949 and how it has been affected by the major policy developments during this period. The repercussions of government policies on various facets of the national economy that constrain the choice of technologies are then examined. These policies have affected industrial

---

ROMEO M. BAUTISTA, of the Philippines, is a research fellow and Co-coordinator of Development Strategy Research at the International Food Policy Research Institute in Washington, D.C. He was formerly professor of economics at the University of the Philippines.

incentives, agriculture's share of economic activity, the trade structure, the potential for small-scale production and regional dispersal of industries, employment, income distribution, and the structure of demand. The paper ends with a discussion of the implications for appropriate technology policy and of the political economy factors influencing past and prospective changes in macro-policies and the external environment in which micro-level technological choices are made.

## Postwar economic performance and economic policies

Until the late 1970s, the postwar performance of the Philippine economy seemed impressive, if judged solely in terms of growth of aggregate output. The gross national product in real terms increased at an average annual rate of about 6 per cent over the three decades from 1949 to 1979. Even with the country's rapid population growth, the average increase in per capita income slightly exceeded 3 per cent per annum.

Philippine economic growth slowed sharply in the 1980s. In fact, during the period from 1980 to 1985, real GNP registered an average annual growth rate of −0.5 per cent; in 1985 the country's per capita GNP had fallen to the 1975 level. Before the foreign exchange crisis in late 1983, the marked deceleration in national income growth was commonly attributed to recessionary conditions in the industrialized economies, the intensification of protectionism in those countries' markets and the steep fall in world commodity prices. The economies of neighbouring Asian countries, however, were not as severely affected by these same factors. The corresponding growth rates are significantly higher not only (as one might expect) for South Korea, Taiwan, Hong Kong and Singapore – the Asian Newly Industrializing Countries (NICs) – but also for the other ASEAN countries with which the Philippines can be more naturally compared, namely, Indonesia (3.5 per cent), Thailand (5.1 per cent), and Malaysia (5.5 per cent). Each of these neighbouring Southeast Asian economies also grew faster than the Philippines in each year since 1980.

In addition to the failure to sustain rapid growth through the 1980s, another major blemish in the postwar development record of the Philippines has been the highly unequal sharing of the benefits of economic growth. Family income distribution has remained heavily skewed (Table 1). Only a relatively small segment of the population benefited from the substantial postwar gains in national income. Income inequality reflected, in part, the severe underutilization of the labour force. High rates of unemployment and underemployment, which characterized the Philippine economy through the late 1970s,[2] worsened in the 1980s.

The increasing number of unemployed and underemployed has been accompanied by growing poverty in an already low-income economy.

110

**Table 1 Distribution of household income, 1956–85**

| | Percentage of total household income | | | |
| Income distribution | 1956 | 1961 | 1971 | 1985 |
|---|---|---|---|---|
| Top 10 per cent | 39.4 | 41.0 | 36.9 | 37.0 |
| Top 20 per cent | 55.1 | 56.4 | 53.9 | 52.6 |
| Top 40 per cent | 74.9 | 75.7 | 75.0 | 72.8 |
| Bottom 20 per cent | 4.5 | 4.2 | 3.8 | 5.2 |
| Gini coefficient | 0.48 | 0.50 | 0.49 | — |

Source: National Census and Statistics Office, *Family Income and Expenditure Surveys* (1956, 1961, and 1971), National Economic and Development Authority, *Medium-Term Philippine Development Plan 1987–1992.*

Indeed, poverty lies at the heart of the employment problem; the conventional measures of unemployment and underemployment are only imperfect indicators of the employment challenge facing Philippine policy-makers. According to government estimates, the incidence of poverty (defined as the proportion of families whose incomes are below specified poverty lines) among Filipino families increased over the period from 1971 to 1985 from 49.3 per cent to 59.3 per cent for the entire country and from 55.6 per cent to 63.7 per cent for rural areas.[3] Since the incidence of rural poverty is higher than urban poverty and nearly 70 per cent of the population live in rural areas, rural families account for nearly 75 per cent of the total poor.

There is also an important regional dimension to the income distribution problem in the Philippines. Historically, economic activity has been highly concentrated in Manila and the surrounding areas. Table 2 shows the income disparities among the country's 13 regions in terms of per capita gross regional domestic product (GRDP) at 1972 prices in 1978, 1980, 1982, and 1984. Metro Manila's per capita GRDP was more than double the next highest, and more than five times the lowest among the remaining regions in each year.

The above statistics suggest that AT in the Philippine context should be directed at three primary objectives: sustainable economic growth, employment and poverty alleviation. Past technology choices have generally not promoted these objectives.

Technological decisions are, of course, not made in a vacuum. As pointed out above, the environment in which technological choices are made is influenced by the macro-policies that the government adopts. The remainder of this section briefly describes the major changes in Philippine economic policy since 1949. Specific policies and the processes through

**Table 2 Per capita gross domestic product by region: 1978–84 (in pesos at 1972 prices)**

| Region/Year | 1978 | 1980 | 1982 | 1984 |
|---|---|---|---|---|
| PHILIPPINES | *1,808* | *1,917* | *1,950* | *1,790* |
| Metro Manila | 4,631 | 4,912 | 4,966 | 4,476 |
| Ilocos Region | 878 | 967 | 1,021 | 974 |
| Cagayan Valley | 1,106 | 1,175 | 1,128 | 960 |
| Central Luzon | 1,517 | 1,615 | 1,735 | 1,561 |
| Southern Tagalog | 2,060 | 2,100 | 2,075 | 1,947 |
| Bicol Region | 823 | 907 | 833 | 781 |
| Western Visayas | 1,612 | 1,684 | 1,769 | 1,596 |
| Central Visayas | 1,629 | 1,769 | 1,771 | 1,665 |
| Eastern Visayas | 770 | 823 | 832 | 733 |
| Western Mindanao | 1,104 | 1,227 | 1,233 | 1,111 |
| Northern Mindanao | 1,509 | 1,591 | 1,606 | 1,416 |
| Southern Mindanao | 1,876 | 1,863 | 1,784 | 1,727 |
| Central Mindanao | 1,237 | 1,305 | 1,483 | 1,411 |

Source: National Economic and Development Authority, *Philippine Statistical Yearbook, 1985.*

which they have affected technological choice will be discussed in more detail in subsequent sections of the paper.

Four phases in the postwar evolution of Philippine economic policy can be usefully distinguished, and they correspond closely to the four decades from the 1950s to the 1980s. The first, spanning the entire decade of the 1950s, was dominated by the comprehensive system of direct controls on imports and foreign exchange introduced in 1949–50 as a policy response to a severe balance of payments problem. In September of 1946, a legislative act had granted special tax exemptions to 'new and necessary industries'; however, it was not until the early 1950s, when the substantial benefits from import and exchange controls became evident, that a significant number of industrial firms registered for the exemptions. Another major aspect of economic policy in the 1950s was the severe overvaluation of the domestic currency (which retained its prewar exchange rate of 2 pesos per $US).

The resulting economic and political environment stimulated the production of import-substituting industrial consumer goods in the early years, but effectively penalized backward integration, agricultural production and exporting. The incentive structure also encouraged large-scale, capital-intensive production and geographic concentration of industries in and around Manila. The chronic trade deficits of the 1950s, particularly severe during the second half of the decade, reflected the

112

increasing import dependence of domestic industries and the inability to stimulate new exports.

The second phase began with the gradual lifting of import controls and exchange rate adjustment to 3.9 pesos per $US, in 1960–62. These policy changes did not qualitatively change the incentive structure, which favoured import-substituting industries, because a highly protective tariff system was enforced. This tariff system had been introduced in 1957 but was made redundant at that time by the import and foreign exchange controls. However, the policy reform gave small producers greater access to imported inputs. Before the reform, importers were able to charge higher prices for restricted import goods; after it, the government was able to collect more revenue from tariffs.

Two important sectoral policy developments occurred during the second half of the 1960s. One was the promotion of modern high-yielding varieties (HYVs) of rice through extension, credit and fertilizer programmes. After their introduction in 1966, the use of HYVs spread rapidly and helped markedly increase rice output through the end of the decade, reflecting a high degree of supply responsiveness among Filipino farmers to a new, demonstrably superior technology. The other significant policy development was the implementation of a new comprehensive approach to stimulate industrial investment, based on the Investment Incentives Act of 1967. This act also created the Board of Investments (BOI) which was empowered to determine preferred areas of investment through its Investment Priorities Plan and to grant incentives to BOI-registered enterprises. Still largely oriented to import-substitution, this approach was also biased toward capital-intensive manufacturing industries.[4]

Expansionary fiscal and monetary policies adopted by the new Marcos government during the second half of the decade resulted in a significant rise in the inflation rate and a sharp deterioration in the trade balance. In late 1969, a foreign exchange crisis again developed.

The third phase, occurring in the 1970s, represented a major effort by the government to adopt an outward-looking development policy while substantially increasing its role in the regulation of various sectors of the economy. In February 1970, a floating exchange rate system was introduced to cope with the balance of payments problem. The 61 per cent *de facto* devaluation over the year improved the price-competitiveness of export industries, which were given a further boost by the enactment of the Export Incentives Act of 1970. Under this act, manufacturing enterprises registered with the Board of Investments were accorded various sorts of tax exemptions, deductions from taxable income and tax credits. Selective financial and infrastructural supports were also provided to non-traditional export producers to compensate for the still pervasive policy bias against exporting. The highly protective and distorted tariff system was the primary source of this bias, but no attempt was made to

113

deal directly with it as part of the export promotion programme in the 1970s.

In response to the external shocks that buffeted the Philippine economy during the decade, the government increasingly regulated and directly participated in production and marketing activities. This was facilitated by the broad powers assumed by the martial law regime imposed in September 1972. The oil industry and the agricultural food and export crop sectors were particularly subject to government interventions in the 1970s. Beginning in 1974 the government resorted to heavy foreign borrowing in order to finance the mounting trade deficits and expansionary macro-economic policies implemented during the rest of the decade.

The fourth phase, beginning in the early 1980s and continuing to the present day, is marked by several policy developments that can be considered either transitional or emergency measures. In 1981, with technical and financial support from the World Bank, the government initiated a programme of industrial structural adjustment aimed at improving the international competitiveness of domestic industry. It included measures to significantly liberalize the foreign trade regime through tariff reform and relaxation of import licensing; to rationalize fiscal incentives; and to revitalize certain industries (eg, textiles) through technical and credit assistance. However, because of the foreign exchange crisis beginning in August 1983, some of its components (including the phasing out of import quotas) were superseded by policy actions such as direct controls on imports and foreign exchange designed to deal with short-term contingencies.[5] What remained relatively intact was the tariff liberalization scheme, which gradually reduced the effective tariff protection of domestic industry from 1981 to 1985.[6] Although a less distorted incentive structure resulted from the tariff reform, quantitative import restrictions and exchange rate overvaluation continued to favour manufacturing over agriculture, consumer goods over intermediate and capital goods production, and import-substitution over export industries.

The foreign exchange crisis itself was precipitated by the political turmoil and massive capital flight following the assassination of opposition leader Benigno Aquino. However, underlying economic factors, reflected in the burgeoning external debt and increasing real exchange rate overvaluation, made a balance-of-payments crisis inevitable.[7] IMF-prescribed stabilization measures adopted by the government during the years 1984–85 led to a 10 per cent reduction in real GNP. Given the highly skewed income distribution, the poor suffered more during the recent crisis that caused a 15 per cent decline in per capita income. A successful revolution took place in February 1986 putting an end to the Marcos regime and installing the new government of Corazon Aquino – lending support to the notion that economic forces can critically influence political developments.

The new political leadership has begun to influence the direction of economic policy. Promotion of employment-oriented agricultural and rural growth was announced in mid-1986 as the centrepiece of an 'Agenda for a People-Powered Development'. A sharp increase in public spending on rural infrastructure and improved prices for agricultural producers are being promoted to raise farm productivity and rural incomes. Further efforts at trade liberalization are also underway. However, opposition is emerging from vested interests, government and non-government, and may significantly impede movement in the direction of policy reform.

## Industrial incentives and relative factor use

As in most developing countries, rapid industrialization has been a major goal of postwar economic policy in the Philippines. Despite the wide variety of policy instruments used over the years to provide incentives for manufacturing investment, the general direction of factor use bias has remained the same.

In the 1950s, the 'essentiality' rule governing the allocation of foreign exchange conferred a large windfall on industries importing capital equipment, which was obtainable at artificially low prices due to the unrealistic exchange rate. Thus, not only were capital-intensive industries favoured, but within these industries the choice of production techniques was skewed toward the use of capital. This bias was reinforced by preferential access to low-interest loans from government financial institutions. Finally, some of the tax exemptions granted to 'new and necessary industries' (for a period of 4 years from date of organization) were related to the acquisition of capital and hence also biased the incentive structure against labour use.

With the lifting of import and foreign exchange controls and exchange rate adjustment in the early 1960s the burden of industrial promotion fell on tariff policy and government lending. However, the highly distorted tariff structure only served to perpetuate the low effective rate of protection on capital goods.[8]

The Investment Incentives Act of 1967 and the Export Incentives Act of 1970 represent two of the most important pieces of postwar economic legislation concerning inducements for industrial investments. The following items in the fiscal incentives package given to manufacturing enterprises registered with the Board of Investments have an obviously capital cheapening effect:

1. Tax exemption on capital equipment imported within seven years from the date of registration of the enterprise. This reduced the cost of acquiring imported capital from 10 to 20 per cent depending on the type of capital good;

2. Tax credit on domestic capital equipment equivalent to 100 per cent of customs duties and compensating taxes that would have been paid on imports of such items;
3. Accelerated depreciation allowances, deducted from taxable income. This permits fixed assets to be depreciated up to twice as fast as the normal rate if expected life is 10 years or less, or depreciated over at least 5 years if expected life is more than 10 years;
4. Tax deduction for expansion reinvestment of 25 to 50 per cent for non-pioneer projects and 50 to 100 per cent for pioneer projects.

Some incentives favour labour use, such as the deduction from taxable income of one-half of the expenses for labour training, but not exceeding 10 per cent of direct wages. Exporting firms, moreover, are provided a wage subsidy equal to the direct labour cost in the manufacture of export products but not to exceed 25 per cent of the export revenue.

In a systematic analysis of the overall effects of fiscal incentives to BOI-registered firms, Gregorio finds that the user cost of capital is reduced from 49 to 71 per cent (depending on whether the project is pioneer or non-pioneer, it is a new or an expansion project, capital is imported or domestically produced, it is exporting or not etc.) while labour cost declines 3.5 per cent for non-exporting firms and as much as 22 per cent for exporting firms.[9] At the assumed economic lifespan of the project, the capital/output ratio fell 35.6 per cent and employment declined by 26.1 thousand workers for the BOI-registered non-exporting firms and by 6.9 per cent and 8.4 thousand workers for exporting firms. These calculated values are based on assumptions of unitary elasticity of the factor substitution, 20-year project lifespan, and 15 per cent discount rate.

Two influences on relative factor prices are not reflected in these estimates. One is the preferential access of BOI-registered firms to low-interest credit – which also has a capital cheapening effect, reducing the cost of capital 9 to 35 per cent.[10] The other is that the required minimum wage and supplementary allowances for workers make the actual wage rate for unskilled labour higher than its social opportunity cost. Based on Medalla's findings, the BOI subsidy on labour use does not fully match the difference between the market wage rate and the estimated shadow price of labour.[11] Significant disincentives to employment caused by minimum wage legislation have been documented by Armas at the firm level (in the pineapple industry) and for two-digit ISIC manufacturing industries.[12, 13]

Changes in the composition of manufacturing output in the 1950s and 1960s are consistent with the hypothesis that the incentive system encouraged the growth of capital-intensive industries more than those using the country's abundant labour resources. Production in the more labour-using industries, eg, garments, footwear, other leather products, wood products and printed materials, did not grow as rapidly during those two decades as in the rest of the manufacturing sector, as evidenced by the declining relative contribution of these industries to total manufacturing value added (Table 2 in Bautista, Power et al[14]). In the 1970s the trend was reversed for some labour-intensive industries, largely because of the rapid growth of non-traditional manufactured products accorded various benefits under the Export Incentives Act.

Based on Hooley's estimates of partial factor productivities in Philippine manufacturing, Table 3 shows the quantitative changes in labour employment relative to the use of capital and intermediate inputs, distinguishing among three sub-periods during the period from 1956 to 80.[15] Apparently use of labour per unit of either capital or intermediate input was decreasing from 1956 to 1970, especially in the years when foreign exchange and import controls were in effect (1956–60). By contrast, from 1970 to 1980 when the exchange rate was allowed to float and labour-intensive manufactured exports were being promoted, labour employment increased relative to the use of intermediate inputs and (particularly) of capital.

**Table 3 Average annual growth in relative input use, 1956–80 (per cent)**

|  | 1956–60 | 1960–70 | 1970–80 |
| --- | --- | --- | --- |
| Labour/Capital | −4.77 | −1.15 | 3.98 |
| Labour/Intermediate Input | −6.06 | −5.49 | .25 |

Source: Basic data from Hooley (1985).

No discussion of postwar industrial policies in the Philippines would be complete without including the so-called eleven major industrial projects (MIPs) which were actively supported by the government from the mid-1970s to late 1983. The projects included a copper smelter, a phosphate fertilizer plant, a diesel engine manufacturing plant, an integrated steel mill, and a petrochemical complex. Two of the arguments used by the Ministry of Trade and Industry in heavily promoting these large-scale, capital-intensive projects were that they 'would produce commodities and intermediate inputs at internationally competitive prices' and that they would 'induce the establishment of downstream, labour-intensive industries'.[16] It was also announced that the projects would be financed mainly from private (domestic and foreign) funds and that they would be implemented only if they were economically viable. Unfortunately, insufficient information was made publicly available to provide a basis for an independent evaluation of the economic feasibility of these projects.

The total cost of setting up the 11 projects was estimated to be close to US$4 bn (at 1981 prices) or about 10 per cent of the 1981 GNP. This would

117

seem a large enough sum to warrant a close examination of the macro-economic implications, especially on demand management and the inflation rate. Another source of anxiety was that, given the country's increasingly limited overall borrowing capacity, these large-scale capital-intensive projects would 'crowd out' imports of capital goods for light industry.

The MIPs were not likely to generate much employment. Some of them, like the aluminium smelter and petrochemical complex, would even import their principal raw materials. Very few, perhaps only those relying on domestic raw materials and not subject to rapid technological change, stood a chance of becoming commercially viable without heavy protection. With shelter from foreign competition, these projects would inevitably produce higher priced and lower quality intermediate and capital goods (compared to what could be imported), which would hinder rather than stimulate the development of downstream user industries. Besides being less energy-using, the downstream user industries are more labour-intensive, more regionally dispersed and have a greater export potential.

The only project completed was the copper smelter, which converts the copper concentrates from all but one of the local copper mining companies into copper cathodes. These companies must contribute about 30 per cent of their current concentrate production. Foreign loans provided 75 per cent of the funding. Of the equity, 32 per cent came from a Japanese consortium (that was guaranteed a 9 per cent minimum annual dividend rate), 29 per cent from the local mining companies, and 5 per cent from the International Finance Corporation. A careful evaluation of this project has indicated that it is at best 'little better than marginal from an economic point of view'.[17]

When the external debt-related foreign exchange crisis began in late 1983, the government's active pursuit of the MIPs had to be dropped, preventing the economy from being saddled with numerous white elephants.

## Incentive biases and the trade structure

While the thrust of economic policy throughout most of the postwar period was to encourage manufacturing, those industries producing import-substitution consumer goods were the principal beneficiaries. In effect, domestic industries producing intermediate and capital goods, and those oriented to the export market, were discriminated against.

In the 1950s changes in the domestic price structure resulting from peso overvaluation and direct controls on imports and foreign exchange created a strong bias toward the domestic production of import substitutes, especially for industrial consumer goods, at the expense of capital goods and export products. In the 1960s, a highly distorted and protective tariff

118

system sustained the qualitative biases against backward integration and export expansion. Tariff escalation, making import duties higher on semi-finished products and higher still on finished products, encouraged assembly and packing operations that depended heavily on imported materials and capital equipment. Manufacturing value added increased very little and industrial employment even less, because of the absence of strong inter-industry linkages normally expected among manufacturing industries. It is not surprising, therefore, that the contribution of the manufacturing sector to total employment in the Philippines remained virtually constant at about 12 per cent through the late 1960s.[18]

An aggregate measure of trade bias (between importables and exportables) caused by domestic price policies is given by $(P_x/P_m)/(P^*_x/P^*_m)$ where $P_x$ and $P_m$ are the domestic prices of exported and imported goods and $P^*_x$ and $P^*_m$ are their respective foreign prices. A proportionate change in this ratio of relative prices would reflect the net movement of the relative domestic price of exportables *vis-à-vis* importables after taking into account the concurrent change in the relative foreign price; hence it can be interpreted to represent the change in the domestic price ratio due to domestic policies. Empirical estimation of the trade bias measure has yielded average values of 0.39 for 1950–61 and 0.60 for 1962–69.[7] Both figures are less than 1.0, indicating that domestic pricing policies favoured producers of import-competing goods over export producers during the two decades. The magnitude of the bias against exports was significantly reduced, however, from the 1950s to the 1960s.

In the 1970s when exporting was being actively promoted by the government, the trade bias measure increased to an average value of 0.76. Since it was still less than one (and significantly so), a substantial price bias existed in favour of import-competing production even during that export promotion phase, in spite of the fiscal and other incentives granted to export producers.

It is useful to distinguish between 'essential' and 'non-essential' consumer goods imports and between 'traditional' and 'new' exports. Most food imports are in the essential consumer good category. On the other hand, imports of most industrial consumer goods are considered non-essential, their domestic production having been promoted through direct trade controls in the 1950s and by high tariffs since the early 1960s. Agricultural and mining exports are classified as traditional; since 1970 the expansion of non-traditional or new exports, largely labour-intensive manufactured products, has been officially encouraged.

A useful indicator of relative production incentives between two categories of tradable goods through domestic policies is the ratio of their effective exchange rates (EERs). EER is the number of units of domestic currency actually paid by importers or received by exporters per unit of foreign exchange, including related taxes and subsidies. Based on the annual EER estimates derived by Baldwin for 1950–71[19] and updated by Senga through 1980,[20] the calculated ratios of the effective exchange rates between traditional exports (TX), new exports (NX) and non-essential consumer (NEC) imports are shown in Table 4. The first two columns indicate a continuing bias in favour of import-competing industrial consumer goods production to the detriment of new exports, especially traditional exports. Also, the last column shows that new exports have

**Table 4 Ratios of effective exchange rates, by product category, 1950–80**

| Year | Effective Exchange Rate Ratio | | |
|------|--------|--------|--------|
|      | TX/NEC | NX/NEC | NX/TX |
| 1950 | 0.976 | 1.093 | 1.120 |
| 1951 | 0.590 | 0.661 | 1.120 |
| 1952 | 0.590 | 0.661 | 1.120 |
| 1953 | 0.590 | 0.684 | 1.160 |
| 1954 | 0.599 | 0.695 | 1.160 |
| 1955 | 0.543 | 0.630 | 1.160 |
| 1956 | 0.518 | 0.601 | 1.160 |
| 1957 | 0.485 | 0.563 | 1.160 |
| 1958 | 0.480 | 0.556 | 1.160 |
| 1959 | 0.395 | 0.455 | 1.150 |
| 1960 | 0.319 | 0.360 | 1.131 |
| 1961 | 0.382 | 0.420 | 1.101 |
| 1962 | 0.314 | 0.336 | 1.070 |
| 1963 | 0.313 | 0.331 | 1.057 |
| 1964 | 0.317 | 0.335 | 1.057 |
| 1965 | 0.326 | 0.346 | 1.059 |
| 1966 | 0.334 | 0.353 | 1.059 |
| 1967 | 0.331 | 0.354 | 1.069 |
| 1968 | 0.327 | 0.350 | 1.069 |
| 1969 | 0.327 | 0.349 | 1.069 |
| 1970 | 0.291 | 0.370 | 1.270 |
| 1971 | 0.299 | 0.377 | 1.260 |
| 1972 | 0.312 | 0.367 | 1.174 |
| 1973 | 0.290 | 0.339 | 1.169 |
| 1974 | 0.280 | 0.366 | 1.308 |
| 1975 | 0.280 | 0.356 | 1.274 |
| 1976 | 0.279 | 0.312 | 1.116 |
| 1977 | 0.279 | 0.328 | 1.173 |
| 1978 | 0.280 | 0.342 | 1.225 |
| 1979 | 0.279 | 0.337 | 1.208 |
| 1980 | 0.279 | 0.337 | 1.207 |

Source: Basic data from Baldwin (1975) and Senga (1983).
Note: TX is traditional exports; NX is new exports; and NEC is nonessential consumer good imports.

been consistently favoured by domestic policies relative to traditional exports, particularly during the 1970s.

The price competitiveness of exportables and importables, relative to home goods (non-tradables), is reflected in the real exchange rate. The relative profitability of producing tradable goods was impaired, especially by Philippine trade policies and, from 1975 to 1983, by aggregate demand management, which continuously overvalued the domestic currency.[7] The first half of the 1970s was the least unfavourable period for producers of tradable goods; even at that time, however, the real exchange rate was overvalued by about 20 per cent.

In significantly reducing the price competitiveness of export production, domestic policies have encouraged an inward orientation of the industrial structure and effectively placed a limit on the size of the market for the products of the favoured industries. The sudden profitability of manufacturing investment directed to the protected domestic market serves to explain the initial spurt of rapid growth in the first half of the 1950s – which dwindled just as quickly when the limits of the narrow market base for the products of import-substituting industries were reached toward the end of the decade. (Thus, the average annual growth rate of manufacturing value added (in real terms) was 12.6 per cent during 1949–56, the so-called exuberant stage of import-substitution, but it plunged to 6.3 per cent during 1957–61.) The inability of those industries to compete in the foreign market reflects the inefficiencies in resource allocation and use that resulted from the control system of the 1950s and the protective tariff policy instituted in the early 1960s.

Despite the labour-surplus character of the Philippine economy, the contribution of labour-intensive manufactured products to total exports throughout the 1950s and 1960s was very small. It may also seem paradoxical, but can be attributed to the nature of economic policies adopted, that export industries with lower (direct and indirect) labour content increased their share in total exports relative to the more labour-using sectors.[21] While labour-intensive manufactured exports expanded rapidly in the 1970s, the incentive structure favoured heavy reliance on imported inputs, reducing the possibilities for intersectoral backward linkages.

Not only would growth have been more sustainable had the foreign trade regime been more neutral, but labour employment and use of locally-produced inputs would have been greater, in view of the country's comparative advantage in labour-intensive production. The choice of products and the choice of productive techniques would have favoured a greater utilization of the unskilled labour force and, because the poor comprise the bulk of the unemployed and underemployed, greater participation by the poor in the growth process.

## Location choice and size structure

Two related consequences of postwar trade and industrial policies are the regional concentration of industries and the underdevelopment of small- and medium-scale enterprises. The system of import and foreign exchange controls in the 1950s, in particular, favoured large enterprises in and around Manila, effectively discriminating against the relatively small and regionally dispersed manufacturing firms. The latter similarly did not benefit much from the tax exemption privileges for 'new and necessary industries' and the wider fiscal incentives granted to BOI-registered firms. Indeed it is difficult for the small and the remote to deal with the requirements of bureaucratic controls and to receive the attention from government offices that come easily to large, Manila-based firms.

Because the favoured industries relied heavily on imported intermediate inputs and capital equipment, there was a strong inducement to locate plants near the source of supply, ie, Manila, the principal port. Infra-structure policy that promoted the idea of Manila as a 'metropolis of international stature' also meant a disproportionately larger allocation of public investment funds relative to the other regions, making Metro Manila more attractive to industries and migrants.[23] Reinforcing these tendencies was the need to obtain tax and credit favours from the centrally-run financial and government institutions in Metro Manila. Indeed even the mining and lumber companies based in the outlying regions found it necessary to maintain large offices there.

Manufacturing growth has been very uneven, therefore, among the country's 13 regions. According to census data, Metro Manila and the adjoining Southern Tagalog region accounted for 49.1 per cent of total manufacturing value added in 1948; this increased to 64.0 per cent in the next census year 1961, and to 81.6 per cent in 1978. The inability of the other regions to substantially expand manufacturing production has contributed to the persistence of large disparities in regional per capita incomes.[24]

In the early 1970s, the government attempted to disperse industrial activity away from the Metro Manila area through various policy measures. For example, a locational ban on new industrial establishments within a 50 km radius of Manila was imposed. Its impact was greatly weakened, however, by the numerous exceptions allowed by the Human Settlements Commission. The exceptions to the rule were based on such criteria as conformity with the development plan of the Metro Manila municipality or city, location within the identified growth centres, and need for the firm to be near an international airport.

Another regional dispersal policy made export enterprises locating in designated areas eligible to receive a tax deduction equal to the sum of the local raw materials costs and double the direct labour costs, but with a

122

maximum allowable deduction of 25 per cent of export revenue. Also, a tax credit was offered covering the entire amount of infrastructure expenses incurred by the firm. Neither of these two fiscal incentives proved effective, as a survey on location choice of industrial firms established after 1970 has indicated.[25] The survey found that a large number of sample firms were unaware of those incentives, as well as the available technical, financial and management assistance, while most of the other firms considered the economic benefits to be relatively insignificant. Most firms indicated that market factors related to output supply and product markets overwhelmingly dominated their location decisions. Not surprisingly, therefore, close to 80 per cent of new firms that registered with the Board of Investments during 1970–71 chose to locate in Metro Manila and the Southern Tagalog region.[26] The findings of another survey conducted in 1985 also indicate 'that the more recently established firms based their location decision on much the same set of factors as did the old firms, whether local or foreign . . . (and that) direct government intervention(s) . . . do not seem to have mattered at all'.[27]

To promote small industry development, as many as twelve government agencies were directly involved in the provision of credit, labour training and technical assistance to small- and medium-scale enterprises as of 1974 – when the Commission of Small and Medium Industries was created to integrate their efforts. A subsequent survey assessing the impact of government assistance programmes for small industries found that:

1. Less than 25 per cent of the firms surveyed were aware of such programmes (except for the credit programme of the Development Bank of the Philippines which was known to 72 per cent of the respondents);
2. Of these, less than 10 per cent actually sought or received assistance; and
3. Those that received assistance had relatively poor performance in terms of efficiency and growth as compared to the whole group.[28]

It was concluded, therefore, that government assistance tended to promote weak firms and that in the future it should be directed toward industries identified as labour-intensive and efficient in the use of capital.

Indeed the relationships between firm size on the one hand and labour intensity and capital productivity on the other are not uniform. Estimates of capital per worker and average capital productivity (ratio of value added to capital) are shown in Table 5, distinguishing among 3-digit ISIC manufacturing industries, and in each industry, four different employment size groups of establishments. It is clear that there are wide variations in both capital intensity and capital productivity across industries within the manufacturing sector and across various size groups of establishments within an industry. Moreover, a mixed pattern is seen with respect to the size structure: small scale appears more labour-intensive and more efficient in capital use in some industries but not in others.

123

# Table 5 Capital intensity and productivity in manufacturing by industry group and employment size, 1970 (in pesos)

| Industry | Kr/N | | | | VA/Kr | | | |
|---|---|---|---|---|---|---|---|---|
| | 20-49 workers | 50-99 workers | 100-199 workers | 200+ workers | 20-49 workers | 50-99 workers | 100-199 workers | 200+ workers |
| Food | 24611 | 19229 | 50990 | 32913 | 0.118 | 0.343 | 0.205 | 0.347 |
| Beverages | 14303 | 45994 | 20613 | 25448 | 0.311 | 0.401 | 1.406 | 1.234 |
| Tobacco | 3923 | 18005 | 81818 | 17066 | 0.578 | 0.301 | 0.053 | 0.655 |
| Textiles | 23650 | 30127 | 17014 | 4665 | 0.090 | 0.060 | 0.145 | 0.501 |
| Footwear | 9157 | 8875 | 10789 | 16439 | 0.329 | 0.495 | 0.316 | 0.208 |
| Wood products | 10104 | 7690 | 12765 | 5014 | 0.464 | 0.921 | 0.494 | 1.210 |
| Furniture | 7559 | 5970 | 22521 | — | 0.355 | 0.484 | 0.158 | — |
| Paper | 51747 | 36711 | 45488 | 87209 | 0.097 | 0.177 | 0.192 | 0.118 |
| Printing | 21745 | 15224 | 12781 | — | 0.362 | 0.740 | 0.701 | — |
| Leather products | 17443 | 15161 | 36534 | — | 0.061 | 0.072 | 0.039 | — |
| Rubber products | 21903 | 24554 | 33449 | 39934 | 0.489 | 0.187 | 0.195 | 0.498 |
| Chemicals | 50800 | 43847 | 53224 | 55009 | 0.333 | 0.492 | 0.408 | 0.603 |
| Petroleum products | 109650 | — | — | — | 0.454 | — | — | — |
| Non-metallic products | 55924 | 157975 | 21729 | 46201 | 0.049 | 0.002 | 0.229 | 0.253 |
| Basic metals | 6831 | 30772 | 29833 | 96586 | 0.655 | 0.289 | 0.280 | 0.147 |
| Metal products | 19992 | 26439 | — | — | 0.138 | 0.177 | — | — |
| Machinery | 19240 | — | 18739 | — | 0.277 | — | 0.517 | — |
| Electrical machinery | 29987 | 35717 | 30930 | 30175 | 0.107 | 0.081 | 0.127 | 0.220 |
| Transport equipment | 16694 | 20876 | 14422 | 49554 | 0.164 | 0.129 | 0.112 | 0.154 |
| Miscellaneous | 19399 | 27835 | 14935 | 14945 | 0.102 | — | 0.156 | 0.207 |

Note: VA = value added; N = employment; Kr = replacement value of fixed and inventory capital.
Source: Table 26 in ILO (1974; p. 145).

No blanket endorsement of either large- or small-scale can rationally be made, therefore, in the promotion of manufacturing industries. What is needed are 'policies that encourage the development of the most efficient industries and the most efficient firms, regardless of size. Blunt policies that are strongly biased toward one size or another are not capable of doing this'.[4] It must be emphasized, however, that the macro-policy biases in the Philippines have favoured the large enterprises relative to the small and the capital intensive relative to the labour-intensive. Therefore, removal of such policy biases would enable efficient small-scale and labour-intensive production in many lines that have not yet been developed.

### Agricultural incentives, public investment and resource transfer

Agriculture has traditionally been a major source of employment, income and foreign exchange earnings in the Philippines. More than two-thirds of the country's population still live in the rural areas, where agriculture and related production activities represent the principal means of livelihood. Although its relative importance has declined over the years, agriculture still accounts for about 50 per cent of the total employment and 25 per cent of the country's gross national product. Also, it provides some 40 per cent of total export receipts (from raw and simply processed agricultural products), while agricultural imports account for less than 10 per cent of the total import bill.

Poverty has been and continues to be widespead among the rural population, which includes over 80 per cent of all families in the poorest 30 per cent of the total population. Rural poverty is attributable to the low agricultural labour productivity and related lack of employment opportunities in the rural areas and to the inability of the industrial sector to expand labour demand rapidly enough. The large size of the rural labour force and high degree of its underutilization argue strongly for the necessity to generate productive employment within the rural sector. This did not take place in the past, owing at least in part to postwar biases against agriculture in the form of price disincentives and inadequate infrastructural investments.

Because agricultural output has a high degree of tradability, the real exchange rate overvaluation that resulted from the restrictive trade regime and occasionally imprudent macroeconomic policies during the postwar period decreased the relative profitability of agricultural production. Trade restrictions and policy-induced exchange rate distortions reduced domestic agicultural prices relative to home goods by 42 per cent during the 'control period' of the 1950s, by 19 per cent in the 1960s, by 11 per cent during 1970–74 and by 12 per cent during 1975–80. For non-agricultural products the corresponding figures are 104, 45, 22 and 20 per cent.[29] Agricultural exports have been more heavily penalized compared to import-competing food products not only in terms of product price disincentives but also in terms of input subsidies and infrastructure support.

In reaction to shortfalls in rice production during 1971–73, which coincided with soaring world foodgrain prices, the government undertook a major effort to promote rice self-sufficiency. Adoption of new technology was encouraged by the Masagana 99 programme, which provided farmers with non-collateral, low-interest loans to purchase fertilizer and seeds at subsidized prices. Public investment in irrigation also expanded substantially from 1973 to 1977, to ten times the 1966–70 level in constant peso terms.[30] Furthermore, irrigation water was made available to food crop producers at subsidized rates ranging from 60 to 90 per cent.[31] These input subsidies were provided at the same time that the domestic prices of rice and corn were being maintained below world prices through government trade monopoly of the staple food grains.

A credit subsidy (of about 12 per cent), low tariff rates on power tillers (19 per cent) and tractors (0 per cent), and currency overvaluation had the unsalutary effect of encouraging rapid farm mechanization to the detriment of rural employment.[32] Also, the small-scale farm implements (portable threshers, hand tractors, etc) available from the IRRI proved economically attractive to rice farmers at prevailing market prices.

Another aspect of the 'green revolution' that has influenced technology choice is the inequitable distribution of the benefits of the new technology. Large producers obtained greater access to the infrastructure investments and effective subsidies on irrigation water and credit.[31,33] Small-scale and rain-fed agriculture has been bypassed to a significant extent. This is unfortunate because small farms and low-income rural households have stronger linkages with labour-intensive domestic industry and the services sector than the large-scale, more prosperous agricultural producers.

Export crop agriculture has also been profoundly affected by postwar policy developments. Trade in coconut and sugar – the country's dominant export crops – has been particularly subject to government regulation since the eary 1970s. An export quota system for sugar has been in effect since 1962 and, beginning in 1970, sugar trading in both domestic and export markets has been taken over by state corporations. During the period from 1974 to 1980, producers received an average of only 77 per cent of the world price.[34] It has been estimated that, due to the domestic and foreign trade monopoly, sugar producers suffered a net loss of between 1 and 14bn pesos over the crop years 1974–75 to 1982–83.[35] Moreover, the additional link in the marketing chain and inefficiencies in government marketing operations meant additional markups and a substantially increased marketing margin.[7]

In the case of coconut, in 1971 the government introduced a production levy that established a dominant coconut milling company and began a programme of coconut replanting. The nominal protection rate for copra (dried coconut meat) was estimated at −8 per cent during the years 1970 to 1972 and 'it became more negative, −24 per cent fom 1973 to 1979 reflecting the introduction of the levy'.[36]

These unfavourable policy-induced price distortions for agricultural products must have significantly reduced farm incomes. It has been estimated, for example, that in the absence of government price interventions agricultural crop income in the Philippines would have been as much as 31 per cent higher during the 1970s.[37] This represented an effective resource transfer out of agriculture. Offsetting this was the amount transferred into the agricultural sector through government spending, which was, however, comparatively small. Calculations of net resource transfers out of agriculture showed an annual average of 15 to 21 per cent of agricultural value added from 1967 to 1982.[33]

Although the extraction of agricultural surplus to finance industrial capital formation is frequently assumed to be concomitant to structural transformation during development, one can question the efficiency with which the transferred resources are used outside agriculture. In the Philippine case, as in most other developing countries where the industrial sector has been highly protected, policy-induced distortions in product and factor markets have led to the inefficient use of investment resources for manufacturing. Nevertheless, agricultural productivity could increase rapidly if the needed capital were provided for rural infrastructure. In addition, non-agricultural production would also be stimulated by increased rural incomes resulting from rising agricultural prices and productivity. This form of rural growth linkage is at the heart of recent proposals for the adoption of an employment-oriented, agriculture-based development strategy in the Philippines.[38,39]

## Demand structure and growth linkages

The anti-employment and anti-equity biases of postwar economic policies must have had a significant effect on the structure and growth of effective demand, so that imported goods and capital intensive products were favoured over locally-produced and labour-intensive goods. This in turn can be associated with weaker intermediate and final demand effects on the domestic economy and an unsustainable growth process. The sudden slowdown in the growth of the manufacturing sector after the first half of the 1950s (representing the exuberant stage of import substitution) demonstrates this hypothesis very well.

A similar relationship applies to agricultural growth. Increases in agricultural output stimulate demand for production related products like fertilizer and farm equipment. However, as observed by Ranis and Stewart,[40] based on the survey findings of four independent studies on rural non-agricultural industries in the Philippines,[40-43] the strongest agricultural growth linkage is with consumer goods industries. From 63 to 80 per cent of the total increase in non-agricultural employment was found to be in consumption-related activities. Overall taking into account both production and consumption linkages, 'the elasticity of nonagricultural employment with respect to growth in agricultural output is greater than one, according to Philippine evidence'.[40]

There are obviously some further ramifications of agricultural growth beyond the local economy. Even in the first-round effects, there are goods produced outside the local economy that will be demanded by farmers and rural households for production and consumption. Among the second-round effects, the forward and backward linkages outside the rural economy, as well as the final demand effects of increased incomes, need to be taken into account. Clearly, to be able to capture the full complexity of agricultural growth linkages, one has to go beyond the effects on the local rural economy. It can also be presumed that the macroeconomic effect will be of interest to policy-makers at the national level.

The economy-wide repercussions of rising agricultural productivity are examined quantitatively in Bautista using a multisectoral, general equilibrium model of the Philippine economy.[44] This model simulation assumes an initial static equilibrium, approximated by the observed conditions in 1978, which is disturbed by a 10 per cent increase in total factor productivity in each of the four agricultural and food processing sectors distinguished in the model. Results of the simulation, reflecting the adjustment of the economy to a new equilibrium position, indicate that simultaneous productivity increases in these four sectors would lead to a significant response in sectoral output, ranging from 3.6 per cent for food crops to 17.1 per cent for livestock and fishery. Macroeconomic effects on government income, total investment, the trade balance and especially national income are significantly positive. The resulting 2.2 per cent rise in national income represents about 40 per cent of the actual national income growth in the Philippines for the benchmark year (1978).

The multiplier effects of a given increase in rural income will be greater the more skewed the consumption pattern is toward labour-intensive products. Households of the less affluent, small agricultural producers are more likely to fit this pattern, whereas families of the more prosperous owners of large farms tend to spend more on capital intensive goods, whether locally produced or imported. Although the structure of the model used in the above-mentioned simulations does not make distinctions between small and large agricultural producers between low- and high-income rural households, it is a safe presumption that the resulting benefits to the national economy would be greater if a larger share of the increases in productivity and income went to the smaller farms and lower-income households. Conversely, to the extent that the

128

productivity and income improvements have favoured the large and the prosperous, the simulation results would have overstated the positive macroeconomic effects.

The magnitude of rural growth linkages is also determined by the labour intensity of agricultural production. As more agricultural labourers are employed and/or as their real wage rates rise, the purchasing power of the low-income rural labouring class increases – which has favourable final demand effects. Labour intensity, in turn, is determined partly by the size of farms. Smaller farms generally use relatively more labour because they are typically less mechanized and adopt more labour-using farm equipment, eg, power tillers rather than four-wheel tractors. There is ample evidence that the adoption of agricultural machinery in the Philippines has had both labour-displacing and wage depressing effects.[40] Unfortunately, it has been effectively promoted by cheap credit and exchange rate overvaluation, as pointed out above. Correction of the policy distortions that subsidize mechanization will serve to enhance the linkage effects of agricultural growth.

The important role of farm size in influencing mechanization and labour absorption was evident in the Philippines during the implementation of a land reform programme affecting rice and corn producers during the 1970s. For example, there was a marked increase in the ratio of power tiller to four-wheel tractors from 1.26 in 1972 to 8.32 in 1976. Additional land reform measures that will further reduce the average size of landholdings are therefore likely to strengthen agricultural growth linkages and enhance labour employment. Apart from this there are other considerations that would associate an effective land reform in the Philippines with greater social and political stability.

The more developed the rural infrastructure the stronger are the growth linkages, other things being equal. Transport, electrification, and other infrastructural facilities reduce marketing costs, increase the access of rural households to marketable products, and generally promote market integration (involving not only rural but also urban and export markets) forming a basis for the development of a wide range of rural activities. Rural infrastructure in the Philippines has unfortunately not been given enough consideration by the government, especially over the last decade. 'Most indicators show that provision of rural infrastructure in Taiwan has been substantially greater than in the Philippines'.[40] The share of utilities and infrastructure' in national government expenditures declined significantly from more than 30 per cent in 1978–79 to less than 20 per cent in the years 1983–85. During the period from 1979 to 1983 less than 25 per cent of total investment in roads and bridges was in the rural sector. The deterioration in rural infrastructure has been such that the Community Employment Development Programme, launched by the new government last year to generate rural employment and increase the purchasing power of the rural population, had infrastructure maintenance as a major activity.

Despite comparably rapid agricultural growth in the Philippines and Taiwan during the 1960s, a much greater impetus was given to non-agricultural activities in Taiwan, encouraging rural industrialization and leading to more rapid GDP growth. This was due to the stronger growth linkages and larger labour absorption in Taiwanese agriculture, which in turn was due to the interrelated influences of smaller landholdings, mechanization, and greater use of more labour-intensive farm machinery and more favourable rural infrastructure policies, interest rates, tariffs, the exchange rate and fuel prices.[40]

## Policy implications and political economy considerations

It is evident from the above discussion that the three primary objectives identified earlier as relevant in the assessment of technology choice in the Philippines, namely, poverty reduction, increased employment and sustainable economic growth, are not independent and to a large extent are complementary. How might government policies affecting the environment at the micro-level be redirected so that they advance these objectives and promote the choice of appropriate technologies? Three main areas for policy reform, which are also not independent but mutually reinforcing are suggested by the theoretical and empirical considerations addressed above. They are discussed below with reference to the political economy forces that have constrained policy-making in the past and the new set of constraints facing Philippine policy-makers at this time.

### Liberalization of trade
Depending on the pattern of domestic demand and in the absence of trade restrictions, a labour-abundant country can be expected to export labour-intensive products and import capital-intensive ones, because of international differences in relative factor prices. It is clear from the preceding discussion that excessive import substitution policies, resulting in significant domestic price distortions (among other things), have violated the comparative advantage principle. Foreign trade restrictions, designed to protect domestic industry, have led not only to a lower utilization of the labour force but also made tradable goods production less competitive internationally, contributing to the country's chronic balance of payments problem.

Apart from the direct effect of raising domestic prices of protected industrial products, import restrictions have the general equilibrium effect of reducing the demand for foreign exchange, leading to real exchange rate overvaluation. This artificially cheapens imports that are allowed to come in, especially capital equipment and machinery. Also, exports are penalized by the lower peso price of foreign exchange; consequently, agriculture and other labour-intensive, export-oriented sectors and firms are discriminated against. Both the industry mix and the composition of micro-units (firms) within each industry, as well as the production technique (capital–labour ratio), therefore become biased toward greater use of the country's scarce capital resources relative to labour employment.

The introduction of import and foreign exchange controls in 1949–50 and maintenance of the prewar exchange rate of 2 pesos per $US (despite the high wartime inflation rate) through the end of the decade, can be partly attributed to external influence. A provision in the Philippine Trade Act of 1946, passed by the US Congress and accepted by the newly-independent Philippine government as an executive agreement, required the permission of the US President for any change in the peso–dollar exchange rate. (A period of applicability until 1973 was stipulated. (This provision was repealed subsequently by a revision of the Act in 1955.) Other onerous provisions in the Act infringing on Philippine sovereignty were also accepted by the government, presumably because a companion legislative piece provided for substantial US compensation for war damages.[45] It was thought that a peso devaluation would be opposed by American investment interests in the Philippines. Because there was an existing free-trade agreement between the two countries and the USA was the source of about 80 per cent of Philippine imports, increasing tariff rates would not have provided an effective means to curtail imports.

Continuing balance of payments difficulties, charges of corruption and poor administration of the control system, and political pressure from traditional exporters for a favourable exchange rate, forced the lifting of controls and peso devaluation in the early 1960s. It was, however, made clear 'to the business community that the government . . . wished merely to substitute tariff protection for the protection provided by the control system'.[46] This reflected a strong political presence of the 'import-substitution' industrialists; indeed, this class of entrepreneurs was well represented in the Cabinet of the government at the time.

Greater attention was given to promoting exports by the Marcos government that assumed power in 1966. The favourable experiences of some East Asian countries (eg, Hong Kong and Taiwan) with outward-looking, labour-intensive industrial development were beginning to be appreciated in the Philippines at that time. Government policy was also being influenced by contemporary academic discussions about the penalties being imposed on export-oriented, small-scale, and regionally dispersed industries.[8]

Indeed, in the late 1960s and in the following decade, the number of senior government officials with strong academic backgrounds (and post-graduate degrees from leading US universities) increased significantly. These 'technocrats', possessing an international perspective on economic development issues, were sympathetic to the idea of export-led industrial growth, and they became the *de facto* political representatives of export producers, especially of non-traditional labour-intensive manufactured products in which the country was thought to have comparative advantage. Export producers comprised a very small class of industrial entrepreneurs at that time, relative to other producer groups being favoured by the protectionist trade regime.

The technocrats were successful, especially during the first half of the 1970s, in implementing policies that selectively subsidized export production of labour-intensive goods. However, such subsidies fell far short of compensating for the pervasive bias against exports caused by the existing import restrictions and indirect tax system. As described above, the attempt to liberalize the foreign trade regime in the early 1980s with World Bank assistance was derailed by the external debt-related foreign exchange crisis beginning in late 1983.

The new government of Corazon Aquino, under pressure from the IMF and the World Bank, has planned to gradually liberalize imports, scheduling 1,232 import items for removal from quantitative controls from April 1986 to May 1988 and substituting tariff rates of up to 50 per cent which are slated for adjustment to a uniform low level over a 5-year period. No exact indication of the eventual level of uniform tariff has yet been officially given, although 10 to 30 per cent rates have been mentioned in policy discussions. However, the programme's implementation has been delayed, leading to doubts about the government's commitment to trade liberalization (cf Medalla[47]). A few key officials are known to be associated with business interests (specifically, in some heavily protected industries producing import-substitutes) that would lose from policy reforms toward a more open trade regime. A frequent journalistic commentary is that the February 1986 revolution has not brought a new ruling class into power that can quickly do away with economic corruption. The opportunities for rent-seeking are reduced by economic liberalization, so it is understandable that there are efforts within the government to resist the movement toward freer trade.

Outside the government, opposition to a liberalized trade regime comes from producer interests in the affected industries, ie, those faced with significant reductions in effective protection. They are more powerful, economically and politically, than other producer groups and general consumer interests. The latter are not well organized and are largely unaware of how they could gain from trade liberalization. Also, self-styled 'economic nationalists' have long been naively arguing for the protection of any and all domestic industries against foreign competition. Some of them are ideologues who, because of past colonial rule, reject anything foreign as anathema to national development. Others, and the more vociferous, have personal and family interests in promoting particular industries.

132

Prospects for trade liberalization can be improved significantly if the public and the newly elected Congress are persuasively informed of the heavy cost of protecting sectoral interests and subsidizing inefficient industries. The extent of additional pressure on Philippine policy-makers exerted by the IMF and the World Bank is also likely to prove critical in any sustained drive toward trade liberalization.

## Promotion of labour-intensive industries

The economic rationale for policy action in the Philippines favouring labour-intensive industry derives from two sources:

1. There are existing biases against relative labour use in the industrial incentive system; and
2. Private profitability understates the social desirability of labour intensive projects in a developing country with a severe underutilization of the labour force.

The latter justifies the promotion of labour-intensive industry even at a cost to the rest of the economy. However, since the social marginal productivity of labour-intensive industry relative to other economic activities is not infinite, the cost-effectiveness of policy measures to promote labour-intensive industry also needs to be explored.

There is a need, first of all, to gradually eliminate the various sources of market distortions that hinder the natural development of labour-intensive industry. As discussed above, substantial disparities in effective protection rates due to trade restrictions have encouraged allocative inefficiency within the manufacturing sector. It has been shown that the more highly protected industries are characterized by less labour employment and a greater proportion are largely located in Metro Manila (Center for Policy and Development Studies, 1986). Trade liberalization measures would then be likely to encourage greater labour use and regional dispersal of manufacturing industries. Improvements in real exchange rate management (including the trade and macroeconomic policies that determine the real exchange rate) will also serve to enhance the international competitiveness of labour-intensive industry.

Fiscal incentives for industrial promotion in the Philippines have an anti-employment bias, as discussed above. Relatively neutral ways of stimulating industrial investments should replace those having distortionary effects on factor use and size structure. The identification of preferred industries in the BOI's present system of industrial priorities, which ostensibly seeks to promote industries with long-term social profitability, is fraught with difficulties. Careful evaluation with the use of shadow price and domestic resource cost measures would help, bearing in mind the need to take into account long-run considerations of future factor supplies, scale economies, learning effects and other externalities. In any case, subsidies to 'priority industries' will serve their purpose only if they are given for a specified, limited duration; otherwise, the cost to the economy is likely to become excessive.

The granting of fiscal and other incentives by the BOI has been rationalized on 'second-best policy' grounds, given existing distortions in the protection system. The system of BOI incentives, however, was relatively insubstantial, favoured capital-intensive industies and failed to significantly reach the small and regionally dispersed enterprises. Indeed the determination of investment priority areas by the BOI necessarily narrows the range of industries for which the offsetting incentives can be provided. As the protection structure becomes more uniform and the various biases diminish with reforms in trade and exchange rate policies, the phasing out of BOI incentives merits serious consideration. The new government can more usefully give greater attention to the provision of industrial infrastructure, particularly credit and technical and marketing assistance to small- and medium-scale industries; this would help meet the need to more rapidly create productive jobs in manufacturing and to promote a wider participation in economic growth, both by income classes and by regions, increasing the upward mobility of the poor.

There were some earlier suggestions to dismantle the system of BOI incentives, including those under the Investment Incentives Act of 1967 and Export Incentives Act of 1970. The widely discussed report of the 'comprehensive employment strategy mission,' sponsored by the ILO at the request of the Philippine Government, specifically recommended 'the gradual dismantling of the system of investment incentives'.[4] The question raised implicitly was whether government bureaucrats were capable of predicting the success of future industries.

The proposal to gradually remove BOI incentives was naturally not received favourably by the engineers and business-trained managers who dominated the bureaucracy at the Board of Investments. It is a reflection of their strong influence on policy-making that this recommendation was not even seriously considered. Existing penalties to labour-intensive and export-oriented enterprises were seen by the BOI as manageable on a case-to-case basis (contrary to conclusions from economic analysis) and the Board continued to promote industrial investments in areas indicated in its annual priorities plans.

Along with the Department of Trade and Industry, the BOI provided active support for the large-scale, capital intensive MIPs (major industrial projects), illustrating the large-industry orientation of the Board. Support from the Department for small industries was lacking, prompting the ILO mission to recommend a 'full-scale Department of Industries, with two co-ordinate divisions – one for larger-scale and the other for medium- and smaller-scale manufacturing'.[4] This proposal again fell on deaf ears.

There is no indication that the Aquino government has eliminated the large-industry bias at the BOI and the Department of Trade and Industry, whose organizational structures have remained intact. Senior officials in both places have been changed, but their replacements come from the same elite social class strongly associated with large-scale industry and its supporting services.

## Policies to improve agricultural incentives and productivity

An important implication of the preceding discussion on demand structure and growth linkages is that expansion of the real incomes of rural households could provide the stimulus to broad-based, employment-oriented economic development. (This is at the heart of recent proposals for an agriculture-based development strategy; see Mellor for an early statement.[48]) A direct effect would be an increased demand for food and other agricultural products as well as for labour-intensive industrial goods and services, setting in motion a sequence of employment and income multiplier effects on the rural, regional and national economies. In countries such as the Philippines, that are predominantly rural and have a high incidence of rural poverty, increasing rural incomes might well be the most effective means to stimulate and, through multiplier effects, sustain 'economic growth with equity'.

Initially at least, the expansion of rural income must depend on growth in agricultural production, which 'is a vital precondition for expansion of nonagricultural activities in the rural areas'.[40] Rural industries in turn are associated with appropriate technology in that they contribute to poverty reduction, labour employment and sustainable growth. This is because the technologies used in rural industries are in general smaller-scale, less capital-intensive, and make greater use of indigenous materials – in comparison with their urban counterparts.

The implication for appropriate technology policy in the Philippines is that rapid growth in agricultural output should be actively promoted. Viewed from the supply side, agricultural output can be increased through movements along the supply function via improvements in agricultural price incentives, and shifts in the supply function via increases in total factor productivity. To provide price incentives, the many sources of policy-induced price biases against agriculture need to be eliminated, perhaps gradually. During this time of historically low world commodity prices, it may even be appropriate to provide protection to some agricultural crops, depending on their long-run comparative advantage, in order to ensure that farmers receive adequate price incentives.

It should be emphasized that the real exchange rate is an important determinant of domestic agricultural prices relative to the prices of both home goods and non-agricultural products. 'Getting prices right' for agriculture then requires that the conduct of trade and macroeconomic policies also be examined for their effects on the real exchange rate.

135

Officials at the Department of Agriculture should play a broader role in promoting farmers' interests. They should be concerned not only with sector-specific policies, but also with the industrial protection system, monetary policy, government expenditure, nominal exchange rate policy, and other aspects of macroeconomic management which, through their effects on the real exchange rate, have a potentially strong influence on agricultural production incentives. It will be necessary to prevent the real exchange rate from being overvalued, so as not to impair the price competitiveness of agricultural tradable goods. This would require liberalization of import restrictions unduly protective of domestic industry and maintenance of a sustainable trade balance.[7,29]

Increases in agricultural productivity can be achieved by shifting the structure of public investment toward the rural areas and away from the past bias toward urban-based, capital intensive industries. Improvements in rural transport facilities, electrification, agricultural credit and irrigation will also serve to increase the agricultural supply response to price incentives.

Greater government support for agricultural research and extension that will generate, adapt and disseminate improved technologies can also be expected to have a very high payoff. Provision of these critically needed 'public goods' has been largely neglected in the past. Philippine government expenditures on agricultural research as a proportion of agricultural value added are known to be one of the lowest among developing countries. The government cannot continue to rely primarily on IRRI's contribution to rice research. Biases in the existing structure of research and extension – by crop, type of farm (eg, irrigated vs rainfed), farm size, etc – need to be corrected. Increased decentralization of the research and extension system is also necessary to better assess local needs and potentials. Finally, it also bears emphasis that farmers will adopt new technologies only if they can expect their incomes to improve. It is therefore important for agricultural technology diffusion and productivity growth that price incentives be in place.

Beyond the direct promotion of agricultural growth, strengthening the multiplier or linkage effects on the rest of the economy will also be necessary. Because food and other labour-intensive goods are major items in the consumption patterns of rural households, sectors efficiently producing such products (presumably, small-scale producers in regionally dispersed areas) will be favoured by the rise in rural expenditure. 'Whether supply will be able to match the increased demand for those products would depend on the availability of production inputs and their prices'.[38] For instance, if intermediate inputs to agricultural and non-agricultural production are made artificially scarce or expensive by a restrictive foreign trade regime and/or an underdeveloped domestic transport system, the full benefits from increased final demand in terms of output growth and labour absorption will not be realized. It is also clear that the development of rural infrastructure will be critical not only to generate and diffuse improved agricultural technologies, but also to develop and integrate rural markets.

The total employment effect of rising rural income will be greater, and output growth more broadly based, the more skewed the consumption pattern is toward food and other labour-intensive products. Because households of the small agricultural and non-agricultural producer are most likely to fit this pattern, it is important that improvements in price incentives, production technologies and infrastructure facilities reach the small producers in regionally dispersed areas. It should also be emphasized that adequate support services are needed to implement an agrarian land reform programme.

Agricultural producers traditionally do not have a strong political voice in the Philippines. Even the much touted 'sugar bloc', supposedly the strongest economic and political interest group in the country, was not able to obtain a favourable exchange rate in the immediate postwar years or prevent the maintenance of a massive peso overvaluation throughout the 1950s. The decontrol measures and gradual exchange rate adjustment were implemented in the early 1960s largely because the 'control system' could not solve the country's balance of payments problem; political pressure from the sugar bloc was not the critical factor. In the 1970s, sugar and coconut farmers were exploited financially by government-installed trading and milling monopolies run by Marcos 'cronies'.[35] It is hardly a coincidence that the Communist insurgency found wide support during the 1970s and 1980s in the regions which grow most of the coconut, sugar and other export crops.

The Aquino Government, as noted above, has taken some significant steps to reduce the policy bias against agriculture. Export taxes were eliminated in mid-1986; for too long they were a direct burden to agricultural producers. Government monopolies in sugar, coconut, grains, and fertilizer have also been abolished. Furthermore, the recently launched programme to markedly increase infrastructure expenditures in the rural areas is not only addressing existing deficiencies in aggregate demand but also promoting growth in agricultural productivity and increasing the purchasing power of rural households. General guidelines for a new agrarian land reform programme have also been written into an Executive Order, the details of which are still to be formulated by the legislature.

What has yet to emerge is the 'true colour' of the new Congress. Only about 30 per cent of the members are newcomers, the rest either belong to 'political dynasties' and/or held legislative positions in the pre-martial law period or the interim national assembly. This may indicate strong conservative leanings and a weak commitment to agrarian reform, which is widely regarded as an important credibility test for the new Congress.

137

President Aquino has yet to use her considerable prestige and political influence to actively push her administration's economic agenda in the legislature.

Financing the rural infrastructure and agrarian land reform programmes may be a problem, because of the fiscal and monetary restraint necessitated by the heavy external debt-service burden. The country's ability to expand export earnings and economize on imports, as well as to negotiate favourable repayment terms (with debt relief, it is hoped) with foreign lenders, will be additional factors bearing on the implementation of government policies to promote agricultural growth and, given the nature of the growth linkages discussed above, the overall development prospects of the Philippine economy.

## Postscript

Because of the debt service and foreign exchange difficulties faced by the Philippines, the external environment has a major influence on the ability of the government to undertake policy reforms, but external factors are not entirely exogenous. Although nothing can be done to prevent deteriorating terms of trade or rising interest rates, the government can (and should) negotiate with foreign governments for improved access to export markets, with the IMF for a less severe macroeconomic adjustment programme, and with commercial bank creditors for concessionary debt repayment. Austere macroeconomic policies, such as those adopted during the recession years of 1984 and 1985 at the insistence of the IMF, are self-defeating because they impair the country's capacity to sustain any improvement in the balance of payments. They are also politically risky because the heavy burden of adjustment falls on low-income groups.

Switching policy regimes entails some transitional costs. Short-run problems in the current account, of revenue loss from trade taxes, and in financing expanded government spending (especially on rural infrastructure to help overcome agricultural supply constraints) associated with trade liberalization and rural development have to be addressed. The large amount of foreign resources pledged recently (in July 1989) by developed country governments and multilateral organizations as additional development assistance to the Philippines may or may not lead to long-run economic benefits. In the past, foreign resources were used to improve the economy's short-term growth performance, to inappropriately increase the capital intensity of domestic industry, and worst of all, to confer illicit economic gains to 'crony capitalists'. If the present administration is to succeed where its predecessors have failed, it should use the increased financial assistance to ensure a speedy implementation of needed policy reforms, and not minimize the urgency of making domestic industries more internationally competitive, promoting labour-intensive industry development and improving agricultural incentives, productivity and income.

# Appropriate Technology and Rural Industrial Development in Bangladesh: The Macro-Context

## Q K AHMAD

### Introduction

The purpose of this paper is to review the effect of the macro-environment on technology and rural industry development in Bangladesh. The three key concepts – macro-context or macro-environment, AT and rural industry – will be clarified at the outset. This section defines the three key concepts; the second section gives an overview of the technological status of the rural industrial sector; the third section discusses national policy, institutions and resources for rural industrial and technological development; the fourth section is concerned with the socioeconomic status of rural industrial enterpreneurs *vis-à-vis* other groups of actors in the economy and their relative position in the national decision-making structure; the fifth section analyses technological developments in paddy husking within the context of the relevant macro-environment; the final section contains concluding remarks.

### The macro-context

The macro-environment provides general guidelines, perspectives and dynamics which influence the way micro-decision-making units operate. Macro-policies (that is, all general government policies) which have relevance for technology and rural industrial development are the basic constituents of the macro-environment with which we are concerned here. Other important elements of the macro-environment include the institutions, procedures and interest group/lobbies involved in implementing these policies.

The terms micro-decision-making units or, simply, micro-units and macro-policies are used here in a broad sense, as by Stewart.[1] Micro-units include conventional private sector firms (with owners, employers and employees), public sector firms, co-operatives, and family and household

---

Q.K. AHMAD, development economist, is Chairman of the Bangladesh Centre for Research and Action on Environment and Development, Dhaka. He was formerly Research Director of the Bangladesh Institute of Development Studies, Dhaka.

organizations. Macro-policies include conventionally understood macro-policies, that is, policies concerning major economic aggregates such as money supply, interest rates, public expenditures, budget deficit and exchange rate as well as such policies as those concerning technology, market access and so on.

## Appropriate technology
The type of technological advancement that should take place in a country depends on such matters as factor endowments, demand for goods and services supplied, scientific knowledge and training, and marketing arrangements. The concept of AT is related to the situation or context of an economy. As the context changes there needs to be a corresponding change in the technology for it to be appropriate to the new context. Thus, AT is a dynamic concept, changing as the situation changes.

Bangladesh is essentially rural and agricultural and is characterized by very low incomes, mass poverty, paucity of investible funds, foreign exchange shortages, large-scale unemployment and underemployment and low levels of scientific knowledge and training. The rural population constitutes over 80 per cent of the total population of the country;[2] per capita annual income in 1985–86 was Tk 4629 or about US$ 150; people below the poverty line account for over 75 per cent of the total population of the country and those critically poor account for over 50 per cent; on average, only 1.64 per cent of the GDP was saved during 1980–85; foreign exchange earnings pay around 30–40 per cent of the merchandise imports of the country; about 40 per cent of the total available labour time of the country remains unutilized. For data and comments on poverty and unemployment levels see, for example, Ahmad and Chowdhury.[3] One may also see this report for somewhat elaborate discussions on the concepts of appropriate technology and rural industry, which were liberally drawn on for ideas presented in this paper.

In view of these conditions, appropriate technology for rural Bangladesh would, in general, be:

○ Labour-intensive (to provide more employment);
○ Low capital-using;
○ Economic in the use of foreign exchange;
○ Simple to produce, run and repair (as skills are generally in limited supply);
○ Productive enough to help alleviate poverty;
○ User of as many local raw materials as possible; and
○ Suited to the prevailing and potential demand conditions.

These characteristics define the basic approach under the present circumstances; but there may be a range of variations in the definition of AT among sectors and activities. ATs are generally low to intermediate level, but in certain cases they may be relatively modern.

The characteristics approach to appropriate technology serves the purpose at hand here. For a critical look at this approach and the alternative welfare-approach to appropriate technology (when it is defined as a set of techniques which makes optimum use of available resources in a given environment) see Stewart.[1] It may be noted that she has also preferred the specific characteristics approach over the welfare approach mainly because of the action orientation of the former as opposed to the latter, but she argues that with a specific characteristics approach, it is also necessary to consider the social efficiency of alternative techniques.

Technologies chosen on the basis of the characteristics enumerated above should help provide employment and income-earning opportunities for the rural poor and, hence, help reduce poverty. Poverty alleviation is the ultimate goal of planned development efforts in Bangladesh, and expansion of productive employment and raising productivity by upgrading the technology base have been enunciated as the principal means to that end.[4] This has also been a major goal of previous governments in Bangladesh. To what extent appropriate technology is actually adopted in any given situation largely depends on how policies influencing technology choice are formulated and implemented. This paper addresses the question of what has actually been happening to rural industrial technology in Bangladesh.

## Rural industry

A manufacturing activity located in a rural area is considered a rural industry. Conventionally, industrialization implies modernization and urbanization. Hence, the terms *rural* and *industry* might seem incompatible. Moreover, cottage and small industries located in rural areas are often considered rural industry. Rural industry is now a fairly widely-used term. However, it should not automatically be used to refer to manufacturing activities located in rural areas or cottage and small industries located in both rural and urban areas. The analytical and policy significance of the concept of rural industry derives from the fact that it encompasses a production system (ownership, organization, management, technology, production processes, procurement of inputs, sale of products) that is rural in character – generally traditional, even rudimentary but, occasionally, relatively improved. These industries are usually very small (with one or two employees), although they may include somewhat larger units. They are frequently characterized by unsophisticated technology and low productivity, generally owned by poor people and largely managed and operated by family workers. Rural industrialization may be seen as a process of improvement and expansion of the rural production system, in the light of rural and national resource endowments and the existing and potential demand structure for the goods and services (such as repairing of machinery, vehicles, etc) supplied by these industries. Technology has a crucial role to play in this process.

## Technological status of the rural industrial sector: an overview

Although the largest segment of the rural industrial sector is characterized by traditional (primitive to low) technology, a small segment uses intermediate to relatively modern technology. The use of relatively more capital-intensive, modernized techniques in certain activities is of recent origin. A major factor behind this development has been the extension of electricity to rural areas. As electricity spread, profit-making opportunities emerged through the availability of new or improved electric-powered technologies, especially in certain activities such as rice and oil milling. The more prosperous people who had access to institutional support mechanisms began to take advantage of these opportunities.

While productive activities based on traditional technologies are generally characterized by low labour productivity and, hence, low or even

**Table 1 Factor productivity in certain activities**

|  | VA/L (Tk) | VA/FC (Tk) | VA/FC$_1$ (Tk) |
|---|---|---|---|
| Rice husking (*dhenki*) | 2,863 | 2.27 | 4.57 |
| Rice husking (small huller)* | 15,186 | 0.44 | 0.48 |
| Rice husking (large huller)* | 20,797 | 0.94 | 3.44 |
| Oil seed crushing (ghani) | 6,435 | 2.2e | 2.62 |
| Oil mill | 106,211 | 4.89 | 5.05 |
| Bakery (traditional) | 18,577 | 1.41 | 2.83 |
| Bakery (modern)* | 24,077 | 3.16 | 3.24 |
| Carpentry | 11,301 | 4.58 | 5.19 |
| Furniture* | 24,151 | 1.17 | 2.18 |
| Saw mill* | 38,927 | 1.40 | 2.40 |
| Lime manufacturing | 6,447 | 10.13 | 19.34 |
| Pottery | 5,518 | 2.85 | 7.10 |
| Blacksmithing | 12,463 | 10.02 | 13.17 |
| Coir fiber | 1,745 | 1.75 | 40.72 |
| Coir string | 2,552 | 3.58 | 48.10 |
| Boat making | 9,937 | 2.94 | 23.15 |
| Hogla mat | 1,601 | 1.22 | 27.23 |
| Fish net | 12,961 | 6.61 | 6.73 |
| *Shital pati* | 6,549 | 5.00 | 5.36 |
| Bamboo and cane | 5,169 | 3.43 | 4.80 |
| Tailoring | 6,372 | 2.18 | 3.35 |
| Eng. Workshop* | 29,916 | 0.71 | 0.92 |
| Foundry* | 51,415 | 0.52 | 0.78 |
| Ice factory* | 81,333 | 0.62 | 0.65 |

Notes: VA = value added per year; L = number of workers; FC = fixed capital; FC$_1$ = fixed capital excluding land. The surveys were conducted during 1985–86.
* relatively modern; others are traditional
Source: Ahmad and Chowdhury.

negative profitability as well as high capital productivity, the activities using relatively modern techniques exhibit relatively high labour productivity but relatively low capital productivity. These characteristics, however, vary significantly across activities within each of the two segments (traditional and relatively modernized) (Table 1).

Traditional techniques are still being used in some activities in which modernized techniques have been introduced. Thus, two or more distinctly different levels of technology have developed side by side in certain activities. Examples are paddy husking (*dhenki*, small huller, large huller, automatic mill); oil seed crushing (animal-powered *ghani* or expellers run by electricity); weaving (pitloom, semi-automatic loom, powerloom); *gur* manufacturing (bullock-driven crusher, electrically or diesel-driven crusher); winnowing (traditional method of throwing paddy into air using a *cula*, Bangladesh-Agricultural Research Institute developed winnower – still experimental, hand-operated Cecoco Japanese-designed machine); wood processing (hand *karat*, saw mill). Other industries employing two or more types of technology include garments, soap, coconut oil, coir products, bakery, furniture making, shoes, boat building, tobacco processing and fish processing.[3]

For the largest segment of the rural industrial sector using traditional technology, AT would mean an upgraded or new technology, but for those activities exhibiting technological dualism or pluralism, the AT may be one of the technologies already in use. Hence, a policy to promote appropriate technology for rural industries in Bangladesh should be concerned with upgrading technologies in general and with choosing among existing techniques in those cases where alternatives are already in existence. In upgrading technologies, it is necessary to consider the extent to which upgrading is necessary and the source (local R & D, import or adaptation from an imported technology) of the upgrading.

## Technology for rural industries: national policy, institutions, and resources – an overview

### National science and technology policy

The policy goal of upgrading the technology base of the Bangladesh economy has been a recurring theme in successive five-year plans. (Not only for the rural industrial sector but to a large extent also for the agricultural and the urban informal sectors, an appropriate technology would normally be an upgraded technology because of the preponderance of traditional technologies in these sectors.) But thus far little progress has been made.[4] In fact, the first national science and technology policy was not formulated until 1980; moreover, little effort was made to implement it. However, since that policy was formulated, there has been a growing

143

awareness about technology issues in the country's policy-making circles;[5] and the *Third Five-Year Plan 1985–1990* (TFYP) calls for the formulation of a comprehensive national science and technology policy to be integrated into national development planning. Consequently, a new science and technology policy was formulated and adopted in February 1986 (1986 S&T Policy) aimed at raising the technology base of the economy through such measures as R & D, integration of technological and socioeconomic planning, development of human resources and technology infrastructure and technological co-operation with other, particularly developing, countries.[5]

The apex body for all technology related decision-making in the country is the National Council on Science and Technology (NCST) chaired by the President of Bangladesh, which has an Executive Committee to oversee the implementation of its directives and decisions. The NCST has also set up a Consultative Committee on Transfer of Technology mainly to advise on how best to transfer technologies developed within the country, or adapted from imported technologies, to the actual users. The Committee has recommended an action programme and an institutional arrangement to implement this programme.[6] But the 1986 S&T Policy proposals and the recommendations of the Consultative committee on Transfer of Technology are still at the recommendation or early stages of implementation, and concrete results may be a long time emerging – that is, if the proposals and recommendations are seriously considered. However, a review of policies and discussions since 1986 within the framework of the NCST and development planning exercises indicates that the issue of technology for rural industries has been given a rather low priority.

The 1986 industrial policy did not include technology for rural industries as a subject for major focus, although certain statements in the policy have implications for such technology. For example, the policy states that the Bangladesh Small and Cottage Industries Corporation (BSCIC) will under-take product development, supply new and improved designs, assist in procurement of raw materials and marketing of products, conduct continued research and disseminate its findings to help producers achieve higher quality and productivity. However, the question of appropriate technology was not explicitly mentioned.[7] Thus, there has never been a clear-cut policy stance in favour of AT for rural industries.

### Institutions

While micro-units are the ultimate decision-makers, agencies and organizations concerned with promoting and supporting rural industries are likely to play a crucial role in Bangladesh in the selection of tech-nologies to be used in rural industries, because the selection will be largely dependent on the technical information, facilities and extension services that these organizations provide. Because most people who make decisions in rural industries have little or no education and their technology-awareness may be low, they need help in making wise technology choices.

The BSCIC is the long-established, premier public sector agency charged with promoting and supporting all small and cottage industries, except handloom and sericulture, for which there are Handloom and Sericulture Boards. There are also many other public sector agencies which are, in one way or another, concerned with small and cottage industries in the country. Even if it is not their main focus, these organizations may be considered part of the macro-environment for rural industries since they implement government policies and may influence policy-making through feedback on the basis of their experiences.

The BSCIC is the only public sector agency concerned in any significant way with technology, because of its key role in the promotion of small and cottage industries, but it is only recently that technology became a major concern of the BSCIC. Traditionally, the organization provided promotional support and extension services. One study found that the BSCIC introduced 18 improved or new consumer and 11 improved or new capital items, or groups of items, since its inception in the 1950s; and that all but four of the consumer items or groups of items came on stream after 1980.[8] Besides its traditional functions, the organization now provides technology information, product designs, prototypes and production processes, as available, to its clients. It now has a technology section with a design centre under its planning, development and technology division. A prototype development unit is also planned. These developments signify changes favouring AT for rural industries in one segment of the macro-environment. However, a clear-cut concern for appropriate technology for rural industries has yet to find a place in the national science and technology policy. Unless that happens, the basic frame of reference for detailed policy-making and allocation of resources will not materialize. There is, therefore, an element of 'ad hocism' about what is being done, for example, BSCIC activities are being pursued, to a large extent, at the initiative of the BSCIC and not as an imperative of the national policy.

A large number of foreign and local non-governmental voluntary organizations (NGOs) are also involved in the promotion of rural industries. However, since the macro-environment does not provide effective co-ordination at policy and operational levels, the activities of these organizations lack coherence, focus, and proper direction. Many of these agencies and organizations have very little technology awareness. However, some are sensitive to the need to upgrade technologies and to choose appropriate technology, and have been active in the field, but even these organizations have often tended not to pursue these objectives extensively. To receive continued donor and government support, they often must show tangible results in a short period of time by promoting

145

income-generating activities which are usually traditional in nature to a large number of people. Thus, only limited results have been shown by the few NGOs which have pursued the objective of upgrading technology for certain rural industries.

The NGOs which have made some contribution toward upgrading technology for rural industries in Bangladesh include Bangladesh Rural Advancement Committee (BRAC), Mirpur Agricultural Workshop and Training School (MAWTS), Micro-Industries Development Assistance Society (MIDAS), Proshika (Centre for Human Development), Rangpur Dinajpur Rural Services (RDRS), Mennonite Central Committee (MCC), Rural Technical School (at Suruj in Trangail *Zila*) and Dhaka *Shishu* Programme (DSP). Again, their technology activities are of relatively recent origin, mostly occurring during the past few years. It has been found that these organizations together have, up to 1987, introduced 20 improved or new consumer and 48 improved or new capital items or groups of items, most of which are either at the experimental stage or in limited commercial use.[8]

**Resources**

Table 2 shows public sector allocation for small and cottage industries in successive five-year plans starting with the first pre-independence 5-year plan (1955–60). This varied between 1 and 2 per cent of the total public sector outlay in the pre-independence period, but has consistently been less than 1 per cent since liberation. The various plans since liberation have allocated to small and cottage industries an average of 4.7 per cent of the total allocated to the industrial sector. (To indicate how meagre these sums are in absolute terms, it may be pointed out that the allocation to small and cottage industries in the *TFYP* for the 1985–90 period was Tk 1350 million (US\$ 43.5 m) or 5.4 per cent, out of an allocation to the industrial sector as a whole of Tk 26,000 m (US\$ 838.7 m).) This does not adequately reflect the contribution of small and cottage industries to the GDP and labour absorption as compared to large-scale industries. According to official statistics, the contributions of large-scale and small-scale industries to the GDP (at current market prices) were, on average, 4.6 and 3.7 per cent respectively from 1983 to 1986. (The full contribution of rural industries to the GDP is not reflected in the contribution of small industries as officially shown. Cottage and tiny activities are unlikely to have been taken into account in the official estimates. Micro-studies show a much higher contribution of rural industries to GDP. For example, the Rural Industries Study Project (RSIP) of BIDS found it to be 8.3 per cent.[9]) In addition, one official estimate shows that 26 per cent of the rural labour force is gainfully employed in rural non-farm activities (of which an important component is rural industries), while micro-studies put the figure at 43–45 per cent.[10, 11]

146

Despite the interest in rural industries demonstrated by the government, various donor agencies and many NGOs, the use of credit by the sector has remained extremely limited, especially from institutional sources. A 1979 survey showed that only 6 per cent of the rural enterprises received credit from various sources to meet their initial capital investment and that, of the enterprises which received credit, only 21 per cent received it from institutional sources, while the remaining 79 per cent used non-institutional sources. The situation was similarly discouraging with respect to expansion and working capital. (The entrepreneurs (well over 90 per cent of all entrepreneurs), who do not receive credit raise the initial capital largely from personal savings out of income from agriculture and other occupations but also from sale of land and other assets, inheritance, and dowry. The expansion capital comes mainly from profits made in the activities concerned, but also from personal savings from other income sources, and sale of land and other assets; and working capital from various sources noted above. Since the capacity of the rural entrepreneurs is extremely limited in respect to all these sources, raising working capital, which is needed on a rolling basis regularly, becomes a very formidable problem.[12] Available evidence suggests that the situation has not improved much.

**Table 2 Public sector allocation for small and cottage industries in successive five-year plans before and since independence**

|  | Percentage of total public sector outlay | Percentage of total allocation for all industries |
|---|---|---|
| First Five-Year Plan, 1955–60 | 1.14 | N.A. |
| Second Five-Year Plan, 1960–65 | 2.17 | 21.60 |
| Third Five-Year Plan, 1965–70 | 1.05 | 7.09 |
| First Five-Year Plan, 1973–78 | 0.62 | 3.24 |
| Two Year Plan, 1978–80 | 0.64 | 3.67 |
| Second Five-Year Plan, 1980–85 | 0.88 | 6.87 |
| Third Five-Year Plan, 1985–1990 | 0.54 | 4.84 |

Source: For the First three plan periods from top: Planning Commission, government of Pakistan, the various plan documents; and for the plan periods since independence: Planning commission, Government of Bangladesh, the various plan documents.

The use of credit by rural entrepreneurs is small for two reasons. On the one hand, they have extremely limited access to institutional credit, which is provided at reasonable rates of interest. On the other hand, the non-institutional lenders such as the *mahajans* charge usurious rates of interest. Some reasons for the limited access of rural entrepreneurs to institutional credit include their inability, in general, to provide a sufficient amount of collateral, a lack of knowledge about sources of credit, intricate official formalities, payment of bribes that often become a 'pre-condition' for getting credit from an institutional source, rather long gestation periods (3 months on average, but in some cases, it may be 5 months or more) from the time the application is completed to the time the money is received, and a substantial cost in terms of days spent (about 12 days on average, but 20 or more days in some cases) pursuing the credit. These problems are often so intractable that when the rural entrepreneurs decide to go for credit, they turn more often to usurious money lenders than to institutional sources.[12]

The 1986 industrial policy contains certain proposals to facilitate resource availability to the small and cottage industry sector by channelling more funds, or reducing the amount of funds required to set up and run industries. These include:

○ Requiring financial institutions and commercial banks to have separate windows for small and cottage industry financing and to set apart a definite percentage of their resources for the development of small and cottage industries;
○ Setting the debt–equity ratio for small and cottage industries at 80:20;
○ Initiating a Small Entrepreneur Credit Guarantee Scheme to be intro-duced under the joint sponsorship of the BSCIC and the *Shadaran Bima* Corporation (General Insurance Corporation);
○ Setting the rate of interest payable by small and cottage industries at 10 per cent;
○ Exempting from income tax all income arising from export of handi-crafts; and
○ Entitling small and cottage industries located in less developed areas to income tax rebates linked to production, to pay an import duty of only 2.5 per cent *ad valorem* on machinery and equipment both for setting up new industries and for existing industries, to be exempt from import permits/LC authorization fees, and to receive subsidies on fuel costs from a special fund to be created by the government.[7]

These policy guidelines are a step in the right direction. However, while some, such as the debt: equity ratio and low import duty on machinery and equipment, are not new measures, others are not yet in place. Moreover, the procedures required to take advantage of such provisions are often complicated and lengthy, and poor rural industrial entrepreneurs may find them extremely difficult. They may also not be aware of the facilities available or how to take advantage of them. If imaginatively implemented, these measures should bring about an improvement in the financial environment facing the rural industrial sector.

If rural industrial entrepreneurs have increased access to funds, one might expect them to decide to use new or improved technology, if

148

available, but, as noted earlier their technology awareness is low. More-over, due to lack of alternative opportunities, the rural poor often enter into rural industrial activities without regard for their productivity or profitability to utilize their own labour and that of the members of their families in order to augment their family incomes as much as possible. This is the main reason why many rural industrial activities continue to exist even though, as noted earlier, they suffer from low productivity and hence low, even negative profitability. Hence, to secure an appropriate tech-nology response, the rural poor need to be mobilized as suggested above, in addition to being ensured of the availability of necessary financial resources. Yet both of these conditions have thus far remained largely unfulfilled.

## The class position of rural industrial entrepreneurs and the national policy response to the needs of rural industries

The rural industrial sector faces the macro-environment described above primarily because of the class position of the segment of the population to which most rural entrepreneurs belong. To elaborate, let us briefly analyse national power relations and the decision-making context.

### The rural poor

The majority of rural industrial entrepreneurs come from groups made up of the rural poor. These include landless farm workers, non-farm workers, sharecroppers, tenants, marginal and small farmers and artisans. Figures on poverty and nutrition levels and data on patterns of land ownership all show that the rural poor constitute 75–80 per cent of the rural population. They live in thousands of villages around the country. They are uneducated or ill-educated and have a low level of consciousness about the nature of their problems and prospects. They are often unable to seek out those assistance programmes that are there for them; and even when they know that certain programmes exist, they often fail to take advantage of such programmes because of their inability to fulfil the necessary formalities. Under these circumstances, to assist the poor effectively the institutional system must reach out to them with simplified assistance programmes.

### The rural elite and non-poor group

The rural elite and non-poor are mainly larger landowners who account for about 10 per cent of the rural households; however, a few come from among the ranks of the land-poor who have been involved in certain vocations such as trade and commerce and/or politics. The households of the rural elite provide land for sharecropping and/or supply loans and/or provide jobs for the rural poor. They dominate the rural economy and rural politics and occupy rural leadership positions as members and

149

chairmen of union and upazila parishads and project committees. Because of their leading socioeconomic positions and consequent access to the political and administrative systems, they usually succeed in appropriating a large share, or even the lion's share, of the resources allocated to rural development programmes and projects. They are also the ones who come forward to invest in relatively modern rural industries, if facilities such as electricity supply and upgraded technology become available and profit-making opportunities present themselves. They are well placed to spot emerging opportunities and are also able to raise the necessary funds for upgraded technologies or larger operations which often cost substantial sums of money. The poor are disadvantaged not only because they may not have the information in time, but also, and more important, because they are unable to raise the necessary funds, as they have meagre means of their own and extremely limited capacity to raise funds from institutional or non-institutional sources.

As a result, even when a new or improved technology becomes available, which is prima facie appropriate, it is controlled by the more wealthy people. The poor not only fail to acquire the improved technology, but many of those who were in business using lower levels of technology become displaced and deprived of their livelihood. Unless alternative employment opportunities are created for the displaced, the new or improved technology might be considered inappropriate in the final analysis, that is, when its adverse impact on the poor is taken into account. Moreover, the wealthier people often tend to upgrade their operations and may thereby introduce further inappropriate technology. Appropriate macro-interventions may be necessary to discourage or even prohibit such tendencies.

### Political authority and bureaucracy at various levels, other elite groups and donors

Political authority and bureaucracy at various levels (national, divisions, zila, upazila, union) are involved in decision-making and implementation of policies and programmes. However, all major decisions are made by the head of the national government, on the basis of his perceptions and perspectives and those of cabinet members, and those manning the top echelons of the bureaucracy, both military and civil, who often tend to represent their own class interests, prejudices and biases.

Various non-government elite groups such as politicians, industrialists, businessmen, consulting engineers, economists, accountants, lawyers, and other professional groups, acting through their channels of personal connections or through associations and groupings, influence decisions in such a way as to be favourable to themselves; and if need be they also act in collaboration with the decision-makers for mutual benefit.

Economic decision-making in Bangladesh is also substantially influenced

150

by the UN and other aid and funding agencies. UN agencies such as FAO, UNESCO, and ESCAP seek to improve the foundation and the capacity for decision-making in Bangladesh by supporting research and training, while other UN agencies, including UNDP, UNFPA and WFP, and other multilateral financial organizations, such as the World Bank, IMF, ADB and IFAD, provide financial assistance for development programmes and projects. In addition, bilateral donors, such as USAID, Canadian International Development Agency, the Swedish International Development Agency and the EEC, support research and training as well as development programmes and projects.

The mandates, imperatives, dynamics and leadership of these aid organizations have their own pulls and pushes bearing on the statement of problems and their solutions. Thus, to alleviate poverty, such organizations as ILO, FAO and IFAD, advocate extensive interventions in favour of the poor, while other organizations such as the World Bank, IMF, ADB and USAID are strongly in favour of increasing reliance on market mechanisms. Since the last mentioned organizations provide the bulk of the aid received by Bangladesh, they are highly influential in economic decision-making, particularly in relation to the activities they support. Rural industries are currently a popular subject for most of these organizations, but R & D for developing and diffusing AT for rural industries appears to be a neglected subject or one of low priority. Moreover, the thrust toward market mechanisms typically strengthens the position of the richer people who, as pointed out earlier, often take advantage of emerging opportunities for profit-making and hurt the poor in the process, and also encourage inappropriate technological upgrading.

On the other hand, feedback from those representing the interests of the poor, particularly at the grassroots levels, is not often available in a well-expressed manner at the highest decision-making level. Even when it is available, it tends to be brushed aside, as the viewpoints of the elites and donors have systemic preponderance in the decision-making process. The poor, although a very large majority, are atomistic and powerless and have no organized lobbies to articulate their interests and influence decision-making in their favour.

The above analysis may provide an explanation for the failure of national S&T policy to deal with technological aspects of rural industries and the neglect of the subject of AT in industrial policy as well as in various programmes to promote rural industries in Bangladesh, even though this sector is recognized to have great potential to provide employment and income-generating potential for the rural poor.

## Paddy husking: technological developments and the role of the macro-environment

In this section, technological developments in paddy husking are reviewed. The appropriateness of those developments and the role of the macro-environment in relation to them are examined in light of the analyses presented in the previous sections.

*The growth of mechanized paddy husking and decline of the* dhenki
Paddy husking is a leading rural industrial activity in Bangladesh. The country's rice production is about 15 million tons, all of which is consumed within the country. Paddy husking is carried out throughout the country, since paddy is produced all over rural Bangladesh. Until the 1960s, almost the entire paddy output was husked using the traditional, manual *dhenki* technique. Although a substantial proportion was husked by the households themselves for their own consumption, this activity provided an important source of employment and income for vast numbers of workers, particularly women, from landless and land-poor families. However, in the last two decades alternative capital-intensive, mechanized methods have made heavy inroads into this activity. Thus, about 17 per cent of the total national paddy output was husked by these mechanized methods in 1967: this proportion rose to 20–25 per cent by 1977, to about 30–35 per cent by 1981 and to about 45 per cent by 1987 (Table 3). The alternative milling techniques include rural or small huller mills, large huller or commercial mills and semi- and fully-automatic mills.

**Table 3 Growth of mechanization of paddy husking**

|  | 1967 | 1977 | 1981 |
|---|---|---|---|
| Crop husked by: |  |  |  |
| *Dhenki* (%) | 83 | 65–75 | 60–65 |
| Small huller mill (%) | 17 | 2–25 | 25–30 |
| Commercial mill (%) | – | 5–10 | 10 |
| Number of small huller mills | 6,500 | 7,600 | 10,493 |
| Number of commercial mills: |  |  |  |
| Total | – | 80 | 320 |
| Fully automatic | – | 1 | 15 |
| Semi-automatic | – | – | 5 |

Source: World Bank, *Selected Issues in Rural Employment*, March, 1983

The *dhenki* is a heavy wooden bar with a pestle fitted at one end. It is balanced on two knee-high poles, with the wooden bar working as a lever.

It is foot-operated. The end without the pestle is pressed down and released so that the pestle goes up and then drops heavily into a mortar set below on the ground. Two to three workers are required to operate a *dhenki*. The most common mechanized paddy husking method is the small or rural mill that uses an Engleberg steel huller driven by a diesel or electric motor (15–20 hp). Such a mill normally provides custom services for neighbouring farmers or small traders, who usually bring in small consignments ranging from a few seers to a few maunds of paddy (1 maund = approximately 36 kg; 40 seers = 1 maund). It also employs two or three workers. Large huller or commercial mills use batteries of four or five steel hullers driven by flat belts from line shafts powered by steam engines (using husk as fuel) or diesel or electric motors. These mills have attached to them non-mechanized soaking, parboiling, drying, pre-cleaning and winnowing operations using scaled-up traditional technologies and they operate as both commercial and service units – that is, they buy paddy, husk it and sell the rice, as well as husking rice brought to them for a fee. An average of 20 workers are employed by this sort of mill. The modern integrated mills use rubber roll hullers and offer a full range of services. Pre-cleaning, soaking, parboiling and drying are handled automatically and rice, bran and husk are automatically separated. Some of these mills are semi-automatic in the sense that sun-drying rather than mechanical drying is carried out. They generally operate as wholesale businesses or work on contract for the government, milling government procured paddy. Such a mill employs about 30 workers.

### Factors behind the spread of mechanized methods
The main factor behind the spread of mechanized rice mills has been the expansion of electricity to rural areas at low prices, which created profit-making opportunities through the use of electrically-powered paddy husking machines. In 1977, the cost differential of husking between the *dhenki* method and the huller mill was 12:1 (Tk 11.8 to Tk 1.0). This enabled the huller mill owners to charge very little for husking (Tk 1.2 to 3.0 per maund) and yet make good profits.[14] In spite of subsequent increases in the operating costs of the rice mills, the husking cost differential between the *dhenki* and the huller mill was still found to be 7 or 8:1 (Tk 27.40 to Tk 3.5–4.04) in 1986 (Table 4). This high profitability attracted investment in rice huller mills which, therefore, spread rapidly along with the spread of electricity. The availability of institutional credit for setting up rice mills facilitated the process.

Other favourable factors included the availability of accelerated depreciation and tax holidays. The 1986 industrial policy does, however, discourage the establishment of automatic rice mills in view of the existing underutilization of installed capacity. It may be noted that the question of the appropriateness of the technique does not seem to have been a

**Table 4 Comparative characteristics of alternative paddy husking techniques**

| | Dhenki | Small Huller Mill | Large Huller Mill |
|---|---|---|---|
| Fixed capital, FC (Tk) | 3,285 | 85,832 | 453,667 |
| Fixed capital excluding land, $FC_1$ (Tk) | 1,630 | 78,832 | 123,767 |
| Fixed capital, excluding land and building $FC_2$ (Tk) | 630 | 39,632 | 62,100 |
| Working capital (at current level of capacity utilization) (Tk) | 816 | 2,456 | 108,479 |
| Employment, L (No) | 2.6 | 2.5 | 20.5 |
| Proportion of family workers (%) | 62 | 19 | 18 |
| Proportion of female workers (%) | 100 | 19 | 4 |
| Number of days of operation per year | 175 | 237 | 195 |
| Average work hours per day | 7.2 | 5.5 | 13.5 |
| Yearly hours worked | 1,260 | 1,304 | 2,633 |
| Output, Q (Tk) | 47,750 | 55,504 | 5,060,918 |
| Gross value added, VA (Tk) | 7,445 | 37,964 | 426,347 |
| Net yearly profit, NP (Tk) | Negative | 22,066 | 281,412 |
| Paddy husked per 8 hours (md) | 1.43 | 50.72 | 124.12 |
| Recovery Rate (%) | 73.14 | 70.00 | 70.00 |
| Proportion of broken kernel (%) | 6.00 | 16.00 | 10.00 |
| FC/L (Tk) | 1,263 | 34,333 | 22,130 |
| $FC_1$/L (Tk) | 627 | 31,533 | 6,037 |
| VA/L (Tk) | 2,863 | 15,186 | 20,797 |
| VA/FC | 2.27 | 0.44 | 0.94 |
| VA/$FC_1$ | 4.57 | 0.48 | 3.44 |
| NP/FC | —— | 0.26 | 0.62 |
| FC/Q | 0.069 | 1.546 | 0.090 |
| FCl/Q | 0.034 | 1.420 | 0.025 |
| Q/L (Tk) | 18,635 | 22,202 | 246,874 |
| Per maund cost of processing (Tk) | | | |
| Husking | 27.40 | 4.04 | 3.50 |
| Other processing | 8.59 | —— | 8.61 |
| Total | 35.99 | —— | 12.11 |

Source: Zaid Bakht and K M Nabiul Islam, *Rural Industrialization in Mirzapur Upazila: Status and Potential*, SRID, Bangladesh Institute of Development Studies, Dhaka, May, 1987.

consideration behind that decision.[7] Clearly, therefore, the macro-environment has favoured the rapid spread of rice mills in Bangladesh.

## Comparison of the appropriateness of alternative paddy husking techniques

### *Advantages of the* dhenki *compared to huller mills*
Relevant data regarding the *dhenki*, small huller mill and large huller mill are presented in Table 4.

1. The expansion of rice mills and the consequent displacement of *dhenki*s has had an adverse impact on employment. Given that a *dhenki* can husk 1.43 maunds per 8-hour day while a small huller mill can husk about 51 maunds and a large huller mill about 124 maunds of paddy, a small huller mill displaces about 35 *dhenki*s and 91 *dhenki* operators and a large huller mill displaces about 87 *dhenki*s and 226 *dhenki* operators. Since each small and large huller mills create jobs for 2.5 and 20.5 persons respectively, the net displacements are approximately 89 and 205 persons per small and large huller respectively;
2. The rice mills are highly discriminatory against women. The *dhenki* operators are all women, while all the employees of small huller mills and about 80 per cent of the employees of large huller mills are male;
3. The rural income distributon is adversely affected by the rapid expansion of huller mills. The displaced *dhenki* workers come mostly from landless and low-income families who often lose their only source of livelihood with the advent of these mills. These mills thus divert income from large numbers of poor families to a small group of economically better-off mill owners;
4. The capital/labour ratio of the *dhenki* is very low compared to the mills. A fixed investment of only Tk 1,263 including land or Tk 627 excluding land is required to employ one person to operate one *dhenki*. In reality the *dhenki* is usually set up within the homestead and does not require additional land and *pucca* or semi-*pucca* structure. Per employee the capital requirement (inclusive of land) for one small huller mill is Tk 34,331 and Tk 22,130 for a large huller mill;
5. The *dhenki* uses capital much more efficiently than a mill. Value added per Tk worth of fixed capital (FC) is Tk 2.27 (when land is included in FC) and Tk 4.57 (when land is excluded from FC) in the case of the *dhenki*, compared to only Tk 0.44 and Tk 0.95 respectively in the cases of the small and large hullers;
6. The *dhenki* is locally produced with local materials, while motors used in the huller mills are of foreign origin, although other parts are locally produced;
7. The other advantages of *dhenki* husking over huller mill husking of

155

paddy are a higher recovery rate (73.4 per cent versus 70.0 per cent for huller mills), a lower rate of broken kernel, a more nutritious although less polished rice and easier separation of bran and husk.

## Advantages of huller mills compared to the dhenki

As noted earlier, compared to the *dhenki*, rice mills are characterized by substantially lower husking costs per unit. While *dhenki* operators earned Tk 17.78 per day or Tk 5,334 per year of 300 working days, annual net profits of Tk 22,066 and 282,412 were earned by small and large huller mills, respectively.

Labour productivity of the mills is substantially higher compared to the *dhenki* – 5.3 times and 7.3 times higher for small and large huller mills respectively. However, it may be noted that compared to the corresponding increase in the capital intensity (27.2 times and 17.5 times respectively), labour productivity gains are proportionally much less.

## Characteristics of automatic and semi-automatic rice mills

No R & D efforts have been undertaken to correct the problems of low recovery rates and broken rice encountered with huller mill use. Instead, a further technological advancement in the form of large automatic mills has been introduced. The mechanized parboiling and drying performed by these mills help achieve uniform paddy with optimally low moisture content. Hence, the recovery rate from these mills is higher (71.9 per cent), the percentage of broken rice is lower and the quality of by-products (bran and husk) is better compared to the huller mills.

However, the capacity of these mills has been substantially underutilized due to short paddy supplies. (A fully integrated automatic mill has a daily capacity of over 1,000 maunds, which is difficult to come by except under contract for husking government procured paddy.) This far outweighs any cost savings arising from higher milling efficiency. In fact, at the current levels of capacity utilization, the cost of paddy processing per maund has been found to be 2.5 times higher for automatic mills compared to large huller mills. Also, the value added per Tk worth of investment has been found to be Tk 0.15 in an automatic mill compared to Tk 0.44 in a small and Tk 0.94 in a large huller mill.

An automatic mill, utilized at full capacity, displaces about 345 *dhenkis* and about 1000 women *dhenki* operators and creates jobs for only 30 persons, mainly men, at a cost of Tk 250,000 per workplace. A very large foreign exchange cost is also involved in setting up an automatic mill.[3]

## Choice between automatic and huller mills

The above analysis shows that on all counts including employment creation, capital costs, efficiency, and foreign exchange requirements, the automatic mill is clearly a case of less appropriate technology compared to huller mills in the present context of Bangladesh.

## Choice between huller mill and dhenki

The choice is not very clear. The *dhenki* has several advantages over huller mills as noted above; but the main comparative disadvantage is its substantially lower labour productivity and hence much higher husking cost per maund. This makes it quite non-competitive compared to huller mills. While the existing *dhenki* has little to offer to *dhenki* operators in terms of growth in their income and, hence, a way out of poverty, their displacement from *dhenki* operation may rob them of their only source of livelihood. There are simply no alternative opportunities existing or emerging in which the large numbers of displaced women may be quickly absorbed. Hence, large-scale displacement of *dhenkis* and *dhenki* operators would imply a high social cost. This possible consequence of the expansion of huller mills was ignored as huller mills were allowed to be set up in large numbers without putting programmes in place to provide alternate employment opportunities for the displaced *dhenki* operators.

It thus appears that while the *dhenki* may be too inefficient to be appropriate, the impact of huller mills on employment may be too adverse for them to be appropriate under the present socioeconomic context of rural Bangladesh, which is characterized by widespread poverty and unemployment.

Under these circumstances, three lines of action in the direction of AT would seem to present themselves. One line of action is to seek to improve the mechanical efficiency of the *dhenki* with the aim of improving its productivity with minimal adverse impacts on employment. Sporadic R & D efforts have been made in this direction. The Bangladesh Institute of Development Studies within the framework of its Studies on Rural Industries Development Research Project (1984–87) has shown that good prospects exist for the development of an upgraded *dhenki*, with substantial productivity increases and cost reductions and a minimal adverse impact on employment in relation to the present *dhenki*. However, there has never been government sponsorship of R & D efforts along this line.

The second line of action would be to seek to alleviate the adverse employment impact of the huller mills, and thereby increase their appropriateness under the present context. Programmes could be put in place to organize the displaced *dhenki* operators to take advantage of the opportunities presented by the higher mechanical efficiency of the huller mills by assisting them with credit and other facilities. So assisted, the displaced women could, by working in groups, purchase paddy in bulk, store it, perform pre-husking operations (soaking, parboiling and drying), develop contractual links with huller mills for regular husking of the preprocessed paddy, perform post-husking winnowing operations, store

157

the rice and finally sell it at a profit. However, no policy stance to that end has been formulated, let alone programmes instituted.

The third line of action would be to provide credit, skill development opportunities and management training to groups of women to enable them to own and operate huller mills jointly. A government agency or NGO could mobilize the displaced women, arrange for the training they need, and provide them with the necessary credit. The credit could be provided under group and individual responsibility, without collateral. Given that the women concerned lack education and experience, it will be necessary for the implementing agency to provide supervision, until the group attains the maturity to operate on its own, to ensure effective management, and proper utilization and repayment of credit. There have been some positive experiences with such group ownership of technologies in economic activities generated by, for example, the Bangladesh Rural Advancement Committee (BRAC).[15]

Given a macro-environment unsupportive of the need for AT for rural industries, shaped by dominant elite interests and buttressed by aid dependence, it is not surprising that appropriate technology for a rural industrial activity like paddy husking has not received proper attention and support through appropriate macro-policies, institutions and resource allocation.

## Concluding remarks

Rural industries are a very important source of employment and income for the rural poor in Bangladesh, but the industries have largely remained characterized by underdeveloped technologies and low productivity. In a number of cases, however, improved and modern techniques have been introduced, although traditional techniques have remained in wide use, side by side in the same industries. In these cases of technological dualism and pluralism, the poor have generally remained stuck with the traditional techniques, while the improved and modernized alternatives have generally been captured by relatively well-to-do people. Some of the improved or new techniques are also inappropriate given the existing situation in rural Bangladesh, especially the lack of alternative employment opportunities for the rural poor, particularly women. How things have been shaping up in one such case, that of paddy husking, has been discussed here. Similar developments have been taking place in other rural industries such as oil extraction, wood works and *gur*/sugar making.

From the analysis presented above, it appears that what has been happening with respect to technology and the development of rural industries in Bangladesh has been, in large measure, consistent with the dictates of the macro-environment, which has its roots in the country's highly unequal socioeconomic structure and the nature of its economy,

158

which works against the interests of the ordinary rural industrial entre-preneurs who belong to the ranks of the rural poor. Micro-interventions to upgrade technology in certain rural industries have made some useful contributions, but their scope and reach have remained very limited.

# Discussion: Policy Approaches Toward Technology Choice and Small Enterprise Development in Asia

*J G Waardenburg*: I have a question for Mr Ahmad. In the long-term development of Bangladesh, would you consider rural industries to be part of a distant future situation in Bangladesh, or a useful vehicle for a few generations that would vanish in the long run?

*W Rasaputram*: I have a question for Mr Ahmad regarding the transfer of technology to the rural poor. Do the efforts undertaken in Bangladesh also take into consideration the differences between regions? The AT for one region is not always appropriate for another. Are policies adjusted on the basis of regional studies undertaken in Bangladesh?

*J Sullivan*: I would like to ask a question of Mr Bautista. The first structural adjustment in the Philippines began in 1979 or 1980, and the country subsequently had several others. What is your view of the impact of those interventions by the World Bank and IMF on the situation of rural industries in the Philippines?

*A Saith*: I have one observation to make and one question to ask Mr Ahmad. The observation is that, given the limited degree of sub-contracting from large-scale firms to small, rural ones in most countries, there could be a high degree of product competition between the small and very small enterprises. Unless this possibility is borne in mind, the objectives of industrialization might not be fulfilled.

My question concerns the issue of AT in agricultural processing in Bangladesh. Given the very wide differences in commercial profitability between the *dhenki* and the modern (small and/or large) hullers, is it really possible to think of an 'appropriate' upgraded *dhenki* as a technology to be promoted?

*Y De Wit*: I have one question for Mr Bautista. How do you interpret the mood of the Philippines Government in the late 1970s and early 1980s *vis-à-vis* small enterprises? Was it lack of will, unwillingness, or lack of insight? What has been done with the results of the ILO report prepared by Mr Ranis? I found it a very useful report; did it have any impact on policy making?

A question for Mr Ahmad, concerning credit to small-scale enterprise in the rural areas, I think none of us will be surprised that interest rates are higher for these small firms, but capital productivity is also higher. Are there any studies or do you have any insight on what the maximum interest rate might be that small enterprises can bear? Even if the interest is high, access to credit is often more important than the interest rate.

*Q K Ahmad*: The first question was about whether the rural industrial sector will be a temporary phase or a long-term feature in Bangladesh. I do not think it can be a long-term feature. It must be a dynamic sector, that grows by improving technology, raising productivity and moving up the scale of operation. The very small activities with very low productivity and profitability that we now find in the rural areas cannot continue; that would mean a perpetuation of poverty.

The second question was about regional differences within Bangladesh that might affect appropriate technology. Bangladesh is perhaps more homogeneous than many other countries, with few differences in the rural economic setup, if one excludes the environs of Dhaka and a few other places. Still, there are some important differences. We conducted a major study during the 1984–87 period to identify activities that could be promoted in different areas of the country. The study came up with a number of potential activities for each selected area. Project profiles were prepared for some of them, which included technological aspects. Through similar studies, activities that can be promoted in other areas, as well as their levels of operation and technological requirements, can be identified.

Another question was about the transfer of technology to rural areas. That is a real problem. A number of improved technologies for different rural industries have been developed by the Bangladesh Small and Cottage Industries Corporation (BSCIC) and other organizations such as the Bangladesh Council for Scientific and Industrial Research (BCSIR). Most of these have remained on the shelves of the organizations. Some are being used commercially but in a still very limited way. No institutional structure has been established to transfer the information about these technologies or provide extension services to the rural areas. As a result, effective transfers of technology to rural areas have not been taking place. ATs must not only be developed and identified, they must also be transferred to help rural industries become productive and viable.

Next, there was a question about competition between small and very small units. In our study, we found that the very small units employing a few workers are relatively more productive than firms employing 5 to 10 workers. Productivity improved again in units employing more than 10 workers. At the very small level, entrepreneurs need assistance to expand their activities. It is not clear why units employing 5–10 workers are comparatively less productive. We have not researched that question in any detail.

In making resource allocation decisions, priorities should be set for activities according to their potential for growth, taking into account both

161

supply and demand. In rural Bangladesh, incomes are very low and the income distribution is highly skewed. Not only the urban people but also the rural rich are often urban-oriented in their consumption pattern. Therefore, the main source of demand for goods produced by rural industries is the rural population, particularly the poor. For rural industries to expand, rural income must rise. Here the importance of agriculture immediately comes into perspective.

Regarding sub-contracting, in general there is not much sub-contracting between large industries and small, rural industries in Bangladesh. There is limited sub-contracting between large and small/cottage industries in the industrial belts of Dhaka and Khulna. The practice is not widespread in the rural areas and I do not think it can be promoted quickly.

On the question of the profitability differential between the *dhenki* and dehuller, it should be noted that in 1977 the husking cost differential per unit of paddy was 12:1 and, by 1986, had decreased but was still 8:1. Hence, the profitability has been much higher for dehullers. One reason for this has been availability of cheap electricity to operate dehullers. If electricity had been priced more appropriately, the figures on the husking cost differential would have been somewhat different, but there would still have been a substantial profitability differential in favour of the dehullers. There is a strong case for the small dehullers on the basis of productivity. The point I wanted to make was that alternative employment should be found for the *dhenki* workers who are displaced by dehullers. Three options could be adopted individually or in combination to assist the displaced workers. These options include promoting other activities to employ the displaced persons, giving them credit so that they can buy paddy, have it processed by dehullers and sell it for a profit, and providing credit and training so that groups can purchase dehullers.

There are a number of studies on the issue of interest rates for rural entrepreneurs, but there is no consensus on what rates should be charged. Some people suggest that interest for this sector should be as high as 30 or 40 per cent because the alternative is 100 or 200 per cent charged by moneylenders. However, to promote the rural sector, it is necessary for small enterprises to generate profits for reinvestment and expansion. As the rate of interest charged to large industries is much lower than the current rate of 16–20 per cent charged rural entrepreneurs, it is unethical to charge even the rate currently charged, and charging 30 or 40 per cent should not even be considered. Although it costs more to administer small amounts of credit to large numbers of rural people, the government should pick up the extra costs to make rural industrial activities more viable and for ethical reasons. Indeed, access to credit is important but, given the need to alleviate poverty, and for ethical considerations, rural entrepreneurs should not be charged higher interest rates than industries. In fact, the government of Bangladesh instituted a 10 per cent rate of interest for the rural sector some time ago but it has not actually been implemented.

*E Hyman*: A question was raised about ATI's palm oil processing experience in Cameroon, which demonstrates some interesting points. First, it shows that what is an AT in one country is not necessarily appropriate in another country. In Cameroon, unlike Bangladesh, there is a shortage of labour, so there is a need for more productive labour-saving technologies. In fact, some arable land in Cameroon is uncultivated for lack of labour and some palm fruit is not harvested for the same reason. Also, the burden of labour time on women, in particular, is very high.

A little bit of background on the case. There is a traditional palm oil extraction process in West Africa, which involves stomping the fruit by foot and using water to separate the oil from the pulp. In Cameroon, unlike most of West Africa, a hand-operated press (the Colin press) also has been in use since the 1930s. This press, imported from France, is no longer being manufactured. Many of the old presses are still in use, but are in deteriorating condition. As a result, ATI actually designed a project to rehabilitate the existing presses. However, it was found that few owners of Colin presses were willing to sell them since they were still usable. The imported spare parts were also too expensive and difficult to obtain. Subsequently, APICA, the implementing organization, decided it would be cheaper to produce a slightly smaller press, the Caltech, with design assistance from ATI. It is available in both hand-operated and motorized versions. The newest model minimizes the use of imported parts. Another reason why small-scale palm oil production is desirable is that West African consumers prefer the sharp taste of artisanally produced oil over the refined oil produced by large-scale industry.

*R Bautista*: A question was raised about whether the 1974 Report of the ILO Comprehensive Employment Strategy Mission that Mr Ranis headed, made an impact on Philippine policy. The book's local edition was made available at an inexpensive price, and it was widely discussed in government and academic circles. A few 'enlightened' technocrats pushed actively for the implementation of the report's policy recommendations, but they proved less influential than others in the Cabinet who opposed major policy reform at that time. The Ministry of Trade and Industry was particularly resistant to changes in trade and industrial policies. However, the ideas articulated so well in the report probably had a beneficial long-term effect as evidenced by the similar policy recommendations made by the World Bank Industrial Mission that visited two years later concerning the need for trade liberalization, export expansion and support for labour-intensive industries.

This has resulted in increasing recognition by the Philippine government of the need to improve the international competitiveness of domestic industry. When the World Bank offered a structural adjustment loan to finance an industrial adjustment programme, the government agreed to liberalize trade by reducing tariff levels and quantitative import restrictions over the 5-year period from 1981 to 1985. Also included in the structural adjustment financing was the technological upgrading of a few inefficient import-competing industries such as textiles and cement.

In late 1983, however, an external debt-related foreign exchange crisis occurred after heavy foreign borrowing that financed sustained trade deficits and inefficient investments after 1974. The trade liberalization measures were then suspended by emergency import restrictions imposed to conserve foreign exchange. Elimination of the infamous 11 major industrial projects supported by the Ministry of Trade and Industry was a blessing in disguise.

Later, a second structural adjustment loan provided by the World Bank helped reduce domestic price distortions in agriculture. The Aquino Goverment dismantled the marketing monopoly for the two major export crops (sugarcane and coconut), which were formerly controlled by Marcos cronies.

Philippine trade and industrial policies are now in transition. Large industry continues to have a strong influence. The dialogues between the Ministry and various industrial sectors have only involved representatives of large-scale industry to address their problems. The government has not been expeditious in following through on its commitment to the World Bank and IMF to liberalize imports. However, rural small-scale industry has still not been adequately promoted.

*B Mansuri*: I detected a note of concern in Mr Ahmad's remark about interest rates in regard to the Grameen Bank. I hope I do not appear to be an advocate of high interest rates. The main concerns should be the rationalization of interest rates and the sustainability of lending institutions. Our experience shows that small-scale enterprises and the rural poor are mostly interested in access to institutional credit, and that the interest rate is only a secondary concern. Some observations in Ethiopia have revealed that transactions totalling about $100 million are made annually in rural areas with some interest rates as high as 100 per cent, so the need for credit is very strong. The 19 per cent interest rate charged by the Grameen Bank also reflects the cost of distributing credit to a large number of very small borrowers. The recovery rate of over 95 per cent indicates, in addition, that the interest rates are acceptable to the target groups, who are usually interested in repeat loans.

I noted that Mr Ahmad found in Bangladesh small enterprises employing 5 to 6 to be more efficient than larger ones with 15 to 20 workers. Micro-enterprises supported by the Grameen Bank are even smaller than that. Our evaluation has shown that the Grameen Bank has contributed positively to the objectives of income distribution and trade in rural areas.

Its contribution to overall economic growth might be rather marginal. That is why an IFAD mission is now taking a comprehensive look at the small enterprise sector in Bangladesh and reviewing both policy and institutional issues.

Finally, it was suggested that IFAD favours an interventionist policy. This is not so. We focus on the poor and small-scale producers. Our main objective is, however, to influence policy directions and institutional orientations in favour of our target groups. We also intervene to assist in developing a structured market. Our approach is a balanced one of helping to develop the markets for small-scale products supplemented by direct intervention to help the poor.

*G Ranis*: I wanted to make two comments, one on the question of the most efficient size of enterprise. If we conclude that a most efficient firm size is to be promoted, I think we should be careful to ensure that the different sizes are facing the same kinds of environments. If there were less of a differentiation in environments, it seems to me that there would be a most efficient size that more or less would emerge. There may be economies of scale. What I am worried about is the notion that we could come up with the ideal size and deploy our agencies and instruments to assist firms of that size. I am not suggesting altering market principles, but these are also affected by choices in infrastructure investments.

Concerning the Philippine experience, I agree with the basic judgment that the results of our mission were somewhat mixed. Even in the 1970s, there was one area where the recommendations were actually implemented – the monetary credit rate sphere. Credit rates became more flexible, although never floating, and exchange rates were liberalized.

The dialogue is now different. In the 1970s, concern over rural development and employment was not broadly based. Now it is a mainstream concern which is a big step forward. Donors and governments are talking about small enterprise development now. I feel that there was a tendency toward more reforms in the 1970s, but the large inflow of foreign capital which occurred then from the commercial banks took the pressure off, so that no one had to do anything. I am concerned that the current discussion of large aid flows to the Philippines may also have this consequence. As tough as the early 1980s were in the Philippines for per capita income, they also led to a serious reassessment of policies by the academic community in the Philippines. In agriculture and industry this is how reforms should be made, not by foreign teams like the ILO, but by citizens of LDCs themselves. That trend, I think, has lost its steam now in the Philippines. The US is spending large sums in return for its bases, money is flowing in, and the Japanese want to increase their development assistance in the Philippines. Foreign capital can be useful, but if it is just used to relieve pressure without insisting on policy improvements, it can have a negative impact. That is one of the problems the Philippines is facing today.

165

*W Rasaputram*: I want to come back to the question of interest rates. First, people in rural areas are sensitive to both cost and availability. It is not only access to credit which is important. Non-institutional credit is expensive. Some people even pay 200 or 300 per cent on loans for mainly consumption purposes when they cannot get institutional credit. If interest rates on institutional credit are high, the people want them to be brought down to reasonable levels. Second, most people are born into poverty, live in debt and die in debt. It is important to relieve their indebtedness so that they can engage in productive enterprises and work for progress.

The third point is that the interest rate should be such that the rate of return is sufficiently attractive to promote non-agricultural enterprises. When the interest rate is high, producers have no incentive to produce more and merely fight for survival, rather than for progress.

# Macro-Policies for Appropriate Technology in Zimbabwean Industry

## DANIEL B NDLELA

### Introduction

Government macro-policies have a wide scope of influence and application in Zimbabwe's economy in general and in the industrial sectors in particular. Historically, Zimbabwe's macroeconomic policies and policy instruments have influenced the pace, structure and location of industrial enterprises. These policies have affected the decision-making of industrial units either directly or indirectly.

Present government policies are mainly focused on the environment immediately affecting the formal industrial sectors of mining and quarrying, manufacturing, construction and energy. In terms of value added these sectors contributed an average of 38 per cent to the gross domestic product (GDP) in the 12 year period from 1974–85. During the same period these four sectors contributed 25 per cent to total average formal employment. Though this is less than agricultural employment (26.6 per cent), there is greater potential for growth and employment generation in the country's industrial sectors.

Decisions about technology take place at the level of the micro-unit. Micro-units include multinational corporations, domestic, corporate and small-scale family firms in the private sector, public sector enterprises (parastatals and state corporations) and small-scale informal-sector firms. Whatever the size of the firm, decisions are made at the micro-level in light of each firm's own objectives and resources. However, as shown in this paper, these decisions are strongly influenced by the external environment and macro-economic policies of the central government.

In the Zimbabwean case, the government has outlined explicit policies and objectives that are meant to influence the environment affecting appropriate technology. The two national development plans that have been published since Zimbabwe's independence in 1980 (the Transitional National Development Plan 1982/83–1984/85 and the First Five-Year National Development Plan 1986–90) propose to restructure the industrial

DANIEL BODA NDLELA, is Regional Adviser on Economic Cooperation for the United Nations Economic Commission for Africa, Addis Ababa, Ethiopia. He formerly taught economics at the University of Zimbabwe.

sector in order to meet the changing patterns of demand for industrial products, increase employment through the adoption of labour-intensive technologies, and encourage geographic decentralization.

Implementing government policies to assist small- and medium-scale enterprises and to encourage decentralization are the objectives of two institutions, the Small Enterprise Development Corporation, (SEDCO) and the Industrial Development Corporation (IDC). However, this government policy initiative has not been successful. About 90 per cent of SEDCO's supported projects are in the commercial sector. Productive enterprises are not the priority of SEDCO. The IDC is still completely involved in medium- to large-scale manufacturing enterprises and has not yet started financing small-scale emerging businesses in Zimbabwe.

The financial resource mobilization instruments and controls which were developed during the UDI period are the most important set of institutional policies that influence the environment in which firms make their technology decisions. The foreign exchange system is probably the most important policy instrument affecting the long-term and short-term decisions of Zimbabwean enterprises. This financial resource mobilization instrument is mainly geared to the needs of formal sector enterprises. Small-scale and especially informal sector firms are invariably bypassed by these macroeconomic policy instruments.

## The scope and characteristics of appropriate technology in Zimbabwe's industrial sector

For purposes of describing government policies and macroeconomic policies that have influenced the adoption or rejection of appropriate technologies, this paper will define industry broadly under divisions 1 to 5 of the International Standard Industrial Classification (ISIC), that is, mining and quarrying (division one), manufacturing (divisions two and three), construction (division four) and electricity, gas and water and sanitary services (division five).[1] Although this is an attempt to cover as wide a spectrum as possible under the official statistical definition of the industrial sector, the present classification still excludes a small but growing set of industrial products manufactured by the informal sector. In the Zimbabwean case, classified manufacturers are registered companies that submit returns to the Central Statistical Office, and the requirement for this is a minimum initial capital outlay of Z\$30,000 (US\$18,300). This means that small formal and informal industrial activities are excluded from the statistical definition.

Mining is included in the industrial sector in the discussion of appropriate technology because in the definition of the manufacturing sector used in official Zimbabwean statistics, the demarcation between mining and manufacturing is somewhat blurred. The definition of the

Table 1 GDP at factor cost by industry of origin (% shares) – constant 1980 prices

| | 1974 | 1975 | 1976 | 1977 | 1978 | 1979 | 1980 | 1981 | 1982 | 1983 | 1984 | 1985 |
|---|---|---|---|---|---|---|---|---|---|---|---|---|
| Agriculture and Forestry | 15.6 | 14.7 | 16.5 | 14.0 | 15.5 | 15.3 | 14.2 | 13.6 | 13.7 | 13.3 | 13.6 | 16.1 |
| Mining and quarrying | 9.4 | 9.6 | 10.5 | 10.7 | 10.2 | 10.1 | 8.8 | 7.4 | 7.8 | 8.0 | 8.3 | 7.6 |
| Manufacturing | 23.5 | 23.3 | 22.1 | 22.7 | 22.0 | 24.1 | 24.9 | 24.2 | 24.1 | 24.2 | 23.0 | 23.4 |
| Electricity and water | 2.9 | 3.0 | 2.7 | 2.0 | 2.5 | 2.2 | 2.2 | 1.9 | 1.7 | 1.9 | 2.0 | 2.1 |
| Construction | 5.3 | 5.0 | 4.0 | 3.8 | 3.2 | 3.1 | 2.7 | 2.7 | 12.4 | 2.5 | 2.4 | 2.3 |
| Transport and Communication | 6.7 | 6.3 | 6.1 | 5.7 | 5.8 | 6.0 | 6.5 | 6.6 | 6.5 | 6.3 | 6.5 | 6.3 |
| Distribution, hotels and restaurants | 12.3 | 12.1 | 11.4 | 11.7 | 8.4 | 11.7 | 14.0 | 14.5 | 12.4 | 11.1 | 10.5 | 10.7 |
| Total material production | 75.7 | 74.0 | 73.3 | 70.6 | 67.6 | 72.5 | 73.3 | 70.9 | 78.6 | 67.3 | 66.3 | 68.5 |
| Finance | 4.5 | 6.1 | 6.2 | 6.7 | 6.0 | 5.1 | 4.9 | 5.7 | 6.6 | 6.0 | 5.6 | 5.1 |
| Real Estate | 3.0 | 2.6 | 2.3 | 2.3 | 1.9 | 1.7 | 1.3 | 1.4 | 1.2 | 1.2 | 1.2 | 1.1 |
| Public Administration | 5.6 | 6.3 | 7.1 | 8.5 | 9.7 | 9.6 | 9.0 | 9.2 | 9.1 | 9.5 | 10.2 | 9.8 |
| Education | 4.1 | 4.3 | 4.3 | 4.8 | 4.4 | 4.4 | 5.2 | 6.5 | 7.8 | 8.8 | 9.4 | 9.1 |
| Health | 1.9 | 2.0 | 2.0 | 2.4 | 2.4 | 2.3 | 2.2 | 2.4 | 2.4 | 2.6 | 2.7 | 2.5 |
| Domestic services | 2.4 | 2.4 | 2.4 | 2.5 | 2.4 | 2.2 | 2.0 | 1.7 | 1.7 | 1.7 | 1.7 | 1.5 |
| Other services | 5.4 | 5.4 | 5.3 | 5.7 | 5.7 | 5.7 | 5.4 | 5.1 | 5.6 | 6.1 | 6.1 | 5.5 |
| Total non-material production | 26.9 | 29.1 | 29.6 | 32.9 | 32.5 | 31.0 | 30.0 | 32.0 | 34.4 | 35.9 | 36.9 | 34.4 |
| Imputed banking charges | -2.6 | -3.1 | -2.9 | -3.5 | -0.1 | -3.5 | -3.3 | -2.9 | -13.0 | -3.2 | -3.2 | -3.1 |
| Total GDP | 100.0 | 100.0 | 100.0 | 100.0 | 100.0 | 100.0 | 100.0 | 100.0 | 100.0 | 100.0 | 100.0 | 100.0 |

Source: Socio-Economic Review 1980–1985, Zimbabwe, Ministry of Finance, Economic Planning and Development, 1986.

169

manufacturing sector states that 'establishments operating on a mining site as refiners/smelters of non-ferrous or precious metals are . . . excluded'.[2] On the other hand, excluded from the definition of mining are 'mines and quarries operated by manufacturers as a source of their raw materials, such as limestone mines operated by cement manufacturers. These form part of the manufacturing sectors'.[2] It is, therefore, obvious that a single treatment of these sectors will contribute to the formulation of a combined strategy for AT.

In terms of value added, mining and quarrying, manufacturing, electricity and water, and construction contributed an average of 38 per cent to gross domestic product (GDP) in the 12 year period, 1974–85 (see Table 1). During the same period, the manufacturing sector, which is the single most important sector in terms of output contributed an average of 23.4 per cent to the GDP, over 8.5 per cent higher than the next important sector, agriculture, which averaged 14.6 per cent over the same period.

However, the agricultural sector has made by far the largest impact on the economy in terms of employment. The agricultural sector's overall contribution to employment is larger than the four industrial sectors combined. During the 20 years between 1965 and 1984, agricultural employment averaged 279,100 per year – 26.6 per cent of average total formal employment (Table 2). During the same period the four industrial sectors combined (mining and quarrying, manufacturing, electricity and water, and construction) employed an average of 240,675 annually – 25 per cent of average total formal employment. This figure excludes self-employment in manufacturing and other industrial activities as these are not recorded by the Central Statistical Office. However, these statistics do not reveal the dynamics of the development and future prospects for employment generation in Zimbabwe. Although agriculture has thus far dominated as the largest employer, the role of the manufacturing and other industrial sectors as a source of employment needs to be emphasized. In the 15-year period between 1965 and 1979, agricultural employment averaged 324,333 per year, which was 23.3 per cent of total average formal sector employment. During the same period, manufacturing employment averaged 122,900 – only 8 per cent of total average formal sector employment per year. By the post-independence period (after 1980), agricultural employment for the years 1982–84 had dropped to an annual average of 269,667 or 7 per cent less than the 1965–69 yearly average. This was 26 per cent of total average formal employment and 1.5 times the 173,400 figure for manufacturing (see Table 2).

Both formal commercial and communal agriculture has declined in relative importance since 1969, while the formal non-agricultural sector grew substantially and informal sectors nearly tripled in relative size.[3] Growth of the informal sector results largely from seasonal and permanent migration of rural populations in communal areas and non-agricultural formal wage sectors.

**Table 2 Employment in manufacturing, agriculture and the national economy (thousands)**

| Year | Agriculture | Total % | Manufacturing | Total % | Total formal sector employment |
|---|---|---|---|---|---|
| 1965–69 | 289.5 | 37.5 | 89.5 | 11.6 | 771.7 |
| 1970–74 | 334.6 | 19.5 | 131.5 | 7.7 | 1,718.6 |
| 1975–79 | 348.9 | 12.8 | 147.7 | 5.4 | 2,731.9 |
| 1980 | 327.0 | 32.4 | 159.4 | 15.8 | 1,009.9 |
| 1981 | 294.3 | 28.2 | 173.2 | 16.7 | 1,037.7 |
| 1982 | 274.3 | 26.2 | 180.5 | 17.3 | 1,045.9 |
| 1983 | 263.5 | 25.4 | 173.4 | 16.8 | 1,033.9 |
| 1984 | 271.2 | 26.2 | 166.3 | 16.1 | 1,035.4 |

Source: Quarterly digest of statistics, June, 1986, Monthly Digest of Statistics, December, 1984, Central Statistical Office and unpublished data provided by the Central Statistical Office.

Potential applications of AT are numerous in the mining and quarrying, energy and water development, and construction sectors. ATs are particularly relevant in the construction and housing sector because they make greater use of local materials, are more labour using, and produce a product designed for lower income groups. In the Transitional National Development Plan (TNDP), a target of 115,000 housing units had been set over a 3-year period; however only 15,500 units were completed (13.4 per cent). During the First Five-Year National Development Plan (1986–90) the government outlined the following objectives:

○ Reduce costs of building materials and construction;
○ Increase government participation in the housing and construction sector;
○ Improve the quality of houses in communal, resettlement, mining and commercial farming areas; and
○ Modernize equipment and expand production capacity in the sector.[4]

The government introduced innovative financing programmes and technologies that were meant to reduce the costs of houses to levels within the reach of the majority of the people. The investment programme for the construction sector amounted to Z$1,040 m (US$634.4 m) or 15 per cent of total investment in fixed assets, the second largest item in the plan.

Through its Public Sector Investment Programme (PSIP), the government has allocated an estimated Z$812 m (US$495 m) for the housing programme for the 5 year period. The private sector is also helping finance the low cost housing programme through a stipulated proportion of building society funds tied by law to financing low-cost housing schemes.

171

On the supply side, the government's appropriate technology strategy includes:

○ Encouraging distributors of building materials to set up outlets in rural areas in order to facilitate availability of materials and reduce transportation costs;
○ Encouraging employers to provide decent accommodations for their workers;
○ Encouraging local authorities to commit a greater proportion of their revenues from income generating projects to housing;
○ Upgrading building brigades and establishing building co-operatives to facilitate speedier provision of housing.

The following macro-development objectives target the appropriateness of technology in production and utilization of energy supplies:

○ To achieve, as far as possible, self-sufficiency in energy supply thereby reducing the degree of dependence on imported fuels;
○ To increase the amount of energy produced from conventional sources such as coal and hydropower;
○ To increase the use of coal and electricity in rural areas, thus raising the quality of life of the rural population, and at the same time slowing environmental degradation caused by the destruction of forests; and
○ To develop the water supplies for rural and urban areas.

For the manufacturing sector, the government proposed a programme to convert industrial furnaces from diesel to gas and coal tar fuel (CTF) derived from coal. The author's research indicates that the conversion to CTF was already underway in 1983/84 for most of the large firms in the metal work industries. The sudden increase in electricity prices in 1982 caused the shift from electric heating to CTF for furnace heating.[5] Also during the plan period, Zimbabwe introduced two types of efficient waste-material burning stoves for rural and urban households. About 60 per cent of rural households are expected to have adopted this type of a fuel efficient wood stove by the end of the planning period in 1990. Also to be introduced are efficient coal-burning stoves in rural households and institutions such as schools and hospitals.

Twenty per cent of Zimbabwe's motor fuel is already blended with ethanol produced from sugar and there are plans underway to increase this to 25 per cent. However, to generate electricity, the government adopted an inappropriate technology with the construction of the Hwange Thermal Power Station Phases I and II. The project was inappropriate because the power station utilizes the more expensive thermal power to generate electricity in spite of the existing excess capacity for inexpensive hydro-power generation in both Zambia's Kafue dam and Mozambique's Cabora Bassa dam.

172

As shown in this section, the potential for the application of ATs in Zimbabwe's industrial sector is tremendous. The mining, manufacturing, construction and water and energy sectors have not yet been fully exploited in terms of growth and employment generation. For instance, because of the historical neglect by colonial regimes of both urban and rural infrastructure, low-cost housing is in great demand. The use of building brigades and building co-operatives offers opportunities for production by the masses as opposed to mass production by large-scale companies. Low capital investment per worker would create greater labour participation rates and encourage participation by the people and thus improve the quality of life at the local and community level. These appropriate technology activities would complement formal sector investments of medium- to large-scale firms.

## The ownership structure and characteristics of Zimbabwean enterprise

In 1985 the ownership structure of the manufacturing sector was divided into the following sub-categories: private companies, 85.5 per cent; parastatals, 10 per cent; government controlled companies (with more than 50 per cent shares held by government), 4 per cent; and local authorities, 0.5 per cent.[6] Central government and parastatals have an influence in three major subsectors of the manufacturing sector, that is, foodstuffs, where the Cold Storage Commission and the Dairy Marketing Board together contributed 25 per cent of total turnover; textiles, where the Cotton Marketing Board contributed 38 per cent of total turnover; and metals and metal products, where ZISCO Steel, Lancaster Steel and F Issels together contributed some 17 per cent to total output of the subsector.

The central government and local authorities have full control over electricity, water and sanitary services, through the Zimbabwe Electricity Supply Authority (ZESA) and local authorities. In the transport equipment sub-sector the government controlled 10 per cent of total output through Willovale Motor Industries, 100 per cent owned by the Industrial Development Corporation.

In all other sectors, private companies controlled over 90 per cent of total turnover. In the manufacturing sector, the only significant contribution by local authorities was in drink and tobacco through municipal beer production. UNIDO recently estimated that 48 per cent of the capital in manufacturing is foreign-owned and 52 per cent domestically-owned.[6] There is also a high degree of local ownership of the textile sub-sector and overall domestic control of foodstuffs, clothing and footwear, and transport equipment subsectors. On the other hand, four sub-sectors have a high degree of foreign ownership, namely drink and tobacco, paper, printing and publishing and chemical products.

173

As shown above, because of the statistical definition adopted by the Central Statistical Office, the only people or groups who are classified as manufacturers are registered companies, and to be accepted as a registered company requires an initial capital outlay of Z$30,000. This classification causes serious underestimations of the number of companies engaged in specific areas of manufacturing and is particularly inadequate when it comes to small-scale, informal and part-time manufacturing. A recent sample study of informal sector activities found 194 firms engaged in some 16 types of manufacturing activities in just four urban and three rural areas of the country. In comparison, official statistics recorded only 46 units with an annual turnover of less than Z$20,000 engaged in manufacturing in 1982. The official statistics explicitly exclude establishments with a gross output of under Z$2,000.[2] It is clear that policy recommendations for small-scale manufacturing cannot be based on the official statistics available.

The situation is more or less the same in the other areas of the industrial sector with the exception of mining and quarrying sector enterprises which must be registered by law. Small-scale and informal sector building firms are not included in the number of registered building and construction firms.

## Structural features of the macro-economic policy framework

The structural features of Zimbabwe's macroeconomic policy framework that influence the choice of technology are divided into two parts: general policies enunciated in national development plans and other policy documents which affect technology and market access more or less directly and institutionalized macroeconomic policies such as those which affect the supply of financial resources (ie, foreign exchange allocation, public expenditure levels and budget deficits). This section will discuss the empirical and analytical aspects of these two broad structural features of macroeconomic policy affecting choice of technology by micro-level units.

### Policies and objectives affecting appropriate technology as enunciated in national development plans

In the Transitional National Development Plan (TNDP) 1982/83–1984/85, Zimbabwe's first three-year proclaimed plan period, the government promised to undertake measures to increase the labour absorption capacity of industry and to rationalize and transform the industrial sector by reorienting it toward external markets. The objectives outlined by the government were the following:

○ To expand and restructure the sector to enable it to meet the growing and changing patterns of demand for industrial products;
○ To promote further linkages with other sectors such as agriculture, mining and the informal sector;

174

o To increase the export capacity and potential of the sector;
o To increase employment through the utilization (where appropriate) of labour-intensive techniques;
o To encourage further import substitution where economically justified (as in energy and fertilizer production);
o To encourage and promote the training, development and upgrading of the Zimbabwean labour force at all levels including managerial, technical and skilled;
o To encourage geographical decentralization of industries;
o To encourage more participation, ownership and control of industries by Zimbabweans or by the state; and
o To encourage and promote the establishment of small- and medium-scale agro-industrial enterprises in rural areas.[6]

To achieve these objectives, the government began to establish institutions that could facilitate local, private and state participation in the industrial sector. Promoting small-scale production and commercial units and decentralization were to be the goals of the Small Enterprise Development Corporation (SEDCO). The objectives of the latter were:

o To encourage and assist in the establishment of co-operatives and small commercial or industrial enterprises;
o To provide assistance to small- and medium-scale commercial and industrial enterprises;
o To promote local participation in the development of the following industries in rural areas and small towns: textiles, metal fabrication, furniture making, brick making, leather industry, tin and blacksmiths poultry dressing, broom and brush making; and
o To encourage labour-intensive technologies in the above industries.

The policy of assisting small- and medium-scale enterprises engaged in processing and manufacturing activities, especially outside of the major cities of Harare and Bulawayo, was to be implemented by SEDCO, the Industrial Development Corporation (IDC), Ministry of Industry and Technology, Ministry of Finance, Economic Planning and Development and ultimately the Cabinet. Implementation of the policy of decentralization are the goals of SEDCO and the IDC, but to date they have not been successful. SEDCO's programme is dominated by commercial rather than manufacturing and processing projects. Thus far, the IDC has not yet begun financing small-scale manufacturing and processing enterprises to be established by the so-called emerging businessmen, although such a programme has been articulated in policy statements. The Zimbabwe Development Bank (ZDB) also finances medium- to large-scale manufacturing projects. (The ZDB finances projects of about Z$100,000 (US$61,000). This minimum threshold was adopted on the understanding

175

that projects below this level were to be financed by SEDCO.) Besides giving financial assistance through SEDCO, the post-independence government has also encouraged some redirection of resources through the partial reorientation of the Agricultural Finance Corporation (AFC) which specifically funds agricultural enterprises.

The question of industrial location and decentralization is central to the appropriate technology discussion in view of the pattern of industrial concentration in Zimbabwe. In 1982, the capital city, Harare (including Chitungwiza), with only 11 per cent of the country's population, accounted for 51 per cent of manufacturing output and 46 per cent of manufacturing employment (Table 3). Bulawayo, the second largest city with 5 per cent of the total population, accounted for 23 per cent of manufacturing output and 28 per cent of manufacturing employment and the Kwekwe-Redcliff industrial complex (ZISCO Steel site) accounted for 7 per cent of manufacturing output and 5 per cent of total manufacturing employment. Together these three centres accounted for 82 per cent of total manufacturing output and 79 per cent of overall manufacturing employment.

Despite clearly articulated government objectives, at least in national development plans, geographic concentration of industries has not dropped; on the contrary it seems to have increased. In the 5-year period from 1977 to 1982 there has been a slight increase in industrial concentration in Harare, Bulawayo and Kwekwe-Redcliff, although the Kwekwe-Redcliff share fell. In the First Five-Year National Development Plan (1986–90), the government further promised to take measures to establish small-scale industries and industrial co-operatives capable of using locally available raw materials as well as indigenous technology or a combination of foreign and local technology.[4] The plan suggested that this policy would be implemented through the Industrial Development Corporation (IDC) SEDCO, and other local authorities. The rationale of this government policy was that co-operatives and small-scale industries would play an extensive role in industrialization, particularly as subcontractors to large companies and as producers of basic consumer goods. The other rationale was that promotion of small-scale industries together with public sector enterprises, especially agricultural parastatals would help encourage a decentralized pattern of ownership and location. By establishing industrial estates the government hoped to achieve the multipurpose objectives of decentralizing industry, to increase local participation and encourage development of entrepreneurial skills, and providing competition to existing monopolistic and other inefficient producers.[4]

According to the government, a certain degree of AT has already been adopted. 'There has been a definite transfer, adaptation, diffusion, and anchorage of technology through licensing agreements and the activities of subsidiaries and associates of foreign companies. However, most of this technology transfer has focused on the mechanisms of transfer cost as well

176

**Table 3 Geographical concentration of manufacturing industry, 1977 and 1982**

| | 1977 | | | | 1982 | | | | | |
| | Gross Output | | Employment | | Gross Output | | Employment | | Change in output % | Change in employment % |
| Location | Value[a] | Per cent | Numbers employed | Per cent | Value[a] | Per cent | Average number employed | Per cent | | |
|---|---|---|---|---|---|---|---|---|---|---|
| Harare | 655,228 | 47.8 | 63,920 | 45.3 | 1,667,983 | 51.6 | 80,849 | 45.9 | 155 | 26 |
| Bulawayo | 299,184 | 21.8 | 40,711 | 28.8 | 748,198 | 23.1 | 50,078 | 28.4 | 150 | 23 |
| Masvingo | 18,444 | 1.3 | 1,147 | 0.8 | 32,501 | 1.0 | 1,247 | 0.7 | 76 | 9 |
| Kadoma[b] | 45,789 | 3.3 | 3,735 | 2.6 | 71,268 | 2.2 | 4,355 | 2.5 | 56 | 17 |
| Gweru | 60,377 | 4.4 | 6,770 | 4.8 | 129,330 | 4.0 | 8,550 | 4.9 | 114 | 26 |
| Redcliff/Kwekwe | 129,169 | 9.4 | 8,320 | 5.9 | 229,447 | 7.1 | 8,844 | 5.0 | 78 | 6 |
| Mutare | 43,539 | 3.2 | 4,962 | 3.5 | 99,861 | 3.1 | 7,882 | 4.5 | 129 | 59 |
| Other | 117,817 | 8.6 | 11,668 | 8.3 | 256,456 | 7.9 | 14,399 | 8.2 | 118 | 28 |
| Total | 1,369,547 | 100.0 | 141,233 | 100.0 | 3,235,044 | 100.0 | 176,204 | 100.0 | 136.0 | 25 |

Source: Census of Industrial Production 1982/83, CSO, Table 10
[a] Figures in thousands of current dollars.
[b] Figures for Kadoma not strictly comparable because of change in geographical reporting by a major company

as appropriateness of the technology.'[4] During the current plan period, the government proposed the formation of a Council for Industrial Research which would assist in the co-ordination of all industrial R & D and in determining how best to develop an indigenous technology capacity to increase complementarities between local and foreign technologies. The Council for Industrial Research will also be involved in research aimed at meeting the changing pattern of demand for industrial products and guiding the technological advancement of the manufacturing industry.[4]

The government's assessment of its success with regard to appropriate technology is viewed in a narrow sense, that is, only with the formal sector in mind. This is so in spite of the explicit formulation of policies toward small-scale industries and industrial decentralization. Lack of action or inertia in grappling with appropriate technology issues might lie in the deep-seated structural features of the broader macroeconomic framework. The latter may often frustrate or hinder the government in achieving its stated and planned objectives.

## Institutionalized macroeconomic policy framework

Government policy can influence firms in a number of ways – directly through government directives to publicly owned enterprises and indirectly through policies enunciated through national development plans which influence deployment of resources and markets. In the Zimbabwean case, the government does have publicly-owned firms in which it makes particular decisions through the choice of management policies, as in the case of IDC, SEDCO, and many parastatal organizations operating in almost all the sectors of the national economy. (A few examples of parastatals operating in the economy are the Agricultural Marketing Authority, Grain and Marketing Board, Cotton Marketing Board, Agricultural Rural Development Authority, Cold Storage Commission and Dairy Marketing Board in the agricultural sector, Zimbabwe Electric Supply Authority, National Railways of Zimbabwe operating within the energy and transport sectors respectively.) These government organizations and parastatals directly and indirectly influence prices, markets, and material and human resource deployment in the economy.

However, the most important category of institutional macroeconomic policies influencing technology choice by Zimbabwean firms are the financial resource mobilization instruments and controls developed during the UDI (Unilateral Declaration of Independence) period. Foreign exchange allocation is probably the most important policy instrument influencing the long- and short-term decisions of enterprises both in the private and public sectors.

The Zimbabwean policy framework for resource allocation involves a high degree of indirect and direct controls over productive activities. Through the existing system of administrative allocation of foreign exchange, the government allocates all foreign exchange to firms for both working capital and investment purposes. The system is administered according to the assessed global foreign exchange available and the perceived priorities of the economy. Current allocations are based upon historical allocations to firms as well as specific assessments of the current needs of enterprises and organizations and foreign exchange shortages.

Investment allocations are screened by three committees: the Industrial Projects Committee (IPC), the External Loans Co-ordinating Committee (ELCC), and the Foreign Investment Committee (FIC). All new investments or expansions involving foreign exchange have to be submitted for approval by the IPC. Projects requiring more than the equivalent of Z\$2.5 m (\$US 1.6 m) in foreign loans require additional approval from the ELCC and projects with more than 15 per cent foreign ownership also require additional approval from the FIC.

In practice, the IPC approval is granted if the project replaces essential imports and/or produces exports and recoups the initial foreign exchange outlay within 12 months and continues saving foreign exchange throughout its lifetime. (There are other IPC criteria such as that the project should not produce goods already in local production unless it also produces for the export market; sell at competitive prices and satisfactory quality; and show firm export orders, preferably on a continuous basis.) In other words, the project should not be a net user of foreign exchange in any 12-month period during its projected lifetime and it should not compete with local production unless it also produces for export.

The criteria that a project be a net non-user of foreign exchange for it to be approved has impeded the establishment of firms that would exploit the domestic market exclusively without either increasing exports or substituting imports. This criteria has led to a high degree of product concentration over the last 20 years. Thus in 1982 half of the over 6,000 identifiable products produced in Zimbabwe were manufactured under monopoly conditions and an additional 30 per cent under oligopoly conditions. Over half of manufacturing output and employment was in the 11 per cent of firms with more than 500 workers. Established firms are not only enjoying protection from foreign competition, but also from actual and potential domestic competitors.

The rationing of foreign exchange through the IPC has also been responsible for the low level of investment, particularly since the mid-1970s. In the early years of the UDI when ample opportunities for import-substitution were still available the rationing of foreign exchange was not an impediment to investment. Investment in manufacturing from 1970 to 1974 grew at 23.6 per cent annually, but began to decline in the post-1975 period though there was a slight recovery in the mid-1970s. Virtually all investment projects require imported capital goods, and therefore, IPC approval. In 1984, the foreign exchange component of industrial projects submitted to IPC was some 70 per cent of total project value. For every

179

project approved, four were rejected. The high rejection rate was attributed largely, though not exclusively, to foreign exchange constraints.

Currently, foreign exchange is allocated on a firm-by-firm basis according to historical shares. Though in theory these shares are modified for new entrants and changes in the needs of existing firms, in practice the system provides absolute protection against established foreign or domestic competition, since no allocation is available to a new entrant if this would lead to competition with domestically produced products. For example, if one or more companies are already established and produce container glass, it is unlikely that a new entry would be allowed in this area of activity. The issues of the appropriateness of the technology in terms of local resource utilization, geographic location, and market acceptability to a low-income clientele may not be considered by the relevant committee or committees. Thus, there is a strong bias toward maintenance of the status quo; those enterprises already in the system are assured continuance of foreign exchange allocations.

While the system effectively protects firms from foreign competition, it has also led to a high degree of protection from potential domestic competitors. Although the government stated after independence that the IPC criteria would be modified to favour local investors and emerging entrepreneurs, this has not yet been the case. Very few emerging entrepreneurs have been allowed to establish themselves without satisfying the strict IPC criteria.

A macroeconomic concern addressed by Zimbabwe's financial resource mobilization policy and its impact on industry is that credit required for the industrial sector could be crowded out by public sector borrowing. The government budget primarily mobilizes its resources from institutional investors (insurance houses and pension funds) and the Post Office while the Agricultural Marketing Authority mobilizes resources mainly from commercial banks. In the past, however, crowding out has not occurred to any significant extent as evidenced by the low interest rates resulting from the lack of credit rationing. However, the primary reason for the coexistence of a large public sector borrowing requirement and the absence of crowding-out is the foreign exchange allocation system. Since over 70 per cent of the value of plant and equipment needs, for either replacement or new plants and machinery, consists of foreign exchange, shortages of the latter lead to less demand for credit by the firms.

Yet another area of concern is the historically conservative bias of financial institutions in their lending policies. Almost all private sector lending by financial institutions goes to well established firms. Zimbabwe's financial institutions generally make their lending decisions on the basis of prior earnings, credit history and the strength of the balance sheets of the borrowing firms. The banks, in particular, lend on a term basis for general expansion, or only to long-standing clients, or require guarantees by a reputable firm of good financial standing. There is very little project-oriented financing undertaken by private financial institutions and, as a result, there are no conditions for aggressive lending to new businesses. These lending policies and procedures tend to limit opportunities for new appropriate technologies as they work against emergent businesses that have little collateral and no connection with the financial community.

Commercial banks which provide short-term lending, primarily for working capital and agricultural finance, and merchant banks or finance company subsidiaries, which, in some instances, provide medium-term lending (three to seven years), generally have no time for small-scale businesses, either in industry or agriculture. The services of merchant banks (technically known as accepting houses), which are geared to corporate needs and large account holders, include financing of foreign trade through acceptance credits, processing commercial letters of credit and foreign bills of exchange, short- and medium-term financing, bridge financing, and foreign exchange transactions and dealings. Insurance companies and pension plans are engaged in long-term financing and usually in Central Government and parastatal securities.

The institutional macroeconomic policy framework in Zimbabwe does not facilitate appropriate technology choice. To encourage use of appropriate industrial technology decentralized small-scale industries need to be developed. This would lead to production of goods and services by the masses of the population with low capital investment per worker and participation by the people in improving the quality of life at the local and community level. The development of small-scale industries would necessitate the improvement of credit facilities, provision of training in technology know-how and establishment of marketing opportunities. In general, rural small-scale industries need to be promoted including the establishment of rural-based industrial estates and marketing opportunities.

Appropriate small-scale manufacturing technologies would complement the technologies developed in the formal large-scale industrial sector of the economy but, as shown in this section, the institutional policy framework under which financial resources for new and replacement investments are provided is still biased in favour of the large-scale sector, in spite of the official rhetoric and pronouncements in support of small-scale industries and decentralization.

## The latent potential for appropriate technology in the rural economic sector

As shown above, Zimbabwe's economic activity has, historically, been dominated by the formal sector and the bulk of economic services and policies have been oriented toward formal sector activities. The thrust of the government's technology policy toward the formal sector is, to a

181

certain degree, appropriate. This is due to the fact that the main characteristics of the economy include heavy reliance on export of raw materials and a high degree of dependence on the outside world for technology. Zimbabwe's technological dependence is illustrated by the fact that 84 per cent of its total imports consist of intermediate and capital goods, with the remaining 16 per cent consisting of consumer goods.[4] Accounting for over 30 per cent of the total imports are capital goods, which range from light- and heavy-duty machinery to precision instruments, while intermediate goods include, among others, simple instruments such as screws, bolts, plate glass and explosives. Production of some of these intermediate goods involves relatively simple processes, most of which are readily available in Zimbabwe. Indeed, some of these intermediate goods are now being produced in Zimbabwe.

In a recent field survey conducted by the author, in which a sample of 30 metalworking firms were interviewed, all the firms were found to have developed new products and made product modifications, particularly in the post-UDI period.[8] Products (mainly capital goods) manufactured by some of the larger firms are listed in Table 4. Agricultural machines and implements range from hoes and axes to tractor-drawn disc ploughs and crop sprayers. Mining machinery includes sinter plants, ball mills and electric travelling cranes. The survey sample included both large and small firms, ranging from multinational to family enterprises. Regardless of the size of the unit, decisions were made by individual units in the light of their own objectives and resources. These decisions are influenced by the external environment, particularly government macroeconomic policies. In this respect, the emphasis of macroeconomic policies on formal sector activities does influence the choice of ATs.

However, since 56 per cent of Zimbabwe's population consists of peasants who live in rural areas, while 23 per cent live in urban areas, the dissemination of appropriate technologies in the rural areas could provide an answer to many economic and social problems, especially the unemployment problem. Experience from elsewhere, particularly Asia, shows the potential for growth in rural output and employment to lie in the selection of appropriate technologies. This experience indicates that there are three factors necessary for successful growth:

○ Sustained growth in agricultural incomes;
○ Extension of economic services, especially transport services between rural and small towns; and
○ A supportive and relatively unregulated economic environment for small-scale entrepreneurs and self-employed urban dwellers.

In the case of Zimbabwe, the colonial government had alienated massive areas of land and developed machinery to provide systematic technical, financial, marketing and infrastructural support to the large-scale white

**Table 4 Zimbabwe's main machinery manufacturers**

| Company | Year of Establishment | Location | Main Products |
|---|---|---|---|
| *Agricultural Machinery/Implements* | | | |
| Zimplow | 1951 | Bulawayo | Ploughs, cultivators, hoes, harrows, ridgers. |
| Imco, Ltd | 1964 | Harare | Fertilizer spreaders, land mills, ploughs, planters, mowers, graders. |
| Bulawayo Steel Products | 1965 | Bulawayo | Ploughs, harrows, ridgers, planters, cultivators, axes, picks, mattocks. |
| Bain Manufacturers | 1968 | Harare | Disc ploughs, disk and spike harrows, tine and spike cultivators, potholders, rollers, rippers, tippers. |
| Tinto Industries | 1968 | Harare | Disc and tine chisel ploughs, mounted offset disc harrows, disc ridgers, tillers, rollers, tine cultivators and graders. |
| Farmquip | 1972 | Harare | Crop sprayers, humidifiers, tobacco curing equipment, grain handling equipment. |
| *Mining and General Machines* | | | |
| WS Craster | 1936 | Harare | Mechanite castings, mining equipment, agricultural equipment, non-ferrous castings. |
| Clarson & Co | 1918 | Harare | Iron and non-iron castings, hammermills (for food, mining and general industries), sinter plants, mine pulverizers, mine filter presses, water cooling towers, effluent and sewage plants, turbines, heat exchangers. |
| Conolly & Co | 1929 | Bulawayo | Castings, ball mills, hammermills, coal pulverizing plant, iron pipes, electric travelling cranes, sugar mills. |
| Hogarths | 1926 | Harare | Mine headgear, steel structures, boiler support structures, water circulation ducts. |

Source: Ndlela, Daniel B 'Technology Imports and Indigenous Technological Capacity Building: The Zimbabwean Case' WEP – Working papers 173, ILO, Geneva, March, 1987.

farmers, who over the decades achieved advanced levels of productivity and made major contributions to the GDP and export earnings. These high levels of productivity contrasted with declining growth in the African 'communal' areas due to soil degradation of marginal lands. This formed the basis for the dualistic production system which was inherited at Zimbabwe's independence in 1980.[9] In the post-independence period (after 1980), the government undertook measures to reverse the dualistic structure of the economy inherited at independence. Resettlement of landless peasants was identified as a major rural development objective. Back-up services, such as extension and credit were provided to ensure that agricultural production improved. The agricultural extension services are primarily oriented toward small-scale farmers by Agritex, a national institution under the Ministry of Agriculture. The Agricultural Finance Corporation (AFC), also under the Ministry of Agriculture, provided loans to small-scale farmers. In 1984 alone, the AFC provided 19,900 loans worth Z$10.2 m ($US6.2 m) to small-scale farmers.

Manpower training for the agricultural sector is the responsibility of the government. In addition to university agricultural training, Zimbabwe has four agricultural training institutes including two colleges producing 300 graduates per year. There are also 375 rural training centres. In further attempts to strengthen the rural infrastructure, at independence the state-controlled estates organization, the Agriculture and Rural Development Authority (ARDA), was given a generalized mandate to develop rural area activities beneficial to the inhabitants of the respective areas including any mining, industrial, commercial, agricultural or forestry undertakings. ARDA's programmes are meant to develop the following types of organizations:

○ State farms, which engage in the production of strategic commodities such as breeding stock, seed and selected food crops;
○ Nucleus estates, which primarily encourage individual tenant farmers to engage in technically sound production;
○ Agro-industrial estates, which integrate commodity production with processing.[10]

In spite of these apparent measures to promote appropriate technologies in the rural industrial sector in Zimbabwe, rural small-scale industries have not been established to a great extent. First, Zimbabwe still lacks an effective 'problem-oriented' approach to rural small-scale industries designed to ease specific bottlenecks and constraints at the enterprise level. As shown above, SEDCO and IDC have not been effective as the official instruments for improving credit facilities, providing training in technology know-how and establishing marketing opportunities. Up to 90 per cent of SEDCO-supported enterprises are still in the commercial sector and as such do not promote small-scale manufacturing or processing enterprises. The directive for the IDC to promote small-scale industries has not yet been implemented. IDC continues to promote medium- to large-scale formal sector enterprises.

The more direct approach to the promotion of small-scale industries at the sector level through assistance to small-scale enterprises, provision of a package of inputs and services, establishment of rural-based industrial estates and marketing co-operatives has had limited success. The resettlement of landless peasants and establishment of agricultural co-operatives have not been accompanied by establishment of small-scale industries.

## Conclusions

The macroeconomic policies that influence choice of technology by enterprises in Zimbabwe are mainly geared toward formal sector units. This has developed historically as a result of the close co-operation between the government and the private sector, especially during the UDI when colonial Zimbabwe faced economic sanctions that were imposed by the international community.

While appropriate technology decisions have been made with regard to firms in the formal industrial sectors, these have not been complemented by similar decisions in the small-scale urban and rural sector industries. Well-articulated government policies designed to influence the environment in which microeconomic units make decisions have not been implemented. There seems to be a contradiction between planned goals and policies and the macroeconomic policies which are institutionalized in the economic system. Thus, while national development plans have elaborated objectives such as promotion of labour-intensive technologies, geographic decentralization of industry and development of small-scale industries, the macroeconomic policies in place strongly militate against these goals.

Well-established industrial enterprises are also well protected by the policy instruments of the foreign exchange allocation system. Firms are given foreign exchange on the basis of historical quotas, which naturally favour the larger and well-established enterprises. Second, no new firm is given foreign exchange to establish itself in an area where older firms are already manufacturing similar products unless the new firm demonstrates its ability and commitment to export its products.

The current macro-policies described in the text have, to a certain degree, contributed to choice of appropriate technologies in the industrial sector, as evidenced by Zimbabwe's development of the capital goods and intermediate goods subsectors, which are vital for the national economy, especially for the agricultural and mining sectors. However, since a large majority of the population consists of peasants who live in rural areas, the use of AT in the rural areas would help alleviate many economic and social problems, especially the unemployment problem. It is, therefore, argued that macro-policies that have an impact on industrial growth in the rural areas and informal sectors have the latent potential to promote AT in Zimbabwe.

185

# Impact of Economic Policies on Technological Choice and Development in Tanzanian Industry

## S M WANGWE and M S D BAGACHWA

## Introduction

This paper examines the role of macro-policies on technology choice and development. According to Stewart, macro-policies influence micro-level decisions of firms by affecting firm objectives, availability and cost of resources, scale and type of markets, and technology.[1] Alternatively, macro-policies may affect the balance of choice in the economy as a whole by altering the composition of units in the economy. The paper briefly reviews developments in the level and structure of industry in Tanzania in the last three decades, presents the evolution of national policy objectives in general and in industry in particular and examines the factors which have influenced the choice of technology with a view to linking them to macro-policies.

## Development in the level and structure of industry

### Level of industrial development 1961–1986
At independence (1961) the level of industrial development was very low. There were only 220 establishments employing 10 persons or more and owning fixed assets worth TzShs 20,000 or more. These manufacturing sector establishments employed a total of 20,000 persons, providing the livelihood for about 1 per cent of the families out of a population of about 9m. In terms of output the manufacturing sector contributed about 4 per cent to the Gross Domestic Product (GDP). The rate of industrial growth has been more rapid than the rate of growth of the whole economy in the 1960s and early 1970s up to 1972. Between 1964 and 1972 manufacturing value added more than doubled with an average annual rate of growth of more than 10 per cent. Even though during this period the actual growth rate fell below the planned growth rate of 13 per cent, by any standards the performance was impressive.

S.M. WANGWE is Professor of Economics at the University of Dar Es Salaam, Tanzania. M.S.D. Bagachwa is with the Economic Research Bureau at the University of Dar Es Salaam.

After 1973 (except in 1976 and 1978) industrial growth was generally lower than overall economic growth. The year 1973 marks the beginning of the oil crisis which caused a shortage of foreign exchange for importing capital goods and intermediate inputs for industry. The coffee boom of 1977 facilitated a relatively adequate allocation of foreign exchange to industries following the improvement in the balance of payments position. The coffee boom is reflected as a boom in industrial production whereby manufacturing value added increased by 24 per cent between 1977 and 1978. In 1978 the balance of payments deteriorated (and through 1988 it has not improved) as evidenced by negative industrial growth since 1979.[2]

The manufacturing sector improved its share of value added from a low of 4 per cent in 1961 to a high of 12.3 per cent in 1978. Following the deterioration of the balance of payments and consequent decline in foreign exchange allocation to purchase imported intermediate inputs, capacity utilization declined. This situation was worsened by the allocation of foreign exchange and foreign finance in favour of new projects rather than utilization of existing projects. Causes of capacity underutilization in the manufacturing sector have been examined in greater detail by Wangwe[3,4] and Ndulu.[5] This situation resulted in a declining share of manufacturing value added from 12.3 per cent in 1978 to 9 per cent in 1984 and 7.6 per cent in 1986 at 1976 prices (Economic Survey 1986). The share of manufacturing value added in 1986 had fallen below the 1964 share of 8.25 per cent (Statistical Series 1951–85). Although new capacities continued to be created in industry in the 1970s and 1980s such investments did not result in additional outputs of industrial goods in the 1980s.[4,5] However, to the extent that new investment was taking place, choice of technology continued to be exercised.

### Structure of industry 1961–87

The structure of industry evolved along two main fronts. First, it was necessary to process primary products for export either to increase the value added or reduce their weight. Second, import-substitution was pursued in response to the growth and pattern of distribution of the domestic market. This led to the predominance of simple consumer goods mainly for the small urban population.

Figures for industrial distribution indicate that in 1961, 25 per cent of all industrial establishments were manufacturing food products, beverages and tobacco and about 30 per cent were in sisal decorticating and cotton ginning.[6] The rest were mainly engaged in wood and furniture (15 per cent) and in repair of machinery and transport equipment (16 per cent). In the processing industries group the main activities were ginning, sisal decorticating, saw milling, vegetable oil extraction, tobacco curing, coffee curing and wattle extract. In consumer goods manufacturing, the most important activities were canned beef, textiles and clothing, footwear, beer, sugar, soft drinks and soap manufacturing.

## Sectoral composition of output

The history of industrialization has shown that as an economy develops the capital and intermediate goods sectors normally increase their contributions to industrial output. Because of the dynamism inherent in the capital goods sector, it has become common to expect the externalities of technical advance to become more important as this sector grows. These externalities may include further breakthroughs in the technology or related technologies or in human resource development more broadly associated with use of the orginal technology. Thus if technology choice is to incorporate effects of technology development one would expect a substantial increase in the share of the capital goods sector in total industrial output. In other words, the correct identification of the appropriate composition of output is a prerequisite toward the choice of appropriate techniques.

In the case of Tanzania, as shown in Table 1, the composition of manufacturing output has changed to some extent during the past two decades. The consumer goods sector still predominates in production while the capital goods sector accounts for less than 10 per cent of the total industrial output measured in domestic prices. In fact, according to World Bank estimates, the share of consumer goods industries for 1984 is even higher when measured in world prices, as it exceeds that of 1965 by about 29 per cent.[7]

**Table 1 Structural change in manufacturing (%)**

|                   | 1961 | 1965 | 1969 | 1974 | 1977 | 1984 |
|-------------------|------|------|------|------|------|------|
| Consumer Goods    | 74   | 59   | 60   | 56   | 56   | 48   |
| Intermediate Goods| 23   | 37   | 34   | 35   | 37   | 43   |
| Capital Goods     | 3    | 4    | 6    | 9    | 7    | 9    |
| Total             | 100  | 100  | 100  | 100  | 100  | 100  |

Source: Economic Surveys (various), Survey of Industrial Production; the 1961 figures have been taken from UNIDO, *The Potential for Resources Based On Industrial Development in the Least Developed Countries, No. 3*, The United Republic of Tanzania, Feb. 1982.

However, the relatively low shares of value added for the capital and intermediate goods sectors do not imply the absence of significant investments in the two sectors. Rather, these shares highlight the gross inefficiency in the use of inputs by the two sectors (eg, capacity under-utilization as indicated in the previous section). In fact, as the World Bank study reveals, the share in total gross output of the two sectors was 60 per cent in 1984, and the two sectors also accounted for two-thirds of the total installed capacity in industry. Within the specific sectors new industrial activities were introduced which may not be reflected in changes in sectoral shares.

The food, beverage and tobacco sector has not changed to any significant level structurally, although in scale the activities have increased. The textile and leather sector has grown, with textile mills, tanneries, a canvas mill, and a number of sisal-based products being introduced in the post-independence period. In the chemical sector major activities were introduced during the 1960s and 1970s. An oil refinery, tyres and tubes, fertilizer, pharmaceuticals, polysacks and cassava starch were introduced during this period. The last three were introduced in the post-1978 period. Notable structural changes have also taken place in the basic metals sector where a steel rolling mill, steel casting (from scrap metal), foundries, farm implements, radio assembly, farm implements, transformers and switch gears, batteries (cells and for motor vehicles), bicycles and machine tools were established after the late sixties.

The industrial structure has, therefore, changed in favour of intermediate and capital goods. In the nine industrial groups, some structural change has occurred, but the changes have not been very conspicuous, with the exception of metals and chemicals which have clearly increased their share, and wood products whose share has declined. Within these groups, however, many new activities have been introduced into the economy. Although the effects of these structural changes, and new activities in particular, may have been mitigated somewhat by the increase in capacity underutilization after the mid-1970s, they are still quite substantial.[2]

**Market orientation of output**
Tanzania has relied on domestic demand growth and import-substitution as the basis for industrial development. As Table 2 shows, an estimated 60 per cent of Tanzania's domestic manufactured products in 1987 were produced locally, 35 per cent were imported while 5 per cent were exported. The corresponding figures in 1961 were approximately 30 per cent (domestic production) 62 per cent (imports) and 8 per cent (exports). As might be expected, import-substitution industrialization has encouraged the use of capital-intensive and import-intensive production technologies.

**Pattern of resource use**
From the resource input side, the structure of industrial production in Tanzania has been characterized by an increase in large-scale production,

**Table 2 Market shares for manufactured products (%)**

| Source of Manufacturing Supply | 1961 | 1965 | 1971 | 1978 | 1984 | 1987 |
|---|---|---|---|---|---|---|
| Production for Domestic Market | 29.6 | 36.0 | 35.4 | 46.7 | 53.9 | 60.0 |
| Production for Exports | 8.2 | 7.8 | 10.5 | 3.7 | 5.0 | 3.0 |
| Manufactured Imports | 62.2 | 56.2 | 54.1 | 49.6 | 41.1 | 35.0 |
| Total | 100 | 100 | 100 | 100 | 100 | 100 |

Source: World Bank (1986), Table 1.6, p. 9 for figures up to 1984, and SADCC estimates for 1987.

deepening capital intensity and intensification of import dependence. Increasingly centralized production has not only occurred in higher technology industries, which might have been more susceptible to scale economies (as is the case with Mufindi Southern Paper Mill), but also in leather processing, sugar processing,[8] shoes, grain-milling[9] and even in bread baking.[10] At the sectoral level increasing capital intensity in industry has been revealed by the consistent rise in the incremental capital–output ratio which more than doubled between 1968 and 1979 and became negative thereafter.[2,7] Resource usage has also tended to be import-oriented. Import dependency, as measured by the ratio of imported input costs to total input costs, rose from 15.1 in 1961 to 52 per cent in 1984 and to 70 per cent in 1987, when evaluated at domestic prices. When provision is made for the overvaluation of the local currency, the import dependency ratio for 1984 rises to 70 per cent. The implied total direct foreign exchange consumption of the manufacturing sector in 1984 has been estimated to be US$365m, which is about six times the value of the sector's export earnings of about US$65m.[7]

### Enterprise organization

In response to the principles outlined in the Arusha Declaration, the government became involved in public sector industrial development by nationalizing the major industrial enterprises existing at that time and by establishing new industrial enterprises with full or majority ownership by the state. In Tanzania these public sector industrial enterprises are more commonly referred to as parastatal enterprises or simply parastatals. Development of the industrial parastatal sector started off under one major parastatal holding, the National Development Corporation (NDC). The NDC was established in 1965 but had to expand very fast in 1967–68 to cope with pace of nationalization.

In view of the growing size and complexity of industrial activities in the public sector it became necessary to rationalize the institutional organization of these activities along sectoral lines. The share of the public sector manufacturing value added (MVA) and employment has increased considerably since 1966. The sharp growth of the public sector in the late 1960s seems to have started to level off in 1975–77 (about 40 per cent of MVA and 48 per cent of employment). After 1979 the share of parastatal sector increased to about 50–56 per cent of MVA and employment in the 1980s.

The extent of public ownership of industry and the consequent role of the public sector in industrial development varies from one industrial activity to another. Within the metal-based industries the public sector is dominant in basic metals, metal construction materials (except nails), metal containers, farm implements and spares and components. Manufacturing of household metal products and nails, and assembly of transport and electrical equipment are predominantly private sector activities. In the chemical-based industries the public sector is dominant in the manufacture of tyres, fertilizers, starch and pharmaceuticals, while the private sector dominates in the manufacture of soap, cosmetics, paints, plastics, mosquito coils and pesticides. The textile, leather, cement and paper industries are mainly public sector owned. In the textile sector, the public sector accounts for 83 per cent of all output. The public sector has a monopoly in the tanning of leather and also manufactures 60 per cent of the total output of shoes. Cement production is wholly within the public sector and it accounts for 74 per cent of total output of paper products.

While the overall share of the public sector in manufacturing shows a rising trend, the dominance of the public sector has been most pronounced in certain industrial activities that are key in effecting structural change. For instance, chemicals, basic metals, cement, paper, textiles, leather and publishing and printing are basic industries that could be stimulated to bring about a qualitative change in the structure of industry. The public sector may have a role in promoting these basic industries either through public industrial enterprises or the private sector. The major expansions are notable in steel rolling, transport equipment, glass and ceramics, farm implements, textiles and chemicals which are all central (at least potentially) in effecting structural change in the industrial sector.[3]

The proliferation of public sector enterprises in almost every sector of the economy has been accompanied by a variety of economic regulatory measures including centralized control of investment, administrative allocation of foreign exchange and price and wage controls. Undoubtedly these must have affected technology choice at both macro- and micro-levels, although since 1984 many of these regulations have been relaxed somewhat.

191

## National objectives and policies

### Goals, objectives and strategies 1961–67

At independence a three-year plan (1961–64) was enacted. The main emphasis of the plan was economic growth. It began to lay the foundations for more rapid growth of the economy. The growth objective for industrial development implied that investments would be made in projects which were capable of yielding quick and high returns in the near future (TYP 1961–64). The implied industrial strategy based on reports by Arthur D Little and World Bank entailed import-substitution mainly in simple consumer goods. Although the government gave some financial assistance to industry through the Tanganyika Development Corporation it was generally taken for granted that foreign private capital would flow into the country if favourable conditions were created. The government made attempts to create these conditions by offering tariff protection, guaranteeing foreign investors against nationalization, publishing existing investment opportunities and by designing a tax incentive structure.[6]

The First Five-Year Plan (FFYP 1964–69) proposed a more ambitious programme of industrial development without essentially changing the inherited strategy. The plan identified the main constraints to industrial development as the size of the market and the availability of capital. The market constraint was to be tackled by changing the rules of the East African Common Market to allow a transfer tax system to provide some protection to the industries of the less developed partners. Another solution would be to set up an industrial licensing procedure that protects key industries in the entire regional market. The capital constraint was to be tackled through encouragement of private investment (local and foreign). In fact about 75 per cent of total industrial investment was expected to come from the private sector over the plan period FFYP (1964–69).

Although the FFYP (1964–69) proposed a wider range of industrial investments along with the policy of import-substitution, it remained silent on the significance of the product-mix, specific ownership patterns, choice of technology, linkage effects, external economies and structural trans-formation.[2] The specific policy instruments which were designed to achieve desired investment targets included accelerated depreciation allowances, tariff protection and guarantees for the repatriation of capital. But as Rweyemamu argues, protection tariffs were not set by the government on its own initiative but by a negotiation process which guaranteed sufficient protection to the (foreign) investor.[6] Normal tariff rates varied among industries but usually ranged between 20 and 50 per cent. Generally, however, tariffs were low for capital and intermediate goods imports and higher for final consumer goods products, resulting in effective rates of protection ranging from negative to well over 500 per cent.

192

The impact of the broad development policies and specific economic policies on the choice of technique and technology development during these early years of independence have been empirically analysed by Rweyemamu.[6] At the sectoral level, the strategy inhibited the development of the capital goods sector, and, as a result, intersectoral linkages were found to be weak. Furthermore, the alleged benefits of foreign investment (ie, automatic transfer of capital, management and technical know-how) were minimal and in fact negative in the long run. As Rweyemamu has documented, between 1961 and 1968, capital outflow exceeded capital inflow by TzShs 3,732 m. At the enterprise level many foreign-owned firms were found to be relatively more capital intensive than locally owned firms. Moreover, because the bulk of the industrial firms were foreign-owned and protected, the development of an indigenous entrepreneurial class was stifled. At the same time the relatively cheap goods produced by the foreign sector further reduced the markets for the local firms and hence, their capacity for self-sustained growth.

## The Arusha Declaration (1967) and the Second Five-Year Plan

The Arusha Declaration of 1967 outlined a new course for development. It contained two main principles – socialism and self-reliance. The policy of socialism implied the eradication of exploitation of man by man, the consolidation of democracy and the ownership of the major means of production and exchange by peasants and workers. These major means of production and exchange were identified as land, forests, minerals, water, oil and electricity, news media, communications, banking and insurance, export–import trade, wholesale trade and major industries.

While the Arusha Declaration was specific on the issue of ownership, it was not specific on the issue of priority industrial activities. In light of the Arusha Declaration major industries were taken over by the public sector and subsequent new investments largely occurred in the public sector. It was realized that foreign investment could not act as the principal agent of industrial investment, not only because of the unreliability of foreign capital inflows but also more importantly on the grounds that it was inconsistent with the principles of socialism and self-reliance. Furthermore, the Arusha Declaration brought to the fore the objectives of employment creation and equity (inter-personal and inter-regional).

The Second Five-Year Plan (1969–74) reflects the impact of the principles of the Arusha Declaration. Regarding the ownership of industry the SFYP (1969–74) came out with arguments explicitly in favour of expansion of the public sector and elaborated on the need to consolidate the institutional foundations for socialistic development. For income distribution objectives the SFYP placed special emphasis on the development of small-scale industries in rural areas.

The establishment of the parastatal known as SIDO (the Small Industries Development Organization) in 1973 reflected the thrust to assist and promote small-scale industries. A statement by the ruling political party emphasized that SIDO should assist and promote the establishment of productive units which employ simple, labour-intensive technologies which utilize locally available human and material resources. The Second Five-Year Plan also provided for the decentralization of industry through the identification of nine growth towns (Dar es Salaam was not one of them). The explicit encouragement of the use of labour-intensive techniques is a reflection of the pursuit of equity and the employment objective.

For the first time the need to effect structural change for sustained growth was mentioned. In terms of the product mix it was proposed that manufacture of export products be increased and that the range of manufactured products be expanded to include not only consumer goods but also intermediate and capital goods. Despite concerns about the product mix, the task of defining a long-term industrial strategy was to provide a framework for the Third Five-Year Plan (TFYP 1976–81).[2]

### The long-term industrial strategy (1975–95)

In the long-term industrial strategy seven national goals were identified. These were industrial growth, structural changes, employment generation, increased equality of income distribution, increased equality of regional development, worker participation in industry and increased self-reliance. The goals were used as a guide to formulate the long-term industrial strategy.

In the process of formulating the long-term industrial strategy at least five alternative strategies were considered. These were the maximum growth strategy, basic industry strategy, small-scale rural strategy, East African strategy and the mixed strategy. In terms of structural change and self-reliance the basic industry strategy appeared superior to the other strategies. It was therefore recommended and adopted.

Under the basic industry strategy resources would be channelled into the manufacture of a broad range of consumer, intermediate and capital goods essentially for the domestic market. Exports of manufactured goods would be seen as an extension of the home market. This meant that the export market would develop after the home market had been fully developed and provided for. The basic industry strategy represented a significant shift toward the development of domestic resources to meet domestic needs whereby most of the material required for industrial development would be produced in the country. The proposed strategy differed from the previous pattern in which local resources were largely allocated to the production of exports and simple consumer goods, while intermediate inputs and capital goods were largely imported.

The basic industry strategy therefore emphasizes two sets of industrial activities. The first set consists of industries which meet the basic needs of the people. Important industrial activities included in this set are food processing, textiles, clothing, footwear, building materials, and materials and facilities required for education, health services, transportation and water supply. The second set of industries consists of activities which can use domestic resources to produce and supply intermediate inputs and capital goods to industries in the first set. There is a core group of industries whose products are used by most other industries.[11] This core group which forms the base of industrial production consists of industries like iron and steel, metal-working and engineering, industrial chemicals, paper, textiles, leather, construction materials and electricity. In the Tanzanian context, for instance, the metalworking and engineering industry is considered important because of its capacity to supply machinery and equipment, while iron and steel is a priority industry because of its capacity to supply inputs to metalworking and engineering industries. For further details on the formulation and implementation of the basic industry strategy see Skarstein and Wangwe.[2]

### The basic industry strategy and technology policy

The basic industry strategy proposed development of the local capital goods sector. It was argued that the local capital goods sector would contribute to greater self-reliance and desired structural change in the economy. It was suggested that in order to reduce dependence on foreign technology it would be necessary to put the bulk of manufacturing investment into industries using simple technologies which could be produced by capital goods industries in developing countries. It was also argued that attempts to produce capital goods locally would require the development of the metal engineering industry to reduce dependence on foreign technology.

Concerning technomanagerial skills training, it was pointed out that in the early stages of industrial development there would be a marked increase in the need for foreign technical assistance and a corresponding delay in control by Tanzanian managers and technicians. To overcome this disadvantage, it was argued, it would be necessary to establish powerful and effective planning institutions which could ensure the fulfilment of the necessarily heavy commitment to training. However, there is no evidence that the proposed stringent control has actually been effected.[2]

While it was accepted that both large and small industries should have a role in the process of industrialization, the precise role of each and the links between them were not clarified. The proposal that small industries be established in activities where they compete reasonably well in price and quality with large-scale industries carries more of a competitive than a complementary tone. It was further proposed that when information on comparative costs and product quality is available, SIDO should work together with relevant parastatals and ministries to outline a plan to develop small-scale production in designated industries.

Choice of technology was not taken up as an explicit policy issue in discussions of the basic industry strategy (BIS). The emphasis of the BIS was on selection of industrial activities primarily to achieve structural change and self-reliance objectives. Therefore the role of choice of technology was to ensure that within the framework of the selected industrial activities the objectives of growth, employment and regional equality would be achieved as much as possible. While the choice between capital-intensive and labour-intensive technologies mainly influences employment generation, choosing between large- and small-scale industries influences employment and regional dispersion of industries (especially the industries that can easily change location). The choice of technology was basically viewed in the context of factor intensity and scale of operation. Although further questions were posed (eg, sacrifices in terms of cost and quality, consumer choice, speed or implementation, organizational demands and information about production techniques), it seems that answers to these questions were unambiguous.

## Factors influencing choice of technology in industry

### Source of foreign finance

Foreign investment during the 1961–66 period was encouraged through a system of tariff protection, tax incentives (such as accelerated depreciation and tax holidays) and the offering of guarantees to prevent the repatriation of capital. This resulted in increased capital and import intensities in industry and favoured the production of consumer goods. After the Arusha Declaration foreign private investment was discouraged and the policy regime increasingly relied on central planning and administrative controls in the regulation of the economy. Over time, however, Tanzania has become more dependent on foreign finance, in particular from aid donors. More importantly, however, throughout the 1970s external aid has increasingly become tied to specific donor-supported projects.

Foreign assistance has encouraged the parastatal sector to continue to invest in new large-scale, capital and import-intensive plants and machinery, despite excess capacity in existing plants. This has happened partly because donors prefer to finance new projects rather than fund plant rehabilitation and recurrent costs in existing projects, but also partly because such capital-intensive projects guarantee the importation of technology from the donor country. This tendency is exacerbated by a number of domestic institutional weaknesses at the planning and project implementation stages. One such weakness is the lack of seriousness in aid co-ordination and scrutiny on the part of the government which tends to approve any public project which has been assured of foreign financial support regardless of whether or not it falls within the nation's priority category. The source of financing has tended to restrict the sourcing of technology to that of a specific country (or countries) or a specific technology supplier. The first type of restriction (by country), allowing choice among alternative technologies in the financing country, has often occurred when funding comes from foreign governments. For example, James' reference to sugar projects (Kagera and Kilimbero) indicates that in the case of the Kagera sugar project, tenders for technology supplies were floated only in India because it was known that financing was available from the government of India, while in the case of the Kilimbero project turnkey tenders were floated in Denmark and Holland, countries which were providing external finance (75 per cent tied to procurement in these two countries).[8] A similar tendency was noted in the case of an automatic bakery[10] and several projects under the Capital Development Authority. The second type of tying often occurs when sources of finance are closely linked with contractors and/or technology suppliers, and leaves no room for the choice of technology. For instance, James has indicated that in the case of the Musoma Textile Mill, the feasibility study was done by the same French contracting company which identified a consortium of financiers and machinery suppliers. This resulted in inflation of the cost of the project about $2\frac{1}{2}$ times that of a similar (size and timing) textile project (expansion of Mwanza textiles).[8] Further evidence of this phenomenon is indicated by Coulson[10], Mihyo[12], Dolman et al[13], UNCTAD[14], Perkins[15], Williams[16, 17] and James.[8] Bagachwa[9] demonstrated a close connection between the source of foreign finance and choice of technology for merchant milling in a case in Tanzania where three British manufactured rollers were financed by suppliers' credit from Britain and three German made rollers were financed by suppliers' credit from West Germany.

Most of the studies on the influence of foreign financing on choice of technology refer to public sector industrial enterprises. The little evidence which is available on the private sector choice of technology indicates that, although private enterprises had some technology preferences based on the profitability criterion, the degree of freedom in the actual selection of technology was limited by the availability of foreign financing.[8] The nature of this limitation, as indicated by James, is that these enterprises are forced to move down their technology preference list according to the availability of foreign financing.

The influence of foreign finance on choice of technology has been explained by Williams[17] on the basis of his 'bureaucratic-man hypothesis'. According to this hypothesis the environment in the parastatal system in Tanzania (cost-plus pricing, replacement of market forces by government controls and weak incentives to management) deprives the managers of any incentive to minimize costs. This induces managers to turn to other goals that appear to offer greater scope for advancement in the eyes of

197

their superiors in the planning hierarchy. In particular the manager tries to initiate as many projects as possible. Because projects with foreign finance are likely to be approved more easily by the planning system and therefore move faster, the manager's attention is drawn toward foreign finance mobilization for projects. For this reason, Williams argues, choice of technology is effectively eliminated from parastatal investment decision making.

The influence of foreign finance on the choice of technology is the result of two forces. First, foreign financiers prefer projects rather than pro-grammes or support for intermediate inputs.[4] This preference is often reflected in the relative emphasis on the provision of initial investment resources without regard for economic and technological implications at the operations stage of the project. However, it is the latter which are important in technology transfer and development issues. Second, the planning system itself leaves much to be desired. For example, if invest-ment financing, especially in foreign exchange, is such a critical constraint why is limiting the foreign exchange costs of initial investment and of the technologies not made an explicit criterion of project planning? This problem has been explained in terms of the weak link between macro-level and micro-level planning.[4] The same resource (foreign exchange) leads to the search for foreign finance with its influence on choice of technology; then foreign finance is often leaked away through technology contracts, overpriced projects and transfer pricing.

A recent change in government policy which may influence the role of foreign finance is the deliberate effort to shift foreign finance from project aid to programme aid. This policy is very recent, thus a conclusive evaluation of it cannot be made at this stage.

### The managerial and technical skills constraint

The shortage of managerial and technical manpower has influenced the choice of technology in at least three ways:

○ The managerial and technical manpower constraint has led to the option of joint ventures in investment which require new and/or relatively complex technology. Joint ventures are often between parastatals and foreign partners. The latter are expected to provide the technical and managerial component to the project in addition to holding the minority equity shares. The main reason for the joint ventures has primarily been technological rather than equity sharing which explains why joint ventures with local capitalists have not taken place. In joint ventures the foreign partners have provided the technical management skills (eg, the Fertilizer Company, Metal Box Ltd., General Tyre Co, Mwanza Textiles);
○ Second, this skills constraint has tended to encourage packaged turnkey projects. The argument in this case has been that it is preferable to opt

for a fully packaged turnkey project in order to minimize the local technical and managerial manpower required to supervise and manage the design, planning, execution, implementation and, to some extent, the actual management of the project. James has indicated that these arguments have been used to rationalize the choice of large-scale projects to avoid managerial and supervisory problems associated with too many plants.[8] This occurred in the case of the Morogoro oil processing project when the project tender specified that tenders must be responsible for the whole package (design, installation and commissioning) and in the case of Morogoro Shoe. On this point Perkins has added that the management of parastatal holding companies usually prefers projects with economies of scale.[15] Often these are the fully packaged turnkey projects;

o  Attempts to fill the managerial and technical skills gap have often resulted in the engagement of foreign technical and management teams through agreements or contracts. It has ordinarily been hoped that after the expiration of such contracts (usually lasting 5–10 years), local technical and managerial skills would be sufficiently developed and the foreign technical and managerial personnel would be phased out accordingly. The engagement of foreign technical and management teams has tended to 'free' local manpower from taking part in making decisions on technology. These decisions have essentially been vested in the technical management teams or foreign consultants. This has meant that the consultants and the technical management teams would recommend the technologies they themselves have experience with. In cases where the technical management teams are also technology suppliers, or linked to technology suppliers in some way, they have preferred to recommend those technology suppliers. The overwhelming influence of these teams/consultants on the choice of technology has been documented for instance by Mihyo in the case of the silos[12] and the fertilizer factory and by James in the case of the printing ink factory.[8]

In the three examples above, in which the technical/managerial manpower constraint influenced the choice of technology, the available evidence suggests that, while local technical/managerial manpower requirements may have been minimized at the time the technology choices were made, the technologies chosen have subsequently hindered the process of alleviating the skills constraint over time through training and learning by doing. The training and learning effects of such technologies have been limited as evidenced by Eze in the case of multinational enterprises[18], Mihyo in the case of Mwanza Textiles and several CDA projects,[12] by UNCTAD in the case of technical management agreements and their failure to implement local manpower training programmes, by Dolman *et al* on the limitations of learning by doing.[14] Mlawa's study on the textile

199

sector in Tanzania, quite clearly exposes this weakness.[19] He points out that when establishing Urafiki and Mwatex textile mills in the late 1960s, all services (ie, feasibility studies, civil engineering works, production start ups, etc) and all machinery supplies were imported. The responsibility for the provision of all buildings and infrastructure also lay with foreign contractors. In addition, in the late 1970s when Mwatex was being expanded, and Musoma, Tabora, Ubungo, Mbeye and Morogoro textile mills were being installed, the only Tanzanian participation was limited to the sub-contracted components in building tasks (eg, roofing and electrical installation). Bagachwa examined the issue of participation by Tanzanian experts in investment decisions at the MNC and found that in all cases of rehabilitation and expansion the foreign financing agency identified, selected and negotiated with the project engineering agency.[9] Indeed there was no active local expertise involved in key technological decisions.

## Production quality and consumption technology

A number of studies have shown that the product quality (or the acquired consumption technology) has influenced the choice of technology. In the case of food manufacturing high standards of hygiene have led to the choice of specific production technologies as indicated by Green in the case of the automated bakery in Dar es Salaam,[20] and by James in the case of Morogoro oil processing and Tanga flour milling.[8] It is conceivable that there are cheaper ways to attain desired hygienic standards but these case studies indicate that production technology was presumably considered the only means available to arrive at the required hygienic standards. In the case of Morogoro oil processing James reported that in order to ensure product quality and a uniform colour product, a more expensive con- tinuous refining process was selected because of reduced dependence on human operation and error.[8]

One of the criticisms of import-substitution industrialization has been that it encourages consumption technologies of the same quality as the imports they replace, without the corresponding process of capital accumu- lation and technological development.[6] Arguing that consumers have been used to the acquired taste of previously imported products, producers of import-substitutes have tended to replicate those same tastes and this has influenced the choice of production technology. For instance, in the case of detergent manufacture in Tanzania the most popular import brand was known as OMO. When a decision was being considered to locally produce a substitute for OMO, tenders were floated to prospective technology suppliers. James reveals that the tender document specified that the desired quality of the detergent to be produced must be the same quality as, or even better than, the previously imported OMO and tenderers were required to send samples of their brands. It is not surprising that the winner of the contract happens to be the supplier of plant and machinery to

Unilever of Kenya, the manufacturer of OMO.[8] The influence of consumption technology on choice of technology has been documented in other cases by James in the case of printing ink, sugar and shoes[8] and by Perkins in the case of sugar, cement, beer and flour milling.[15]

There has been very little government intervention in choice of consumption technology. However, Bagachwa pointed out that in grain milling the government banned the production of sembe superior (flour of about 80 per cent extraction rate) in order to encourage the public to consume sembe standard (about 98 per cent extraction rate).[9] This was done in 1979 at a time when there was a grain shortage in the country. This policy indirectly favours the choice of custom mills rather than merchant roller mills thus altering the composition of units away from roller mills.

## Foreign exchange market

The foreign exchange market in Tanzania has been characterized by excess demand for foreign exchange and an increasingly overvalued exchange rate. The overvaluation of the official exchange rate has been exacerbated by escalating domestic rates of inflation (which averaged about 15 per cent and 28 per cent per annum during the 1970s and 1980s respectively), deterioration in the terms of trade (and the subsequent increasing current account deficits) and increasing debt accumulation. It is thus estimated that the real effective exchange rate appreciated by 56 per cent between 1970–78 and by 120 per cent between 1979–85.

The government, through the Central Bank of Tanzania (BCT), and the People's Bank of Zanzibar, has, since 1970 relied on a system of foreign exchange rationing which uses administrative allocation and import licensing as the major means to contain excess demand. On paper the system is quite elaborate with broad guidelines on how to prioritize sectoral demands (using various criteria such as the extent of linkages, basic consumer needs, revenue generation, and foreign exchange earning). In practice, however, the system is vulnerable to the lobbying strength of the applicant, the crisis nature of the application, overall foreign exchange availability and other political considerations.

Although the system of foreign exchange rationing has spread imports thinly across sectors to even out the effects on capacity use rates across sectors, the primary beneficiaries of the system have been the large-scale parastatal sector. Because of their political and economic power, parastatal enterprises have received a disproportionate share of allocations of foreign exchange, not only through the budget and external project aid, but also since 1984 through the export retention scheme. In addition, given the overvalued exchange rate, the relatively high rates of domestic inflation, low real interest rates and the concessional nature of project aid, the structure of protection provides an implicit subsidy to direct large-scale public sector importers at the expense of the private and small-scale

201

industrial sectors. The implications of the system of import rationing as far as product choice is concerned is that, due to increasing budgetary pressures, firms generating fiscal revenues (especially beer and cigarettes, and to some extent soft drinks) have been allocated the largest proportion of foreign exchange.[21,22] This has reinforced the bias against the development of a capital goods sector.

Another and probably unexpected technological effect resulting from imited accessibility and/or availability of foreign exchange has been some shifts in production lines from import dependence to increased use of domestic resources. Although the scarcity of foreign exchange is widely reported to be the major cause of capacity underutilization in the manufacturing sector in Tanzania,[4,5,23,24] the subsequent raw materials shortages have stimulated the search for alternatives. This search has taken various forms:

1. Active search for local raw materials to substitute for imported materials in the production of existing products (eg, Fabrication and Wire Products Manufacturers (FAWPMA) based in Arusha; Afro Cooling System which substituted local brass and bronze fittings for imports);
2. Increased efficiency in the utilization of imported inputs (eg, FAWPMA);
3. Development of new products that economize on imported inputs (eg, Sunguratex has reduced production of Khangas in favour of more profitable and less import-dependent bedsheets; Bora Shoe Company has reduced output of rubber sandals in favour of higher-priced shoes using local leather; some textiles have also changed production lines from those relying on synthetics to those using local cotton);
4. Rationalization in process, product and industrial engineering. A number of firms have instituted preventive maintenance and rehabilitation programmes, standardization of designs and the manufacturing of in-house spares to solve the problem of scarcity of spares. (Examples in this category include Afro Cooling Systems Ltd which manufactures car radiators of high quality and has standardized the designs for radiator tubes and structures; Auto Mech Ltd which rehabilitates automotive engines, gearboxes, differentials and electricals.)

### Effects of economic policies on factor markets

In a competitive setting, the cheapening of capital inputs relative to other inputs will tend to encourage the use of more capital-intensive technologies. Policies influencing relative factor prices have therefore been instrumental in influencing the direction of technology choice. The most important policies that have influenced the price and availability of capital in Tanzania include a system of credit rationing, interest rate ceiling, tariff protection and other forms of quantitative restrictions on imports and tax incentives.

**Effects of credit policies**

The domestic capital market has been heavily subsidized by high rates of domestic inflation and low interest rates. The banking sector in Tanzania is exclusively government controlled with interest rates and loan structures being controlled by the government through the Central Bank of Tanzania (BOT). Credit is also allocated quantitatively according to government policy priorities as specified by the Finance and Credit Plan.

Though this arrangement is intended to channel credit to the 'high priority' sectors it has led to two undesirable side effects. One is that credit rationing has led to the bulk of loanable funds being allocated to the large-scale public sector firms which are both the most politically and economically adept of the eligible recipients. The small-scale industry (SSI) sector, which is predominantly privately owned, has thus been discriminated against by the institutional market for credit on the basis of higher risks and administrative lending costs. The bulk of small-scale establishments are therefore forced to rely on self-financing (which is nevertheless not sufficient to satisfy the major needs) and informal sources where the rates of interest are higher than official interest rates.[25]

Moreover, to the extent that credit policies result in interest rates which are below the opportunity cost of borrowing domestic capital, as a second side effect they may have biased choice of technology toward greater capital intensity. The BOT, which maintains ceilings on deposit rates as well as floors and ceilings on commercial lending rates, maintained almost fixed nominal rates between 1966 and 1982. At the same time, prices rose at an average annual rate of about 5 per cent between 1966 and 1973 and accelerated to about 22 per cent annually between 1978 and 1983. Thus, the real cost of borrowing has been declining over time and has been negative since 1978. This has not only affected the capital intensity of production but also has resulted in reduced domestic savings and incentives for capital flight. Although one objective of the Economic Recovery Programme is to raise real interest rates to positive levels, this has yet to be achieved. However, over the 1986–88 period the extent of negativity of real interest rates has been reduced.

**Tariff structure**

Tariff protection was used extensively during the 1961–66 period to cushion foreign investors from domestic and international competition. Over time, however, the government has increasingly relied on import licences, administrative allocation of foreign exchange and the confinement system to protect domestic industry. With the partial liberalization of these quantitative controls (through own-funds importation) and devaluation

203

since 1986 the potential role of tariffs has tended to increase over time.

Since independence Tanzania's tariff structure has not changed significantly. Most intermediate and capital goods imports are subjected to a 20 per cent tariff or less, while for the majority of consumer imports, the applicable tariff rate averages about 60 per cent. Most finished consumer goods are subject to a tariff rate of between 60 and 120 per cent, much higher than that placed on intermediate and capital goods. For that reason and because of the overvalued exchange rate, domestic producers of intermediate and capital goods products have a greater incentive to import capital goods rather than search for domestic alternatives.

The structure of protection in Tanzania has also tended to overprotect (and hence channel large resources to) large-scale inefficient firms at the expense of small-scale efficient firms which are in a sense being penalized. A World Bank study has revealed that, while a small-scale firm employing less than 25 workers has an effective rate of protection below 10 per cent, the large enterprise which employs over 250 workers enjoys a rate of effective protection of well over 2,000 per cent. This is so despite the fact that the economic rate of return on capital is normally positive for firms of less than 25 workers as opposed to the larger firms which have a highly negative economic rate of return.[7]

The capital-based tax benefits of accelerated depreciation not only tend to encourage capital intensity in production but also do not accrue to smaller firms. Most small firms escape the official tax net and at times their capital inputs are mistakenly classified as consumer goods and hence subjected to higher tariff rates.

In the 1983/84 Budget, a provision was made for the semi-liberalization of imports under the 'own-funds import scheme'. Under this scheme, importers use foreign exchange earned through private remittances, direct investments, parallel market proceeds and returning capital to import commodities, without declaring the sources of such funds. Own-funds imports have doubled between 1984 and 1986, having increased their share of the total imports from about 20.4 per cent in 1984, to about 41 per cent in 1986.[21] This scheme generally favours intermediate goods and capital goods producers. On the positive side, it has also induced some quality improvements and price reductions in similar domestic items.

### Effects of policies on labour markets

Policies such as minimum wage legislation, mandated fringe benefits and public sector wage policies, have been instrumental in some countries in pushing up the price of labour. In Tanzania, prices, wages and income policies have been used to reduce income disparities among workers and between urban and rural sectors of the economy. Consequently the freeze in wages has been accompanied by a progressive income tax structure. The acceleration of inflation since the late 1970s (at about 25.5 per cent annually between 1979 and 1984) has caused a significant drop in real wages. At the same time, the output supply constraint on the economy as a whole, manifested in underutilization of capacity in the industrial sector, has resulted in falling profit rates. Consequently the share of the wage bill in value added has remained more or less constant. However, due to a government directive which restricts the authority of employers to lay off workers when production declines, the expected wage costs per unit of value added have risen. This acts as a disincentive to the employment of labour and tends to promote capital-intensive technology.

## Policies affecting the development of small industries

### Agricultural policies

There are normally strong potential production and income linkages between agricultural and industrial activities. This is particularly true for rural small-scale industries whose products primarily fill demand from the rural sector. Since the available evidence suggests that, generally, in most developing countries, rural household income elasticity of demand for rural industrial goods is positive and that agriculture generates the largest share of rural incomes, policies designed to increase agricultural output and income would tend to bolster demand for products of small firms.[26,27]

In Tanzania the agricultural pricing and marketing policies have, to a significant degree, contributed to the agricultural sector's poor perform-ance particularly before 1985. These policies have resulted in declining real producer prices and the state's marketing arrangement has been char-acterized by high collection, administrative and transportation unit costs.[28] Thus it may be argued that agricultural policies in Tanzania have not promoted the development of small-scale industries.

### Special SSI promotional programmes

In principle, Tanzanian industrial strategy places a significant weight on the role played by the small-scale industry (SSI) sector in the process of industrialization. The National Small-Scale Industry Corporation was formed as early as 1965 to promote small-scale industries. This was superceded by the Small-Scale Industry Development Organization (SIDO) in 1973. SIDO has been entrusted with the overall co-ordination of all policies and programmes (eg, in project preparation, financing, basic infrastructure, and consultant services) intended for promotion of SSI.

SIDO has designed and implemented a number of promotional programmes including:

1. Provision of 16 industrial estates with 154 sheds;
2. Provision of financial support at relatively subsidized (8 per cent interest) rates through its Rural and Urban Hire Purchase Scheme;

3. Promotion of technology transfer through the Sister Industry programme whereby Swedish firms (senior sisters) provide training
   facilities for local firms (junior sisters) and help to select machinery and
   raw materials;
4. Provision of extension and training services; and
5. Support and promotion of handcrafts.

By 1984, 24 firms employing 600 persons were involved in the sister
industry programme. Technology transfer has also been affected through
the Indo-Tanzanian programme which began in 1977 and supported 48
Tanzanian firms through provision of materials and training.

Reasonably modest success has been achieved by SIDO through these
programmes. The implicit effects of these programmes in relation to
technology choice and development have been discussed in detail by
Havnevik *et al.*[29] Briefly, the industrial estate programme has always been
confined to urban regional headquarters apparently because of lack of
basic infrastructure in the rural areas. They are also heavily capitalized.
Second, over two-thirds of SIDO's assisted investments are located in
urban areas. In fact, by June 1984 SIDO's loan approvals stood at TzShs
53.3m compared to TzShs 256.5m set for urban schemes. Third, a
preponderance of foreign finance in SIDO's aided projects has not only
tended to direct investments toward urban areas but also encouraged
capital and import-intensive techniques, as was the case with the Sister
Industry programme.[30] Finally, in most SIDO-foreign donor negotiations,
the recipient local entrepreneur is not usually involved in the early but
crucial stages of product design and technology selection.[30] The development of indigenous entrepreneurship is thus stifled because of the lack of
opportunities for training and learning by doing.

## Conclusion

Starting from a very low initial level, the growth of industry in Tanzania
was quite rapid in the 1960s and the 1970s. Industrial output, however, has
declined in absolute terms since 1979, following the failure to utilize the
capacity which had been created through large investments in the 1970s.
Capacity expansion, however, continued into the 1970s and 1980s in spite
of the problems of capacity underutilization. For this reason, choice of
technology continued to be relevant even during this period of decline.

The structure of industry has been altered somewhat in favour of
intermediate goods and capital goods, although it remains predominantly
consumer goods oriented. The absence of a strong local capital goods
sector is still quite conspicuous. While industrial output has become
increasingly oriented toward the domestic market rather than the export
market, the import intensity of industrial production has tended to
increase.

The basic industry strategy (1975–95) was formulated to replace the conventional import-substitution industrialization policy. The BIS placed high priority on basic industries, notably capital goods and intermediate goods. However, it did not elaborate on scales of production or choice of technology. Its implementation seems to have been distorted by the deteriorating balance of payments position and the consequent over-dependence on foreign finance which ultimately had considerable influence on which projects would be implemented and at what speed.

The source of foreign finance is a most important factor in the choice of technology in Tanzanian industry. Sourcing of technology has largely favoured the country providing foreign finance and/or the technology supplier who is also providing supplier's credit or other forms of financing. The influence of foreign consultants (who are often tied to source of finance) has tended to reinforce the influence of source of finance on choice of technology. This occurs partly because foreign financiers prefer projects rather than programmes or support of intermediate inputs and partly because the planning system does not deliberately counter this influence.

The shortage of managerial and technical manpower has influenced choice of technology. In response to these constraints, the tendency has been to opt for joint ventures with foreign partners, turnkey projects, and technical and management agreements with foreign agents. The measures used to handle the manpower constraint have deprived local manpower of the opportunity to upgrade their skills through learning by doing. The training effects of these arrangements have been minimal. This reflects the absence of a government policy to encourage participation of techno-managerial personnel in investment decisions and in various project implementation tasks.

Product characteristics have influenced choice of technology in the direction of replication of the imports they replace and toward capital intensity. In general, government policy has been silent on the appropriateness of products or their product characteristics. In one case, however, the government banned the milling of sembe superior; a decision which favours custom mills rather than merchant roller mills.

The overvalued exchange rate tended to favour imported capital-intensive technologies while the foreign exchange allocation system favoured the large-scale, often capital intensive technologies. The foreign exchange allocation system favoured the large-scale, often capital-intensive technologies in the parastatal sector. Although the import squeeze has forced some import-substitution activities, these have emerged in an *ad hoc* rather than systematic manner. Credit allocation has favoured large-scale public sector firms while the negative real interest rates charged on capital have tended to favour capital-intensive technologies. The structure of industrial protection in Tanzania favours large-scale enterprises at the expense of small-scale firms.

The government's restrictions on laying off workers during production declines have tended to act as a disincentive to labour employment and a promoter of capital-intensive technology. There is no doubt that agricultural incomes are closely related to the successful development of small rural industries. The fact that the agricultural sector has stagnated in the past decade suggests that demand-driven small industries could not be established.

Even the small-scale industry programme has tended to be urban biased, highly dependent on foreign finance, capital-intensive and import-intensive. These characteristics have been observed in the case of the industrial sector as a whole (small and large firms).

# Discussion: Policy Approaches Toward Technology Choice and Small Enterprise Development in Africa

R Bautista: I would like to talk about the repercussions of the nominal exchange rate adjustment in the Tanzania study. As we know, only the nominal exchange rate can be affected by the stroke of the pen, not the real exchange rate. Yet structural adjustment may require a devaluation in real terms and whether that can be sustained is a critical issue. Other components of domestic policy also need to accompany the nominal exchange rate adjustment to avoid undercutting the cost competitiveness of producers of tradable goods and to give them sufficient time to assess the effect on the real exchange rate.

*E Doryan-Garron:* I feel that there are various pervasive aspects related to the introduction and implementation of an AT policy. There is a large amount of inertia that makes it very difficult to incorporate science and technology. First, there is a cultural aspect to this inertia in many LDCs. Culturally, we may feel there is no need for a pool of knowledge of science and technology. Embedded in this cultural perception is a view that science and technology is for the developed countries. In a certain sense, we face a self-fulfilling prophecy. Because if we are not convinced that science and technology are building blocks for economic development, and that everything we do requires a process of adaptation, then we are not going to make technology an instrument for development.

Second, there are the economic aspects. For 20 years, at least in Latin America, a policy of import substitution prevailed. Import substitution did not require a science and technology policy, because generally mature technology was imported. In general, the major purpose of import substitution was the final product, not the process used in manufacturing that product. Export promotion would probably not have required an explicit science and technology policy either if we had stayed in the first stages of export promotion and the linkages between sectors were not deepened through a real process of industrialization. Either development strategy (import substitution or export promotion) may or may not need a strong domestic technology component. In either case, there is a need for an explicit science and technology policy for development. If we can formulate such a policy, then appropriate technology will be much more viable.

209

Regarding the preconditions for appropriate technology, there is a need for innovations to link educational policies, infrastructure development and government/private efforts. Development and transfer of appropriate technologies require greater intellectual and technical resources in the population than adoption of imported turnkey technology. How we build this infrastructure and how we link sectors, and how we create a dialogue between the universities and the private sector and the government are part of the process of developing AT.

Furthermore, there is a cultural dependence factor in how we approach science and technology. We thought that we would get technology from science and production from technology, but that did not work. Those who were engaged in basic science remained in basic science, those in technology remained there, and those in production bought technology from abroad. We will have to reverse the process so that production will need appropriate technology, which in turn will depend on increasing the numbers of people involved in basic and applied sciences. Most LDCs have not yet built up this human resource infrastructure to increase the capacity to develop appropriate technologies.

*G de Kalbermatten:* My question concerns the financing of small-scale enterprises and the technologies they use. The excellent RSIE study mentioned this morning did not support supply-side credit mechanisms for small-scale enterprises; however, it indicated that those programmes that focus on well-targeted beneficiary groups can be successful. The study gave the example of a rice milling project in Senegal financed by UNCDF. This project was interesting because it was based on a locally developed appropriate technology prototype, which allowed Senegalese rural women to save long hours of labour and earn additional income.

UNCDF is now financing a second phase of the Senegal project that provides rural credit to women's groups. It may be difficult to institutionalize the original successfully tailored programme to expand the benefits. Often, attempts to do so fail because they add another layer of institutions to existing structures. This leads to my question concerning small-scale enterprise development in Africa. Instead of the bottom-up approach that UNCDF tends to favour but which reaches its limits when we try to institutionalize it, what can we achieve in this area through assistance to the banking sector in Africa? We have conducted our own thematic review of our credit activities and our conclusions are the same as the RSIE study. We found that a great deal of management assistance has to be given to financial intermediaries and extension support services when credit is provided for agricultural inputs. We would like to know how improvements in services can be developed through the banking sector. The findings also noted the importance of having positive real interest rates and covering transaction costs.

*F Stewart:* I would like to know what happened to the basic industry strategy of Tanzania, which formed such an important part of the country's earlier development strategy. This is related to the question of the extent to which regional trade forms an element in the plans of Tanzania and Zimbabwe. In my opinion, the basic industry strategy was impossible for such a small country because it was asking for independent development of certain basic industries, which is just not feasible given the economies of scale. I also feel that regional trade offers a great potential to combine some protection with efficiency and also for the sale of appropriate products and the use of appropriate technology.

Second, reflecting on Mr Doryan-Garron's comments on science and technology, I concluded that new technologies in micro-electronics and biotechnology are going to be very important for developing countries. It will be important to master these technologies to remain competitive, and especially in biotechnology, it is impossible to do so without a local science base. Many countries are too small to create this scientific capability by themselves, particularly in Africa. So the question is, what are the prospects for regional co-operative efforts in science and trade?

*S K Gupta:* I would like to discuss the issues of cost of capital and the need to sustain institutions and micro- and small enterprises targeted by assistance programmes. The whole debate on capital costs and interest rates is one sided. Access to capital and interest rates are only the supply aspects, capital productivity is more important. Without productive use of capital, the institutions dealing with micro-enterprises will not be sustainable.

Mr Mansuri's concern about micro-enterprises and Mr Rasaputram's comment suggest that there is a trade-off between the sustainability of institutions and their clients. We cannot afford to neglect either sustainability of enterprises or sustainability of institutions. If we address the capital productivity issue, we are really addressing the technology dimension of the enterprises, which ensures the sustainability both of the institutions and their clients. It is in this context that ATI has experimented with risk sharing based on a modified venture capital mechanism, which we have introduced in some Asian countries.

This brings me to Mr de Kalbermatten's question. Is there a banking answer to the needs of micro-enterprises? The answer is do not supply financing as credit. Instead, share risks and benefits with the farmer and the micro-entrepreneur – the risks originating from new products, new inputs, and dealing with new systems and institutions. Dealing with risk at this level addresses the capital productivity aspects of micro-enterprises. ATI has experimented on a small-scale with this approach in Indonesia, the Philippines and in Thailand. We want to widen this experiment in co-operation with formal banking institutions. The focus here is to promote innovations in the banking industry and introduce risk sharing mechanisms, which can bring about tremendous productivity improvements.

Regarding the sustainability of institutions and micro-enterprises, Mrs Stewart mentioned the need to change the project appraisal system itself from its exclusive focus on returns to capital. The conventional approach misses the most important thing – the returns to labour. If returns to labour are emphasized, appropriate technologies are more likely to be selected. Therefore, we need to change the selection criteria used by financing institutions and introduce equity financing for micro-enterprises.

*G Ranis*: I am very puzzled about how one diffuses information to rural entrepreneurs. When you do not want to imitate the agricultural extension service, the suggestion is always made to do something with the banking system, but how can this capacity be embedded in a commercial banking system? My experience involves building on co-operative banks. Rather than bringing in resources from outside the locality, co-operative banks have their own credit base in the rural areas. Other members of the co-operative have an incentive to monitor repayment by their peers. This amounts to a type of supervised credit. This approach seems to have worked in East Asia, but I do not know whether it would work in Africa.

Concerning the regional potential, Mrs Stewart is right scientifically, but it may be too difficult politically to expect a lot from regional co-operation. I do not foresee many regional arrangements of this type. I agree with Mr Doryan-Garron's notion that in the import substitution phase, firms do not demand appropriate science and technology. But I do not agree that this capability is also not needed with an export orientation. How can you be competitive abroad if your technology is not appropriate? Adaptation is important, but so is stimulation from outside. You want to use outside technology selectively and adapt it. That may be difficult to achieve, because although most countries have some science policy, the system for carrying out that policy may not be well matched to the needs. Decisions are usually based on short-term financial and nationalistic considerations. The costs of imported technology must be considered in relation to willingness to pay for all scales of enterprises.

*D Ndlela:* My first comment concerns Mrs Stewart's question about whether regional trade and science and technology strategies are being planned by Zimbabwe, Tanzania and other countries in the region. Although regional aspects of science and technology should be quite important in planning the scale of industry, they are not being explicitly considered at this time, from the standpoint of the regional organizations like the South African Development Co-ordination Conference (SADCC) and Preferential Trade Area for Eastern and Southern African States (PTA). Through the sub-regional organization, the PTA, tariff and non-tariff barriers have been reduced and this has helped in the planning of a fertilizer plant in Tanzania, for example. Ideally, such plans must take into account national and regional needs. While some efforts have been made along these lines, these countries are not obligated to actually trade with each other. In some cases, one country imports something from as far as Australia, when that product could have been imported from a neighbouring country.

On the issue of science and technology there is not much going on. However, since 1987 SADCC has been putting in place a policy framework for implementing a science and technology centre for the region, although this has not yet been implemented.

On the question of assistance through the banking sector in Africa, in some cases, such as Zimbabwe, the banking system is quite effective, but so far only in agriculture. Small-scale cotton farmers in Zimbabwe have actually displaced large-scale farmers because of the credit facilities provided. Yet, this was not due to the credit system alone because credit to small farmers was only given after long experience with appropriate extension services. This has made the farmers respond to credit and become quite efficient in facing both local and export markets. We do not have similar services for the mining sector and industrial sector. It is taken for granted that new entrepreneurs in these sectors will apply technology without assistance from extension services. One cannot expect a small-scale miner to be successful without adequate training and support in this field. Why should the banking system be reoriented when there is also a need for more extension services than the present system offers to the small-scale industrial sector?

*S M Wangwe:* On the problem of exchange rates, some of the effects of adjustment can be seen, although not enough time has passed to make conclusive observations. Export prices have increased considerably in local currency terms and this has been accompanied by a number of non-price incentive mechanisms. As a result of these changes, output has increased. Most imports have become much more expensive and capital-intensive enterprises are finding it difficult to replace their equipment. Companies starting new firms are seeing that it is very expensive to acquire imported technologies. Some entrepreneurs try to mobilize the large amount of financing necessary for this, but others realize they must make smaller-scale, less expensive investments. Policy mechanisms have not yet been put in place to move firms away from capital-intensive technologies. For example, the head of the sugar development corporation believes that it is difficult to secure finance to start large-scale sugar plants now, but does not know how to assist entrepreneurs interested in setting up alternative small-scale technologies. No financing is available to promote the small-scale technologies. It is a new challenge to promote alternative technology without a push from financiers and donors.

213

The real exchange rate has also been reduced in Tanzania so that the exchange rate has become less overvalued. Negotiations are proceeding on further devaluations, but even changing the nominal exchange rate is politically sensitive.

Science and technology policy is relevant in both import-substitution and export promotion, unless you define import-substitution so narrowly that automatically it excludes technology questions. If you define import-substitution broadly, you must define what imports should be substituted and how to do it. In import-substitution, the question of what to produce and how to produce it is loaded with science and technology policy issues. Therefore, it is difficult to make a convincing case that the science and technology policy is necessarily excluded from consideration under either import-substitution or export-oriented industrialization.

The question of how to reform the finance and banking system to cope with the requirements of small-scale industries remains a challenge. There must be a way to meet the needs of small-scale industries by mobilizing financial resources. In the African context, I am not sure whether the Grameen Bank's model is applicable. Substantial education would be necessary and also restoration of the idea that credit is not free money, but a resource for the whole community. Where monitoring of the repayment is by the people themselves and borrowers lose credibility in the community if a loan is not repaid, the chances of a successful credit system are better.

The basic industry strategy was formulated in the mid-1970s in Tanzania to encourage greater use of local resources for industrial development and increase production to meet the basic needs of the people directly and through intermediate and capital goods. The question of whether the national market is too small to produce some products has been raised. In the long run, market constraints could be a bottleneck if the basic industry strategy is pursued at a national level. Nevertheless, experience in Tanzania so far suggests that market constraints were not significant from the late 1970s to date. Supply bottlenecks arising from use of inappropriate technologies and foreign exchange shortages that blocked imports of intermediate inputs were the major problems.

The principles of Tanzania's basic industry strategy were quite simple, but implementation required control of resources. Issues of linkages and technology choices were neglected due to overdependence on foreign finance. The few industries established during this period, such as consumer textiles and shoe manufacturing, have not satisfied the domestic market. There are still shortages of textiles and shoes, as a result of technology problems in these industries and the failure to utilize the created capacity. The way the plants were designed and the types of technology used seem to be the major problems. For example, two cement plants and two large tanneries were built in this period, but neither of these

214

industries has satisfied the market. So the situation has not really come to a stage where the domestic market is the bottleneck.

The basic industry strategy has become difficult to implement, even without market constraints. Product design, the control of resources, technology choice, the failure to sequence the establishment of plants and weak linkages between industrial activities were the main problems. These problems cut short the implementation of the strategy well before the market constraints came into play.

Mr Ndlela has responded to the question of regional constraints. I can only add that scrutiny of the development plans of nine SADCC countries shows that most projects are planned with the national rather than regional market in mind. In very few cases will you find a small mention in the plan of the regional market. Although it is discussed, the subject of regional markets has not filtered down to the planning process. Although the process of considering regional trade is starting, thus far it has not been sufficiently incorporated in national planning mechanisms.

# Macroeconomic Policy, Technological Change and Rural Development: The Costa Rica Case

## EDUARDO DORYAN-GARRON

### Interrelationships between macro-policies and technological change in the rural areas

The experience with lime and coffee production in Costa Rica shows the importance of policies affecting economic, social and technological aspects of the sector. However, in the medium-term and beyond, general macro-policies can have an even larger influence that should be evaluated.

For example, whether coffee is consumed domestically or exported, it must be processed for storage and sale. The specific type of processing technology used by a plant will affect the employment generated, income distribution and price incentives available for producers.[1] A range of local and foreign technologies exists for drying coffee, and some are more labour-intensive than others. A change from one technology to another requires investment decisions that can be expressed in what economists call isoquant diagrams, defining the optimal combination of production factors.

Processors do not make their production decisions solely based on farmer's production costs since they are also influenced by the institutional framework of social agreements among the various interest groups in the sector. Calculations to determine the profitability of entry, exit, or expansion decisions in processing depend on macroeconomic variables such as currency exchange rates, interest rates, salaries, and world market prices for coffee and traded inputs. The exchange rate affects the cost of imported machinery in processing plants and the farmgate price of coffee. Interest rates comprise part of the cost of machinery for processing and equipment for harvesting. Labour costs affect both the processors and the

---

As Deputy Minister for Science and Technology of the Government of Costa Rica, EDUARDO DORYAN-GARRON has been responsible for linking scientific and technological policies with macroeconomic policies. As an author of books in areas such as energy planning, project appraisal and technology policy, he draws on his training as an electrical engineer and Ph.D. in political economics and government.

**Table 1 Macropolicy factors and their influence on coffee production techniques**

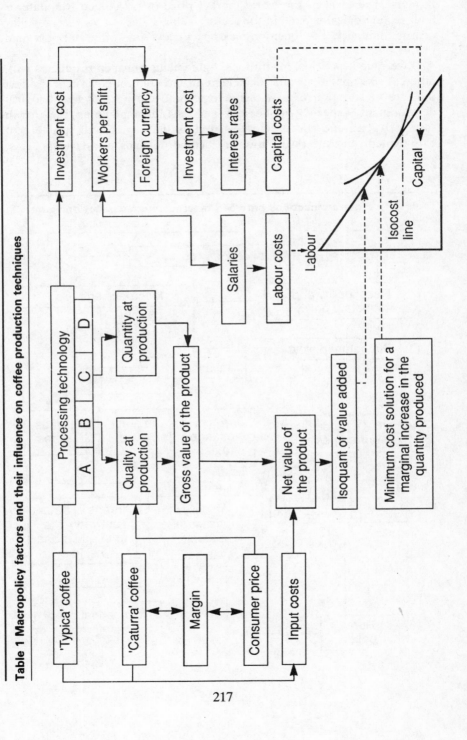

217

farmers. The level of the world market price of coffee can stimulate or limit technological change in the sector. Table 1 shows how macro-policy factors influence the decision-making process of coffee farmers and processors.[2]

Government policies, institutional agreements between producers with different size operations and the general macro-political environment affect the rate of adoption of new technologies and the pace of technological development. Especially in medium- and long-range planning, the growth rates of urban and rural sectors as well as the degree and structure of employment and the distribution of income depends on macro-policies.

**Table 2 The interconnections between macroeconomic policy and rural policy**

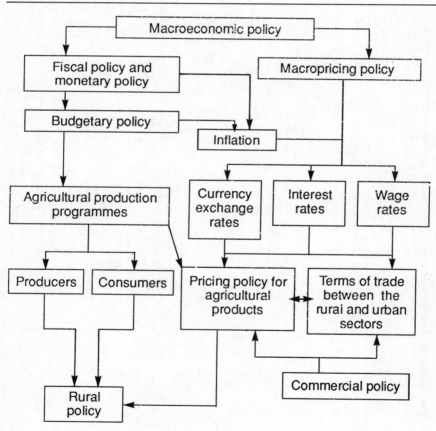

Four macro-policy areas include: budget policies, fiscal policies, monetary policies and pricing policies (foreign currency, interest rates, and wage rates). These macro-policies can have a major effect in terms of trade between the urban and rural sectors.

Table 2 shows the connections between macroeconomic policies and rural production. Fiscal and monetary policies can have a dual effect on prices directly and through feedback via the inflation rate. The relationship between consumers and producers, and the rural and urban sectors, is demonstrated in the connections.[4] These relationships influence the adoption of technology by farmers and, therefore, the rural productivity. Nevertheless, to understand the links between rural productivity and the adoption of technology, it is necessary to describe the economic policies that characterized Costa Rica in the past.

---

**Table 3**

---

*Geographic Information*
- Location: Central American isthmus, between Nicaragua and Panama.
- Total: 51,100 km$^2$
- Political divisions: 7 Provinces, 81 Counties, 421 Districts and more than 6,000 communities.
- Capital: San Jose, at 1,161 metres above sea level

*Demographic information*
- Total population: 2,800,000
- Population density: 55 inhabitants per km$^2$
- Birth rate: 30.6 births per 1,000 inhabitants
- Population growth: 27.0 per 1,000 inhabitants
- Urban share of population: 49%
- Rural share of population: 51%
- Rural population in communities of less than 2,000 inhabitants: 32%
- Population younger than 15 years of age: 36.5%
- Population older than 65 years of age: 4.1%

*Economic information*
- Per capita income: US $1,708 (1985)
- Economically Active Share of Population: 35.8%
- Unemployment rate: 6.2%
- Total exports (thousands U.S. $): 1,121,272
- Total imports (thousands U.S. $): 1,044,643
- External debt (thousands U.S. $): 3,739.000
- Ratio of external debt to exports of goods and services: 48.6%
- Ratio of external debt to annual public expenditures: 80.9%
- Wholesale price index (1978 = 100): 808.01
- Consumer price index (1975 = 100): 733.78

---

### Costa Rica: Macroeconomic context

Costa Rica has a land area of 51,100 km², making it the smallest Central American Republic after Belize and El Salvador. It borders Panama on the South and Nicaragua on the north. Table 3 shows the country's principal geographic, demographic and economic characteristerics.

From the incorporation of Costa Rica in the Central American Common Market in the early 1970s to the present, the social and technological organization of the production in the country has changed significantly. The use of human and natural resources, the output of goods and services, and the socio-political structure have adjusted in response to internal and external factors. Costa Rica's economic history over the last 26 years can be divided into three periods: import substitution (1962–79), crisis (1980–82) and recovery (1983–88).

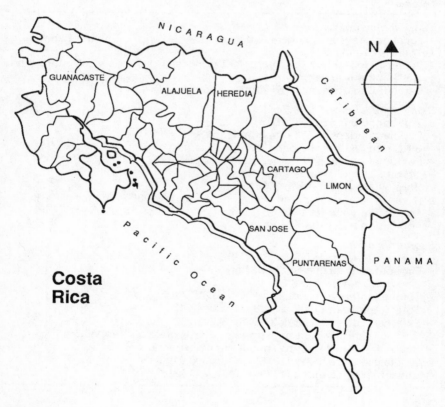

Figure 1

## The period of import substitution

In the period of import substitution, the development model sought to cushion the inherent difficulties of a small economy dependent on the export of a few cash crops through the production and export of industrial products to other countries in Central America. The adopted policies facilitated development of a manufacturing sector, which in turn,

**Table 4 Costa Rica: Share of aggregate supply and demand (%)**

|  | Average share 1962–64 | Average share 1977–79 | Average annual growth rate |
|---|---|---|---|
| Gross National Product | 78.1 | 69.6 | 6.0 |
| Total Imports | 21.9 | 30.4 | 9.1 |
| SUPPLY = DEMAND | 100.0 | 100.0 | 6.8 |
| Internal Demand | 82.1 | 74.4 | 6.2 |
| Final Consumpton | 68.6 | 55.8 | 5.5 |
| Private | 57.7 | 46.7 | 5.4 |
| Public | 10.9 | 9.1 | 5.9 |
| Gross Fixed Investment | 14.1 | 18.3 | 8.5 |
| Private | 10.9 | 12.4 | 7.8 |
| Public | 3.2 | 5.8 | 10.4 |
| Variation of Goods | −0.6 | 0.3 | —— |
| External Demand | 17.8 | 25.6 | 9.1 |

Source: Compiled with data from BCCR. MIDEPLAN, National Development Plan 1986–90.

**Table 5 Composition of exports in Costa Rica**

|  | Average 1962–64 (%) | Average 1977–79 (%) |
|---|---|---|
| *Traditional by Type* | *87.1* | *66.1* |
| Coffee | 47.1 | 36.1 |
| Banana | 26.8 | 19.4 |
| Cacao | 4.4 | 1.6 |
| Sugar | 4.3 | 1.9 |
| Meat | 4.5 | 7.1 |
| *Non-traditional by Destination* | *12.9* | *33.9* |
| Central America | 6.9 | 20.1 |
| The remainder of the world | 6.0 | 13.8 |
| TOTAL | *100.0* | *100.0* |

Source: Compiled from data from the BCCR. MIDEPLAN, National Development Plan 1986–90.

influenced the government to superimpose a policy of import substitution on the old model of agricultural exports. During this time, agricultural exports expanded and were gradually diversified. The principal results of the policy on aggregate supply and demand are shown in Tables 4 and 5.

Regarding supply, the Gross National Product (GNP) grew by an average annual rate of 6.0 per cent, one of the highest rates in the region. At the same time, imports grew at an average annual rate of 9.1 per cent from 21.9 per cent of GNP at the beginning of this period to 30.4 per cent. Capital investment also increased substantially, especially for public investment.

Total exports of goods and services constituted the most important dynamic element in GNP. The export share rose 17.8 per cent from 1962 to 1964, and 25.6 per cent from 1977 to 1979. This was equivalent to an average annual increase of 9.1 per cent. Moreover, exports became more diversified in type and destinations.

Although this development model allowed the economy to grow at an accelerated rate and improved the general population's living conditions in the short-run, it was not sustainable. This fact was demonstrated in the crisis of 1974–75 which was initially caused by the increase in petroleum prices. A temporary improvement in terms of trade occurred in 1977 primarily as a result of an increase in the coffee prices and access to foreign financing. Yet, though production had diversified and exports increased, it was insufficient to finance the economic model of import substitution.

*Economic policies during the crisis*
The convergence of structural problems posed by the failure of the import substitution model, external factors that negatively affected the balance of payments; and an inadequate, internal economic policy drove the economy into a profound crisis between 1980 and 1982. Actual production decreased by 9.1 per cent; prices increased by 179.5 per cent, the unemployment rate increased up to 9.4 per cent, the total underemployment rate reached 21%, real salaries were reduced by 40 per cent, and the proportion of poor families increased to 53 per cent. The imbalance of public finances showed a deficit in the public, non-financial sector of 14.3 per cent of the GNP. The indebtedness level reached 114.5 per cent of the GNP and service payments for the external debt required more than 50 per cent of exports.

A combination of external and internal factors brought on the crisis. The external factors included:

o Deterioration of the exchange rate as petroleum prices increased a second time;
o The international recession that affected Costa Rican exports;
o Instability of the international financial system and rising interest rates;
o Political and economic problems in Central America.

The internal factors included:

o A fiscal policy that allowed an unsustainable acceleration of government expenditures;
o A monetary policy of net internal credit expansion which increased demand excessively and resulted in inflation;
o An overvalued exchange rate policy that kept imports high, followed by speculations against local currency that helped force a devaluation of 350 per cent;
o The doubling of the external debt from 1979 to 1982.

*Economic policies during the recovery*

After 1982, the main concern of the government was to stabilize the economy. It did this by re-establishing international financial relationships, balancing public finances, regulating the exchange market and renegotiating the external debt. To correct the imbalance in public finances, direct and indirect taxes were increased and the expansion of public spending was limited. The most important element of this adjustment was an increase in prices and tariffs for goods and services under the government's control to stabilize demand.

The foreign exchange market was stabilized through strict controls by the Central Bank. Also, operations of stock speculators were regulated. The foreign debt was renegotiated to gain more favourable terms. To avoid a further deterioration in the standard of living and reduce the social costs of the adjustment, a Social Compensation Programme was established to assist those groups in the most desperate financial situations. At the same time, a drastic decrease in productivity was avoided by the establishment of a programme to help businesses.

The relative stability attained by 1983 permitted the reorientation of the government's efforts for a gradual transformation of the structure of production. The promotion of exports was identified as a priority. Through regional negotiations, the Central American Common External Tariff was reduced. New subsidy and tax exemption systems were created, and institutional support for non-traditional exports to markets outside of Central America was reorganized. By the mid-1980s, production was growing at an annual rate of about 3 per cent; inflation had declined by 10 – 15 per cent per year, and non-traditional exports rose from approximately $150 m to more than $450 m in 1987. In addition, the unemployment rate in 1987 fell to 5.5 per cent, the lowest in the region.

Some structural factors also limit the future economic growth of Costa Rica. The growth of non-traditional exports continues to be an important source of hard currency; however, demand for these types of products is declining, resulting in lower and more unstable prices. The Central American market is still weak, impeding an easy route for economic

**Table 6 Quality of life, 1986.**

*Health*

| | |
|---|---:|
| Hospital beds per 1,000 inhabitants | 2.9 |
| Expenditures per 1,000 inhabitants | 126.5 |
| Life expectancy at birth (years) | 73.7 |
| General mortality per 1000 inhabitants | 3.8 |
| Infant mortality per 1000 live births | 17.8 |
| Mortality of children 1–4 yrs. old per 1000 | 0.8 |
| Deaths due to contagious diseases (%) | 3.6 |
| Proportion of mortality of those less than 5 years old (%) | 17.3 |
| Per capita expenditures for health (US$) | 101.6 |
| Expenditures on health services as part of GNP (% of budget) | 17.0 |
| Availability of potable water (%) | 93.0 |
| Availability of sewage facilities (%) | 94.8 |
| Daily calories consumed per inhabitant | 2,653 |
| Newborns born underweight (less than 2,500 g) (%) | 7.5 |
| Children with midlevel and severe malnutrition (%) | 4.1 |
| Hospital births (%) | 96.0 |
| Population covered by health and maternity insurance (%) | 89.5 |
| Vaccination rate in children below 1 year old (%) | 89.5 |
| Doctors per 10,000 inhabitants | 10.0 |
| Nurses per 10,000 inhabitants | 7.0 |
| Nurses aids per 10,000 inhabitants | 22.7 |
| Number of medical consultations per inhabitant per year | 2.6 |

*Education*

| | |
|---|---:|
| Illiteracy (%) | 7.5 |
| Levels of school achievement (%) | |
| Preschool | 53.8 |
| Cycles I and II | 104.1 |
| Cycle III | 46.2 |
| Diversified (vocational/technical) | 22.5 |
| University | 20.6 |
| Post-graduate | 1.9 |
| Number of primary schools | 3,137 |
| Number of secondary/high schools | 241 |
| Number of universities | 5 |
| Public expenditure on education as a % of the GNP | 5.2 |

*Communications*

| | |
|---|---:|
| Newspapers | 6 |
| Radio stations | 156 |
| Television networks | 9 |
| Telephones per 100 inhabitants | 12.2 |
| Automotive vehicles in circulation | 246,458 |
| Length of highways (km) | 35,313 |
| Length of railroad tracks (km) | 468 |

recovery. The capacity for export to Third World markets is limited because their spending power is constrained by protectionist practices in developed nations and their position along the learning curve in highly competitive markets. Another problem is a high dependency on imported imputs and external financing.

One of the primary characteristics of the current production structure is the low level of intersectoral integration, which limits economic growth in the hinterlands and results in a high dependency on imported imputs. In the past, the agribusiness sector has shown the largest linkages to the rural economy and also the lowest proportions of imported inputs after agriculture. Thus, the expansion of agricultural product processing could promote the urban–rural integration of production. Finally, expertise in science and technology has been a constraint.

Although many of these problems still exist, the government has been able to promote a development policy that is concerned with both economic and social impacts. This policy has helped to maintain an atmosphere of peace and democracy despite the crisis. The results of this social policy can be seen in Table 6. In particular, the government sought to strengthen co-operatives and community development associations. As a result, 600 co-operative organizations exist and are generating 10.4 per cent of the GNP and 13.2 per cent of exports. Over 1,240 community associations now exist and are in the process of transforming themselves to play a larger role in economic production, while still carrying out their social responsibilities.

## The present strategy for development

The present development strategy of Costa Rica seeks to expand exports because the domestic market is small. It also attempts to reduce reliance on production and consumption technologies that are highly dependent on imported goods. Three alternative strategies were considered to increase exports. The first strategy was based on free markets, where international prices are used to allocate resources, and automatic market mechanisms are assumed to achieve social objectives. This strategy would reduce government participation in regulating prices.

According to Costa Rican government officials:

This focus is not capable of directing us toward equitable development, in the search for peace and democracy. First, the costs in the medium and long range are very high in comparison to the expected benefits. For this reason, this plan would generate opposition from most social groups. Second, the distortions of international commerce (e.g. oligopolies and protectionism), imply that market signals do not always lead to an optimal allocation of resources. Third, the market by itself does not assure that social objectives such as equity, reduction of extreme poverty, and increased social mobility are achieved[3]

The second strategy would have the government participate actively in supporting the export sector as an end itself through subsidies, exemptions, preferential access to credit, and other policies.

Costa Rican officials noted that,

'This option implies high subsidies for the export sector and would require growing and perhaps unsustainable fiscal policies. Also, this would be inefficient, since it promotes the growth of certain sectors that would not grow without government concessions and would not necessarily transfer funds to the rest of the economy. The social cost of the strategy is high because this strategy depends on low salaries to compete in international markets'

The third strategy which was chosen by the Government is called exports for development. This strategy uses the expansion of exports as part of an integral plan for economic and social progress. It is characterized by the use of policies to increase the amount of added value in processed exports. The goal of this strategy is to attain more economic democracy and social mobility.

Four areas of action were identified to implement the third strategy:

1. Increase national savings;
2. Create a new scientific and technological style;
3. Increase labour productivity; and
4. Encourage the vertical integration of the production system.

However, these actions are not sufficient to guarantee equitable access to productive resources. Reduction of poverty, protection of the environment, satisfaction of basic needs and greater social mobility are all important. In implementing this strategy, the social problems that need to be addressed include: housing, employment, economic democracy, geographic democracy, and equal participation of women in the development process. These have been given importance in the government's priorities.

### The role of small-scale industry

Small-scale industrial production has been given a high priority because it constitutes a large share of rural industry.[10] One example is the small-scale lime production industry in Costa Rica. More than 50 per cent of total industrial employment in the country is found in the 15,000 small-scale workshops and businesses.[11] Small-scale industry also plays an important role in the distribution of wealth since it allows a larger number of people access to the means of production.

In small firms, the ratio of capital investment to the number of people employed is very small in comparison with big business. Thus, many jobs are generated at low cost. Important labour-intensive industries specialize in the manufacturing of such basic goods as clothing, shoes, furniture, and foods. For the most part, local raw materials are used in these industries. The amount of imported material required is only 0.5 per cent of that required by large industry.

In addition, these enterprises use a large percentage of indigenous technology. By utilizing their own creativity, entrepreneurs can take advantage of local equipment and machinery, thus saving foreign currency.

Of the total number of enterprises in the country, 85 per cent can be categorized as small (less than 20 employees). These firms represent 60 per cent of the gross value of total industrial production and absorb 75 per cent of total industrial employment. A programme covering 38 of the country's subdivisions, urban as well as rural, has been directed toward small enterprises during the better part of this decade. It has provided credit and technical assistance to 2,291 businesses (approximately 15 per cent of the total). As a result of greater access to financing for fixed capital expenses and technical assistance, these businesses have increased their employment by 25 per cent.

Small enterprises were less seriously affected by the crisis than large ones because they did not have debts in dollars and were less dependent on imported raw materials. Also, small-scale enterprises do not have large financing costs for maintaining large inventories and marketing. The loan default rate for small enterprises is only 10 per cent compared to 50 per cent for big business. Finally, in times of crisis, specialized workers, with access to a small amount of credit, can start their own workshops.

However, a number of problems that affect small enterprises can be seen in the experience of farmers and lime producers. These problems include:

o Little access to bank credit;
o Insufficient technical and administrative assistance;
o Marketing problems;
o Problems with raw materials supply;
o Limited access to centralized services; and
o The absence of an information system for transferring technology to the sector.

The financing needs of the small-scale sector exceed the amount that banks have been willing to loan. Also, there is no special division within the bank for handling loans for this sector, which are largely subsidized. This makes it more difficult for small-scale entrepreneurs to streamline their operations.

The collateral requirements demanded by commercial banks are a major difficulty for small enterprises because their capital equipment is inexpensive, and they are often located in rural areas. For loans of more then US $2,000, guarantors with goods, securities, or mortgages, are required.

Of 1,707 credit applications recommended by the Small-Enterprise

227

Division of the Ministry of Labour, 1,025 applications were approved; the rest were not, mostly due to a lack of guarantees.

To date, only 10 per cent of small-scale businesses have received technical or managerial assistance in general accounting, inventory control, plant distribution, production processes, quality control, label design, and other areas. The greatest bottlenecks in production by small firms include disorganization in production flow, low capacity use rates, and lack of planning.

The primary marketing problems observed are weak organization, lack of working capital to offer purchaser credit or sales on consignment, high prices for raw materials that are often purchased in small quantities from retailers, poor product quality, and poor product presentation.

Information on the best technological options is basically restricted to those enterprises that receive support from some public entity or a producers' organization. Only 20 per cent of small enterprises fall into this category.[13] Also, small enterprises are characterized by less dynamic technological change than that observed in larger enterprises. Sometimes, the technologies used are old and inefficient, but could be upgraded at relatively low cost, as happened in coffee production.

## Scientific and technological policies[4]

A programme of scientific and technological development was made possible by the participation of the public sector, the research and teaching centres and the production sector. A three-part policy through the year 2000 was defined in this area. First, for four years, the emphasis will be on achieving an organized process for the transfer of technology and the adaptation and generation of local technology. This will require development of the science and technology infrastructure and increased investment in those activities. During this stage, leading enterprises in key sectors will be assisted to set an example for other less dynamic enterprises and sectors.

A second stage will consist of technological assimilation. This five-year programme will be directed at obtaining better control over the acquired technologies. In this phase, the innovative capacity of the country will be strengthened for the transfer and creation of technology. Exports of goods and services with a greater technological content will be encouraged consistent with development of comparative advantage.

A third stage, lasting through the year 2000, will be the generation of appropriate technologies for industries and agriculture with a broad national, scientific base. Efforts will be directed toward the formation of a highly qualified human resource base and also to increase basic and applied research.

The policies and programmes underway and planned will seek to promote modernization for more efficient use of installed capacity, and technological change that combines the rational selection and adaptation of technology for export production with the development of appropriate technology.

The government's policy is:

to support the formation of the scientific capacity associated with the process of adapting and generating appropriate technology to create a broad scientific base, with which Costa Rica can become a country that exports goods and services with a high technological content by the twenty-first century. Technological policies, alone, directly support the export effort and import substitution. This policy will create the tools to induce technological change in the production through financing of institutional infrastructure, planning and coordination, and the development of human resources, research, and legislation to promote industrial technology.[3]

The government is currently working in three areas to achieve these goals. The first approach is to encourage efficient substitution of imports with high technological content by using the government's buying power and supplying science and technology services to the business sector. The expected results are a strengthening of local technological capacity, creation of employment in the private sector, a reduction in public expenditures and the drain on foreign currency, and building up the entrepreneurial experience required for successful exportation in external markets. Particular priority has been placed on the mechanical, electronic, and chemical–pharmaceutical industries.

A second area of importance is the competitive production of non-traditional products for export with a high technological content. To achieve this goal, labour-intensive technologies are to be promoted, such as biotechnology in health and agricultural applications. Key sectors in this regard will be agronomy, agribusiness, fisheries and aquaculture, and housing. Attention will be paid to product and process standardization and quality control.

Third, technologies for efficient production for the domestic market will be supported, especially those that are widely applicable in the rural areas for housing, agriculture, and agricultural product processing. Priority will be given to innovative technologies for use by co-operatives and other similar social organizations, and to projects with regional impact.

The following two programmes are relevant in this category. The first is the Regional Technology Project directed by the Ministry of Science and Technology, which attempts to support technological change in organizations such as co-operatives and sustainable businesses in rural areas of the country. The programme focuses on diagnosing the technological bottlenecks that impede some productive processes. Regional leaders, government technicians, small-scale enterprises and organized farmers all participate in these diagnoses.

The second project is called Social Product Development. This project attempts to support 1,200 community organizations in the establishment, management, and incorporation of technological change generated nationally to assist small- and medium-scale enterprises. The expected results of the work of community associations include encouragement of economic democracy, technological modernization at the most basic level, and the active presence of associations in the national productive livelihood.

The coffee industry in Costa Rica is an example of the successful diffusion of technology and support to small farmers. This case also shows how macro-policies affect production and the way that social agreements and producer organizations can increase productivity and the rate and depth of technological change. However, before focusing on this example, it is useful to examine the context of the whole agricultural sector.

## The agricultural sector

### General situation

The agricultural sector contributes about 20 per cent of Costa Rica's Gross National Product, although its share has dropped from 24.1 per cent in 1970 to 18.0 per cent in 1980. The recent recovery in agriculture may be due to short-term speculation.[4] Within the agricultural sector, crop production is the largest sector with an average participation rate of 69 per cent, followed by the livestock sector with 24.5 per cent and the fisheries, forestry and other sectors comprising 6.5 per cent. Only in the last few years has the fisheries sector recovered.

Agriculture remains the source of 70 per cent of the country's foreign currency earnings. However, the export earnings are concentrated in the coffee, banana, sugar cane and cattle sub-sectors. Agriculture is also the largest source of employment for the economically active population although the level has been decreasing. In 1978, 38.2 per cent of the economically active population worked in agriculture, but this declined to 27.0 per cent in 1984. The growth of agricultural employment has increased at an average annual rate of 0.2 per cent, while overall employment has increased at 3.3 per cent per year. This relative lack of dynamism in agricultural production is due to competition for resources from other growing economic sectors. Solving the problems of agriculture will require modernization of cultural practices, perhaps through mechanization which may reduce employment in the sector.

### Rural development

Concerns over social problems that affect rural inhabitants, such as low income, unequal land distribution, and lack of basic services, have been gradually included in the country's development strategy since the 1950s.[56] Before then, public investment programmes emphasized development of the central region. To increase inter-regional integration, highways were built to the Pacific coast and between the north and south, allowing the spread of activities related to cattle and grains production in those regions. The government also supported rural electrification and telecommunications. By 1987, highways were extended to the Atlantic region, and communications between the north-central and north-east regions had improved, to the benefit of banana, coffee and grain production.

The opening of new areas through infrastructure development stimulated agricultural settlement. This process increased the availability of farm land because of the low population density of the outlying areas.

In the 1960s, monopolization of land and intensive colonization exhausted the easily accessible agricultural areas and created strong pressures on land use. This obliged the government in the 1970s to intervene directly with land tenure programmes, and purchase land for transfer to peasants. Land redistribution lessened the adverse social effects of market forces.

Two decades of industrial development had been concentrated in the central region of the country. During the 1960s, this led to rural–urban migration to the modern, manufacturing sector. In response, the state started social programmes to encourage the rural inhabitants to stay in their regions. This flight to the city meant quantitatively that in 1963, agriculture comprised almost 50 per cent of total employment but dropped to 29 per cent in 1979. The secondary industry sectors of construction in 1963 made up 17 per cent of jobs, increased to 24 per cent in 1979; which the third level industrial sector increased from 33 per cent to 47 per cent in this same period. In 1974, the Social Security system rapidly established medical services in the rural areas. Later, a programme of social services for the rural population was initiated. This programme provided health, food and nutrition services, as well as rural housing, training, community help and villager organization programmes.

The programmes established in those years allowed the rural population to survive the effects of the crisis from 1980–82 in relatively better conditions than the inhabitants of the urban areas, except for the lowest income levels. In the rural areas, in 1983 a significant increase in total income of 21.2 per cent could already be seen. All strata participated in this increase, except for the poorest 10 per cent whose income decreased by 16.3 per cent.[3]

The adjustment of prices for services, a reduced deficit of the public institution that stabilizes the prices of agricultural products, and the process of liberalizing the economy from 1983 on have had major effects on agricultural production and rural employment. While the metropolitan areas of San Jose and the Central Valley both show substantial improvement in economic growth, the outlying rural regions still lag behind. This could accelerate rural–urban migration again. This is so even with a policy of subsidized interest rates for small rural and urban producers, currently 15 per cent compared to 25 per cent for other activities.

The repercussions of this situation have been noted by the Costa Rican Ministry of Planning:

> There exists a rapidly growing pressure on the land and increasing rural–urban migration, which is a product of spontaneous colonization, exhaustion of available agriculture frontiers, a decrease in agriculturally related employment, the process of consolidating the land owned, and of the poor use of soils.

> The agrarian problem has not been addressed from an integrated point of view. The agrarian policy of the country has been characterized by a special emphasis on the distribution of land, while the provision of support services appears to have been affected by a lack of human resources, materials, financing and poor co-ordination among the institutions that deal with agrarian problems.[3]

The change to the current strategy of exports for development could provide for a transition and consolidation period, that would increase agricultural productivity and rural stability. As can be seen in Table 7, the agricultural sector was among the least affected during the crisis of 1981–82. It is also the sector that has still not achieved complete recovery and appears to face more difficulties than the other sectors of the economy.

**Table 7 Annual rates of actual growth, 1980–87**

|  | 1980 | 81 | 82 | 83 | 84 | 85 | 86 | 87 |
|---|---|---|---|---|---|---|---|---|
| *GROSS NATIONAL PRODUCT* | 0.8 | −2.3 | −7.3 | 2.9 | 8.0 | 0.7 | 5.4 | 3.9 |
| Agriculture, forestry, hunting and fishing | −0.5 | 5.1 | −4.7 | 4.0 | 10.1 | −5.5 | 4.2 | −2.5 |
| Mining and minerals | 0.8 | −0.5 | −11.4 | 1.8 | 10.4 | 2.0 | 7.2 | 5.5 |
| Electricity and water | 11.8 | 7.8 | 4.2 | 20.2 | 3.2 | −7.4 | 6.1 | 6.0 |
| Construction | −1.1 | −21.7 | −31.9 | 4.7 | 23.6 | 5.6 | 2.7 | 4.4 |
| Wholesale and retail, restaurants and hotels | −3.0 | −10.6 | −11.7 | 3.2 | 11.4 | 4.6 | 9.7 | 7.1 |
| Transportation, storage and communications | 5.2 | −0.7 | −0.8 | 1.5 | 3.6 | 2.3 | 4.9 | 6.6 |
| Financial estab., insurance and other services | 2.9 | −2.0 | 0.8 | 5.6 | 5.7 | 3.9 | 6.0 | 9.5 |
| Fixed goods | 2.4 | 1.7 | 0.9 | 1.0 | 1.6 | 1.6 | 2.5 | 3.6 |
| Central government | 3.6 | 1.8 | 2.9 | 1.6 | 1.5 | 0.5 | 1.0 | 1.5 |
| Other personnel services | 0.7 | 0.3 | 3.6 | 2.0 | 3.0 | 2.8 | 2.8 | 2.0 |

Source: Central Bank of Costa Rica.

## Rural productivity and technological change[4]

The increase in agricultural production over the last 5 years has been based more on the expansion of land under cultivation than on an increase in yields. Disaggregation of data by type of crop and time period, shows that increases in productivity have not played a relevant role in agricultural growth. In fact, a tendency toward stagnation has contributed to the loss of dynamism in this sector.

However, there exist the following differences between the two periods. During 1973–80, agricultural GNP grew at about 2 per cent annually. At the same time, the land under cultivation decreased slightly, which is an indicator of an increase in productivity. From 1980 on, agricultural GNP only grew at the same rate as the amount of land under cultivation.

In part, these changes were due to difficulties in obtaining modern inputs, most of which are imported. Although the amount of fertilizer used increased at an annual rate of 12.5 per cent in the earlier period, it declined by 15.3 per cent in the later period. Similarly, pesticide use had earlier increased by 21.8 per cent and only went up 6.7 per cent after that.

Productivity changes have varied by product. Rice production grew until 1980 and then levelled off. In this decade, corn production increased 7.5 per cent per year but only due to an increase in the cultivated area. The same is true for beans, sorghum, beef, dairy cattle, and other products. The major exception to this pattern is coffee production.

The level of technology is a key factor in situation. The agricultural sector relies heavily on traditional technologies for the majority of farmers. The bulk of production is generated by a relatively small number of operations that use intensive technology. For rice, 4 per cent of the farms produce 59 per cent of the total harvest. The situation is similar for sorghum and dairy cattle. In the cultivation of corn, 98 per cent of the farms use traditional technology and generate 87 per cent of the production. Until three years ago, all of the cassava growers were traditional operations and the same was true for 99 per cent of cacao producers.

For operations that comprise more than 75 per cent of agricultural GNP, 23 per cent of the production is generated by operations that use traditional technology. About 13 per cent use intermediate technology and 64 per cent have adopted intensive technology. The majority of the producers, especially the small-scale ones, are those that use traditional technologies. The main reason for this is the differential access that producers have to modern inputs and services such as credit and insurance.

There are extensive gaps in technology in the production of export crops such as sugarcane and cacao, as well as domestically consumed ones like corn, beans, cassava, potatoes, beef, pork, and some tropical fruits. The gap has been reduced considerably in the production of bananas and especially coffee due to extensive research on cultural practices, and renewal of high quality planting stock.

233

Imbalances in the structure of production are a constraint on change in agriculture. The adoption of advanced agricultural technologies often necessitates the purchase of imported inputs since the local industry is not oriented to produce these inputs. Imports of raw materials for animal feeds, and industrial inputs and capital goods for agriculture, represent almost 20 per cent of the fob export value of the sector. Table 8 shows the import component by crop. In times of crisis it is difficult to obtain foreign currency for the corresponding imports.

Technological advances have been limited in other aspects, such as control of soil erosion, sustainable conversion of forest areas into agricultural and grazing lands and better management of forest resources.

**Table 8 The relative importance of imported inputs**

| Product | Import component of production inputs (%) |
|---|---|
| Banana | 31 |
| Coffee | 23 |
| Sugar cane | 16 |
| Cacao | 9 |
| Grains | 30 |
| Cotton | 18 |
| Tobacco | 24 |
| Livestock | 13 |
| Other agricultural products | 21 |

Source: Edgar Briceno, *The Results of the Realization of an Input-Product Mode for Costa Rica*, San Jose: Institute of Investigations in the Economic Sciences No 91, University of Costa Rica, 1986.

The public sector has tried to stimulate producers to adopt actions in the national interest. Government policies have included the direct and indirect modification of relative prices of products and inputs used in agriculture. Table 9 groups the policies used in this sector.[5] These policies produced variable results, and in other cases, critical problems continue without a solution.

## The process of technology adoption

Over the past 5 years, the process of technology adoption has been dualistic. Some crops such as bananas and coffee use modern technology while others are very backward, for example, cacao, corn, tomatoes and dairy cattle, with resulting low yields (more than 30 per cent below world averages).

For a particular crop, the adoption of technology has not been very

**Table 9 Classification of policies that affect the agricultural sector**

| Categories | Policies |
|---|---|

*Economic policies that encourage production*

| CREDIT | . Regulation of total credit through interest rates, etc.<br>. Credit from SIN for agriculture and distribution by sectors.<br>. External credit for farmers<br>. Crop insurance |
|---|---|
| FOREIGN AND<br>INTERNAL<br>COMMERCE | . Official purchase of products<br>. Minimum purchase prices<br>. Maximum sales prices<br>. Temporary storage in deposit warehouses<br>. Subsidies or equipment and inputs for production<br>. Production and/or distribution of production input<br>. Quality standards for inputs and products<br>. Establishment of services<br>. Incentives for traditional and non-traditional exports<br>. Regulation of exports through quotas<br>. Participation in international marketing agreements<br>. Negotiation of entry into preferred markets |
| FISCAL AND<br>MONETARY | . Land taxes<br>. Internal trade taxes (products and imports)<br>. Foreign trade taxes (imports and exports)<br>. Exchange restrictions |
| STATE<br>PRODUCTION | . Creation of state enterprise for production and marketing |
| DEVELOPMENT OF<br>THE PHYSICAL<br>INFRASTRUCTURE | . Construction of highways<br>. Rural electrification<br>. Rural telecommunication<br>. Irrigation and drainage works |

*Distribution of income and properties policies*

| SALARY | . Minimum Salaries |
|---|---|
| SOCIAL SECURITY | . Insurance for health, retirement and others<br>. Family policies |
| ACCESS TO<br>PROPERTY | . Agrarian reform<br>. Guarantee of land ownership |

*Policies on the organizational structure of the sector*

| LINKAGES<br>BETWEEN<br>DIFFERENT SOCIAL<br>GROUPS | *. Regulation of linkages between producers and workers and between those parties and the state* |
|---|---|
| DEVELOPMENT OF<br>PRIVATE<br>ORGANIZATIONS | *. Stimulus for the formation of agricultural and agribusiness enterprises*<br>*. Stimulus for the development of small and family enterprises*<br>*. Incentives for co-operatives*<br>*. Establishment of producer associations and chambers*<br>*. Establishment of syndicates* |

*Source: Leon et al., 1982.*

| PUBLIC SECTOR ORGANIZATION | . Functional specialization of institutions<br>. Establishment of autonomous entities<br>. Coordination between institutions<br>. Planning and programming of state activities within the sector<br>. A mechanism for producer participation in the State decision-making process |
|---|---|

Source: Leon *et al.* 1982.

uniform across producers, with the exception of coffee. Typically, the process of technology adoption follows a cycle in which the innovations are first adopted by a small innovative group that is willing to accept the risks of a new technology. Once the benefits of these innovations have been proven, a progressive group of farmers also adopts them. There is usually a group of traditional producers that lags behind.

The speed of adoption of innovations varies substantially by crop. For coffee, 80 per cent of the farmers adopted improved technologies. By contrast, the percentage is still only 10 per cent for corn producers.

The CONICIT study concluded that there was a strong relationship between the change in price of the products and the adoption of new technology. Improvements in product prices provided incentives for the use of more productive technology. Under conditions of declining or stagnant prices, few changes in technology occurred and in some cases there was a reduction in the level of technology employed. Product prices are heavily influenced by macroeconomic policies. Macroeconomic policies have favoured some factors of production over others, influencing the adoption of technology. However, the results varied from crop to crop due to specific organizational and social conditions.

As summarized in Table 10, changes in relative prices have made labour more expensive than machinery. This phenomenon is partly a consequence of the import substitution policy that exempted capital equipment from tariffs. At the same time, the relative cost of labour has increased as a result of payroll taxes and benefits. As a result, labour-saving technologies have been encouraged in some cases. For some crops, innovations have increased the use of labour.

The innovations were also land saving because intensive use of fertilizers and pesticides allowed an increase in planting density. The resulting increases in productivity allowed intensive use of land and increased its price substantially. Farm land prices also rose as a result of the expansion of cultivated area with population growth and competition with other land uses such as extensive grazing of beef cattle and urban expansion.

In general, the adopted innovations were congruent with the changes in prices. Increases in the price of labour and land induced the adoption of technologies that substitute for those factors.

Figure 2 Changes in Relative Prices of Factors of Production in Agriculture, 1950–78

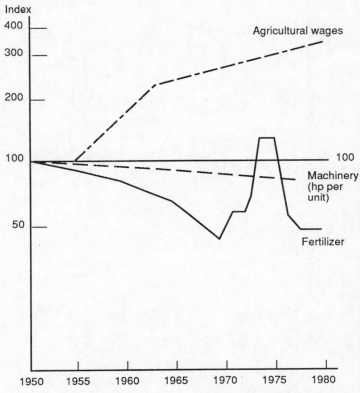

However, the process of adoption was influenced by the market structure for the product, availability of credit, human resources, and organization of production, which in some cases inhibited the entry of producers. In some cases, agreements between small and large producers or between contract growers and processors allowed barriers to technology adoption to be overcome.

## Technological change in the production of coffee.[4]

### The legal–institutional context
Macroeconomic policies cannot be viewed in isolation from the legal–institutional and organizational context of production. This institutional focus explains differences in terms of the adoption of technology across crops. John Kenneth Galbraith following Veblen and other institutionalists at the beginning of the century, emphasizes how institutions develop and

# Table 10 Relationship between technological change and change in the use selected crops and activities. (1950–1978)

| Crop or activity | Adopted innovations in the production process | Type of technology | Effect of the innovation on: | | | Observations |
|---|---|---|---|---|---|---|
| | | | Labor | Land | Capital | |
| 1. COFFEE | Fertilization | chemical | + | − | ++ | The adopted technology requires significant amounts of labour as well as capital |
| | Selection of varieties | biological | + | − | 0 | |
| | Disease control | chemical | + | 0 | + | |
| | Weed control | chemical | − | 0 | + | |
| | Increased planting density | agronomic | ++ | − | 0 | |
| | Coffee breeding systems | agronomic | ++ | 0 | 0 | |
| | Shade regulation | agronomic | + | 0 | 0 | |
| 2. BANANA | Fertilizers | chemical | + | − | ++ | The adopted technology is especially labour and capital intensive, in some cases |
| | Resistant varieties | biological | + | − | 0 | |
| | Control of 'sigatoka' | chemical | + | 0 | + | |
| | Control of nematodes | chemical | 0 | 0 | + | |
| | Weed control | chemical | − | 0 | ++ | |
| | Irrigation | mechanical | 0 | − | ++ | |
| | Drainage | mechanical | 0 | 0 | ++ | |
| | Wrapping of roots | agronomic | + | 0 | + | |
| 3. SUGAR CANE | Irrigation | mechanical | 0 | − | ++ | The adopted technology demands large increases in capital and some increases in labour |
| | Improved varieties | biological | + | − | 0 | |
| | Fertilization | chemical | + | − | ++ | |
| | Increased planting density | agronomic | + | − | 0 | |
| | Determin. of a maturity scale | chemical | 0 | − | 0 | |
| | Weed control | chemical | − | 0 | + | |
| 4. CACAO | Disease control | chemical | + | 0 | + | The recommended technology is also labour intensive |
| | Hybrid development | biological | + | − | 0 | |
| | Renovation systems | agronomic | + | − | + | |

| Crop or activity | Adopted innovations in the production process | Type of technology | Effect of the innovation on: Labor | Land | Capital | Observations |
|---|---|---|---|---|---|---|
| 5. RICE | Improved varieties | biological | + | – | 0 | Adopted technology is highly capital intensive |
| | Mechanization of production | mechanical | – – | 0 | ++ | |
| | Fertilization | chemical | + | – | ++ | |
| | Disease control | chemical/biological | 0 | 0 | + | |
| 6. CORN | Introduction of hybrids | biological | + | – | 0 | Adopted technology still is labour-intensive among the majority of producers. A small group have mechanized production and capital intensive technology |
| | Improved varieties | biological | + | – | 0 | |
| | Increased planting density | agronomic | + | – | 0 | |
| | Fertilization | chemical | + | – | ++ | |
| | Pest control | chemical | + | 0 | + | |
| 7. BEAN | Vegetative planting | agronomic | + | – | 0 | Adopted technology is for the most part traditional (land extensive). Some producers use labour-intensive technology. A few others have begun to use capital-intensive technology |
| | Selection of varieties (MC) | biological | + | 0 | 0 | |
| | Disease control (MC) | chemical | + | 0 | + | |
| | Weed control (MC) | chemical | – | 0 | + | |
| | Controlled irrigation (MC)/(PN) | mechanical | 0 | 0 | ++ | |
| | Fertilization | chemical | + | 0 | ++ | |
| 8. POTATO | Improved varieties | biological | + | – | 0 | Adopted technology is capital-intensive |
| | Fertilization | chemical | + | – | ++ | |
| | Pest control | chemical | + | 0 | ++ | |
| | Production of improved seed | agronomic | 0 | 0 | + | |
| 9. AFRICAN PALM | Introduction of hybrids | biological | + | – | 0 | Adopted technology increases the demand for labour |
| | Fertilization | chemical | + | – | ++ | |

239

implement economic policies. According to this view, even the market itself is an institution created by long-term agreements arising out of a particular historical and social structure. In the case of coffee, the organizations and groups participating in this process include small- and large-scale farmers, workers, consumers, roasters, exporters, and the Coffee Institute – ICAFE.

In this model, the government represents a stabilizing and regulating factor for the economic behaviour of the other agents. The rules and criteria defined by law establish relatively equitable relationships among those agents and modify the distribution of income and demand. However, the price of coffee is determined in international markets. At a certain international price level for a determined harvest, the distribution of the revenues is based on rules setting fixed percentages for the agents in charge of the harvest, the processing and marketing, and a variable proportion for the government, which varies inversely to the price variations. The rest goes to the farmer, normally, 70 per cent or more of the world price.

The function of the state in this activity derives from its regulatory and advisory roles, including the protection of the interests of various groups, through the development of technologies, financing of processing and marketing and risk sharing.

In 1933, three laws were promulgated, creating the predecessor organization to ICAFE and aiming at ensuring equitable relations among the various agents. After more than five decades, the system of relation-ships between the government, farmers, producers, processors and exporters has been well established.

The institutional context includes the following institutions:

o ICAFE, which monitors implementation of coffee regulations;
o The Ministry of Agriculture, responsible for research and extension work;
o The Ministry of Economy and Trade, charged with setting the price for domestic consumption;
o The National Banking System, which finances investments in production, processing, and marketing; and
o The University of Costa Rica's Centre for Agronomic Research, which supports coffee research.

In the private sector, the farmers are organized by the National Chamber of Coffee Producers and local co-operatives, which in turn make up the Federation of Co-operatives. The co-operatives manage the production of their members, run some processing plants and even do export marketing. Co-operatives process a little less than half of the total national production of coffee (Table 11).

**Table 11 Coffee processed by Cooperatives according to size of harvest*/year of harvest**/comparison with national production**

| Year harvested | Small | % | Medium | % | Large | % | Total production of co-operative sector | Total national production | % Participation co-operative sector |
|---|---|---|---|---|---|---|---|---|---|
| 1982–83 | 77,306 | 3.5 | 172,848 | 7.6 | 2,015,129 | 88.9 | 2,265,283 | 5,463,503 | 41.5 |
| 1983–84 | 73,544 | 3.2 | 247,242 | 10.7 | 1,984,096 | 86.1 | 2,304,912 | 5,214,149 | 44.2 |
| 1984–85 | 112,053 | 3.8 | 81,732 | 2.7 | 2,805,975 | 93.5 | 2,999,760 | 6,719,550 | 44.6 |
| 1985–86 | 97,216 | 5.1 | 328,064 | 17.4 | 1,464,363 | 77.5 | 1,899,643 | 4,194,006 | 45.0 |
| 1986–87 | 33,558 | 1.2 | 190,493 | 6.6 | 2,656,724 | 92.2 | 2,882,775 | 6,462,786 | 44.6 |
| 1987–88 | 74,912 | 2.8 | 222,790 | 8.5 | 2,384,931 | 88.7 | 2,688,633 | 6,370,958 | 42.6 |

Note: * Size      Capacity (Double Hectolitre)
      Small      Less than 23,000
      Medium   23,0001–50,000
      Large      Larger than 50,000
     ** From April 1 to March 31

Source: Developed using information from the Coffee Institute (ICAFE) as a base.

### The technological change in coffee production

Technological change in coffee production has evolved over the last four decades.

In 1948, the average production was less than 2,580 kg per hectare. The area of land planted to coffee was frozen at 85,000 hectares in 1963, and the yield rose to 5,126 kg per hectare, while the international price stabilized at US $0.80 per kg of dry coffee at the railroad side. Four distinct periods can be identified in this history:

1. Relative stagnation of yields and cultivated areas prior to 1948;
2. Growth in both yields and cultivated areas between 1948 and 1962;
3. Continued growth in yields coupled with a freeze in the land under cultivation between 1963 and 1972 following an International Agreement; and
4. Growth in yields and planted areas from 1973 to the present despite significant fluctuations in market prices.

In the first phase, the farmers used both land and labour extensively. About 80 per cent of the coffee planted was the 'Typica' variety, which was set out in relatively low densities of 800 to 1,500 plants per hectare. By the end of the fourth phase, the predominant technology became labour- and land-intensive, complemented by the use of agrichemicals and improved crop management. Selected varieties have been planted in higher densities of up to 3,200 plants per hectare under integrated plantation management. Other changes include better means of disease treatment and greater exposure to sunlight. As a result, high yields have been achieved.

These technological changes occurred continually over the second, third, and fourth phases. At the beginning of the second phase, a general revision of the production technology took place, through the efforts of the Ministry of Agriculture, the InterAmerican Technical Service for Co-operation in Agriculture (STICA), the Inter-American Institute for Agricultural Science (IICA) and the National Production Council of Costa Rica.

In the second phase, new varieties such as the Tico Hybrid were planted. Also, new pruning systems, higher planting densities and a better use of chemical fertilizers were promoted. The third phase was characterized by a refinement of technological practices and greater diffusion of the technology by the Ministry of Agriculture and the Coffee Department. In this phase, the variety Caturra was promoted because of its compact growth characteristic, which allowed further intensification of the planting density. Also, the results of a research programme on the use of herbicides and insecticides were disseminated.

In the fourth phase, the work of the Ministry of Agriculture's Coffee Department was expanded. The Catuai and Caturra varieties became more predominant with substantial decreases in the Typica variety. Table 12 shows the evolution of production, area under cultivation, and yields.

242

**Table 12 Comparison of the increase in area planted and the amount of coffee produced**

| Harvest Period | Total harvest in DDH* | Area planted in hectares | Yield DDH/ha. | % Increase in area | % Increase in production |
|---|---|---|---|---|---|
| 1950–51** | 384,533 | 48,837 | 7.87 | —— | —— |
| 1955–56 | 498,243 | 57,543 | 8.66 | 17.83 | 29.57 |
| 1960–61 | 1,147,434 | 63,533 | 18.06 | 30.09 | 198.47 |
| 1965–66 | 1,221,868 | 69,523 | 17.58 | 42.36 | 217.75 |
| 1970–71 | 1,559,988 | 75,513 | 20.66 | 54.62 | 305.68 |
| 1975–76 | 1,700,178 | 83,406 | 20.38 | 70.78 | 342.14 |
| 1980–81 | 2,624,176 | 89,306 | 20.39 | 82.87 | 582.43 |
| 1984–85*** | 3,360,266 | 95,000 | 35.37 | 94.52 | 773.86 |
| 1985–86 | 2,096,920 | 110,000 | 19.06 | 125.24 | 445.32 |
| 1986–87 | 3,225,538 | 110,000 | 29.32 | 125.24 | 738.82 |

&ast; Fanega is a measure of capacity equal to 1.6 bushels or 1.59 acres
&ast;&ast; Harvest year 1950–51 was the initial period for the cultivation research
&ast;&ast;&ast; Harvest for 1984–85 was highest in national history.
Source: *La Nacion*, 26 July 1988

## The process of technological diffusion

The availability and cost of new inputs are important factors in the rate of transformation of traditional agriculture.[7,8] Where these inputs are distributed at low prices, producers have a greater incentive to accept them, although the inputs might not be used efficiently if relative prices become too distorted.

However, other factors affecting the diffusion of technology include the mechanisms for communication with farmers and the characteristics of local leadership and channels for information within the community. The accessibility of appropriate technology depends on the supporting infrastructure (access to credit, supply of new inputs, information on new varieties adapted to the region, etc). The conditions under which the farmers receive the information as well as their motivation and socio-cultural values affect decisions on technology use.

In short, the rate of diffusion depends on the accessibility of the information to the producer and the extent of socio-cultural resistance to adoption of the information. However, the simplicity of this focus on communicating available technical knowledge has been questioned. Also needed is a means of expanding participation in production and establishing more equitable arrangements for the distribution of the benefits of the increases in productivity.[9]

This more integrated focus is a departure from the assumption that technology is a social product and that innovations occur within determined groups of clients, with their own values and available resources. Thus, the social organization and legal/institutional framework are variables that must be understood in the relationship between agricultural technology and development. Sectoral policies are filtered through this network of social agreements, client–patron relationships and organizations involved in research, extension and production.

Chacon *et al*, reached the following conclusions about technological change in two coffee producing communities:

○ Producers who are associated with groups are more innovative than those that work independently;
○ The existence of producer associations that act as lobbying groups facilitates the process of technological change; and
○ Producer associations also put pressure on the government to facilitate dissemination of technologies.

Coffee producer co-operatives played a definite role in technology diffusion and most farmers saw this as an important reason for joining a co-operative. Also, the complementary services provided by co-operatives help explain the higher level of technology used by associated producers than the independent ones. Community studies have shown the impact of the co-operatives as a means of diffusing technologies recommended by the Ministry of Agriculture.

Chapman *et al*. noted that coffee production in the region has experienced an important technological change, especially if one considers the perennial nature of the crop which makes it difficult to adopt new techniques, as well as the inappropriate ecological conditions that it is exposed to. Therefore, it makes more sense to attribute this development to the existence of the following:

○ Public policies that fixed the distribution of the income from the product to favour the producers;
○ Appropriate marketing and finance channels;
○ Technologies within reach of the small producers.

This group of factors made coffee production very profitable and provided incentives for the adoption of technology and the expansion of the area planted.[10]

These special characteristics of coffee do not hold true for other products such as corn and beans even in the same area. Public policies have kept prices low for basic food crops for domestic consumption. Consequently, technologies suited to the economic and ecological conditions in the region have not been developed. Even the organization needed to facilitate the diffusion of technologies for these crops and social agreements between producers and marketers are unavailable.

## Conclusions.

### Lessons about technological change in coffee production

The key to successful technological change in coffee production and an equitable distribution of the benefits is due to public policies. Some policies have a direct effect on the research and extension activities for coffee growing and processing. Research and extension programmes achieved a critical mass of experts working on this crop, and focused on information retrieval and development. Channels of diffusion for this information included government agencies and co-operatives.

Indirect policies of the government supported the development of public institutions charged with the generation and diffusion of technologies for coffee production, and providing farmers with financing and more profitable production inputs. The government also promoted a macro-policy environment that encouraged the improvement of coffee production. It regulated the economic participation of farmers, processors and marketers to enable greater harmony among these groups. Another important factor was the availability of a public financing system for coffee production from harvest to export. Credit programmes allowed the introduction of new higher cost technologies. Tax policies were flexible, since part of the surplus was transferred to the state in years when the price was good. Yet, taxes did not reduce the minimum return to the producer in periods of low prices.

From 1962 to 1973, national limits on the area of coffee planted were established in accordance with the International Coffee Agreement which promoted increases in yield as a result of higher product prices. This opportunity required the rapid adoption of new technology to generate surpluses in production that could be sold to countries that did not subscribe to the agreement.

On the other hand, the emphasis on carrying out on-farm trials allowed producers to evaluate the feasibility of the recommended technology on-site. Finally, it is important to remember that those policies operate within the general context of national development and government price stabilization activities for coffee that minimize price fluctuations in years of excess supply or shortages in production.

The case of coffee illustrates the potential of programmes that concentrate on technological change to induce economic growth. This case also shows that each activity demands certain organizational systems compatible with the local social, political and economic conditions. The diffusion of technology has major impacts on the distribution of income, degree of economic democracy and social harmony.

## Macro-policies, micro-policies and technological change

Technological change in the agricultural sector can be promoted by crop-specific policies for the country as a whole or particular regions, given the economic context. The relationship among interest groups is an integral part of the dynamics of technological change.[6] Some policies are more closely associated with particular components of the system than others. Science and technology policies influence the components of demand in an important way and are developed and implemented by a relatively small number of specialized institutions in the public sector. While sectoral policies are important, other types of policies also affect decisions on technology use.

Macroeconomic policies strongly affect producers' interests. These include policies on prices, taxes, credit, distribution of land, and highway construction. Moreover, the application of macro-policies can promote changes in the production technology used and the benefits to producers.

The explicit as well as the implicit policies that have an effect on scientific and technological development are directed toward a group of active and passive agents (organized groups of producers, individual producers, agro-industry entrepreneurs, officials from public institutions, university professors and researchers, etc.). At the same time, these agents respond to stimuli from certain policies or the omission of such policies. Their response is determined not only by the policies themselves but also by the socioeconomic conditions within which they act. These contextual aspects are important to consider in policy analysis, since the success or failure of these policies will depend on whether the policy formulators have adequately foreseen such conditions.

Last, it is important that a policy for technological change not be self-determined but function within a strategy for general development that the country designs for its advancement. Therefore, the general focus, priorities, and selected instruments of the development strategy are the factors that will determine the form in which technological change and increases in productivity will be realized.

# The FUNDAP/Momostenango Project: A Strategy for Development Promoted by the Private Sector (The Guatemala Case)

## ROBERTO GUTIERREZ

### Introduction

The purpose of this paper is to analyse thoroughly how institutional and macroeconomic polices have affected rural development in a case study in Guatemala. From this knowledge base, changes in institutional and macroeconomic policies could be proposed to create conditions that can provide the most benefits for rural areas. The case study presented here is of the Momostenango project. This project was started in January 1986 by the Foundation for the Integral Development of Socioeconomic Programmes (FUNDAP) with financial support from the members of the Foundation, the US Agency for International Development (USAID), and Appropriate Technology International (ATI). The project's purpose is to assist sheep farmers, weavers and wool product vendors in the Western Highlands of Guatemala. So far, over 60,000 sheep farmers have received assistance and over 1,200 families involved in wool processing and weaving have received financial or technical assistance.

To provide an understanding of the context, this paper begins by discussing rural Guatemalan society as a whole and in the project area. A systems approach is taken to examine the various components of the Momostenango project. The results obtained to date are analysed, focusing on the relationships among macro-policies, institutional policies and the problems of rural development in the area.

### National frame of reference

#### Poverty in rural Guatemalan society
The socioeconomic crisis that has affected the whole Latin American region has reinforced the poverty of the majority of the Guatemalan

FRANCISCO ROBERTO GUTIERREZ MARTINEZ is Regional Director of the Foundation for the Integral Development of Socioeconomic Programmes (FUNDAP) in Guatemala. Mr Gutierrez is a chemical engineer who is also the general manager of a commercial enterprise and director of five businesses.

population. Extreme poverty in Guatemala is primarily a problem of rural areas and 80 per cent of the indigenous population lives in the rural zone. The portions of the population most subject to poverty are the 'campesino' (rural peasant) sector and unskilled agricultural workers. Some 250,000 families living on small farms of less than 6.9 hectares and 200,000 families of unskilled paid agricultural workers make up the bulk of households living in poverty. In fact, 86 per cent of the poorest families of the country who earn a total annual income of less than $1,200 live in rural areas. There is a pronounced disparity between urban and rural incomes. The average income of urban families is 2.7 times that of rural area families and in Guatemala City the average income is four times higher than incomes in rural areas.

It can be difficult to estimate incomes in rural areas because the survival strategy of the peasant family is based on a combination of various economic activities. Usually, poor rural families raise animals and crops, earn some wages off the farm, are involved in handcraft production, do their own construction, and look for potential commercial activities and services to supplement their incomes. This is especially true for families with very small land holdings.

However, agricultural work predominates in rural areas. More than half of the economically active population directly depends on the agricultural sector as their primary source of income. Although the relative importance of securing a job in agriculture continues to decrease, Guatemala still has a strong focus on agriculture.

A large percentage of the families that depend on agriculture live in poverty. The National Survey of Income and Expenses (1980–81) defined poverty in terms of the income needed to provide basic human requirements. By this definition, the survey found that 83 per cent of the rural population is poor. Half of the population which earns an insufficient income to meet basic needs cannot fulfil minimum recommended dietary requirements.

Definitions of poverty can be debated, and the income threshold used in this survey is relatively high. Also, surveys often underestimate income because some respondents underreport their earnings and produce some of their own food for basic subsistence. Nevertheless, there is no question that poverty in the rural Guatemalan areas is extensive. Other social indicators in education, health and housing reinforce the diagnosis that a large majority of the rural population lives in an extremely precarious situation. Another study of the income distribution in rural areas corroborates this finding. For the year 1970, the Secretariat of Economic Planning (SGNPE) estimated that 60 per cent of rural families earned an income of less than $400. Only 10 per cent of the families had an annual income greater than $1,000, which could satisfy basic needs.

## Agriculture

Agriculture in Guatemala is heterogeneous. Productive units of different sizes and technologies coexist, resulting in a large disparity between productivity and the capital density per person. Large-scale farms may have 44 or more hectares and may be operated as multifamily businesses. Small farmers own or work on less than 6.9 hectares of land. There is a large correspondence between the production structure and the existence of these socioeconomic strata. Crops and livestock geared toward export are concentrated in the large- and medium-sized farms, while the small farmers generally produce for the local market. Almost all of the cotton crop and 75 per cent of the coffee and sugar production are carried out on farms larger than 44 hectares. On the other hand, around 65 per cent of corn production and more than 50 per cent of bean production takes place on small farms.

Consequently, the medium- and large-scale farms have benefited the most from expansion policies for export-oriented crops. These policies have stimulated growth of the agricultural sector. Yet, small-scale farms do not have the capacity to make the necessary investments for introducing new crops or upgrading technologies for traditional farm products. Larger operations have greater access to quality land and capital, and can afford larger risks.

Analysis of the use of capital goods and materials shows a significant change in farming technology for non-traditional crops. However, the basic characteristic of this rapid expansion in production has been a marked inequality in results by size of farm and type of production. In 1980, 70 per cent of the large farms regularly used chemical fertilizers. However, cotton farms absorbed most of this input. The difference in input use shows up in the variation in yields. In 1964, multi-family farm businesses had a 40 per cent higher corn yield and 100 per cent higher coffee yield in comparison with the peasant farms. The difference is even greater in the value of production per hectare because the income generated from one hectare of coffee or cotton is over nine or ten times, respectively, that from one hectare of corn.

Structural heterogeneity is also evident at the regional level. The areas of greatest relative development produce most of the export crops. For example, the South Coast only covers 13 per cent of the national land area, but contributes more than 40 per cent of the total value of farm production. In this region, more than three-quarters of the agricultural production is exported.

In other regions, food production for the domestic market has grown slowly. For example, agriculture in the Western Highlands is characterized by production of basic grains on small farms. The region's production has grown at the same rate as the demographic expansion. One third of the population economically active in agriculture is concentrated in the

249

Highlands, although it only has 18 per cent of the total national land area for agriculture and forestry. Poverty has plagued the peasant population in this mountainous zone for centuries. Today, the average income of the families in this region is only two-thirds of that of rural families in the South Coast and only 18 per cent of the average for urban families. In the 1970s, the percentage of rural families classified as 'poor' residing in this region increased to 40 per cent.

Changes in the agricultural sector have created an economic barrier that prevented the peasants from modernizing. Public investment in infrastructure and the expansion of more profitable crops have increased land values, preventing tenant farmers from being able to save enough money to buy land. Without land for collateral, families cannot usually obtain agricultural credit. In addition, the increased minimum capital required to develop a viable business in cotton, sugarcane or livestock breeding has eliminated these possibilities for the small-scale farmer.

Another important point is that the chronic scarcity of resources makes it impossible for campesinos to have enough of a reserve in money or in goods, that would let them grow riskier high-valued crops. The mere task of producing exclusively for sale is a difficult task to assume due to marketing difficulties and price instability. Since the risk grows as a function of investment and since more profitable crops require relatively higher levels of training and material costs, small farms are precluded from these opportunities.

In conclusion, economic and social barriers that impede access to an adequate area of land, lack of access to improved inputs, transportation difficulties, problems in conservation or marketing of perishable products and lack of credit are barriers to the introduction of technological changes or more profitable crops. Thus, most rural families are motivated by the undeniable need to assure subsistence nourishment by producing the traditional food staples.

Agricultural growth in Guatemala has come from the modern capitalized sector. Despite its high productivity, it only absorbs a relatively small quantity of the available work force. About 30 per cent of the agricultural work force is securely employed on farms dedicated to export crops. The bulk of rural labour remains underutilized on the small farms producing traditional crops at low productivity. Only a small fraction of the rural labour force has the option of obtaining temporary work during harvest season. Consequently, the surplus of labour keeps agricultural salaries relatively low.

Export agricultural businesses do not offer many full-time year-round jobs. Most of the seasonal agricultural unemployment is transferred from the modern sector to the peasant sector, where scarce resources result in narrow production margins.

Not surprisingly, the Survey of Incomes found that 30 per cent of the labour force in rural areas in 1980–81 was underemployed, the equivalent of more than 300,000 workers in 1980–81. Given that the seasonal changes for agricultural activities are more profound than for rural activities as a whole, the instability in employment is even greater for farm workers.

Finally, it is interesting to emphasize the consequences that the marked seasonal changes have on the agricultural work force. The expansion and increased technological sophistication of export crop production has heightened the seasonal variations in labour requirements. Often, the production from small farms or the wages obtained in seasonal work on large farms during the harvest months by themselves cannot assure subsistence for the farmer and his dependents. Both sources of income are needed.

## Handcrafts

There is relatively little published literature on self-employment and rural incomes in Guatemala. However, it is known that the rural people often take up other economic activities to supplement agricultural incomes. Handcrafts constitute a very important source of this income. Either as a supplementary or principal activity, handcraft production is a source of income for 17.7 per cent of the economically productive population. In 1986, this represented employment for 449,528 artisans. In that year, the value of artisanal production amounted to 4.3 per cent of the Gross Domestic Product (GDP).

There are approximately 60,080 artisan workshops throughout the country. In 1986, 15,826 artisan workshops were identified in the Western Highlands and a large percentage of them were operated by the indigenous population.

During the period 1960–75, employment in the artisanal sector grew by an average of 3.52 per cent per year while total employment only increased 2.38 per cent per year. This reflects the dynamic contribution of the artisanal sector to employment generation. In the early 1980s, the absorption of labour by the artisanal sector decreased, which meant lower employment generation rates compared to the preceding period. However, in recent years, this sector picked up once again.

Guatemalan handcrafts have roots in the folklore of pre-Columbian culture. Popular crafts include textiles, weaving, embroidery, ceramics, basketry and rope products. This work is done in small workshops in rural zones or cities in the interior of the country. Much of the production is for the domestic market. The indigenous population is also an important consumer for these products. Indian women still wear the customary regional outfits made out of embroidered cloth produced by the handcraft industry. Because of this tradition, these sleeveless blouses and skirts ('guipiles' and 'cortes' in Spanish) have a potential market of about 1.5 m Guatemalan women.

251

In addition, the mestizo population of the urban centres also buys decorative and utilitarian artisanal products marketed through intermediaries. Guatemalan handcrafts also accounted for 2.1 per cent of the total non-traditional exports in 1985, rising to 3.1 per cent in 1987. Foreign sales of typical articles totalled Q2,195,000 (1 US$ = 2.5 quetzales).

Development of this sector is currently hindered by several factors. Artisanal products are being displaced by cheaper subsitutes, for example plastic pots instead of ceramic ones and industrial textiles for handmade items. Also, the lack of standardization among the artisanal products and the limitations of individual production make it difficult to market the products. Institutional help to the artisans has been minimal for technical assistance and credit is only offered to a very limited number of producers. The artisans have little opportunity to capitalize and increase their output or upgrade their production technology. The sector is unorganized and government does not have adequate policies for its development. Yet, this neglected sector has a significant potential to generate employment and help the peasant economy.

## Development policies

In the last three decades, various Guatemalan governments have used macroeconomic and institutional policies to promote general economic growth and rural development. However, these policies have not had a significant impact and have not overcome the serious problems of the rural population. Macroeconomic policies have imposed a bias on the use of factors of production, emphasizing the production of agricultural export products that are capital intensive. The emphasis on promotion of traditional exports has been unable to satisfy the need to generate employment and income in rural areas, even in periods of greatest expansion.

The Ministry of Agriculture and various decentralized institutions that provide research, technical assistance, credit and marketing services have targeted the small- and medium-scale farmer in special development programmes. However, the level of assistance has not been enough to improve the rural sector's productivity. Capital, skilled labour, and entrepreneurial ability are particularly scarce in rural areas, but there is an abundance of low-cost, unskilled labour.

The structure of agricultural production has increased the gap between the commercial export sector and the weaker traditional sector. The traditional sector has not been able to obtain the same level of technology as the modern agricultural sector. Furthermore, there exists a large gap between the traditional sector and the modern sector in credit availability, marketing of services and final products. Small-scale farmers do not have easy access to conventional credit for lack of financial guarantees or collateral. They are forced to obtain small amounts of working capital from large producers, processors and marketers at high cost, often repaid through their products.

In summary, the agricultural sector policies as a whole have not encouraged the modification of the sector's structure and therefore have been unable to significantly alleviate the underdevelopment of rural areas.

## Industrial policies

Beginning in 1960, Guatemala's industrial policy emphasized import substitution and integration through the Central American Common Market. The rationale for this policy was to create a larger market for manufactured articles to stimulate industrial development of the country. The government promoted industrial development through protectionist tariffs, controls, tax policies, credit policies, subsidies for production of food, certain materials and raw materials, and foreign exchange controls designed to permit the importation of capital equipment and inputs for industrial expansion. The commercial sector played an important complementary role in these policies.

The import substitution policy began with the production of consumer goods and later focused on the manufacturing of luxury items. This strategy was dependent on imported machinery and, to a lesser extent, on financial resources from abroad. The industrial development policy showed considerable success in increasing production and exports until the beginning of the 1970s. Reasons for its decline include external factors such as the increase in oil prices and trade protectionism of industrialized countries. The industrial policy had little positive impact on artisanal production. Given the differences in productivity, availability of capital, technology and other factors, the artisanal producers were clearly at a disadvantage compared to the industrial producers. Consequently, the industrial policy did not directly benefit the bulk of the rural population.

## Summary

1. The poverty problem in Guatemala is more acutely seen in the rural areas, where the bulk of the peasant population lives.
2. Agriculture is the principal means of sustenance for the rural people and small-scale farm production is oriented toward the supply of basic food staples, using low-level technology that only yields a low income for the farmers. The modern agricultural export sector does not generate enough employment to provide jobs for the landless poor and seasonal migrants.
3. To assure their livelihoods, the rural inhabitants have to undertake economic activities to supplement their agricultural income. Handcraft production is one of the most important activities for rural people, but governmental policies have ignored this sector.
4. The macroeconomic policies applied by different governments over the

253

last 30 years have not been able to improve the problems of poverty and underdevelopment in the rural areas.

5. The policies of industrial development have benefited the large-scale and urban industrial sector, but have not helped the handcraft sector much.

## Momostenango case study

### General characteristics

The municipality of Momostenango is located in the department of Totonicapan in Western Guatemala. It is situated in a rugged mountainous zone that has little available arable land. About 98 per cent of the population is from indigenous groups. Approximately 89 per cent of the population lives in rural areas and 11 per cent in urban areas. In 1985, there were 59,843 inhabitants in the 305 km$^2$ area of the municipality. This high population density puts a lot of pressure on the land resources.

Momostenango is connected to two important centres, which are located relatively close by – the departmental capital of Totonicapan is 37 km away, and the departmental capital of Quetzaltenango, the most important city in the western region, is 38 km away.

### Economic activities

Historically, the Momostenango people have dedicated themselves to business and artisanal activities as principal sources of work, although these activities are not among their traditional customs. This is due to the fact that agricultural prospects are not good because of the limited availability of agricultural land and the small average size of the land parcels. Typically small farms are less than 0.2 hectares and rely on technologies of low productivity for the production of the traditional crops such as corn, wheat, kidney beans and lima beans. Thus, small farm yields and incomes are low.

A study by the University of San Carlos in 1978 has shown that 43 per cent of the economically active population in the area was dedicated to business. Of this group, 71 per cent are rural inhabitants. About 27 per cent of the economically active group is involved in handcraft production and 26 per cent in agriculture. This study refutes the common belief that the villages of the highlands rely mainly on agriculture for their sustenance. Second, it implies that the small farm has atomized to such an extent that the bulk of the population has been displaced to other activities. Third, the fertility of the land has been depleted, resulting in low yields. Of the commercial activities that take place in Momostenango, 11 per cent of the products are of local origin and 89 per cent of the products are produced outside of the municipality. The commercial sector exerts a strong influence on consumers to buy certain types of product generated by the industrial sector.

The artisanal sector is also the most important in the value of annual production in the area, contributing 65 per cent of the gross value of production. Weaving is the most important activity among the handcrafts with 36 per cent of the gross production value. About 89 per cent of the value of woven products is for ponchos, 9 per cent for blankets, and the remaining 2 per cent is distributed among bags, vests, woollen shawls and scarves.

The artisanal sector contributes 32 per cent of the value of local commerce. In a positive trend, the production is mostly marketed outside of the municipality to markets in the interior of the country. Some is exported to other countries, principally in Central America. However, the artisanal sector is highly dependent on foreign sources of raw materials, dyes and even wool, despite a tradition of sheep production in Guatemala.

### Sheep development

Sheep production in Guatemala began during the period of Spanish Colonization. The Spanish brought over the White Castillian and Black Castillian breeds which were primarily used for milk production. Today, one can find Creole sheep in the highlands with some characteristerics of their ancestors. However, due to inadequate nutrition and care, these sheep are not good producers of milk.

The sheep production zone in Guatemala is relatively small, occupying less than 2 per cent of the total land area. It is located on the highest parts of two major mountain ranges, the Sierra Madre and the Sierra de los Cuchematanes. This zone, considered marginal for agriculture, has an altitude of 2,700 to 4,000 m.

Until a few years ago, a large part of the sheep production zone consisted of extensive areas of communal and municipal land. Gradually, the land has been divided into family-owned lots. The area has become so segmented that it is now difficult to find economic agricultural activity there.

The sheep population in Guatemala totals more than 600,000 head. An average flock consists of 15 sheep. Some 40,000 families own sheep for wool production, with an average of five people per household at least partially dependent on this activity. Sheep producers obtain an average yield of two pounds per year of wool per head, which is low. Another product is the meat, which constitutes an important source of animal protein in the highlands. The manure is used as fertilizer for subsistence crops. The hide is used for leather. The ownership of sheep can also be considered the only method for savings available to the peasants of this zone to cover emergencies. There are few other productive alternatives for peasants living in this zone.

However, in the last few decades, sheep production has decreased due to the expansion of land in subsistence crops. Demographic pressures have forced the planting of much of the plains, steppes and pasture in corn and beans. This gradual expansion of subsistence agriculture has pressured the sheep farmers to go to higher elevations, resulting in a large decrease in sheep production. Business and trade activities have also contributed to the decline in wool production by absorbing some of the most productive members of the labour force. Since sheep farmers were not adequately organized, efforts had not been made to improve their productivity through technical assistance programmes, introduction of improved genetic stock, new pasture techniques, pasture improvement, or animal health services programmes.

In Momostenango cattle only comprise 2 per cent of total annual livestock production, because sheep production predominates. The local sheep provide 22 per cent of the wool required by weavers in the municipality. Of all the wool that is produced in the country, 40 per cent is used in Momostenango, 40 per cent by the textile industry of Quetzaltenango and 20 per cent by the sheep farmers themselves. The wool produced in Momostenango is used to make ponchos, blankets, jackets and other manufactured articles. In fact, the wool handcraft industry in the municipality is more important than the local sheep production as a source of income.

## Wool technology

The technology used in processing the rough wool into the finished products developed from colonial techniques was adapted by the Momostenango weavers. The only major changes in the techniques over the last few decades have been the substitution of manufactured soaps for locally produced ones and chemical colourants for vegetable dyes. The process can be categorized into washing, pre-weaving, and weaving techniques.

### Washing techniques

After the wool is removed from the sheep, it is cleaned by washing and carding. Washing removes the dirt and grease from the wool. Washing is done in cold water from flowing rivers using soaps and detergents.

Carding consists of untangling, smoothing and loosening the fibres, guiding and cleaning them of the foreign material and converting it to textile fibre. Carding is done with a type of thistle known as 'cardo'.

### Pre-weaving phases

Spinning converts the pads or tufts of wool prepared in the carder into yarn. This is accomplished with a spinner known as a 'Batz Ibal', in the Quiche language. The yarn is wound into balls. Another technique of spinning uses a spindle. This technique is mainly done by shepherds as they tend their flocks.

Skeining consists of joining the twisted yarn.

Until recently, the wool was treated with natural dyes, which are now being replaced with chemical dyes. Dyeing is carried out in large clay jars and some dyes are heated before use.

Warping consists of systematically winding the yarn. In Momostenango, two forms of warping are used, the traditional and an upgraded traditional method.

## Weaving

Weaving is done on artisanal pedal or foot looms. These looms have not undergone substantial changes since their introduction. Small looms are usually one metre high and large ones are twice that size. The Momostenango weavers use three different techniques: 'pepenado', wooden looms with shuttles, and blanket knotting.

'Pepenado' refers to an old type of weaving done completely by hand, without a shuttle. This technique is common among the weavers who use traditional waist looms or looms of little sticks. The Momostenango weavers do pedal weaving using the fingers from both hands.

The most common weaving technique in the area uses a wooden shuttle. The woof of the fabric is placed over the base of the loom and the yarn is carried horizontally by a shuttle. Blanket knotting is done by hand.

The weavers use a variety of designs strongly influenced by the culture of the Quiches. The traditional designs in Momostenango include volcanoes, lightning, snakes, the moon, the sun, deer and quetzals. Other common designs are codes and ornaments from Mayan symbols. The weavers can also reproduce whatever designs are presented to them. Each weaving workshop has its own warping machine, wheel, yarn spool, skein stand and other accessories.

### Marketing

The Momostenango market is a very important centre for wool from other areas. The intermediaries mostly inhabitants of Momostenango, buy wool in the producing areas, wash it and then transport it to the market. Wool is sold to spinners and weavers in balls of 80 ounces or more, in the natural colours of white, black and grey. The prices range between quetzales 12.50 to 13.50. Wool is sold in two grades: the 'fine' and the cheaper 'ordinary' quality.

Usually a weaver buys enough wool at one time to last him a week. Weavers do not purchase larger quantities due to the lack of financing. Working capital for the wool business is rarely kept separate from the family's own finances.

Woven articles are sold in the local market or in the artisans' own

257

workshops. The best business days are Sunday and Monday, the local market days. About 90 per cent of the local production is marketed in Momostenango and the rest along the roadside in neighbouring villages. The wool market is picturesque because of the variety of colours used in the ponchos. Vendors gather in two lines in front of the municipal gate, one at each side of the street. There, buyers stock up at wholesale prices. Buyers generally are middlemen who buy at least three to five articles at a time. Direct contact with the artisan in the workshop assures the buyers of the quality and variety in the work. Typically the middlemen own stands in the capital, at tourist sites, or in the main cities.

Exporters also buy the Momostenango products either directly from the artisan producers or through intermediaries. The major export destination is Central America but some are also sold in the USA and Europe.

The market for woollen handcrafts is characterized by competition among producers. The intermediaries always apply pressure to lower prices. Sometimes, artisans accept lower prices because they need immediate cash for the family or working capital. Most artisans do not have access to credit or enough savings to increase production or adopt more productive technologies. The artisans are unaware of prices in different markets, and how the export market functions.

## Summary
The topographic characteristerics, high population density and traditional customs make handcraft production and trade rather than agriculture the principal economic activity of Momostenango. This municipality is the centre for artisanal production of wool products in Guatemala. Sheep farming takes place in areas where the altitude is high and the terrain and soils are marginal for agriculture.

Momostenango is the most important market for raw wool produced for domestic consumption. It is also a key market for finished wool products for both the national demand and export markets. The technology used in producing the artisanal wool products is rudimentary and has undergone little change. Also the structure of production and marketing put small-scale producers at a disadvantage.


## The Fundap/Momostenango Project

### Project description
To help solve the problems of rural areas, Guatemalan businessmen formed a foundation. This foundation, FUNDAP, sponsors economic development activities that incorporate social groups in rural areas who have limited resources. FUNDAP did several studies to identify groups meeting its criteria of having a productive capacity, but lacking skills in training, technology, marketing and finance. FUNDAP decided that the people

involved in wool processing have the basic skills and artisanal traditions, and latent business skills that would allow them to profit from assistance.

The Momostenango Project was conceived, to assist sheep farmers, wool weavers and those marketing the finished wool products. The project began in January 1986 in the area where the majority of wool weavers in Guatemala are concentrated. About 1,200 households in the project area work as a family in washing, spinning, dyeing, weaving, beating the material and selling the finished products.

The Momostenango Project was undertaken by FUNDAP with financial and technical support from US AID, ATI and the Guatemalan Ministry of Agriculture. The project has involved Guatemalan businessmen in improving private initiatives in sheep production and artisanal wool processing and marketing. In the first phase of the project, emphasis was placed on increasing the quality and quantity of wool by genetic improvement of sheep and better animal husbandry practices. Credit aid and technical assistance is also available for the weavers. Assistance is being provided in identifying domestic and international markets where the finished wool products could be sold at higher prices.

FUNDAP will have a direct presence in the project for five years. After that, FUNDAP will indirectly participate in the marketing business for another 5 years.

## Objectives
The general objectives of the project are to:

- Increase the income of the people who are involved in the production, transformation and marketing of wool and other products derived from sheep in the western part of the country;
- Encourage the participation of those involved in the different phases of the project to establish their own permanent organization so they can achieve sustained development;
- Strengthen and stimulate production, transformation and marketing of products derived from sheep in the project area;
- Increase employment through boosting sheep production and building on existing handcraft skills;
- Identify the lessons learned from a private sector development strategy which could be used as a model for other projects elsewhere in the country.

The basic activities of the project include sheep production, the buying and selling of wool, wool processing and weaving, and marketing of finished products. The specific objectives in these areas are listed below.

## Sheep production and buying and selling of wool
- Improve the quality of wool through technical assistance;
- Increase the production of wool per head of sheep;

- Increase the number and quality of sheep flocks;
- Implement a national sheep development programme which could sustain the continuity of the work in the project area;
- Establish and strengthen individual businesses and associations buying and selling wool;
- Establish a system of wool buying that takes into account the product's quality.

## Processing and weaving

- Stimulate the production of wool articles that are in demand in national and international markets;
- Improve the productivity of the different phases of processing and weaving wool products;
- Expand and increase the number of artisanal units producing wool articles;
- Research adequate techniques for weaving and disseminate knowledge on these techniques to improve the artisans' skills more efficient.

## Marketing

- Widen the market for wool products, nationally, in Central America, and in other markets;
- Improve the efficiency of wool product marketing;
- Establish a marketing enterprise to buy and sell raw wool and finished products.

### Project components
The project has four basic components: technical help, formation and development, access to credit, self-organization, and applied research.

## Technical assistance, formation and development
Wool producers, buyers and sellers receive technical assistance in sheep improvement, pasture and animal production improvement, administration, financial management, wool selection, and quality assurance. The weavers receive technical assistance to improve the quality and quantity of production and the designs. The marketers receive help in commercialization. Wool producers receiving training at the sheep research stations. A school for weaving has also been established.

## Access to credit
One of the principal obstacles to development of the wool handcraft industry is the limited access to financing. Reasons for this problem include the limited ability of the rural population to offer collateral and other guarantees and lack of financial knowledge. Therefore, the project provides

financing to producers, transformers or weavers and marketers, charging the same interest rates as the average bank rate. It accepts fiduciary guarantees, pledges or mortgages. Credit is available to individual or group businesses and co-operatives. The local field presence provides supervision of credit.

## Organization
The organizational goals of the project are to make personnel training more effective, sustain financial and technical assistance, and help the businesses function more effectively. To achieve these goals, the project strengthens existing organizations and organizes new groups involved in the different phases of wool production and commercialization. FUNDAP's specialized personnel act as facilitators so that groups develop the capacity to define and implement their own projects.

## Applied research
Applied research is needed to increase productivity, establish quality norms, improve the development and quality of products, and increase demand through marketing techniques.

### Results obtained to date
A recent evaluation of activities in 1986–87, the first stage of the project, noted the following achievements:

## Sheep farmers
To date, 14 technical assistance centres have been organized with 239 members and a pre-association of sheep farmers has been established. As a result of these changes, new wool buyers have entered the market, breaking the oligopoly that kept wool prices low. The transfer of new techniques has added value to the local production of wool. The technical assistance has had a positive impact on the sheep farmers' economic situation by increasing wool production and the number of head of livestock. The total sheep population in the area rose by 5,000 during this period.

## Weavers
The development of new designs and products that are in high demand has permitted many weavers to increase the amount of time they spend in wool handcraft production. A materials bank has been established which acquires raw material at wholesale for resale to the artisans at a low profit margin. A raw materials bank has been a great help in providing access to wool at a low cost. The availability of credit allowed weavers to expand production. The amount of credit loaned exceeded Q20,400.

There has been limited success in increasing productivity through development and introduction of new techniques. Some improvements have been achieved in dyeing, but little in equipment.

So far, export volumes have not increased much because weavers are not yet accustomed to work to fill orders. However, 11 weaver groups have formed, with a total of 160 members. A national association of weavers has also been established. There has been only a slight increase in the number of workshops, mainly by weavers who had abandoned the craft who have reinitiated work. Some weavers have increased the number of hours that they spend in this activity.

**Marketers**
Marketers have a close relationship with the weavers. FUNDAP has tried to involve wool suppliers in the sale of products and promote an organization capable of developing the Momostenango product market. Product sales have been made to handcraft buyers for the national and international markets. About 90 per cent of the sales were for export. After working with weaver groups in calculating production costs, buyers permitted the product price to rise by 25 per cent. One of the most important marketing outputs has been the formation of a commercial enterprise of 102 associated weavers, with a permanent exhibition and sales room. This enterprise has sold Q60,000 of products.

One of the common causes of project failure in rural areas is local people's rejection of the project and lack of trust of foreigners. This problem has been overcome by the project; however, it is recognized that improvements in communication are needed at all levels.

## The impact of macroeconomic policies on the project

The following analysis of the impact of macroeconomic policies on the project focuses on the policy actions of the Christian Democratic Government in the last two years. On gaining power in January 1986, the Democrats developed a three-stage work plan.

### The social and economic reorder stage
A period of 12 to 16 months for social and economic reordering was anticipated in the work plan. Its goals were to increase service coverage, promote national level dialogue, reduce inflation, achieve a stable currency exchange rate, protect employment, and permit basic consumption for the people through greater efficiency in public spending.

After the re-ordering stage, the plan sought to achieve economic development by maintaining stability and achieving gradual modernization of the productive sectors; establish mechanisms that could improve the distribution of property, wealth and social benefits; promote domestic savings; and reduce the vulnerability of Guatemala's export markets.

The third stage of the plan focused on social development, including the achievement of an adequate distribution of wealth and social justice.

## Exchange policies

The official value of the quetzal was maintained and a simplified exchange system was established which reduced the nearly 30 existing exchange rates to only three different rates of exchange. These three markets are:

1. The official market (with a rate of exchange of 1 quetzal per $US) would be for payments of public and private external debt, registered in the Guatemala Bank and for materials to make generic medicines.
2. A regulated exchange market (with a fixed rate of exchange of Q2.50 per $US) subject to adjustments by the Guatemala Bank would be used for income for the external debt, and certain other transactions.
3. A controlled, floating rate would be needed to convert income and expenses for tourism, consumer goods, and foreign investments. This would fluctuate within a range established by the Guatemala Bank in response to changes in the supply and demand of foreign currency.

A commission of foreign refinancing was established to renegotiate the external debt in accordance with the country's ability to pay. The Monetary Board maintained bank interest rates at 12 per cent.

Until the late 1970s, Guatemala had maintained a stable exchange rate on par with the $US, under relatively low inflation. However, the government of General Romero Lucas (1978–85), had an expansionary policy that supported many large investments. As a result, currency devaluation brought the quetzal to a rate of 4 per $US on the black market in 1983–84. By 1986–87, the currency had recovered, and an exchange of 2.50 per $US was maintained. This devaluation reduced the purchasing power of local wages with respect to imported goods.

In Momostenango, the devaluation reduced the affordability of modern inputs for agriculture. The chemical dyes used in wool processing increased in price by 200 per cent, resulting in a 30 per cent increase in the prices of finished products. Wool prices increased, but did not keep pace with inflation, a situation that made the sheep farmers' economic situation precarious. However, the inflation and exchange rate policies affected people in Momostenango less than urban residents, since rural people produce most of their own subsistence foods.

The structure of the banking system and its policies have limited access to credit in rural communities. Rural credit is only available through the National Bank of Agricultural Development's programmes for production of basic grains. To get this credit, farmers have to go to Totonicapan. Most small-scale farmers have little use for this financial source. There were no credit programmes for rural micro-enterprises.

As a result, the FUNDAP project had to provide its own credit so that weavers could increase their production. This credit has had a positive effect on wool article production.

263

## Fiscal policies

The fiscal policies of the government sought to reduce the public deficit, and reduce inflation and pressure on the exchange rate. Revenues would be increased through a provisional tax of 30 per cent on agricultural exports. This tax would gradually diminish from 1987 on. Industrial exports were subject to a 4 per cent tax. Telephone service tariffs and fees for other government services were raised as were import taxes for luxury articles. A tax was established on real estate.

The effects of these fiscal policies on the Momostenango area were limited since most of these direct taxes were not imposed on rural people. The tax on agricultural exports did not affect Momostenango because it only produces basic grains for subsistence. The tax on land was not applicable in the majority of cases because of the threshold based on average property size.

Taxes on luxury products are irrelevant in the area given the population's income level and consumption patterns.

The only direct tax applicable to Momostenango was the one for industrial exports, but this did not have a significant effect since it was borne by intermediaries farther down the marketing channel. Indirect taxes have had a negative impact on the population, increasing the cost of transportation by more than 100 per cent over the past few years. In turn, this has increased the price of locally consumed goods and raw materials.

## Price policies

The government has gradually liberalized price policies. So far, over 3,000 products have been eliminated from the list of ceiling prices. Of these products, 225 are basic items consumed by most households.

Artisanal crafts had not been subject to price controls before. The results of this policy were positive. The annual rate of increase in consumer prices which had reached 43 per cent in June 1986, decreased to 26 per cent in December and remained lower in 1987. The price liberalization also discouraged hoarding and speculation. However, in remote rural areas such as Momostenango, many price controls had not been effectively enforced anyway.

## Monetary and credit policies

The government's monetary and credit policies over this period tried to counteract the effects of the Guatemala Bank's exchange losses on the money supply and to stimulate private sector financing. To contribute to the economic revitalization of the country, lines of credit were established for basic grains. Local and foreign investment and exports of goods and services were also promoted.

To complement the monetary policies, the following actions were anticipated:

264

o Applying an open airspace and fishing ground policy;
o Creating a fund for the promotion of export;
o Creating a fund for credit guarantee for export;
o Providing credit security for exports;
o Establishing duty-free zones;
o Studying the possibility of removing taxes on non-traditional exports.

The latter policy change could have a direct effect on this project, although planned removal of taxes on non-traditional exports has not yet happened.

A private sector Guild of Exporters of Non-traditional Products has been created. This trade association's regional office in Quetzaltenango has co-ordinated some of its activities with the project. The Guild could facilitate the search for new markets and take advantage of government measures to develop exports. Expanding exports of wool products would give producers the opportunity to obtain better prices for their goods and allow more entry into the profession.

### Science and technology policies

To date, Guatemala does not have a national policy for science and technology and the government has not promoted the development of appropriate technologies. There seem to be few links between various institutions and universities/colleges in production, distribution and commercialization of technologies. Government involvement in technology development and transference is the responsibility of the Central American Research and Industrial Technology Institute (ICAITI) and the Agricultural Science and Technology Institute (ICTA). Neither of these organizations has been active in the Momostenango area. Because of this gap, FUNDAP found it necessary to seek the assistance of other organizations.

### Rural development policies

Historically, the Guatemalan government has had a centralized administration. As a result, infrastructure investment and economic development have been concentrated in the capital city and its environs. The government's national reorganization plan seeks to reverse this situation. Proposals have been made for greater decentralization of authority, establishment of a regional development policy, and urban and rural planning.

One component of this policy has been provision of financial aid to municipal governments amounting to 8 per cent of the national budget. This transfer of funds has permitted municipalities that have not had funds for infrastructure development to implement projects benefiting the local people. In particular, this policy has considerably increased Momostenango's financial capacity to execute projects.

265

## Conclusions and recommendations

FUNDAP started the Momostenango project with the vision that the wool handcrafts sector can contribute more to the economic development of Western Guatemala, boost sheep farming, and stimulate trade.

Making handcrafts is a traditional activity, which has the potential to become even more important in Guatemala. Handcraft production can be a principal or complementary activity to reinforce the rural economy, especially where farm sizes are small and the land is poor. This sector can help provide an adequate income to peasants and generate stable employment; however, it has largely been ignored by governmental policies.

In its two years of operation, the wool project has obtained promising results and gained the confidence of the indigenous people in the area.

Macroeconomic policies of various Guatemalan governments have encouraged national economic growth over regional development. The groups with economic power were the main beneficiaries of these policies, whereas the majority of the population experienced a deterioration in the standard of living.

The macroeconomic policies planned by the government focus more directly on the masses of the population with scarce resources. Concrete measures to make development more dynamic in the interior of the country are expected.

The structure and administrative conditions of government agencies make it difficult to use financial resources at a grassroots level. With its characteristics of political interference and paternalism, the government has demonstrated little capacity to efficiently implement development projects for the benefit of the rural poor.

The private sector has a responsibility to assist rural development in the country. It has the means, experience, and ability to channel financial resources to benefit low-income groups.

Well-formulated macroeconomic policies are not sufficient to promote rural development.

High levels of unemployment and poverty in Guatemala justify giving priority to projects that build the productive base of the rural and urban poor.

Non-governmental organizations have demonstrated skill and efficiency in the management of grassroots development projects, and deserve more resources from governments and international development agencies.

Specific sectoral and institutional policies directly concerned with problems of rural areas are needed.

Multilateral financial organizations, such as the International Monetary Fund and the World Bank, have played an important role in influencing the macroeconomic policies of Latin American countries, but have not effectively addressed the problems of poverty. Regional actions are required to sensitize these organizations to this problem.

Guatemala and other Latin American countries are characterized by weak technology development and poor implementation of policies. More work needs to be done in developing and disseminating technologies. Collaboration with international organizations may be necessary in this regard.

Rural development projects need to be monitored and evaluated thoroughly so that the accumulated experience can be useful in the design of similar projects elsewhere.

| Statistical information on Guatemala | |
| --- | --- |
| Territory (km$^2$) | 108,889 |
| Total population in 1986 | 8,195,118 |
| Urban share of the population (%) | 32.7 |
| Annual rate of demographic growth | 2.8 |
| Birth rate in 1986 | 40.8 |
| General mortality per thousand inhabitants in 1986 | 8.9 |
| Infant mortality per thousand live births in 1986 | 57.1 |
| Literacy rate in 1986 | 56.6 |
| Labour force by sector in 1985 (%) | |
| Agriculture | 58.1 |
| Manufacturing | 13.6 |
| Construction | 4.1 |
| Other | 24.2 |
| GNP total growth rate in 1986 | 0.0 |
| Exchange rate in 1986 (quetzales per $US) | 2.5 |
| Public external debt payment in 1986 ($US) | 2,178,000 |

# Discussion: Policy Approaches Toward Technology Choice and Small Enterprise Development in Latin America

*W Nash*: I would like to ask a question about a basic assumption of this conference. How can we sustain growth systematically in a limited system which does not grow in terms of energy and resource availability?

*E Doryan-Garron*: That is a difficult question, which I am going to answer with an example. There is a Costa Rican firm that sub-contracts with small firms and co-operatives. This firm exported a high quality door to Europe and the USA. It was made from a traditional cheap wood that is now depleted throughout most of the country. So this company, in conjunction with a co-operative, bought a large parcel of land. The land has been well distributed to many people. They have begun to exploit the wood using methods that could sustain the supply, after obtaining the advice of technologists on how to harvest the wood without destroying the forest. Sustainable development is possible with the wide use of natural resources through different organizational arrangements and the help of co-operatives, scientists, and technologists. There are no general recipes. On different levels and with different crops innovative ways to reinforce sustainable development must be found.

*L de la Rive Box*: I was very interested to hear your comments on the Costa Rican coffee case. In my research over the past three years, I have been trying to apply that case to other crops in Costa Rica such as cacao and have found it difficult. The question is, why isn't this transferable? You have quite explicitly shown that this is a special case embedded in the history and political organization of Costa Rica. Could you expand on the relevance of the coffee grower model to other crops in Costa Rica?

*F Stewart*: I would like to make two comments on the issue of sustainable development and poverty. First, we have to consider the ecological effect of various alternatives before we come to any conclusion. One alternative is doing nothing for the poor, which has a devastating effect on their welfare and on the ecology. The environment does not stay constant if the poor remain in poverty because they will be forced to deforest land to earn a living. We must also consider what are the alternative ways of promoting development. One alternativ is to centralize industrial development, but that has a more devastating effect than the use of small-scale technologies.

268

Second, I do not feel that it is the responsibility of the most deprived people in the world to take on the burden of the world's ecology. It is much more the responsibility of those who have standards of living far above subsistence. The rich countries cause the most environmental damage in the world and should take action first without placing the burden on the less developed countries.

*W Nash*: I was not suggesting that the most deprived should carry the ecological burden. But if, as you say, some small forestry practices are sustainable for a thousand year period then that fulfils an essential requirement of matching the demand on resources to the natural recovery of the environment. If it was not fulfilling this requirement, then we could not assume it to be sustainable.

I, of course, agree with the need to alleviate poverty, especially poverty linked to our affluence. People in the developed countries are consuming most of the resources of the world and creating most of the ecological damage. If development means bringing the poor to a level of unsustainability, as is prevalent in developed countries, long-term problems of poverty and ecological crises will only be multiplied. The development of the Third World and alleviation of poverty must be connected to the alleviation of affluence and unrealistic expectations. We should make a serious shift to technologies that balance ecological demand with natural recovery.

*E Doryan-Garron*: Mr de la Rive Box's question is difficult to answer. There are cycles and steps that could facilitate the possibility of translating the experience in coffee to other crops. Twenty or thirty years ago, the co-operatives involved in coffee production were not very powerful. However, concrete policies and institutional arrangements were developed, satisfying the different actors and enabling co-operatives and technology to develop. Cultural factors contributed to these changes. Today, co-operatives control 50 per cent of the coffee production and are very politically powerful.

If we had done a similar thing with other crops, their productivity would now be much higher. Will it take as long to bring about the elements necessary to reproduce the coffee experience with maize or beans? No, because the work with coffee was an experiment. It took a long time to consolidate a framework for rapid technological change in coffee production. We should do the same with new crops. Now is the time to organize an infrastructure to enable the small producers to participate in the productions of non-traditional exports such as fruits and vegetables, which are increasing at a rate of 25 per cent per annum. An overall framework of administrative and technological innovations needs to be established to transfer the experience of coffee to other crops and sectors. I am sure a lot of problems will arise, but we cannot wait as long to see what is going to happen.

*W Gschwend*: I would like to comment, having had the chance to observe both these experiences. In both cases, the FUNDAP/Momostenango case and the Costa Rican case, they focused on the market and what products it wanted. Thus, they were able to communicate that to the producers who geared the technology and production to the market. I think that this linkage is very important, because it is also related to prices and incomes.

*E Doryan-Garron*: Yes, I agree, but with a comment. For example, 20 years ago it was clear that the world market for coffee was evolving and that higher priced and premium varieties would be in greatest demand. So, most plantations have changed from the old varieties to the newer, higher priced ones. There was a sign from the market, but institutional arrangements and a whole framework of support were needed for small producers to take advantage of the projected new market demand. Many obstacles needed to be overcome. Sometimes, markets give false signals based on temporary trends and one must be alert for these.

If the new coffee varieties become obsolete rapidly the next step might be to make applications from biotechnology available to the small coffee producers. For example, the genetic structure of the plants could be altered so that the coffee matches changing market tastes. Californians might like coffee with less caffeine and New Yorkers might like triple the caffeine content.

I am concerned that biotechnology could allow coffee to be grown in Kansas in the not too distant future. Last week, a group of biotechnologists told me that this could be a possibility in less than twenty years. It could also happen with other tropical crops such as bananas. New technologies can provide opportunities, but can also be dangerous. Therefore, it is necessary to establish a system of innovation in LDCs.

It is too soon to tell whether biotechnologies will be to the benefit or detriment of tropical producers, but whether it becomes appropriate or not it is here to stay. Costa Rica is beginning to take steps to obtain the agrochemicals recommended for new genetic varieties of plants. The impact of new technologies on appropriate technology is a topic that needs to be discussed seriously.

*L de la Rive Box*: Mr Doryan-Garron has made a case for a fairly small-scale industry but now you are talking about biotechnology. In this context, what type of research do you think countries like your own should engage in – fairly small-scale technologies or highly specialized ones such as biotechnology?

*E Doryan-Garron*: In reply, I would like to stress that there are many niche markets for production in small quantities according to consumer tastes. New technologies are opening new windows for niche goods. One of the most important new technologies is organization, allowing firms to be more flexible and creative.

270

As Professor Dominguez from Harvard said, 'Everybody knows the cold war has ended between the US and USSR. Japan won'. A new form of organization based on 'just in time' production techniques is currently the fashion. This will provide opportunities and dangers for the economies of developing countries. Opportunities will open up for small countries to get into the market. Organizational restructuring and new technologies can be managed on a small-scale, if they are matched to the resource endowments of each country. Conceivably, a small firm in Costa Rica with only one experienced researcher in biotechnology could produce new varieties of banana plants at a much lower cost. Such varieties could be produced through in vitro cultivation and exported to many countries. So, the firm might export the technology of banana growing instead of bananas themselves.

A similar strategy could be used for other crops and there is room for regional co-operation in this regard. In the last 6 months regional conferences have been held in Central America during which interest was expressed in regional co-operation in biotechnology. Many opportunities have been opened which demand explicit policies. To take advantage of them we must maintain or create an infrastructure based on this new technology.

*C Schmal-Vogelaar*: I would like to return to the FUNDAP case. I heard of it in Mexico and was very impressed, because it is an example of how to develop an area where the resources are poor and the population density high in relation to the land available. On the one hand, you are developing the wool sector through modern technologies such as genetic engineering. On the other hand, you are encouraging people to take up non-farm employment. This is significant, because I think that the artisanal sector is often seen as not viable or sustainable.

Perhaps you can tell us a little more about how you succeeded in helping the wool sector to grow. Did you provide a lot of market support? Most of the time this is a problem for the artisanal sector, especially when they produce traditional products. How has FUNDAP helped these people located in a remote mountainous area market their products?

*F R Gutierrez*: In all of our projects, FUNDAP has started with market research. Then, we find out how many jobs can be created or maintained by improving production. After that, we look for possibilities to promote the organization of the people by themselves and the technology that could be used to develop the products.

In marketing, we find out who is interested in these products by sending samples and letters. We have been lucky because the artisanal products of Guatemala are competitive in quality and price. Through specialty stores, we have reached the market of people interested in the cultural aspects of these products. Since we are not talking about a large quantity of articles, this is not too difficult.

*T de Wilde*: I would like to make a few comments on the earlier question of Mr de la Rive Box. First, another example of a successful project is the Plan Puebla in Mexico. Farmers were able to increase corn production from one ton per hectare to three tons per hectare over seven years. This was mainly accomplished by changing the institutional framework, organizing groups of farmers and bringing them together with researchers, extension agencies and later banks. Farmers became the researchers on their own land, and the researchers worked on actual farms. This change in institutional structures led to a revamping of the way that science and technology for agriculture is organized in Mexico. Rather than just focusing on plant diseases or other technical issues affecting particular crops, the researchers now focus on region-specific problems in the production system.

Second, concerning the question of biotechnology, I would like to share some of ATI's experiences. We have started to work with the Thailand Institute for Scientific and Technological Research. We have developed a small-scale production process for rhizobium inoculant. Since different strains of rhizobium work best with particular types of leguminous crops and soil types, a small-scale production unit is the most flexible.

Clearly, the whole question of implementation of biotechnology seems to be very much related to the niche markets that were already mentioned. We have run into problems in Thailand because of the lack of standardization. The inoculant has become so popular that people are starting to sell little packages mislabelled as rhizobium. The legitimate producers cannot prevent this because there is no legislation to mandate that such a packet contain a certain number of bacteria of that particular type. Thus, we could not implement commercial production of the inoculant because we ran into the problem that the legislation is lagging behind the development of the technology.

*G Ranis*: My question concerns the market niches in western countries and other developing countries. Entry into niche markets is often hampered by quotas for the products. Thus, how do you allocate the coffee quota in a way that allows small new exporters into the business? If the large producers or existing ones have a lock on the quotas, this is a major impediment to entrepreneurial science and technology induced through blue-collar innovations.

*E Doryan-Garron*: The question of Mr Ranis about market niches is more relevant to other crops than coffee. Since the coffee market is very structured at present, major negotiations are underway to determine whether the London coffee agreement will be continued or not. The agreement would have impacts on the fulfilment of diverse consumer tastes and choices on types of coffee produced by different countries.

The world market for coffee still allows some scope to upgrade the type

272

produced. So, there are shifts in resources from one type of coffee with respect to the country's quota. Costa Rica has changed from the old to the new types of coffee over the last 5 to 6 years. It is less viable to try to produce outside the quota and export processed coffee. That part of the negotiations must be done case by case.

For products that are not controlled through an international marketing agreement, there are more possibilities in filling market niches. It is important for small producers to have a flexible organization to enable them to change their product type according to shifts in market tastes. Since market niches are much smaller for vegetables, production and marketing can be geared to the demand in a nearby city. To do this, the producer needs direct feedback from the market to change the type of vegetable planted. The producers would have to be flexible and in tune with direct information from the market. This is part of the process of creating a much more innovative infrastructure in the country.

*G Ranis*: That answers part of my question, but does not address the role of government policy in allocating the quota. If, for example, this year's quota on coffee or textiles is based on last year's, then the flexibility is not there for the innovations you are talking about. Some countries auction their quotas, what does Costa Rica do?

*E Doryan-Garron*: With coffee, the quota is for the country as a whole. The country produces up to the quota and no more. If someone with a new product or variety wants to get into the market, there is space because the quotas are not fixed in Costa Rica and there is no office where quotas are allocated. Instead, there are negotiations between small and large producers, exporters, and the government. The negotiating process is very complex. As far as I know no one has ever been left out because the structure of what was planted in the last few years remained very near the quota. However, there could be a problem later on. For other products that are not subject to quotas at the international level, Costa Rica hopes to export a whole new set of products over the next 5 to 10 years.

*A Berry*: I would like to return to a comment by Mr Doryan about the impacts of structural adjustment in Costa Rica. The context of structural adjustment raises important new questions about the role of small enterprise. I am concerned with manufacturing, although the issues are similar in other sectors. In the past, structural adjustment has generally led to a shortage of foreign exchange, savings, investment, and an employment problem. Thus, whatever arguments previously existed for small enterprise are magnified. So, one would hope that the structure of the economy would shift in that direction. In Argentina and Chile, the process of structural adjustment was unusual in that it was imposed with a high degree of ideological purity. In Argentina, the structure of industry moved toward the large-scale and the main victims were small- and medium-scale

273

enterprises. Some people interpret that as being rational, moving toward efficiency in terms of economies of scale, but I question that interpretation.

In any case, we need to be concerned about a fairly new area – the dynamics of structural adjustment. How likely is it that producers who are basically efficient will not survive an unusual transition during structural adjustment? Anecdotal evidence indicates that the simple lack of financial flexibility does firms in, where their basic economic characteristics may be quite appropriate. What has happened to the size structure of manufacturing in Costa Rica since the economic crisis of the early 1980s?

*E Doryan-Garron*: When the stabilization programme started in 1982–83 with the support of the IMF and later the World Bank, there was an explicit programme for 'Industry Recovery'. This programme provided credit and wrote off the debt in dollars of any firm. It prevented a major bankruptcy of many small- and medium-sized firms. Although the first treatment to the economy was a severe austerity and liberalization programme, this programme helped compensate. Even with the programme, a small group of firms went bankrupt. But, in general, there was a clear policy to prevent that from happening.

The government also instituted a 'social compensation programme'. During the worst of the crisis this programme gave free lunches to 40,000 families, while the macroeconomic corrections were taking place. Such a scheme was not applied in Argentina or Venezuela and that explains their recent problems.

Now, for the second time in this decade, there is a need for a specific programme for industry. Tariffs have already been reduced by half and they will be much lower in the next few years. That is why the government, in conjunction with the private sector, has started a comprehensive programme of industrial structuring. At the level of general policy and in sub-sectors such as metal, plastics, and chemicals, special programmes were developed. One pilot project involving at least 100 firms is investigating ways to prevent firms from going bankrupt and to help them recover through credit, marketing, technology management, quality control and technological innovation. This programme is targeted at both small and large firms. In general the small firms in Costa Rica are organized by sector, which would make the process easier. It would also be similar to the process with coffee, because there is already an organized group and experience with co-operatives. If the appropriate measures are taken, the process of industrial reconversion can bring small enterprises new opportunities, rather than greater risk of bankruptcy.

*D Ndlela*: In my view, the whole objective of revisiting the debate on industrialization is to reduce the historical dependence of developing countries on primary products and to turn to the dynamism of appropriate

274

production technology in these countries. With this assumption, I have a problem with the low-income elasticities of demand for products like coffee, cacao and sugar for developing countries for the medium to long term. African producers of these crops face international quotas in their traditional markets in Europe. How do you expect these countries to increase their production of these products with the help of AT when they already supply the market at the maximum of their quotas?

Therefore, the best option is to use appropriate technology to encourage rural industrialization for the domestic market because concentration on exporting primary products is not the game of the future. How does the situation compare in Asia and Latin America?

*E Doryan-Garron*: First, I am not convinced that any of our countries are going to develop by producing what we do today. If we plant all suitable areas of Costa Rica in high-yielding coffee, the most we could export is $US 2bn worth. Now, we are exporting various products worth about $US 1.4bn. For the long run, we need to diversify our export portfolio for a greater increase in earnings. Where there are quotas, we need to produce more efficiently so that land and other resources can be devoted to other products. Furthermore, diversification may allow payment of higher wages and greater linkages with other sectors.

In the long run, a much more diversified portfolio is needed to reduce the susceptibility to fluctuations in the prices of any one export. Presently, when the price of coffee goes down, the Costa Rican economy experiences an earthquake.

I would like to see Costa Rica industrialize some of its export products and export caffeine, tannin, or other substances derived from basic products. By exporting 1,000–2,000 new products for small market niches, the country can respond more flexibly to market demand. This does not mean we must stop exporting traditional products; they can still provide a stable cash flow. New products face a different set of market conditions and can be chosen to build linkages in the economy. To accomplish this, a strategy based on ATs and sustainable development is needed. This strategy could substantially increase national and family incomes.

# III

*Policies and Rural Industrialization*

# Macro-Strategies and Rural Industrialization in Comparative Perspective

## ASHWANI SAITH

I would like to begin by discussing the two objectives normally associated with rural industrialization: developing linkages to economic activities of the poor and increasing linkages with agriculture. If these two objectives are not firmly kept in mind, one can easily make policy decisions that are not supportive of small enterprise development. A satisfactory growth performance in rural industrialization could be established without significant spin-off effects for agricultural development.

Furthermore, the majority of employment in non-farm, small-sector industries is located in rural areas. Manufacturing provides only a small fraction of total employment in this sector, compared to the services, trade, transport and commerce sectors. This distribution of activities has implications for policies that deal with the rural poor. Although small manufacturing enterprises do not have large capital requirements for entry, the costs of entry are generally higher than for services or commerce.

Most theories of economic growth emphasize the shift in occupations and percentages of GNP from agriculture and resource extraction to large urban industries during development, but often do not deal with small-scale rural industries. Yesterday someone asked whether the rural industrial sector will progress or disappear as economic growth occurs.

I would like to distinguish between different categories of rural non-farm employment: proto-industrial products and inferior goods. Proto-industrial products are associated with new technologies and markets. In the Japanese case or the Industrial Revolution, there was a progression of industries from rural agrarian household activities to large-scale firms. Initially, there was a greater division of labour and specialization as well as a movement to towns and, in Japan, a switch to export products. Japan also had some special factors, such as a strong domestic market based on stable cultural preferences. Some of these factors are less prevalent in LDCs because of colonization. Frequently, development strategies have assumed that most rural industries produce proto-industrial products and that with the right

ASHWANI SAITH is Professor of rural economics at the Institute of Social Studies, The Hague. His current research concerns rural industrialization and poverty, particularly in Asian countries.

technology or the right policy changes, industrialization would occur naturally. I do not think that this is likely to happen.

Inferior goods tend to disappear when superior substitutes take their place as incomes rise. This process is influenced by the development of superior substitutes outside the rural economy. Support of rural industries through long-term subsidies is not a good idea, although it is difficult to say that an enterprise that cannot survive without subsidies in the face of an otherwise unfavourable policy environment is inefficient.

There are several reasons why rural industrialization has become popular. First, there is the shift in donor and government attitudes on rural agrarian reform. The issue of agrarian reform is not raised very often now in most parts of the Third World even where there is a problem of acute rural poverty. Second, in countries that have been reasonably successful in reducing poverty, the ability to absorb a growing number of labour force entrants is a concern. Third, the kinds of policies being recommended for structural adjustments could encourage rural industrialization and use of more labour-intensive technologies. Fourth, rural industrial enterprises are small and less complex than large-scale firms and can be assisted through small NGOs.

Rural employment problems are increasingly being recognized. Studies in Bangladesh have estimated that even with growth of agricultural output of approximately 4 per cent a year, only a quarter of the growth of the labour force can be absorbed through existing technologies. In India, this figure is one-third. A World Bank report on Kenya presents an alarming picture of the rural and urban informal sector by the year 2000, despite respectable overall economic growth rates. If you look at the actual growth performance rather than the distribution, Bangladesh has not done badly compared to many African countries. Economic growth has kept pace with population growth. Yet, successful growth and employment in the cities is not enough to absorb all the excess labour. Rural industries can play an important part in this area because they usually are less capital intensive than urban industries. However, I question the extent to which technology interventions alone can solve the problem of labour absorption.

As an economy grows over time, there is a shift in consumption patterns from domestically produced, unprocessed foods to manufactured ones and imported commodities. Although food production may keep up with the demand, without attention to the technology side, agriculture may become less labour-absorbing. This change is partly a result of sectoral shifts in the pattern of output.

In many Asian countries over the long run the solution for poverty will change from food production to income generation and provision of entitlements. If rural industrialization takes the form of enterprises that only employ small blocks of the rural population, the rest of the population will have to be assisted through entitlements. The labour absorption capacity of growth may increase to some extent, but not by enough.

There are two other kinds of approaches to reach the rural poor. The first, is to set up special programmes targeted at the rural poor. However, this is not a sectoral approach. The second approach is to restructure institutions to encourage sharing of resources. An extreme example of this approach is that of the Chinese commune.

These two approaches, targeting and institutional sharing are critical if rural industrialization is to achieve more than just efficient growth. Economists who are mainly concerned about economic efficiency do not talk about labour absorption, except in terms of reducing distortions from minimum wage laws and mandated social benefits. Rural enterprises are often exempt from the wage laws and thus face lower labour costs. Occupational safety hazards and exposure to economic exploitation can be greater in unregulated industries. Since development is not just a matter of labour costs and inefficiencies, there is a profound need to protect labour in these enterprises. I am not advocating protection of wages at unsustainable levels that will cost other people their employment, but workers need to be protected from occupational hazards and given other fundamental rights. Failure to do so will bring political risks.

Concerning the policy framework, it is important to distinguish between supply-side, demand-side, and institutional approaches. The supply side can be associated with technological interventions. The demand side is less often discussed. The institutional side goes beyond just credit or market institutions. It includes the pattern of ownership and the sharing of employment and assets. In my view, fundamental problems in rural industrialization in LDCs arise most often from the demand side. Where rural industrialization is succeeding but does not reach the poor, the institutional side is likely to be the problem.

Within this framework, one can learn from the experience of South Asia; however, the literature often makes selective use of these lessons. It concentrates on things that fit certain aspects of present policy scenarios and tends to forget about how the situation arose in the first place. For South Korea and Taiwan, it is often overlooked that development began 40 years before the end of World War II. The period of rural industrialization between 1950 and 1970 was based on agricultural growth, agrarian reforms, and a strong export-orientation which had its roots in earlier decades. The development of exports was essentially connected to colonialism. The colonial presence in South Asia had a lesser influence on the same sectors.

The timing of these factors is also important. When Japan began vacating its position in a wide range of labour-intensive proto-industries, South Korea and Taiwan entered this market. The size of these markets was large enough to drive economic growth in these countries. At this point in time, other Asian countries face greater competition in entering these markets. Although many Asian economies are doing relatively well in agriculture and industrial exports, they are constrained by an external market. Although the situation may differ for individual countries, I question how far one can take the export-oriented strategy for the Third World as a whole. It raises the question of where the demand will come from. The East Asian countries, with their externally defined demand and high GNP growth, need growth in both the domestic and export sectors. It is important to remember that there has not yet been a successful case of rural industrialization without a high growth rate in agriculture and industrialization at the same time. China also fits this pattern.

If we compare the Asian cases with others, how is the demand side managed? The present growth rates of Third World economies with acute rural poverty problems are not high enough to enable the rural sector as well as other sectors to gain. There are trade-offs in the industrial strategy itself. Even when you do not have high growth rates, you could reallocate demand within the growth process, as Mellor suggests. When there is a shift toward agriculture, there may also be an increase in the incomes of wealthier farmers who have more linkages to the rest of the rural economy. Yet, to reach the poor it is necessary to reach them directly, as Adelman has found.

A strategy to reach the poor does not necessarily encourage general linkages between agriculture and rural industry. That is one way to restructure demand within a slow growth rate. Another way to restructure demand is to shift the pattern of demand in favour of locally produced products. In China, the rural sector is protected in relation to urban products through the institutional framework.

This strategy is less feasible for Bangladesh. Bangladesh has a ratio of manufacturing of less than 10 per cent of its GNP. In India the proportion is 17 per cent, an increase from 13 per cent in 1960. That is not a rapid rate of industrialization. If that pattern of industrialization continues the markets for a wide range of industrial products will be cut off.

In Bangladesh, it has been argued that there is less conflict between growth and equity in rural areas because the rural rich have almost as high a propensity to consume rural industrial products as the rural poor. There is a poverty trap and if the products do not exist, one cannot buy them. On the other hand, many firms are trying to set up small-scale enterprises.

Sub-contracting is a way of demand sharing that can benefit rural, small-scale industries. However, little has been done on the policy side to promote sub-contracting to link growth in rural and urban enterprises. When small enterprises are a small percentage of total employment, sub-contracting can only be taken so far.

There is another approach to reach the rural poor which consists of institutional sharing mechanisms and special programmes with linkages to the poor and agriculture. One example, the Chinese commune, was based on a lease model. People in the enterprises were paid at a rate similar to the average consumption level generated by agriculture. The prices they received for their products were much higher and the profits automatically accumulated. About one-third of the profit went into a higher level of accumulation. Another third was spent to expand enterprises and the remaining third went into agricultural development. These are institutionalized ways to use the higher productivities of successful rural enterprises to further agricultural development and rural industrialization.

This institutional sharing does not happen automatically in Third World economies. We are always asking ourselves what happens to agriculture if rural industrialization takes place. Even if linkages between rural industry occur, and the inequality aspect improves to some extent, it would be a slow route to reach the agricultural poor. It can certainly not be assumed that capital accumulated in rural industries will go into agriculture. There may be faster gains to be made in trade, particularly in South Asia.

Another type of institutional sharing was done with the *dhenki*. An institutional framework was proposed in which the women displaced from the traditional technology became the owners of the modern technology. This sharing approach has the advantage of both efficiency and equity in technology transfer.

Special programmes are another way of reaching the rural poor. Examples include the Grameen Bank, and rural public works and rural self-employment programmes. Sometimes self-employment and wage employment are viewed as competing, but since the target groups are very different, these may be complementary programmes.

There is another type of complementarity. Special employment programmes that create a large number of small non-farm enterprises at the household level will pump a lot of money into the economy. However, what will happen to entitlements and food production? Will it be necessary to have matching food aid or some sort of agricultural production programme? Rural public works programmes can have a tremendous impact on agricultural productivity. As a package, these two types of programmes can be very efficient and should be emphasized more.

Finally, I would like to return to what I regard as a key feature – the institutional dimension. In rural public works programmes, the rural poor go from site to site. The work on these schemes stops as soon as the project is finished and the rural poor lose their jobs. A great deal of the investment and employment in these programmes stops with the end of the contruction project. Evaluation of the benefits of these programmes in Bangladesh and India, often show that only 10 to 15 per cent of the total stream of benefits go to the target group, the rural poor. In Bangladesh, for instance, the target group includes all labour drawn from farms of up to 2.5 acres –

well above the poverty line. In addition the rural rich often get free use of the infrastructure.

Infrastructure investments are often politically convenient for governments. Public works programmes bypass some of the potential conflicts, because they generate incomes for the poor and go through the political middlemen. In India, money is now being given to local communities to buy local power. There is little local initiative in matching the funds with local participation and finding the most efficient ways to do things.

Even with high leakages both the rural rich and poor benefit from public works programmes. From the perspective of rural non-farm activities, they can bridge the production and entitlement gap. The only problem is the scale aspect. India has devoted a lot of resources to these interventions; however, only a small percentage of the rural poor have actually benefited from them. By contrast, large entitlement programmes would require big tax increases. The public works programmes are politically useful and are often announced at election times. Later, many of these promises are quickly forgotten.

In conclusion, agricultural development expenditures can be reallocated, but the data often are not accurate enough with respect to these desicions. In Malaysia, for example, non-farm expenditures include health, transport, and government services for both the rich and the poor. In the South Asian case, there are enormous leakages. A different pattern of agricultural growth can generate more employment. Rural non-farm activities are not the only way of reaching the rural poor.

# Discussion: Macro-Policies and Rural Industrialization in Comparative Perspective

*F Stewart*: I thought Mr Saith's presentation was very interesting and I certainly agree that institutions and demand are both important factors. The review I have done suggests that programmes in Bangladesh are a particularly extreme example of maldistribution of the benefits from public works. According to a study in Maharashtra, India, the benefits from their public works programmes are more well distributed. Secondary effects have resulted in more employment.

Second, the issue of scale was mentioned. Some of the schemes have been very large scale. For example, the Mahararashtran Employment Scheme establishes a minimum income for the poor for counter-cyclical purposes. If the economy improves in the locality, the scheme becomes less important. It is difficult to develop effective public works schemes that are ready to be implemented when there is a cyclical need. Scale may not be an important problem because if the returns are high the costs are reasonable. So the scale problem should not frighten one from exploring public works schemes further.

*G Ranis*: Mr Saith stated that output mix changes, technology changes, and decentralized decision-making (both public and private) can only solve a small part of the problem of poverty and that a large part can be solved by targeting direct programmes. I disagree with this view. I am not against the institutional devices mentioned by Mr Saith and Mrs Stewart, but I do not think the problem can be solved with direct action alone.

*A Saith*: I may not have adequately conveyed my views. The way I sketched rural industrialization is the way governments are viewing it. There are constraints to appropriate interventions because of political, institutional, and technological problems. Thus, it is convenient for governments to use the targeting approach. I actually share your views.

First, I am not criticizing public works schemes as such. However, I do think that the problem of poverty is too large in South Asia and the resources available too few to solve this problem in a broad assault. What makes these schemes so attractive to rural people is the free money provided. In the Indian case, I would say that if local taxes had to be raised to support these investments, the whole momentum would collapse. Maharashtra is a special case; none of the other schemes has been as successful. The targeting of the Maharashtra scheme is not very strong. Both the poor and more affluent farmers have benefited. Rural poverty programmes usually cannot go far enough and I do not believe that this is the way to build a society of egalitarian principles and development. A permanent handout to the poorest and subsidization of the capital formation of the rural rich would further entrench those institutions that stand in the way of other needed interventions at the local level. These schemes can be a way out from a government point of view. From the bottom up, they may appear to be a windfall, but they are not the way to solve the problem of poverty.

*Q K Ahmad*: First, I would like to emphasize the importance of demand and its linkages with agriculture. A large proportion of rural industrial goods are bought by rural people and unless rural incomes rise, rural industries face a serious demand constraint. Rural incomes are largely from agriculture. Public works programmes have been of marginal impact in raising rural incomes in Bangladesh.

Second, exploitation of hired labour is common in the rural sector. The question of exploitation can be related to the question of interest rates. To maintain their profit, while paying a high interest rate, entrepreneurs may lower wages to the hired workers. Self-employment activities account for a large proportion of rural industries and a high rate of interest might not help the people involved to escape poverty. It is also ethically wrong to charge higher rates of interest to small rural operators than large industries, as is the case in Bangladesh. Moreover, in Bangladesh, repayment rates by the large borrowers have been extremely poor compared to the small-scale sector.

The speaker stated that it is not possible to criticize the Grameen Bank because the people in Bangladesh do not like that. There have always been critics of the Grameen Bank approach in Bangladesh. If one believes that credit is the main problem, as the Grameen Bank does and if the bank is judged on that score, it has succeeded to a very large extent. Given the magnitude of the problem, in spite of the very fast expansion of the Grameen Bank, it has thus far covered less than one per cent of the target population. If one judges the bank on other criteria such as sustained development and employment of the poor, then certainly the Grameen Bank approach cannot be the answer.

*C Liedholm*: I would like to emphasize the importance of demand. First, the BIDS study that Mr Ahmad mentioned is one of the few expenditure surveys that actually distinguished the location of production by size. Products were also differentiated by income class and the location of production. We did a similar study in Sierra Leone for a wide array of locally produced products.

Second, Mr Mead of Michigan State University recently completed a survey of sub-contracting in Bangladesh and Thailand. One of the surprising findings was the extensive amount of sub-contracting, much of which was from urban to rural small-scale enterprises. This is a very important finding.

Third, on a point unrelated to demand, Mr Saith pointed out in his Malaysian work that manufacturing was not as important as some of the other rural non-farm categories. In our work in a number of other countries manufacturing is the most important rural non-farm activity, based on studies by Chuta and myself. Recent studies from the World Bank show similar results.

*W Rasaputram*: I would like Mr Saith to clarify a point. In the Malaysian example, you indicated that no matter what is done, there is a tendency for a small share of the benefits to accrue to the poor while most goes to the rich. This is disheartening for policy-makers. Even when the institutional approach is used, a similar situation arises as vested interest grow and political factors aggravate the problem. Particularly when the institutions become larger, the big producers, vested interests, or politicians will interfere to allow the rich to benefit more than the poor. Can taxation correct this? I doubt it and would like Mr Saith's view on how we can redistribute resources from the rich to the poor in a feasible manner for the short run.

*A Saith*: First, I would like to make one or two points about the Grameen Bank. I think it has succeeded to a great extent. The only problem is the criteria against which it is evaluated. A lot of people have tried to declare it to be a successful model based on certain criteria that it does not achieve, such as national economic impact. However, one cannot expect everything from a credit organization. For instance, the Bank does not care how the poor use the money as long as it is repaid. Thus, most of the money goes into trade. So, instead of buying cigarettes from a shop, you can buy cigarettes from a little fellow sitting out on the street. This is good for the little fellow but does not increase GNP much. We would need a very complex model of how trade builds up, its investments and its reallocation to have any long-term impact on the development process.

Second, the Bank has a tendency to organize small groups from village to village. The fundamental problem of removing poverty in Bangladesh is really a problem of inequality in the power structures at the local level. The Grameen Bank likes to make agreements on a strictly non-political level. Political organizations or general associations of all the poor in a village are not offered credit.

Also, I am not entirely impressed by the recorded repayment rates. More evidence from surveys is needed. The loan is given to an individual, but a group is held responsible. I have heard many stories about people borrowing from others to repay because if one person cannot repay,

287

somebody else in the group will not get a loan. So there are many problems in reference to the high rate of repayment.

The points about the BIDS study in Bangladesh are very important. This is one of the rare cases of location-specific demand analysis. Are we interested in seeing what is going to happen to the demands of certain groups of consumers or just certain groups of producers? I believe we are talking about the latter. I would estimate that half of the production of the rural non-farm sector is bought by the urban sector. Studies of the urban sector in the same report indicate a tremendous substitution away from rural industrial products in the urban demand.

Second, if one were to establish a poverty level on the basis of food intake or a wider set of basic needs, one would find that the average incomes of the richest quarter in Bangladesh are below that level. The entire production pattern is in the inferior category. So, incomes could rise for quite some time without leading to major substitution effects.

The third point concerns the source of national economic growth. To some extent it should come from industry. This is where the proto-industrial approach again becomes relevant. When Pakistan separated from India, most of the industry was in India. Pakistan had to build its industry up from scratch. When Pakistan and Bangladesh separated, most of the industry was on the Pakistan side. Now industries are being promoted in the same way in Bangladesh through state enterprises and the small-scale sector. It cannot be done on a grand scale. But I think there will be problems if modern industrialization is pursued in this manner. Although the range of options of goods available will widen, rural people have a very limited choice of rural products and often prefer the cheaper products of large-scale firms or imports, such as nylon rope instead of sisal rope.

Fourth, if the income elasticity of demand for a product is less than one, per capita consumption of that product may then decline. I have found that the income elasticity of demand for 14 urban products was far greater than that of the rural ones. Mustard oil was one exception. But if you look at these data more carefully, the case we want to make is far from being established. This becomes even more clear from data on other countries.

# Small-Scale Industrialization Policies and Industrial Development in Rural Regions

## FRANCISCO URIBE-ECHEVARRIA

### Introduction

In most developing nations, industrial development is extremely concentrated in a few, or even only one metropolitan area. With a few exceptions, rural regions have become more dependent on primary economic activities despite advances in the total production of industry and services at the national level. In many cases, this had led to the deindustrialization of rural areas and their surrounding regions.

Reducing the severe inter-regional income inequalities and excessive urban concentration accompanying such patterns of industrialization is an objective of most LDC governments. Surveys indicate that close to 80 per cent of these governments consider their spatial patterns of development unsatisfactory and share the view that 'radical' or 'substantial' intervention is necessary to improve this situation.[1] A variety of strategies has been tried, but the results have generally been frustrating. During the 1950s and 1960s, most LDC policies aimed at speeding up the modernization outside the main metropolitan regions. Developing the urban environments of peripheral regions was deemed necessary given the roles of:

1. Economies of scale and agglomeration in the process of cumulative economic growth;
2. Urban contact networks in accelerating the diffusion of growth-inducing innovations and;
3. Political changes associated with urbanization and resulting pressures on distribution.

Industrial development was the backbone of most of these policies, either in the form of 'growth-pole/centre' strategies or in spatial dispersion

FRANCISCO URIBE-ECHEVARRIA is a Senior Lecturer in urban and regional planning at the Institute of Social Studies, The Hague. His research has focused on the role of small-scale enterprises, particularly in Colombia. An Appendix with further details on the analytical and statistical basis of this paper can be obtained from the author upon request. Please address inquiries to Dr Francisco Uribe-Echevarria, Institute of Social Studies, PO Box 90733, 2059 LS The Hague, The Netherlands.

programmes. In general, the results were disappointing and sometimes showed undesirable side-effects [2,3]. In consequence, development policies shifted in the 1970s with rural development becoming the new focus of regional development policies. Failure to increase labour absorption and productivity in agriculture has also resulted in greater interest in the potential for non-farm employment. Small-scale industries have acquired a new relevance based on the assumption that they are better suited for rural conditions than large industries.

This paper contains preliminary evidence on these claims and conditions for an effective small-scale, rural industrialization strategy. It is part of an ongoing research effort on regional industrialization. The paper explores an alternative view of the nature of the policy problems posed by industrial development in rural regions. It suggests that only an integrated concern for both sectoral and spatial factors can provide a relevant framework for the analysis of such policy problems. A second, more concrete objective, is to assess the effectiveness of the dominant form of small-scale industry promotion schemes in meeting rural industrial development objectives.

The paper is organized in three sections. The first section modifies the usual definition of the policy problems in rural industry promotion. It discusses the limitations of rural industrialization approaches. It emphasizes the importance of a more integrated view of development processes within a region, encompassing both rural and urban areas.

The second presents some background information on Colombia and the findings of a regional–sectoral study. Two main areas of analysis are covered:

1. Identification and analysis of inter-regional patterns and processes of industrial development and their linkages with national industrial and agricultural development;
2. Observations about the role of small-scale production systems.

This section finds than an implicit spatial model characterizes certain industrialization processes and strongly influences the feasibility of alternative inter-regional industrial patterns.

The final section reflects on the implications of these findings for the formulation and effectiveness of rural programmes for promotion of small-scale manufacturing.

## Rural industrialization or industrialization of rural regions?

Small-scale rural industrialization is currently being touted as an important strategy in creating employment, alleviating poverty and redistributing resources to poorer economic groups and areas. However, its ability to meet these expectations and help slow urbanization is questionable.

Despite many enthusiastic statements, the problem of population

290

concentration has not been thoroughly analysed in the literature. Neither the conceptual nor the practical aspects of the problem has been seriously considered. Yet, the usual simplistic assumptions about the modest requirements for starting up small-scale industries, and a strong trust in the effectiveness of supply-side interventions have resulted in an overemphasis on extending service delivery systems in the regions concerned.

The presumed potential of small-scale manufacturing to contribute to the development of the periphery is based on the following assumptions. Small-scale industries supply small markets, demand modest amounts of capital, use local resources and raw materials, and do not require costly and sophisticated infrastructure.[4-10] Therefore, small-scale industrialization may appear to be an obvious strategy for governments trying to increase employment and self-reliance and simultaneously achieve balanced regional growth.[11] However, this reduces the rural development problem almost entirely to locational issues and ignores the most crucial issues of industrial and regional development processes.

Moreover, this strategy may only apply to those rural industries that can tap small, localized, spatially protected markets, but it can hardly be assumed to hold for other kinds of small-scale industries. The growth potential and employment-generating capacity of such industries is doubtful given the subsistence nature of the market for their products and the uncertainty of future demand.

Currently, a rural industrialization bias exists, which ignores strong arguments that viable industrial development in rural areas is associated with urbanization. Research has repeatedly shown the importance of external economies for the efficiency of small-scale production. Other important factors include the advantages of spatial clustering for vertical disaggregation of industrial production and easier access to product and factor markets.[12-15] Empirical assessments of the potential of rural industry often highlight the limited scope for future development and the difficulties of competing with larger, more centrally located industries as markets grow and become more integrated.[16-22] Evaluations of rural industrialization policies and programmes indicate that their impacts have been limited.[20,22-27]

Misgivings about the potential of rural industrialization schemes are not based solely on the unsettled controversy about the income elasticity of demand for the products of rural cottage and household industries.[28-39] These misgivings are also supported by evidence of drastic changes in the spatial patterns of supply structures as transport and communications costs decline and marketing systems are extended and upgraded. These changes are not limited to the shift from small- to large-production scales. Therefore, the urbanization of industrial production also occurs because of increased spatial agglomeration of the small-scale sector.

Certainly, scope for growth exists in rural industries serving small, localized markets, especially in countries with lower levels of industrialization.[5] Nevertheless, it would be difficult to prove that small firms can contribute significantly to increased industrialization in rural areas.

Increasing the industrial share of employment in rural areas implies a sustained process of industrial development, which must have a rationale at the inter-regional level such as simultaneous urbanization. Much of the industrialization will take place in urban agglomerations.

The economic advantages of urban environments are critical in achieving the efficiency levels required to resist the pressure from inter-regional competitors. In the long run, whenever the linkages from agricultural growth begin to diminish in importance, the continued expansion of regional employment and income opportunities will increasingly depend on the capacity of industries to compete in markets outside the region.

There is a potential role for intermediate and small cities in rural industrialization, although in a different way than is conventionally stated in regional development policies. The development of dynamic intermediate cities is a consequence of successful economic diversification within rural regions rather than its cause. Investment programmes to improve the infrastructure of secondary cities may be necessary to reduce development constraints, but cannot be used to promote industrialization by enhancing their locational attraction.

To some extent, this view is reflected in the Chinese conception of the role of small-scale industries in preventing metropolitan concentration. The Chinese policy was not to decentralize small plants at the village or small town level. Instead, it followed a two-tier model whereby larger plants were decentralized to intermediate cities within each province to 'help create a suitable environment in which other small industries can survive'.[40]

In summary, rural industrial development must be achieved in the context of increasingly integrated inter-regional industrial systems. This fact has important consequences for the conceptual framework for policy formulation. Simplistic policies based on a static appraisal of locational advantages and existing supply conditions are a weak basis for predicting the potential value of rural small-scale industrial promotion.

By contrast, the participation of rural as well as urban regions in the national economy depends largely on the roles their industrial sectors can effectively play in national industrialization processes. The variety of such roles and their geographic allocation differ with specific industrialization processes and the national policy environment. The pattern of industrial development in a particular rural region depends on its economic structure and basic organizational and physical infrastructure.

A framework for formulating and evaluating small-scale industrialization policies must be capable of explicitly associating industrial and regional development processes. None of these issues is addressed in the supply-side, firm-centred and nationally uniform policy or project formats that have dominated small-scale manufacturing policies. The lack of a comprehensive sectoral–regional framework makes it difficult to predict success or failure and may cause misallocation of resources. Indiscriminate support of a particular industry may jeopardize the achievement of regional or national economic objectives. Incompatibility between regional objectives and sectoral policies has often rendered policies ineffective.

## Industrial development in rural Colombia 1960–75

Policy problems may be broken down into two interrelated issues. The first issue is the more general problem of industrial development in rural regions. The second refers to the role small-scale production systems play in rural industrialization. This section deals with both issues, although more attention is paid to the first due to the lack of integrated sectoral and regional models of industrialization.

Despite their importance, spatial patterns have remained one of the least studied aspects of industrialization.[41] Widespread concern about spatial concentration has been approached in a normative manner relying mainly on descriptive and monitoring studies. The few attempts to uncover the mechanisms that generate industrial change spatially are recent and have mostly taken place in developed countries.[42,43]

It has long been assumed that unbalanced access to factors of production is the key factor determining industrial location. Evidence about the lack of infrastructure, difficult access to credit and scarcity of trained entrepreneurs and skilled manpower in the periphery seemed to provide a rational explanation. Armed with this diagnosis, many governments have attempted to correct this situation by launching programmes to encourage industrial deconcentration. The main instruments used have been credit quotas, lower interest rates, longer repayment periods for loans, direct or indirect subsidies and special infrastructure programmes.

For the most part, these policies failed to change the trends to any measurable degree. The first reaction to this observation was to blame flawed implementation, but in the light of almost unanimous frustrations, such a hypothesis has become untenable.

An alternative explanation concerns the neglect of rural and agricultural development. This new 'urban bias approach' assumed that the declining importance of manufacturing industries in rural areas results from the slow rate of income growth. This seems to be the main argument for a demand-side approach to policy formulation.[44] In practice, a demand-side approach implies the introduction of policies to stimulate agricultural production.

Certainly, the more income generated by the agricultural sector, the higher will be the aggregate consumption of industrial goods. Nevertheless, it is not altogether clear what impact this might have on the supply

293

side. For example, to what extent and under what conditions would the propensity to import from urban regions or abroad change or would export-oriented industries develop?

This section presents the results of an analysis of inter-regional patterns of industrialization in Colombia during the 1960–75 period. The process of industrialization in Colombia during that period progressed through a number of dynamic phases. The easier import-substitution phase was exhausted by the end of the 1950s. The intermediate goods industry, and, to a lesser extent, the capital goods industries, began to appear during the 1960s. By the 1970s, a weak export-oriented industrial sector was emerging at the same time that some dynamism was returning to the domestic consumer goods sector.

During the same period, the agricultural sector underwent major transformations. Agriculture became more sophisticated, commercially and technologically, and the development of this sector changed the economic profile of several rural regions. Therefore, it is useful to explore the impacts of both the national policy environment and sectoral changes on regional industrial development during this period. The next part of this paper discusses the role played by small-scale production in these processes. Then, the policy implications of the main findings will be analysed and the limitations of conventional approaches are discussed.

## A typology of regional industrial sectors

A typological approach can be used to analyse regional industrialization processes because a variety of regional features exist, resulting in different inter-regional distributions of industrial activities and characteristic sets of linkages. Such patterns are the territorial expression of an economic structure defined as the 'spatial' or geographic model of an industrialization process. This structure can be represented by the types of regional industrial sectors and their linkages in factor and product markets.

These types of regional industrial sectors function as units of national–sectoral industrial systems and also as aggregations of regional (territorial) industrial sectors. For this reason, they are the key links between regional and sectoral aspects of industrialization processes and the main unit for the analysis of regional industrialization processes.

Each regional industrial sector can be described as the aggregation of different types of firms in each industry. Industries were divided into four main groups: basic consumer goods, consumer durables, intermediate goods, and capital goods. For some specific purposes, it was necessary to disaggregate the basic consumer goods sector into food and simple consumer goods (clothing, shoes and leather, and furniture). Also, the intermediate sector was divided into agro-based goods (wood, paper and

294

textiles) and other industrial goods (metallic, oil and petrochemicals, non-metallic basic, and chemical).

Three types of firms were considered:

1. Micro-enterprises with fewer than 10 workers, often in the informal sector;
2. Small-scale formal production units employing 10–49 workers; and
3. Medium and large factories employing more than 49 workers.

This crude categorization could be improved in future studies. Here, the inter-regional aspects of industrialization and the scope for industrial development in rural regions are discussed. Then, some aspects of the role played by small-scale production are analysed.

The following expressions synthesize the above statements:

$$T = \sum_1^M \sum_1^N In$$

where T = Total industrial output (employment)
1.....N = Types of regional industrial sectors
1.....M = Regional industrial sectors of type $n$
In = Industrial output (employment) of region $n$

$$In = \sum_1^I \sum_1^J S_{ij} * C_i$$

where $S_{ij}$ = proportion of output in industry i produced by firms of type j

$C_i$ = share of industry i in total regional manufacturing industry

For Colombia, the typology was achieved via cluster analysis for 23 regions. A nearest neighbour method with Euclidean distances was used. The variables selected after pairwise analysis were:

○ Level of industrialization – measured by the per capita value of total manufacturing production;
○ Degree of diversification – measured by the Gibbs-Martin Index estimated for a set of 23 industries;
○ Product orientation – measured by the proportion of basic consumer goods in the total manufacturing production;

The period of analysis was 1960 to 1970. Three types of industrial regions were identified in the national economy. These regions were the following: metropolitan regions, intermediate regions and rural regions.

Metropolitan regions include the departments of Bogota DE (3), Antioquia (1), Atlantico (2) and Valle del Cauca (23). These regions are characterized by the highest degree of industrialization. Their diversified industrial structure includes basic consumer goods, consumer durables, and variable proportions of intermediate and capital goods.

The metropolitan regions are highly urbanized (averaging 69 per cent in 1960 and 84 per cent in 1970) and the non-farm sector is clearly predominant. Real per capita income in these regions grew an average of 3.5 per cent per year and was 1.25 times greater than the national average income, both in 1960 and 1975. No new metropolitan regions emerged over the period of analysis and the areas within these regions became more homogeneous, narrowing their differences in per capita values of manufacturing production and ranges of diversification. Industrialization deepened in these regions since the per capita value of manufacturing production increased by one third, as diversification increased and the share of basic consumer goods production decreased.

Intermediate regions include the departments of Bolivar (4), Boyaca (5), Cundinamarca (11) and Santander (20). These regions were economically defined in 1960, but became more distinct by 1974. By that year a fifth region had moved into the intermediate range but because of its similarities with the third group it was not included in this category.

The overall degree of urbanization of the 4 intermediate regions increased from 39 per cent in 1960 to 58 per cent in 1975, ranging from 25 per cent to 50 per cent at the beginning of the period, and from 45 to 65 per cent at the end. The real per capita income in these regions increased at a rate slightly superior to the national rate.

By 1974, the main characteristics of the intermediate regions were moderate levels of industrialization (about two-thirds of that of metropolitan regions) and a substantially lower index of diversification (by about one-half). Per capita production increased substantially, although it became less diversified. (See Table 1, Figures 1–4.)

Rural regions include Caldas (6), Cauca (7), Cesar (8), Cordoba (10), Choco (9), Guajira (12), Huila (13), Magdalena (14), Meta (15), Narino (16), Norte de Santander (17), Quindio (18), Risaralda (19), Sucre (21), and Tolima (22). These regions are characterized by a low level of industrialization, 25 per cent of metropolitan regions. In millions of 1970 pesos, per capita values of industrial production fluctuated between 0.21 and 0.72 in 1960 and 0.17 and 0.65 in 1974. They also exhibit a lower level of diversification with Gibbs-Martin indexes ranging from 0.30 to 0.75 in 1960 and 0.26 to 0.64 in 1974.

The level of urbanization in rural regions is similar to that of the intermediate regions, 36 per cent in 1960 and 52 per cent in 1974. Real per capita income grew at an average annual rate of 3.1 per cent and was the lowest among the three groups of regions. In 1960, it was about 80 per cent of that of intermediate regions and remained at that level over the period.

The economies of rural regions are dominated by agriculture. Agricultural production amounted to 40 to 70 per cent of total production. However, this does not mean that there is little or no urbanization in these regions.

Due to the split in the intermediate group, the homogeneity of each of the larger remaining groups of rural regions increased, as can be observed in the plot of the clusters. However, greater diversity within the remaining group can also be observed as the range of values for level of industrialization and diversification became wider.

On the whole, the evolution of the manufacturing sector of rural regions was far from favourable. The value of per capita production barely increased, the degree of diversification decreased, and the share of basic consumer goods increased. In general, there was a slow process of deindustrialization, resulting in greater dependence on primary production. (See Table 1, Figures 1–4.)

**Table 1 Types of industrial regions (mean values)**

|  | Type I | | Type II | | Type III | |
|---|---|---|---|---|---|---|
|  | 1960 | 1974 | 1960 | 1974 | 1960 | 1974 |
| Level of industrialization (value of p/cap output) | 1.80 | 2.40 | 0.90 | 1.40 | 0.30 | 0.40 |
| Degree of diversification (Gibbs-Martin index) | 86 | 88 | 74 | 70 | 48 | 42 |
| Product orientation (share of value added by non-durable industries) | 43 | 40 | 56 | 55 | 95 | 97 |

## Patterns and processes of regional industrial development

The first part of this section organizes the industrial space of Colombia using the typology outlined in the previous section. The second part of this section presents the results obtained in the analysis of the spatial model of regional industrialization during the period 1960–75. These conclusions are based on the following areas of analysis:

1. Output composition and its evolution over the period of analysis – patterns of distribution of industries and the output structure, and diversification. In the case of rural regions, some attention is paid to the variations observed within that particular group.
2. Inter-regional trade and its evolution. The lack of data on inter-regional flows of manufactured products necessitates the use of indirect indicators such as location quotient analysis. Two modifications have been made in this analysis. First, for consumer goods, where demand is

297

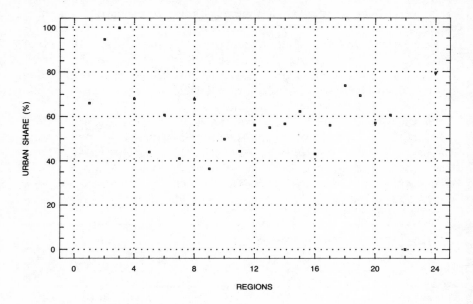

Figure 1   Urban share of population by region, 1976

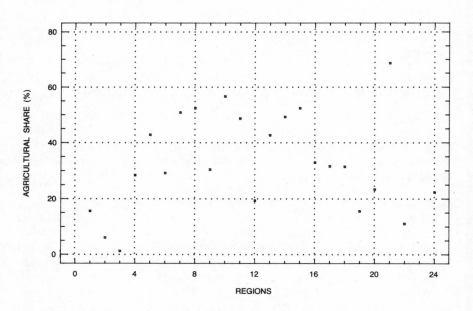

Figure 2   Agricultural share of total production

## Figure 3 Characteristics of regional industry, 1960

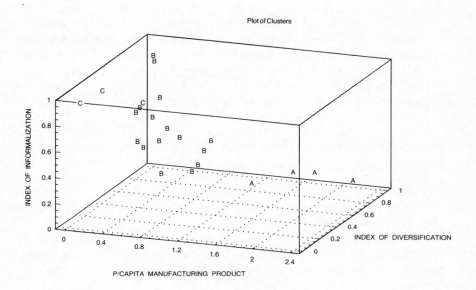

## Figure 4 Characteristics of regional industry, 1974

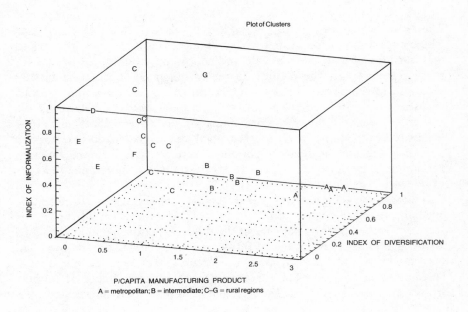

A = metropolitan; B = intermediate; C–G = rural regions

299

related to income levels, the likelihood of inter-regional exports has been estimated by comparing the value of manufactured goods produced in each region by the unit of regional income. Second, for intermediate and capital goods, where demand is related to the level of output in final goods industries, the likelihood of exports has been estimated on the basis of regional output per unit of consumption goods produced. However, this is still an approximation since it does not take into account differences in the structure of demand due to differences in income distribution or industrial output composition.

Some aspects of economic performance and linkages were also explored: the growth implications of inter-regional flows, linkages to agriculture and market linkages.

The growth implications of the inter-regional flows were studied using cross-correlation analysis. This method was applied to two variables, the total and the per capita yearly increments in the value of manufacturing production by regions in 1960–75.

Linkages with the agricultural sector were considered through an index of agricultural income/productivity. This index included the value of the product divided by rural population and the level of industrialization measured by per capita production.

Market linkages were handled through cross-correlation analysis for per capita income levels and per capita production levels.

The following section presents some of the conclusions and policy implications suggested by these analyses.

*The composition of output*
The composition of output in metropolitan regions is the most diversified and includes capital, intermediate and consumer goods. In consequence, these regions enjoy the highest degree of independence. The industrial sector in intermediate regions is made up of domestic consumer goods industries and intermediate goods producers. These two sub-sectors have few inter-industrial links because most of the intermediate industries originated exogenously and have remained an enclave linked to economic processes outside the region. Although there are inter-sectoral linkages through income/demand generation, there is a lack of horizontal linkages in industrial development.

Industrial development in rural regions has been limited to basic consumer goods industries. In 1960, formal and informal industries in this sector produced over 80 per cent of the industrial output, and in six out of 15 rural regions they produced 90 per cent. By 1974, this pattern had become more pronounced. With the exception of two regions, simple consumer goods accounted for over 85 per cent of industrial output; in seven regions it was 95 per cent. Formal food processing and

300

micro-industries (which also include a large proportion of food industries), account for almost all of the rural industrial output. Agro-based intermediate industries (paper, wood, and textiles) accounted only for 10–15 per cent of the output in four rural regions and less than 5 per cent in the rest.

## Diversification of regional industrial sectors
The index of diversification and the level of per capita production are high and have continued to increase in metropolitan regions. This suggests increasing economic interindustrial multipliers and self-sufficiency in production. The evolution of diversification in intermediate regions reflects the disjointed character of their industrial structure, with increasing per capita production and less diversification. In rural regions, the diversification index indicates a slow process of deindustrialization. With few exceptions, increasing specialization was accompanied by lower levels of per capita production in the rural areas.

## Inter-regional trade
In 1960, inter-regional trade in manufactured products was dominated by a downward flow of processed intermediate and final consumption goods to non-metropolitan regions and unprocessed rural products to the metropolitan regions.

By 1974, these relationships had become more complex due to the emergence of an upward flow of exports of basic intermediate (non-agrarian) industries from four of the intermediate regions. Additionally, some exports developed from a few rural regions; basic consumer goods (clothing and shoes and leather products) in Risaralda and Santander and food industries in region 7, Cauca; region 18, Quindio and, especially, in Tolima 22.

The exports from rural regions are still limited. Rural industries essentially supply their own intra-regional demands. The high and increasing ratio of location quotients between metropolitan and rural region suggests low and decreasing levels of self-sufficiency in the rural areas as well as an increasing propensity to import.

## Economic performance
During the 1960s, the output growth rates were increasing in all types of regions, but the trend reversed in the early 1970s. Growth rates in metropolitan regions fluctuated around a level above the national average, while those of intermediate regions fluctuated around the national rate and those of rural regions were below the national mean.

However, four distinct time periods can be identified. From 1960–63, the share of metropolitan industry increased from 67.8 per cent to 69.9 per

301

cent. It fell slightly between 1963–67, increased steadily to a peak of 71.2 per cent in 1973 and decreased to 69.9 per cent in 1975.

Intermediate regions demonstrated no net increase over the period, with the 1960 figure of 15 per cent unchanged by 1975. However, fluctuations similar to those observed in metropolitan regions also occurred. Output decreased slightly until 1964, increased continuously until 1973, and fell again in 1974 and 1975. The domestic sub-sector showed a different dynamic, falling continuously from 11.0 per cent in 1960 to 9.8 per cent in 1975.

The evolution of the participation of rural regions in national manufacturing production contrasts sharply with the other regions. With the exception of 1967, there has been a continuous fall in their share of the national manufacturing output from 17.4 per cent in 1960 to 14.2 per cent in 1975.

## Linkages

Industrial growth in the metropolitan regions pulls the intermediate sub-sector of intermediate regions through backward linkages, but has no direct impact on the domestic sector of these regions, nor on the industrial sector in rural regions. The latter two sectors are associated with the agrarian sectors in their own regions through market linkages. Over time, the impact of increased agricultural productivity on industrialization diminishes, but is suggests some stimulation of agro-processing industries.

The use of different agricultural technologies has had a significant bearing on the size of intra-regional linkages on industrial production because of the weak effect of increases in agricultural productivity and income resulting from the development of commercial agriculture. A proportionate change in the level of industrialization did not occur unless export-oriented regional industries emerged. In all other cases, increased industrial consumption generated a higher propensity to import rather than stimulating regional production.

The contribution of each rural region to national manufacturing output during the study period correlated highly with the contribution of agricultural output to the Gross National Product. This suggests that, in aggregate terms, the industrial sector in rural regions is a derived demand of the agricultural sector. For each percentage point reduction in the contribution of the agricultural sector of rural regions to GNP, their industrial sector output decreased by 0.65 of a percentage point.

At the national level increases in the level of industrialization were stimulated by per capita income growth. The forward impacts of industrialization on income were less important. In this demand-driven industrialization, the propensity of industrial production to increase with national income was small, but significant in metropolitan regions and far less responsive in intermediate and rural regions.

In general, the propensity of per capita industrial production to respond to variations in the level of national as well as regional per capita income levels was lowest in rural regions. Three main factors may be considered responsible for this phenomenon:

1. Import-substitution during the period was oriented to non-agro-based intermediate industries. Expansion of this type of industry had no significant role in rural regions;
2. Modernization of agriculture increased the propensity to import in rural regions; and
3. The bulk of the intermediate goods consumed in industrial production in rural regions are imported from metropolitan areas except in food processing industries.

A comparison of the rates of growth at the national and regional levels supports the above interpretation of linkages. The 1959–63 period showed dynamic annual rates of growth for employment, productivity, and output of 3.6 per cent; 8.4 per cent and 12.3 per cent respectively. By contrast, these figures were 1.2, 2, and 4.3 per cent for the 1964–67 period.[45] Between 1953 and 1963, import-substitution contributed 38 per cent to industrial growth, while this figure dropped to 4 per cent between 1963 and 1968. Production for domestic markets became dominant in the second half of the 1960s, along with a strong decline of the overall rate.[46]

Between 1959 and 1963, the rate of growth of metropolitan industries was above average and their share of national output increased. The opposite occurred over the period 1963–67. This indicates a close relationship between import-substitution induced growth and metropolitan industrial expansion. The recovery of the growth rates of output and employment (8.1 and 6.6 per cent respectively) between 1968 and 1974 led to a new expansion in metropolitan industries. During the less dynamic period between 1975 and 1980, output growth fell to 5.6 per cent and employment growth to 2.3 per cent.

Despite these variations, the participation rate in the industrial sector in intermediate regions tended to decline validating the hypothesis about this sector's weak direct links with industrialization in the metropolitan regions. The greater stability of industry in intermediate regions is a consequence of its linkages with the agricultural sector. However, some fluctuations in intermediate region industrialization occurred generally in the opposite direction of the trends in metropolitan industries.

Industries in rural regions managed to at least sustain their shares of national output from 1963 to 1967 and from 1970 to 1975. This is a result of the greater stability of rural industrial production during periods of low growth in the national–metropolitan system. In the 1970–73 period rural industries did gain from the small export boom associated with the introduction of incentives in 1967 (Plan Vallejo). This was possible due to the active trade in regions bordering Venezuela and Ecuador, benefiting the regions of Norte de Santander, Risaralda and Narino.

## Key emerging issues

The above findings indicate that the role of the manufacturing sector in the rural regions narrowed and often declined during the period of the analysis. The composition of industrial output suggests that horizontal integration through intra-regional product markets is the most important linkage for stimulating economic growth.

On the other hand, the capacity of these product market linkages to stimulate the regional economy is relatively limited. There are few backward linkages with the agricultural sector because intermediate industries are primarily located in metropolitan regions. Although data about inter-regional trade are non-existent, indirect evidence suggests that flows of manufactured products from rural to metropolitan areas are small and confined to a narrow range of agro-based products in a limited number of regions. By contrast, industrial imports from the metropolitan centres to other regions are large and growing. They consist of consumer goods, intermediate goods and capital goods. The role of the industrial sector in rural regions remained limited to satisfying a decreasing proportion of the intra-regional demand mostly for simple consumer goods produced by small and micro-scale firms.

## Constraints to industrial development in rural regions

During the study period of 1960–75, the limited role of small-scale rural industries in national industrial development was a structural phenomenon resulting from general constraints to the viability of industrial development in these regions. Some of the most important constraints were built into the predominant form of industrial expansion, vertical integration. After the period of import-substitution of basic consumer goods lost its momentum, the process continued in the intermediate goods and, to a lesser degree, the capital goods industries. The main impacts of this orientation were an increase in industrial development in intermediate regions where the necessary resources were available and reinforcement of the dominant position and the degree of regional integration of metropolitan industries as a result of the development of a new range of intermediate industries.

Rural regions only benefited from these developments indirectly and to a lesser extent. Most of the reduced rural development resulted from increases in demand for food, other agricultural consumer products, and agro-based raw materials. However, this increase in intra-regional demand was also associated with the income growth resulting from agricultural expansion. The increased demand for agro-based intermediate inputs did not stimulate such industrial development in rural regions, as such industries tended to locate in metropolitan regions.

The chronological order in which industries usually develop under an import-substitution strategy was a key factor in the emergence of these location patterns. Metropolitan concentration was favoured because of locational advantages (proximity to markets for established metropolitan consumer goods) and the attraction of external economies implied by existing intermediate industries in metropolitan areas that used imported inputs.

**Table 2 Changes in the output composition of manufacturing industry in Colombia**

|  | I | II | III | IV | V |
|---|---|---|---|---|---|
| *1951–1968* | | | | | |
| Consumer goods | 100 | 68.1 | 25.2 | 3.6 | 3.1 |
| Intermediate goods | 100 | 24.1 | 47.7 | −0.5 | 28.7 |
| Capital goods | 100 | 50.4 | 2.9 | 0.6 | 46.1 |
| TOTAL | 100 | 49.9 | 34.3 | 1.1 | 14.7 |
| *1968/70–1978/80* | | | | | |
| Consumer goods | 100 | 72.5 | 11.7 | 22.7 | −6.9 |
| Intermediate goods | 100 | 116.9 | 31.5 | 16.7 | −65.1 |
| Capital goods | 100 | 106.4 | 3.7 | 4.6 | −14.7 |
| TOTAL | 100 | 108.4 | 17.0 | 15.6 | −41.2 |

Source: Montes and Candelo 1981.

Column I   = Changes in output
Column II  = Changes in final domestic demand
Column III = Changes in intermediate demand
Column IV = Changes in exports
Column V = Changes in imports

In addition, by 1970, the effective rates of protection for industries discriminated against simple consumer goods and processed agro-based products. These two sectors make up the bulk of the industrial sector in rural regions. Trade policies strongly favoured capital-intensive industries located in metropolitan regions and, to a lesser degree, those in intermediate regions. Hutchenson calculated that this effective rate of protection was low or negative for agriculture and many traditional industries such as shoes, wood, furniture and non-metallic products. Almost 50 per cent of the two-digit ISIC industries including food products, textiles, clothing, leather and paper products received modest protection. However, industries producing beverages and tobacco, chemicals, basic metals, electrical machinery, and transport vehicles were heavily protected.[47]

Active border trade with Ecuador and Venezuela made it possible for some regions in the periphery to join in the small export boom of 1972–73. The development of traditional and agro-processing industries under low levels of protection was an important element in the capacity of such industries to take advantage of the new incentives. This phenomenon accelerated in the mid–1970s due to the oil boom in neighbouring countries and demonstrates a new facet of the national and inter-regional industrial interface.

In general, import-substitution reinforces trends toward metropolitan concentration, while a stronger reliance on domestic demand or export to neighbouring markets by traditional and agro-processing industries has the opposite effect. The export component of the economy was small and tended to bring about industrial concentration in some specific regions.

### The weakness of inward-looking, input-dependent industrialization in rural regions

The economies of rural regions experienced stagnation and slight de-industrialization during the study period. Their relative contributions to both national output and employment fell during this period. Most importantly, increases in the value of manufacturing production per capita only occurred in a few regions and were relatively small. In most regions. this indicator of industrialization tended to stagnate or decline. This structural phenomenon reveals the weakness of inward-looking regional industrialization schemes.

Colombia's regional industrial structure, composed of small-scale units producing basic consumer goods, depends upon intra-regional growth in demand through the expansion of the agricultural sector. In the long run, the importance of this demand at the national level may fall, causing a proportionate reduction in the share of national industrial production in rural regions. The share of industrial output located in rural regions is mainly a function of their shares of agricultural output in national GNP, which tends to fall along with economic growth.

In addition, the slope of the relationship between regional per capita income and the value of regional per capita industrial production during this period was small although positive. It was also lower than in the other two types of regions, averaging 0.103 for rural regions, 0.392 for intermediate regions, and 0.347 for metropolitan regions. This phenomenon is probably due to a combination of a lower income elasticity of demand for industrial products and a higher propensity to import. Thus, industrial decentralization policies based solely on stimulating intra-regional growth have limitations.

The evidence indicates that the level of self-sufficiency tended to decrease as the propensity to import increased. Two mechanisms seem to underlie this observation. First, increased per capita income reorients the demand profile toward large-scale production or relatively sophisticated

306

small-scale production that is only feasible in large urban agglomerations. Second, increased industrial production in rural regions has very few intra-regional impacts. The backward linkages are small given the location of intermediate industries and forward linkages are practically non-existent. The cross-correlation analysis found that industrial output growth had no significant relationship to income growth in the future. Yet, this relationship was only of importance in metropolitan regions.

The data show that significant increases in the level of industrialization only took place in those two rural regions where specialized, export-oriented industries emerged. This strategy may deserve more attention in the future since larger specialized outputs may create better conditions for a parallel process of import-substitution of intermediate inputs and the creation of external economies. This strategy has been used successfully in the clothing industry in Risaralda.

### The differentiation of industrial development in rural regions

The transformations experienced by the agricultural sector influenced the changes observed in industrial production in rural regions. Growth in cattle breeding had a very small and delayed impact on industrial production. Increased agricultural productivity and income resulting from greater commercialization of agriculture elicited a less than one-to-one response in industrial production.

Commercial agriculture and/or cattle breeding expanded in the departments of Sucre, Cordoba, Cesar, Tolima, Magdalena and Meta. In these areas, gains in the value of agricultural product per rural individual gave rise to smaller increases in levels of per capita industrial production than in areas characterized by a different agricultural output mix. Increases in the productivity and income generated through mixed cultivation and coffee production (typical of small-scale farming) had larger positive impacts on per capita industrial production. One of the reasons for these changes is transformation of the structure of household consumption associated with changes in income distribution. Another reason is intermediate consumption by the agricultural sector resulting from a different pattern of demand associated with the new technology. The net effect was a higher propensity to import.

Location quotient analysis of inter-regional trade flows revealed that the low impact of increased demand was offset in some cases by the emergence of specialized export-oriented food industries. This phenomenon occurred most notably in Tolima, where substantial advances in per capita industrial production were achieved.

307

### The role of small-scale production in industrial development of rural regions

As industrialization progresses, small-scale production becomes increasingly concentrated in industries that are innovative, have a comparative advantage from being small, are protected by their location, or that are able to maintain a particular niche. New industries normally require a period of experimentation and rapid innovation. When small scale they have greater flexibility and incur less of a risk. However, this may be a temporary phenomenon in which these firms grow to their optimal size as the industry becomes established. Some industries offer a competitive advantage to small-scale firms. These industries generally do not use methods that generate significant economies of scale. These industries can be characterized by one or more of the following features:

- Commodities produced by labour-intensive technologies;
- Commodities that are diverse and/or require frequent changes in design and are therefore characterized by fragmented markets;
- Highly personalized services and repairs;
- Highly specialized intermediate products for further assembly in large-scale plants or labour-intensive assembly operations;
- Markets protected by a combination of transport and marketing costs that result in a locational advantage insulating them from competition;
- A niche in an oligopolistic market due to the lack of interest of the dominant firms or as part of a lower pricing strategy.

Small-scale production in rural regions is often limited to basic consumer goods due to the narrow extent of industrialization in those regions rather than problems at the firm level. Some of these firms have survived due to market protection, but others operate in at least partly competitive environments. Their markets are often fragmented markets and in urban areas.

### Relative participation of small-scale production

In 1973, the small-scale informal industries (1–9 workers) and formal enterprises (10–49 workers) provided a very high proportion of manufacturing employment in rural regions of Colombia – 74–100 per cent of industrial employment. The negative correlation between the level of industrialization, as measured by the per capita value of production, and the importance of small-scale industry in employment suggests that 'market protected' industries still constitute a sizeable component of the industrial structure. This relationship is largely due to informal industry since employment in small-scale factories has a positive association with levels of industrial development. Thus, the relative importance of informal employment within small-scale employment is smaller the higher the level of per capita industrial production.

Figure 5   Regional share of employment in micro-enterprises with less than 10 employees, 1973–74

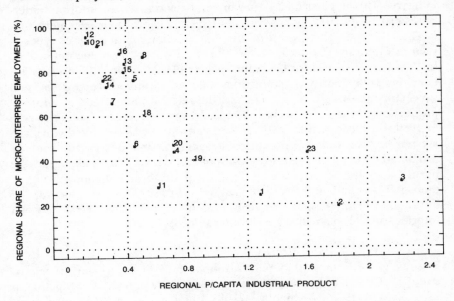

Figure 6   Regional share of manufacturing employment in small enterprises with 10–49 employees, 1973–74

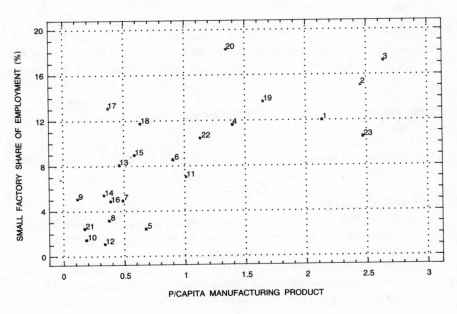

A comparison of Figures 5 and 6 indicates that employment by formal small manufacturing units is only a fraction of the employment by informal industry. This is particularly true in rural regions where informal enterprises provide 60–100 per cent of the total employment in small enterprises.

The relative importance of informal production fell in all three types of regions for an overall decline from 19 per cent of total production in 1960 to 13 per cent in 1974 for Colombia as a whole. However, the process has been faster in metropolitan regions than in intermediate regions, and slowest in rural regions. As a result, the relative importance of informal production in rural regions has increased from an estimated 44.5 per cent in 1960 to 51 per cent in 1973. In comparison, it has remained constant, around 15 per cent for intermediate regions and decreased from an estimated 40 to 34 per cent for metropolitan regions. These changes were mostly a result of an increase in growth of formal manufacturing in metropolitan and intermediate regions. In 1973–74, the degree of informality in small-scale production, as measured by the ratio between informal and total small-scale employment, declined.

## Urban and rural micro-firms

Figures 7 and 8 show that relative importance of the output of micro-enterprises fell at a decreasing rate with per capita industrial production in 1964–65 and 1973–74. Similar results obtained in cross-country comparisons suggest a common rationale for this phenomenon, such as the substitution of formal production methods as markets integrate and become more urban-focused.

As rural micro-enterprises decline, urban micro-enterprise production increases, but the overall effect is a decrease in production by micro-enterprises relative to formal producers. Such an interpretation is supported by the small but positive association between increases in per capita informal production and the level of urbanization of rural regions. This result points to qualitative differences in the role played by the two types of firms and the convenience of distinguishing both for policy analysis.

While rural micro-enterprises often have spatially protected markets, their urban counterparts can best be understood as a successful adaptation to a policy environment that is hostile to small-scale, labour-intensive production.

## Formal industry: small and medium/large scales of production

As expected, the relative importance of medium- and large-scale production in employment has a positive relationship to per capita production that is almost identical to that observed for formal small-scale units. This points to a close association of the two types of industry and the dependence of small-scale production on the external economies generated by higher levels of regional industrial development.

310

Figure 7　Regional share of output in micro-enterprises with less than 10 employees, 1960

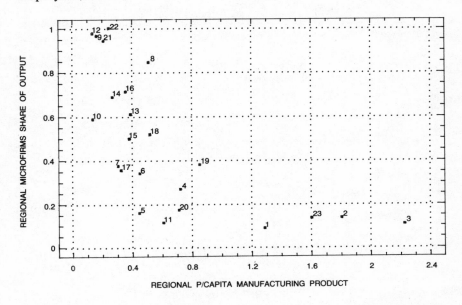

Figure 8　Regional share of output in micro-enterprises with less than 10 employees, 1973–74

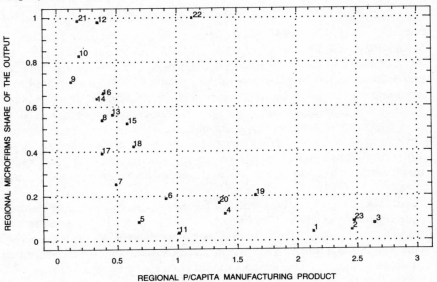

Figure 9    Relative importance of medium-/large-scale industries and per capita manufacturing production in employment, 1973–74

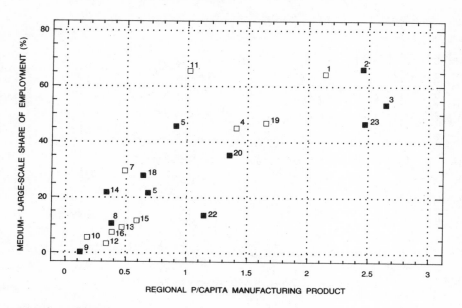

## Policy implications

### Regional industrialization patterns and forms of industrial development

Conventionally, the lack of dynamism observed in rural industrial development has been blamed on supply-side constraints. However, the limits of the 'spatial-institutional planning perspective resulting from this approach are evidenced in many of the problems LDCs have experienced in attempting to slow regional industrial concentration.

Numerous case studies have shown that financial resources allocated to decentralization strategies are often underutilized or misused. Industrial parks built to promote non-metropolitan locations have remained empty and state-planned industrial complexes have behaved as enclaves rather than growth poles. Moreover, these strategies have rarely achieved their targets.[48-50]

Attempts to explain these failures have highlighted the role of national macroeconomic policies in making industrial dispersal policies ineffective and indicated many contradictions between policies at the two levels. Although this is a limited explanation, it acknowledges the role of sectoral variables in the determination of spatial patterns of development.

Regional patterns of industrialization cannot be explained simply by deficiencies in the supply side and/or sluggish demand. On the contrary, they appear to be a basic outcome of the national industrialization process. In fact, the problems of rural industrialization stem from the inherent weakness of an inward-looking, input-dependent industrial development strategy. This inward-looking strategy is essentially a result of national macro-policies implemented in conjunction with an import-substitution strategy, which remained unchanged until the late 1960s.

This strategy favoured concentrated (metropolitan) industrial development through high levels of protection for final consumer goods, and non-agricultural based, capital-intensive intermediate industries and low rates of protection for traditional industries and the processing of indigenous natural resources.

The concentration effect has been reinforced by the competitive advantage obtained through industrial agglomeration (Kaldor-Verdoorn effect), or the growth centre effect. It was also reinforced by structural trends toward the oligopolization of capital-intensive industries and the increasing informality of labour-intensive industries. As a result, metropolitan industries were able to move into peripheral markets, but rural regions found it difficult to develop export capacity.

The sequence of industrial development that characterizes import-substitution processes caused rural industries to become more dependent on inputs from metropolitan regions. By the time intermediate goods industries were substituted the final consumer goods industries had already been consolidated in metropolitan locations. In addition to making transport more difficult and costly, the concentration of end-users and the resulting external economies led to concentration of intermediate input industries.

In this sense, the spatial and sectoral trends were essentially shaped by the same set of variables affected by the macro- and sectoral policy environment. In turn, regional variables mostly had an impact on the geographical pattern of industrialization and linkages.

The problem of the viability of small-scale rural industries is dominated by the more general issue of industrialization in rural regions. A policy to promote small-scale industries will not succeed if better conditions for industrial development are not created. Without an appropriate national policy environment and the availability of suitable technologies for both industrial and agricultural development, small-scale rural industries are unlikely to become extensive despite efforts to make institutional, capital, and infrastructural resources available.

### Limitations of conventional approaches to the promotion of small-scale rural industries.

Conventional approaches to the promotion of small-scale industries are supply-side oriented, centred around particular firms and undifferentiated by regions. They may either be characterized by a 'business-like' approach or a 'welfare' approach. The supply-side orientation is based on the belief that the efficiency and growth potential of small firms is limited because of their lack of sufficient access to inputs, factors, and markets. Consequently, governments develop policies, programmes and projects to correct this situation by creating special delivery systems.

A firm-centred approach emphasizes dealing with constraints to small-scale industrial development as they are experienced within the enterprises. These approaches ignore industrial development beyond the level of the firm in the sector or region.

A regionally undifferentiated approach does not take into account differences in economic structures across regions. Each region is characterized by a particular set of potentials and constraints for industrial development. Typically, spatial patterns of development are not taken into consideration and little effort is made to identify the places where industrial development might have the greatest potential for success.

The welfare approach is often justified by weak arguments about its potential to curb rural–urban migration. A business-like approach means that the potential of any industry is judged on the basis of anticipated conditions without assuming increased investment in infrastructure or complementary industries. The limitations of such approaches to industrial development in rural regions are apparent from the Colombian analysis.

It is clear that industries in rural regions often face demand constraints. These constraints can only be overcome by stimulating the economic base, most likely agriculture. However, given the limitations of inward-looking, input-dependent industrial development, encouraging growth of the agricultural sector may not be enough for two reasons:

First, the impacts of agricultural development are highly dependent on the technology used because of the income distribution and demand patterns generated through intermediate inputs.

Second, growth in demand may have a lower than expected impact on economies that have followed import-substitution strategies. Such strategies favour capital-intensive industries and penalize traditional and region-based processing industries that rely on indigenous raw materials. Consequently, they lead to a high degree of spatial concentration of production. Increases in income under these conditions may result in a higher propensity to import goods to rural regions rather than higher levels of production within the regions. Demand stimulation may be a necessary condition for broader industrialization but it is often not sufficient.

A firm-centred, region-wise, regionally undifferentiated policy ignores the structural nature of the problems faced by industrial development. The inward-looking, input-dependent model distorts the comparative advantages of the various types of regions, especially rural ones. To correct this situation, a different focus at the industry level is necessary guided by sectoral–regional policy principles and supported by infrastructure and human resource development.

The business-like approach is based on resource allocation criteria derived only from economic performance at the firm level. It does not take into consideration the overall impacts on the regional economy. Thus it concentrates resources on the economically stronger firms despite the possibility that other firms may be pushed out of the market as a consequence. By contrast, a broader approach to expand the range of opportunities for industrial investment may prove useful in rural regions.

## The policy environment and the organization of production

There are many weaknesses in rural industrialization strategies based on the natural protection offered by spatial barriers. In the long run, the development of manufacturing in the rural regions must take place in spatially integrated competitive markets, unless governments are prepared to create internal tariffs and protect traditional technologies.

In a vertically integrated competitive market, the development of rural industries depends on their capacity to check the expansion of metro-politan industries and compete in national markets that mainly produce products for metropolitan markets. Certainly, this requires a strong commitment to production efficiency and a favourable policy environment. The conditions that foster the oligopolization of capital-intensive industries and the polarization of labour-intensive industries by production scale may have to be reduced. Approaches that can achieve these goals range from correcting segmented factor markets to the development of suitable technologies.

## The alternative of selective, outward looking strategies for rural regions

It is doubtful that most regions of a country could substantially increase their levels of industrialization on the basis of their internal markets, especially in the presence of strongly integrated and expanding metro-politan industries. It may be important to explore an alternative strategy based on developing a regional system of industrial specializations. This would require a number of enabling operations and reorientation of small-scale promotion schemes.

The main reorientation would be the introduction of a sectoral–regional framework, based on comparative advantages. This would imply a complementary focus on the industry level and a shift in emphasis toward structural changes. Inter-regional deconcentration of agro-based inter-mediate industries could form the core of successful specialized regional industries oriented to extra-regional markets. Although it may be difficult to achieve this objective in practice, this approach may be more sound that other approaches used in the past.

315

# On the Dynamism of Small and Medium Industry in Colombia: Some Possible Lessons

ALBERT BERRY, MARILUZ CORTES and ASHFAQ ISHAQ

## Introduction

While there can be little doubt about the importance of industrialization in the development process, uncertainty surrounds the question of what sort of industrialization best advances development and what policies best lead to a healthy industrialization. Modern industrialization is generally understood to involve, ultimately, the attainment of high labour-productivity, so a large traditional handicrafts sector with low labour productivity could not be a permanent feature of that process. High labour productivity is usually associated with high capital-intensity and with large scales of production. It is evident, though, that many establishments which eventually become large and modern have their origins as small plants, and some small establishments are themselves modern in the sense that they use sophisticated technology and have high labour-productivity.

The last couple of decades have seen a burst of interest in small-scale manufacturing in less developed countries (LDCs), but viewpoints remain disparate on its potential contribution to the growth of the manufacturing sector and to development in general.[1,2] The important issues may be conveniently classified into those involving the static characteristics of the small-scale sector, especially its economic efficiency as traditionally defined, but also its employment and income distribution implications, and the dynamic aspects – its own growth patterns and the ways it affects the overall development process. Much debate has centred around the static efficiency or productivity of small establishments. Perhaps the discrepancy between competing views comes in part from different implicit definitions of efficiency or from different inclusions in the terms 'handicraft' or 'small'. It is important to distinguish at least three size categories of plants or firms: household activities, small non-household establishments, and large industry (LI). What we refer to here as small and medium industry (SMI) is significantly different from household industry or micro-enterprise.

ALBERT BERRY is Professor of Economics at the University of Toronto. He specializes in Latin American issues and his research has focused on small enterprise, agrarian structure, labour markets and income distribution.

The possible long run contribution of small enterprise to development does not depend solely on its present static efficiency. In some industries small establishments have been able to contribute in one or more dynamic ways,[8,9] that is, by growing into larger, more modern firms, becoming more productive themselves though remaining small, or contributing directly to the capital and skill formation and the technological improvements which raise overall industrial productivity in the long run.[10] In some industries, household and other craft enterprises may play no role in the growth of manufacturing beyond the very indirect contributions which any sector can make, such as, generation of transferable savings and creation of a market.

The chief task in the study of small-scale industry in developing countries is to ascertain in which industries small enterprises are most likely to make contributions to the overall growth process, what conditions foster these contributions, and how public policy affects them. This paper reviews relevant evidence from Colombia, focusing primarily on the 1970s. We define small industry (SI) and medium industry (MI) as plants with 5–49 workers and plants with 50–99 workers, respectively. While necessarily arbitrary, these categories are designed to focus on the size range above what is traditionally known as household or cottage industry. Aggregate data on the evolution of small and medium industry (SMI), together with micro-level data from sample surveys of small and medium firms in the metal-working and food-processing industries permits us to evaluate some aspects of the sector's performance, and to suggest possible reasons for its impressive boom during the 1970s. During this decade the downward secular trend in SMI's share of factory employment was reversed. (Factory employment as defined here includes SMI and large industry (ie, plants of 100 or more workers) and excludes the very small establishments of less than five workers.)

## Colombia's small/medium industry boom of the 1970s

Before 1970, SMI's share of factory manufacturing employment in Colombia was falling, following the usual pattern in the process of development;[11] it was approximately 57 per cent in 1953 and 47 per cent in 1970 (Table 1). (Its share of total manufacturing employment was a shade higher in 1970 (22 per cent as against 20 per cent in 1953) as the employment share of establishments with less than 5 workers fell from 61–54 per cent.) By 1978, however, this share had moved back up to 52–54 per cent. Total factory employment was growing at a high rate of 7.5–8 per cent per year from 1970 to 1978, and employment in SMI at a remarkable 9 per cent per year or more. Growth appears to have been fastest in plants of under 50 workers. How does one explain such impressive growth? What are its portents for the future? Unfortunately data for the 1980s are

**Table 1 Employment in the Colombian manufacturing sector by size categories, selected years, 1944–45 to 1978 (thousands of workers)**

| Year | Total manufacturing | Establishments of less than 5 workers | Factory sector[a] | Small and medium establishments[b] | Large establishments[c] | Employment in small and medium establishments as a percentage of | |
|---|---|---|---|---|---|---|---|
| | | | | | | All manufacturing | Factory manufacturing |
| 1944–45 | 455 | 314 | 141 | 78 | 63 | 17.0 | 55.0 |
| 1953 | 485 | 295 | 191 | 108 | 83 | 20.3 | 56.8 |
| 1964 | 637 | 327 | 310 | 159 | 151 | 24.9 | 51.2 |
| 1970 | 853 | 458 | 395 | 185 | 210 | 21.7 | 46.8 |
| 1978 | 1232–1417 | 524–669 | 708–748 | 368–408 | 340 | 28.7–29.9 | 52.0–54.5 |

[a] Establishments of five or more workers.
[b] Establishments of 5 – 99 workers.
[c] Establishments of 100 or more workers.

Source: Mariluz Cortes, Albert Berry and Ashfaq Ishaq, *Success in Small and Medium-Scale Enterprises: The Evidence from Colombia*, Oxford University Press, 1987, Table 2.21, pp. 44–45. Details of the methodology are explained in the source. The range of estimates for 1978 reflects the possibility that there was some (as yet unidentified) non-comparability between the 1978 figures and those for earlier years.

considerably less complete than for the 1970s, so we do not know in detail how SMI fared during the recession of the early 1980s. What are the relevant lessons for other countries?

This Colombian SMI boom appears to have been a result of both contextual factors and the specific characteristics of small and medium establishments. Available evidence suggests that the average economic efficiency of medium-sized plants may be greater than that of small ones, though average profit rates appear to have been high during the 1970s for both groups, approximating those of large plants. Many SMI firms grew rapidly, using past profits as an important source of funds. They showed innovative capacity, both in terms of product and design modifications and in terms of process modification. The entrepreneurs came from a wide variety of backgrounds, including skilled blue-collar workers, white-collar workers, and professionals. It appears that the dynamism of the Colombian economy, whose GDP grew at an average rate of about 6 per cent from 1967 to 1979, was important in fostering this growth. Demand for many manufactured goods rose rapidly, and although large industry was also expanding reasonably quickly, especially in the early 1970s, part of this growth was shifted to the external market under the incentives provided by a depreciating real exchange rate. A number of factors, discussed below, contributed to an increasing supply of entrepreneurial talent for SMI.

We review first some of the features of SMI establishments in Colombia, then return to a consideration of the special features of the economy in the 1970s.

## Productivity, technology and factor proportions of Colombian SMI

Small and medium establishments are found in many branches of Colombian industry, but are concentrated in food processing, clothing and footwear, metal products, transportation equipment (including repairs) and, to a lesser degree, chemicals and textiles. In 1964 the total share of employment by small and medium establishments exceeded 35 per cent – in metal products (excluding machinery) it was 44 per cent; printing, 42 per cent; food processing, 39 per cent; non-metallic mineral products, 35 per cent; and chemicals, 35 per cent.[12] In only a few sectors was the SMI employment share less than 20 per cent; these included several sectors dominated by capital intensive technologies and large plants – beverages, textiles, rubber, petroleum and coal products and base metals, and several where employment was concentrated in very small cottage/shop activities – clothing/footwear, wooden furniture, and transportation equipment.

SMI appears to have a somewhat greater regional dispersion than does LI, and is perhaps a little less concentrated in large cities. It is, nevertheless, a distinctly urban phenomenon. In 1975, 72 per cent of

# Table 2 Characteristic differences across Colombian manufacturing plants by size category, 1975–77

| | Household and other very small establishments of ≤ 5 workers | Small industry (5–49 workers) | Medium industry (50–99 workers) | Small and medium (5–99 workers) | Large industry (≥ 100 workers) | All |
|---|---|---|---|---|---|---|
| 1. Labour productivity, 1975 (thousands of Pesos/yr.) | 28.56 | 75.19 | 120.10 | 85.56 | 222.30 | 97.62 |
| 2. Wages, 1975 | | | | | | |
| (a) Blue-collar[a] | 18.00 | 19.00 | 22.15 | | 33.60 | |
| (b) White-collar[a] | 23.44 | 36.00 | 53.00 | | 73.62 | |
| (c) Both | 19.10 | 23.08 | 28.75 | 25.35 | 43.48 | |
| 3. Per cent of 1976 labour force who were: | | | | | | |
| (a) Unpaid workers[b] | 5.62 | 1.44 | 3.95 | 0.21 | | |
| (b) White collar | 19.53 | 21.18 | 20.19 | 25.89 | | |
| (b1) Clerical | 14.78 | 16.56 | 15.49 | 21.92 | | |
| (b2) Other | 4.75 | 4.62 | 4.70 | 3.97 | | |
| (c) Blue collar | 74.82 | 77.38 | 75.84 | 73.91 | | |
| 4. Labour share of gross value added,[c] 1976 | 33.9 | 32.2 | 33.5 | 30.3 | | |

320

| | Household and other very small establishments of ≤ 5 workers | Small industry (5–49 workers) | Medium industry (50–99 workers) | Small and medium (5–99 workers) | Large industry (≥ 100 workers) | All |
|---|---|---|---|---|---|---|
| 5. Indicators of the ratio of physical capital to labour | | | | | | |
| (a) Inventories plus book value of fixed assets per worker, 1976 | 96.2 | 136.9 | 112.7 | 257.0 | | |
| (b) KWH consumed per worker, 1977 | 3691 | 4338 | 3953 | 11,871 | | |
| (c) Inventories plus book value of fixed assets in relation to labour costs, 1976 | 2.67 | 2.74 | 2.71 | 2.98 | | |
| 6. Indicators of the ratio of physical capital to output, 1976 | | | | | | |
| (a) Inventories plus book value of fixed assets in relation to value added | .875 | .870 | .873 | .903 | | |
| (b) KWH per peso of value added | .031 | .039 | .035 | .042 | | |
| 7. Indicators of profitability, 1976 | | | | | | |
| (a) Before direct tax profits as a per cent of value added | 32.11 | 27.24 | 29.41 | 32.33 | | |
| (b) Before direct tax profits as a per cent of inventories plus book value of fixed capital | 36.72 | 31.30 | 33.61 | 35.79 | | |

[a] Excluding fringe benefits, whose inclusion would increase the difference across plant size.
[b] Self-employed proprietors and unpaid family workers.
[c] DANE definition, which includes some items which are, in fact, not part of value added.
Sources: Cortes, Berry and Ishaq, Row 1 from Table 2.10; Row 2 from Table 2.12; Row 3 from Table 2.15; Row 4 from Table 2.18; Row 5 from Table 2.16; Row 6 from Table 2.17; and Row 7 from Tables 2.18 and 2.19. Details of the methodologies used to arrive at the figures are given in that source.

employment in large industry and probably about 65 per cent of SMI employment was in the four largest metropolitan areas. Only cottage/shop employment was widely dispersed geographically.[13]

SMI is typified by intermediate technology and a capital intensity which falls between that of household and other very small establishments on the one hand and large industry on the other. These aggregate differences come partly from the different industrial composition of each of the three broad size categories, with household activities being concentrated in the relatively labour-intensive industries and large industry focused disproportionately in the capital-intensive ones, but they appear also to come substantially from intra-industry differences. This is, at any rate, true when 'industry' refers to the two-digit level of classification. The share of the variance in factor proportions across size categories of manufacturing as a whole which comes from intra-industry variance is likely to diminish the more narrowly industries are defined. In Colombia's manufacturing sector, that share is still high (around 40–50 per cent depending on exactly how measured) when a three-digit classification is used, but we have not undertaken the calculation at a four- or five-digit level. Ho has done so for average wages in Korea; the tendency to a positive association with size is less marked at that level of disaggregation; but the tendency is still there, and Ho's figures do not allow any simple conclusion about whether the relationship in the aggregate figures is primarily due to aggregation or to intra narrow branch associations.[14] In 1975, average labour productivity of SMI's was about 40 per cent of that of large industry, while average labour remuneration was 58 per cent. In large industry, with its more complex hierarchy and administration, a higher share of the labour force are white-collar (26 per cent to 20 per cent for SMI) and there are almost no unpaid workers. The ratio of physical capital to labour force is probably about one-half as high in SMI as in large industry. (There are no fully adequate figures. It is of interest that in 1977 electricity consumption per worker was about a third as high in SMI as in large industry.)

The size of the labour force is not a good measure of labour inputs, since appropriate weights must be given to different skills. Were relative earnings an accurate reflection of relative worker productivity, then labour costs would measure labour inputs correctly and, the capital–labour ratio would differ by only 10 per cent between SMI and large industry. (Clerical workers in manufacturing receive on average about twice as much as blue-collar workers (1976) and other white-collar workers (managers and technicians) nearly five times as much.) But if, as appears to be the case, large industry pays somewhat better for a given level of skill, the gap would be greater than this. In any case, in terms of the implications for income distribution and employment, the ratio of unskilled workers to each of the other factors of production may be of more interest than the traditional worker/capital ratio.

322

According to the figures in Table 2, the ratio of physical capital to output varies little between SMI and large industry. (One necessary qualification to this conclusion, on which we say more below, involves the assumption that the ratio of price to value is the same across plant sizes. There is evidence that this is not true, and it seems probable that on balance the ratio is higher in large industry than in SMI, so the true gap in capital output ratios may be greater than shown in the Table.)

In addition, the measurement of capital is no doubt somewhat in-accurate. Whereas the measure of capital stock used in our analysis of metal-working and food-processing firms was market value, the aggregate data on fixed capital shown in Table 2 refer to book value. Given the rapid inflation suffered by Colombia since the early 1970s, this would seriously understate true value (even commercial value). In 1976 the profit rate before direct taxes was 31 per cent of physical capital (as measured here) in SMI and 36 per cent in large industry. Figures on factor proportions and profits are not readily available for the household and very small shop sector, but one may fairly safely surmise that capital intensity is con-siderably lower than in SMI; average profitability is much harder to judge.

In summary, then, the aggregate data reveal an SMI sector which uses simpler technology than large industry, has a somewhat lower level of capital per unit of labour input, pays moderately lower wages and winds up, on average, with approximately the same rate of return to capital, though with greater variance across firms (see below). SMI may employ less efficient technology than large industry (information is lacking) or reap fewer economies of scale. However, it brings its profit rates up by paying somewhat lower wages and salaries. Although this is not reflected in our average profit rate figures for SMI, which are high (at least in 1976), the opportunity cost of capital may also be lower if many entrepreneurs have few other productive ways of using their own capital. It is also evident (see below) that although management problems are frequent in SMI, many small firms are better able to compete with large firms because of their capacity to innovate.

Recent (1978–79) surveys of small and medium metal-working and food processing firms, ranging in size from 3 to about 100 workers, permit analysis of such correlates of economic efficiency as firm size, character-istics of the entrepreneur, technology used and market conditions. The average economic payoff to resources used in the sampled firms was very high (possibly higher than in earlier and probably higher than in later years; 1978 was a year of very fast GNP growth, and came at the end of over a decade of striking economic growth in Colombia). Both the private benefit–cost (BC) ratio (defined as current revenues divided by the cost of all resources used, measured at private opportunity cost)

**Table 3a Estimates of average benefit-cost ratios for metal-working and food processing firms, by firm size[a] and by private v social (Standard deviations in parentheses)**

| Private | | Basic Estimate[b] | Social — Adjustment to Basic Estimate | | | |
| --- | --- | --- | --- | --- | --- | --- |
| Firm Size (No. of Workers) | No. of Firms | | Replacement Value of Capital Instead of Commercial Value | Capital Costed at 8% | Opportunity Cost of Entrepreneur Set Equal to Earnings of Skilled Mechanic | Product Prices Adjusted[c] |
| *Metal-working Firms* | | | | | | |
| 1–10 | 13 | 1.47 (0.63) | 1.22 (0.52) | 1.02 | 1.28 | 1.18 | 1.40 |
| 11–20 | 17 | 1.76 (0.93) | 1.41 (0.68) | 1.19 | 1.49 | 1.44 | 1.38 |
| 21–40 | 15 | 1.55 (0.75) | 1.43 (0.63) | 1.28 | 1.49 | 1.47 | 1.38 |
| 41–60 | 12 | 1.90 (0.96) | 1.72 (0.81) | 1.58 | 1.82 | 1.80 | 1.65 |
| 61+ | 8 | 2.07 (1.36) | 1.73 (1.07) | 1.53 | 1.88 | 1.77 | 1.68 |
| All | 65 | 1.71 (0.91) | 1.47 (0.73) | 1.29 | 1.56 | 1.50 | 1.47 |
| *Food-Processing Firms* | | | | | | |
| 1–7 | 9 | 2.11 (1.11) | 1.72 (0.90) | — | 1.83 | 1.56 | — |
| 8–15 | 10 | 2.62 (1.90) | 2.24 (1.73) | — | 2.39 | 2.10 | — |
| 16–29 | 4 | 2.87 (2.00) | 2.58 (1.76) | — | 2.71 | 2.09 | — |
| 30+ | 3 | 3.08 (1.78) | 2.85 (1.63) | — | 3.05 | 2.76 | — |
| All | 26 | 2.60 (1.66) | 2.26 (1.50) | — | 2.40 | 2.04 | — |

[a] Figures are unweighted averages across firms in a given size category.

[b] Assumes real opportunity cost of capital is 12 per cent for all capital; capital is measured by its reported commercial value; entrepreneur's opportunity cost is based on the income generating function estimated by R. Mohan for Bogota, 1978 (Rakesh Mohan, *The Determinants of Labour Incomes in Developing Metropoli: Estimates from Bogota and Cali, Colombia*, World Bank Staff Working Paper # 498, October 1981), and no adjustment is made to value added to allow for differences in product prices across firms.

[c] When the respondent indicated his prices were lower (higher) than his competitors, his firm's value added was raised (lowered) by 25 per cent.

Source: Calculations based on the authors' surveys of metalworking firms in 1978 and food processing firms in 1979.

and the social benefit–cost ratio were well above one in each industry (Table 3). The main difference between the private and social ratios is the assumed cost of capital (12 per cent from all sources) in the social BC ratio. The private payoff to the entrepreneur was on average a multiple of what his inputs would be expected to yield elsewhere. But the variance of all these measures across firms was high and, according to our calculations, a number had BC ratios below one (Table 3b). The relationship between average BC and firm size is shown in Table 3a. Both the private and the social BC ratios tend to be highest for the largest firms in each sample, though the average exceeds one for all size classes. This broad conclusion appears to be robust in spite of the various data problems plaguing these sorts of estimates; estimates of social benefit-cost (SBC) ratios using a variety of alternative assumptions are shown in Table 3. It appears that the positive association with size in the metal-working case could be significantly weakened only if product price were a quite poor indicator of value. We had the entrepreneur's assessment of whether the quality of his product was better or worse than that of his competitors, and when we assumed that better (worse) meant 25 per cent better (worse), the gap in SBC between the smallest and the largest sampled firms diminished considerably.

The wide inter-firm differences in BC ratios appeared, especially in the metal-working sector, to be more closely related to differences in technical efficiency (the ratio of outputs measured at given prices to inputs measured at given prices) than to differences in price or allocative efficiency[15] or to

Table 3b Distribution of metalworking and food processing firms by benefit-cost ratios

|  | Metal-working Firms | Food-Processing Firms |
|---|---|---|
| Private Benefit–Cost Ratio | | |
| < 1 | 11 | 5 |
| 1–1.5 | 25 | 4 |
| > 1.5 | 29 | 27 |
| All | 65 | 36 |
| Social Benefit–Cost Ratio | | |
| < 1 | 20 | 6 |
| 1–1.5 | 17 | 8 |
| > 1.5 | 28 | 22 |
| All | 65 | 36 |

Source: Calculations based on the author's surveys of metalworking firms in 197 and food processing firms in 1979.

**Table 4 Results of linear regression to explain variation in the private benefit cost ratio among small and medium metal-working and food-processing firms.**

| Independent variables | Metal-working firms coefficient (t) | | Food-processing firms coefficient (t) | |
|---|---|---|---|---|
| Constant | 3.973 | | 3.438 | |
| Relative wages | −1.650 | (−2.78)[a] | | |
| % of workers attending courses in year prior to survey | 0.015 | (2.41)[b] | | |
| % of equipment purchased 2nd hand | 0.0041 | (1.01) | −0.0115 | (−1.13) |
| *Entrepreneur's education*[1] | | | | |
| Primary | 0.788 | (2.96)[a] | −0.967 | (−1.49) |
| University | 0.565 | (2.24)[b] | −0.783 | (−1.22) |
| *Entrepreneur's main skills*[2] | | | | |
| Production only | −0.663 | (−2.52)[a] | 2.028 | (1.93)[c] |
| Administration/production | 0.130 | (0.35) | — | |
| Sales/administration | −0.276 | (−0.62) | −0.251 | (−0.32) |
| Administration only | | | −0.296 | (−0.34) |
| *Main source of complementary finance*[3] | | | | |
| Private banks | 0.270 | (0.89) | 2.027 | (2.99)[a] |
| Public banks | −0.317 | (−1.33) | 0.199 | (0.10) |
| Money lenders | −0.598 | (−2.29)[b] | 1.840[d] | (1.70)[c] |
| *Firm's prices compared with competitors*[4] | | | | |
| Higher | 0.333 | (1.23) | | |
| Lower | −0.594 | (−2.49)[a] | | |
| *Type of technology*[5] | | | | |
| Simple | −0.612 | (−2.35)[b] | −1.154 | (−1.62) |
| 'Sophisticated' | −0.517 | (−2.13)[b] | −2.222 | (−3.11) |
| *Labour mobility*[6] | | | | |
| High | 0.0049 | (0.03) | | |
| Low | 0.707 | (2.09) | | |
| *Production group*[7] | | | | |
| Agricultural implements | −0.498 | (−1.96)[b] | | |
| Ovens, stoves, kitchens | −0.369 | (−1.37) | | |
| $R^2$ | 0.61 | | 0.55 | |
| $R^2$ (adjusted) | 0.44 | | 0.34 | |
| DOF | 43.00 | | 23.00 | |
| F | 3.59[a] | | 2.59[b] | |

Note: The regressions are linear; all variables were dummies except relative wages, percentage of workers taking courses, and percentage of equipment, which was second hand. For further details see Cortes et al Tables 3.9 and 3.10.

Symbols: The (t) statistic;
[b] Significant at ≥0.01 to ≤0.05;
[d] Money lenders and suppliers.
[2] In the base, Administration only.
[4] In the base, same prices as competitors.
[6] In the base, moderate labour mobility

[a] Significant at the 0.01 level or less
[c] Significant at ≥ 0.05 to ≤ 0.1;
[1] In the base, secondary education;
[3] In the base, self-financing only.
[5] In the base, moderate technology.
[7] In the base, pumps & agricultural capital goods.

*Definitions and variables*
*Relative wages*:
A weighted average of the skill specific wages paid by the firm, compared to the average for all the firms in the sample.

*Type of technology*:
Categorical variable indicating the relative level of sophistication of the equipment in the firm's main production stages: simple technology – most of the firm's equipment is manual; intermediate technology – the firm uses a combination of manual and simple powered equipment; sophisticated – most of the equipment is powered and includes some special or more advanced machines.

*Labour mobility*:
Relative mobility of the firm's labour force according to whether most of the workers have been in the firm for: less than one year (high), one to five years (medium), more than five years or from the beginning (low).

---

differences in the absolute levels of output or input prices. Both BC ratios and technical efficiency were significantly related to the entrepreneur's education. In metal-working the primary and university levels were associated with higher BCs than the secondary level, while in food processing exactly the opposite was the case. (Table 4 presents the results of multiple regressions to explain the value of the private benefit–cost ratio and Table 5 gives the average for that variable across firms with selected characteristics.) In metal-working, where the entrepreneur's technical expertise is important, it may be that university training pays off in better understanding of relevant abstract principles, whereas primary education is correlated with having productive skills based on past experience; the skilled metalworkers usually have no more than a primary education. In food processing entrepreneurs do not seem to know the technical details of the production process; even quite small firms usually hire a technician or a skilled worker who knows the production process. Though the technical aspects of production are of obvious importance in the metal-working sector, entrepreneurs whose main skills lie only in production and who hence lack administrative skills tend to have lower BC ratios and technical efficiency indices, especially when the firm is of medium size or larger. Despite a lack of skills in these areas, such entrepreneurs are usually responsible for administration anyway.

One way that the entrepreneur's skills and education affect the firm's economic efficiency is through the selection of technology; technical efficiency tends to be highest for firms with an intermediate level of technological sophistication. (The term 'sophisticated' is used in a relative sense here; very few of the firms sampled use technology approaching the complexity common in large Colombian firms, let alone the developed countries.) (Table 6). Both the entrepreneur's formal education and his

327

**Table 5 Small and medium metal-working and food-processing firms, grouped by entrepreneurial characteristics: average private benefit–cost ratio**

| Entrepreneurial Characteristics | Metal-working Firms | | Food-Processing Firms | |
|---|---|---|---|---|
| | Number of Firms | Private BC Ratio | Number of Firms | Private BC Ratio |
| *Entrepreneur's Main Skills* | | | | |
| Production | 40 | 1.52 | — | — |
| Administration | 12 | 2.09 | 4 | 3.09 |
| Production/Administration | 5 | 2.12 | 25[e] | 2.53 |
| Administration/Sales | 4 | 2.05 | 5 | 1.91 |
| *Entrepreneur's Previous Job* | | | | |
| None (This is first Job) | 4 | 2.29 | 4 | 2.57 |
| Father's Firms | 5 | 2.09 | — | — |
| Mechanic/Technician | 30 | 1.49 | 5[c] | 2.65 |
| Independent Professional | 5 | 1.71 | | |
| Sales/Management | 12 | 1.80 | } 10[b] | } 2.73[b] |
| Sales | 9[d] | 2.33 | | |
| Owner of Enterprise | 9 | 1.91 | 4 | 3.15 |
| *Entrepreneur's Education* | | | | |
| Primary | 19 | 1.84 | 12 | 2.17 |
| Secondary | 19 | 1.25 | 16 | 3.24 |
| University | 27 | 1.96 | 8 | 1.95 |
| *Way Firm Was Acquired* | | | | |
| Founded by Present Owner | 9 | 2.07 | 22 | 2.92 |
| Bought | 56 | 1.66 | 12 | 2.21 |
| *Sources of Entrepreneur's Skills* | | | | |
| Working in Large Firms | 9 | 1.69 | | |
| Working in Small and Medium Firms | 13 | 1.51 | } 9[a] | } 2.01 |
| Training Institutions | 13 | 1.46 | | |
| University | 17 | 1.83 | | |
| Self-Taught | | | | |
| Previous Job & Courses | 3 | 3.51 | | |
| By Himself/Courses/Assistance | 7 | 2.36 | | |
| All of the above | 65 | 1.72 | 14 | 2.68 |

[a] The sources of entrepreneurial skills 'in previous job'.
[b] The entrepreneur's previous job is 'management or professional'.
[c] The entrepreneur's previous job is 'skilled worker'.
[d] The entrepreneur's previous job is 'salesman'.
[e] Includes persons whose main skill is in production control.
Source: The authors' surveys of metalworking firms in 1978 and food processing firms in 1979.

previous occupation are associated with type of technology. (Note that in the regressions reported in Table 4 both type of technology and entrepreneurial characteristics are included as separate 'determinants' of the PBC; the statistical significance of both indicates that education's impact is not exclusively through its effect on technological choice.) In the

328

Table 6 Average private benefit-cost ratio and technical efficiency index for metal-working and food-processing firms, by firm size and type of technology

| Firm size (No of workers) | PBC by Type of Technology | | | | TEI by Type of Technology | | | |
|---|---|---|---|---|---|---|---|---|
| | Simple | Intermediate | Sophisticated | All | Simple | Intermediate | Sophisticated | All |
| *Metal-working Firms* | | | | | | | | |
| 1–10 | 1.60 (9) | 0.91 (3) | 2.00 (1) | 1.47 (13) | 0.42 (9) | 0.24 (3) | 0.44 (1) | 0.38 (13) |
| 11–20 | 1.66 (7) | 1.96 (6) | 1.86 (2) | 1.80 (15) | 0.55 (7) | 0.64 (2) | 0.48 (2) | 0.57 (15) |
| 21–40 | 1.59 (3) | 2.11 (3) | 1.35 (9) | 1.55 (15) | 0.55 (3) | 0.80 (3) | 0.42 (9) | 0.52 (15) |
| 41–60 | 1.54 (2) | 2.42 (4) | 1.68 (6) | 1.90 (12) | 0.53 (2) | 0.87 (4) | 0.62 (6) | 0.69 (12) |
| 61+ | — (0) | 0.89 (2) | 2.47 (6) | 2.07 (8) | — (0) | 0.55 (2) | 0.78 (6) | 0.72 (8) |
| All | 1.61 (21) | 1.79 (18) | 1.78 (24) | 1.73 (63) | 0.49 (21) | 0.64 (18) | 0.56 (24) | 0.56 (63) |
| Standard Deviation | 0.61 | 1.18 | 0.93 | 0.91 | 0.23 | 0.38 | 0.30 | 0.29 |
| *Food-Processing Firms* | | | | | | | | |
| 1–7 | 1.91 (5) | 2.43 (5) | 1.53 (1) | 2.11 (11) | 0.40 (4) | 0.62 (5) | — (0) | 0.53 (9) |
| 8–15 | 1.98 (1) | 3.30 (6) | 1.76 (4) | 2.62 (11) | — (0) | 0.71 (6) | 0.59 (4) | 0.66 (10) |
| 16+ | 2.71 (4) | 3.18 (5) | 2.94 (5) | 2.96 (14) | 0.45 (2) | 0.93 (2) | 0.34 (3) | 0.54 (7) |
| All | 2.24 (10) | 2.99 (16) | 2.33 (10) | 2.60 (36) | 0.42 (6) | 0.71 (13) | 0.48 (7) | 0.58 (26) |
| Standard Deviation | 1.51 | 1.78 | 1.63 | 1.66 | 0.24 | 0.28 | 0.18 | 0.27 |

Note: Figures in parentheses are the number of firms.

metal-working sector, university-educated entrepreneurs employ a wide range of techniques (generally with success). Entrepreneurs who were previously production workers, and who usually have lower levels of education, use mostly simpler technologies; when they use more sophisticated technologies their technical efficiency is lower. Entrepreneurs with sales and administrative skills have a tendency to use more sophisticated technologies.

In the food sector firms using intermediate technologies have higher benefit–cost ratios for all size categories distinguished (there are not many medium or large firms in this sample), though this pattern is more marked for the smaller firms (Table 6). In the metal-working sector the pattern is more complicated; technological sophistication pays off more the larger the firm. Thus, among the smallest firms (1–10 workers), the efficiency indicators are above average for those using simple technologies, while firms with 11–60 workers do best with intermediate technologies, and firms with over 60 workers are more successful with sophisticated technologies (though in this last case only two firms use anything other than the sophisticated technologies). The larger the firm, the more sophisticated the technology tends to be – none of the large firms in this sample uses the simplest techniques and only one of the very small firms uses the most sophisticated techniques – but what Table 6 suggests is that at each size some firms use technology which is too sophisticated for their size while others use technology which is too simple. It is possible that firm size is affected by efficiency; an inefficient firm attempting to use sophisticated technology might become small due to its inefficiency. Our interpretation – that a small firm made the mistake of adopting a too sophisticated technology – would then be reversing the direction of causation. Our data did not permit adequate probing on this point. The standard deviation of PBC (the private benefit–cost ratio) is least for simple technologies, with the result that, although their average PBC is a little lower than that of the other two groups, only one of the firms with a PBC less than one uses simple technology while six use intermediate and three use sophisticated technologies.

Although BC ratios were associated with the firm's main source of finance, in both sectors those with access to private banks had the highest BCs. We did not attempt to discover why this was so; access could raise the BC ratio or a high BC ratio could facilitate access; or both. A number of other independent variables tested in our analysis did not have strong explanatory power (Table 4). It is noteworthy that in the presence of the independent variables discussed above, firm size was not significantly related to BC.

## SMI growth patterns

The growth performance of the firms in our metal-working sample was particularly striking. From 1973 to 1977, a buoyant period for this industry, average annual employment growth was 15 per cent; it was highest for the firms which were smallest in 1973. Although such growth rates are perhaps deceptive for firms which start with less than 20 workers, the average for those with over 30 workers in 1973 was still a striking 10 per cent per year. During the economy's fast growth period of the 1970s, aggregate data for Colombian manufacturing also show a tendency for small plants to grow faster than large ones; average annual employment growth from 1970 to 1975 was 4.8 per cent for plants with 10–49 workers in 1970 and 3.3 per cent for those with 100 or more workers in 1970.[16] In contrast, during the slow growth period from 1962 to 1966, Todd found that plants with under 25 workers in 1962 had virtually no employment growth while those with 100 or more workers grew at about 5 per cent over the period (1.2 per cent per year).[17] The tendency for smaller firms (or plants) to grow faster than large ones may be particularly characteristic of periods of rapid overall growth of manufacturing or of the economy as a whole.

Judging from the metal-working sector, on which we have reasonably detailed information, young firms usually start small, whether measured by the initial capital stock or the initial labour force. For those firms in our sample providing historical data, the average initial labour force was 15 workers, sales were about 7m 1977 Pesos ($US185,000) and capital 2.5m Pesos ($US67,000). The medians were considerably smaller: 8.5 workers, 2.3m Pesos ($US62,000) and 0.55m Pesos ($US15,000). Initial firm size was evidently associated with access to capital; for persons who had not completed primary school, usually a good reflection of low family income and status, initial investment was under 200,000 Pesos (about $US5,500) whereas at the other end of the spectrum the figure for persons with higher education was 5.2m Pesos ($US140,000). Most firms reported having had technical difficulties at the start and nearly half cited problems in getting raw materials, responsible workers, and an adequate level of working capital. Lack of clients was not a frequent problem (only one-quarter cited it). Lack of working capital, unlike the other early obstacles, was considerably more severe the smaller the initial size of the firm.

The formal capital market was of very limited importance in the start-up of small and medium firms. The recently created metal-working and food processing firms in our samples used own funds (including that from relatives and friends) for about 80 and 95 per cent, respectively, of investment undertaken during the 3–4 years before the sample. At inception, this share was probably higher still.

The process of firm growth was typically characterized not only by increases in capital stock and the work force but also by the addition of new products, design changes, and a variety of technological improvements.

Eighty per cent of firms reported design changes; smaller firms were most likely to do this to improve quality. Introduction of new products was associated with fast firm growth. These small and medium firms often displayed inventive and innovative ability, as well as responsiveness to consumer needs, and these traits permitted them to compete successfully against large, established plants. In agricultural implements, for example, the success of SMI firms was based largely on a series of significant improvements to implement design, based in part on their having greater familiarity with the problems of existing models than did their larger rivals.

A good part of the success of firms in our metal-working and food-processing samples seems to have been due to innovative capacity, though it is also true that some inputs, especially labour, may be cheaper for SMI than for large industry. The impression of technological progress is supported somewhat by aggregate figures on SMI labour productivity trends, which indicate a difference of about 40 per cent between the firms falling in this size category in 1953–57 and the (partly different set of) firms of the same size in 1977–79.[12] The figures must be viewed with some suspicion in light of the strange finding that labour productivity rose by 45 per cent in small plants (5–49 workers) and not at all in medium ones (50–99 workers).

### Explaining the SMI boom of the 1970s

Many of the features of the food-processing and metal-working firms included in our surveys of the late 1970s hold for SMI in general.[6] However, we do know that the decade beginning around 1970 was one of unusual dynamism for SMI as a whole. The firm growth rates we observed over the mid-1970s were not true of Colombian SMI during most of the 1960s, for example, nor probably of the 1980s. It is a matter of great interest why the 1970s were special.

A number of demand and supply factors appear to have contributed to the resurgence of SMI. On the demand side, the rapid growth of national income, at an annual average of 7 per cent over the years 1967 to 1978, created a rapidly expanding domestic market for the products of SMI. The growth of SMI in turn contributed to the overall economic boom, though probably not in a major way.

An increase in the competitive potential of SMI may have been as important as the favourable demand conditions. Investment funds, capital goods, entrepreneurship and labour all became available to a significantly greater degree than in any earlier period; this simultaneity makes it difficult to assess the relative importance of each of these factors in the creation of the boom. Three events underlying much of the improved input availability were the improved balance of payments situation beginning in the late 1960s, the related fast overall growth, and the declining real wages of the early 1970s.

The increase in the number of small and medium manufacturing establishments was facilitated by an expanding pool of potential SMI entrepreneurs, reflecting both improvements in educational achievement and the cumulative work experience of large-scale and SMI employees; in the metal-working industry, a significant minority of entrepreneurs were previously skilled workers in other firms, most frequently large firms. A final probable factor was a decline in real wages of 15–20 per cent during the first half of the 1970s in most occupational categories, including blue- and white-collar workers in manufacturing. This sharp decline, occurring at a time of economic buoyancy and rapidly increasing average per capita incomes, would be expected to encourage skilled blue-collar, white-collar, and professional workers to start their own businesses, either on a full-time basis (the usual case for former blue-collar workers) or as a side-line (more often the case with professionals). The ratio of wage or salary earnings to potential SMI profits must have fallen sharply indeed during the early 1970s; the paid labour share of gross value added in the manufacturing sector fell sharply from 40.2 per cent in 1972 to 30.4 per cent in 1974. The same decline in wages and salaries which encouraged some individuals to become entrepreneurs by lowering the opportunity cost of their time also meant that labour costs in SMI establishments were falling. An inflation-induced wage price lag seems to explain the initial sharp wage decline of the early 1970s. Even by 1980, however, after 5 to 6 years of adjustment to the new higher level of inflation (20–30 per cent compared to a typical rate of about 10 per cent per year in earlier decades), real wages in many occupations had barely recovered their 1970 levels. This sluggishness probably reflects downward pressure resulting from the record fast growth in the urban labour force during the 1970s (5.5 per cent compared to 4 per cent in the 1950s, for example) as the population of prime working age rose and participation rates rose as well.

The SMI sector appears very much to have fed on its own growth during the 1970s; its investment to value added ratio rose sharply to surpass that of large industry (Table 7). The high profits reaped by manufacturing as a whole throughout the booming 1970s were probably shared by SMI. (Profit figures by plant size are available only for 1976 – see Table 8.) There is considerable evidence, from our metal-working and food sector surveys and other sources, that SMI firms get started almost entirely with their own capital and rely on credit only in a very limited way until reaching medium size. Large industry, on the other hand, has good access to credit, often at subsidized rates. Under these conditions, SMI investment for purposes of expansion is likely to be based mainly on past profits and, given sufficient demand, to be high when profits are high, as in the 1970s. The more stable supply of funds (including credit), available to large industry would make

333

its investment rate less sensitive to the profit rate. Accordingly, during the 1960s and 1970s the investment to output ratio was virtually constant in large industry whereas in SMI it was rising.

### Table 7 Investment-output ratios, by plant size, 1962–78

| Plant Size | 1962–66 Gross | 1967–71 Gross | 1972–76 Net | 1972–76 Gross[b] | 1977–78[a] Net | 1977–78[a] Gross[c] |
|---|---|---|---|---|---|---|
| SI | 10.23 | 11.63 | 9.31 | 15.91 | 10.88 | 19.19 |
| MI | 10.33 | 12.75 | 8.84 | 15.10 | 10.75 | 18.96 |
| LI | 14.14 | 13.29 | 8.01 | 13.70 | 7.99 | 14.09 |
| 100–199 workers | 8.96 | 10.05 | 5.47[d] | 9.35[d] | 7.48 | 13.19 |
| 200+ workers | 15.90 | 14.33 | 8.53[d] | 14.58[d] | 8.08 | 14.25 |
| SMI | 10.27 | 12.09 | 8.26 | 14.11 | 10.82 | 19.08 |
| All of the above | 12.91 | 12.95 | 7.87 | 13.45 | 8.15 | 14.37 |

Note: Data for the four groups of years are not fully comparable. Those for 1967–71 are gross figures for legal depreciation; the rest are net but with the additional adjustment mentioned in note a.
[a] Data in 1978 include revaluation of fixed assets, whereas those in 1977 do not.
[b] Based on application of the sector wide average gross-net ratio of 1.709 to each size category.
[c] Based on application of the sector wide average gross-net ratio of 1.764 to each size category
[d] Assumes the same figure for firms with 100–199 workers and for those with 200+ in 1974, as we had only the average of these two categories for that year.
Source: Dane, *Anuario General de Estadistica* for years through 1967; *III Censo Industrial* for 1970; and *Industria Manufacturera* for other years.

### Table 8 Profit[a] rates in Colombian manufacturing by plant size, 1976

| | Profits[a] as a percentage of Gross Value Added | Profits[a] as a percentage of Book Value of Fixed Assets Plus Inventories |
|---|---|---|
| Small Plants (5 to 49 workers) | 32.1 | 36.7 |
| Medium Plants (50–99 workers) | 27.2 | 31.3 |
| Large Plants (100 workers or more) | 32.3 | 35.8 |
| All | 31.6 | 35.2 |

[a] After indirect taxes, before direct taxes.
Source: Unpublished DANE statistics, made available to the authors.

While the formal capital market continued to play a limited role in support of SMI expansion, the evolution of a broad non-formal credit market during the 1970s may have been beneficial to it. This market was fostered by the low real rate of interest on most traditional assets resulting from the higher inflation rate of the 1970s, and by the large inflow of funds from illegal drug activities and from the coffee bonanza. SMI makes more extensive use of this market than does large industry, though exactly how important a role it plays is not known.

Directly and indirectly, the absence of balance of payment problems during the 1970s made it easier for small and medium plants to acquire the capital equipment they needed. The tight rationing of foreign exchange during most of the previous two decades is presumed by most observers to have worked against SMI.[18] During the 1970s they had easier access to imported equipment; the ample supply of foreign exchange and the lowering of tariffs on capital goods also induced large firms to bring in new machinery and place their used equipment on the secondhand market at prices affordable to SMI. The improving market in secondhand equipment was a further boon to SMI in the 1970s. Both the metal-working and food-processing firms included in our sample and SMI firms in general purchased approximately a quarter of their machinery and equipment second-hand in the late 1970s. For younger firms the ratio was higher; in our samples it averaged about 40 per cent for those created within the previous 5 years.[12] During the 1970s the number and scope of firms specializing in supplying secondhand machinery to interested buyers increased, as did the repair capacity associated with the use of such machinery.

## Lessons from the Colombian experience

The recent experience of small- and medium-scale manufacturing in Colombia suggests a number of lessons relevant to other developing countries, and also raises a number of issues. The major lessons would appear to be:

1. The normal experience of declining SMI importance with increasing industrialization does have exceptions, as in the case of Colombia in the 1970s. This case demonstrates that SMI output and employment may continue to grow rapidly, even after some reversals, as a country joins the ranks of newly industrialized nations. This is an optimistic note with regard to the overall employment creating potential of the industrial sector. In particular, the success of intermediate technology in SMI means that such potential is not yet seriously challenged by modern sophisticated technology requiring a great deal more capital and employing far fewer workers;
2. The very rapid growth of SMI output and employment achieved by

Colombia in the 1970s did not have the precondition of dramatically rapid growth in large-scale manufacturing at rates like those achieved by Korea, Taiwan or Brazil. SMI was not essentially pulled along by linkages with large industry. Probably the key ingredients in its performance were a rapid growth of domestic demand, fairly extensive experience in non-handicraft manufacturing, fairly well developed educational and training systems, and a good market for secondhand machinery;

3. SMI establishments can be efficient resource users in the short-run, and also dynamic over time as they grow, improve their technology, and introduce innovations in response to constraints and problems;

4. The extent to which SMI establishments are created and grow to a moderate size with little credit from formal channels suggests that the absence of a well developed credit system need not be a very serious obstacle to a flourishing SMI sector. Own savings, social security benefits, severance pay and money lenders have all played a role in Colombia and elsewhere. It is not impossible that the opportunity cost of the entrepreneur's own savings is relatively low in comparison with those flowing through the formal capital markets. That is, in some cases if an alternative productive use is not found, the funds are used instead for consumption purposes;

5. Monopoly/oligopoly characteristics of an industry in its early stages in the face of import-substitution policies may give way to a more competitive structure at a later phase when an expanding market coincides with the necessary entrepreneurial capacity to generate a dynamic SMI sector. This pattern was very clear, for example, in the agricultural implements industry;

6. The combination of a good market for secondhand equipment and workers skilled in repair and maintenance is important and may be pivotal to the development of SMI in some branches, especially in the first years after founding.

Among the more interesting hypotheses suggested by the Colombian experience, but requiring more analysis to assess their validity are:

1. The growth rate of SMI firms and of SMI output and employment in the aggregate depends very heavily on the profit rate of the sector, since outside sources of funds are not available (or at any rate not used) to any significant degree. This suggests that SMI is likely to grow faster when the economy as a whole is buoyant, when labour and input costs are relatively low and when taxes impinging on it are not too high. It would be interesting to compare SMI growth performance in Colombia in the 1970s with that in other countries (for example, Japan) where SMI can draw more extensively on the capital market or where

its linkages with large industry give it better access to outside funds;

2. SMI performs well when wages are low or falling, either in absolute terms or relative to wage expectations or returns to capital. The beginning of the boom decade in Colombia was characterized by these features, but we did not have the detailed information necessary to judge how important they were in inducing individuals to become entrepreneurs;

3. SMI may be encouraged when large industry moves increasingly into the export market.

# Discussion: Rural Linkages

*L de la Rive Box*: Can you give an example of the changes in government policy toward small industries in Columbia? Were there different credit policies for rural regions? Can you link such policies to the data you have seen?

*F Uribe-Echevarria*: By the end of the 1960s, the Colombian government was very concerned that industry was becoming too concentrated in urban areas and began making an effort to slow the rate of urbanization and industrial concentration. There was a policy to provide special credit terms including subsidized interest rates for investors in secondary cities located in rural regions. This was part of a more elaborate scheme for investment in secondary cities with measures to facilitate the construction of infrastructure, and industrial parks and a prohibition against foreign investment in the industrial sector in the four metropolitan areas.

We analysed some of the credit demand data for a ten-year period (5 years before and after the above measures were taken). Although one should be cautious about making causal links between credit schemes and credit demand, the data show no change in rural demand for credit for industrial investment.

Second, approximately three-quarters of the few industrial parks that were built went bankrupt and many others did not materialize. Eventually in 1980–82, the government cancelled the prohibitions against foreign industrial investment in metropolitan areas because they did not have any impact. Two reasons can be given for the ineffectiveness of these policies in broadening regional development:

1. The investment went primarily toward expansion of existing firms and relocation was a non-issue;
2. Most of the firms could demonstrate that their performance would be jeopardized if they were not located near a major metropolitan area.

In general, investment decisions may not be that sensitive to policy objectives built into credit schemes. After all, a large proportion of industrial investment (perhaps 40 per cent in Colombia) is from domestic resources.

*A Berry*: An additional reason why credit policy did not have a significant impact on industrial investment is that part of the investment was financed by outside funds. A lot came from the financial corporations that were not clearly under the control of the monetary authorities.

I would also like to comment on the relationship between the trade regime and the development of small- and medium-scale industry. The usual hypothesis is that an equilibirum in the foreign exchange rate is good for small- and medium-scale enterprises because it gives them better access to foreign exchange than in rationed foreign exchange trade regimes. The Colombian experience is broadly consistent with this hypothesis. With the switch to a more realistic (and floating) exchange rate, the substantially greater availability of foreign exchange presumably gave the small and medium sector better access to foreign exchange than it had in the 1960s. It is uncertain to what extent this additional foreign exchange was a direct source of the boom in small- and medium-scale enterprises. Certainly the change in the performance of the Colombian external sector was an indirect cause of much that happened. The growth boom was associated with an improved trade policy, but I am not sure whether there were direct effects on the small- and medium-scale sector. Certainly the boom generated a huge inflow of capital to this sector, but data were not available to support this hypothesis.

*G Ranis*: Mr Berry has mentioned that the rest of the economy's growth did affect the boom in the small- and medium-scale sector. Since we are talking about linkages, what about agricultural growth and the feedback to agriculture?

*A Berry*: We were never able to develop figures showing the extent to which the small- and medium-scale sector was exporting in Colombia. We knew of individual firms that were exporting, but our impression was that this sector was mainly producing for the domestic market. In at least a few cases, we speculated that there was an indirect effect on exports. In the agricultural machinery sector, a number of small firms grew rapidly because they were able to identify the needs of local farmers better. When they began to compete, they sold a better product at half the price charged by the larger firms. As a result, the largest firms in this industry moved into the export market. I have not had a chance to see how long this situation persisted or how important the phenomenon was.

On the question of linkages, I have no quantitative feel for the extent to which products of the urban small and medium sector were purchased by rural people. Many products (eg, gas stoves) were bought by the lower middle class, because cheaper versions were produced. So, there is no doubt that some products were going to rural areas, but probably not in large quantities.

*F Uribe-Echevarria*: The export trade may have had something to do with the industrial boom of the seventies. The oil boom in two neighbouring countries (Venezuela and Ecuador) stimulated an active trade along the border areas. Large quantities of mostly labour-intensive products were exported.

I did a small study of one of these areas on the border with Venezuela. By the end of the 1970s, the unregistered export trade between those two regions was approximately three hundred million dollars. Based on a detailed inventory at transport crossings, this stream of trade was even bigger than official trade between Colombia and Venezuela, excluding oil.

These goods were recorded as produced in Colombia but not registered as exports. To some extent, the same thing happened along the southern border with Ecuador. Thus, exports may have had a larger contribution than is often acknowledged.

*C Liedholm*: What role has the illegal drug trade played in these linkages?

*F Uribe-Echevarria*: The drug trade has boosted the Colombian economy for many years. Initially, it was more a regional phenomenon which generated income for small farmers but also created a very high rate of inflation in those regions. The cocaine traffic today is a different issue altogether, one that is bigger and less localized. The economic significance of the phenomenon is somewhat exaggerated because a large part of that money does not come back to Colombia. Nevertheless, it has an impact since some of this money is finding its way into investments, such as in the construction sector and more recently in agriculture and livestock production. The latter is especially true in areas where social unrest has reduced the real price of land.

Given the size of the returns to narcotics traffic, there is no doubt that part of that money is being channelled through financial institutions. However, I do not think that has influenced regional patterns of industrialization to any significant degree. Only very recently has a larger proportion of the profits returned to Colombia due to increasing difficulties in retaining the money outside the country. The concentration of drug money on cattle breeding may soon end and have some impact on other regional economic specializations.

*G Waardenburg*: I am wondering about the character of research on small enterprise development. How much insight do you think has already been gained compared to what you expect could be obtained in this field of research? Could more complex theories provide a firm grip on the phenomena we are talking about and would they be hard to test? Will there always be a large amount of uncertainty about this sector due to random factors and situation-specific social and cultural factors?

*A Berry*: The important thing about the research done thus far is that it established that the smaller enterprises are not necessarily inefficient. This is paralleled by the first burst of research on small farms. I think it will be a lot tougher to do further research to shed more light on this sector. There

340

are several key areas that we do not know enough about at this time. One is the complementarities linking different size or technology categories to each other, in other words, what is really competing with what? We also need to know a lot more about what happens to small- and medium-scale enterprises in macroeconomic crises. When the economy is doing well overall, how this sector performs does not matter as much in terms of national economic growth. When the economy is sputtering, it matters much more.

At present, we do not have enough information on how the sector can be encouraged through policy. Some say that the best thing to do is to leave this sector alone since policies designed to help it will backfire. That is an extreme view, but in general we understand a lot more about how these firms behave than how they respond to policy initiatives.

*A Saith*: I would like to ask Mr Berry a question about the rapid growth of the small- and medium-scale sector in Colombia. How important is sub-contracting from large-scale firms? Frequently, large-scale companies sub-contract work out but this does not show up in official credit records or second-hand machine sales. How has the performance been in sub-contracting orders, component manufacturing, and final product manufacturing?

*A Berry*: I do not know how important sub-contracting is in the small- and medium-scale sector in Colombia because there have been few studies of this topic. Ten years ago, most of us did not think there was much sub-contracting in comparison to other countries. Although I have heard that there is a lot more than meets the eye, the common view is that there is little.

Among the firms we surveyed, there was very little sub-contracting and their growth had nothing to do with sub-contracting. The nature of the products in our surveys did not suggest such links.

In looking at the composition of employment growth in the small- and medium-scale sector as a whole, our impression is that sub-contracting was not prominent during that phase of growth. It might have been more prominent earlier, but this is not known.

*F Uribe-Echevarria*: Sub-contracting does not seem to be very important. Putting out is probably more important. Some large firms organize some of their operations to distribute work to households, especially from the metropolitan areas into the surrounding areas. But this is not really sub-contracting, because independent firms are not involved.

*J Sullivan*: I am interested in the roller-coaster ride that these companies face. It suggests to me that if they can sharply cut back their hired labour, they must not have organized trade unions. Obviously, labour codes in many countries either allow employee lay-offs or else the regulations are not being observed.

341

*A Berry*: Certainly there are labour codes which, in principle, should have made it difficult to drop so many workers. If we had been aware beforehand of this roller-coaster trend, we would have tried to find out more through our questionnaires. It is true that the legislation does not legally cover firms below a certain size, but most of the firms studied were above that size. In these companies, manoeuvres like firing and rehiring workers on the same day to keep them from getting on the permanent payroll were undoubtedly going on. That would be an important set of questions to ask in the future.

*S M Wangwe*: I would like to talk about linkages on the supply side. The extent to which rural industries are linked to the agricultural sector in supplying inputs and agricultural implements and other capital goods is not very clear. In Tanzania, attempts to encourage these linkages involved establishing rural craft workshops in every region. This was done in the hope that location appropriate equipment could be produced by scattered, small rural industries so that simple things like oxcarts would not have to be transported over hundreds of miles. In a number of regions, these workshops reproduced prototypes developed in the larger R & D institutions, in some cases, modifying some of the equipment to suit local conditions. Eventually, however, the pattern of demand led to the transformation of some of these workshops into producers of other goods such as furniture.

Although the purpose of these activities was to develop linkages to support agriculture, agriculture itself does not always generate enough demand for those products. How widespread is this problem of insufficient effective demand? The limited production of inputs for agriculture also reflects a weak link between agricultural production, producers of agricultural equipment, and R & D institutions. It would be useful to draw lessons from experiences where this link has been strengthened.

My next question concerns the extent to which R & D institutions link up with rural small- and medium-scale industries to assist them in their technological innovations. As enterprises grow and new problems emerge, do they use technologies developed by the R & D departments of the larger enterprises or do they have links with R & D institutions and universities elsewhere? Our experience is that the demand for R & D is so small that it is normally handled by craftsmen and a few technicians instead of engineers.

*J Sullivan*: My experience in several countries is that the R & D activities that are set up to assist small and rural enterprises are often too academic and do not really explore the questions and issues that actually affect people trying to keep an enterprise going. Government-run technology centres are often too bureaucratic and their activities are often off target.

342

*G Waardenburg*: I am familiar with one country where it is obvious that the mentality of people devoted to science and technology is totally different from that of people interested in small-scale industries. Any question of small-scale industry alternatives is immediately referred to another department. This is fortunate because then other people who are really interested in the area can deal with it. You should not expect technologists who are interested in other things to also deal with such questions. Fortunately, there are some exceptions.

*A Berry*: The institutes in Colombia charged with providing technology assistance and developing new products have done something. They are not weak relative to their counterparts in other countries, however, they do not play a large role in the process of technological change in small- and medium-scale enterprises in Colombia. As with financing, the firms themselves provide the bulk of this activity and many entrepreneurs have been quite ingenious.

Anecdotal information indicates that entrepreneurs are often able to locate people who have done some relevant research. Such people often have nothing to do with the R & D institutions. Sometimes they work for a university. Many entrepreneurs pick up ideas from catalogues and exhibitions. We were struck by the amount of aggregate technological change that is occurring, but still only have a vague idea about where it comes from. However, we are sure that the majority of R & D does not come from the R & D institutions.

*G Ranis*: Concerning the qualitative importance of linkages, FAO did a survey of some of the literature and there is also some work that Mrs Stewart and I did on the Philippines. This research indicated that consumer linkages are the most important quantitatively. The production linkages (backward and forward) are smaller, but may still be important.

However, a minority also feels that backward linkages to agriculture are important in generating new incentives as well as awareness of the market. The work in this area is very limited, but it might be interesting to compare the African and Asian situations. Since Africa has a much lower population density than Asia, the rural demand pattern is very different. The typical market is much larger in Africa than in Asia because it services a larger area, which also means that transport distances are greater.

*F Stewart*: Since the data on economic linkages are limited in Africa, in contrast to Asia, these generalizations are based on piecemeal evidence. Although total linkages are smaller, consumption linkages tend to be more important in Africa than in other places because there are fewer backward linkages. African agriculture uses fewer inputs than Asian agriculture. Why total linkages are lower is difficult to explain, but is probably related to both demand and supply factors. Second, services are far more important than manufacturing in African rural linkages.

343

*C Liedholm*: Recent studies by Hazell, Haggblade and Brown, based on very limited data, indicated that the linkages in Africa are only 60 per cent of the levels in Asia. They also noted that forward production linkages are greater than the backward linkages by a factor of eight. Some of the reasons noted for the smaller production linkages in Africa included less irrigation and machinery use in agriculture.

*G Ranis*: What specific actions could governments take to strengthen linkages where they do not seem to be very strong, particularly in transport, the public sector, and infrastructure? Who decides what infrastructure is needed and where it is to be placed? How can direct private linkages be strengthened?

*F Stewart*: First, governments could emphasize the supply-side variables but the low demand for agriculture inputs also needs to be addressed. The Mellor school has claimed that consumption linkages are greater where there is an unequal income distribution in agriculture. However, those studies have neglected savings behaviour and how much people of different income levels spend on locally produced products in comparison to those produced in urban areas. Consequently, I think their evidence is not relevant to this question and suspect the linkages go in the other direction. The smaller farmers are likely to spend more on local products. I am studying this further in Africa.

One of my students has written an essay on another supply-side issue, the importance of telecommunications for rural appropriate technology in Africa. Worldwide, telecommunications are largely concentrated in urban areas. Many countries literally have no telecommunications infrastructure in rural areas. The availability of rural telecommunications could make a tremendous difference in technology identification and access to credit institutions. We need more empirical work on this issue.

*A Saith*: I would like to discuss the demand side. I agree with you that some of the Mellor school studies suffer from misinterpretation. I would like to emphasize one other aspect – what are we talking about when we speak of rural industrialization and rural non-farm employment? With a focus on target groups, poverty alleviation and rural labour force absorption, the concern is with the objectives, not the linkages. While local linkages are important, what does it matter if the middle-income farmers buy something produced by rich entrepreneurs in the countryside? The distributional aspect is the critical one, not the locational aspect. Location is important to the extent that it is associated with other distributional aspects. What is really needed is a profile of what is locally produced – the value added, the structure of production and the dynamics of the local sectors.

I would like to mention a few case studies on dynamics because I think it is very difficult to make general statements on linkages. Infrastructure development, such as electrification, can have a dramatically different impact on local poor producers depending on the context. Consider the example of an industry that is doing very well in India, costume jewellery. People from department stores buy local designs in the villages. As soon as they start selling well, the production process is motorized and moved to a small town often with bank financing. Often, the firm is later bought out by someone from the outside. What started initially as a local linkage disappears. Without examining the distribution question and the stability of linkages, it is not obvious whether linkages can be converted into capital accumulation in the rural areas.

Another example is agricultural processing. The growth in agricultural productivity, from the Green Revolution in parts of North India, made small-scale, mechanized agricultural processing technologies viable along the main roads. Infrastructure now links the villages, but a whole range of traditional activities has disappeared from the villages.

This raises another question. Where will a middle-scale landowner reinvest the profits from increased agricultural productivity – in the village or in trade? Questions about relative profitabilities and risks of different sectors are important. More studies are needed on this to understand the implications for income distribution.

*G Ranis*: I agree that the demand side is important, though we still need more information. I emphasize the supply side because many bottlenecks offset these linkages. Substantial scope exists for productivity gains in agriculture and rural industry that are currently inhibited by shortages on the supply side. However, the necessary infrastructure must be in place and this is a real problem that often results in poor allocation of scarce resources.

*A Berry*: The concept of linkages has most relevance in countries where there is an untapped supply potential in the 'linked' sectors. The savings potential and sometimes the entrepreneurial potential is often substantial in these countries. In parts of Latin America where changes are occurring in the financial systems, the potential impact of financial liberalization on the small-scale sector needs to be examined. Then, there are general equilibrium questions about where the savings will go. This is a new area that needs attention.

*G Waardenburg*:
In our research over the last few years, we found that:

1. Rural enterprises in China were unrelated to agricultural production per capita, but strongly related to industrial production and income per capita;
2. In Sri Lanka, there was no direct link between agriculture and funds for investment in industry. Few people shifted from agriculture to industry.

345

Instead, they often went into trades or urban manufacturing as labourers. Later, some moved back into rural industries. Thus, the agricultural surplus only went into rural industrial investment indirectly.

*C Liedholm*: I have a few comments on the supply response of micro-enterprises in rural areas. In virtually all of the enterprises that we examined in our studies, there was excess capacity. With small increases in demand, they could produce much more. What are the constraints to futher expansion? We need much more information on the dynamics of how existing firms evolve and expand over time and whether there are policy or managerial bottlenecks to this expansion.

*G Ranis*: A recent study on China's 'responsibility system' in agriculture showed that what are called 'side jobs' are often the only way for farmers to invest in non-agricultural enterprises. In that country, urban non-agricultural enterprises are not yet open except for a small collective sector. Thus, urban areas are cut off from this dynamic change. Rural areas are getting richer, but poor urban dwellers have not profited from the reforms. This is the opposite of the usual case elsewhere.

# Appropriate Technology in Publicly Owned Industries in Kenya and Tanzania

## JEFFREY JAMES

### Introduction

Despite the divergent approaches to development that have been adopted in Kenya and Tanzania – with the explicitly capitalistic orientation of the former usually regarded as standing in sharp contrast to the type of socialism espoused by the latter – public enterprises have come to assume an important position in the manufacturing sectors of both countries. Motivated perhaps primarily to expedite Africanization (that is, to rectify the marked racial imbalance in positions of power and privilege that existed at independence), direct participation in manufacturing activity by the Kenyan Government increased sharply during the 1970s, leading a recent World Bank mission to observe that: 'Financial participation by government in industrial ventures has been an important feature in the expansion of Kenya's manufacturing sector'[1], and according to a government report published in 1979, the investments of these and other enterprises in which government has participated in Kenya accounted 'for a very sizeable proportion of the total capital formation in the country'.[2] In Tanzania, the rapid expansion of public enterprises in the manufacturing sector was of course far more ideologically motivated, forming an integral part of the transition to socialist ownership of the means of production after the Arusha Declaration of 1967. By 1974, the public sector accounted for as much as 50 per cent of manufacturing value added and employment.[3]

In view of the rise to prominence of public enterprises in the manufacturing sectors of the two countries, an understanding of the technological choices made by these firms is central to explaining what happened to output, employment and other major macroeconomic variables during the 1970s. An adequate explanation of these choices is also needed because

JEFFREY JAMES is Professor of Development Economics at Catholic University of Brabant, Tilburg, The Netherlands. This article is reprinted by permission of Westview Press from *Macro policies for Appropriate Technology in Developing Countries*, edited by Frances Stewart, copyright Westview Press, 1987, Boulder, Co. Funded by the U.S. Agency for International Development under Co-operative Agreement DAN-5428-A-00-3047-00.

they do not appear to have conformed to what one might have expected. In particular, the highly disparate development strategies that were adopted could reasonably have been expected to produce a correspondingly diverse pattern of technological behaviour by the public enterprises concerned, for these enterprises are often considered an extension, or creature, of the states, so that the divergent goals of Kenya and Tanzania would presumably be reflected to a high degree in their technological choices. But even if this were not the case, and the firms in the two countries had similar goals, their choices might still be expected to differ because of the contrasting macro-environments in which these choices are made; in particular, in Tanzania, market forces are replaced by administrative (or non-market) forms of resource allocation to a greater extent than in Kenya.

Yet, from available evidence one is struck not only by the *similarity* rather than the *differences* in technological behaviour between the two sets of firms, but also by the outcome of this behaviour which diverges from many important national development goals of both countries. The purpose of this chapter is to explain these unexpected findings, using data from a detailed study of how technology decisions were made in a sample of publicly-owned firms in the manufacturing sectors of Kenya and Tanzania. It is contended that, in general, technology decisions are dominated by a single objective which the parastatal holding companies are able to pursue without countervailing pressures from either the macro-environment or from other government agencies. This objective pre-disposes managers to search for investment projects in which, through various mechanisms and with varying degrees of directness, developed-country patterns of scale, factor-intensity and product characteristics are invariably closely reproduced.

The second section describes and compares data on the technological characteristics of public enterprise in the two countries. In the following section, a framework is proposed to explain these observations. In the fourth section, the framework is applied to the case studies. The final section considers the main policy implications of the findings.

## The technological characteristics of public enterprises in manufacturing in Kenya and Tanzania: an overview of a common problem

Parastatals in Tanzania have been analysed more than in Kenya. With respect to the technological aspects of the behaviour of these enterprises in particular, the two major studies of the Tanzanian experience are more extensive than the corresponding evidence for Kenya.[3, 4] As a result, the assertions based on these studies juxtaposed in Table 1 differ in the degree to which they can be said to accurately characterize the manufacturing sector as whole. But what comparative data does exist, strongly suggests an interesting paradox common to *both* countries – that the essentially

348

*unplanned* character of the technological behaviour of public enterprises coincides with, and is largely produced by, the *systematic* tendency for large-scale and (often inefficient) capital-intensive technologies to be associated with each other and with excessively sophisticated products. It is this paradoxical combination of features that underlies the striking *similarity* of what has occurred in Kenya and Tanzania. This paper is designed to contribute to an understanding of this similarity.

## The analytical framework

According to Gillis, the traditional view in economics is that managers of public enterprises are 'cosmic maximizers'. That is, they are 'motivated solely by a desire to maximize a clearly defined measure of social welfare, as defined by the parent government, under conditions of perfect information on all shadow prices, externalities, and risk'.[5] However, it is apparent even from the brief description of the common problem presented in the previous section that this idealized model (which assumes not only that government is able to provide the firm with a clear set of goals but also that managers actually seek to maximize according to them) will not do. In both Kenya and Tanzania, what has to be explained is why the technological behaviour of public enterprises *diverges* so sharply from many of the most important objectives of their governments. Therefore, an alternative theoretical framework is needed which both posits an alternative behavioural assumption at the level of the enterprise and also contains an alternative and more realistic model of the relationship between the firm and government agencies. Both these modifications are necessary for an alternative framework, for even if public enterprises pursue goals different from those articulated by government, leading to the technological outcomes observed in Kenya and Tanzania, it is necessary to explain the relationship between the firms and the government agencies that enables this to occur.

With respect to the behavioural aspect of an alternative framework, our point of departure is the view that conditions in both Kenya and Tanzania in the 1970s were basically such as to produce what David Williams has termed the bureaucratic-man mechanism, a hypothesis that differs from the neo-classical approach and the engineering-man mode.[6]

Formulated specifically to explain the choice of technology in Tanzanian public enterprises, the bureaucratic-man thesis takes off from the connection between the economic environment and managerial goals.[7] In the environment in which parastatals for the most part operate in that country, market forces have been substantially replaced by government controls.

The price-controls system, for example, is in many cases based on a cost-plus formulation which both shelters the inefficient and gives only a

349

weak incentive to become more efficient ... The incentive structure to which the parastatal manager responds offers little in the way of personal financial rewards and, in any case, may focus on surpluses which are more related to windfall gains from the pricing system than to productive efficiency.[7]

Thus deprived of much of an incentive to minimize costs, the manager turns to other goals that appear to offer greater advancement in the eyes of his superiors in the planning hierarchy. In particular, he is said to shift his attention to initiating as many projects as possible. But the manager is constrained in pursuing this goal by financial needs (especially foreign exchange), and he accomplishes this by searching for aid-related projects rather than seeking funds from the planners.

The project which can be secured, presented, moved past the planner, delivered, and staffed fastest and at the least effort to the parastatal is the one that is chosen.[7]

The key element of this hypothesis is that, given the goals of the Tanzanian manager, securing finance becomes critical to achieving his objective. And since the technology for projects is usually closely associated with the financial source (for example, aid donors or export credits), it follows that 'the choice of technique in any particular project *is often merely a fallout from the chosen source of finance and related project inputs*'.[7] The bureaucratic-man hypothesis may be expressed more strongly as 'the bureaucratic decision-maker attempts to achieve objectives which *eliminate* the choice of technology from the decision process'.[7]

What can be said about the characteristics of the technological choices that emerge from this process? According to Williams, it is large-scale, turnkey projects that usually best meet the requirements of rapidly raising finance for projects and ensuring their rapid delivery and construction. Such projects also have the advantage of providing economies of scale in terms of scarce managerial resources at headquarters.

But while the bureaucratic process has, therefore, a systematic bias associated with large-scale production (that is also highly packaged), it does *not*, according to Williams, have a systematic factor-intensity bias. Instead, the factor-intensity of the technology that results from the bureaucratic-man process is thought to be random.

This hypothesis accounts for some of the observed characteristics of the choices made by parastatals in Kenya and Tanzania. But, it fails to explain the tendency toward capital intensity that was noted above in relation to both countries and the sophisticated nature of the products that invariably appear to accompany this tendency. It is possible, however, to modify the implications of the basic model in a direction that is more consistent with these empirical observations by incorporating a more realistic view of the

350

finance bias that is imparted to the technological features of the projects that are selected. And central to this modification are the systematic historical links between the various dimensions of technology that Frances Stewart has described in relation to the experience of the developed countries.[8]

The first point that needs to be recognized is that most of the offers of foreign finance to Kenyan and Tanzanian parastatals that seek this means of expanding investment emanate from the developed market economies. Thus, despite its socialist orientation, even in Tanzania in the mid-1970s, 'Almost 35 per cent of Tanzania's assistance is in the form of bilateral aid from Western capitalist countries, while another third comes from the World Bank'.[9] And in Kenya, not surprisingly, aid from these same sources is a much higher percentage of the total. Secondly, the 'fall-out' (to use Williams' phrase) from this type of finance normally produces a combination of technological characteristics that is not at all random but rather has evolved systematically out of the socioeconomic circumstances prevailing in the developed countries with which the finance is associated.

Stewart first elaborated the view that a technology was a 'vector' of characteristics (comprising, among other things, the nature of the product and the scale of production) and that changes in these characteristics in the developed countries (where almost all technical change occurs) are mutually interrelated. On the one hand, 'As incomes rise, wages rise, making existing technology uneconomic compared with labour-saving innovations. Rising incomes allow greater expenditure on investment per employee'.[8] On the other hand:

> Technical change in products in developed countries occurs in line with the rising incomes (and is partly responsible for those rising incomes), so that the balance of characteristics offered by new products corresponds to the changing demands of consumers as their incomes rise. The rising incomes have the effect of shifting demand toward different products with more sophisticated, labour-saving, higher-quality, etc. characteristics.[8]

Moreover, since an increase in the size of the market is another consequence of the rise in average incomes, the scale of output tends to increase with economic growth. 'Historically, in the advanced countries the typical size of plant has grown faster than the market as a whole'.[8]

Therefore, insofar as the argument of the two previous paragraphs has validity, the finance bias that defines the bureaucratic-man hypothesis has implications not only for the scale of output, but also for the factor-intensity of technology and the nature of the product. In this way, the behavioural implications of the theory become more consistent with the empirical observations described in Table 1. But even this version of the bureaucratic-man mechanism does not adequately describe the relationship

351

**Table 1 Comparative summary of the technological characteristics of public enterprises in manufacturing**

| | Tanzania | Kenya |
|---|---|---|
| *Degree of Conformity to National Development Goals* | 'The failure of the post-Arusha companies to distinguish themselves significantly and favourably from the pre-Arusha companies points to one of the most important conclusions which can be made about the performance of the manufacturing parastatals, indeed about all parastatals. *There has been as yet no developmental innovation on the part of parastatals to make themselves more consistent with the Tanzanian ideology.* They have tended to want the most modern plants. Turn-key projects … have not been uncommon'. (Clark 1978, p. 140) <br><br> 'In general the observed pattern of technological choice … only reflects to a limited degree Tanzania's articulated development goals'. (Perkins 1980, p. 408) | 'This study suggests that the parastatal investment companies have done little or nothing to push the manufacturing sector in the directions specified by the policy statements of government. Rather, they appear to have *aided and abetted some of the least appropriate features of the Kenyan industrial structure'.* (Hopcraft and Oguttu 1982, p. 193) <br><br> 'While too large a proportion of the development budget has been diverted to investments, the balance of that budget has not been effectively utilized either. The pattern of development outlined in Development Plans has often been ignored in practice in favour of unplanned projects'. (Ndegwa 1982, p. 14) |
| *Relation to the Planning System* | 'The present system of investment decision-making in the parastatal sector is essentially one of *unplanned socialism* … The results bear only an incidental relation to any formal development plan or to the proclaimed goals of industrial development'. (IBRD 1977a, p. 125) | 'Parastatals have played a large and increasingly important role in Kenya's life in recent years. Growth of this sector has been, in many respects, *unplanned and uncoordinated'.* (IBRD 1983, p. 105) |

352

| | | |
|---|---|---|
| *Technological Characteristics of Public Enterprises* | 'Despite the rhetoric, Tanzania's industrialization programme has, in general, promoted the establishment of enterprises using large-scale capital-intensive, often technically, and almost invariably economically inefficient techniques' (Perkins 1983, p. 231). <br><br> 'Almost one-third of parastatals have chosen to manufacture products ... for which a simpler, less technologically specified substitute exists' (Perkins 1983, p. 226). <br><br> 'There is a strong tendency for parastatals to adopt the most advanced techniques, and build the most modern buildings. In manufacturing this tendency is exhibited as an inclination towards large-scale, capital-intensive, 'transformation' projects .... There has been very little change in the orientation of the parastatal sector since the Arusha Declaration ... There has been no significant development of small-scale rural industries' (Clark 1978, p. 125). | 'The parastatal client firms tend to be large, capital intensive, import intensive and almost exclusively oriented toward a protected, over priced local market' (Hopcraft and Oguttu 1982, p. 193). <br><br> 'Despite the emphasis in policy statements on assistance to small, African owned and export-oriented firms, firms with government participation tend to be large (half of all Kenya's industrial firms employing more than 200 people have government financial participation', (IBRD 1983, p. 85) <br><br> 'Examples of unsound and poorly controlled investments can readily be found in such areas of activity as fertilizer, sugar, textiles and power alcohol. ... this has resulted in uncontrolled cost escalations, inefficient technologies and unprofitable enterprises'. (Ndegwa 1982, p. 42) |
| *Relation to Foreign Finance* | 'Public investment today remains about as *heavily dependent* on foreign funds as it did ten years ago. About one-half of public investment has been foreign financed'. (Clark 1978, p. 173) | 'A major characteristic of most of the parastatals in Kenya is that they *depend heavily* on foreign financing and management advice'. (Oyugi 1982, p. 64) |

between the parastatals and the government agencies that permits the pursuit of a managerial goal, the technological implications of which are, for the most part, inimical to the proclaimed goals of development. The remaining part of the conceptual analysis is devoted to this issue.

Apart from specific problems that vary from one country to another, there are intrinsic difficulties in ensuring that public enterprises are effectively used for implementing government policies. Much of this inherent difficulty can be explained in terms of agent–principal theory.

Raymond Vernon expressed the basic problem in this branch of theory as follows: 'How does the principal ensure that the agent acting for him responds to the same information and the same congeries of objectives as the principal would do if acting on his own behalf?'[10] While by definition this problem pervades all organizations in which agents act on behalf of principals, its severity depends largely on the degree to which the behaviour of the agents can be made accountable to. Without an adequate system of accountability, control of the agent by his principal becomes extremely difficult.

Howard Raiffa correctly observed that the problems of accountability and control are usually less acute in private than publicly-owned firms. In private firms, 'Managers usually have a bottom-line figure that holds them accountable to some extent. In private enterprise, that profit motive is strong and serves as a sieve through which gross incompetents are weeded out and others rewarded'.[11] In public enterprises, however, as is well-known, the objectives are usually far more diffuse because these firms are formed to fulfil a variety of different functions.

*In itself*, however, the diversity of objectives of the public enterprise creates no particular problem for the accountability and control system. If, as is assumed in the 'cosmic maximization' model described above, the numerous objectives of the enterprise are combined into an unambiguous objective function, managers could be judged and held accountable, according to this function, in the way that the private enterprise manager is held accountable in terms of profits. In practice, however, a clear objective function is rarely presented to the managers of the public enterprise and the multiplicity of goals consequently creates severe problems of enterprise accountability and control.

The difficulties in aggregating multiple objectives into an operational composite index have been lucidly described by Raiffa, in relation to the chief executive officer (the principal) of a public enterprise, whose problem it is to communicate the multiple conflicting objectives of the firm to his agents so they can act as the principal would in the same situation. The dilemma facing the chief executive is this: on the one hand, if he is to control his agents he will need to formalize the trade-offs between the conflicting objectives of the firm (for only with such formalization can an unambiguous objective function be derived). On the other hand, because

354

there is unlikely to be any kind of consensus among the board members about the various trade-offs, whatever formalization of these that he enunciates will get him into 'political trouble' with at least some members of the board. 'Thus, the chief executive officer is in an uncomfortable squeeze; he is damned if he formalizes his trade-offs and damned if he does not'.[11]

Raiffa's example can be extended to the case where the government is the principal and the public enterprise its agent; the problem of distilling from the different government agencies a comprehensive set of trade-offs among conflicting goals is likely to be no less serious than it is for the board or directors in the firm. Vernon points to, 'the disconcerting fact that, where conflicting and mutually inconsistent goals seem to exist, politicians may find it undesirable, even dangerous, to try to clarify ambiguity'.[10]

The political difficulties of formalizing trade-offs (and consequently of controlling public enterprises effectively) may be severe in open, participatory democracies where there are diffuse and opposing interest groups. Fewer difficulties might be predicted in less participatory regimes where political power is more concentrated among a small group of decision-makers. But even then, considerable disagreement about fundamental trade-offs among development goals can exist.

What we have shown in this section is that there are some inherent (and perhaps intractable) difficulties in making public enterprise conform to national goals. These difficulties often confer substantial autonomy on the enterprises. But there are also measures that can be actively pursued by managers to further their autonomy. The degree to which managers are successful in these endeavours is a further determinant of the likelihood that the outcomes of the behaviour of public enterprises will be at variance with what is intended by government. According to Aharoni, a variety of variables bear on the ability of the manager to increase his autonomy.[12] Among the most important of these are finance, the legal organization of the firm, and the efficacy of the control functions exercised by government.

### Application to Kenya and Tanzania

It follows from the discussion of the previous section that to apply the analytical framework to Kenya and Tanzania we shall need to concern ourselves with three major issues in these two countries:

1. Conditions that give rise to the operation of the bureaucratic-man mechanism;
2. Technological fall-out from this mechanism, that is, the manner in which the factor-intensity, scale of output, and type of product are

355

**Table 2 The industrial objectives of government in the 1970s**

| | Tanzania | Kenya |
|---|---|---|
| National Goals | 'The major objective ... is to achieve a greater degree of economic self-sufficiency'. (Third Five Year Plan, p. 43) | 'The overriding industrial strategy of the Government. ... is to *accelerate* industrial growth'. (Second Five Year Plan, p. 326) |
| | 'The present plan has placed a high priority on the satisfaction of domestic basic needs. Thus the production of food, textiles, shoes and construction materials will have particular emphasis'. (Third Five Year Plan, p. 43) | 'The target [for 1974] is an increase in output of over 70 per cent compared with 1967'. (Second Five Year Plan, p. 12) |
| | 'The strategy puts a premium on the *earliest* feasible development of a basic industry'. (Roemer *et al.* 1976, p. 269) | 'The attainment of the income and employment targets in this Plan depends to a significant degree on the country obtaining physical resources from abroad to supplement its own effort. Without making use of these physical resources ... the country cannot develop as *rapidly* as planned. The Government will therefore endeavour to obtain from abroad the resources necessary to achieve the national goals'. (Second Five Year Plan, p. 329–330) |
| | 'New projects will have to be consistent with the basic industrial strategy'. (Third Five Year Plan, p. 47) | 'The crucial point in the drive for accelerated industrial development is that highest priority be accorded to projects which make the greatest contribution to improving Kenya's balance of payments position'. (Annual Reports and Accounts of the Industrial Development Bank, 1974, p. 9) |

356

|  | Tanzania | Kenya |
|---|---|---|
| The Sugar Industry | 'The national goal is to achieve self-sufficiency in sugar production at *the earliest opportunity*, sustaining self-sufficiency at all times and resources and economics permitting produce surplus sugar for export'. (Sugar Development Corporation Annual Report and Accounts, 1976–77, p. 33)<br><br>'*Rapid* progress in this area is required to satisfy domestic demands'. (Third Five Year Plan, p. 46) | 'Bearing in mind the sugar production deficit and the need for foreign exchange to purchase additional sugar for the country's consumption requirements, the Government requested funds … for a study to be made of the industry and the development of a programme for the country to become self-sufficient if economically possible *within a period of 10 years*'. (Government of Kenya, Kenya Sugar Industry, *Expansion Study*, Vol V, Nyanza Sugar Belt Improvement Project, Tate and Lyle, May 1976, p. 8)<br><br>'Kenya's commitment to meeting the consumer demand for sugar by attaining self-sufficiency in its production. The latter theme has been consistently stated as central to agricultural and industrial policy during recent years. Satisfaction of consumer demand has remained a high political priority for the Government'. (Barclay 1977, p. 61–2) |
| The Textile Industry | 'In order to satisfy projected local and export demand in 1985, it will be necessary to produce 220 million square metres of cloth. To achieve this *four mills must be established between 1977/78 and 1980/81*'. (Third Five Year Plan, p. 47) | 'The Government attaches great importance to the *rapid* development of the textile industry'. (from the correspondence files of the Rift Valley Textile Project)<br><br>'Our keen determination to move with utmost *speed* (to complete the project) as desired by the Kenyan authorities', (from the correspondence files of the Rift Valley Textile Project) |

357

**Table 2 continued**

| | *Tanzania* | *Kenya* |
|---|---|---|
| The Parastatal Holding Companies and New Projects | 'NDC's (the National Development Corporation's) interest is not to run companies for the purpose of profit maximization, but rather to implement projects in certain sectors. In fact, NDC seems to be evaluated by the *number* of projects it implements ... *The unofficial goal of NDC as expressed by* some of its employees, to push through as *many* projects as possible'. (Quoted in O'Brien 1982, p. 22)<br><br>'The management (of NDC) is anxious to show success. Lever Brothers will come and erect a detergent factory in a year. ... Despite the poor economics of such a project from a developmental point of view, NDC appears more successful than if it had spent the year trying to organize Ujamaa village work shops'. (Clark 1978, p. 189) | 'One of IDB's (the Industrial Development Bank's) important aims has been to attract investment funds from abroad'. (Annual Report and Accounts, 1977, Industrial Development Bank, p. 13)<br><br>'Since December 1974 total investments approved ... have grown by an average of nearly 25% a year ... The *total number of projects* investigated and considered for investment has increased even more *rapidly* because of IDB's search for new business'. (Annual Report and Accounts 1977, Industrial Development Bank, p. 12) |

358

derived from financial and other inputs embodied in the sample projects; and

3. Relationships between the parastatals and relevant government agencies that bear (theoretically and in practice) on this fall-out.

## The common origins of the bureaucratic mechanism

It will be recalled that bureaucratic-man tries to start up as many projects as possible. For, it is this focus that is said to be 'the way to survive and prosper'. But what pressures produce this sort of managerial motivation is not clear from Williams' statement of the hypothesis. It is argued here that the source of these pressures in both Kenya and Tanzania can be traced to the extent of, and rapidity with which, output increases were sought (especially in key sectors) and the ease with which this objective of government could be assumed by managers of the parastatals. It will be argued, furthermore, that the goal of rapid (and sizeable) increments in output was pursued by managers in both countries without much pressure for cost-minimization from the macroeconomic environment.

The juxtaposed entries in the first half of Table 2 dealing with national goals and goals for the textile and sugar industries support the view that a common desire for rapid growth in domestic output (of wage goods in particular) can be discerned from a study of official and other documents from the 1970s. In both Kenya and Tanzania, this desire was shaped by both political and economic factors. In Kenya this was due to the significance attributed to meeting the excess demand for many wage goods (see, for example, Barclay's view of this for the Kenyan sugar industry in Table 2). In Tanzania the cause was the foreign exchange crisis that beset these countries during much of the decade. In the Tanzanian case it should be noted that there was also an ideological basis for the quest for self-reliance in basic goods that formed an essential part of the so-called basic industry strategy.[13]

The admittedly rather sketchy evidence in the second part of Table 2 suggests that these political and economic imperatives underlying the national goal for industries such as textiles and sugar translated themselves, at the level of the parastatal holding companies (in which most important decisions regarding manufacturing subsidiaries are made), into a predisposition to initiate a large *number* of projects. The manner of this translation as well as its effects derive from the facts that maximizing current output is an objective that is easily measured (and in terms of which, therefore *kudos* can be *unambiguously* earned). It is also a goal that can be rapidly achieved (as the last quotation for Tanzanian Table 2 suggests) on the basis of the foreign-financed projects – the more so given that, as Table 3 clearly indicates, pressures from the macro-environment to minimize costs were largely absent from both countries. This common

359

**Table 3 The macro-environment and pressures for cost-consciousness in the choice of technology**

| Tanzania | Kenya |
|---|---|
| 'Both product and factor markets in Tanzania are nominally under the control of planners. In both areas several aspects of the competitive model have been replaced with devices which operate in quite different directions from market forces. The price-control system, for example, is in many cases based on a cost-plus formulation which both shelters the inefficient and gives only a weak incentive to become more efficient. ... The incentive structure to which the arastatal manager responds offers little in the way of personal financial rewards and, in any case, may focus on surpluses which are more related to windfall gains from the pricing system than to productive efficiency'. (Williams 1975, p. 7) | 'Financial participation by Government is the best guarantee obtainable that a firm will make high and secure financial profits *regardless of its economic efficiency or of its international competitiveness*'. (Hopcraft 1979, p. 18)<br><br>'Firms with Government participation use it to make Government behave in the firm's interest. The complete range of special concessions, licenses, guarantees, and the whole edifice of protective measures, are far more accessible to the firm that has Government financial participation than to one that does not'. (IBRD 1983, p. 149)<br><br>'The monopsonist position of most parastatals means that there is no competitive pressure to keep operations efficient, whereas their political connections make them immune to the ultimate commercial sanction of bankruptcy and dissolution'. (Schluter 1984, p. 93) |

absence of pressures on costs stemmed largely from government interventions that broke the link between economic efficiency and profitability at the level of the enterprise.

Of course, maximizing output could be achieved by the fuller use of existing projects, and, to some extent, this method was used by parastatal managers (for example, in the attempted reduction of excess capacity). But given the often severe foreign exchange constraints on the efficient operation of these enterprises and the difficulty of raising foreign capital for a fuller utilization of existing capacity – foreign aid, for example, is usually not available for repairs and spare parts – output maximization tended to translate in practice into a concern with new projects.

In brief, then, the parastatal holding companies searched for foreign finance (as was explicitly stated by the Kenyan Industrial Development Bank in the final quotation of Table 2) and were receptive to offers of such finance. In practice, this usually meant finance from the developed market economies for two main reasons. First, it was this type of finance that, even in Tanzania, tended to be most abundant. Clark observed,

> The socialist overtones, far from repelling Western donors, attracted them. ... What it meant to most donors was that the elite in Tanzania, because of the leadership code, would not enrich themselves on foreign aid, and would in fact strive to enact programmes to better the mass of the population. The Nordic countries, Canada, and the World Bank all found this a striking contrast to the situation in most of the Third World.[3]

The second reason is the relative speed (and certainty) of the output increases that are associated with Western finance: 'Western firms offer quick, reliable delivery of capital-goods. To buy from countries like China takes time and involves uncertainty'.[3] (Perhaps a third reason is that developed-country suppliers are more able than their counterparts in the Third World to afford the hard-currency bribes that are not infrequently made to government officials in these countries).

### The technological fall-out from the bureaucratic mechanism: case studies from Kenya and Tanzania

In each country a small sample of publicly-owned firms was selected for analysis. The purpose of these case studies was not to attain statistically significant explanations; rather, it was to study the subtleties of how decisions on technology are made in public enterprises through a detailed study of the decision-making process. The selection of firms was made first for Tanzania from among industries where, for the most part, a considerable data base already existed – sugar, textiles, footwear, detergents, printing ink, grain, and oil milling. The selected cases generally relate to the Third Five Year Plan period from July 1976 to June 1981.[14] In Kenya, an attempt was made to select government majority-owned firms from some of these same industries for a comparable period. These criteria, and formidable problems of data availability and access, produced a sample of enterprises drawn from the following industries: textiles, sugar, salt manufacturing, bottling, cashew processing, ceramics, furfural and power alcohol. In both countries, data were sought from a variety of documents, such as feasibility studies, board minutes, annual reports, ministerial papers, and tender bids. There was greater access to these documents in Kenya, permitting a more complete reconstruction of the technology decision process in the Kenyan sample than in Tanzanian firms, which should be borne in mind in interpreting the results.

## Kenya

The case studies from Kenya provide clear confirmation of the decision-making process for technology envisaged by the notion of bureaucratic-man. They also clearly disprove the implication drawn by Williams that the technological fall-out from this process tends to be random. The confirmatory evidence is contained in Table 4 which shows the predicted link between the choice of managing agents (who were generally also minority partners) and the source of technology for the sample enterprises. Table 5, however, suggests that when, as is the case for most of the examples studied here, developed-country collaborators are involved, the technological fall-out from this collaboration is more likely to be systematic

**Table 4 Managing agents/minority partners and the source of technology in Kenyan parastatals**

| Firm | Managing agents/ minority partners | Main source of technology |
|---|---|---|
| Rift Valley Textiles | Seditex (Germany) | Germany |
| Yuken Textiles | Jugotekstil (Yugoslavia) | ? |
| Salt Manufacturers | Saltec International (Italy) | Saltec |
| Nyeri Bottling Plant | Coca Cola Africa | ? |
| Nzoia Sugar | Technisucre (France) | France |
| South Nyanza Sugar | Buckau Wolf (Germany)[1] | Germany/India |
| Kenya Furfural | Escher Wyss | Escher Wyss |
| Kenya Cashewnuts | Oltremare (Italy) | Oltremare |
| Ceramic Industries | Ceramic Industries (private owners) | UK/Italy |

Notes: [1] One of the turnkey contractors.
Source: Correspondence files of the Industrial Development Bank and the Industrial and Commercial Development Corporation.

than random. That is, Table 5 points to some tendency for the large-scale of output to go with high capital intensity on the one hand and a sophisticated type of product, often intended for export, on the other.

One could infer from Tables 4 and 5 an underlying decision-making process in which, because of the lack of concern with the technological aspects of the projects that is assumed to be exhibited by bureaucratic-man (in the form of the parastatal holding companies), the fall-out from the developed-country collaboration proceeded entirely unquestioned, a process in which the appropriateness of the technology to national development goals might, therefore, never be raised. But a close scrutiny of the actual negotiations reveals that this depiction of what occurred is only part of a more complex story.

It is only a partial explanation, not so much because the parastatal holding companies were generally more active technologically than the theory posited, but because other institutions frequently questioned the desirability of the technology proposed. What is interesting, therefore, is the question of how the evident closeness of the fall-out was sustainable in the face of the various challenges to its desirability. Four of the cases are especially revealing in this regard.

Consider first the salt refining and Nzoia sugar projects. In both cases, the World Bank was critical of the lack of attention the Industrial Development Bank paid in appraisals of the technological choice aspects of the project. In relation to the salt refining project, the World Bank drew attention specifically to what it regarded as the excessively capital-intensive equipment selected. The Industrial Development Bank's unenthusiastic response to the suggestion that more labour-intensive alternatives be considered is worth quoting in full because it reveals this institution's perception (and arguably, to some degree, rationalization) of the limits of technological choice, given the constraints imposed by the scale of output and the prior selection of developed-country collaborators.

As IDB is involved mainly in fairly large-scale industrial projects, for which technology has to be imported from the developed countries, the possibility of maximizing employment (mainly unskilled labour) is severely limited by the inability of the foreign technical collaborator to adapt the technology involved to local needs. We do try to make changes in project design but our experience has so far shown that the scope to make substantial changes is limited, partly because of the technological environment to which the technical participants or sponsors are used. Some of the processes in any case have naturally to be sophisticated, for example a salt refinery or fertilizer plant.[15]

Apparently not satisfied with this response, the officials of the World Bank offered a rejoinder to the effect that a less capital-intensive technology, even if less profitable, ought nevertheless to form part of the holding

**Table 5 Scale, products and technology – Kenya**

| | Scale | Technology | Products |
|---|---|---|---|
| Rift Valley Textiles | 'Annual capacity of 11,500,000 linear metres ... 'a complete modern integrated textile mill'. | 'All machinery and equipment selected are brand new, the most modern and of very high quality and reputation'. | 'Very high quality ... an annual production of approximately 23 m square metres, of which about 7 million metres shall be exported'. |
| Yuken Textiles | 'The largeness of premises and their division is a result of the conception of the whole factory and up-to-date technology as well as its flexibility.... The biggest manufacturer of this line in Yugoslavia'. | 'Highly developed productive technology ... to compete with the European standards'. | 'The technological part of the project provides a very high quality of the output (European level') ... 'Activities of the newly established enterprise would be concentrated during its first phase above all on the Kenyan market and on the markets of East African countries, later-on also on other markets'. |
| Molasses Plant | 'The plant will be capable of producing 7,300 tons per annum of 99.5% Power Alcohol'. | 'The Installation shall conform to the latest and most modern technology and development currently available as of the date of this contract as to the Installation and the *volume* and *quality* of *products* produced. ... The opportunities to sell the surplus factory's products ... are fully appreciated and exploited'. | |

|  | Scale | Technology | Products |
|---|---|---|---|
| Nyeri Bottling Plant | | 'The plant will be equipped with a new sophisticated bottling line with ancillary equipment with a capacity for bottling 500 cases per working hour. ... The bottling equipment to be installed is very sophisticated'. | 'a standard quality product'. |
| Kenya Furfural | | 'The high capital intensity of the project – due mainly to the high cost of the proposed plant'. | 'Most of the end products would be mainly for export'. |
| Cashew Processing | 'Mechanical processing in large-scale units with relatively high capital investment costs'. | 'Equipment considered the best in this field. ... Though mechanized, the project is still labour-intensive. ... All the machinery will be new'. | 'producing high quality products. ... The project would generate significant additional foreign exchange earnings for the country'. |

Source: Correspondence files of the Industrial Development Bank and the Industrial and Commercial Development Corporation.

company's frame of reference. The question, as the World Bank officials saw it, was 'by how much (it was less profitable) and whether it would be worthwhile to accept the trade-off'. They added, however, that:

the project is far too advanced to raise this question at this stage; this question should be raised in the context of the government industrialization and employment policy and should be discussed between the government, the IDB and the promoters in the early stages of project preparation.[15]

In the Nzoia sugar project, the World Bank's admonition (regarding the inadequate attention that IDB's appraisal had paid to the suitability of the technology selected by the French collaborators) seemed well founded because IDB's management 'was not able to assess the technical suitability of the proposed plant or to establish whether the price agreed on was reasonable and competitive' and has therefore, 'to make do with assurances received regarding Fives-Cail Babcock's many years of experience in supplying similar plants to various countries'.[15] But here, as in the previous case, the late stage in the negotiation at which this issue was raised seemed to make any effective countervailing action very difficult.

It was noted in Table 4 that Seditex, the German managing agents of the Rift Valley textiles project, chose German-made equipment for this project. This firm had, however, been asked (apparently by the International Finance Corporation as a minority shareholder and lender) also to consider bids from Japanese and American machinery suppliers. Although these bids were considerably cheaper than the German quotations, they were rejected by Seditex on the following grounds:

From our viewpoint, two vital aspects have to be considered. The first is operational costs, involving quality and efficiency; the second is the practical and psychological conditions. By opting for the cheapest, we have no doubt the mill's efficiency and fabric quality will be lower, that supervision, labour and maintenance costs, as well as consumption of electricity and spares will be higher. On the other hand, as European promoters, with our main office in Hamburg, it would undoubtedly be more difficult and costly to plan and coordinate with Japanese or American suppliers the multitude of details before and during the construction period. Loopholes in tight coordination and planning can have grave financial consequences.

We shall equally have considerable difficulties in coping with urgent problems that would probably require the manufacturer's assistance, once the mill is in operation. Moreover, our natural source of recruiting technicians is Europe. Such European technicians will have to become acquainted with Japanese or American equipment; this would involve more expenses and, in general, contacts would be more difficult and complicated.[16]

366

In the case of Kenya Furfural, both the Agricultural Development Corporation and the Industrial and Commercial Development Corporation (ICDC) raised strenuous objections to the technological (and other) aspects of the project. The former noted that, 'one or two of the intended equity holders and/or lenders whatever the case may be are also the suppliers of the plant' and sought reassurance that the plant would be purchased 'on an international tender basis'. Such reassurance did not, however, materialize as the project leader argued that the plant and equipment, because of its specialized design, 'could only be supplied by Escher Wyss', and consequently, an international tender was not possible. The ICDC objection focused on the high capital cost of the project and on an inability to obtain a detailed breakdown of this cost from the sponsor. In spite of these criticisms, other government agencies, (the IDB, the Treasury and the Development Finance Company of Kenya) favoured the project, which was approved in apparently unmodified form.

Due to the fragmented government involvement, the attitude of the holding company, the stage at which objections were raised and the alleged hidden costs of cheaper machinery – the closeness of the technological fall-out was able to be preserved in these cases. But apart perhaps from the hidden costs argument, these reasons offer little basis for supposing that the preservation had anything whatsoever to do with economic efficiency. Rather, it is probable that the outcome was inimical to this objective (the continuous financial losses made by all these enterprises are consistent with, though not proof of, this assertion).

### Tanzania

We have seen that the Kenyan case studies generally conformed closely to the bureaucratic-man notion with respect to its prediction of a role for technology that is essentially derivative of the source of foreign (mostly developed-country) finance and related managerial inputs into the project. And in this derivative process there was a tendency for the technological characteristics of the project (scale of output, factor-intensity, and type of product) to take on a systematic form. While some cases in Tanzania (mostly in sugar and textiles) also followed this general pattern, other cases did not.

In these other cases, though there was still a large-scale bias arising from the search for foreign finance, the type of finance obtained for these projects happened not to be closely tied to any particular source of technology and because this permitted the technological choice aspects of the projects to assume a more central role, other factors, not allowed for in the bureaucratic-man formulation, came to be important. These other factors worked, as we shall see, through the same tendency toward interrelatedness of the various aspects of developed-country technology with which it was necessary in the Kenyan cases to supplement the original formulation of the bureaucratic mechanism. But the tendency was not merely appended to the mechanism as a derivative. Rather, it was set in motion by an active set of preferences. That is, the basic components of the explanation of these cases remain the same, but the manner of their combination into an integrated approach differs from what has so far been the case.

Let us, however, first deal briefly with the case studies in Tanzania that closely followed the Kenyan model.[17] These were drawn mostly from the textiles and sugar industries, which were particularly emphasized in the Third Five Year Plan (Table 2). Interviews with the managers of the parastatal holding companies responsible for these industries revealed that the emphasis of the Plan on rapid import substitution had been incorporated into, and seemed to dominate, the objective functions of these institutions. For example, one manager in Texco (the holding company for the textiles industry) described his primary concern as being 'to clothe the nation as fast as possible'. He stressed that if his concern was simply to maximize profits, he would prefer second-hand machinery to the turnkey projects that were thought best to promote the rapid expansion of output. Similarly, what emerged from interviews with managers at the Sugar Development Corporation could be described as an objective function embodying the primary goals of meeting national excess demand as rapidly as possible subject to the constraint of avoiding losses. From this overriding objective there followed the implication that particular types of products and techniques were ruled out of consideration *ab initio*. The managers stressed that the rapid expansion of the sugar industry based on jaggery and OPS sugar (the small-scale alternative to the large-scale production of refined sugar) would not have been feasible. In the case of the OPS alternative, they pointed out that some 200 small plants would have been required to replace the output of five large ones. The managerial and supervisory problems associated with this alternative, not to mention the training of operatives in the OPS method and the difficulties of raising finance for small-scale techniques, meant to the managers that this method could at best supplement a strategy based on large-scale factories.

In many of the large-scale projects in these industries, to which the objective described in the previous paragraph gave rise during the Third Five Year Plan period, the technology fall-out was closely tied (as in the Kenyan cases) to the sources of finance (and other inputs) that were secured for the (highly packaged) projects. In the Musoma textile mill, for example, with a capacity of 25m square metres of cloth, a general French contracting company was responsible for financing and constructing the plant on a semi-turnkey basis. This company identified not only the consortium of financing institutions in Europe (whose loans were effectively tied to procurement in each particular country) but also the machinery suppliers. Similarly, in the expansion of the capacity of the sugar mills at Kilombero, Kagera and Mtibwa, turnkey tenders were floated in the countries to which the external finance was tied.

There were, however, other large-scale projects initiated during the Third Five Year Plan period in which the technological fall-out did not conform at all to this derivative pattern. In these cases, in contrast, technological choice came to comprise a more central element of the decision that had to be made for the projects. Three examples, all financed directly or indirectly (through the Tanzanian Investment Bank) by the World Bank, illustrate this point and demonstrate how other factors impart an independent upward bias to the capital intensity.

The most important of these factors is product choice, the bias from which, as the recently established Morogoro Shoe Company shows, can be imparted through the alleged need to produce exports conforming to international standards. The choice of product for this project was dictated almost entirely by its orientation to exports, as is made quite clear in the Bank's Appraisal Report. Thus,

> One fairly modern shoe factory presently produces leather and canvas shoes for the internal market. The output is of acceptable quality within Tanzania, but does not meet international standards. The new shoe factory ... would produce about 4 million pairs of shoes which meet international standards, primarily for export, but it is expected that a small part of the production will be sold internally.[18]

The same report also makes explicit the link between production for export and the nature of the technology that is required. To quote again from this document,

> During the detailed engineering design phase, efforts will be made to substitute labour for capital without compromising product style, quality, and cost competitiveness but the extent to which this can be done is limited in export-oriented industries.[18]

Sabuni Industries Limited, the only parastatal in Tanzania which produces powdered laundry detergent, is a clear example of a second main influence on product choice, that which originates in historically determined tastes. The Sabuni project was conceived in the 1960s, when, following the break-up of the East African Community, supplies of the detergent Omo from Kenya were discontinued. It seemed clear to the National Development Corporation (the holding company responsible for the detergent industry at the time), that local production of a substitute was required. In the decision to replicate, or even improve, the brand that had been imported, what appears to have been crucial was the consideration that:

369

Since most of the people in the country had used the Kenyan brand of detergent (Omo), which is of very high quality, it was envisaged to produce a detergent of the same standard or even better, in order to capture the market previously supplied by the Unilever Company in Kenya. The intention was also to produce a product which could be exported to neighbouring countries by competing effectively with other high quality brands.[19]

That the choice of this particular type of product had a decisive influence on the choice of technology for Sabuni, can be inferred from the impact it had on the tender process. The tenderers were apparently asked to supply, with their quotations, a sample of their brands. These samples were then analysed by the research staff of the National Development Corporation. It is surely not without significance that the Italian firm which was awarded the tender, also happens to be the plant supplier to Unilever in Kenya, the manufacturers of Omo.

The final example, the multi-purpose oil mill at Morogoro, illustrates how engineering-man type factors, in addition to those arising from product choice, operated at different stages of the decision process to exacerbate the capital-intensive bias of the technology that was chosen. First, the tender document specified that all the equipment should be new.[20] This prohibition against second-hand equipment is not unique to the acquisition of oil-milling equipment; on the contrary, it is a practice which is endorsed in the bidding rules of the World Bank and by the governments of both Tanzania and Kenya.

In a second respect as well – which concerns once more the link between products and techniques – the specification of the tender document appears to have imparted a bias against the use of more appropriate techniques. Specifically, the document embodies requirements for buildings that require relatively sophisticated products and techniques. Thus, to quote from the document, 'Building and construction work must meet local building and hygiene requirements and standards, which to a great extent are of British origin'.[20] Or, to take another example, the use of locally produced roofing tiles is precluded by 'the minimum requirement for roofing material – corrugated aluminium sheets or corrugated asbestos sheets'.[20]

If there were therefore biases in the manner in which the tender document was specified, it was also true that in the next stage – the evaluation of the tenders received – engineering-man type factors further reduced the pressures for cost minimization in the choice of technology. At the very outset of the evaluation procedure, for example, we find that most of the numerous quotations were rejected on the grounds that they had not come 'from potentially competent and internationally-known companies'.[21] And in the selection from among the five contractors that

370

did conform to this description, considerable emphasis was laid on the following factors (in addition, of course, to costs): goodwill of the bidder in his country and abroad, competence and capability of the bidder to successfully complete the project, quality of the end products, experience in export, and establishment of plants in foreign countries.[21]

One of the major technological issues that confronted the sub-committee formed by Moproco to evaluate the bids, was the choice between a batch and a continuous refining process. Despite the relatively high cost of the latter, this was nevertheless the method selected. With respect to the bleaching component of the refining process, the sub-committee explained its choice with what amounts to a statement of the engineering-man hypothesis. Thus, 'continuous bleaching plants have gained wide acceptance as they are now feasible, but they are relatively costly owing to their expensive control instruments ... Continuous bleaching units are favoured by processors because they render a finished product of uniform colour'.[21] In the opinion of the general manager of Moproco, a member of the sub-committee for evaluating the tenders, the last reason, the uniformity of product quality associated with continuous refining, was perhaps most influential in the process.

The conclusion from these three cases is that active biases in selection led, through the close link between product choice and technology, to the same tendency toward reproducing developed-country technologies that was shown in the derivative process with which the other case studies were associated. An essential difference, however, lies in the implications for policy that seek to alter this outcome. In the one case it is the active biases that need to be tackled directly and in the other it is the prior forces that give rise to the derivation of developed-country technological characteristics. More on this important policy issue will be contained in the concluding section.

## The direction of parastatal managers in Kenya and Tanzania

So far this paper has described the common origins of the bureaucratic mechanism in Kenya and Tanzania and the nature of the technological fall-out from this mechanism in case studies from the manufacturing sectors of the two countries. The analysis has been concerned with how the chosen technologies in the case studies acquired characteristics that rendered them inconsistent with many important development goals (as stated in the respective 5-year plans). Following the conceptual framework, it remains to consider briefly the relationship between the parastatal holding companies and government agencies that allowed these outcomes to occur.

Table 6 summarizes these relationships, which, when juxtaposed, reveal a remarkable similarity between the two countries. In both countries it appears that the failure of the elaborate control system has invested

371

**Table 6 Managerial discretion and the failings of the parastatal control system**

| | Tanzania | Kenya |
|---|---|---|
| Overall Character- izations of the System | 'The elaborate internal and external control system over parastatal activities, which exist on paper are in reality very weak'. (Ministry of Planning 1982, p. 42) | 'The President identified ineffective Government supervision as one of the factors contributing to the unsatisfactory performance of parastatals'. (Ndegwa 1979, p. 10) |
| Managerial Discretion | 'It [the party] has remained an institution capable of directing the system only on the most general plane'. (Loxley and Saul 1975, p. 62) | 'The weakness of the party system means that the bureaucratic elites are left *on their own* to determine the major developmental policies'. (Oyugi 1982, p. 70) |
| | 'There was no clear policy especially as regards science and technology. At enterprise level, each corporation remained *free to choose* its own techniques'. (Mihyo, undated (a), p. 3) | 'Functionally, parastatals do enjoy a very large degree of *autonomy* with respect to investment decisions'. (Oyugi 1982, p. 71) |
| | 'Parastatals are quite *autonomous* institutions. Control by their parent ministries is often slight'. (Clark 1978, p. 185) | 'The parent ministries tend to leave the organizations pretty much *on their own*'. (Oyugi 1982, p. 67) |
| | 'There is still a large question mark over the ability of boards effectively to control foreign management'. (Loxley and Saul 1975, p. 69/70) | 'In many parastatals, the boards of management have failed to discharge the duties expected of them'. (Oyugi 1982, p. 72) |
| | 'In most of the subsidiaries of the National Development Corporation, the management has taken over the policy decision-making function'. (Mihyo undated (b), p. 16) | 'Most of the parastatals have management contracts with foreign based firms or locally based foreign owned management consultancy firms. They have a lot of influence on the operational policies of the organizations'. (Oyugi 1982, p. 69) |

| | Tanzania | Kenya |
|---|---|---|
| Investment Criteria and Accountability | "in the absence of a clearly defined strategy for the socialist transformation of Tanzania there have been *no rational criteria* by which public sector investment and other spending decisions could be *assessed*'. (Loxley and Saul 1975, pp. 65–6) | 'At the moment it is difficult, in the case of many parastatals, to say who is ultimately *accountable* to the Board, the Government and the public for the proper management of their affairs'. (Ndegwa 1979, p. 9) 'Because of the confusion which exists, it is becoming increasingly difficult to say where *responsibility* for inefficiency or waste lies'. (Ndegwa 1979, p. 3) |
| | 'both the proposing parastatals and the central planning authorities *appear to lack clear criteria* on which to assess the alternative projects which they develop and evaluate'. (Perkins 1983, p. 236) | 'The *criteria* for accepting or rejecting projects are *vague* and have not included rigorous economic analysis'. (IBRD 1983, p. 104) |
| The Limited Capacity for Control | 'The central planning ministry does not have the manpower to effectively scrutinize parastatal operations'. (Clark 1978, p. 186) | 'While government financial involvement has been expanding, the machinery to control and examine proposed investments in parastatals is inadequate'. (IBRD 1983, p. 42) |
| | 'The country's already weak planning capacity'. (IBRD 1978, p. 10) | |
| Orientation to Social vs. Private Profitability | 'Most parastatals have used commercial profitability . . . discounted cash flow . . . as their investment yardstick. . . . It is, however, apparent that . . . the use of DCF will almost inevitably give results which have little meaning in social terms'. (Loxley and Saul 1975, p. 67) | 'Firms with Government or parastatal involvement find that such agencies behave like any other investor, concerned with the protection and profitability of their portfolio'. (IBRD 1983, p. 416) |

373

parastatal managers with almost complete autonomy and that the weaknesses of the system come from the same fundamental source.

On the one hand, neither government has been able and willing to specify the trade-offs between the multiple and conflicting goals of development that are required for forming a national objective function and without which the agents of government cannot effectively be controlled. One manifestation of this inability is in the lack of clear criteria for project appraisal by the holding companies in both countries (and perhaps also in the orientation to private, rather than social, profitability that is generally exhibited in the appraisals). On the other hand, even if there was no such problem of formulating a clear national objective function, the efficacy of the control system in Kenya and Tanzania would still be severely constrained by managerial and administrative resources that were inadequate to the burgeoning tasks imposed on them during the 1970s.[14] Following Killick, it is plausible to argue that such a constraint is necessarily entailed in a strategy that makes major demands on limited skilled manpower.[22]

## Conclusions

Although there are many important respects in which the divergent development strategies adopted by Kenya and Tanzania have produced correspondingly different outcomes, with regard to the factors that are thought to have determined the technological behaviour of public enterprises in the manufacturing sectors of these countries, this paper has stressed instead the striking similarities between them. It was suggested not only that the two groups of enterprises adopted the same predominant policy goal, but also that the relevant aspects of the policy environment (both domestic and foreign) in which this goal was pursued were similar. Moreover, the achievement of this common goal of rapid and sizeable output increases in key sectors – took place in the macro-environment that prevailed in the two countries. There were similar constraints on achieving the objective on the basis of small-scale production. The tendency for developed-country offers of finance to be dominant in both countries, and these offers tended to be associated with the reproduction of technologies from these same countries (either merely derivatively when the tie to finance was direct or through an active set of biases when the tie was much less close). Both countries exhibited a similar weak government capacity for control, which meant that the resulting technologies were in most respects inconsistent with major goals of development. The rapid and substantial increases in manufacturing output that were achieved during most of the 1970s in Kenya and Tanzania through large-scale, capital-intensive and highly packaged techniques appear to have had adverse consequences for employment, economic efficiency, income distribution, regional policy, products suitable for meeting basic needs, learning effects and the balance of payments since the exports that were intended often failed to materialize from these projects while their import requirements were extremely heavy.[1]

It could be argued that this outcome reflects the fact that national goals other than output maximization were not in fact accorded much weight by either government. While this interpretation may explain part of what occurred, it assumes that an explicit (or implicit) trade-off between goals was actually made by policy-makers. It may be more realistic, however, to posit an alternative decision-making process in terms of which policy-makers were essentially unaware of the conflicts (and especially the extent of the conflicts) with other goals that output maximization would entail. In relation to Tanzania, Hyden, for example, suggested that, 'policy-makers often decide on matters without first having obtained full and detailed knowledge of the possible consequences of their decisions. They start "running" and take the consequences as they occur'.[23]

There are two broad implications for policy that follow from this interpretation of what occurred. One is that a less rapid and more moderate target increase in output would tend to make more feasible a strategy of relying more heavily on small-scale, labour-intensive techniques, since the managerial and organizational constraints on such a strategy would then become binding less quickly (and to this extent dependence on foreign sources of finance would also be reduced). The second broad policy option arises from the fact that even if this goal cannot be altered (for instance because of political factors), one can still seek to alter aspects of the environment in which the goal is pursued, so as to render its achievement more consistent with a different and more appropriate set of techniques than those with which it has been associated in the past.

The components of such an alteration, in turn, can be grouped into two broad categories, comprising policies to enhance the role of small-scale, labour-intensive projects on the one hand, and those seeking to alter the choices that are made by given large-scale projects on the other. Since the goal of rapid and large increases in output is assumed to remain essentially intact and, consequently, there is no diminution in the existing constraints on an enlarged role for the small-scale sector, these constraints will need to be surmounted. For this purpose, it is not sufficient merely to advocate intensive training schemes that will produce additional entrepreneurs. In addition, policies will be required to strengthen the regional, district, and village organizations in which the expanded numbers of small-scale projects will have to operate.

The need for simultaneous efforts to improve the technological component of large-scale projects derives from the fact that one cannot realistically expect any rapid and substantial progress from even effective policies indicated in the previous paragraph. A parallel set of policies for the large-scale sector first ought to comprise efforts to restore the link between efficiency and profitability at the enterprise level. In Tanzania, this would require reform of the price-control system. In Kenya it would mean, among other things, ending privileges to public enterprises in financial difficulties. Particularly if they are combined with more emphasis on profitability in the incentive (and accountability) systems, and a move toward a more competitive environment (as is now occurring in Kenya), these policies ought to reduce the slackness in the decision-making procedures of the holding companies, in relation to their search behaviour and appraisal methods. In this way, the behaviour of managers will be subject to a discipline that will make it more difficult for them to ignore the technological choice aspects of projects.

Secondly, a set of policies will be required to address the problems of the finance bias that tend to be especially pronounced when there is a close fall-out from developed-country sources of finance. One way to overcome this bias is to encourage donors, multinational development banks and governments to search for technologies from other developing countries (for example, India and China), which are more likely to be appropriate. But in the latter case, unless the active biases that were found in the selection mechanism can be overcome, little will be gained from the wider choice that this type of finance potentially affords. Policies to correct these selection biases will have to pay particular attention to the various influences that govern product choice. For one thing, any rationale of the choice of sophisticated products that is based on the need for exports (especially to developed countries) ought to be very carefully evaluated. In many of the sample projects in Kenya and Tanzania this argument was advanced in feasibility studies (partly to rationalize particular product and process choices) but in most cases the intended exports failed to materialize and the output ended up being sold to local consumers, for most of whom it was highly inappropriate. Where the source of the product choice bias originates, instead, in historically conditioned tastes for advanced country imports, countervailing pressures, exercised for example through promotional campaigns for local goods, are required. While product policies of this kind may help combat engineering-man type biases, other parts of this problem, such as the prohibition of used equipment, need to be tackled directly. Finally, because there are limits to the extent to which the sources of finance can be altered along the lines suggested above, dependence on developed-country technologies that are closely tied to sources of finance in these countries will remain an important problem for Kenya and Tanzania. In these cases, independent technological advice that is taken early in appraising the project (from say the United Nations Industrial Development Organization), using some

**Table 7 A matrix of gaining and losing interests**

| Interest Groups Policy | Major interest groups that stand to lose | Major interest groups that stand to gain |
|---|---|---|
| Reform of the macro-environment | For Tanzania, those dependent on inefficient firms (public and private) that are sheltered by the price-control system. | Efficient firms, firms purchasing inputs from currently inefficient enterprises, consumers in general. |
| | For Kenya, those currently gaining most from government concessions to inefficient public enterprises | Competing (mostly private) firms, firms purchasing inputs from currently inefficient public enterprises, consumers in general. |
| Altered composition of output in favour of small-scale enterprises (particularly those in rural areas) | Urban elites (managers, highly-paid workers, bureaucrats, consumers), foreign interests that are allied to urban elites (investors, machinery sellers, managers, skilled workers, etc). | Rural interests (small-scale firms, the unemployed/underemployed), consumers of products made by small-scale firms (ie, mostly the poor). |
| Altered technological choices made by large-scale public enterprises | Developed country interests (aid donors, managers, machinery sellers, workers), consumers of products of developed country technologies, and local interests that most benefit from the presence of developed country interests (eg, local politicians serving on the boards of joint ventures between foreign and state capital). | Developing country interests (aid donors, financiers, sellers of machinery), sellers of used equipment, the unemployed, consumers of products produced by the alternative technologies. |

377

social, rather than private mode of project appraisal, can help reveal grossly inappropriate choices and increase the bargaining strength of the government *vis-à-vis* foreign collaborators.

Finally, the political economy aspects of these policy proposals need to be considered. In particular, our concern is to indicate that each of the different sets of prescribed policies will be associated with a different – though to some degree overlapping – profile of gaining and losing interests. And insofar as the political significance of these interests varies within and between the two countries, so too will the feasibility of the different policies.

Table 7 represents a crude matrix of likely gainers and losers for the three policy areas identified earlier: reform of the macro-environment; enlargement of the role of small-scale, labour-intensive projects; and improved choices for large-scale projects.

Reform of the macro-environment would generally shift the distribution of gains from inefficient enterprises toward more efficient ones and toward consumers and firms previously reliant on the expensive output of the inefficient firms. Some evidence for Kenya indicates these potential gains could be substantial if protectionist policies are eliminated or reduced, since, 'It is possible to document high local prices and/or low or deterioriating quality for virtually the complete range of products for which there are import restrictions'.[1] The ban on competing imports of lead pencils, for example, amounts to an implicit tariff of 208 per cent, while domestically produced ballpoint pens sell for KSh 0.75 as against a comparable import price of half a shilling.[1]

Whereas reform of the macro-economic environment indirectly pro-motes small-scale projects to the extent that these are relatively efficient, the second policy area shown in Table 7 seeks directly to alter the composition of output in favour of these units. If this is pursued in a context of rural industrialization, it poses a challenge principally to urban and allied foreign interests on behalf of rural groups. In this case, as with macro-reform, gains accrue to consumers, but because the gains derive here from the altered characteristics of the products produced on a small-scale, rather than from a fall in the price of existing goods, they tend to be concentrated on those consumers with low incomes.

Unlike the policy prescription considered in the previous paragraph, which challenges the interests associated with large-scale, the final policy alternative impinges only on the form that these interests currently take, namely, those based on the predominance of developed-country finance and techniques. As such, policies to alter the techniques that are chosen by large-scale public enterprises threaten a narrower set of interests than those that seek to undermine the enterprises themselves.

Assessing the relative political strengths of the gaining and losing interests shown in the table – and hence the feasibility of different policies

378

within each country – is far from easy, not least because of the substantial disagreement among students of political economy issues in Kenya and Tanzania.[24-26]. Nor, despite the socialistic orientation of Tanzania's leaders, can one cogently argue that the challenges to existing interests that are required will necessarily be easier to effect in that country than in Kenya. For,

> What is clear in Tanzania is that the conversion to socialism occurred essentially at the top, indeed at the very top, and has not yet permeated the whole society. As a result there remain many anti-socialist forces in the society. . . . The importance of the urban elite in derailing attempts at radical change has been emphasized by many writers.[3]

But one should not infer from this that all the areas of policy intervention will be no more feasible politically in Tanzania than in Kenya. It may be that because of its greater political independence, Tanzania is better placed to implement the switch from predominantly developed-country to alternative (notably developing-country) sources of finance and technology.

# The Impact of Macroeconomic Policies on Small-Scale Industry: Some Analytical Considerations

## E V K FITZGERALD

### *Macroeconomic policy and small-scale industry*

The patient accumulation of empirical microeconomic research in recent years has revealed the crucial role of the national economic environment in influencing small enterprise decisions on production, employment, technology and investment. Meanwhile, the preoccupation with structural adjustment in the face of external shock has focused macroeconomic debates – somewhat more dramatically – on the efficacy of factor pricing policies and the consequences of aggregate demand management. This paper attempts to advance our understanding of the analytical link between these two concerns, as a contribution to the debate on the impact of macroeconomic policy on small-scale industry.

The 'neo-orthodox' paradigm for macroeconomic policy, as defined by the World Bank[1] and the IMF,[2] suggests that adjustment should involve both the establishment of market-clearing factor prices and reductions in the fiscal claim on resources in order to release scarce savings for private investment. Small-scale industry (SSI) characterized by labour-intensive technology and capital shortages would benefit automatically from these policy shifts. Profit maximization by independent firms (within given factor endowments and uncongested capital markets) would thus automatically link microeconomic resource allocation decisions to a macroeconomic equilibrium that favours SSI because it is more efficient and competitive.

In contrast, the AT approach suggests that the link between macro-economic conditions and firm-level decisions is much more complex.[3] Factor price distortions and capital rationing are not just due to government policy; but also to the operation of market forces within the existing industrial structure. Developing economy markets dominated by large-scale industry (LSI) do not promote the adoption of technologies suitable for local resource use and thus do not promote SSI, for systemic reasons. This 'specific characteristics' approach and recent work on the structural

---

VALPY FITZGERALD is professor of development economics at the Institute of Social Studies, The Hague. His current research concerns structural adjustment and its implications for development. This paper will also be published in *Oxford Economic Papers*, Oxford University Press.

and distributive aspects of LDC finance[4] provide the point of departure for this paper.

For the purposes of macroeconomic analysis it is not very helpful (or easy) to define SSI quantitatively in terms of 'size' as measured by parameters such as fixed capital or number of employees.[5] It is customary therefore, to define SSI in terms of specific technological characteristics – smaller enterprises are held to be both relatively labour-intensive (low capital–labour ratio, K/L) and have relatively high capital productivity (output–capital ratio, O/K). Low labour productivity (output–labour ratio, O/L) is thus also a characteristic of SSI. Two more features emerge from the argument that SSI involves a more AT – the greater use of *local* materials and resources and thus less use of imported inputs (ie, lower M/O); and the production of a 'simpler' product suitable for lower income consumers.[3]

However, the empirical evidence from recent research indicates that there is no reason to believe that, in practice, SSI necessarily possesses all these characteristics, especially when household or artisan workshops are compared to small *capitalist* (ie, medium-scale) industry.[7, 8] Little concludes that 'small firms are *not* reliably more labour-intensive than their larger counterparts; nor are they consistently more technically efficient in their use of resources'.[6] Moreover, there are severe econometric problems in specification of production functions because dimensions such as working capital requirements and use of family labour may imply higher capital–labour ratios than appear at first sight.[9] Finally, of course, the tastes of even the poorest consumers are moulded in practice by transnational advertising designed (successfully) to raise the income-elasticity of demand for mass-produced industrial consumer goods.

Nonetheless, these 'stylized characteristics' are obviously helpful in exploring the effects of different macro-policies. The consequences for employment, for example, can quite easily be derived from them; but they do not define the role of SSI in product and factor markets (unless *all* firms are small profit maximizers as the neoclassical model assumes) or in the sectoral investment-savings behaviour which lies at the heart of macroeconomic adjustment. Because of this lack of specificity on enterprise forms, analytical writing on SSI still contrasts markedly with agrarian economics, where different types of economic organization with distinct objective functions, forms of market power, resource constraints and relationships to the state are always explicitly considered.[10]

In the second part of this paper, the two key assumptions of the neo-orthodox model of the macro–micro relationship are outlined: the direct optimizing effect of 'clearing' factor prices upon the choice of technique in industry; and the causal relationship between fiscal deficits on the one hand and the balance of payments and private investment funding on the other. The essentially 'meso-economic' critique from the AT viewpoint of the first proposition is shown to have significant macroeconomic implications, particularly if enterprise heterogeneity is taken into account.

In the third part it is argued that the second proposition is not really tenable either – or at least that it must be radically modified – once the evidence on the macroeconomic response of the private sector to external shock is taken into account. When the distinct investment and savings behaviour of large and small industry are included in the analysis, the paper argues that neo-orthodox adjustment programmes may well affect SSI adversely.

In the fourth part, a clearer analytical distinction is drawn between the corporate large-scale industrial sector (LSI) and the non-corporate small-scale industrial (SSI) sector made up of competitive small/medium firms (often unincorporated) and household enterprise (including artisans). The relationship between the two sectors reflects the heterogenous industrial structure of the private economy and thus helps define macroeconomic response.

Finally, some tentative conclusions are drawn about the policy implications of this 'structuralist' approach for the relationship between policy toward small-scale industry and macroeconomic adjustment.

## *The Neo-Orthodox Model and the appropriate technology critique: macroeconomic implications*

The theoretical link between macroeconomic adjustment policy and SSI in the Neo-Orthodox Model (NOM) is not always entirely explicit. Programmatic statements do however identify two main themes – the effect of factor prices on choice of production technique; and the effect of the fiscal imbalance on private sector savings and investment.[1,2,11] Although the theoretical argument tends to be presented schematically, and international financial institutions such as the Bank and the IMF inevitably take a somewhat more pragmatic view in the field, the thrust of the policy argument is clear.

On the one hand, it is held that SSI is more labour-intensive and less capital (and import) intensive than LSI. Thus, given the supposedly general surplus of labour and shortage of savings in the typical under-developed economy, SSI would use resource endowments more effectively and allow production to be raised without balance of payments strain (ie, indebtedness) while redistributing income through increased employment. On the other hand, SSI is held to be more competitive than LSI, adapting itself to market demand, while LSI is sheltered behind tariff protection and government subsidies. Moreover, the most inefficient category of LSI in this context is said to be state-owned enterprises (SOEs), followed implicitly by 'rent-seeking' domestic oligopolies. Multi-national corporations (MNCs) are not mentioned, presumably because they are efficient *ex hypothesi* due to their global reach.

Two major macro-policy assumptions accompany this picture of industrial organization in LDCs. The first is that inappropriate technology choice is the result of distorted factor pricing of labour and capital – including foreign exchange. These distortions are largely the result of misguided (albeit possibly well-meaning) government intervention in these factor markets. If more efficient market-clearing prices were to be established in order to give the correct signals to firms, then technical choice and resource utilization would move in the right direction, thereby strengthening SSI. The second assumption is that if the size of the state were to be reduced, not only would privatization force LSI to be more efficient, but the fiscal deficit would be reduced. This would ameliorate balance of payments pressures and releasing domestic resources for private investment – and SSI would benefit in particular from price stability and increased credit availability.

The first NOM assumption, on factor pricing, is strictly neoclassical in origin – although it can at times assume a moral tone reminiscent of the classical political economists inveighing against mercantilism. Wages are held above the market clearing level by trade union power and government welfare legislation. In effect labour 'prices itself out' of industrial employment.[11] Especially in LSI, this distortion is exacerbated by social security charges on employers and other regulations (such as job security) which raise labour costs. Exchange parities are held administratively at overvalued levels by governments keen to protect inefficient LSI, a problem related directly to factor pricing through the strong influence of wages on the real exchange rate.[12] This depresses exports and leads to import rationing and 'rent seeking'. Interest rates are held down to promote industrialization, but the result is that domestic savings are discouraged and leads to excess investment demand generated in a process known as 'financial repression'.[13] This in turn leads to credit rationing[2] which favours LSI over SSI because it has more leverage with the banks.

The second NOM assumption, on fiscal imbalance, is monetarist in origin – although it is usually expressed in Keynesian categories of aggregate demand management. It is argued that the root cause of external account deficits – and thus indebtedness – is the fiscal deficit caused by the government's own borrowing abroad for investment programmes and the effect of budget expenditures on aggregate domestic demand and imports.[1, 12] 'Crowding out' of the domestic private sector also takes place – if the budget deficit is financed by borrowing from the banks under a fairly strict monetary policy; then credit to the private sector will be reduced and private investment fall. 'Unprotected' SSI would presumably suffer disproportionately in this process. If the deficit is funded by creating high-powered money, the subsequent inflation generates government seigniorage (sometimes known as an 'inflation tax') on the cash balances of

383

firms and households, which reduces real private sector incomes and thus the capacity to save and invest. It is not clear whether SSI would suffer more from inflation than LSI.

On the question of industrial structure, the NOM is somewhat ambiguous. The discussion of factor price distortions in the first assumption implies considerable market power (at least in influence over government regulations) on the part of LSI and proprietary technological superiority over SSI. However, the discussion of macroeconomic balance under the second assumption implies that *all* firms are discrete profit-maximizing units constrained only by savings (own profits and household surpluses on loan) in their investment decisions.

At the heart of the neoclassical formulation of the 'choice of technique' problem lies the proposition that profit-maximizing firms will choose production technologies from a freely available range according to the market prices of capital and labour. Alterations in the relative factor prices (particularly lower wages and higher interest rates) can thus induce technology shifts toward the desired position of full employment and efficient use of capital. As SSI already uses labour-intensive technology its profitability relative to LSI rises and it can expand more rapidly once policymakers have got 'factor prices right'.

The critique of this model from the AT viewpoint is as long-standing and almost as well known and focuses on the lack of realism in neoclassical assumptions about the production function.[3,14] In particular it is pointed out that the production function is not continuous, so that alternative efficient technologies to the dominant one, that is, large-scale, do not exist. SSI often has old and absolutely inefficient (in terms of capital and labour inputs per unit of output) technology; this is the argument for creating *new* appropriate (or 'intermediate') technologies. This 'lack of access' is exacerbated by the patenting of industrial technologies so they are not available to all firms. In particular, new foreign technologies are dominated by LSI (ie, MNCs and their local partners) which not only exclude SSI but also limit the potential for export except within markets determined by the international strategy of that MNC.

Analysis of the dynamics of technical progress indicates that 'organizational' scale economies exist in industry (as opposed to agriculture), so that while labour-intensive techniques may be as efficient as capital-intensive ones for small production runs at the *plant* level, as output increases larger *firms* are more efficient (or at least, more profitable) due to factors such as marketing and finance.[15] Moreover, industrial products are not homogeneous, for while SSI generally produces traditional unbranded items, LSI explicitly introduces new models and relies on advertising in order to ensure product identification in the market. In other words, modern product-cycle arguments necessarily assume *imperfect* markets and industrial accumulation based on technological quasi-monopoly.

The implications of this critique for macroeconomic policy are not entirely clear, beyond the general point that under these circumstances the proposed shift in relative factor prices will not have the desired effect because of technological and organizational inflexibility. In a sense, the stress placed by AT on 'fair access' to capital and technology for SSI could be seen as consistent with the spirit of the NOM emphasis on open factor markets. However, the AT insistence on 'meso-economic' market intervention by government to modify the relationship between enterprise units implies a need for comprehensive industrial planning.[3] Moreover, historical analysis of successful industrialization shows that monopoly profits in protected markets may be needed to stimulate industrial investment, although to be effective such support must be conditional upon the attainment of international competitiveness (the 'Korean' model) – a point which even the proponents of the NOM have been obliged to accept.[11]

These lines of critique are essentially directed at the production function contained in the 'choice of technique' model. In practice, the critique of the 'cost' side of the model (or the 'budget line' as it is often called in diagrammatic exposition) has focused upon the wider effects of 'controlled' wage-rate reductions on overall employment, taking the objective function as a given. The assumed behavioural function for firms seems to have been less discussed in the literature, even though it too is highly relevant to the issue of the impact of macroeconomic policy on SSI.

First, the logic of the neoclassical approach to the choice-of-technique means that 'if the production functions are homothetic and profits are maximized, then the (NOM) claim that the small-scale enterprise is characterized by a more effective use of capital and labour . . . implies that small firms face a lower price of labour relative to capital than larger'.[6] Indeed, labour market segmentation implies that increased wages in the 'formal' sector (ie, LSI) could actually *increase* total employment, for although higher 'controlled' wages might well reduce employment in LSI as now-unprofitable marginal output is withdrawn, the shift in market shares from LSI to labour-intensive SSI could result in new employment (from more labour-intensive production, albeit at the lower informal wage) greater than the initial loss.

Second, the structuralist critique originated by the Economic Commission for Latin America and developed with some effect by Stewart and Weeks, suggests that increased 'controlled' (ie, LSI) wage levels will stimulate the effective demand for the labour-intensive consumer goods produced by SSI.[16] In other words, the real wage rate reductions urged by the NOM would actually *reduce* total employment by diminishing demand for SSI output, even if LSI employment were to increase – which is unlikely due to the absence of continuous factor variability in production. This argument is strongly supported by the empirical evidence – 'recent studies have revealed without exception a strong positive relationship between changes

385

in household income and changes in the demand for a range of small-scale industry goods and services'.[9]

Third, it should be noted that variations in the wage rate also affect the cost of capital and thus lead to ambiguous 'Cambridge type' results even if all the other NOM assumptions hold. In terms of the familiar choice-of-technique diagram a wage rise not only increases the slope of the budget line in the usual way but also moves the production function upwards – by 'stretching' the K-axis so to speak – so the direction in which the resulting tangent point moves becomes indeterminate. On the one hand, this is due to the fact that half of the fixed capital formation in LDCs consists of labour-intensive construction[17] so that higher (lower) wages mean higher (lower) investment costs as well. On the other hand, the effect of the wage rate on the real exchange rate is such that if the real exchange rate (RER) is kept stable as policy, then higher (lower) wages mean higher (lower) local currency costs for imported capital goods.[12]

In sum, the AT critique of the NOM clearly does have significant heterodox implications for the effect of adjustment policies on SSI. However, to advance the corresponding macroeconomic analysis it is necessary to explore the investment-savings mechanisms of each of the two sectors explicitly.

## The macroeconomic balance: demand adjustments and SSI

Adjustment policy based on the NOM combines the aim discussed above of more efficient resource use through factor price clearing with specific 'expenditure changing' policies (fiscal and monetary) on the one hand, and 'expenditure switching' policies (trade and exchange rate) on the other.[12] The structuralist (or 'heterodox') critique of adjustment to external shock based on the NOM holds that in practice it has involved undesirable reductions in imports (rather than increased exports) through lower economic activity, combined with cuts in public welfare provision and declining real wages.[18-19] Such critics not only stress the need for active demand management to sustain investment and welfare, but also have far less faith in factor prices as an effective mechanism for resource reallocation. It is even suggested that increased interest rates and devaluation, far from increasing savings and exports, actually stimulate inflation by increasing production costs in economies characterized by mark-up pricing, supply constraints and effectively indexed wages.[21]

However, as Haggblade and colleagues point out, neither the NOM or its critics appears to take SSI explicitly into account in designing or evaluating adjustment.[22] On the contrary, in its canonical form the neo-orthodox 'financial decompression thesis' suggests that the objective of deregulating capital markets was to mobilize savings *out* of the informal sector by enhanced financial intermediation (including higher interest rates) in order to make better use of them in formal sector investment.[23] Neither have the underlying 'real' balances determining poverty – particularly the employment and food balances which have significant implications for small-scale enterprise[24] – been used by the structuralists to build up an alternative policy framework.

What Dornbusch and Helmers call the 'basic balance of payments equation'[12] – more correctly termed the 'accumulation account'[25] – is seen by the Bank as a 'good starting place' to analyse adjustment.[1] This logic is also closely followed by the Fund in its financial programming methodology.[2] The accumulation account records the ex-post identity between a country's aggregate savings and investment on the one hand, and foreign exchange receipts minus foreign exchange expenditures (the surplus on the current account of the balance of payments) on the other. The domestic accumulation balance is made up of the fiscal balance (which broadly corresponds to the budget) and the balance between private savings and investment – which in fact reflects the difference between private income and expenditure because private consumption is netted out.

Fiscal balance + Private balance = External balance (Increase in Net Foreign Assets)

$$(T - G - I_g) + (S_p - I_p) = (X - M)$$

By definition, the three accounts (fiscal, private and external) must reach an *ex post* balance. Exogenous changes – external shocks in particular – in one must be absorbed by the other two.[12] This section of the paper focuses on the way in which institutions and markets adapt their *ex ante* intentions and distribute the burden of adjustment between large firms (LSI), small firms (SSI) and households (ie, wage-earners and artisans).

The NOM model holds that the fiscal balance must be the prime mover in adjustment because budget deficits are the root cause of the external imbalance, and thus of foreign indebtedness.[1] Not only does this ignore what has happened to the external shock itself during the adjustment period (eg, commodity price collapse, increases in world interest rates and international credit rationing), it also assumes that private sector savings ($S_p$) are inherently stable; that even if the private sector is not entirely passive in the adjustment policy it is essentially *reactive* to policy. Another assumption is that the part of fiscal deficits not covered by foreign borrowing will cause a shortage of capital funds (if the government borrows from the banks under a tight monetary stance) and consequently will either involuntarily crowd out private investment ($I_p$) due to a lack of credit or force the private sector to borrow abroad in order to finance its investments. Alternatively, under a lax monetary stance, inflation sets in and private savings are used to maintain working capital (the real balance effect) or are used to finance capital flight as a reflection of the lack of business confidence. Here too, private investment will decline in both cases; to which can be added the depressive effects on investment of inflationary expectations.

Sucessful NOM adjustment would thus reduce both the fiscal and the external deficits in parallel, and the reverse process to that just described should occur. The NOM tacitly assumes that not only are such processes reversible in the short or medium term, but also that the positive effect of adjustment on the private sector benefits small and large firms equally, particularly if financial liberalization is also included.

In practice, adjustment to external shock – particularly over the past decade – has been a difficult and as yet incomplete process. The accumulation balances for nearly one hundred countries were examined by FitzGerald and colleagues.[26] Drastic efforts have been made, with and without NOM inspiration, to reduce aggregate expenditure, but government capacity to manage demand is largely confined to the budget rather than, for example, luxury consumption, so policy-makers can only try to adjust the budget in the hope of restoring the overall accumulation balance. Experience shows that this is made extremely difficult by structural rigidities in taxation and expenditures and the weight of debt servicing in the budget itself, so that a substantial part of the residual shock must necessarily be absorbed by the private sector. This is sometimes known as the 'transfer problem'. In any event, tax pressure does appear to have risen somewhat and real government expenditure to have fallen as a share of GDP in most LDCs, so the 'primary budget deficit' *has* fallen.[1] However, the interest charge on external debt is so large that the overall fiscal balance has declined *less* than the external balance – which has been forced to close because of lack of new aid, debt repayments and capital flight.

As a consequence, the private sector savings surplus $(S_p - I_p)$ has risen considerably (by some 3–5 per cent of GDP for LDCs as a whole over the last decade). Private sector investment rates have slightly declined, which is hardly surprising in view of the depressed level of activity and capital goods imports; although public investment has not fallen as much as might be expected, due to project lags and tied aid.

The somewhat unexpected conclusion is that the private savings rate has generally *risen* during the adjustment period in most LDCs. This is probably not due to financial reform (for the reasons indicated below) but rather to what might be called a 'forced solution to the transfer problem', by which resources are squeezed out of the private sector. This almost certainly takes place through a net increase in enterprise profits and a reduction in household consumption, although the mechanisms can be complex. The simple 'post-Keynesian' model, where profits and wages have fixed (but different) savings ratios, so that a redistribution of income from the latter to the former raises the overall savings rate is insufficient to explain this experience.[27] Rather, because so much investment is self-financed in LDCs, it is a question of *enterprise* response – whether this be a large corporation, the small firm or the artisan household – to macro-policies.

To understand this, we must disaggregate the private sector accumulation account, which is made up of large (subscript 1) and small (subscript 2) enterprises and households (subscript 3). On the one hand, we must look at the investment reaction of firms ($I_{p1}$, $I_{p2}$) and that of households ($I_{p3}$). Broadly, expansion of larger firms is constrained only by the market for their product, as they are able to adjust their sources of funds to cover profitable investment decisions and maintain profit rates through mark-up pricing. Small firm investment is constrained by both demand (ie, sales expectations) *and* savings – and in particular by credit. Household investment (mainly in housing and farm improvement) is constrained by savings; which can be raised only by reducing the non-essential components of consumption or obtaining credit (itself a function of income). On the other hand, savings in the firm sector depend on the availability of retained profits (R); while for households, savings in national accounting terms are the difference between aggregate personal income ($Y_3$) and consumption ($C_3$).

$$\text{Private Sector Balance} = \text{Large Firm Balance} + \text{Small Firm Balance} + \text{Household Balance}$$
$$(S_p - I_p) \qquad = (R_1 - I_{p1}) \qquad + (R_2 - I_{p2}) \qquad + (Y_3 - C_3 - I_{p3})$$

It is the contention of this paper that the burden of forced adjustment placed on the private sector by external shock and incomplete fiscal absorption, is transferred in varying degrees by the large firms to be absorbed by households and small firms, depending on the institutional structure of markets.

The adjustment process over the past decade has involved considerable fiscal changes, despite the continuing deficits. Unfortunately, the transfer problem does not appear to have been tackled through taxation – still less through the taxation of luxury consumption along Kaleckian lines[28] – but through real expenditure cuts in salaries, purchases of goods and services, and construction. With respect to taxation, there is evidence of a reduction in trade duties and a shift toward value added tax (VAT).[1] This has considerable advantages for overall fiscal efficiency, but from the point of view of SSI it may imply inclusion in the 'tax net' for the first time and a net charge on its accumulation balance.

As a component of expenditure cuts the reduction in subsidies is no great loss to SSI; and if state owned enterprises are dismantled there might be some market gain – although the main beneficiaries are likely to be the former state managers who take over the privatized portions. More serious, however, are the effects of reducing direct expenditures. On the one hand, the widespread decline observed in the real level of government wagebills sharply reduces urban demand for SSI consumer goods.[1] It may also reduce the 'protected wage' with the consequences discussed above. On the other, the reduced government expenditures on social services clearly affect SSI employees (and owners) directly[20]; but even more significantly, reduced provision of roads, electricity and water holds back the expansion of rural SSI.[24] On balance, therefore, the reduction in fiscal deficit caused by adjustment is likely to *reduce* SSI profits and investment.

Restrictive monetary policy is a feature of all adjustment policies: ideally the reduced credit/GDP ratio should be the result of a falling personal savings balance ratio (PSBR) and thus allow for slightly larger real credit to the private sector. The NOM holds that SSI benefits, particularly if real interest rates are imposed to clear financial markets and eliminate the necessity for discriminatory credit rationing. However, no empirical evidence exists that in developing economies the interest rate does significantly affect savings,[29] although it does alter the propensity to acquire financial instruments as opposed to productive investment or real estate.[30] The observed tendency for private savings to rise can thus be seen as a combination of the response of profits to the inflationary pressures of excess demand, devaluation and (imported) supply shortage on the one hand, and the real balance effect on the other.

Obtaining investment funds is clearly easier for LSI than for SSI. Credit supervision costs for banks when lending to SSI are intrinsically high, and it is inevitable that larger entrepreneurs have closer contacts with local bank managers.[31] These are essentially normal aspects of industrial organization rather than government policy; indeed, official SSI loan systems are designed to *counteract* them. Further, in rural areas at least,[32] the 'informal' credit system acts as a means by which small firms (especially peasant families) are controlled by larger ones. LSI itself generates large amounts of retained profits, and is usually linked to banks and other firms through membership in 'ownership groups' which span sectors and have their own international connections.[33] Thus preferential access to funds is not the result of financial repression, but of a perfectly rational capitalist accumulation strategy on the part of LSI: not exclusive to developing countries – and insufficient collateral (substantial property or a larger businessman as guarantor) on the part of SSI. In itself, financial liberalization will not solve these problems because higher interest rates will increase production costs and only LSI can pass these costs on to the market through price increases. Moreover, only the richest households holding a significant amount of financial assets will benefit from the income effect.

Expenditure-switching policies under adjustment have mainly been related to the external sector. Regarding external trade, there has been a general movement towards liberalization of quantitative import controls, reduction of effective protection and increases in the real exchange rate. In effect, this has been accompanied by somewhat increased export volumes and sharply reduced import volumes. It is not clear whether this closing of the trade gap is the result of these new policies or the consequences of restricted foreign finance, cuts in domestic demand, and the drive to export (against – or perhaps causing – declining world commodity prices) in order to meet debt service obligations.[18] Nonetheless, from the point of view of domestic markets, there have been substantial changes.

One of the key objectives of import liberalization is to reduce protection for LSI which (as in the case of credit) also enjoys preferential access to import quotas, foreign exchange allocations and trade credits. Such liberalization would tend to reduce LSI profits and improve SSI access to imported inputs and producer goods (particularly spare parts), although it would also open up the market to imported consumer goods, many of which compete directly with SSI. Moreover, to the extent that import demand is kept under control by monetary deflation, the consequent fall in the demand for basic consumer goods will have a negative effect on SSI as discussed earlier.

The Real Exchange Rate (RER) can be usefully although unconventionally defined as the ratio between the nominal exchange rate and the wage rate.[12] – The increase in the RER has one directly beneficial effect on SSI because it is less import-intensive than LSI, the increase in unit costs is smaller. If LSI can pass on higher costs in prices, SSI also benefits. However, a higher RER implies a decline in real wages, and therefore reduced spending by workers on SSI products. Further, the internal terms of trade are likely to improve with import liberalization and increased RER. This is likely to reduce the profits of urban SSI, but it could have a favourable indirect effect on rural SSI.[24] The net impact of orthodox trade strategies is ambiguous in its direction, therefore.

There are two kinds of policies to deal with the balance of payments. First, there are official debt renegotiations and attempts to encourage new loans and aid. Debt renegotiation clearly helps SSI to the extent that it reduces the scale of the transfer problem, even if the conditionality has ambiguous effects on SSI in the ways we have seen. New loans, especially if channelled directly to the private sector, directly benefit LSI, while new aid increasingly contains specific provisions for SSI.

Second, there are policies that can deal with private capital movements. It is reasonable to assume that capital flight as such is mainly conducted by LSI; the SSI equivalent is usually hoarding of gold or hard currencies. On the contrary, remittances of money from abroad are mainly generated by family labour and are often used to set up small businesses. Overall, it is unlikely that policies on interest rates or exchange rates have much effect on capital flight;[34] while the flow of remittances for SSI accumulation are mainly a function of employment opportunities abroad.

Although private sector response patterns will naturally vary according to national economic and institutional structures, it is reasonable to conclude that, far from NOM adjustment policies automatically favouring SSI over LSI, the reverse is just as likely to be the case. LSI is better able to maintain its investment and savings plans, and thus sustain its *ex ante* accumulation account into the *ex post* macroeconomic equilibrium, due to its being a price maker and part of larger financial groupings. LSI thus has considerable potential to force onto SSI and households the burden of adjustment generated by external shock and only partly absorbed by the fiscal sector.

## The macroeconomic consequences of LSI–SSI linkage

In order to construct a complete macroeconomic framework reflecting this institutional heterogeneity, it is necessary to define the behaviour of the sector properly. This is a task beyond the scope of this paper. However, some initial points might help to indicate how this might be done. In particular, it is necessary to specify the relationship *between* the LSI and SSI.

The neo-orthodox model (NOM) assumes that all firms face the same price in their output market, and that they have equal access to inputs at the clearing price. In practice neither of these propositions is valid for systemic reasons arising from industrial organization and not government policy alone – the latter may reinforce or counterbalance the former, depending on the circumstances. In the output market it is generally correct to say that LSI is a 'price maker' while SSI is a 'price taker'.[4] Large firms are usually located in highly concentrated industries producing differentiated products. These products often are priced by 'markup pricing' or government-regulated prices based on negotiated profit margins.[35] In the case of LSI exporters, the exchange rate (including tax incentives, etc) will also be negotiated in terms of an acceptable markup as well. In contrast, SSI usually faces a highly competitive market and accepts a clearing price over which it has no control.

Access to labour is more complex. LSI may be more attractive than SSI to well-trained professionals as it can offer career opportunities; it may also be preferred by skilled labour due to higher wages and fringe benefits. In addition, LSI wages appear to be linked to capital-intensity (that is, the wagebill is a fairly stable share of value-added across branches), rather than clearing the labour market.[36] Nonetheless, LSI firms in more labour-intensive branches (eg, textiles) do appear to have difficulties in maintaining and controlling large work forces effectively, which is one reason why labour-saving technologies are preferred.[6] In contrast, SSI tends to pay low wages, but has preferential access to members of the extended family of the owner–manager (often with only imputed wages or subsistence), women from nearby households, seasonal workers and so on; the costs of labour administration, social security and training are also much lower or non-existent.[37]

Finally, the NOM assumes profit maximization by firms, or in the case of households, utility maximization, as the logical basis of production decisions. This implies expanding production up to the 'socially efficient' point where price is equal to marginal cost. However, modern business theory indicates that LSI is likely to attempt to maximize size – measured by sales or capital stock – subject to a minimum profitability constraint. This can be interpreted as an expression of managerial capitalism, or of corporate power in the case of owner-controlled firms – it is clearly a rational strategy. Curiously, there appears to have been little theorizing on the true objectives of SSI or its relationship to local social and economic organization – this contrasts markedly with the modern theorization about the agrarian enterprise. The need to survive and diversify, the desire to maximize family income – profits *plus* wages, if the two are distinguishable at all – possibly subject to the constraint of family labour – all seem plausible.[16] Indeed, casual observation would indicate that over the 'life' of SSI, stability may be found only in achieving *medium* size, with its managerial economies of scale, or by retreating to artisan status. For artisan SSI, where minimal subsistence requirements may oblige the family to engage in other activities in order to reduce risk, output is still viable as long as price exceeds marginal *material* costs.

Large firms working on a markup are not closely constrained by savings in their investment decisions. They enjoy accumulated profits and access to bank credit particularly when they belong to large 'groups'. Investment decisions are taken on the basis of anticipated profitability, which (political considerations apart) depends on existing capacity, expected market demand growth, export prospects and so on. Corporate investment decisions are made on the basis of expected profitability. Even in the presence of a well-functioning capital market, retained profits are first employed along with bank credits for physical and working capital. The rest of the profits are distributed to shareholders, to be used in non-essential consumption, real estate or capital flight.

The situation of SSI is quite different. Here the firm is clearly more likely to be constrained by lack of capital, and to be less concerned with strategic considerations – as evidenced by the high birth and death rates for small business. Own profits are the main source of funds – indeed household budget surveys indicate that only households with self-employed members save much at all, which is all the more true when investment in own housing is netted out.[38] Bank credit may not only be hard to obtain, but also tends to create an element of inflexibility in costs which may be undesirable in a fluctuating market. The logical sequence for a small-scale firm would be to save the balance between the enterprise margin and a socially acceptable consumption level for the family; take on available bank credit up to a level determined by expected ability to repay (or collateral value); and invest this sum in business expansion, unless market prospects are poor or family labour is a constraint.

Thus far, we have assumed that LSI and SSI are separate entities with distinct rules of economic behaviour. They respond to changes in factor prices or to aggregate demand shocks in different ways, implying a heterogeneous private sector, but without any connection between the two. The next and final step in the paper is to examine possible connections between LSI and SSI and their macroeconomic consequences. Clearly there exist[25] an almost infinite number of possible relations between the two forms of production. Here I shall focus on three key categories: competition between LSI and SSI for the same product market; sub-contracting by SSI as part of the LSI production process; and complementary provision of basic consumer goods by SSI to the LSI work force.

Other linkages clearly exist – SSI provision of labour to LSI, credit from LSI to SSI, or the final processing by SSI of LSI output – but much the same analytical approach could probably be applied. The point is that private sector responses to macroeconomic variables will depend crucially on the transmission of market signals between the two sectors.

The main operating characteristics for SSI and LSI are taken to be the following:

1. SSI has a higher labour intensity (L/O) than LSI;
2. SSI has a lower imported raw material (M) utilization coefficient (M/O) than LSI;
3. LSI employs labour at an institutionally defined wage rate and maximizes sales as long as profits remain above an acceptable level; SSI uses family and informal labour, and maximizes income net of raw material costs and wages;
4. LSI can fix prices on the basis of labour and raw material costs, plus a markup; SSI accepts the price set on the market.

The first case is that of *competition* between LSI and SSI firms producing similar products and selling on the same markets. The market price is set by LSI; this price will in turn determine SSI income per head. As LSI works on a markup, any increases in its costs will drive up the market price, and thus benefit SSI. A policy of reducing real wages may help to control inflation but it will not help SSI. Nor will such a policy increase employment in the LSI because there is no technology shift as a consequence. A similarly heterodox result would emerge if increased interest charges on capital were taken into account. This too would drive up LSI costs and prices; again SSI would benefit, not from a change in the relative profitability of different techniques of production, but because of higher market prices.

A decrease in aggregate demand as part of a stabilization package would, by forcing LSI to reduce output, raise its unit costs – which have a large fixed component compared to SSI – and thus push up the market price, to the advantage of competitive SSI. The reverse applies to expansionary demand policies, until LSI capacity constraints (which may be defined by import shortages) are reached. After this point the industrial economy moves from a 'Keynesian' to a 'Kaldorian' phase and prices are driven up again by excess demand. Although much of these scarcity rents will be captured by commercial intermediaries, it is reasonable to suppose that SSI will benefit too.

In this first case market shares are not endogenously defined. To some extent they will be determined by factors such as product quality and access to productive resources and not by relative prices. 'Quality' in turn depends not only on the superior technology of LSI, but also on advertising which shifts consumer preferences toward LSI products as such. Access by competitive SSI to resources can be limited by LSI (often through pressure on government) using methods ranging from differential credit supply to urban zoning regulations.

The second case is that of *sub-contracting* where one or more stages in the LSI production process is 'put out' to SSI. Examples abound, ranging from the assembly of sports shoes for export, to small engineering shops supporting the capital goods industry. The relevant price for the SSI product will be determined by the potential cost savings to the LSI through sub-contracting the process rather than carrying it out itself. The extent of sub-contracting thus depends upon cost conditions within LSI. A decrease in real wages will hurt SSI in two ways – on the one hand, LSI will not be willing to sub-contract more work; on the other, the price paid to SSI will fall.

In this case the volume of SSI output will depend on that of LSI, which in turn will vary with macroeconomic policy. An adjustment programme which depresses domestic industrial output by reducing domestic demand more than any increase in export possibilities would clearly have this effect and be damaging for SSI.

The third case is that of *complementarity*, expressed here in terms of SSI providing wage goods (basic consumer goods) for the LSI labour force. The price would be determined by the clearing of a competitive market, with demand coming from the proportion of workers' budgets spent on these goods – the wagefund itself being determined by the wage level and the level of LSI employment. For a given wagegoods supply (constrained, for example, by food supply to the towns), an increase in wages or in LSI employment will clearly benefit SSI through higher prices. An increased food supply from the farmers would increase SSI output (and thus

395

employment possibilities), but for a given level of LSI employment and wages it would *depress* SSI prices and incomes.

Another variant within this case is to consider elastic raw materials supply (from LSI by-products for instance) used by household-based SSI of limited size. For a given increase in the level of demand for wagegoods (generated by increased employment or wages) the number of SSI firms will increase, raising output but depressing prices. The equilibrium point will be reached when average income in SSI is brought down to the opportunity cost of labour, which can be taken for analytical purposes as the average level of rural incomes.[39] For *established urban* SSI, rural to urban migration is detrimental as it reduces margins; for the new arrivals the situation is the reverse. From the point of view of national economic policy, the implications are obvious.

These three simple models obviously cannot capture fully a complex industrial reality, but they do serve to show that even within a polarized industrial structure different forms of SSI–LSI articulation can lead to quite distinct macroeconomic policy impacts on SSI.

## Concluding remarks

In an exploratory exercise such as this it is extremely difficult to come to firm conclusions, let alone policy recommendations. All that I have tried to do in this paper is point out the shortcomings of the 'neo-orthodox' model (NOM) of the macro–micro relationship, and to suggest how more realistic modelling of industrial behaviour might yield a more plausible 'heterodox' analysis. To achieve more concrete results, far more detailed modelling on empirical data for specific country cases would have to be carried out; perhaps within the structuralist frameworks established by Taylor and Pyatt.[27,40]

The main argument contained four main points: first, the neo-orthodox model of the macro–micro relationship is based on two propositions:

o Direct and determinate causal effect of factor prices (wages, interest rates and real exchange parities) on the choice of technique in industry; and

o Direct relationship between fiscal deficits and the balance of payments, which would favour the private sector during adjustment programmes;

Second, although the first proposition would favour SSI, it is not tenable in practice, as is shown both by the 'appropriate technology' critique and an examination of the assumptions as to firm behaviour. Third, the second proposition is not tenable either, as is shown by the experience of macroeconomic response to external shock in practice, and by the theoretical analysis of the distinct accumulation behaviour of LSI

396

and SSI. Fourth, plausible characterizations of the articulation between LSI and SSI all yield heterodox macroeconomic response to adjustments in aggregate demand and factor prices.

This paper has argued that simply reducing real wages will not create more employment, nor favour SSI in general. Similarly, higher interest rates alone will not have the desired technological effect. This is not to imply that the wage rate can be safely raised to any level, nor that negative real interest rates are desirable; but rather that their consequences must be seen in terms of income transfers, demand effects and price formation. The negative effect of allowing wages to rise too rapidly is not really a question of industrial profitability or labour 'pricing itself out of a job'. Rather it is a question of:

o Pressure on the real exchange rate, which will divert tradables from exports to the home market;
o Inflationary effect on aggregate demand when full industrial capacity is reached (although wages are usually only a minor part of national expenditure); and
o Impact on basic needs prices when food supply is limited.

This conclusion implies that a more careful macroeconomic planning of both wage levels and of wagegoods supply would benefit not only workers but also SSI; while recognizing that this has inevitable consequences for tax regimes and non-essential consumption if aggregate demand is to be kept under control.

Similarly, the elimination of subsidized credit will not increase aggregate savings or make SSI more competitive. However, negative real rates do have serious consequences in terms of the large subsidy from the fiscal sector to LSI (in the case of development banks) and the limitation on the total revolving credit fund available if commercial bank loans are not fully recovered allowing for inflation. In fact, as far as SSI is concerned, the volume of credit available rather than the price is probably the limiting factor; so that adjustment of the capital market through institutional reform rather than prices is indicated.

This conclusion implies that banks should not just move toward real interest rates but also develop different systems of collateralization that would permit loans to be made to SSI on a normal business basis.

In view of the incapacity of the state to absorb the whole impact of external shock by increasing its own savings–investment balance (especially in the absence of tax reform) without abandoning the welfare objectives from which SSI also benefits, neo-orthodox adjustment policy means that the private sector is forced into involuntary savings surplus. Private consumption is depressed even more than private investment, and given the superior capacity of LSI to protect itself by price rises or access to credit, SSI and households will take a disproportionate part of the burden.

This conclusion implies that greater care must be taken in designing structural adjustment programmes to take into account the heterogeneity of the private sector, the linkages between its component parts and the differential impact of fiscal activities. In sum, macroeconomic policy should be combined with an integrated industrial programme – even if the objective is financial stabilization after external shock rather than economic development proper – to avoid unintended negative impacts of adjustment policy on SSI.

# Notes on Income Distribution, Growth and Demand

## CHARLES COOPER

This paper will explore relationships between income distribution, growth and demand in developing countries. They focus on assumptions that seem to be very common in discussions of the employment effects of income redistribution (ie, that it results in higher unit labour inputs and increased employment) and of the role of small-scale industries (that they benefit from redistribution because they produce mainly low income goods).

In development economics it has long been thought that income redistribution in favour of the poor would have positive effects on employment. This line of argument was particularly common in the 1970s – though it no doubt has much earlier origins. In 1970 Dudley Seers wrote the following in the ILO Report on Employment in Colombia:

> ... Basic goods which are widely purchased by those on low incomes, essentially food and rather simple manufactures like clothing and footwear – are precisely the goods which are (or can be) produced with techniques considerably more labour-intensive than those used in the production of goods demanded by the rich. ... A given amount of income will thus generate more employment when spent in the purchase of wage goods than in the acquisition of consumer durables ... Since ... these goods for mass consumption can be produced with simple techniques, the greater the increase in their sales the greater the demand for unskilled labour which is in particularly ample supply.[1]

Seers' adherence to this idea probably reflects the influence of ECLA structuralism, though many structuralists would have been much more sceptical than he about the possibilities of using income redistribution to expand employment. For many, the political economy of most Latin American countries, has meant that economic growth would inevitably involve increasing unemployment and a deterioration in income distribution. Taylor contrasts the Latin American assertion that high growth would be associated with inequitable distribution with an Indian view that inequity had contributed to stagnation.[2] On the Indian argument, for example,

---

CHARLES COOPER is Professor of Development Economics at the Institute of Social Studies, The Hague. His research has concentrated particularly on the role of technology in development processes.

Nayar.[3] In fact, Seers argued, on essentially Keynesian grounds, that a more equitable distribution in Colombia would be expansionary.[1]

This starts a virtuous circle. In the first round income redistribution toward the poor causes increases in employment especially of the unskilled, resulting in further improvement in income distribution during the second round. This pattern of growth, characterized by increasing participation of unskilled labour and improvements in equity, is presently associated with increasing 'social articulation', a concept discussed later on in this paper.[4] More recently Ian Little has made the same assumption:

> ... Measures to make income distribution more equal will probably shift production in a labour-intensive direction, for the things demanded by the poor – food, clothing, and shelter – are made in a relatively labour-intensive manner. These aspects are self-reinforcing, in that the use of labour-intensive production methods benefits poor, unskilled workers and their dependents ...[5]

The Seers concept of a simple relationship between income distribution, the nature of demand, and the labour intensity of production makes no mention of small-scale industry as such. It is, however, quite commonly assumed that the small-scale sector has a special part to play because (it is said) small-scale firms produce 'goods for mass consumption ... with simple techniques'. The small-scale sector, therefore, appears to have an especially important part to play in the virtuous circle. It is seen by some as the link between the first round impact of income redistribution on demand and the second round in which expansion of labour-intensive production further improves the distribution of income through its effects on the employment of the unskilled.[6]

There are, in short, two assertions about economic reality which are used to link redistribution policies to labour intensity in production and labour intensity to the small-scale sector; both need to be further examined. These assertions are the following:

○ Redistribution of income toward the poor results in a relative increase in the demand for goods which are labour-intensive in production; and
○ These labour-intensive goods are produced predominantly by small-scale industries.

### Redistribution and labour intensity of demand

The empirical evidence linking income redistribution to an increase in labour-intensity of demand and hence a greater volume of employment at given levels of income is in fact rather sparse. Perhaps the boldest tests of this relationship were done during the 1970s using input–output methods to explore the employment effects of changes in the final demand vector in various economies, in relation to simulated changes in the redistribution of income. A number of such studies were reviewed some years ago by Morawetz and independently by Tokman in two well-known articles.[7,8] These studies showed unexpectedly limited second round employment effects, that is, the increase in employment resulting from an initial redistribution was found to be disappointingly small. The studies generally showed a shift toward higher consumption and output of the more labour-intensive agricultural and industrial products, as was expected, but the positive effect of this on employment was offset in part by decreases in service employment by the high income classes and also by negative 'indirect' employment effects. The latter arose from the fact that labour-intensive final outputs may make use of capital-intensive input materials. For example, textile weaving for low-income consumers may use low-cost synthetic fibre yarns which are highly capital-intensive in production; or low-cost leather-substituting plastic materials which are made in very capital-intensive production systems may be used as inputs by labour-intensive artisanal producers of leather goods for low-income consumers; or metal or plastic products used in low-income housing construction may be very capital-intensive in production. Obviously, not all materials used in labour-intensive production for final demand are capital-intensive goods, but apparently enough are to cause appreciable reductions in the employment effects of increases in low-income consumption.

Such studies (which presently seem to be somewhat out of vogue) are not necessarily decisive evidence against the existence of a virtuous link between equitable redistribution and the level of employment. For one thing, the results are contingent upon the structure of the economies in which they occur. Most of these were in Latin America. It may be that in Africa, where the rich are absolutely less rich and (possibly) demand fewer labour-intensive services than the Latin American elites, the reductions in service employment would be less decisive – and overall employment effects of redistribution more decisively favourable. Furthermore, in countries where industrialization is less deep, the negative 'indirect' employment effects arising from the need for capital-intensive intermediate materials may be less pronounced, simply because the intermediates are not locally made. In this case, however, import content would be increased. It remains to be shown whether the 'disappointing' input–output results would be seriously modified for economies where structural conditions are significantly different from the conditions in the Latin American countries of the 1970s.

There is, however, a more important methodological case against the input–output studies which arises from the way in which industries are aggregated and then treated as having constant input coefficients.[6] It may be that a redistribution of income would produce a shift in the pattern of demand *within* the industry groups as they are defined in the input–output table. After all, the industries defined in input–output tables include many different outputs – some substitutes for one another in the consumption basket. Thus, if there were a shift toward more labour-intensive outputs within the aggregated 'industries' so defined, its employment effects would not show up in the calculation. There is, therefore, at least a possibility that these studies underestimate employment effects of redistribution. However, the implications of disaggregation for the 'indirect' employment effects discussed above cannot even be inferred.

There have been some attempts to deal with the problems of aggregation by carrying out studies on industrial branches which are more narrowly defined than is manageable in input–output systems. Some disaggregated studies were done in the ILO–WEP research programme.[9-11] The major problem remains, however, that it is very difficult to infer much about aggregate effects from such studies – especially since the evidence does not unambiguously support the idea that aggregation systematically underestimates employment effects. Results go in either direction. Moreover, the many studies that have shown the existence of efficient technological choices in a wide variety of industrial sectors usually do not address the question of the effect of redistribution on demand and technical choice at the 'technique' level.

In short, the evidence available at present on the likely employment effect of redistribution is incomplete. This makes it difficult to generalize about the existence of a positive second round effect on employment following redistribution, as assumed by Little.[5]

There is at least one other reason to be cautious in assuming that the poor tend to consume goods which are inherently labour-intensive. This is simply that at any given moment the relative factor intensities of production for various output categories are the product of economic and technological history – and it is not particularly clear why one should expect *a priori* that the historic evolution of technology should guarantee that low-income goods will be produced by more labour-intensive methods than high-income goods. Moreover, the largely impressionistic empirical evidence available on this point does not really give much support to the idea. The textile, dyestuff and basic organic and inorganic chemical industries of the Industrial Revolution supplied significant amounts of final outputs to low-income demand, and were in their time relatively highly capital-intensive. There are many examples. In fact the existence of mass low-income markets has often been a spur to innovation, which is very frequently accompanied by increasing capital intensity and reduced labour inputs per unit of output. Accordingly it should not be at all surprising that the things which are consumed by low-income classes should, at least sometime in the historic process, be produced by capital-intensive methods and quite conceivably by more capital-intensive methods than the things which the rich consume. Historically this was most probably the case. Furthermore, as the Industrial Revolution extended to the mechanization of machine-making and the large-scale production of intermediate goods, the industries involved in what we have called 'indirect' employment effects also became very capital-intensive. It would be plausible to suggest, therefore, that in the middle quarter of the nineteenth century, the capital intensity of production of basic goods consumed by the poor began increasing very sharply. During that period a redistribution of income in favour of the poor easily might not have increased employment per unit of output, (aside from effects on high income demands for service).

If it is agreed that there is no apparent reason why the history of technology should lead to a situation where low-income goods are inherently more labour-intensive in production than high-income goods, then perhaps we need to take another look at the present state of affairs. It might be true that in the Third World at the present time there is a systematic bias toward relatively labour-intensive production of low-income goods. But, even if this happens to be true (and the evidence is not decisive), technological history should make us cautious about assuming that it will somehow always remain true. On the contrary, we should expect the situation to change under the impact of technological change.

This may well be happening. At the present time many industries which have been regarded as 'traditional' (because technological change in them happened to be slow for a few decades) are likely to experience accelerated technological change. Textiles production, for example, under the combined impact of devices like the aerodynamic loom, open-end spinning and new systems of automation will certainly change a great deal. No doubt there are many other examples, especially where new 'generic' technologies like microelectronic innovations are likely to be incorporated into production. Hoffman and Rush, for example, suggest that garment manufacturing may well be automated soon.[12] Others have noted with concern the effective intrusion of multinational producers in traditional markets like soap-making, at the cost of local firms. These 'traditional' industries are, for the most part, the ones which produce for low-income consumers. Technical progress will decrease labour inputs per unit of output in these industries and it is also likely that the labour coefficients will decrease more rapidly than the labour coefficients in production of goods for high-income consumers. In these circumstances our comfortable, though questionable, generalization about the links between income redistribution and employment may have to be abandoned. In particular, the possibility of virtuous circles in which growth is based on production for the poor who are as a result employed in increasing numbers in the labour-intensive sectors – growth with 'social articulation' as de Janvry and Sadoulet have called it,[4] may be less of a possibility than we would wish to believe. The factor patterns associated with microelectronics innovation have been researched by Soete.[13] But, indeed, as the bits of empirical evidence discussed above suggest, we may not have to wait on history. It is quite possible that we are there already.

Certainly it would be helpful to have more detailed empirical knowledge of the relative factor intensities of low- and high-income consumption patterns (including of course inter-industry effects).

## Small-scale industry and the labour intensity of production

The second assertion above was that the small-scale sector is an important source of labour-intensive goods associated with the final demand patterns of the poor. Aside from the doubts about the inherent labour intensity of low-income final and intermediate demands explored above, this generalization about the role of small-scale industries needs to be qualified. In the first place, not all small-scale firms are producing for final demand. In sectors like metal goods and mechanical engineering small firms are usually involved in producing intermediate goods – quite often as sub-contractors to larger enterprises. Second, even where the small-scale sector is engaged in producing goods for final demand (whether for low- or high-income groups) it is not necessarily doing so in the most labour-intensive way. Little has shown that in India (and in a comparative study on Colombia), the smallest firms which produce printed matter, soap and shoes are not the most labour-intensive producers in the sectors to which they belong.[5] There must, however, be some doubt about this result since it is based on a comparison of factor productivity and capital–labour ratios measured as size group averages. As Little himself points out, the variances associated with the means are so large that the comparison of size group averages runs into problems of statistical significance. However, this in itself points to the difficulty of generalizing about the relative labour intensity of small-scale production. Last, Little has noted some (rather superficial) evidence of economic and technological inferiority in the small-scale sector, as compared to medium-sized firms.[5] This conclusion is based on size group comparisons which in some cases show the small-scale sector as having higher capital *and* higher labour input coefficients than middle-sized firms.[5] It must be kept in mind, however, that there are significant differences in product characteristics between the sub-sectors which undermine simple comparisons. The point is, however, that even if there are product differences, the smaller firms would appear to be making the more capital-intensive products – somewhat against the general run of assumptions made about the nature of small-scale outputs.

Therefore, caution should be exercised in relying on the 'stylized facts' often used in discussing small-scale production. For example, it is not necessarily true that a prior income redistribution is needed in order to increase demand for small-scale outputs. No doubt this holds for some outputs, but for other small-scale products – capital goods like light machinery, or intermediate goods, for example – an income redistribution may not be at all helpful. It is even likely that the expansion of these types of small-scale output will be favoured by inequitable income distributions. It must be remembered that small-scale sub-contracting enterprises in Japan grew rapidly without any redistributive policies to help them.[14] Nor is it necessarily true that small-scale industry as such will provide a way to generate virtuous circles of equitable growth along the lines of the 'social articulation' models. There will be cases where small-scale firms are not the most labour-intensive and hence not those which will generate the highest employment of unskilled labour at a 'second round'. Small-scale firms are, of course, among the most labour-intensive, and no doubt effective policies to increase the labour intensity of industrial production would in many cases result in a relatively high rate of growth in the small-scale sectors. But, it does not follow that interventions to stimulate the growth of small-scale firms are the most effective way to increase labour intensity. As Little has remarked '... size of firm, ... is a very poor indicator of those characteristics of firms that may be of interest to policy-makers ...', and somewhat more to the immediate point: '... such differences in labour intensity as there are between size groups in an industry ... are dwarfed by differences between industries. ...' The upshot is that policies which change the pattern of inter-industry outputs are likely to be more effective ways of increasing labour intensity than the promotion of small-scale production per sè '... small and very small firms are often labour-intensive, because labour-intensive industries have a relatively high proportion of small enterprises. ... However, small modern factories may be very capital-intensive. Many smaller firms are relatively labour-intensive of course, but quite a few are not and it may be inappropriate to aim employment policies at small firms per se.'[5]

## Concluding remarks

The main purpose of these notes is to express a degree of scepticism about the assumptions which lead to the notion of a simple virtuous relationship between equitable income distribution and the labour intensity of production. It also expresses scepticism about the assumption that small-scale firms are particularly important in generating 'second round' effects following an initial income redistribution, or more straightforwardly that general promotion of small-scale industry is the best way to increase the labour intensity of production. The customary 'stylized facts' may need another look. It is a pity that all one does is express scepticism on these matters. Firm conclusions in either direction depend on more and better evidence than we presently have at hand. In the meantime we might take Alfred Marshall's caution about long chains of argument more seriously: 'There is no room in economics for long chains of reasoning. . .'.[15] Some of the chains of reasoning which connect the distribution of income with the labour intensity of production and the role of small firms are rather long.

# Discussion: Small-Scale Industrial Policies

*W Gschwend*: Was the use of second-hand plant equipment important in any of the industries you studied?

*J James*: Used equipment normally requires selection by people with technical capabilities. However, the people who make technology decisions in parastatals are often not well versed in technology. In any case, they have no incentive to make the most cost-effective technology choices. Risks are higher in buying used equipment and risk-averse managers usually avoid this option.

*F Stewart*: I think Mr James' research is very valuable, but too pessimistic about the possibilities for change. How can we push public companies to make wise management decisions? For instance they can be turned into profit maximizers. Both public and private sectors should be made to face a more competitive environment. Technology appraisals should become a systematic part of decision-making in the public sector. Furthermore, public enterprises should not necessarily be modelled after huge enterprises. A decentralized model based on smaller enterprises could force more appropriate decisions.

*J James*: Attempts to improve decision-making processes in public enterprises have not been very successful thus far. I agree with some of the things you have mentioned, but the aid donor motivation is hard to change. The large donors would need more staff to administer smaller projects.

The other policy direction that could be pursued would be to search for technologies that originated in other developing countries. The classic example is the labour-intensive textile plants built by the Chinese in Tanzania. Another example is the small-scale, Pan-African papermill in Kenya, which was adapted to the local environment by the Indian venture partners.

Other successful cases have minimized foreign exchange requirements. Juma compared ethanol production plants in Kenya and Zimbabwe. The Kenya plant's technology was influenced by the source of finance. In Zimbabwe, the government required the private firm to repay the foreign exchange investment in six months. As a result, the Zimbabwe plant was much less costly and more appropriate than the unsuccessful Kenya one.

At the Kiltex textile plant in Tanzania, managers faced with the problem of foreign exchange shortages decided to minimize foreign exchange requirements. At the same time, they successfully adapted and innovated the production process.

*E Doryan-Garron*: Two different paths could be followed to make public enterprises more efficient. First, when a public enterprise plans to construct a plant, the manager must identify various alternative technologies available in the world market and define which one is most appropriate. Alternatively, parastatal managers could choose technologies that had been successfully tried in other countries in the region.

As long as they look at technology as a whole package, most managers will be less receptive to appropriate technology. Instead of dealing with technology as a black box, the technology package should be disaggregated as much as possible and components of the package should be produced and bought locally. This would build a constituency with an incentive to use local technology and increase the domestic manufacturing capacity. It would also require the manager to have a more sophisticated level of technical knowledge to be able to appraise technologies.

*J James*: Usually, the question of technology choice and labour-intensive alternatives is never posed in the first place. The point raised by Mr Doryan-Garron is interesting in another way. Judith Tendler found that donor-funded energy/power projects in Brazil maximized foreign exchange use and bypassed local industry. Yet, in Latin America, there is a local alternative. In Africa, as local technical capabilities are more limited, there are fewer local manufacturers to say, 'we could have made that'.

*H Thomas*: Usually, in Africa, there is not a choice between working with a few large public enterprises and a large number of small ones because there are not many small entrepreneurs. In Latin America and South Asia this is less of a problem.

It is still quite early to design policies and draw conclusions of this kind for small enterprises, because we know relatively little about them and how they choose technology. In Pakistan, small entrepreneurs are generally reluctant to invest in technology because they cannot sell a better quality product to customers or cannot obtain credit with a long enough repayment period. If the private entrepreneur is not motivated to invest in technology a new rationale should be explored, particularly with donor interventions.

*J James*: The findings of my paper do not apply to regions other than Africa. Even in Africa, there are large differences across countries. Organization is a very serious constraint in some African countries but not in others.

*D E van de Poel*: Mr James' diagnosis is clear, but I would like to hear more about the policy 'medicine' needed to solve these problems. Second, it is not surprising that parastatals are important in Africa considering its cultural background. Even if African countries shift more toward private enterprise development, parastatals will continue to exist for some time.

*J James*: Regarding the policy implications, the connection needs to be broken between the suppliers of machinery and finance in preparation of project feasibility studies. Botswana, for example, has managed its public sector fairly well. The government has kept the public sector at a manageable size and it is explicit about priorities, making it easier to exercise control. Something being tried in other parts of Africa is to develop a contract that explicitly arranges the communication between the Ministries and the parastatals to narrow down their objectives.

A recent paper released by the World Bank describes the experience with this type of contract in developed as well as in developing countries. However, the World Bank tends to recommend social cost–benefit analysis as a panacea and criticize the reliance on more limited financial analysis in decision-making by many donor-financed companies and governments. The World Bank feels social cost–benefit analysis could eliminate many poor investment decisions. In fact, this would not solve the problem because by the time you get to the cost–benefit stage, it is often too late in the decision-making process for more than incremental differences in the technologies analysed. Cost–benefit analysis is good only in choosing between what is available. If there is no mechanism to search for alternative technologies, it will not help.

David Leonard argued that the World Bank solutions do not work in the African context because African management is very different from the model that underlies the policies of the World Bank. He argues that the correct approach is to begin with a realistic model of how managers behave within the political economy of African countries. Policies should explicitly take these factors into account.

*Y de Wit*: Having participated in many meetings of development finance companies in Africa, I think your picture is rather fair. A number of these companies did a social cost–benefit analysis, but it was too late. In addition, the responsibility of the board members is to choose the most financially rewarding project, not the most appropriate technology from a development point of view.

Neither the finance companies nor the World Bank can be blamed for that. The real problem in the African countries I am familiar with is that a single government agency is not responsible for approving project investments. In Indonesia, at least two agencies have a central function. The Central Planning Bureau deals with public investments issues, while another bureau is responsible for technology. These agencies have an active interest in and sometimes supply the knowledge needed to find the right technology, but they do not influence private investment decisions.

In some countries many government bureaus have been the strongest advocates for changes in technology choice, because they have seen so many wrong decisions in private investments. When correct price signals are built into the system, the effect can be amazing. Isn't it possible to centralize investment decisions through licensing, and then help these agencies with correct price signals?

Many wrong decisions are made because foreign exchange is too easy to get. Once a manager, a board, or an owner sees that the original proposal is very expensive, they will look for another one.

*J James*: I agree in part. Some critics argue that social cost–benefit is not used that much in the World Bank either. They argue that the real decisions in developing countries are not made about projects but about sectors. Moreover, cost–benefit analysis is complex and time consuming.

Some African countries do have a central institution that is supposed to deal with technological issues, but I do not think they have been effective. For the most part, African governments have been concerned with maximization of output in a short period. They have tended to disregard technological issues which could slow down the process and require a lot of scarce, skilled manpower. Moreover, many governments simply have not felt that technology choice is so critical in development.

*V FitzGerald*: These public enterprise problems are a familiar story, not just in Africa. We have the same problems in Europe. Ten years ago in England a Royal Commission on the topic could not specify the objective function for the government. As the then Chancellor of the Exchequer pointed out, if any government specified its objective function, politics would be over! Politics is about negotiations and about processes.

My criticism is that your image of what a normal or well functioning enterprise should be is rather idealized. Large enterprises everywhere behave similarly if they get a chance. In Eastern Europe, there is the same complaint about very large 'white elephants', requiring excessive investment. This systematic problem is usually known as 'accumulation bias'. Large companies in Western Europe work the same way if they can. The usual objectives of a large corporation are growth and increased market share. What makes large firms in the West efficient is the fear of bankruptcy or takeover, not price signals. Thus, the issue is not one of different objectives, but rather the penalties for failure. That is what *perestroika* is about, providing some form of stick as well as carrot. The formula for incentive contracts between Ministries and parastatals comes from eastern Europe, but if the contract cannot be enforced, what can you do about it?

*G de Kalbermatten*: In the years to come, there will probably be even greater demands on LDC governments to meet all kinds of aid requirements. The availability of local policy-makers to devote attention to AT cannot be taken for granted. Introducing technologies to central decision makers or planning authorities might not be feasible. It might be better to introduce appropriate technology at the project level in a kind of organized disorder. Let the various technologies compete on the tests of technical and commercial viability. The initial investment would provide a laboratory to see whether proposed activities are compatible with local absorptive capacity. After a few years of successful activities, a proposal for appropriate technology will then have more influence.

*J James*: Learning by mistakes is very important, but one of the difficulties with this is getting donors to allow for this in their procedures.

*E Hyman*: Mr FitzGerald's paper makes the useful contribution that the real world is much more complex than simple theories and models indicate. However, there are certain assumptions embedded in his analysis that also may not generally be the case. Three examples follow.

First, he stated that structural adjustment programmes that reduce real wages of government employees would cut the demand for small-scale goods and services. On the contrary, where government employees are predominantly located in urban areas and have had relatively high incomes compared to the rural population, a cut in their wages may shift consumption toward more basic goods. These goods are usually produced by the agricultural and small-scale industrial sectors at the expense of imported and import-substituted goods.

Second, he stated that a reduction in government infrastructure expenditures would have a negative effect on small-scale rural industries that could not obtain electricity or water supplies. Yet, small-scale firms using AT and available energy sources may not need this type of infrastructure as much as large-scale firms using conventional technology.

Third, the assumption was made that small firms sub-contracting for large firms would be hurt by any structural adjustments that adversely affect the large firms. This is not necessarily the case. The small firms might shift from being sub-contractors to become competitors of the large firms or new small-scale firms may enter the market. It is not necessarily the import sector that would benefit, especially where structural adjustment includes devaluations that make imports more expensive.

*V FitzGerald*: I agree with Mr Hyman's points completely. It is all a case of *where* the cutting of government expenditure takes place. The decline of the government wage rate may also affect rural areas, where government employees are a substantial part of the local middle class.

The argument is especially true if there is an increase in the real exchange rate and import liberalization. Particularly in Africa, this has generally had the effect of improving the internal terms of trade – increasing agricultural prices relative to industrial prices. It has had an income depressing effect on small-scale industries in urban areas, but a

410

large positive impact on the demand for products of rural small-scale industries. The lack of infrastructure such as electricity might not affect rural small-scale industries if people have alternative energy, but in my own experience, small-scale industrialists in rural areas often state that what they really need most is adequate power supplies.

Of course, everything depends on the case in question and that is my basic point. It is necessary to look at sectoral response to macroeconomic change. One cannot blindly assume that reducing government deficits will automatically have positive effects on small-scale industries.

*C Cooper*: Mr Fitzgerald's paper is an important one. He has set the large-scale and small-scale sector into a full macroeconomic context. I do not think this has been done so explicitly elsewhere. I want to make a few points about mechanisms you introduce that need more elucidation.

My first point is that the model includes small-scale industries in the informal sector at some times, but not others. A more systematic statement about the relationship between small-scale industries and informality and a more systematic differentiation of the characteristics of small-scale and large-scale industries are needed.

A second point concerns the interesting discussion about private sector balances. This is the critical point at which the link between macro-economic adjustments and the sectoral structure of industry is made. I am puzzled that agriculture was left out here. What happens to agricultural savings and investments must affect balances significantly. A case must be made for excluding agriculture in discussing the relationship between small- and large-scale industry.

Finally, I was surprised by the assertion that increased interest rates would have very large effects on production costs. The first mention of this in the paper is ambiguous about Taylor's incorporation of interest into the cost structure of firms. A clarification is needed about the importance of Taylor's argument.

*V FitzGerald*: Conceptually, two different kinds of small-scale enterprise exist – small capitalist firms and the artisanal or household sector. The key issue for many observers is whether they use wage labour or predominantly household labour. The main difference I wanted to emphasize is that large-scale industry is basically a price-maker in the market or in negotiations with the government, while small-scale industries are price takers. There-fore, changes in interest rates can be passed on in prices by large firms more easily than by small firms.

On financial liberalization, the paper suggests that taking resources away from the 'curb market' was McKinnon's argument, and thus lies at the foundations of the World Bank approach. This is not my argument; it is just the orthodox view. My argument is that a segmented credit market will continue to exist whatever the monetary or financial policy, precisely because there are so many different forms of enterprise organization. Empirical sociological research on rural credit clearly reveals how loans are used to control labour and marketing. On the other hand, theoretical neoclassical work (eg, Stiglitz) shows how credit rationing is Pareto-optimal in a world of uncertainty and incomplete information. In our 'Money, Finance and Development' project at the Institute of Social Studies, we are setting up social accounting matrices that distinguish production sectors in one direction and enterprises, corporations, small-scale industries, and households in the other direction. We will also look at the effect of international financial flows on these different sectors.

*E Hyman*: Mr FitzGerald noted that higher interest rates would pose a major burden on firms, amounting to costs as high as 60–70 per cent of total production costs. This is unlikely, as few people are advocating increasing interest rates as high as those in the informal sector, ie, 100–200 per cent per annum. Reform recommendations are usually to raise interest rates to a level at least equal to the inflation rate or a small positive real interest rate. Such rates are not likely to be burdensome given the reported profitability of small firms. Usually, small-scale firms are more concerned about access to credit than the interest rate. If a revolving credit fund is maintained by realistic interest rates, more firms can borrow money.

The speaker argued that small firms are more likely to be adversely affected by higher interest rates than larger firms as large firms can raise their prices more easily than small ones. Yet, most small firms do not rely on formal sector credit at all. If small firms can get credit and are competitive with large firms who manufacture similar products, the small firms would also benefit from product-price raises imposed on the market by the large firms.

Finally, the impression is given that it is unclear what policy-makers should do. Nevertheless, 'getting prices right' and reducing distortions in economies would make it more likely that the policy reforms would have the expected impacts on 'levelling the playing field' for large and small firms, rather than the possible counter-intuitive impacts.

*V FitzGerald*: I agree that it is essential to maintain a positive, real interest rate, but it would not solve the lack of credit for small-scale industries if interest rates are allowed to reach market levels, let alone raise national savings.

*J James*: I am wondering whether what you are saying is a wider critique of macro-politics. Is this critique specifically about the straw man of the IMF and the World Bank models, or is it a general attack on macroeconomics which fails to be based on a realistic microeconomics?

*V FitzGerald*: A number of economists in Europe, the USA, and the Third World are trying to construct a new macroeconomics on sound micro-economic foundations. After ten or so years of research, we have a good microeconomic picture of the public sector, a wealth of peasant studies, and a legacy of multinational enterprise studies. However, we have very little information on large private firms.

The work we do at the Institute of Social Studies is very closely related to the various other attempts at producing these sectoral models, but differs in two aspects. First, the Dutch tradition of statistics leads to sounder social accounting matrices for such models. Second, we pay more attention to financial flows, (ie, fiscal and monetary aspects) and much less attention to disaggregation of production.

*S K Gupta*: My question concerns the relationship between small and large firms. There is much evidence that the inefficiencies of the large enterprises are transferred to the small sector. These inefficiencies should be attacked; how do you treat this in your model?

Second, incremental capital–output ratios have increased as a result of trade liberalization and structural adjustment policies. Particularly in West Africa, the incremental capital–output ratio increased seven to eight times during the last two decades because of a shortage of financing for working capital. The large investment in physical capacity resulted in excess capacity in large-scale industry and forced some enterprises out of business. This interaction between the small and large enterprises needs attention.

*V FitzGerald*: An easy answer to Mr Gupta's first point is that anything can be added to the model. I do not know much about transmitted inefficiency whether through costs or credit. It would appear that in India and probably elsewhere, medium firms are more efficient than either large or small firms. I also suspect that a successful small firm becomes a medium-sized firm or else it disappears.

As for your second point aid flows mostly to the non-traded sector, which tends to raise the incremental capital–output ratio. Productive sectors have problems getting foreign exchange, and even investment banks gear loans to large projects in the non-traded sector. Measurement of the incremental capital–output ratio is a problem because it depends on GDP growth, which is strongly affected by world prices and not just by the inefficient use of capital. The Institute of Social Studies has recently done some work on Central America for the EEC, which concluded that new large investments are not needed. Central America needs funds for its working capital to enable it to export products to repay loans. Most agrarian economies and small-scale enterprises, in particular, need working capital more than fixed capital.

On an empirical level, I do not fully accept the micro-arguments made by the ATI group. All I am saying is that we must look at macro-policy with a micro perspective.

413

*J James*: Morawetz observed in 1974 that income redistribution may be necessary before more appropriate products could be sold. In the early 1980s, I looked at the aggregate data, which included categories like transport and textiles and the different factor intensities within these categories. We found that low-income people do consume labour-intensive goods. Then, I used household spending data to simulate an income redistribution in favour of the poor. The disaggregated approach predicted a higher level of employment than the aggregated approach did, but this is not a universal mechanism because the rich often buy labour-intensive luxury goods such as handmade carpets and Meerschaum pipes.

I agree also that there is no deterministic relationship between labour intensity and consumption patterns. Historically, however, higher product quality has been associated with greater automation. Sometimes, greater automation produces better quality, but not always. The only micro-evidence I know of is the ILO series of studies on products. Although not specifically addressed to this question, the ILO studies showed that some of the relationships worked in the predicted directions, while others did not. I am currently collaborating with an expert on social accounting matrices in Indonesia on the use of disaggregated data in a macro-framework.

*C Cooper*: Today's technology is the product of technological history. The literature argues that the poor use traditional goods, but this does not always seem to be the case. Therefore, the fact that traditional goods are more labour-intensive is not the point because the poor do not necessarily consume those goods. Where incomes are high, the foreign and domestic rich often buy labour-intensive products. The things that poor people consume are sometimes inappropriate by most definitions, but we do not have effective policies for dealing with the inappropriateness of products.

*G de Kalbermatten*: My question is about the relationship between income distribution and new technologies. Do we not need more research on the impact of new technologies (such as electronics and biotechnology) on income distribution? I wonder about the theory that new technologies generate new labour forces, replacing the work force. The possibility of obtaining the new technologies seems to be very limited for a number of countries. On the other hand, new technology does eliminate part of the traditional labour market. One computer might put 12 bank employees in Nepal out of jobs. Is there some notion of how this issue can be resolved in the overall context of North–South dependency?

*C Cooper*: I have no clear solution for this problem. It seems that countries will face conflicting pressures. To be competitive they will need to use the new technologies to maintain their export positions. On the other hand, they will not improve the amount of employment generated per unit investment. There is evidence from the Newly Industrializing Countries

(NICs), that the rapid adoption of micro-electronic systems can produce extraordinary export growth.

A long time ago I was told that Japan was very special and its increase in exports could not be reproduced in other countries. Today, several other economies are doing as well. I doubt that we could apply the same argument we made about Japan to South Korea today.

# IV

## *Policy Experience and Policy Problems*

# Reflections on Development Aid Policies

## BAHMAN MANSURI

Discussions of rural linkages and their impacts on small-scale enterprise development and rural industrialization constituted a major part of the deliberations of this conference. There is now a consensus among us that a sustained and more egalitarian pattern of agricultural growth will facilitate the development of non-farm enterprises in rural areas.

My presentation begins with a review of the agricultural sector in sub-Saharan Africa. It then examines the impact of the present transformation of policy and the development of the private sector as the primary source of growth in the economies of the region. I will then discuss farm and non-farm linkages with particular reference to small-scale rural enterprises. Finally, I will share with you my perceptions regarding actions needed to achieve balanced rural growth through development of small-scale enterprises in African countries.

The macroeconomic policies generally pursued in African countries have adversely affected agricultural growth. These adverse effects have been borne most heavily by the majority of smallholders. Over the last 30 years, agricultural production in Africa rose by only 2 per cent annually. Exports have declined and food imports are now increasing at about 7 per cent per year. This weak agricultural growth is the basis of the economic crisis in Africa. Without a doubt, many external factors are also responsible for this crisis. My remarks here will be confined to the internal factors. Structural adjustment programmes adopted by governments in response to the present economic crisis emphasize shifting incentives toward the more productive sector of the economy, which is usually agriculture. Within the agricultural sector in Africa, the supply response is expected to come from smallholders who constitute about 70 to 90 per cent of the population. The primary supply side objectives of structural adjustment will not be achieved if the agricultural sector does not grow.

The majority of the poor in Africa live in rural areas. Any structural adjustment efforts should, therefore, help the smallholders increase their productivity. Structural adjustment programmes do not necessarily

---

BAHMAN MANSURI is Director, Africa Division, International Fund for Agricultural Development (IFAD).

guarantee income parity for small-scale producers. With the help of the Overseas Development Institute in England IFAD undertook five country studies to guide us in improving lending programmes. Included in the studies were Kenya, Malawi, Niger, Madagascar and Ghana. The studies examined the impacts of structural adjustment on the rural poor and the importance of nonfarm activities in rural areas in African countries.

The studies found that the impact of the reforms depends substantially on the access of smallholders to complementary resources and services that enable them to take advantage of improved macroeconomic conditions. The main conclusion is that recovery programmes have made some progress in reallocating resources toward agriculture in several of the countries under review. In these cases, the programmes have improved the prospects for production and income growth, but many of the other conditions necessary to achieve and sustain this growth are not yet in place. As a result, the potential of the reforms to contribute to economic growth and increased equity is diminished because many smallholders are poorly placed to participate in the economic recovery.

Cutbacks in public expenditures might be expected to reduce the number of agricultural services available to small farmers, with adverse effects on their ability to respond to new incentives. The studies found that in many instances these services were of little value to most small-scale farmers before the expenditure cuts and so the adverse effects were minimal. Yet, with such limited support, farmers cannot increase aggregate production and potential benefits from greater profitability are partially lost. The challenge is, therefore, to support rural services that can reach smallholders and the rural poor. These services should be able to be implemented with the financial, human and organizational resources available to the public and private sectors.

In promoting the development of capital markets, governments and donors have generally emphasized the provision of formal credit through parastatal banks while neglecting the wider informal market and the mobilization of local savings. Despite this emphasis, only a small minority of rural households in the countries studied had made use of formal credit.

The role of product markets in public sector agencies has decreased markedly in the five countries. The impact of these marketing reforms is negligible where the role of the agencies was previously limited. Where they were more active, the effects of the reforms depend greatly on whether marketing alternatives exist. Therefore, the ability of the private sector or co-operatives to provide services is an important element in successful adjustment. Unfortunately, the private sector frequently lacks the capacity to fulfill these functions effectively and the lack of competition reduces the benefits to rural producers and consumers.

In all five countries, rural low-income groups rely significantly on the rural and urban (formal and informal) labour markets for supplementary off-farm earnings. Their economic welfare depends largely on the performance of the economy and, in particular, measures to promote growth of labour-intensive industry. The impacts of recovery programmes have been uneven, depending on the extent of their implementation, other features of the economy and especially household characteristics. The overall evidence suggests that there has been a modest positive impact. Impacts have been most positive when:

1. Substantial groups of smallholders are producing commodities whose prices have improved because of the reforms;
2. Labour markets are well-integrated so that growth can generate income-earning opportunities more widely;
3. Underused factors of production, particularly land, are available; and
4. Physical infrastructure, and formal or informal agricultural support services are widely available through the private or public sectors.

These findings have important policy implications. First, strong support should be given to economic recovery programmes designed to improve the incentives and resources for smallholders over the long-term. In designing such programmes, explicit attention needs to be given to creating a wide base of participation among the rural population for both equity and growth. Priority should also be given to policies that can stimulate the demand for labour, especially unskilled labour. Many low-income groups have few saleable assets other than family labour; this is especially true for the increasing number of landless people in the more densely populated countries. Adjustment measures that increase the returns to land and capital will not benefit such people directly.

Policies for employment generation should include the creation of a framework to encourage linkages between agriculture and other sectors and stimulate the use of agricultural inputs produced in the domestic economy. They should also promote local processing of agricultural produce, labour-intensive public works, and education and training geared to income generation. New relationships between public and private sector operations in production, processing or distribution are generally needed. Promotion of the private sector should be encouraged; at the same time its currently weak capacity should be strengthened. However, a whole range of functions can only be effectively carried out by the public sector; for example, construction of rural infrastructure, assuring national food security, and provision of health and education services.

An improved transport system has been highlighted in the study as a necessary condition for economic growth, especially in some isolated areas. In addition, interventions should be designed to support the informal sectors that supply services used by small farmers and provide income-earning opportunities. Rural financial markets generally need to be developed, not just formal credit. Many financial intermediaries (including banks, the informal sector, credit unions and credit groups) need to be used more fully. The development of effective mechanisms to do this requires a much better understanding of the linkages between different aspects of the capital markets. Linkages between agricultural producers and other sectors and between rural consumers should be exploited.

In considering the type of actions required to facilitate the development of nonfarm activities, we should first review the composition and characteristics of non-farm enterprises in rural Africa. Available data indicate that commerce and services are the predominant types of enterprises. Less than 25 per cent of the manufacturing labour force is located in the rural areas. The service and commerce sector is, therefore, the key growth sector for rural structural transformation in African economies. A common mistake in the past has been exclusion of these activities in any promotional activities. Second, the overwhelming majority of nonfarm enterprises are very small, employing less than ten workers and the average is only two workers. Third, the average capital requirements of rural nonfarm enterprises are rather modest, ranging from a few hundred to a maximum of five thousand dollars.

Women play an important role in agriculture in the rural economy in Africa. Many nonfarm activities dominated by women will increasingly be in demand as agriculture grows. For example, processing facilities and tailoring are female-dominated activities. A wide range of services, especially those relating to the financial market, are performed by self-help organizations and farmer associations.

In these countries, forward linkages from agriculture to processors and distributors tend to be far larger than backward linkages to rural input suppliers due to the low level of input use in African agriculture. With greater development of agriculture and more intensive methods of cultivation, such backward linkages will be strengthened, but probably not to the same extent as in Asia. Finally, the development of the nonfarm sector is hindered by some of the same policy factors that affect the agricultural sector. Most macroeconomic policies that favour smallholder farming are generally beneficial to small-scale rural enterprise.

The study made some recommendations for policy changes. First, structural adjustment packages and sectoral programmes should be carefully scrutinized to ensure their conduciveness to the participation of small-scale producers. This objective could be achieved through consultative groups, donor meetings, joint consultations in policy co-ordination, and most importantly by government promotion policy analyses. In light of the significant role women play in the rural economy, gender issues should receive more attention in policy analyses.

In the institutional arena, a number of measures should be taken. Since various types of entrepreneurs have different skills and business

422

requirements, their training and technical assistance requirements vary. Many businesses face common needs for infrastructure and a more flexible and responsive financial system. For example, innovative approaches could promote co-operation between informal and formal credit givers.

Africa has a large number of informal financial intermediaries. NGOs are well suited to provide support such as technical assistance, and advice and intermediation between the formal banking institutions and the target groups. NGO activities are not co-ordinated within many countries and adhere to different standards and criteria. Many NGOs treat income redistribution as their main objective and do not recognize the realities and economic requirements of the financial markets. To solve this problem, aid donors should try to set up an effective dialogue with NGOs or provide formal training in planning and project formulation if needed.

Government decentralization policies are important tools to promote greater participation by the people. In reality, this may prove to be more difficult than expected. Our experience in Kenya shows that it was difficult to implement policies at the district government level because of lack of clarity in objectives and inadequate guidelines for implementation. Training programmes for government officials could help change their attitudes toward small entrepreneurs and farmer organizations.

Research and development to assist small-scale industry is non-existent in many countries and different approaches could be tested on a pilot basis. University research in LDCs is usually hindered by lack of funding. It would be more cost-effective if countries shared the results of their research with others. The import regime of the government should be examined to ensure that small-scale producers, both on and off farms, receive the inputs, spare parts, and implements that they need for their work.

There is a need for increasing co-ordination between aid donors. A comprehensive, balanced approach toward rural development that avoids the pitfalls of integrated rural development is important. This objective could be pursued by introducing pilot private sector programmes. Closely co-ordinated multilateral action is important. The International Finance Corporation provides credit in LDCs for enterprises that have capital requirements above US$1 m. The African Enterprise Project (AEP), jointly administered by the African Development Bank and the International Finance Corporation provides support for enterprises with a capitalization between $100,000 and $250,000. However, small- and micro-enterprises with their needs ranging from a few hundred dollars to a few thousand dollars are not served. This leaves a gap to be filled. Finally, I would like to highlight the importance of a consistent and sustained effort. This could be attained through a multilateral mechanism, not subject to bilateral politics.

# The UNCDF Programme

## GREGOIRE DE KALBERMATTEN

The United Nations Capital Development Fund was established in 1966 by the United Nations General assembly as an autonomous organization within the UN system. With donor countries concentrating on other multilateral financing agencies, the UNCDF got a slow start and in 1967 the General Assembly decided to make the UNDP responsible for managing the Fund. After the first oil crisis in 1973/74, the UNCDF focused on bringing direct benefits to lower income groups in the least developed countries more rapidly. In the 1980s the Fund specialized in delivering grants for small-scale capital assistance projects for economic infrastructure, agricultural activities, micro- and small-scale enterprises and basic needs infrastructure. During this period, voluntary contributions to the Fund increased steadily to a level of about US$40 m a year for 1989. The main sponsors of the Fund traditionally have been the Nordic countries and The Netherlands. Whenever feasible, the Fund seeks to build into the project design ways to empower people to become the main agents of their own socioeconomic development. Approaches for this include participatory mechanisms for managing the inputs delivered by the Fund, credit facilities, or appropriate technologies.

People-focused projects are not easy to formulate or implement. Small-scale investment projects can be useful in policy experimentation. A combination of specialized NGO and small-scale multilateral investors represents the kind of appropriate delivery system that developing countries will need in the 1990s. This collaboration will allow implementation of projects well-suited to the absorption capacities of the recipient countries. Funds involved in projects of this type have a better chance of reaching target groups than large projects.

The Fund's projects range between $200,000 and $5,000,000. UNCDF welcomes the opportunity to work in partnership with competent NGOs and has launched joint ventures with ATI for alpaca wool production in Bolivia and venture capital promotion in Nepal.

In conclusion, there has been much talk about inclusion of a human face

---

GREGOIRE DE KALBERMATTEN is Chief of the Policy, Planning and Evaluation Unit, UN Capital Development Fund.

in an improved structural adjustment policy package. We should assess how to achieve the social goals and identify key elements of policies and strategies. We have to ensure that the target groups we want to serve will not be bypassed again.

# The Pros and Cons of Policy Changes

## TON DE WILDE

Rapid population growth in developing countries is causing an employment crisis, which is expected to intensify in the 1990s. Although precise figures are difficult to obtain, it is predicted that between now and the year 2000 an additional 1.2 bn new jobs will be needed just to match the labour force growth.

In the 1970s, economists advised governments that the most efficient way to create employment and increase economic growth was to establish large-scale industries. Recent experience, in both developed and developing countries, shows that this is no longer true. For example, in the USA in 1987, 75 per cent of new employment was generated in the small-scale sector, a significant shift from the previous decade. Yet, ILO studies indicate that small-scale enterprises in themselves do not create more employment than large-scale enterprises. It is the technology utilized by the enterprise that determines the number of jobs created.

Economic theories hold that large-scale enterprises may be more efficient because of economies of scale, but myth has become mixed with fact there also. Large enterprises are not automatically more cost-effective than small ones, and small may be beautiful and powerful, but it is not always more profitable.

Since 1982, ATI's demonstration and replication projects have created over 1,600 small and micro-enterprises. These projects and the macro-policy studies ATI has supported, show that appropriate technology can be found in both large and small-scale enterprises. Both are necessary for economic growth. Depending on the particular market niche, a large-scale, capital-intensive or a small-scale, labour-intensive technology may be more appropriate.

The science of development might learn from the example of the physical sciences. Before Einstein, the Cartesian/Newtonian model was extremely useful in developing laws and models to help us understand how things work on earth and its direct atmosphere. Yet, these laws and models are not effective in space outside the planet earth. In the theory of relativity, Einstein showed that the Cartesian/Newtonian paradigm, which

---

TON DE WILDE is president of Appropriate Technology International. Prior to joining ATI in 1982, Dr. de Wilde was executive secretary of the Sarvodaya Shramadana Movement (SSM) in Sri Lanka.

had served humanity well for 200 years might literally cause us to fall flat on our noses if applied in space or on the planet Pluto. A similar shift is needed in development because of the failures of traditional economic models.

Presentations at the three regional macro-policy conferences ATI organized in 1988 and discussions during this conference have demonstrated the enormous potential for economic growth in the informal and rural sectors of developing countries. As indicated in Stewart's paper, current structural adjustment policies might help eliminate the unfavourable business climate for small enterprises that is a result of the hidden subsidies to the large-scale sector. However, structural adjustment will not be sufficient to realize the opportunities that exist in the informal and rural sectors. Scarce science and technology resources are too often directed at a very small percentage of the producers. For example, in the early 1970s, 90 per cent of the agricultural R & D in Mexico was directed at improving the productivity of irrigated crops, while only 6 per cent of the arable land was under irrigation.

Government price controls on food have consistently favoured urban consumers over rural producers. However, if the economic costs of implementing these pricing policies had been directed to improving producers' access to large markets in cities, the same objective could have been achieved more efficiently. The consumer would have been able to buy foods at low prices, but the producers would also have benefited.

During the 1970s and 1980s, there were two prevailing schools of thought in development theory. One group of development specialists focused on economic growth and creation of wealth. The second group emphasized alleviating poverty by sharing resources that were already available. The first group looked at large issues first, while the second group looked at last things first.

To use another analogy from the hard sciences, development strategies for the 1990s should be characterized by fusion, that is, a blending of economic growth and poverty alleviation. Development programmes that will bring together macro-, meso- and institutional policies to support growth with equity are needed. The main task for government is to create an enabling environment for the use of appropriate technology and to increase productivity in both large and small-scale enterprises through infrastructure development at the national, regional, and village levels.

One of the lessons learned from the 1970s was that without sustainable economic programmes subsidized basic human needs programmes cannot be implemented. I hope that five years from now I will not have to say that one of the lessons learned from the 1980s is that we cannot afford structural adjustment programmes with a human face.

A key issue is how can we stimulate the fusion needed to blend the informal sector with the formal sector and to integrate policy analysis with policy-making? I would like to make some suggestions to consider in designing country programmes to implement some of the policy recommendations generated from the macro-policy studies presented at this, and earlier, regional conferences.

A competitive environment makes it more difficult for firms exhibiting non-maximizing behaviours to be successful or simply to survive. In most countries, parastatals are permitted to operate at a loss or are indirectly subsidized. For example, parastatals do not include depreciation expenses as part of the production costs of a unit of output (this is also true for some donor-supported NGOs). Another factor that affects the choice of technology is the assumed advantages of economies of scale. In many cases, these economies of scale are offset by higher transportation costs.

A country programme should begin with a study of the resource base that addresses such questions as:

1. What domestic raw materials or agricultural produce are now being processed in the country?
2. Do small-scale technologies that produce the same quality of product as the large-scale exist? Can these technologies be used in rural areas where the raw materials or agricultural products are being produced?
3. Is the small-scale technology more profitable than the large-scale urban-based alternative or the traditional method currently used in the village? Technologies should be compared using the same standards for depreciation expenses; demonstrated underutilization of capacity due to equipment breakdowns, maintenance difficulties, or lack of parts; and the cost of transporting and marketing raw materials or other inputs.

ATI's work has shown that small-scale industries are often more competitive than large-scale industries, at least in the following areas: extraction of vegetable oils such as palm oil, sunflower seed oil, and shea nut butter, and under certain conditions, coconut oil; sugar processing; rice milling; sorghum and millet dehulling and milling; maize milling; wool spinning; shrimp farming; some forms of fertilizer production (eg, rhizobium inoculant for soybeans); and production of lime for construction.

A country programme should review the credit and foreign exchange needs of small-scale enterprises. Important factors to investigate include the following:

1. Administrative procedures that are often too complex and based on unrealistic lending criteria such as collateral requirements that preclude the rural poor from taking advantage of the financing;
2. Risk sharing as a means of disseminating technologies. Simple agricultural equipment such as multibars, seeders or water pumps could be introduced through lease/purchase arrangements. Maintenance of the equipment could be handled by the bank or NGO that provides the

lease or, alternatively, by providing a rebate to farmers who maintain their own equipment to a certain standard of quality;

3. Equity financing as a way to share risks. Shareholder agreements between a company that provides equity and the other owners should stipulate that once a positive cashflow is reached, a certain percentage of the profits must be used to buy out shares held by the bank or NGO or that the equity would be recycled in more conventional loan programmes.

A country programme should review the research and development needed to support small enterprises in the informal and rural sectors. Mechanisms are needed to get the results of the R & D into the hands of rural-based small entrepreneurs. These mechanisms could include:

1. Grants awarded to local universities and/or research institutions for proposals that focus on and are implemented with the active involvement of farmers and/or small entrepreneurs. Examples of ATI's activities that have actively involved local producers include the lime kiln project in Costa Rica (the local university worked with a co-operative of lime producers), and the farm support project in Mexico (the Postgraduate College worked with local farmers);

2. Establishment of a national research council for AT and small enterprise development consisting of leading researchers and small entrepreneurs. ATI has established such a council in Thailand, which contributed to the development of two technologies: small-scale production of rhizobium inoculant and a fermentation process to produce protein enriched cassava for animal feed;

3. A review of the patent and copyright system and procedures. Lack of intellectual property protection discourages many people from developing their ideas. For example, since Kenya has no local system of patent registration, patents have to be registered in London, which is only feasible for more sophisticated technologies. The utility system used in Japan and recently introduced in the Philippines should be considered as an alternative.

Country programmes need to review the marketing networks for agricultural produce and forest and mineral products:

1. Some products are only available in rural areas despite potential urban markets. Storage and transport problems should be identified and solutions found so that farmers do not remain captives of the immediate market. For example, in some areas, artisanal cheeses may only be marketed in villages near where they are made because lack of refrigerated transport precludes them from being sold in urban markets. Small-scale dairy operations such as the Anand cooperative's efficient milk collection schemes in India have dramatically increased villagers' incomes through improved industrial capacity. Appropriate local

technologies have increased the value of milk and yoghurt in Sri Lanka, cottage type cheese in Mexico, and fermented milk beverages in Kenya. ATI projects for potato storage and processing in India and annatto processing in Peru have tapped inherent efficiency advantages by moving the processing of perishable products to sites closer to the source of the raw materials;

2. The possibility of creating market promotion boards for domestic and export products should be considered. Markets in other developing countries and exports to low-income consumers in industrialized countries offer potential for increased trade in more appropriate products.

Other factors that merit consideration include publicity, training and extension services:

1. In most countries, government and private sector decision makers have little faith in the capacity of both entrepreneurs and public officials in rural areas. For the most part, the mass communication media are located in cities. Getting publicity for success stories in rural areas is costly and time consuming. Language differences may also present communication problems. To remedy this situation, educational programmes could take the form of awards to journalists who report on successful rural enterprises and seminars for policy-makers and politicians;

2. Conventional training programmes for rural entrepreneurs have yielded few results. Studies conducted by the ILO and others have shown that few rural entrepreneurs benefit from these programmes. Mostly, trainees have found jobs in urban enterprises or local banks and formal sector commercial establishments. On-the-job training and product-specific training such as ATI's computer video training to improve villagers' production of spices in Sri Lanka can be successful;

3. Few effective extension services exist for rural industries anywhere in the Third World. ATI has helped to fill this gap on a small scale. With a total investment of approximately $11,600,000 over a recent three-year period, ATI has provided support for the establishment of more than 63 small and 1200 micro-enterprises, the creation of 5,000 sustainable jobs, and has indirectly increased the incomes of more than 150,000 people.

# Dilemmas for Research

## HENK THOMAS

Two years ago, the closing sessions of a policy research workshop on small-scale industrialization with an urban employment perspective were held. The aim of the workshop was to examine 10 country case studies. Each of the studies included a policy paper prepared by an expert from the government and a critical analysis by an independent researcher on the relevance and impact of the policies implemented. This approach illustrated that small enterprises could not be examined in isolation and could not be promoted through single interventions such as management training, industrial estate programmes, or subsidized credit schemes.

While an emphasis on the policy environment for small- and micro-enterprises was still novel and controversial at that time, this topic has since become a dominant theme in the study of small enterprises, as we have seen during this conference. Here, we have highlighted the importance of rural linkages and regional analysis as one of the central problem areas for analysis and policy recommendations.

Research on development policy issues affecting small-scale enterprises faces a considerable number of challenges. White noted that there are two basic approaches to this research, each characterized by a certain type of 'rhetoric'.[2] The first approach is characterized by 'a positive, action-oriented' jargon with 'little concrete meaning'. This approach emphasizes local resources, employment creation, the efficiency of small enterprises, and improvements in the balance of payments. The second approach is characterized by a high degree of frustration and pessimism about the dismal poverty in which small enterprises generally are found.

The small enterprise field is an area that must be examined using a holistic, multidisciplinary approach. According to Bienefeld research on small-scale industrialization is too often characterized by 'narrow focus' and 'inadequate analytical framework'.[3] As a result, this research has not made much of a contribution in identifying 'the circumstances under which the informal sector can be a major source of accumulation and growth'. Research on the behaviour of small industrial enterprises should address the complexity of this sector.

---

HENK THOMAS is Professor of Labour Studies at the Institute of Social Studies, The Hague. His research and policy advisory work has focused on small-scale industrialization, particularly in Pakistan.

431

In other words, any particular set of internal characteristics can ensure the sector's success only when it is combined with certain external conditions and these must also be specified if research is to identify the circumstances and policies that could promote the successful development of this sector.[3]

I would like to discuss a few issues that are generally not prominent in the literature on small-scale enterprise development. These include the labour perspective, the behaviour and characteristics of the firm, and the wider socio-political setting of economic systems. Lastly, I will address the research dilemmas faced by development agencies.

## The labour perspective

The current strong interest in policies to promote small labour-intensive production results from the weak employment creation record of past industrialization strategies. In the late 1960s Griffin warned of the inefficiency of Pakistan's industrial strategy and its unfavourable effects on employment.[4] More recently, Tokman reviewed the lessons from the Latin American experience with industrialization strategies and found that economic information on employment impacts is extremely weak.[5] Most of the data treat labour as if it were a homogenous production factor and information on earnings is rarely available in surveys on small enterprises.

Most of the research has ignored the special labour market situation of workers in small and micro-enterprises, whether unpaid family labour, apprentices, or labourers. It is usually assumed that a job created in a small enterprise is equivalent to a job created in a large-scale, modern industrial enterprise, although that is not generally the case. In reality, labour markets are heterogenous and segmented.

Because of the tremendous adjustments that have taken place in labour markets under conditions of rapid development, I assume that disequilibrium is the correct starting point for any analysis of these markets. Kanappan described how certain segments of small enterprise labour belong in the category of 'unprotected' workers.[6] Apparently efficient but inequitable social hierarchies and divisions in the small-scale sector foster employment clusters of widely varying productivity. Recent labour research, such as Harrod's work on social relations of production and Standing's examination of different categories of 'vulnerable workers', show how work relationships in small-scale enterprises fall largely into a special category of labour market relationships. Work relationships, motivations, productivities, and the policy environment differ across categories of enterprises (eg, self-employment, small-scale modern and small-scale informal).[7,8] Small enterprises generally are highly dependent and vulnerable. Most of the state involvement in the sector is harassment rather than support. The workers receive no protection through labour legislation and are not organized through trade unions. As Standing stated, 'vulnerable groups emerge because a structure needs them to emerge', and 'to believe that small-scale businesses can be turned into the engine of growth, equality and development is to ignore history. It has not happened'. In my opinion this is unlikely to happen given the fundamental disturbances in urban labour markets related to long-run supply factors, especially demographic pressures.

Small enterprises contain a high percentage of socially disadvantaged workers and often use child labour. Apprentices may be forced to stay on far beyond the period of time during which any new learning would take place. Unpaid family workers are called on at irregular times to sustain production. In certain sectors, women compose the majority of workers. Working conditions are often unfavourable in small enterprises – earnings are low, workers do not have the right to organize, working hours are long, hygienic conditions are poor, and the work environments may be hazardous.

This does not necessarily mean that policies should discourage small-scale enterprises. Rather, the development policy agencies and researchers must include fundamental labour and distributional issues in their analysis of any policies oriented toward blending AT and small-scale enterprises.

AT may be one of the few policy instruments that can achieve some improved labour conditions through upgraded production methods. Without consideration of the impacts of technology in a small-scale industrialization strategy, nineteenth century labour and working conditions may persist in small enterprises in the twenty-first century.

## Behaviour and characteristics of small industrial firms

There has been relatively little theoretical and empirical research on the behaviour of small industrial enterprises compared to what has been done on small farms and large-scale or public enterprises. FitzGerald's paper, presented at this conference, covered the relationships between macro-policies and small-scale enterprises and recognized that the objective function of small enterprises may differ from that of medium and large-sized ones.[9] The paper clearly illustrates the urgent need to blend neo-classical economic analysis with institutional economics. It also proves that much work needs to be undertaken before the role of small enterprises within the broader context of the organization of economic sectors is well understood.

Theoretical and applied research in this area is important for two reasons. First, policy makers need to understand the objectives and constraints of entrepreneurs. Development professionals involved in designing industrialization strategies sometimes wonder why small-scale industry does not make major strides despite favourable demand and the absence of supply side barriers. In certain cases, stagnation of the small-scale industrial sector may be related to widespread smuggling, which makes foreign commodities available at lower prices than domestic goods. It can also make investments in speculation and trade more lucrative than in industrial production.

Sometimes, technological innovations are found to be unacceptable to entrepreneurs, even when the technology could improve the quality of the product and potentially benefit both producers and consumers. One reason for this may be that customers are not inclined to pay for higher quality. Thus, the entrepreneur may only be willing to make small investments that can be profitably recovered over the short term. This entrepreneurial behaviour may only allow marginal technological innovations. Nevertheless, when introduced in a well-planned manner over a long span of time, marginal improvements may add up to a major increase in productivity. Since some innovations may push a producer into a higher market segment, temporary marketing support may be needed for a profitable adoption of the innovation.

Second, there are major variances within informal industry. For example, in a major industrial programme in the Northwest Province of Pakistan, three categories of enterprises were distinguished: 'urban survivors', of limited profitability; 'expanders', which have limited potential to grow; and 'graduators', which have the potential to grow into larger or more modern firms.[10] There may also be differences in behaviour among 'starters' of new enterprises, depending on whether they are unemployed graduates, returning migrants, or workers from existing medium and large enterprises. Thus, policy interventions should differentiate among such categories. Weijland pursued this subject in Indonesia.[11] At present, not enough is known about the possible differential impacts of policies on different kinds of small enterprises in various country settings. More insight is needed on the dynamic behaviour of small enterprises. For example, how does technological change affect enterprises? Who innovates and who does not?

Another issue concerns macro-policies. This conference has raised questions about earlier optimistic expectations about the impact of macro-policies on small enterprises. Theoretical and empirical evidence indicates that mechanisms influencing small-enterprise development are much more complex than was originally envisaged.[9,12] More information at the micro-level is clearly needed before present controversies may be solved. Research, such as that undertaken by Dawson on Ghanian enterprises, and by the ILO on the impact of trade liberalization on small enterprises at the micro- and branch-specific level, is still quite rare.[13] The role of sub-contracting needs to be spelled out much more precisely. With reference to India, Nagaraj concluded that little detailed information was available on how sub-contracting is organized and the logic of its growth.[14]

Major uncertainties and gaps in knowledge make it difficult for policy-makers to implement optimal macro-policy measures to promote small-scale industry. For example, the evidence on the relative efficiency of small-scale industry has thus far been rather light. The Indian and Colombian country cases are among the few studies to provide adequate data on this issue. The role of factor markets and linkages also needs attention.

## The role of institutions: public involvement, private sector, and co-operative self-management

The pivotal role of institutions is now widely recognized. Studies of small enterprise development and appropriate technology must take into consideration markets, and the planning and decision-making mechanisms. For example, Dr Doryan-Garron argued that institutions supporting small enterprises may be important instruments in fostering economic democracy.[15] This leads to the important issue of convergence between command and market-type economies or a 'third system'. It is interesting that Hungary and Yugoslavia are now attempting to provide a strong niche for small enterprises within their economic systems.[16]

Surveys indicate that many nongovernmental organizations have a preference for co-operative implementation of income-generating activities especially those at a 'survival' level of operation. This preference for co-operatives over individualized market competition is somewhat ideological. The history of co-operatives is characterized by contradictions and 'compulsory' introduction of co-operatives may not be a good way to organize small enterprises. On the other hand, research indicates that when small enterprises organize it may contribute considerably to their chances for economic survival and growth as well as their political leverage.

At a macro-level, this dilemma can be seen in present-day Yugoslavia which operates under a system of self-management. The Government realized the importance of private small enterprises operating in open markets in preventing further deterioration or stagnation of the economy. It recognized that there might be constraints to co-operatives as a form of organization at a small-scale level of production. Nevertheless, the Mondragon co-operative system in Spain provides an example of an attempt to achieve a precise balance between large, medium and small enterprises through a co-operative system composed of 20,000 members in production and more than 100,000 in other co-operative organizations. Over the past decade, this system has performed strongly during both economic expansion and recession, including structural adjustment periods.[17]

At present, particularly given the widely held preference for private entrepreneurship, the role of the state in direct interventions to support small enterprises is still in question. For countries with many parastatals, breaking up of large public enterprises into smaller units may become an important issue. In this respect, Eastern Europe, Hungary and Yugoslavia in particular, are providing important evidence. Much heralded reforms to allow the development of small enterprises have taken too long to produce even modest results as Laky has proven. Examination of the Eastern European experiences may indicate ways to strengthen the small enterprise domain in mixed capitalist economies. It is important to find out whether earnings levels and working conditions in small enterprises can be improved through interventionist policies. In South Korea, the earnings levels of small enterprises are linked with those of large ones. ILO is searching for ways to improve working conditions that can favour both workers and entrepreneurs and the public sector role may require better definition.[18]

## The organization of research

New primary data on a relatively large scale is needed on the characteristics of small enterprises, the status of their workers, and policy options. Buzzard and Edgcomb provide methods for data collection.[19] Nevertheless, funding must be budgeted to enable collection and analysis of data. A database for project impact analysis could be broadly divided into four compartments: social, technological, micro-level cost- and benefit indicators and economic. This database can be used by various groups including project and programme management and academicians.

Dr Liedholm's presentation of the findings of ten years in a set of countries, based on some 20,000 interviews, provided important lessons for the implementation of future research programmes on small enterprises and AT.[20] One of the key findings, which has far-reaching policy implications, concerns the main cause of price distortions in factor markets. Convincing evidence was accumulated to conclude that the main cause of irrational allocation of capital and labour in LDCs was distorted capital market prices rather than high minimum wage laws. The research format of this study is characterized in particular by its long-term nature, the in-depth character of research designs, and the wide coverage of its activities.

Independent research can contribute to the performance of projects and programmes while safeguarding academic independence and allowing the collection of the required primary data without jeopardizing the independence of those executing projects. In carrying out this research, the different roles of programme implementing agents and academic institutions must be recognized. If local research capabilities do not exist, then institution building in this area must be given a high priority.

The Netherlands government has recently completed the preparatory work to implement such a research policy design. The Advisory Council for Scientific Research in Developing Countries published a study on priorities and conditions for research on LDC industry. The National Advisory Council (NAR) is about to publish its advice to the Government of The Netherlands on its involvement with the 'informal sector' in foreign assistance activities.[21] A Policy Workshop funded by the Department of Development Co-operation was held at the ISS in 1987. More recently, in the Hague this department organized a Workshop on Small-Scale Enterprise Development. All these efforts will culminate in a major policy note on the different aspects of the 'Quality of Development Co-operation' to be sent to Parliament by the Minister for Development Co-operation. A Policy Note on Small-Scale Developmental Involvement will follow early in 1990.

# Synthesis

## FRANCES STEWART

I would like to make a few comments on the conference as a whole. First, I will restate the generally accepted views. There was remarkably little debate about the definition of appropriate technology and whether it is efficient. It was also generally accepted that rural linkages are an important part of the development strategy. We agree that macro- and meso-policies are very relevant to the success of small- and micro-enterprises. There was general agreement that the policies in place in many developing countries have had distorting effects. There was also agreement that the current macroeconomic package of the World Bank and IMF has elements that support AT, but not sufficiently.

Second, some important, but controversial issues were raised that need to be studied further. For example, the significance of demand was emphasized in the rural linkages generated by agricultural growth and in relation to trade policies. The importance of demand was underlined by evidence from Mr Liedholm that most small firms have excess capacity and could expand with greater demand. There was some controversy about the best mechanism for increasing demand. One issue was the relationship between income distribution and demand for small-scale industrial products. Questions were raised about whether a more egalitarian agricultural sector would lead to more linkages. Mr Cooper disputed whether income redistribution would increase the demand for small-scale output at the macro-level. I and others disagreed with his view that income redistribution would not increase the demand. More research on this question would be valuable.

Another controversy relating to demand was the relationship between the formal and informal sector under various policy settings. Do measures that benefit the formal sector improve the position of the informal sector and vice versa? The answer to this question depends on whether the relationships between the sectors are complementary or competitive. In fact, both relationships hold. There are complementary relationships in subcontracting and in the expenditures of formal sector employees on products from the informal sector. In the competition for capital the two sectors may have a competitive relationship. More empirical work needs to be done to sort out the net effect in particular locations.

A second area of major interest was the institutional aspect. For example, what is the best way to provide credit for small-scale technologies or to develop and transfer technology for the small-scale sector? What is the best way to form producer organizations, from below or above? I support the idea of a structured market. Some people disagree with this idea, but most people would agree that additional changes in the current structural adjustment package are needed.

Mr Saith questioned the way the institutional structure of production influences income distribution. Clearly, a co-operative will allow a more equal distribution of income than a capitalist firm. That is an important issue, if we are concerned with how to get incomes to poor people. Some of us have worked on this issue a lot in the past, but it has been less in vogue recently because it is a political issue. There is no question that capitalist institutions are here to stay. Alternative institutions such as parastatals have not been successful.

The dynamics of AT is an important issue. Growth is needed, but it is not clear how this should be achieved. What are the sources of technological change? How can the dynamism of technology be increased? What are the sources of savings and investment? What is the natural evolution and how is it best achieved, both in terms of size and location? Another dynamic issue that was not discussed is the impact of new technologies from developed countries. Do they replace ATs or can they be used to improve them? In micro-electronics, we have seen a blending of old and new technologies.

The political economy is a matter of fundamental importance. If a first-best solution in a certain economy may be impractical for political reasons, we may have to use a second-best solution. For example, the best solution to rural poverty in Bangladesh would probably be land reform, while a programme like the Grameen Bank is a second-best solution. We have identified appropriate rural policies, but they are a long way from being put into effect. Policy changes on paper can be made with a stroke of a pen, but there is a big difference between moving the pen and making a change actually happen.

Third, there are some new issues that need more study. One issue is education and training for appropriate technology development. This should be relatively easy to accomplish because there are fewer political economy obstacles to this path. The question of environment was raised and it should be incorporated in our work. What are the environmental consequences of using various technologies and of poverty and more conventional approaches to development? How can incentives be structured to incorporate environmental considerations into decision-making?

Fourth, I have suggestions for follow up activities. One suggestion is to target a particular country, taking the ideas we have developed and identifying the policy changes that would be needed to encourage AT use there. A lot obviously has to be done at the dissemination level to get these ideas rolling. You might reflect on the absence of the World Bank from this meeting. We have to look at what the donors and multilateral agencies do, not what they say, and what they do is not so good.

More work is needed to formulate rural adjustment packages that incorporate the above issues on both the general and country level. The developing countries themselves need to have a much more coherent and articulate view to be able to put forward alternatives that can gain the support of the international community.

There is also a need to change the quality of aid; the bulk of it continues to be inappropriate. Again and again, technology concerns are put in a small corner of the aid budget. Aid needs to be reformed throughout to be much more poverty-related.

# Observations by Participants

## W RASAPUTRAM, S M WANGWE AND E DORYAN-GARRON

Our discussions in this conference pointed out that AT varies from country to country, from industry to industry, from region to region, and from time to time. AT is a dynamic concept that takes into consideration the need to raise the efficiency of producers on a broad basis and thereby increase incomes and employment for more egalitarian development.

Policy priorities of successive governments often change. Sometimes policies are changed when ministers are replaced in the same government. Rapid changes can cause confusion and uncertainty for rural entrepreneurs. Therefore, policies must be stable, consistent, and forward looking.

However, since policy-makers often consider short-term political gains more important than long-term growth, inappopiate macroeconomic policies frequently are promoted. Such policies can prevent the rural sector from contributing to the economy most effectively. Although the potential of this sector is substantial, sustained development has not occurred because most development schemes and policy approaches favour urban areas and the richer classes.

As development benefits do not easily trickle down to the lowest level, distortions in income distribution and barriers to structural changes in the rural areas persist. Policies that favour the rural poor should help stimulate growth in rural areas.

Both supply and demand factors need to be carefully considered in formulating general and specific policies. Specific policies may include tax concessions and interest rate subsidies for enterprises that invest and remain in rural areas.

Besides economic factors, there are many sociological constraints that affect sectoral and subsectoral growth. These constraints may have to be overcome gradually by decreasing impediments to economic growth.

Bureaucracies have often discriminated against small- and micro-enterprises. Their management styles may lead to serious delays in the formulation and implementation of policies. It is often said that decisions are made quickly but implementation is painfully slow. Entrepreneurs need a higher degree of freedom than bureaucrats can provide, but the small-scale sector may need more guidance in production and distribution.

---

WARNASENA RASAPUTRAM is the former Governor of the Central Bank of Sri Lanka.

441

Import-substitution programmes have caused excess capacity and inefficiencies in many industries. Lending policies can lead to over-investment that is not justified by demand conditions. When banks extend credit without proper feasibility studies, the resulting financial burdens on borrowers may be passed on to the consumers in the form of higher prices in a protected market.

Lack of co-ordination of micro-policies has wasted scarce resources. Small-scale industry policies are pursued by many countries, but research and evaluation studies have not given a clear picture as to whether small enterprises increase employment and incomes more than large ones. What about the quality and productivity levels of small enterprises? If these enterprises are to have good survival and growth rates they must improve their quality and productivity and remain competitive. Consumers are becoming more sophisticated and their preferences will also change as their incomes rise.

It is a difficult task to prove that small-scale enterprises can increase rural unemployment and raise the effective demand of rural people. Can credit availability help make the small-scale sector more dynamic? Donors and credit agencies have not done much in this direction. When loan repayment rates are high, they consider credit policies to be successful. Donors and credit agencies should play a more responsible role. Credit has to be delivered at the correct time and its utilization and supervision are important. Training schemes for lending agency staff must go beyond credit management to include project planning, evaluation, and marketing.

Structural adjustments supported by the IMF and World Bank are meant to achieve economic stability with growth, but small producers can suffer heavily in the process. After accepting the IMF remedies, some countries have had to face riots. More study is needed on the effects of these policies on small-scale industry and the rural poor. The IMF argues that the adjustments take place along the path of a J-shaped curve. How far the downward slope of the J-curve extends and how it affects the small-scale sector need to be studied.

Sociological factors influence the policies formulated by decision-makers and rural people. Ethnic, religious and caste differences exist in many societies. Special interest groups that influence government policies often exploit the situation to their benefit. Studies of the sociological factors that affect economic forces need to be undertaken. Research is also needed to influence the choice of technologies to raise production and productivity.

Individual country studies have been presented at this conference. Comparative studies of regions or groups of countries might be valuable, but can be difficult to arrange because some countries do not have reliable information to facilitate these studies. The findings and conclusions of this conference should be made widely available to government and donor officials.

Most small- and micro-scale entrepreneurs do not have information about new products, technologies, and policies. Many research organizations have not communicated this information to the users effectively. Although involvement of users in research has been talked about, little has been done in that direction. People at the grassroots must be able to participate effectively in decision making.

# S M WANGWE

This conference has brought out the ongoing struggles and lessons learned in confronting development problems. In the 1970s, clear distinctions were made between macroeconomic policies and theories and between the work of policy-makers, politicians and field staff. Now, people at the project or grassroots level are questioning what is going on at the macro-policy level because they are more aware of the implementation difficulties that can arise from inappropriate policies.

In many African countries, the institutional structures created extensive market failures. As a result, most African countries went through a phase of government interventions such as import controls, price controls, and creation of parastatals to try to deal with these problems. The experience of the 1980s now indicates that intervention does not solve the development problem.

One response to the current understanding is to discontinue interventions and return to a free market system. Another response is to realize that neither reliance on the market alone nor extensive interventions will provide the answer to development. It is the appropriate use of interventions and market forces that will provide the answer. Why should intervention be necessary? What kind of intervention is needed and what impact is that intervention likely to have on various groups in the society? It is important to keep in mind the groups targeted by development programmes. In addition, the institutional framework to mediate these interventions must be appropriate. In developing countries, the institutional framework to deliver goods such as credit to small entrepreneurs is often inadequate.

The importance of political economy has come across quite clearly. When the African countries achieved independence in the 1960s, many ministries did not have sufficient expertise in carrying out development programmes and formulating policies. In some countries, policy-making and planning were initially products of studies supported by the World Bank and other donors.

Over time, this paternalistic type of development led to conflicts. In the 1980s, the multilateral organizations insisted that many LDCs carry out structural adjustments as a condition for further lending. Recently, at a meeting in Addis Ababa, many African countries agreed that the structural adjustment programmes will not solve their basic problems. They also noted that the political structure is one of the areas that needs rethinking. In other words, are developing countries sufficiently democratic? Do they involve the people in decision-making? Are present political structures and institutions legitimate? Increasingly, country nationals are questioning decisions of the policy-makers and have blamed multilateral and bilateral donors as a convenient scapegoat.

We have come to a point where all parties in development are ready to rethink past actions. The World Bank and the IMF are beginning to address the social dimensions of adjustment. Countries facing structural adjustments are demanding greater participation in decision-making. Governments themselves are beginning to rethink their policies. They are realizing that the structural adjustment programmes are not panaceas. Even if there were a positive balance of payments, a balanced budget and low inflation, there would still be a serious poverty problem in LDCs. Structural adjustment programmes have not specifically addressed issues in technology, small-scale enterprises and rural linkages. These issues were being addressed to some extent in previous programmes and policies. This conference has clearly shown that the real development problems at the grassroots level, particularly in rural areas, have not been addressed by the structural adjustment programmes in their present form.

## E DORYAN-GARRON

I am reminded of a phrase that used to appear on the navigational maps of areas east of Europe during the late Middle Age: 'Beware of dragons'. This conference has identified several dragons. The first is that each country has its own reality. When addressing issues of technology policy or development in general, policy-makers must keep the differences between countries in mind. There are no general recipes.

The second dragon is related to structural adjustment loans. Several experts have warned that it is not clear that small enterprises will be automatically assisted by structural adjustment programmes. Nevertheless, we have to proceed in the same way as the sailors of the sixteenth and seventeenth centuries by being wary of dragons, but moving forward, knowing what type of vessel you are in. It turned out there were no dragons in the Atlantic Ocean, but there were storms and a new continent to discover. We must recognize the opportunities provided by new programmes, but also the dangers. The main danger is a failure of local elites, the government, the private sector and labour union members. There should be a long-term plan to take advantage of the new opportunities. If complementary programmes are not expressly put into place to address issues of small enterprises, technology transfer, industrial restructuring, and agricultural modernization, the magic of adjustment may not necessarily bring development.

Often, countries that are successful seem to have done things in a different way from everyone else. For example the British government of the nineteenth century created the institution of the market, which we now think is natural. In 1947, most international advisors counselled Japan to continue producing cheap lighters and cameras for the next 30 years. One of the Japanese leaders of that time said, 'We are not just going to develop; we are going to be a technological power within 20 years' and they did, but everybody else laughed. They did things that seemed at that moment completely different from what was expected. We should understand that diversity and take advantage of it.

The Economic Commission for Latin America (ECLA) did an interesting study last year relating the degree of equity of each country and economic growth. In general, the countries that have been relatively stable politically, and have achieved high rates of economic growth have combined efficiency and equity. AT can only exist in a framework where the policy environment is equitable.

How resources are used in a society is also important. There is a saying that developed countries have 10,000 arrows, but only shoot at just a few targets. LDCs, by contrast, have only 10 arrows, but try to throw them at 10,000 targets including a large military sector, luxury goods, clientelism and inefficient parastatals. For better development, we should aim at just a few targets and concentrate dispersed resources.

It is also important to understand and address the changing world political economy. What is needed to compete in the world economy today might be completely different in 10 or 15 years. Governments and the private sector can help build comparative advantages, by strengthening the science and AT infrastructure. In addition to the traditional concept of economies of scale, two other concepts may be useful to developing countries. The first is the concept of 'economies of scope', as the work of Carlotta Perez in Venezuela has shown. Economies of scope can be achieved by having a small plant produce a large number of different products. For example, a team of 10 biotechnologists could produce hundreds of different virus-free plant varieties in a single laboratory at lower cost than the traditional methods of plant propagation. Technology can open up a wide range of possibilities with a small number of resources.

The second concept is that of economies of specialization, which is

445

linked to the concept of market niches. Small-scale technologies can be used in producing for a market niche. In this way, small can be economically viable as well as beautiful and poor countries can concentrate their meagre resources in a few key areas. Old interventionist government policies would be ineffective in replacing these economies of specialization, but a weak state would not be helpful either. The government can assist by fostering communication among the private sector, the labour movement and universities for efficient resource use.

To put the ideas discussed during the past two days into practice, I propose a five-point national programme. First, we need to develop a backbone and a central nervous system by constructing institutional arrangements that can join dispersed efforts together. In Costa Rica, there are at least twenty such institutions, private and public. Better institutional integration would enable countries to concentrate their efforts in one direction and provide a basis for a national consensus and long-term policy.

Second, it is important to identify where the key policies are made that adversely affect small enterprises. That is where a programme to change things should be located. Depending on the country, it may be within the Treasury Department, the Central Bank, or the boardrooms of the private sector or the co-operatives.

Third, human capital should be emphasized. Appropriate technology is impossible without appropriate people behind it. In contrast to the usual view, appropriate technology demands more highly trained people than inappropriate technology. Less qualified people often choose turnkey technological packages that are available commercially because they do not require creativity and innovation.

Fourth, small-scale technologies have to be efficient and flexible to make a change in society. Fifth, countries should be particular in programme implementation, but have a wide general scope. Pilot programmes can provide a basis for other programmes later. Simon Rodriguez, the teacher of Simon Bolivar, the Latin American liberator in the early nineteenth century said, 'We innovate or we err'. Now is the time to apply what Simon Rodriguez taught us and be creative.

# Adept: Adapt

## LUC DE LA RIVE BOX

A triptych, a rice thresher, development policy, and a Japanese motorcycle repairman in the Dominican Republic are the subjects I am now going to discuss. My presentation is in the form of a triptych, an altarpiece with a central panel and two half-sized side panels. The central panel will be small because Frances Stewart and our colleagues have provided an excellent summary of the conference. One of the side panels depicts the future and how it can be shaped by policies. The other side panel depicts the past and deals with my interpretation of one case in small enterprise development and technology adaptation. Let me start with that case, which illustrates the failure of an ideal.

### The failure of an ideal

In 1983, while I co-ordinated an Adaptive Agricultural Research Programme in the Dominican Republic, a small portable rice thresher was introduced in the country. It happened in this way. While visiting a farmers' association in Nagua, in the northeast of the country, a researcher from our programme asked about problems in rice production and processing. The farmers offered many suggestions, but one problem struck him as fairly easy to solve – the hard labour involved in manual rice threshing. This was still being done by hand with sticks on the small land-reform parcels of the cultivators. Young men had to do this low-paying work for hours under a hot sun. They also risked being blinded by flying rice grains.

A small Dutch firm, in collaboration with the Agricultural University at Wageningen, had developed the VOTEX rice thresher, and this machine had shown promising results. It reduced the occupational risks, the harshness of labour, and yield losses. It did not reduce labour requirements. The capital costs were relatively low although it did require an increased investment. The design has some advantages over the IRRI rice thresher discussed by Duff.[1] We decided to aim the technology at the poor, but organized, rice cultivators. We started with the farmers' association that had identified the problem in the first place and, by 1984, the prototype was in use.

---

LUC DE LA RIVE BOX is Director of the Development Policy Department at the Ministry of Foreign Affairs, Government of the Netherlands. Ideas formulated in this address are personal views and do not necessarily reflect the policy of the government of the Netherlands.

Dutch Aid designed a monitoring and evaluation system to track the technology. The feedback on the thresher was laudatory. The machine was in continuous use and the farmers' association had appointed a special operator for it. The association's chairman handled the financial aspects of its use together with the treasurer. We had suggested that funds be set aside to allow for maintenance and savings, and that others be trained to use the thresher. In 1986, we walked the hot roads around Nagua, evaluating the experience with the first thresher and the ones subsequently introduced.

Suddenly a huge combine harvester crossed our path. I asked my Dominican Republic colleague who worked with a local NGO, what it was doing there. He replied, 'It must be one of those capitalists making a quick buck on the backs of our campesinos', and walked on. I walked back to speak to the capitalist or his representative. The man had spotted me, stopped his huge engine at the wayside and greeted me, 'Remember, I was the operator of the small thresher you people brought two years ago. The association made the down payment on this one and another one with the savings from the one you gave us. The bank takes care of the rest'.

So much for our ideals. Here we saw what nobody had predicted. In two years, our little thresher had been used until it was completely worn down. We later found it, dismembered, reduced to a relic, just like our ideals. We had come to bring small-scale technology to the poorest of the poor. Within 2 years they had saved enough to make the down payment on two giant pieces of equipment that represented the exact opposite of what we had set out to do. They were capital-intensive, labour-displacing, had negative income distributional effects and could not be made or repaired in local shops. Did we fail? Not in the eyes of the farmers involved nor the Dominican Republic policy-makers with whom I discussed the case, who said, 'Dominican Republic rice production needs to be cheap and plentiful; small-scale threshers are small-scale solutions for a large-scale problem'.

Three aspects of this case deserve attention. First, the political economy of technological development in the Dominican Republic cannot be viewed in the static terms of one interest group ('campesinos'), or associated with one type of technology ('small-scale'). It is best viewed as a complex interaction between economic and technological differentiation, which often proceeds unplanned.

Second, national macro- or agricultural sector policies still reflect urban biases. They are loaded against rural priorities such as local employment, local technology maintenance or local capital accumulation. If development planning exists at all, it should counteract such biases.

Third, development agencies, large or small, have a double job to do if they are convinced that technological differentiation is needed. They would have to work at the top to undo particular biases and work at the technological base to allow technological differentiation.

448

## The conference

This leads me to the centre panel of the triptych – the discussions and conclusions of our conference. For a number of us, this conference brought together experiences already discussed in three regional conferences in Africa, Asia and Latin America. For all of us, the other objective was new – to compare and contrast these experiences and formulate recommendations relevant to policy-makers in development agencies. Some of us can compare the results with a workshop on development policies held 7 years ago. What have we learned since then?

The tone of this conference was set by Frances Stewart, who also wrote the central paper for the 1982 workshop. She compellingly argued that a favourable macro-policy environment is a necessary condition for appropriate technology to exist. In most poor countries, this supportive environment is absent and therefore, appropriate technology interventions tend to be shortlived.

In her conference paper with Gus Ranis, Stewart concluded paradoxically that in the countries studied:

> Efficient, small-scale and labour-intensive technologies do exist in many industries (yet) most investment in Third World countries is in large-scale and often inappropriate technologies.

This is what I will call Stewart's paradox: we know that appropriate technologies are available and can be used efficiently, yet policy-makers and investors do not stop pushing inappropriate technologies. Stewart specified the relations between policy environments and small enterprise development. In her discussion with Little, she discussed the empirical validity of the concepts used during this conference.

In the past, at least part of the problem lay with conceptual confusion. In this conference, I have heard terms like appropriate technology, small-scale industry and rural industrialization. This difference in terminology does not matter. It may just reflect the blossoming of many intellectual flowers. What does matter is whether we understand each other. Are we able to see the various realities through our diverse lenses and fruitfully compare our conclusions? I have my doubts, but am happy to see that we did not get lost in terminological discussions. What matters is conceptualization and the testing of different propositions against theoretical models.

The theoretical underpinnings for our understanding have been strengthened by FitzGerald's work reported in this conference. His analysis of small-scale industrialization and structural adjustment policies focused our attention on technological change and macro-policies.

Both FitzGerald and Stewart have reduced the gap between scientific and political discourse in this area. Stewart and Ranis suggested three ways to get around the political economy problems surrounding policy reforms.

449

○ Adapt the recommended policy package to the local political situation;
○ Increase the power of the impoverished, through organization and education so they may influence priority setting in their favour;
○ Use aid funding to ease the short-term costs of policy changes.[2]

Aid cutbacks in the 1980s have generally had a negative impact on appropriate technology development by reducing rural programmes and funds. Moreover, structural adjustment packages often do not contain favourable macro-policies for appropriate technology, particularly with respect to science and technology, and redistribution of income and assets. This was most clearly noted in the Latin American conference.

If we are serious about developing ATs, macro-policies clearly need to be made 'appropriate technology friendly' both at the national and international level. Such policies should not just focus on the informal or small-scale sector, but must be '. . . formulated together with policy toward the large-scale sector. In most countries, removing privileges enjoyed by the large-scale enterprises would do much more for small-scale enterprises than the special schemes and regulations currently adopted'.

The macro-context has been spelled out well at this conference. The earlier workshop held at ISS 7 years ago was called 'Macro-Policies for Appropriate Technology'. The present conference dealt more broadly with policy and technology development. Both were aimed at small enterprises, mostly rural ones. I would like to end by discussing two themes: the relevance of the conference conclusions for Dutch development assistance policy and some areas that could be covered in subsequent meetings.

### Dutch policy

Mr Tinbergen reminded us recently that every debate about development should be clear about the final aim of increasing incomes. He argued in favour of a doubling of incomes in LDCs within 20 years.[3] Dutch development policy is predominantly oriented to rural and agricultural change. Dutch government interest in industrialization is relatively recent, but is likely to grow. Earlier this year the Rural Small Industrial Enterprise study[4] was discussed at a workshop in The Hague. Its conclusions are similar to those of this conference. A thorough report on industrialization has been prepared by the Netherlands National Council for Scientific Research on Development and, shortly, the National Advisory Council will submit a report on the informal sector in LDCs.

My personal conclusions about the implications of this conference for development policy follow:

1. The diversity of the small enterprise sector has to be recognized in policy formulation as few generalizations can be made. Some parts of

450

the informal sector are quite dynamic, but others remain stagnant. Macro-policies are needed, but their effects on different sub-sectors will differ;

2. Regionalization of policies is also needed because of large differences within regions. Nevertheless, certain problems such as access to particular production factors tend to cluster in a region. Decentralization of development policy-making is needed as well. Donor missions in country will need to develop expertise on the relationship between macro- and sectoral policies and development projects;

3. Donor co-ordination is more than just a cliché. Small donors have little clout to counteract the major policies and programmes that place small-scale enterprises at a disadvantage in poor countries. Small donors can make a contribution by sharing information in international consultations and by forming coalitions;

4. Donor policies need their own structural adjustments to fit diverse realities. This conference showed that small-scale industry suffers when large-scale development is promoted. As Mr Gupta argued during this conference, small enterprises should not have to adjust to the idiosyncracies of donors;

5. Linkages to private industry should be emphasized in policy formulation. Policy-makers do not produce development, but can generate a favourable or unfavourable environment. The knowledge needed for development is often with private industry, rather than with government or NGO officials. This was my experience with the VOTEX rice threshers project in the Dominican Republic;

6. NGOs should play a larger role in providing the necessary linkages with small-scale private sector firms. This was the case with FUNDAP in Guatemala and the Association para el Desarrollo in the Dominican Republic. These NGOs are representative of a special breed of industry-led non-profit organizations. Development policy-makers will have to learn to work together with such NGOs and evaluate whose interests they serve. There is a danger of faddism in NGO-linked approaches and parastatals should not be left out of the picture. After all, many donors are at least partly responsible for the existence of parastatals and NGOs cannot simply take the place of these firms;

7. Basic research in developed countries will continue to be important for small enterprise development in poor countries, provided it is well connected with local applied researchers. Mr Doryan-Garron made an eloquent plea in favour of such research when referring to particular applications of biotechnology in coffee production. Development policy-makers need to be informed on both the availability of alternative technology and the demand for them. Development assistance agencies can be technology brokers, but may need strengthening to carry this out.

8. Appropriate technology is often generated through user experimentation in a given environmental and socioeconomic context. An understanding of such interactions with the local context is essential. For example, the VOTEX rice thresher was adapted by a Japanese motorcycle repairman in the Dominican Republic. This is called 'blue collar innovation', to use Ranis' term. At the root of many technological developments there is a need for sound empirical studies of technological development and adaptation.

Economists have set the tone of this conference in arguing for the importance of macroeconomic policies. Now it is up to technologists, users, social scientists and policy-makers to show how other factors affect the potential for appropriate technologies in small-scale enterprise development. The scientists have to adapt to the requests of policy makers and small-scale entrepreneurs in the field. Policy-makers must adapt the insights of scientists and intended beneficiaries. In this way we may be able to accomplish Tinbergen's goal of doubling incomes in the next 20 years.

# Notes

## Stewart and Ranis

1 Carr (1986)
2 Stewart (1987)
3 Katz (1980), Westphal (1982), Lall (1987)
4 Eckaus (1955), Kaldor (1965), Emmanuel (1982)
5 Little (1988), Little, Mazumdar and Page, forthcoming
6 Ranis (1973)
7 Fisseha and Milimo (1985)
8 Ahmad (1988)
9 Haggblade (1983)
10 Ranis and Stewart (1987)
11 van Ginneken and van der Hoeven (1989)
12 Cornia, Jolly and Stewart (1987)
13 Santikarn (1988)
14 Lecraw (1979)
15 Bell and Scott-Kemmis (1987)
16 James (1987)
17 Wangwe and Bagachwa (1988)
18 ILO (1977)
19 Bautista (1988)
20 Ndlela (1988)
21 Liedholm and Mead (1987)
22 World Bank (1975)
23 Siamwalla and Setboonsarng (1987)
24 Stewart (1985)
25 Nogues (1980)
26 Haggblade, Liedholm and Mead (1986)
27 World Bank (1986)
28 Bhagwati (1978)
29 Ncube (1987)
30 Stewart and Weeks (1975)
31 Berry and Sabot (1978)
32 Kaplinsky (1987)
33 Duff (1987)
34 Carranza (1988)
35 Andrade no date
36 Hyman (1988)
37 Beranek and Ranis (1978), Crane (1977)
38 Green (1988)
39 Ranis (1973)
40 Bates (1981)
41 Helleiner (1988)
42 Reddy (1979)

## Ranis

1 Schultz (1953), Nicholls (1964), Tang (1958)
2 Mendel (1982)
3 Oshima (1984)
4 Ranis, Stewart and Angeles-Reyes, forthcoming
5 Ranis and Stewart (1987)

## Haggblade, Liedholm and Mead

1 Steel and Takagi (1983)
2 Squire (1981)
3 Page and Steel (1984)
4 Chuta and Liedholm (1979)
5 Liedholm and Mead (1986)
6 King and Byerlee (1978)
7 Berry (1978)
8 Berry and Sabot (1978)
9 World Bank (1983)
10 Krueger et al. (1981)
11 Knight and Sabot (1980)
12 Kannappan (1983)
13 Page (1979)
14 Mazumdar (1979)
15 Child (1977)
16 Byerlee et al. (1983)
17 Steel (1977)
18 Mazumdar and Ahmad (1978)
19 Watanabe (1976)
20 Gregory (1975)

21 ILO (1970)
22 Frank (1968)
23 Kannappan (1977)
24 Joshi *et al.* (1974)
25 Atasi (1968)
26 Fapohunda *et al* (1975)
27 Guisinger (1978)
28 Bertrand and Squire (1980)
29 Reynolds and Gregory (1965)
30 Kannappan (1977)
31 Anderson and Khambata (1981)
32 Akrasane (1981)
33 Squire (1981)
34 Krueger *et al.* (1983)
35 World Bank (1975)
36 Wai (1957)
37 Wai (1977)
38 Liedholm (1985)
39 Haggblade (1984)
40 Monson (1981)
41 Hong (1981)
42 Nogues (1980)
43 Bhagwati (1978)
44 Leith (1974)
45 Bhagwati and Srinivasan (1978)
46 Guisinger (1981)
47 Jansen (1980)
48 Lizondo (1985)
49 Harberger (1962)
50 Wozny (no date)
51 Government of Jamaica (1981)
52 Kilby (1982)
53 Krueger (1978)
54 Frank *et al.* (1978)
55 Carvalho and Haddad (1981)
56 Westphal and Kim (1977)
57 Scitovsky (1985)
58 Streeten (1985)
59 Anderson and Khambata (1981)
60 Hiemenz and Bruch (1983)
61 von Rabenau (1976)
62 Little *et al.* (1970)
63 Leibenstein (1957)
64 Dougherty and Selowsky (1973)
65 de Melo (1977)
66 White (1978)
67 Bruton (1972)
68 Morawetz (1974)
69 Morawetz (1976)
70 Behrman (1982)
71 Page (1984)
72 Kim (1984)
73 Akrasane (1976)

74 Hooley (1981)
75 Gaude (1975)
76 O'Herlihy (1972)
77 Pack (1972)
78 Roemer (1975)
79 Eriksson (1970)
80 Williams College (1972)
81 Wolgin *et al.* (1983)
82 Fields (1984)
83 Lipton (1978)
84 Williamson (1971b)
85 Krishna (1976)
86 Mellor and Mudahar (1974)
87 Rangarajan (1982)
88 Byerlee (1973)
89 Gibb (1974)
90 Bell, Hazell and Slade (1982)
91 Hazell and Roell (1983)
92 Balassa *et al.* (1982)
93 Krueger (1966)
94 de Melo and Robinson (1980)
95 Harberger (1959)
96 Ho (1980)
97 Berry (1972)
98 Weiskoff (1973)
99 Soligo (1972)
100 Jimenez (1972)
101 King and Byerlee (1978)
102 Paukert *et al.* (1974)

*Bautista*

1 Stewart (1987a)
2 Tidalgo and Esguerra (1984)
3 NEDA (1986)
4 ILO (1974)
5 Lamberte *et al.* (1985)
6 Bautista (1981b)
7 Bautista (1987)
8 Power and Sicat (1971)
9 Gregorio (1979)
10 Mejia (1979)
11 Medalla (1979)
12 Armas (1973)
13 Armas (1975)
14 Bautista *et al* (1979)
15 Hooley (1985)
16 Government of the Philippines (1981)
17 Emerson and Warr (1981)
18 Bautista (1973)
19 Baldwin (1975)

20 Senga (1983)
21 Bautista (1975)
22 Bautista (1975)
23 NEDA (1982)
24 Moran (1978)
25 Moran (1979)
26 Bautista (1981a)
27 Herrin and Pernia (1987)
28 Hife (1979)
29 Bautista (1987b)
30 Barker (1984)
31 David (1983a)
32 David (1983b)
33 Intal and Power (1987)
34 Nelson and Agcaoili (1983)
35 Canlas *et al.* (1984)
36 Clarete and Roumasset (1983)
37 Bautista (1986a)
38 Alburo *et al.* (1986)
39 Bautista (1988)
40 Ranis and Stewart (1987)
41 Gibbs (1974)
42 Sander (1979)
43 Wangwaracharakul (1984)
44 Bautista (1986b)
45 Golay (1961)
46 Baldwin (1975)
47 Medalla (1986)
48 Mellor (1976)

### Ahmad

1 Stewart (1987)
2 Government of Bangladesh (1986)
3 Ahmad and Chowdhury (1987)
4 Government of Bangladesh (1985)
5 Government of Bangladesh (1986a)
6 Government of Bangladesh (1987)
7 Government of Bangladesh (1986b)
8 Ahmad (1987)
9 BIDS (1981)
10 Government of Bangladesh (1980)
11 Ahmad (1985)
12 Ahmed (1984)
13 Ahmad (1986)
14 Scott and Carr (1985)
15 Ahmad (1988)

### Ndlela

1 Sutcliffe (1971)
2 Government of Zimbabwe (1982)
3 CSO (1985)
4 Government of Zimbabwe (1983)
5 Ndlela *et al.* (1984)
6 Government of Zimbabwe (1983)
7 Government of Zimbabwe (1986)
8 Ndlela (1986)
9 Ndlela (1987)
10 Moyo (1986)

### Wangwe and Bagachwa

1 Stewart (1987)
2 Skarstein and Wangwe (1986)
3 Wangwe (1977)
4 Wangwe (1983)
5 Ndulu (1986)
6 Rweyemamu (1973)
7 World Bank (1986)
8 James (1983)
9 Bagachwa (1987)
10 Coulson (1974)
11 Thomas (1974)
12 Mihyo (1981)
13 Dolman *et al.* (1981)
14 UNCTAD (1981)
15 Perkins (1983)
16 Williams (1975)
17 Williams (1976)
18 Eze (1977)
19 Mlawa (1983)
20 Green (1982)
21 Osoro (1987)
22 World Bank (1988)
23 URT Economic Survey (1986)
24 Wangwe (1979)
25 Bagachwa (1983)
26 Liedholm and Mead (1987)
27 Stewart (1987)
28 Odegaard (1985)
29 Havnevik *et al.* (1985)
30 Alange (1987)

### Doryan-Garron

1 Timmer *et al.* (19   )

2  Timmer (1986)
3  MIDEPLAN (1987)
4  MICIT (1987)
5  SEPSA (1986)
6  Leon *et al.* (1982)
7  Chacon *et al.* (1982)
8  Schultz (1964)
9  Saint and Coward (1977)
10  Chapman *et al.* (1986)

### *Uribe – Echevania*

1  UN (1979)
2  Sthor and Todtling (1978)
3  Higgins (1978)
4  Staley and Morse (1965)
5  Anderson (1982)
6  Page and Steel (1984)
7  Elkan (1987)
8  Alcantara *et al.* (1984)
9  Baroin and Fracheboud (1982)
10  von Dewall *et al.* (1985)
11  Miller (1974)
12  Ho (1979)
13  Bar-El (1985)
14  de Haan (1989)
15  Scott (1986)
16  van der Hulst and Steffens (1975)
17  Miller (1975)
18  Uribe-Echevarria and Forero (1985)
19  Wicramanaye (1988)
20  Sandesara (1988)
21  Ngethe and Wahome (1987)
22  Gasper (1989)
23  Mathur (1975)
24  Vepa (1987)
25  Gamaya (1988)
26  Dutting (1988)
27  Gasper (1989)
28  Hymer and Reswick (1969)
29  Massel (1969)
30  ILO (1972)
31  ILO (1974)
32  ILO (1976)
33  Mellor (1976)
34  Liedholm and Chuta (1976)
35  King and Byerlee (1977)
36  Chuta and Liedholm (1985)
37  Jhaveri (1981)
38  Saith (1986)
39  Liedholm and Mead (1986)

40  American Rural Industry Delegation (1977)
41  Uribe-Echevarria (1989)
42  Sayer (1982)
43  Taylor and Thrift (1983)
44  UNDP (1989)
45  Azevedo *et al.* (1985)
46  Wogart (1978)
47  Hutchenson (1973)
48  Wescott (1981)
49  Reyes and Pederanga (1983)
50  Uribe-Echevarria (1983)

### *Berry, Cortes and Ishaq*

1  Anderson (1982)
2  Schmitz (1982)
3  Nelson (1971)
4  Schumacher (1973)
5  Gold (1981)
6  Liedholm and Mead (1987)
7  Little *et al.* (1987)
8  Felix (1977)
9  Felix (1974)
10  Mendel (1982)
11  Parker (1979)
12  Cortes *et al.* (1988)
13  DANE (1978)
14  Ho (1980)
15  Farrell (1957)
16  Berry and Pinell-Siles (1979)
17  Todd (1972)
18  Diaz-Alejandro (1983)

### *James*

1  IBRD (1983)
2  Ndegwa (1979)
3  Clark (1978)
4  Perkins (1980)
5  Gillis (1980)
6  Wells (1975)
7  Williams (1975)
8  Stewart (1977)
9  Okumu (1979)
10  Vernon (1981)
11  Raiffa (1980)
12  Aharoni (1981)
13  IBRD (1977a)
14  James (1985)
15  IDB, Project correspondence files

16  ICDC, Project correspondence files
17  James (1983)
18  IBRD (1977b)
19  National Chemicals Industries document
20  ISDC (1975a)
21  ISDC (1975b)
22  Killick (1978)
23  Hyden (1979)
24  Fransman (1982)
25  Swainson (1980)
26  Coulson (1982)

### FitzGerald

1   World Bank (1988)
2   IMF (1987)
3   Stewart (1987)
4   FitzGerald and Vos (1989)
5   Anderson (1982)
6   Little (1987)
7   Little et al. (1988)
8   Cortes et al. (1988)
9   Liedholm and Mead (1986)
10  Ellis (1988)
11  World Bank (1987)
12  Dornbusch and Helmers (1988)
13  McKinnon (1973)
14  Stewart (1972)
15  Cooper (1972)
16  Stewart and Weeks (1975)
17  Wells (1986)
18  Dell (1987)
19  Taylor (1988)
20  Cornia et al. (1987)
21  Taylor (1988)
22  Haggblade et al. (1986)
23  Galbis (1977)
24  Saith (1989)
25  UN (1968)
26  FitzGerald et al. (1988)
27  Taylor (1983)
28  FitzGerald (1988)
29  Giovanni (1985)
30  Virmani (1986)
31  Schmitz (1982)
32  Badhuri (1983)
33  Leff (1976)
34  Lessard and Williamson (1987)
35  Sylos-Labini (1969)
36  Lydall (1979)
37  Laenen (1988)

38  Lluch (1977)
39  FitzGerald (1976)
40  Pyatt (1985)

### Cooper

1   ILO (1970)
2   Taylor (1983)
3   Nayar (1978)
4   de Janvry and Sadoulet (1983)
5   Little (1987)
6   Thirsk (1979)
7   Morawetz (1974)
8   Tokman (1974)
9   House (1980)
10  Aryee (1981)
11  Forsyth and Mubin (1980)
12  Hoffman and Rush (1986)
13  Soete (1985)
14  Watanabe (1983)
15  Marshall (1966)

### Thomas

1   Thomas and Uribe-Echevarria, forthcoming
2   White (1986)
3   Bienefeld (1987)
4   Griffin and Enos (1973)
5   Tokman (1987)
6   Kannappan (1983)
7   Harrod (1987)
8   Standing (1987)
9   FitzGerald (1989)
10  IDTC (1989)
11  Weijland (1988)
12  Mihyo (1989)
13  Dawson, forthcoming
14  Nagaraj (1984)
15  Doryan-Garron (1989)
16  Laky, forthcoming
17  Thomas and Logan (1982)
18  Kogi (1985)
19  Buzzard and Edgcomb (1987)
20  RAWOO (1989)
21  Gosses et al. (1989)

### de la Rive Box

1   Duff (1987)
2   Stewart and Ranis (1987)
3   NRC Handelsblad (1989)
4   UNDP, UNIDO, Govt of the Netherlands (1988)

# Bibliography

Acebedo, A., Quiros, G. and Restrepo R. (1985) 'Una Aproximacion Sobre el Desarrollo Industrial Colombiano. 1958–1980', in Bejarano J. A. (ed) *Lecturas Sobre Economia Colombiana*, Nueva Biblioteca Colombiana de Cultura, Procultura, Bogota, DE.

Adelman, I., Hopkins, M. J. D., Robinson, S., Rogers, G. B. and Werj, R. (1979) 'A Comparison of Two Models for Income Distribution Planning', *Journal of Policy Modelling*, Vol. 1, No. 1.

Aharoni, Y. (1981) 'Managerial Discretion', in *State-Owned Enterprise in the Western Economies*, Vernon R. and Aharoni, Y. (eds) New York, St Martin's Press.

Ahmad, Q. K. (1987) *Upgrading of Technology for Rural Industries in Bangladesh: A Review of Experience*, ILO/ARTEP, New Delhi.

Ahmad, Q. K. (1988) 'Appropriate Technology and Rural Industrial Development in Bangladesh: The Macro Context', paper prepared for Conference on Implications of Technology Choice on Economic Development, Pattaya, Thailand, March 21–24.

Ahmad, Q. K. *et al.* (1988) *The Role of Women in Rural Industries*, Vol. 2 (Bangladesh) and Vol. 3 (Nepal), CIRDAP, Dhaka.

Ahmad, Q. K. and Ahmed, M. U. (1985) 'A Review of Rural Non-farm Activities in Bangladesh', in Mukhopadhyay, S. and Chee Peng Lim (eds) *Development and Diversification of Rural Industries in Asia*, Kuala Lumpur, APDC

Ahmad, Q. K. and Chowdhury, F. A. (1987) *Rural Industrialization in Bangladesh: a Synthesis Based on Studies on Rural Industries Development in Selected Upazilas*, Bangladesh Institute of Development Studies, Dhaka.

Ahmed, M. U. (1984), 'Financing Rural Industries in Bangladesh', in Ahmad, Q. K. (ed) *The Bangladesh Development Studies: Special Issue on Rural Industrialization in Bangladesh*, Dhaka, BIDS.

Akrasane, N. (1976) 'Industrialization and Trade Policies and Employment Effects in Thailand', University of the Philippines, Council for Asian Manpower Studies. *Discussion Paper Series No. 76–11*.

Akrasane, N. (1981) 'Trade Strategy for Employment Growth', in *Trade and Employment in Developing Countries*, Krueger, A. *et al.* (eds) Chicago, University of Chicago Press.

Alange, S. (1987) 'Acquisition of Capabilities Through International Technology Transfer: The Case of Small-Scale Industrialization in Tanzania', PhD dissertation, Chalmers University of Technology, Gothenburg.

Alburo, F. A. *et al.* (1987), *Economic Recovery and Long-Run Growth: Agenda for Reforms*, Makatil, Philippine Institute for Development Studies.

Alcantara, B., Altnick, T., Carre, D., de Bandt, O., Lemettre, J. F., Nichon-Altnick, C. and Roncin, A. (1984) 'L'analyse demographique des petites et moyennes entreprises dans les pays de la Communaute Europeenne', Institut de Recherche en L'Economie de la Production, Nanterre.

Ali, M. S. (1984) 'Employment Expansion – Import Substitution or Export

Promotion? A General Equilibrium Study of Pakistan', *Indian Economic Journal*, Vol. 31, No. 3.

American Rural Industry Delegation (1977) *Rural Small-Scale Industry in The People's Republic of China*, University of California Press.

Anderson, D. (1982) 'Small Industry in Developing Countries: A Discussion of Issues', *World Development*, Vol. 10, No. 11.

Anderson, D. (1982) 'Small Industry in Developing Countries', *World Bank Staff Working Paper No. 518*, World Bank, Washington DC.

Anderson, D. and Khambata, F. (1981) 'Small Enterprises and Development Policy in the Philippines: A Case Study', *World Bank Staff Working Paper No. 468*. World Bank, Washington DC.

Anderson, R. (1972) 'Taxation and Economic Development in Sierra Leone', PhD dissertation, Department of Economics, University of Illinois.

Armas, A. (1973), 'Implications of Legislated Minimum Wages on the Choice of Technique in the Agro-Canned Pineapple Industries in the Philippines: A Micro-approach', *Philippine Economic Journal*, Vol. 12.

Armas, A. (1975), 'The Constraint of Minimum Wage Legislation on the Long-Run Choice of Technology in the Canned Pineapple Industry,' *Philippine Review of Business and Economics*, Vol. 12.

Arriaga Jerez, B. (1988) *Sheep Production and the Development of Capitalism in the Peasant Economy of the Guatemalan Highlands,* Guatemala, University of San Carlos.

Aryee, G. A. (1981) 'Income Distribution, Technology and Employment in the Footwear Industry', *WEP Research Working Paper*, ILO, Geneva.

Atasi, N. (1968) 'Minimum Wage Fixing and Wage Structure in Syria', *International Labour Review*, Vol. 98, No. 4.

Auciello, K. E. *et al.* (1975) *Employment Generation Through Stimulation of Small Industries: An International Compilation of Small-Scale Industry Definitions*, Atlanta, Georgia Institute of Technology.

Badhuri, A. (1983) *The Economic Structure of Backward Agriculture*, London, Academic Press.

Baer, W. and Herve, E. A. M. (1966) 'Employment and Industrialization in Developing Countries', *Quarterly Journal of Economics*, Vol. 80, No. 1.

Bagachwa, M. S. D. (1983) 'Small-Scale Industry Technology and Resource-Use in Manufacturing: Evidence from Tanzania', *Third World Seminar Publications*, No. 38.

Bagachwa, M. S. D. (1987) 'Choice of Technology in Grain-milling Industry in Tanzania', University of Dar-es-Salaam, unpublished.

Bagachwa, M. S. D. (1988) 'Technology Choice in Industry: A Study of Grain-milling Techniques in Tanzania', paper prepared for Conference on the Implications of Technology Choice on Economic Development, Nairobi, August 29–31.

Baland, P. (1989) 'Social Articulation: A Generali', *Journal of Development Studies*, forthcoming, July.

Balassa, B. (1971) *The Structure of Protection in Developing Countries*, Baltimore, Johns Hopkins University Press.

Balassa, B. (1977) *Policy Reform in Developing Countries*, New York, Pergamon Press.

Balassa, B. *et al.* (1982) *Development Strategies in Semi-Industrialized Economies*, Baltimore, Johns Hopkins University Press.

Baldwin, R. E. (1975), *Foreign Trade Regimes and Economic Development: The Philippines*, New York, National Bureau of Economic Research.

Banerji, R. and Reidel, J. (1980) 'Industrial Employment Expansion under

Alternative Trade Strategies: Case of India and Taiwan: 1950–1970', *Journal of Development Economics*, Vol. 7.

Banskota, M. and Ligal, P. R. (1984) 'A Study on Non-Agricultural Private Sector Enterprises in Nepal', Kathmandu: Development Research and Communication Group for USAID/Nepal.

Bar-El, R. (1984) 'Rural Industrialization Objectives: The Income–Employment Conflict', *World Development*, Vol. 12, No. 2.

Bar-El, R. (1985) 'Industrial Dispersion as Instrument for the Achievement of Development Goals', in *Economic Geography*, Vol. 61, No. 3.

Barclay, A. H. (1977) 'The Mumias Sugar Project: A Study of Rural Development in Western Kenya', PhD thesis, New York, Columbia University.

Barker, R. (1984), *The Philippine Rice Program: Lessons for Agricultural Development*, Cornell International Agricultural Monograph 104, Ithaca, N.Y., Cornell University.

Barnett, S. and Engel, N. (1982) 'Effective Institution Building: A Guide for Project Designers and Project Managers Based on Lessons Learned from the AID Portfolio', *AID Programme Evaluation Discussion Paper No. 11*, Washington DC, AID.

Baroin, C. P. A. and Fracheboud, P. (1982) 'Le contribution des petites et moyennes enterprises a l'emplois en Europe', Centre de Recherche de Travail et Societe, Paris.

Bates, R. E. (1981) *Markets and States in Tropical Africa: The Political Basis of Agricultural Policies*, Berkeley, University of California Press.

Bates, R. H. (1983) 'The Private Sector: The Regulation of Rural Markets in Africa', *USAID Evaluation Special Study No. 14*, Washington DC.

Bautista, R. M. (1973), 'Employment Promotion in a Small, Open Economy: The Philippines,' in *Effective Anti-Poverty Strategies*, Bangkok, Friedrich-Ebert-Stiftung.

Bautista, R. M. (1975), 'Employment Effects of Export Expansion in the Philippines,' *Malayan Economic Review* Vol. 20.

Bautista, R. M. (1981a), 'The Development of Labour Intensive Industry in the Philippines,' in R. Amjad (ed.), *The Development of Labour Intensive Industry in ASEAN Countries*, Bangkok, ILO-ARTEP.

Bautista, R. M. (1981b), 'The 1981–85 Tariff Changes and Effective Protection of Manufacturing Industries,' *Journal of Philippine Development* Vol. 8.

Bautista, R. M. (1986a), 'Domestic Price Distortions and Agricultural Income in Developing Countries,' *Journal of Development Economics* Vol. 23.

Bautista, R. M. (1986b), 'Effects of Increasing Agricultural Productivity in a Multisectored Model for the Philippines,' *Agricultural Economics* Vol. 1.

Bautista, R. M. (1987), *Production Incentives in Philippine Agriculture: Effects of Trade and Exchange Rate Policies,* Research Report 59, Washington, D.C., International Food Policy Research Institute.

Bautista, R. M. (1988), 'Agricultural Growth as a Development Strategy for the Philippines.' *Philippine Economic Journal* Vol. 27.

Bautista, R. M., Power, J. H. and Associates (1979), *Industrial Promotion Policies in the Philippines*, Makati, Philippine Institute for Development Studies.

Bautista, R. M. (1988) 'Macro-Policies and Technology Choice in the Philippines', paper prepared for Conference on Implications of Technology Choice on Economic Development, Pattaya, Thailand, March 21–24.

Behrman, J. R. (1982) 'Country and Sectoral Variations in Manufacturing Elasticities of Substitution between Capital and Labour', in *Trade and Employment in Developing Countries*, Vol. 2, *Factor Supply and Substitution*, Krueger, A. O. (ed), Chicago, University of Chicago Press.

Bejarano, J. A. (1978) *Ensayos de Interpretacion de la Economia Colombiana*, Bogota, Editorial La Carreta.

Bejarano, J. A. (1979) 'Industrializacion y Politica Economica. 1950–1975', in Arrubla, M. *et al.* (ed), *Colombia Hoy*, Siglo Veintiuno Ediciones.

Bell, C., Hazell, P. and Slade, R. (1982) *Project Evaluation in Regional Perspective*, Baltimore, Johns Hopkins University Press.

Bell, M. and Scott Kemmis, D. (1987) 'Transfers of Technology and the Accumulation of Technological Capability in Thailand', World Bank, Washington DC.

Beranek, W. and Ranis, G. (1978) *Science and Technology and Economic Development*, New York, Praeger.

Berg, E. (1969) 'Wage Structure in Less Developed Countries', *Wage Policy Issues in Economic Development*, Smith, A. D. (ed), London, Macmillan.

Berg, E. and Batchelder, A. (1984) 'Structural Adjustment Lending: A Critical View', paper prepared for the World Bank Country Policy Department, Alexandria, Virginia, Elliot Berg Associates.

Berry, A. (1972) 'The Rate of Interest and the Demand for Labour', *Yale University Economic Growth Centre Discussion Paper No. 144*, New Haven, Yale University.

Berry, A. (1972) 'The Relevance and Prospects of Small Scale Industry in Colombia', *Yale Economic Growth Centre Discussion Paper No. 142*, New Haven, Yale University.

Berry, A. (1978) 'Price of Capital, Income, and Demand for Labour in Developing Countries', *Southern Economic Journal*.

Berry, A. and Eriksson, J. R. (1972) 'Summary of Yale University Economic Growth Centre Research Papers on Employment and Unemployment Problems', Washington DC, USAID.

Berry, A. and Pinell-Siles, A. (1979) *Small-Scale Enterprise in Colombia: a Case Study*, Studies in Employment and Rural Development, No. 56, World Bank, Washington DC.

Berry, A. and Sabot, R. H. (1978) 'Labour Market Performance in Developing Countries: A Survey', *World Development*, Vol. 6.

Bertrand, T. and Squire, L. (1980) 'The Relevance of the Rural Economy Model: A Case Study of Thailand', *Oxford Economic Papers*, Vol. 32, No. 3.

Beveridge, W. A. and Kelley, M. R. (1980) 'Fiscal Content of Financial Programme Supported by Stand-By Arrangements in the Upper Credit Tranches, 1969–78', *IMF Staff Papers*, Vol. 27, No. 2.

Bhagwati, J. D. (1978) *Anatomy and Consequences of Exchange Control Regimes*, Cambridge, Mass, Ballinger Publishing Co.

Bhagwati, J. D. and Srinivasan, J. W. (1978) *Foreign Trade Regimes and Economic Development: India*, Cambridge, Massachusetts, Ballinger Publishing Company.

Bhalla, A. (ed) (1975) *Technology and Employment in Industry*, Geneva, ILO.

BIDS (1981) *Rural Industry Project*, Dhaka.

Bienefeld, M. (1987) *Industrial Policy Research and Aid: The Need to Retreat in Order to Advance*, paper presented at a meeting of Industrialization in Developing Countries, The Advisory Council for Scientific Research in Development Problems, RAWOO, The Hague.

Biggs, S. and Griffith, J. (1987), 'Irrigation in Bangladesh', in Stewart, F. (ed) *Macro-Policies for Appropriate Technology in Developing Countries*, Boulder, Col., Westview Press.

Bremer, J., Cole, E., Irelan W. and Rourk, P. (1985) 'A Review of AID's Experience in Private Sector Development', *AID Programme Evaluation Report No. 14*, Washington DC, AID.

Brewer, Gary D. and deLeon, Peter. (1983) *The Foundations of Policy Analysis*. Homewood, Illinois, The Dorsey Press.

Bruton, H. (1972) 'The Elasticity of Substitution in Developing Countries', *Research Memorandum No. 45*, Williamstown, Massachusetts, Centre for Development Economics, Williams College.

Bruton, H. (1973) 'Economic Development and Labour Use: A Review', *World Development*, Vol. 1, No. 12.

Buzzard, S. and Edgcomb, E. (eds) (1987) *Monitoring and Evaluating Small Business Projects: A Step by Step Guide for Private Development Organizations*, New York, NY, Private Agencies Collaborating Together (PACT).

Byerlee, D. (1973) 'Indirect Employment and Income Distribution Effects of Agricultural Development Strategies, A Simulation Approach Applied to Nigeria', *African Rural Economy Paper No. 9*, East Lansing, Michigan, Michigan State University.

Byerlee, D., Eicher, C., Liedholm, C. and Spencer, D. S. C. (1977) 'Rural Employment in Tropical Africa: Summary of Findings', *African Rural Economy Working Paper No. 20*, East Lansing, Michigan, Michigan State University.

Byerlee, D., Eicher, C., Liedholm, C. and Spencer, D. S. F. (1983) 'Employment–Output Conflicts, Factor–Price Distortions and Choice of Technique: Empirical Results from Sierra Leone', *Economic Development and Cultural Change*, Vol. 31, No. 2.

Caballero, J. M. (1984) 'Unequal Pricing and Unequal Exchange between the Peasant and Capitalist Economies', *Cambridge Journal of Economics*, Vol. 8, No. 4.

Camposeco, J. and Ortiz, D. (1988) *Wool Handcrafts in Momostenango*, Regional Sub-Centre of Handcrafts and Popular Art, Guatemala.

Canlas, D. B., *et al.* (1984), 'Analysis of the Philippine Economic Crisis: A Workshop Report,' Quezon City, University of the Philippines School of Economics, (mimeo).

Carr, M. (ed) (1986) *The AT Reader: Theory and Practice in Appropriate Technology*, London, Intermediate Technology Publications.

Carranza, F. Pacheco (1988) 'Modification of a Traditional Process of Lime Production', paper prepared for the first Latin American Conference on Economic Policy, Technology and Rural Productivity, Mexico City.

Carvalho, J. and Haddad, C. L. S. (1981) 'Foreign Trade Strategies and Employment in Brazil', in Kreuger, A. O. *et al.* (ed) *Trade and Employment in Developing Countries*, Chicago, University of Chicago Press.

Center for Policy and Development Studies (1986), 'Pragmatic Import Liberalization and Constructive Protectionism', *The Philippine Economist*, Vol. 1.

Chacon, E., Coto, Z., Aguilar, J. and Barboza, C. (1982) *Sociological Aspects of the Technology Adoption Process in Coffee Production in Two Costa Rican Communities*, San Jose, Conicit.

Chambre de Commerce, d'Industrie et d'Artisanat du Burkina Faso (1985) 'Symposium sur L'enterprise Burkinabe: Bilan Critique du Commerce et Perspectives d'Avenir', Ouagadougou: Ministere du Commerce et de l'Approvisionnement du Peuple.

Chandavarkar, A. G. (1971) 'Some Aspects of Interest Rate Policies in Less Developed Economies: The Experience of Selected Asian Countries', *IMF Staff Papers*, Vol. 18, No. 3.

Chander, R., Robless, C. L. and Teh, K. P. (1981) 'Malaysian Growth and Price Stabilization', in Cline *et al.* (eds) *World Inflation and the Developing Countries*, Washington, The Brookings Institution.

Chapman, J. *et al.* (1986) 'Cambio Tecnologico y Relacciones Sociales de

Produccion: Los Pequenos Productores del Distrito de Pejibaye, Costa Rica', in
Pineiro, M. E. and Llovet, I. (ed), *Transicion Technologica y Diferenciacion
Social*, San Jose, Servicio Editorial IICA.

Child, F. C. (1977) 'Small Scale Rural Industry in Kenya', *Occasional Paper No.
17*, Los Angeles, UCLA, African Studies Centre.

Child, F. C. and Kaneda, H. (1975) 'Links to the Green Revolution: A Study of
Small-Scale Agricultural-Related Industry in the Pakistan Punjab', *Economic
Development and Cultural Change*, Vol. 23, No. 2.

Chuta, E. and Liedholm, C. (1976) 'The Economics of Rural and Urban Small-
Scale Industries in Sierra Leone', *African Rural Economy Paper, No. 14*, East
Lansing, Michigan, Michigan State University.

Chuta, E. and Liedholm, C. (1979) 'Rural Non-Farm Employment: A Review of
the State of the Art', *MSU Rural Development Paper No. 4*. East Lansing,
Michigan, Michigan State University.

Chuta, E. and Liedholm, C. (1985) *Employment and Growth in Small Industry:
Empirical Evidence and Assessment from Sierra Leone*, London, Macmillan.

Chuta, E. and Liedholm, C. (1985) *Employment and Growth in Small-Scale
Industry*, New York, St Martins Press.

Clarete, R. L. and Roumasset, J. A. (1983), 'An Analysis of the Economic Policies
Affecting the Philippine Coconut Industry,' Working Paper 83–08, Makati
Philippine Institute for Development Studies.

Clark, W. E. (1978) *Socialist Development and Public Investment in Tanzania*,
Toronto, University of Toronto Press.

Clay, E. J. and Singer, H. W. (1982) 'Food Aid and Development: The Impact and
Effectiveness of Bilateral PL 480 Title I Type Assistance', *AID Program
Evaluation Paper No. 15*.

Cline, W. and Weintraub, S. (eds) (1981) *Economic Stabilization in Developing
Countries*, Washington, The Brookings Institution.

Cline, W. *et al.* (1981) *World Inflation and the Developing Countries*, Washington
DC, The Brookings Institution.

Cody, J., Hughes, H. and Wall, S. (1980) *Policies for Industrial Progress in
Developing Countries*, New York, Oxford University Press.

Cohen, J., Grindle, M. S. and Walker, S. Tjip, (1984) 'Policy Space and
Administrative Systems Research in Donor-Led Rural Development', *Development Discussion Paper No. 166*, Cambridge, Massachusetts, Harvard Institute
for International Development (May).

Cohen, J., Grindle, M. S. and Walker, S. Tjip, (1985) 'Foreign Aid and Conditions
Precedent: Political and Bureaucratic Dimensions', *World Development*, Vol.
13, No. 12.

Cohn, E. J. and Eriksson, J. R. (1972) 'Employment and Income Distribution
Objectives for AID Programmes and Policies', Policy Background Paper,
Bureau for PPC, Washington DC, Agency for International Development.

Cooper, C. (1972) 'Science, Technology and Production in Underdeveloped
Countries', *Journal of Development Studies*, Vol. 9, No. 1.

Cornia, G. A., Jolly, R. and Stewart, F. (1987) *Adjustment with a Human Face*,
Oxford, Oxford University Press.

Cortes, M., Berry, A. and Ishaq, A. (1988) *Success in Small and Medium Scale
Enterprises: The Evidence from Colombia*, New York, Oxford University Press.

Coulson, A. (1974) 'The Automated Bread Factory', in *African Socialism in
Practice: The Case of Tanzanian Experience*, Coulson, A. (ed), Nottingham,
Spokesman Books.

Coulson, A. (1982) *Tanzania: A Political Economy*, Oxford, Oxford University Press.

Crane, D. (1977) 'Technological Innovation in Developing Countries: A Review of the Literature', *Research Policy*, Vol. 6.

CSO (1985a) *Census of Production 1982/83*, Harare.

CSO (1985b) 'Main Demographic Features of the Population of Zimbabwe: An advance report based on a 10 per cent sample', Harare.

Culbertson, R., Jones, E. and Corpeno, R. (1983) 'Private Sector Evaluation: The Dominican Republic', *USAID Evaluation Special Study No. 16*, Washington DC, AID.

Dahlman, C. J., Ross-Larson, B. and Westphal, L. E. (1987) 'Managing Technological Development: Lessons from the Newly Industrializing Countries', *World Development*, Vol. 15, No. 6.

DANE (1978) *Industria Manufactureia 1975*, Bogota.

David, C. C. (1983a), 'Economic Policies and Agricultural Incentives,' *Philippine Economic Journal* Vol. 11.

David, C. C. (1983b), 'Government Policies and Farm Mechanization in the Philippines,' in *The Consequences of Small Rice Farm Mechanization in the Philippines*, Workshop Papers, Development Academy of the Philippines.

Dawson, J. 'Small-Scale Industry Development in Ghana: A Case Study of Kumasi', in Thomas, H. and Uribe-Echevarria, F. (eds) *Small-Scale Industrialization; Urban and Regional Perspectives*, Institute of Social Studies, The Hague, Forthcoming.

de Haan, H. H. (1989) *Alternatives in Industrial Development*, Newburg Park, CA, Sage Publications.

de Haen, H. (1974) 'Aggregate Policy Models of the Sierra Leone Economy with Special Emphasis on the Small-Scale Economy', unpublished.

de Janvry, A. and Sadoulet, E. (1983) 'Social Articulation as a Condition for Equitable Growth', *Journal of Development Economics*, 13, pp. 275–303.

de Melo, J. A. P. (1977) 'Distortions in the Factor Market: Some General Equilibrium Estimates', *Review of Economics and Statistics*, Vol. 59, No. 4.

de Melo, J. A. P. (1978) 'Estimating the Costs of Protection: A General Equilibrium Approach', *Quarterly Journal of Economics*, Vol. 92.

de Melo, J. A. P. and Robinson, S. (1980) 'Impact of Trade Policies on Income Distribution in a Planning Model for Colombia', *Journal of Policy Modelling*, Vol. 2, No. 1.

de Melo, M. H. (1979) 'Agricultural Policies and Development: A Socioeconomic Investigation Applied to Sri Lanka', *Journal of Policy Modelling*, Vol. 1, No. 2.

Dell, S. (ed) (1987) *The International Monetary System and Its Reform*, Amsterdam, North-Holland.

Diaz-Alejandro, C. F. (1983) 'Trade and the Import Control System in Colombia: Some Quantifiable Features', in Berry, A. (ed) *Essays on Industrialization in Colombia*, Centre for Latin American Studies, Tempe, Arizonia State University.

Dixon, P. B., Parmenter, B. R. and Powell, A. A. (1984) 'Trade Liberalization and Labour Market Disruption', *Journal of Policy Modeling*, Vol. 6, No. 4.

Donald, G. (1976) *Credit for Small Farms in Developing Countries*, Boulder, Colorado, Westview Press.

Dornbusch, R. and Helmers, F. (eds) (1988) *The Open Economy: Tools for Policymakers in Developing Countries*, New York, Oxford University Press.

Doryan-Garron, E. (1989) 'Macroeconomic Policy, Technological Change and Rural Development: The Costa Rica Case', paper presented at a Conference on Policy Approaches Toward Technology and Small Enterprise Development, Institute of Social Studies, The Hague.

Dougherty, C. and Selowsky, M. (1973) 'Measuring the Effects of the Misallocation of Labour', *Review of Economics and Statistics*, Vol. 55.

Duff, B. (1987) 'Changes in Small Farm Paddy Threshing Technology in Thailand and the Philippines', in Stewart F. (ed) *Macro-Policies for Appropriate Technology in Developing Countries,* Boulder, Col., Westview Press.

Dunlop, D. W. (1983) 'A Comparative Analysis of Policies and Other Factors Which Affect the Role of the Private Sector in Economic Development, *AID Programme Evaluation Discussion Paper No. 20,* Washington DC, AID (December).

Dunlop, D. W., Adamczyk, C., Ohen, H. and Hammergren, L. (1983) 'A Comparative Analysis of Five PL 480 Title I Impact Evaluation Studies', *AID Programme Evaluation Discussion Paper No. 19.*

Eckaus, R. S. (1955) 'The Factor Proportion Problem in Underdeveloped Areas', *American Economic Review,* Vol. 45.

Edwards, E. O. (1974) *Employment in Developing Countries,* New York, Columbia University Press.

Ellis, F. (1988) *Peasant Economics: Farm Households and Agrarian Development,* Cambridge, Cambridge University Press.

Emerson, C. and Warr, P. G. (1981), 'Economic Evaluation of Mineral Processing Projects: A Case Study of Copper Smelting in the Philippines,' *Philippine Economic Journal* Vol. 20.

Emmanuel, A. (1982) *Appropriate or Underdeveloped Technology,* John Wiley, Chichester.

Eriksson, J. R. (1970) 'Wage Change and Employment Growth in Latin American Industry', *Research Memorandum No. 36,* Williamstown, Mass, Williams College.

Fapohunda, O., Reijmerink, J. and van Dijk, M. P. (1975) 'Urban Development, Income Distribution and Employment in Lagos', *Urbanization and Employment Programme Working Paper No. 13,* Geneva, World Employment Programme, ILO.

Farrell, M. J. (1957) 'The Measurement of Productive Efficiency', *Journal of the Royal Statistical Society,* Series A, Vol. 20.

Felix, D. (1974) 'Technological Dualism in Late Industrializers: On Theory, History and Policy', *Journal of Economic History,* Vol. 34.

Felix, D. (1977) 'Latin American Power: Take Off or Plus C'est La Meme Chose', *Studies in Comparative International Development,* Vol. 12, No. 1.

Fields, G. S. (1984) 'Employment, Income Distribution and Economic Growth in Seven Small Open Economies', *Economic Journal,* Vol. 94.

Figueroa Ibarra, C. (1976) *The Rural Proletariat in Agro-Guatemala,* Institute of Economic Research, University of San Carlos of Guatemala.

Fisseha, Y. (1982) 'Management Characteristics, Practices, and Performance in the Small-Scale Manufacturing Enterprises: Jamaica Milieu', PhD dissertation, Department of Agricultural Economics, Michigan State University.

Fisseha, Y. and Milimo, J. (1985) 'Small Enterprises in Zambia: Summary of Survey Results', paper presented to African Studies Association Meeting, New Orleans.

FitzGerald, E. V. K. (1976) 'The Urban Service Sector, the Supply of Wagegoods and the Shadow Wagerate', *Oxford Economic Papers,* Vol. 28, No. 2.

FitzGerald, E. V. K. (1988) 'A Kaleckian Approach to the Macroeconomics of the Semi-industrialized Economy', *Working Paper (Sub-series on Money, Finance and Development),* No. 28, The Hague, Institute of Social Studies.

FitzGerald, E. V. K. (1989) 'The Impact of Macroeconomic Policies on Small-Scale Industry: Some Analytical Considerations', paper presented at a Conference on Policy Approaches Toward Technology and Small Enterprise Development, Institute of Social Studies, The Hague.

FitzGerald, E. V. K., Jansen, K. and Vos, R. (1989) 'Structural Asymmetries, Adjustment and the Debt Problem', in *Dealing with the Debt Crisis*, Fisher, S. (ed), Washington DC, IBRD.

FitzGerald, E. V. K. and Vos, R. (1989) *Financing Economic Development: a Structural Approach to Monetary Policy*, Aldershot, Gower.

Fletcher, L. B. (1982) *Improving Planning and Policy Analysis Capabilities in Developing Countries*, Ames, Iowa, Iowa State University Press.

Fletcher, L. B., Artero, R. P., Ibanex-Meier, C., Jiron, R., McCormick, K. and Larson, K. H. (1981) *'Manuals for Policy Analysis: Price and Market Intervention Policies'*, Ames, Iowa, Iowa State University Press.

Flores Alvarado, H. (1971) *Proletarization of the Peasant in Guatemala*, Guatemala, Editorial Rumbos Nuevos.

Forsyth, D. and Mubin, A. K. A. (1980) 'Appropriate Products, Employment and Income Distribution in Bangladesh: A Case Study of the Soap Industry', *WEP Research Working Paper*, ILO, Geneva.

Foxley, A. and Whitehead, L. (1980) 'Economic Stabilization in Latin America: Political Dimensions', *World Development*, Vol. 8, No. 11.

Frank, C. R. (1968) 'Urban Unemployment and Economic Growth in Africa', *Oxford Economic Papers*, No. 3.

Frank, C., Kim, K. S. and Westphal, L. E. (1978) *Foreign Trade Regimes and Economic Development: South Korea*, Cambridge, Ballinger.

Frank, C. R. and Webb, R. C. (1977) *Income Distribution and Growth in Less Developed Countries*, Washington DC, The Brookings Institution.

Fransman, M. (ed) (1982) *Industry and Accumulation in Africa*, London, Heinemann.

FUNDAP (no date) *Handcrafts and Popular Arts on the Rise*, Momostenango, Guatemala, FUNDAP Brochure.

FUNDAP (1986) *Momostenango Project*, Foundation for the Integral Development of Socioeconomic Projects, Quetzaltenango.

Galbis, V. (1977) 'Financial Intermediation and Economic Growth in Less Developed Countries: A Theoretical Approach', *Journal of Development Studies*, Vol. 13, No. 2.

Gasper, D. R. (1989) *Growth Points and Rural Industries: Ideologies and Policies*, RUP Occasional Paper No. 18, Department of Rural and Urban Planning, University of Zimbabwe.

Gaude, J. (1975) 'Capital-Labour Substitutions Possibilities: A Review of the Empirical Evidence', in Bhalla, A. S. (ed) *Technology and Employment in Industry*, Geneva: ILO.

General Secretariat of the National Council on Economic Planning, (1988) *Socio-Demographic Characteristics of the Population*, Guatemala, Government of Guatemala, Project GUA-85-PO2.

General Secretariat of the National Council on Economic Planning, *Characterization of Region VI*, Guatemala, Government of Guatemala.

Gibb, A. (1974) 'Agricultural Modernization, Non-Farm Employment and Low Level Urbanization: A Case Study of a Central Luzon Sub-Region', PhD Thesis, University of Michigan.

Gillis, M. (1980) *The Role of State Enterprises in Economic Development*, Harvard Institute for International Development, Discussion Paper No. 83.

Giovanni, A. (1985) 'Savings and the Real Interest Rate in LDCs', *Journal of Development Economics*, Vol. 18.

Golay, F. H. (1961), *The Philippines: Public Policy and National Economic Development*, Ithaca, Cornell University Press.

466

Gold, B. (1981) 'Changing Perspectives on Size, Scale and Returns: An Interpretative Survey', *Journal on Economic Literature*, Vol. 19, No. 1.

Gomez, E. (1974) *Structure and Level of Development of Business in Momostenango*, Guatemala, University of San Carlos.

Gosses, A., Molenaar, K. and Teszler, R. (eds) 'Small-Scale Enterprise Development in Search of New Dutch Approaches: Proceedings of a Workshop, March 6–7, 1989', Directorate General International Cooperation, Ministry of Foreign Affairs, The Hague.

Government of Bangladesh (1980) *Pilot Manpower Survey*, Bangladesh Bureau of Statistics.

Government of Bangladesh (1985) *Third Five Year Plan 1985–90*, Planning Commission, December.

Government of Bangladesh (1986a) *Industrial Policy 1986*, Ministry of Industries.

Government of Bangladesh (1986b) *National Science and Technology Policy*, Ministry of Education.

Government of Bangladesh (1986) *Statistical Pocket Book of Bangladesh*, Bangladesh Bureau of Statistics.

Government of Bangladesh (1987) *Report of the First Meeting of the Consultative Committee on Transfer of Technology*, Ministry of Education.

Government of Botswana (1980) *National Development Plan, 1979–1985*, Gaborone, Ministry of Finance and Development Planning.

Government of Botswana (1982) 'The Development of Productive Employment: A Policy for Financial Assistance', Interministerial Working Group, Gaborone: Ministry of Finance and Development Planning.

Government of Botswana (1982) 'Financial Assistance Policy, 1982', *Government Paper No. 1 of 1982*, Gaborone, Ministry of Finance and Development Planning.

Government of Jamaica (1981) *National Income and Production, 1981*, Department of Statistics.

Government of the Republic of Guatemala (1987) *Second Presidential Memorandum of the Republic*, May.

Government of Zimbabwe (1983) 'Transitional National Development Plan (TNDP) 1982/83–1984/85', Vol. 2, May.

Government of Zimbabwe (1986), First Five-Year Development Plan 1986–90, Vol. 1, April.

Green, R. (1988) 'Operational Relevance of Third World Multinationals to Collective Self-Reliance: Some Problems, Provocations and Possibilities' in Singer, H., Hatti, N. and Tandon, R. (eds) *Technology Transfer by Multinationals*, New Delhi, Ashish Publishing House.

Gregorio, R. G. (1979), 'An Economic Analysis of the Effects of the Philippine Fiscal Incentives for Industrial Promotion,' unpublished Ph.D. thesis, University of the Philippines.

Gregory, P. (1974) 'Wage Structure in Latin America', *Journal of Developing Areas*, Vol. 8, No. 4.

Gregory, P. (1975) 'The Impact of Institutional Factors on Urban Labour Markets', *Studies in Employment and Rural Development No. 27*, Washington DC, World Bank.

Gregory, P. (1980) 'An Assessment of Changes in Employment Conditions in Less Developed Countries', *Economic Development and Cultural Change*, Vol. 28, No. 4.

Griffin, K. B. and Enos, J. L. (1973) 'Policies for Industrialization', in *Underdevelopment and Development: The Third World Today*, Bernstein, H. (ed) Harmondsworth, Baltimore and Ringwood, Penguin Books.

Grindle, M. (ed) (1980) *The Politics of Policy Implementation in the Third World*, Princeton University Press.

Guisinger, S. (1978) 'Wages, Capital Rental Values, and Relative Factor Prices in Pakistan', *World Bank Staff Working Paper No. 287*, Washington DC, World Bank.

Guisinger, S. (1981) 'Trade Policies and Employment: The Case of Pakistan', in Kreugér, A. O. *et al.* (eds) *Trade and Employment in Developing Countries*, Chicago, University of Chicago Press.

Gulick, C. S. and Nelson, J. M. (1965) 'Promoting Effective Employment Policies: AID Experience in Developing Countries', Washington DC, AID/PPC.

Gutierrez, R. (1988) 'The FUNDAP-Momostenango Project', paper prepared for the first Latin American Conference on Economic Policy, Technology and Rural Productivity, Mexico City.

Hageboeck, M. and Allen, M. B. (1982) 'Private Sector: Ideas and Opportunities: A Review of Basic Concepts and Selected Experiences', *AID Programme Evaluation Discussion Paper No. 14*, Washington DC, AID.

Haggblade, S. (1983) 'The Shebeen Queen or Sorghum Beer in Botswana: The Impact of Factory Brews on a Cottage Industry', East Lansing, Michigan State University, PhD thesis.

Haggblade, S. (1984) 'Private Sector Assessment: Synthesis Report for Burkina Faso', Ouagadougou, USAID, unpublished.

Haggblade, S., Liedholm, C. and Mead, D. C. (1986) 'The Effect of Policy and Policy reforms on Non-Agricultural Enterprises and Employment in Developing Countries: A Review of Past Experiences', Employment and Enterprise Analysis Discussion Paper, 1, Washington DC, USAID.

Hansen, B. and Radawan, S. (1982) *Employment Opportunities and Equity in a Changing Economy: Egypt in the 1980's*, Geneva, ILO.

Hanson, J. A. and Neal, C. R. (1985) 'Interest Rate Policies in Selected Developing Countries, 1970–82', *World Bank Staff Working Paper No. 753*, Washington DC, World Bank.

Harberger, A. (1959) 'Using the Resources at Hand More Effectively', *American Economic Review*, Vol. 49 Supplement.

Harberger, A. (1962) 'The Incidence of the Corporation Income Tax', *Journal of Political Economy* Vol. 70, No. 3.

Harrod, J. (1987) *Power, Production and the Unprotected Worker*, New York, Columbia University Press.

Harvard University Development Advisory Service (later, Harvard Institute for International Development), *Annual Reports*.

Hassan, M. F. (1975) *Economic Growth and Employment Problems in Venezuela*, New York, Praeger.

Havnevik, K. J., Skarstein, R. and Wangwe, S. (1985) 'Small-Scale Industry Sector in Tanzania', Report to Ministry of Industry and Trade.

Hazari, B. R. and Krishnamurty, J. (1970) 'Employment Implications of India's Industrialization: Analysis of an Input–Output Framework', *Review of Economics and Statistics*, Vol. 52, No. 2.

Hazell, P. and Roell, A. (1983) 'Rural Growth Linkages: Household Expenditure Patterns in Malaysia and Nigeria', *International Food Policy Research Institute Report No. 41*, Washington DC.

Healey, D. T. (1972) 'Development Policy: New Thinking About an Interpretation', *Journal of Economic Literature*, Vol. 10, No. 3.

Helleiner, G. K. (1983) 'The IMF and Africa in the 1980s', *Essays in International Finance No. 152*.

Helleiner, G. K. (1988) 'Growth-Oriented Adjustment Lending: A Critical

Assessment of IMF/World Bank Approaches', paper prepared for the South Commission, Geneva.

Herrin, A. and Pernia E. M. (1987), 'Factors Affecting the Choice of Location: A Survey of Foreign and Local Firms in the Philippines,' *Journal of Philippine Development* Vol. 24.

Hi Hermann, W. (1986) *Ovine Reports in Guatemala*, Quetzaltenango, Guatemala, FUNDAP.

Hi Hermann, W. (1988) *El Redileo Programme of Ovine Development*, Quetzaltenango, Guatemala, FUNDAP-DIGESPE.

Hiemenz, U. and Bruch, M. (1983) 'Small and Medium Scale Manufacturing Establishments in ASEAN Countries: Perspectives and Policy Issues', *Asian Development Bank Working Paper No. 14*.

Hifo, E. A. (1979), 'Survey Results on the Impact of Industrial Policies on Small Industry Development,' in Bautista, Power and Associates, *Industrial Promotion Policies in the Philippines*, Makati, Philippine Institute for Development Studies.

Higgins, B. (1978) 'Development Poles: Do They Exist?', in Lo, F. C. and Salih K. (eds) *Growth Pole Strategy and Regional Development Policy*, Oxford, Pergamon.

Hintermeister, A. (1985) 'Agricultural Modernization and Rural Poverty in Guatemala', *Revista Polemica*, San Jose, Costa Rica, ICADIS.

Hirschman, A. O. (1963) *Journeys Toward Progress: Studies of Economic Policy-Making in Latin America*, New York, Greenwood Press.

Ho, S. P. S. (1979) 'Decentralized Industrialization and Rural Development: Evidence from Taiwan' in *Economic Development and Cultural Change*, Vol. 28, No. 1.

Ho, S. P. S. (1980) 'Small-Scale Enterprises in Korea and Taiwan', *World Bank Staff Working Paper No. 384*, Washington DC, World Bank.

Hogg, M. (1978) 'Contributions of Industrialization to Rural Development', in *Industrialization and Rural Development*, UNIDO, Vienna.

Hogwood, Brian W. and B. Guy Peters (1983) *Policy Dynamics*, New York, St. Martin's Press.

Hong, Wontack (1981) 'Export Promotion and Employment Growth in South Korea.' In *Trade and Employment in Developing Countries* edited by Anne O. Krueger *et al.* Chicago, University of Chicago Press.

Hooley, Richard (1981) 'An Assessment of the Macroeconomic Policy Framework for Employment Generation in the Philippines', a report submitted to USAID/Philippines. Manila, USAID (April).

Hooley, Richard (1985), *Productivity Growth in Philippine Manufacturing: Retrospect and Future Prospects*, Monograph Series No. 9, Makati, Philippine Institute for Development Studies.

Hopcraft, P. (1979) 'Industrialization, Balance of Payments and Trade Policy in Kenya: Effects of Protectionism and Government Intervention on Prices, Exports and Income Distribution', Institute for Development Studies, University of Nairobi, unpublished.

Hopcraft, P. and Oguttu, J. (1982) *Parastatal Development Agencies and Their Relationship with the Private Sector*, Institute for Development Studies, University of Nairobi Occasional Paper No. 39.

Hopkins, M. and van der Hoeven, R. (1982) 'Survey: Policy Analysis in a Socioeconomic Model of Basic Needs Applied to Four Countries', *Journal of Policy Modelling*, Vol. 4, No. 3.

House, W. J. (1980) 'Technological Choice, Employment Generation, Income Distribution and Consumer Demand: The Case of Furniture Making in Kenya', *WEP Research Working Paper*, ILO. Geneva.

Howe, G. N. (1984) 'The Small-Scale Enterprise Sectors in Egypt: A Critical

Analysis of Seven Selected Studies', Washington DC, AID/NE Office of Technical Support, Social Analysis and Rural Development Division.

Hutchenson, T. L. (1973) *Incentives for Industrialization in Colombia*, dissertation, University of Michigan, Ann Arbor.

Hyden, G. (1979) 'Administration and Public Policy', in Barkan, J. and Okumu, J. (eds) *Politics and Public Policy in Kenya and Tanzania*, New York, Praeger.

Hyman, E. (1988) 'The Design of Micro-Projects and Macro-Policies: Examples from Three of ATI's Projects in Africa', paper prepared for Conference on the Implications of Technology Choice on Economic Development, Nairobi, August 29–31.

Hymer, S. and Resnick, S. (1969) 'A Model of an Agrarian Economy with Non-Agricultural Activities', in *American Economic Review*, Vol. 50.

IBRD (1977a) *Tanzania: Basic Industry Report*.

IBRD (1977b) *Tanzania: Appraisal of the Morogoro Industrial Complex*.

IBRD (1978) *Employment and Development of Small Enterprises*, Washington DC, World Bank Sector Policy Paper.

IBRD (1978) *Tanzania Second Cashewnut Development Project, Staff Appraisal Report*.

IBRD (1983) *Kenya: Growth and Structural Change*.

IDTC (1989) 'Industrial Development and Technical Change, Mission Phasing PAK Holland Metal Project-2', Directorate General International Cooperation, Ministry of Foreign Affairs, The Hague.

Ilchman, W. F. and Uphoff, N. T. (1969) *The Political Economy of Change*, Berkely, University of California Press.

ILO (1970) *Towards Full Employment: A Programme for Columbia*, Geneva, ILO.

ILO (1971) *Matching Employment Opportunities and Expectations: A programme of Action for Ceylon*, Geneva, ILO.

ILO (1972) *Employment, Incomes and Equality: A Strategy for Increasing Productive Employment in Kenya*, Geneva, ILO.

ILO (1973) *Employment and Income Policy for Iran*, Geneva, ILO.

ILO (1973a) *Strategies for Employment Promotion: An Evaluation of Four Inter-Agency Employment Missions*, Geneva, ILO.

ILO (1973b) *Strategies for Employment*, Geneva, ILO.

ILO (1974) *Sharing in Development: A Programme for Employment, Equity and Growth for the Philippines*, Geneva, ILO.

ILO (1975) *Generacion de Empleo, Productivo y Crecimeinto Economic: El Caso de la Republica Dominicana*, Geneva, ILO.

ILO (1976) *Growth, Employment, and Equity: A Comprehensive Strategy for the Sudan*, Geneva, ILO.

IMF (1987) 'Theoretical Aspects of the Design of Fund-Supported Adjustment Programmes', *Occasional Paper No. 55*, Washington DC, IMF.

Industrial Studies and Development Centre, (1975) *Tender Document for a Turnkey Project for a Multi-Purpose Oil Mill Company*, Dar-es-Salaam.

Industrial Studies and Development Centre, (1975b) *Evaluation of Tender Bids for a Multipurpose Oilseed Processing Plant for Morogoro*, Dar-es-Salaam.

Ingram, W. and Pearson, S.R. (1981) 'The Impact of Concessions on the Profitability of Selected Firms in Ghana', *Economic Development and Cultural Change*, Vol. 29, No. 4.

Intal, P. S. and Power, J. H. (1987), 'Government Interventions and Philippine Agriculture,' paper prepared for the World Bank (mimeo).

Inter-American Development Bank, (1987) *Economic and Social Progress in Latin America*, Washington, DC.

Isaacsson, J., Kaplinsky, R. and O'Dell, M. (1984) 'Report on Evaluation on FAP, unpublished.

Islam, N. (1986) 'Non-Farm Employment in Rural Asia: Issues and Evidence', in Shand, (ed), *Off-Farm Employment in the Development of Rural Asia*, National Centre for Development Studies Conference, Australian National University, 1983.

James, J. (1980) 'Employment Effects of an Income Redistribution', *Journal of Development Economics*, Vol. 7.

James, J. (1983) 'Bureaucratic Engineering and Economic Men: Decision-Making for Technology in Tanzania's State-Owned Enterprises', ILO, World Employment Programme Research, Technology and Employment Programme, Working Paper No. 125.

James, J. (1985) 'Bureaucratic, Engineering and Economic Men: Decision-Making for Technology in Tanzania's State-Owned Enterprises', in Lall, S. and Stewart, F. (eds) *Theory and Reality in Development: Essays in Honour of Paul Streeten*, London, Macmillan.

James, J. (1987) 'The Choice of Technology in Public Enterprise: A Comparative Study of Manufacturing Industry in Kenya and Tanzania', in Stewart, F. (ed) *Macro-Policies for Appropriate Technology in Developing Countries,* Boulder, Col., Westview Press.

Jansen, D. (1980) 'Agricultural Pricing Policy in Sub-Saharan Africa in the 1970s', cited in Bates, R. H. (1983) *The Private Sector: The Regulation of Rural Markets in Africa,* Washington DC, USAID Evaluation Study No. 14.

Jenkins, J. B. (1974) 'Policy Impact Evaluation', Washington, DC, AID/PPC/E, unpublished.

Jhaveri, N. J. (1981) 'Needs and Strategy for Industrial Development of Backward Areas', in Industrial Development Bank of India *Industrial Development of Backward Areas*, Bombay.

Jimenez, G. (1972) 'The Capital, Labour and Import Content of Urban Consumption Patterns in Colombia', MA thesis, Houston, Tx, Rice University.

Johnson, O. and Salop, J. (1980) 'Distributional Aspects of Stabilization Programmes in Developing Countries', *IMF Staff Papers*, Vol. 27, No. 1.

Joshi, H., Lubell, H. and Mouly, J. (1974) 'Urban Development and Employment in Abidjan', *Urbanization and Employment Working Paper* No. 4, Geneva, World Employment Programme, ILO.

Kaldor, N. (1965) in Robinson R. (ed) *Industrialization in Developing Countries*, Cambridge Overseas Committee.

Kalmanovitz, S. (1978) *El Desarrollo de la Agricultura en Colombia*, Bogota, Editorial La Cavreta.

Kaneda, H. and Child, F. (1975) 'Small-Scale Agriculturally Related Industry in the Punjab', *Economic Development and Cultural Change*, Jan. 23:2.

Kannappan, S. (1977) *Studies of Urban Labour Market Behaviour in Developing Areas*, Geneva, International Institute for Labour Studies.

Kannappan, S. (1983) *Employment Problems and the Urban Labour Market in Developing Nations*, Ann Arbor, Division of Research, Business Administration, University of Michigan.

Kaplinsky, R. (1987) 'Appropriate Technology in Sugar Manufacturing', in Stewart F. (ed) *Macro-Policies for Appropriate Technology in Developing Countries*, Boulder, Col., Westview Press.

Karunatilake, H. N. S. (1982) 'The Impact of Sri Lanka's Economic Reforms in 1977 on Employment and Income Distribution', *Philippine Review of Economics and Business*, Vol. 19.

471

Katz, J. (1980) 'Domestic Technology Generation in LDCs: A Review of Research Findings', IDB/ECLA Research programme in Science and Technology, Working Paper 35, Buenos Aires.

Kilby, P. (1967) 'Industrial Relations and Wage Determination: Failure of the Anglo-Saxon Model', *Journal of Developing Areas*, Vol. 1, No. 4.

Kilby, P. (1982) 'Small Scale Industry in Kenya', *Working Paper No. 20, MSU Rural Development Series*. East Lansing, Michigan, Department of Agricultural Economics, Michigan State University.

Killick, T. (1978) *Development Economics in Action: A Study of Economic Policies in Ghana*, London, Heinemann.

Killick, T. (ed) (1982) *Adjustment and Finance in the Developing World: The Role of the IMF*, Washington DC, IMF and Overseas Development Institute.

Killick, T. (ed) (1984) *The Quest for Economic Stabilization: The IMF and the Third World*, New York, St Martin's Press.

Kim, J. W. (1984) 'CES Production Functions in Manufacturing and Problems of Industrialization in LDCs: Evidence from Korea', *Economic Development and Cultural Change*, Vol. 33, No. 1.

King, R. P. and Byerlee, D. (1977) *Income Distribution, Consumption Patterns and Consumption Linkages in Rural Sierra Leone*, African Rural Employment Paper No. 16, East Lansing, Michigan State University.

King, R. P. and Byerlee, D. (1978) 'Factor Intensities and Locational Linkages of Rural Consumption Patterns in Sierra Leone', *American Journal of Agricultural Economics*, Vol. 60, No. 2.

Knight, J. B. (1968) 'Earnings, Employment, Education and Income Distribution in Uganda', *Bulletin of the Oxford University Institute of Economics and Statistics*, Vol. 30, No. 4.

Knight, J. B. and Sabot, R. (1980) 'Why Wages Differ', Washington DC, World Bank, unpublished.

Kogi, K. (1985) 'Improving Working Conditions in Small Enterprises in Developing Asia', Geneva, ILO.

Krishna, R. (1976) 'Rural Unemployment – A Survey of Concepts and Estimates for India', *World Bank Staff Working Paper No. 234*, Washington DC: World Bank.

Krueger, A.O. (1966) 'Some Economic Costs of Exchange Control: The Turkish Case', *The Journal of Political Economy*, Vol. 74.

Krueger, A. O. (1978) *Foreign Trade Regimes and Economic Development (11 Volumes)*. Cambridge, Ballinger.

Krueger, A. O., Lary, H. B., Monson, T. and Akrasanee, N, (eds) (1983) *Trade and Employment in Developing Countries: Individual Studies*. Chicago: University of Chicago Press for the NBER.

Laenen, A. (1988) *Dinamica y Transformacion de la Pequena Industria en Nicaragua*, Amsterdam, CEDLA.

Laky, T. 'Small Business Organizations in the Hungarian Economy', in Thomas, H. and Uribe-Echevarria, F. (eds) *Small-Scale Industralization*, forthcoming.

Lall, S. (1987) *Learning to Industrialize: The Acquisition of Technological Capability by India*, London, Macmillan.

Lamberte, M. B. *et al.* (1985), *A Review and Appraisal of the Government Response to the 1983–84 Balance of Payments Crisis,* Monograph Series No. 8, Makati, Philippine Institute for Development Studies.

Lecraw, D. C. (1979) 'Choice of Technology in Low-Wage Countries: a Non Neoclassical Approach', *The Quarterly Journal of Economics*, Vol. XCIII.

Leff, N. H. (1976) 'Capital Markets in the Less Developed Countries: the Group

Principle', in McKinnon, R. I. (ed) *Money and Finance in Economic Growth and Development*, New York, Dekker.

Leibenstein, H. (1957) 'The Theory of Underemployment in Backward Economics', *Journal of Political Economy*, Vol. 65.

Leith, J. C. (1974) *Foreign Trade Regimes and Economic Development: Ghana.* New York, National Bureau of Economic Research.

Leon, L., Aguilar, J. and Barboza, C. (1982) *A Scientific Technological Analysis of the Agricultural Sector of Costa Rica*, San Jose, Conicit.

Leon, J., Aguilar, J. and Barboza, C. (1982) *An Analysis of the Scientific-Technological Development of the Agricultural Sector of Costa Rica*, Conicit, August.

Lessard, D. and Williamson, J. (eds) (1987) *Capital Flight and Third World Debt*, Washington DC, Institute for International Economics.

Levine, R. A. (1981) 'Programme Evaluation and Policy Analysis in Western Nations: An Overview', in Levine, R. A., Salomon, M. A., Hellstern, G–M. and Wollman, H. (eds) *Evaluation Research and Practice: Comparative and International Perspectives.* Beverly Hills, Sage Publications.

Levitsky, J. (1985a) 'Policy Issues in Relation to Assistance Programmes for Small and Medium Enterprise Development' Industry Department, World Bank, paper presented at the Regional Meeting of Donor Agencies on Small-Scale Enterprise Development in Latin America, Quito, Ecuador.

Levitsky, J. (1985b) 'Review of World Bank Lending to Small Enterprises', Financial Development Unit, Industry Department of the World Bank.

Liedholm, C. (1985) 'Small Scale Enterprise Credit Schemes: Administrative Costs and the Role of Inventory Norms'. *MSU International Development Working Paper No. 25.* East Lansing, Mi, Michigan State University.

Liedholm, C. and Chuta, E. (1976) *The Economics of Rural and Urban Small Scale Industries in Sierra Leone*, African Rural Economy Paper No. 14, East Lansing, Michigan State University.

Liedholm, C. and Mead, D. C. (1986) 'Small Scale Enterprises in Developing Countries: A Review of the State of the Art' *MSU International Development Working Paper*, East Lansing, Michigan State University.

Liedholm, C. and Mead, D. C. (1987) 'Small-Scale Industries in Developing Countries: Empirical Evidence and Policy Implications', *MSU International Development Papers No. 9* Michigan State University.

Lipton, M. (1978) *Employment and Labour Use in Botswana*, Gaborone, The Ministry of Finance and Development Planning.

Lipton, M. (1978a) 'Impact of Minimum Wage Rise in July 1977 on Employment Summary of the key findings of the IDM-Szalwelski study)' in Lipton, M. (ed) *Employment and Labour Use in Botswana, Vol. II.* Gaborone, The Ministry of Finance and Development Planning.

Lipton, M. (1980) 'Family, Fungibility and Formality: Rural Advantages of Informal Non-Farm Enterprise Versus the Urban-Formal State', in Amin, S. (ed) *Human Resources, Employment and Development, Vol. 5: Developing Countries.* London, Macmillan.

Little, I. M. D. (1987) 'Small Manufacturing Enterprises in Developing Countries', *World Bank Economic Review*, Vol. 1, No. 2.

Little, I. M. D. (1988), 'Small Manufacturing Enterprises in Developing Countries', *The World Bank Economic Review,* Vol. 1, No. 2.

Little, I. M. D., Mazumdar, D. and Page, J. M. (1988) *Small Manufacturing Enterprise: A Comparative Study of India and Other Countries*, New York, Oxford University Press.

473

Little, I. M. D., Scitovsky, T. and Scott, M. (1970) *Industry and Trade in Some Developing Countries*. London, Oxford University Press.

Lizondo, J. S. (1985) 'Unifying Multiple Exchange Rates', *Finance and Development*, Vol. 22, No. 4.

Lluch, C. *et al.* (1977) *Patterns in Household Demand and Saving*, New York, Oxford University Press.

Lowi, T. J. (1964) 'American Business, Public Policy Case Studies and Political Theory', *World Politics*, Vol. 16, No. 4.

Loxley, J. and Saul, J. (1975) 'Multinationals, Workers and the Parastatals in Tanzania', *Review of African Political Economy, No. 2*.

Lubell, H. (1980) 'Egypt: Employment Issue'. Cairo, USAID.

Lubell, H. and Eriksson, J. (1981) 'Employment Generation in AID Country Strategies and Project Design'. Washington DC, AID/PPC, unpublished.

Lydall, H. F. (1975) *Trade and Employment: A Study of the Effects of Trade Expansion on Employment in Developed (and Developing) Countries*. Geneva, ILO.

Lydall, H. F. (1979) *A Theory of Income Distribution*, Oxford, Clarendon Press.

Marsden, K. (1981) 'Creating the Right Environment for Small Firms,' *Finance and Development*, December.

Marshall, A. (1966) 'Uses of Abstract Responding in Economics', Appendix D in *Principles of Economics (1890)*, Macmillan, p. 644.

Mason, E. S. (1985) 'The Harvard Institute for International Development and its Antecedents', *Harvard University Development Discussion Paper No. 187*.

Massel, B. F. (1969) 'Consistent Estimation of Expenditure Elasticities from Cross-Section Data on Households Producing Partly for Subsistence', *The Review of Economics and Statistics*, Vol. 51, No. 2.

Mathur, O. P. (1975) *Small Scale Industry in India: A Structural Analysis*, New Delhi.

Mazumdar, D. (1979) 'Paradigms in the Study of Urban Labour Markets in LDCs: A Reassessment in the Light of an Empirical Survey in Bombay City', *World Bank Staff Working Paper No. 366*, Washington DC.

Mazumdar, D. (1980) 'A Descriptive Analysis of the Role of Small-Scale Enterprises in the Indian Economy', Washington DC, World Bank, unpublished.

Mazumdar, D. and Ahmed, M. U. (1978) 'Labour Market Segmentation and the Determination of Earnings: A Case Study', *World Bank Staff Working Paper No. 366*, Washington DC, World Bank.

McKinnon, R. I. (1973) *Money and Capital in Economic Development*, Washington DC, Brookings.

McPherson, M. F. (1980) 'Essays on the Employment Problem in Zambia', PhD dissertation, Harvard University.

Medalla, E. M. (1979), 'Estimating the Shadow Price of Labor,' in Bautista, Power and Associates, *Industrial Promotion Policies in the Philippines*, Makati, Philippine Institute for Development Studies.

Medalla, E. M. (1986), 'Some Clarifications and Comments on the Issues on Import Liberalization Raised by Minister Conception,' *The Philippine Economist*, Vol. 1.

Mejia, W. (1979), 'Some Effects of Financial Policies on Industrial Promotion,' unpublished M. A. thesis, University of the Philippines.

Mellor, J. W. (1976), *The New Economics of Growth: A Strategy for India and the Developing World*, Ithaca, Cornell University Press.

Mellor, J. and Mudahar, M. (1974) 'Simulating a Developing Economy with Modernizing Agricultural Sector: Implications for Employment and Economic

Growth in India', *Cornell Agricultural Economic Occasional Paper No. 76*, Ithaca: Cornell University.

Mendel, F. (1982) 'Proto-Industrialization: The First Phase of the Industrialization Process', *Journal of Economic History*, Vol. 32.

MICIT, (1987) *The Evolution of Scientific-Technological Policy in Costa Rica and Other Successful Experiences in Technological Change*, Ministry of Science and Technology of Costa Rica, presented before the Fifth Extraordinary Meeting of the Commission for the Development of Scientific-Technological Policy for Central America and Panama (CTCAP), November.

MICIT, (1987) *National Programme of Sciences and Technology: 1986–1990*, Government of Costa Rica, National Press.

MIDEPLAN, (1987) National Development Plan 1986–1990, Vol. 1, Government of Costa Rica, San Jose, April.

Mihyo, P. (no date) The legal environment and the performance of public enterprises in Tanzania, University of Dar-es-Salaam.

Mihyo, P. (1981) 'Bargaining for Technology in Tanzania's Public Enterprises: Some Policy Issues', Dar-es-Salaam, University of Dar-es-Salaam, unpublished.

Mihyo, P. (1989) 'The Economic Crisis, Recovery Programmes and Labour in Tanzania', paper presented at Workshop on Change in the Labour Process in the Third World and Advanced Capitalist Countries, Institute of Social Studies, The Hague.

Ministry of Planning and Economic Affairs, (1982) *Structural Adjustment Programme for Tanzania*, Dar-es-Salaam.

Mlawa, M. M. (1983) 'The Acquisition of Technological Capability and Technical Change: A Study of Textile Industry in Tanzania', PhD Dissertation, University of Sussex.

Molina, J. J. (1988) *The Situation of the Artisan in Guatemala*, Quetzaltenango, Guatemala, FUNDAP.

Monson, T. (1981) 'Trade Strategies and Employment in the Ivory Coast', in Krueger *et al.*, *Trade and Employment in Developing Countries*. Chicago, University of Chicago Press.

Montes, G. and Candelo, R. (1981) 'El Crecimiento Industrial y la Generacion de Empleo en Colombia: entre la Substitucion de Importanciones y la Promocion de Exportaciones', in *Revista de Planeacion y Desarrollo*, Vol. 13, No. 1–2.

Moore, M. (1985) 'On the Political Economy of Stabilization', *World Development* Vol. 13, No. 9.

Moran, P. B. (1978), 'Regional Structure of Philippine Manufacturing, 1948–1974,' *Philippine Review of Business and Economics*, Vol. 15.

Moran, P. B. (1979), 'The Impact of Regional Dispersal Policies on the Location Choices of Some Manufacturing Firms,' in Bautista, Power, and Associates, *Industrial Promotion Policies in the Philippines*, Makati, Philippine Institute for Development Studies.

Morawetz, D. (1974) 'Employment Implications of Industrialization in Developing Countries: A Survey', *Economic Journal*, Vol. 84.

Morawetz, D. (1976) 'Elasticity of Substitution in Industry: What Do We Learn From Them?', *World Development*, Vol. 4.

Morley, S. A. and Williamson, J. G. (1973) 'The Impact of Demand on Labour Absorption and the Distribution of Earning: The Case of Brazil', *Rice University Programme of Development Studies Paper No. 39*, Houston, Tx, Rice University.

Morrison, T. and Arreaga-Rodas, K. (1981) 'Economic Liberalization in Developing Countries: Some Lessons from Three Case Studies: Sri Lanka, Egypt and Sudan', AID Discussion Paper No. 40, Washington DC, AID.

Mosley, P. (1987) 'Conditionality as Bargaining Process: Structural Adjustment Lending 1980–86', in *Essays in International Finance*, Princeton University, No. 168

Moyo, S. (1986) 'The Land Question', in *Zimbabwe: The Political Economy of Transition, 1980–86*, Mandeza, I. (ed), Codesria Book Series.

Muscat, R. (1984) 'AID Private Enterprise Policy Dialogue: Forms, Experience and Lessons', paper prepared for the President's Task Force on International Private Enterprise.

Nabli, M. (1981) 'Alternative Trade Policies and Employment in Tunisia', in Krueger *et al.*, *Trade and Employment in Developing Countries*, Chicago, University of Chicago Press.

Nagaraj, R. (1984) 'Subcontracting in Indian Manufacturing Industries: Analysis, Evidence and Issues', *Economic and Political Weekly*, Vol. 19.

Nagel, S. S. (1980) *Policy Evaluation: Making Optimum Decisions*. New York, Praeger.

Nayar, Deepak (1978) 'Industrial Development in India: Some Reflections on Growth and Stagnation', *Economic and Political Weekly*, Special Number, August.

Ncube, P. D. (1987) 'The International Monetary Fund and the Zambian Economy', in Havenik, K. J. (ed) *The IMF and the World Bank in Africa*, Uppsala, Scandinavian Institute of African Studies.

Ndegwa, P. (1979) *Review of Statutory Boards*. Report and Recommendations of the Committee appointed by His Excellency the President, Nairobi.

Ndegwa, P. (1982) *Working Party on Government Expenditures*. Report and Recommendations of the Committee appointed by His Excellency the President, Nairobi.

Ndlela, D. B. (1981) *Dualism in the Rhodesian Colonial Economy,* Lund Economic Studies, No. 22.

Ndlela, D. B. (1987) 'Technology Imports and Indigenous Technological Capacity Building: the Zimbabwean Case', in *Technology and Employment Programme Series, World Employment Programme Research Working Papers 173*, ILO, Geneva, March.

Ndlela, D. B. (1988) 'Macro-Policies for Appropriate Technology in Zimbabwean Industry', paper prepared for Conference on the Implications of Technology Choice on Economic Development, Nairobi, August 29–31.

Ndlela, D. B., Kaliyati, J. W. G., Zwizwai, B. M. and Mutuungwazi, D. (1984) 'A Study of the Transfer of Technology and Technology Acquisition in the Metals and Metal Goods Sector in Zimbabwe', East African Technology Policy Studies Projects.

Ndulu, B. J. (1986) 'Investment, Output Growth, Capacity Utilization in an African Economy; The Case of Manufacturing Sector in Tanzania', *Eastern African Economic Review* (New Series) Vol. 2.

NEDA (1981), *Five-Year Philippine Development Plan, 1978–82*, Manila, National Economic and Development Authority.

NEDA (1982), 'Regional Development: Issues and Strategies on Urbanization and Urban Development,' *Philippine Development Planning Studies*, Regional Planning Studies Series, No. 8, Manila, National Economic and Development Authority.

NEDA (1986), *Medium-Term Philippine Development Plan 1987–1992*, Manila, National Economic and Development Authority.

Nelson, G. C. and Agcaoili, M. (1983), 'Impact of Government Policies on Philippine Sugar,' Working Paper 83–04, Makati, Philippine Institute for Development Studies.

Nelson, J. M. (1984a) 'The Political Economy of Stabilization in Small, Low-Income, Trade-Dependent Nations', Washington DC, Overseas Development Council.

Nelson, J. M. (1984b) 'The Political Economy of Stabilization: Commitment, Capacity and Public Response', *World Development*, Vol. 12, No. 10.

Nelson, J. M. (1985) 'Reply', *World Development*, Vol. 13, No. 9.

Nelson, R. R. (1968) 'The Effective Exchange Rate, Employment, and Growth in a Foreign Exchange Constrained Economy'. Santa Monica, CA, The Rand Corporation.

Nelson, R. R., Schultz, T. P. and Slighton, R. L. (1971) *Structural Change in a Developing Economy: Colombia's Problems and Prospects* Princeton University Press, Princeton, Mass.

Newberg, R., Morton, A. and Harmon, D. (1985) 'PL480 Pilot Case Studies: Tunisia Title I and Mali Title II, Section 206', Washington DC, Ronco Consulting Corp.

Ngethe, N. and Wahome, J. (1987) *The Rural Informal Sector in Kenya* Institute for Development Studies, University of Nairobi.

Nicholls, W. (1964) 'Agriculture in Regional Economic Growth', in Eichner, C. and Witt, L. (eds), *Agriculture in Economic Development*, New York, McGraw-Hill.

Nogues, J. (1980) 'Trade Distortions and Employment in the Argentine Manufacturing Sector', PhD dissertation, University of Minnesota.

*NRC Handelsblad* (1989) Supplement Economic, 16 March, Rotterdam, Vol 1, p. 1.

O'Brien, P. (1982) 'Relations between Transnational Corporations and Public Enterprises in Developing Countries, with Particular Reference to Technological Development: A Preliminary Analysis', Vienna.

O'Herlihy, S. St. J. (1972) 'Capital-Labour Substitution and the Developing Countries: A Problem of Measurement', *Bulletin of the Oxford University Institute of Economics and Statistics*.

Odegaard, K. (1985) 'Cash Crop Versus Food Crop Production in Tanzania: An Assessment of Major Post-Colonial Trends', *Lund Economic Studies*, No. 33.

Okumu, J. (1979) 'Foreign Relations: Dilemmas of Independence and Development', in Barkan, J. and Okumu, J. *Politics and Public Policy in Kenya and Tanzania*, New York, Praeger.

Oshima, H. (1984) 'The Significance of Off-Farm Employment and Income in Post-War East Asian Growth', Asian Development Bank *Economics Paper No. 21.*

Osoro, N. (1987) 'The Impact of Foreign Exchange Allocation Management on the Performance of Manufacturing Sector in Tanzania', Paper presented at IDRC Workshop, Nairobi, December.

Oyugi, W. (1982). *Government and Public Enterprises: Some Observations on Kenya*, Institute for Development Studies, University of Nairobi, Occasional Paper No. 39.

Pack, H. (undated) 'AID and the IMF', unpublished.

Pack, H. (1972) 'Employment and Productivity in Kenyan Manufacturing', *Eastern African Economic Review,* 4:2.

Pack, H. (1976) 'Policies to Encourage the Use of Intermediate Technology', paper prepared for USAID. Swarthmore, Pa, Swarthmore College, Department of Economics.

Pack, H. (1982) 'Aggregate Implications of Factor substitution in Industrial Processes', *Journal of Development Economics*, Vol. 11.

Page, J. R. (1979) 'Small Enterprises in African Development: A Survey', *World Bank Staff Working Paper No. 363*, Washington DC, World Bank.

477

Page, J. R. (1984) 'Firm Size and Technical Efficiency: Applications of Production Frontiers to Indian Survey Data', *Journal of Development Economics*, Vol. 16.

Page, J. R. and Steel, W. (1984) 'Small Enterprise Development: Economic Issues from African Experience', *World Bank Technical Paper No. 26*, Washington DC.

Palumbo, D. J. and Harden, M. A. (eds) (1981) *Implementing Public Policy*, Lexington, DC Heath and Co.

Parker, W. N. (1979) 'Industry', in Burke, P. (ed) *The New Cambridge Modern History*, Vol. 13.

Paukert, F., Skolka, J. and Maton, J. (1974) 'Redistribution of Income, Patterns of Consumption and Employment', *Income Distribution, Employment and Economic Development in Southeast and East Asia*, Vol. 1.

Pederanga, C. W. and Pernia, E. M. (1983) 'Economic Policies and Spatial and Urban Development: the Philippine Experience', in *Regional Development Dialogue*, Vol. 4.

Perkins, F. (1980) 'Technological Choice, Industrialization and Development: The Case of Tanzania', PhD thesis, University of Sussex.

Perkins, F. C. (1983) 'Technology Choice, Industrialisation and Development: The Case of Tanzania', *Journal of Development Studies*, No. 19

Petrin, T. and Vahcic, A. 'The Development of Small-Scale Industry: The Key Element in the Development Strategy of The Yugoslav Economy Over the Next Ten Years', in Thomas, H. and Uribe-Echevarria, F. (eds) *Small-Scale Industrialization,* forthcoming.

Picard, L. A. (1979) 'District Councils in Botswana: A Remnant of Local Autonomy', *Journal of Modern African Studies*, Vol. 17.

Pick, F. (1978) *Pick's Currency Yearbook, 1976–77*. New York, Pick Publishing Company.

Pitt, M. (1981) 'Alternative Trade Strategies and Employment in Indonesia', in Krueger *et al.* (eds) *Trade and Employment in Developing Countries*, Chicago, University of Chicago Press.

Posada, C. E. (1983) 'Dinamica Industrial en la Decada del Setenta' in *Revista Antioquena de Economia*.

Power, J. H. and Sicat, G. P. (1971), *The Philippines: Industrialization and Trade Policies*, London, Oxford University Press.

Pratt, R., Adamczyk, C., Audic, F., Esteve, H., Clark, J. and Tugendhat, E. (1983) 'Private Sector: Costa Rica', *USAID Evaluation Special Study No. 9*, Washington DC, USAID.

Pyatt, G. and Round, J. (eds) (1985) *Social Accounting Matrices: a Basis for Planning*, Washington DC, IBRD.

Raiffa, H. (1980) 'Decision Making in the State Owned Enterprise', in Vernon, R. and Aharoni, Y. *State-Owned Enterprise in the Western Economies*, New York, St Martin's Press.

Ramirez, N. (1987) *The Businessman and His Economic State*, San Jose, Costa Rica, Editorial Universitaria Centroamericana.

Rangarajan, C. (1982) 'Agricultural Growth and Industrial Performance in India', International Food Policy Research Institute, *Research Report No. 33*, Washington DC.

Ranis, G. (1973) 'Industrial Sector Labour Absorption', *Economic Development and Structural Change*, Vol. 21.

Ranis, G. (1975) 'LDC Employment and Growth: A Synthesis of Economic Growth Centre Research', *Economic Growth Centre Research Discussion Paper No. 231*, New Haven, Ct, Yale University.